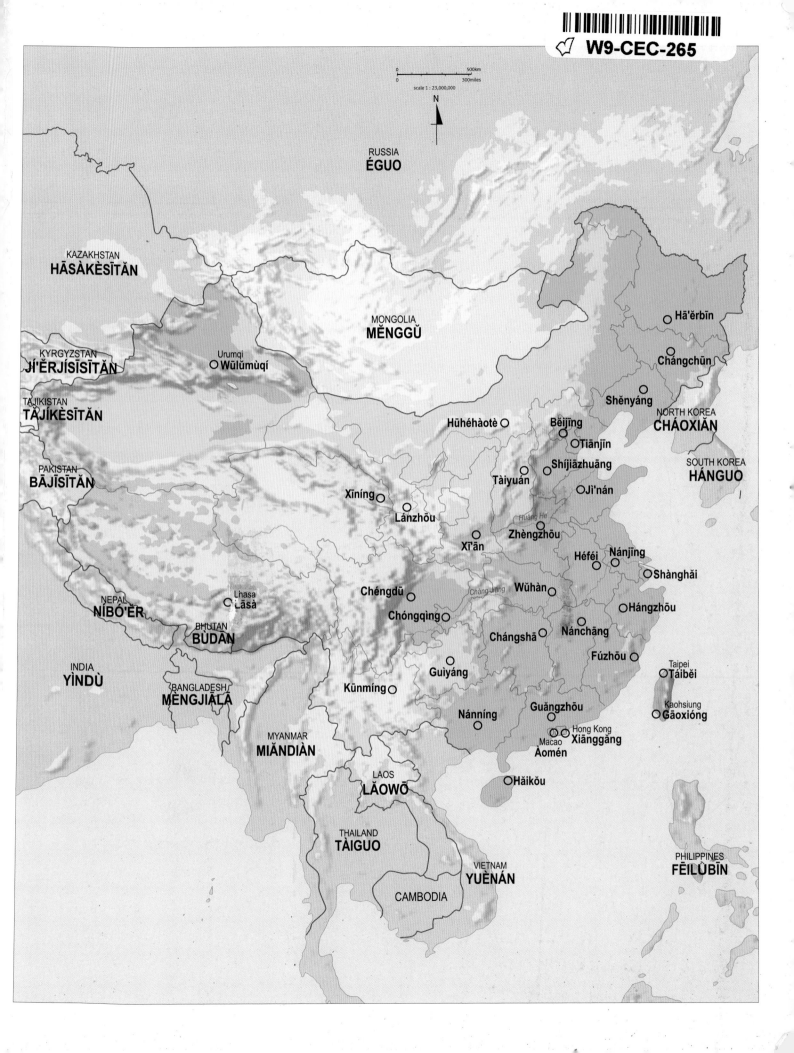

W9-CEC-265

scale 1 : 23,000,000

N

RUSSIA
ÉGUO

KAZAKHSTAN
HĀSÀKÈSĪTĂN

KYRGYZSTAN
JÍ'ĚRJÍSĪSĪTĂN

TAJIKISTAN
TĂJÍKÈSĪTĂN

PAKISTAN
BĀJÍSĪTĂN

MONGOLIA
MĚNGGŬ

Urumqi
Wūlǔmùqí

Hā'ěrbīn

Chángchūn

Shěnyáng

NORTH KOREA
CHÁOXIĂN

Hūhéhàotè

Běijīng

Tiānjīn

Shíjiāzhuāng

Tàiyuán

Jǐ'nán

SOUTH KOREA
HÁNGUO

Xīníng

Lánzhōu

Huáng He

Zhèngzhōu

Xī'ān

Héféi

Nánjīng

Shànghǎi

NEPAL
NÍBÓ'ĚR

Lhasa
Lāsà

BHUTAN
BÙDĀN

Chéngdū

Chóngqìng

Cháng Jiāng

Wǔhàn

Hángzhōu

INDIA
YÌNDÙ

BANGLADESH
MÈNGJIĀLĀ

Chángshā

Nánchāng

Fúzhōu

Taipei
Táiběi

Guìyáng

Kūnmíng

Kaohsiung
Gāoxióng

MYANMAR
MIǍNDIÀN

Nánníng

Guǎngzhōu

Hong Kong
Xiānggǎng

Macao
Àomén

Hǎikǒu

LAOS
LǍOWŌ

THAILAND
TÀIGUO

VIETNAM
YUÈNÁN

PHILIPPINES
FĒILǙBĪN

CAMBODIA

BASIC SPOKEN CHINESE

AN INTRODUCTION TO SPEAKING AND LISTENING FOR BEGINNERS

CORNELIUS C. KUBLER

TUTTLE Publishing

Tokyo | Rutland, Vermont | Singapore

Cornelius C. Kubler is Stanfield Professor of Asian Studies at Williams College, where he teaches Chinese and for many years chaired the Department of Asian Studies. He was formerly Chinese Language Training Supervisor and Chair of the Department of Asian and African Languages at the Foreign Service Institute, U.S. Department of State, where he trained American diplomats in Chinese and other languages, and he served for six years as Principal of the American Institute in Taiwan Chinese Language & Area Studies School. Kubler, who has directed intensive Chinese language training programs in the U.S., mainland China, and Taiwan, has been active in Chinese language test development and has authored or coauthored nine books and over 50 articles on Chinese language pedagogy and linguistics.

Published by Tuttle Publishing, an imprint of Periplus Editions (HK) Ltd.

www.tuttlepublishing.com

Copyright © 2011 Cornelius C. Kubler
All photos © Cornelius C. Kubler except for:

Front cover/title page: Top Right, © iStockphoto.com/Zhang Bo. Bottom Left, © Arenacreative, Dreamstime.com. Bottom Right, © Yang Yu, Dreamstime.com. p. 167: © Otnaydur, Dreamstime.com. p. 195: © 2009 Robert Kim. p. 253: © J. Henning Buchholz, Dreamstime.com.

Assistance received from the following in the filming of conversations is gratefully acknowledged:
Unit 2, Part 1: The Mandarin Training Center, National Taiwan Normal University, Taipei; Part 3: Shangrila Hotel, Beijing; Part 4: Hilton Hotel, Taipei. Unit 3, Part 4: Beijing West Railway Station, Beijing. Unit 4, Part 1: The Mandarin Training Center, National Taiwan Normal University, Taipei; Part 2: Jianquan Clinic, Taipei; Part 3: Swisshotel, Beijing. Unit 5, Part 3: Yuelong Restaurant, Beijing. Unit 7, Part 4: Fortune Garden Restaurant, North Adams, Massachusetts.

Library of Congress Cataloging-in-Publication Data
Kubler, Cornelius C.
  Basic spoken Chinese : an introduction to speaking and listening for beginners / Cornelius C. Kubler.
     p. cm.
  Includes index.
  ISBN 978-0-8048-4015-6 (pbk.)
  1. Chinese language--Textbooks for foreign speakers--English. 2. Chinese language--Spoken Chinese. 3. Chinese language--Sound recordings for English speakers. 4. Chinese language--Self-instruction. I. Title.
  PL1129.E5K83 2010
  495.1'83421--dc22
                    2010036320

ISBN 978-0-8048-4015-6

Interior design: Anne Bell Carter

Distributed by

North America, Latin America & Europe
Tuttle Publishing
364 Innovation Drive
North Clarendon, VT 05759-9436 U.S.A.
Tel: 1 (802) 773-8930 Fax: 1 (802) 773-6993
info@tuttlepublishing.com
www.tuttlepublishing.com

Asia Pacific
Berkeley Books Pte. Ltd.
61 Tai Seng Avenue #02-12
Singapore 534167
Tel: (65) 6280-1330 Fax: (65) 6280-6290
inquiries@periplus.com.sg
www.periplus.com

First edition
14 13 12 11   5 4 3 2 1

Printed in Singapore

TUTTLE PUBLISHING® is a registered trademark of Tuttle Publishing, a division of Periplus Editions (HK) Ltd.

A Note to the Learner

Welcome to the first volume of an unusual, and highly effective, two-volume course in spoken Chinese.

As a native English speaker, your working hard to learn Chinese is not enough: you have to work smart in order to learn this very different language efficiently. No matter why you've chosen to learn Chinese—for business, travel, cultural studies, or another goal—the *Basic Chinese* approach of two separate but integrated tracks will help you learn it most efficiently, and successfully.

There are no Chinese characters to be found here because you don't need characters to learn to speak Chinese. In fact, learning the characters for everything you learn to say is an inefficient way to learn Chinese, one that significantly slows down your progress.

To help you learn to speak and understand Chinese as efficiently as possible, *Basic Spoken Chinese* gives you the Chinese language portions of this course not via characters, but instead through **video** and **audio** featuring native speakers (on the accompanying disc and audio files). And in the pages of this book, the Chinese is represented in Hanyu Pinyin, the official Chinese romanization system.

- *Basic Spoken Chinese* should be used in conjunction with the accompanying **Basic Spoken Chinese Practice Essentials**.
- If you wish to learn Chinese reading and writing, which is certainly to be recommended for most learners, you should—together with or after the spoken course—use the companion course **Basic Written Chinese**. It corresponds with *Basic Spoken Chinese* and systematically introduces the highest-frequency characters (simplified and traditional) and words in context in sentences and reading passages as well as in realia such as street signs, notes, and name cards.
- For instructors and those learners with prior knowledge of Chinese characters, a *Basic Spoken Chinese* **Character Transcription** is also available. It contains transcriptions into simplified and traditional characters of *Basic Spoken Chinese*. Please note that the character transcription is not intended, and should not be used, as the primary vehicle for beginning students to learn reading and writing.
- The *Basic Chinese* **Instructor's Guide** contains detailed suggestions for using these materials as well as a large number of communicative exercises for use by instructors in class or by tutors during practice sessions.

请注意

《基础中文：听与说》为专门练习口语的教材，内附有两张光盘，因此全书内只列有汉语拼音和英文注释，不使用汉字。学习者宜与配套的《基础中文：听与说》练习册一起使用。

此套中文教材另编有《基础中文：读与写》及《基础中文：读与写》练习册，专供读写课使用。《基础中文：听与说》另配有汉字版，将《基础中文：听与说》中所有对话和补充生词的拼音版转为汉字，并分简繁体，供教师和已有汉字基础的学习者参考、使用。

此套教材亦包括一张光盘的《基础中文：教师手册》，指导教师如何使用此教材，且提供大量课堂练习，极为实用。

請注意

《基礎中文：聽與說》為專門練習口語的教材，內附有兩張光盤，因此全書內只列有漢語拼音和英文注釋，不使用漢字。學習者宜與配套的《基礎中文：聽與說》練習冊一起使用。

此套中文教材另編有《基礎中文：讀與寫》及《基礎中文：讀與寫》練習冊，專供讀寫課使用。《基礎中文：聽與說》另配有漢字版，將《基礎中文：聽與說》中所有對話和補充生詞的拼音版轉為漢字，並分簡繁體，供教師和已有漢字基礎的學習者參考、使用。

此套教材亦包括一張光盤的《基礎中文：教師手冊》，指導教師如何使用此教材，且提供大量課堂練習，極為實用。

Contents

Acknowledgments

I am indebted to a great many people in Beijing, Taipei, Hong Kong, Macao, Singapore, Malaysia, and the United States for their assistance in the preparation of this course. It is not possible to mention everyone who participated, but special thanks are due the following for their contributions:

For assistance with the preparation of the basic conversations that serve as the core of this course: Lu Zhi, Wu Zong, Jerling G. Kubler, and Amory Yi-mou Shih. Mr. Shih deserves special recognition for working closely with me on developing early drafts of many of the conversations in the first eight units as well as compiling a corpus of basic vocabulary which served as the basis for all of the conversations.

For recording situational dialogs used as source material for some of the basic conversations: Cao Jianying, Chang Ling-lan, Li Yueying, Liu Shu-yen, Eileen H. Seng, Amory Yi-mou Shih, and Yang-Hou Kun.

For assistance in preparing the accompanying drills and exercises: Huang Ya-Yun, Su-Ling Huang, and my student research assistants Jenny Chen, Hoyoon Nam, Alexander T. Ratté, and Tron Wang.

For assistance in preparing the accompanying audio recordings: Han Bing, Hou San, Huang Ya-Yun, Jerling G. Kubler, Kuo Ching-wei, Li Chunwei, Li Nini, Lu Chün-hung, Jackson Guangnan Lu, Ma Jing, Yuzhong Meng, Yang Wang, Jun Yang, Yuan Ye, Zhang Chun, Shaopeng Zhang, and over one hundred other native speakers in Beijing, Taipei, Hong Kong, Macao, Singapore, and Malaysia. Of these, Dr. Jun Yang, now Senior Lecturer in Chinese at the University of Chicago, deserves special recognition for the many hours he spent painstakingly recording the "Build Up" sections for the basic conversations.

For serving as actors in the accompanying video recordings: Jan Anderson, Patricia Austin, Flora Banker, Lindsay Benedict, Chen Limin, Chiu Ming-hua, Chou Shu-yen, Cynthia Cramsie, Darryl Crane, Anne Marie Decker, Thomas Dornacher, Dorjee, M. O. Danun, Chris Dungharth, Feng He, Chris Folino, Jesse Frey, Fu Zhongyuan, Duarte Geraldino, Ho Tsu-chi, Brad Hou, Mr. and Mrs. Hsueh Fu-hua, Huyen Giang, Kalia Glassey, Christopher Godzicki, Gu Anqi, Patrick Dowdey, Susan Harmon, Hou Lanfen, Deborah Hsu, Ingrid Hsue, Hu Weiguo, Angie Huse, Huang Sheng, Huang Yu-chun, Jonathan Isaacs, Jia Aihua, Rex Krakaw, Jerling G. Kubler, Kuo Chih-chie, Kuo Chih-hsiung, Kuo Chih-wei, Gene Kuo, James Lambert, Gavin LaRowe, Siu-lun Lee, Roger Levy, Debbie Lee, Heidi Lee, Li Chen, Li Chunwei, Li Han, Li Mei, Li Qunhu, Li Yingyou, Li Zhenqiang, Li Zhenwen, Liang Chunshen, Liao Hao-hsiang, Liu Jifeng, Liu Longjun, Liu Xiaodong, Liu Xue, Kevin Lo, Michelle Lopez, Lü Lin, Ma Ke, Ma Yung-Yu, Ma Yulan, Rachel MacCleery, Mao Hui-ling, Maja Mave, Max Mayrhofer, Nicholas Minekime, Emily Murray, Gwendolyn Pascoe, David Rieth, Todd Roma, Thomas Rowley, Andrew Ryan, Colleen Ryan, Michael Saso, Harvey Sernovitz, Mr. and Mrs. Amory Shih, Peter Stein, Su Weiming, Sun Hui, Beth Sutter, Tang Chu-shih, Tang Wei-ying, Gretta Thomas, Alex Tsebelis, Natasha Tyson, Wang Guoli, Wang Lixin, Michael Warres, Tim White, Wong Ho Put, Wu Hsian-jong, Wu Shu-fen, Zondy Wu, Xu Danyan, Yang Chunxue, Yang Ping, Charles Yonts, Zhao Feng, Zhou Lei, and others.

For performing and granting permission to record and use their classical Chinese music for the audio and video recordings: Bai Miao, Chang Jing, and Tian Weining. Note that in the audio and video recordings, Part One of each unit features the **gǔzhēng**, a 21-stringed plucked instrument similar to the zither; Part Two features the **èrhú**, a two-stringed bowed instrument; Part Three features the **yángqín** or dulcimer; and Part Four features the **sānxián**, a three-stringed plucked instrument.

For assistance with the editing and dubbing of the accompanying video recordings: An Zi; Bruce Wheat and Philip Remillard of Audio Visual Services at Williams College; Richard Lescarbeau, Art Department, Williams College; and student research assistants Hoyoon Nam, Negeen Pegahi, Amy Sprengelmeyer, and Freeman Ningchuan Zhu.

For assistance with computer-related work: Adam Jianjun Wang, Senior Instructional Technology specialist at Williams College; student research assistants Feng Jin, Daniel Gerlanc, Hoyoon Nam, Daniel Nelson, and Freeman Zhu; and Carl E. Kubler. Of these, Daniel Nelson and Daniel Gerlanc deserve special recognition for their continued support of the project over a period of several years.

For clerical assistance with various tasks related to the preparation of the manuscript: Donna L. Chenail, Rebecca Brassard, Margaret M. Weyers, Shirley A. Bushika, and Loraine L. Tolle of the Faculty Secretarial Office at Williams College; and my student research assistants Jenny Chen, Steven P. S. Cheng, Angie Chien, Niki Fang, Hoyoon Nam, Amy Sprengelmeyer, Tron Wang, and Freeman Zhu.

For assistance in checking the Chinese contained in this volume and/or providing helpful comments and suggestions: Cecilia Chang, Songren Cui, Jingqi Fu, Guo Wei, Han Bing, Hsu Yu-yin, Jerling G. Kubler, Liao Hao-hsiang, Nicholas Minekime, Eric Pelzl, Cathy Silber, Tseng Hsin-I, Chen Wang, Yang Wang, Tony Chung-yan Yang, and Li Yu. I also wish to thank the students in my Chinese 101-102 courses at Williams College from 1992 through 2006 for numerous suggestions and corrections, as well as for their inspiration and encouragement. Students at St. Mary's College of Maryland, where the course was field-tested with the assistance of Professor Jingqi Fu, and at Wisconsin Lutheran College, where the course was field-tested with the assistance of Professor Eric Pelzl, similarly provided helpful comments. Professor Pelzl deserves special thanks for his many perceptive comments and excellent suggestions.

For meticulous editing and many other helpful suggestions during the production of this course: Sandra Korinchak, Senior Editor at Tuttle Publishing. I also wish to express my appreciation for their enthusiastic support of the project and its development to Tuttle's Publisher Eric Oey and Vice President Christina Ong; and my heartfelt thanks for their expertise and assistance throughout to Nancy Goh, Tan Cheng Har, and the entire Tuttle Sales and Marketing team.

It will be obvious to those familiar with the field of Teaching of Chinese as a Foreign Language how this course builds upon the work of others. I would like to single out the following, whose work has been especially valuable to me: Y. R. Chao, Chien Wang-Chen, John DeFrancis, Charles F. Hockett, Beverly Hong, Thomas E. Madden, Martin Symonds, Shou-hsin Teng, M. Gardner Tewksbury, Galal Walker, and A. Ronald Walton. I wish also to acknowledge my debt to my teacher of Japanese, Eleanor H. Jorden, whose innovative contributions to the field of Teaching of Japanese as a Foreign Language have served both as inspiration and example during the development of this course.

I wish to express thanks to my wife, Jerling G. Kubler; my son, Carl E. Kubler; and my mother, Gisela H. Kubler, for their advice, support, and patience over a period of many years.

Financial or logistical support from the following is gratefully acknowledged: Hong Gang Jin at the Associated Colleges in China Program at Capital University of Economics and Business in Beijing; Wu Jingjyi at the Foundation for Scholarly Exchange in Taipei; Weiping Wu at the Yale-China Chinese Language Center of the Chinese University of Hong Kong; Michael Saso at the Institute of Asian Studies in Beijing; Shouhsin Teng, Hsin Shih-Chang, and Tseng Chin-Chin at the Graduate Institute of Teaching Chinese as a Second/Foreign Language at National Taiwan Normal University in Taipei; Tuttle Publishing; the Mellon Foundation and the Center for Educational Technology at Middlebury College; and, last but not least, Williams College, especially the Center for Technology in the Arts and Humanities, the Oakley Center for the Humanities and Social Sciences, and the Office of the Dean of the Faculty.

I should state here that the ultimate rationale behind the preparation of this course is to improve communication between Americans and the citizens of the various Chinese-speaking societies and thereby contribute, in however small a way, toward promoting understanding and peace between our peoples.

Cornelius C. Kubler
Department of Asian Studies
Williams College
Williamstown, Massachusetts, USA

Orientation

About This Course

Basic Spoken Chinese and *Basic Written Chinese* constitute an introductory course in modern Chinese (Mandarin), the language with the largest number of native speakers in the world, which is the official language of mainland China and Taiwan and one of the official languages of Singapore. The focus of this course, which is designed for adult English-speaking learners, is on communicating in Chinese in practical, everyday situations. We have tried to keep in mind the needs of a wide range of users, from college and university students to business people and government personnel. With some adjustments in the rate of progress, high school students may also be able to use these materials to their advantage. By availing themselves of the detailed usage notes and making good use of the *Practice Essentials* book, the video, and the audio, it is even possible for motivated self-learners to work through these materials on their own, though it would be desirable for them to meet with a teacher or native speaker for an hour or two per week, if possible. Although users with specialized needs will, in the later stages of their study, require supplementary materials, we believe this course provides a solid general foundation or "base" (hence the title of the course) that all learners of Chinese need, on which they may build for future mastery.

The course is divided into spoken and written tracks, each with various types of ancillary materials. The following diagram will clarify the organization of the whole course:

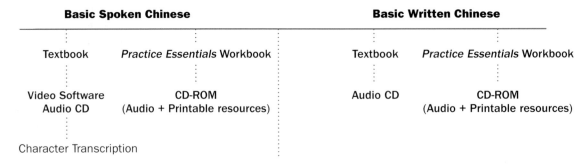

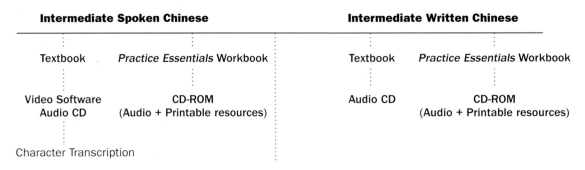

Several modes of study are possible for these materials: (1) the spoken series only; (2) a lesson in the spoken series followed a few days, weeks, or months later by the corresponding lesson in the written series; and (3) a lesson in the spoken and written series studied simultaneously. What is not possible is to study the written series first or only, since the written series assumes knowledge of the pronunciation system and relevant grammatical and cultural information, which are introduced in the spoken series.

Students embarking upon the study of Chinese should be aware that, along with Japanese, Korean, and Arabic, Chinese is one of the most difficult languages for native English speakers. This course makes no pretensions of being an "easy" introduction to the language. However, students can be assured that if they make the effort to master thoroughly the material presented here, they will acquire a solid foundation in Chinese.

The proficiency goals in speaking and reading by completion of the *Intermediate Spoken Chinese* and *Intermediate Written Chinese* portions of the course are Intermediate-Mid on the American Council on the Teaching of Foreign Languages (ACTFL) Chinese Proficiency Guidelines, which correlates with S-1/R-1 on the U.S. government Interagency Language Roundtable (ILR) Language Skill Level Descriptions. By the time they attain this level, learners will be able to conduct simple, practical conversations with Chinese speakers on a variety of everyday topics (cf. Table of Contents). They will also be able to read simple, connected texts printed in simplified or traditional Chinese characters and recognize about 600 high-frequency characters and common words written with them. Of course, they will not yet be able to conduct conversations on professional topics or read newspapers or novels, skills that in the case of Chinese take a considerably longer time to develop.

Some of the special features of *Basic Spoken Chinese* and *Basic Written Chinese* include:

Separate but integrated tracks in spoken and written Chinese. Most textbooks for teaching basic Chinese teach oral and written skills from the same materials, which are covered at a single rate of progress. Students typically study a dialog, learn how to use in their speech the words and grammar contained in the dialog, and also learn how to read and write every character used to write the dialog. But the fact is that, due to the inherent difficulty of Chinese characters, native English speakers can learn spoken Chinese words much faster than they can learn the characters used to write those words. As East Asian language pedagogues Eleanor H. Jorden and A. Ronald Walton have argued,* why must the rate of progress in spoken Chinese be slowed down to the maximum possible rate of progress in written Chinese? Moreover, in Chinese, more than in most languages, there are substantial differences between standard spoken style and standard written style, with many words and grammar patterns that are common in speech being rare in writing or vice versa. For all these reasons, this course uses separate but related materials for training in spoken and written Chinese. However, reflecting the fact that written Chinese is based on spoken Chinese, and so as to mutually reinforce the four skills (listening, speaking, reading, and writing), the written track is closely integrated with the spoken track. A day's spoken lesson is based on a conversation typically introducing one to three new grammar patterns and 15 to 20 new spoken words, while the corresponding written lesson introduces six new high-frequency characters and a number of words that are written using them, chosen from among (but not including all of) the characters used to write the basic conversation of the corresponding lesson. Experience shows that the learning of written skills in Chinese proceeds more efficiently if learners study for reading and writing the characters for words they have previously learned for speaking and comprehension. Under this approach, when students take up a new lesson in written Chinese, they already know the pronunciations, meanings, and usages of the new words, needing only to learn their written representations—which considerably lightens the learning load. Such an approach also allows students and instructors maximum flexibility concerning at which point, how, and even whether, to introduce reading and writing.

Graduated approach. There is so much to learn to become proficient in Chinese that Chinese language learning can easily become overwhelming. By dividing large tasks into a series of many smaller ones, the learning of Chinese becomes more manageable. Therefore, each spoken lesson consists of only one fairly short (five- to twelve-line) conversation, while each written lesson introduces only six new characters. An added bonus to this approach is the sense of accomplishment learners feel through frequent completion of small tasks, rather than getting bogged down in long lessons that seem never-ending.

Naturalness of the language. A special effort has been made to present natural, idiomatic, up-to-date Chinese as opposed to stilted "textbook style." This will be evident, for example, in the use of interjections, pause fillers, and final particles, which occur more frequently in this text than in most other Chinese language textbooks. Occasionally, for comprehension practice, we have included recordings of slightly accented Mandarin

---

* Cf. Eleanor H. Jorden and A. Ronald Walton, "Truly Foreign Languages: Instructional Challenges" in *The Annals of the American Academy of Political and Social Science*, March 1987.

speech, so as to familiarize learners with some of the more common variations in pronunciation they are likely to encounter.

Authenticity of the language. Chinese, like English, is a language spoken in a number of different societies, with multiple standards and varying usages. Although the emphasis of this course is on the core that is common to Mandarin Chinese wherever it is spoken, linguistic differences among the major Chinese speech communities as well as recent innovations are taken up where appropriate. Of the 96 basic conversations in *Basic Spoken Chinese* and *Intermediate Spoken Chinese*, the audio and video for 56 of them were recorded in Beijing, with another 31 recorded in Taipei, 3 in Hong Kong, one in Macao, 2 in Singapore, 2 in Malaysia, and one in the U.S. The relatively small number of terms that are restricted in use to a particular speech area are so indicated.

Emphasis on the practical and immediately useful. We have tried to present material that is high in frequency and has the most immediate "pay-off value" possible. An effort has been made to include the most useful words, grammar patterns, situations, and functions, based on several published frequency studies as well as research by the author. The units of this course have been arranged in order of general usefulness and practical importance. Although the course is designed to be studied from beginning to end, learners with time for only, say, the first five or ten units will at least be exposed to many of the most useful vocabulary items and structural patterns.

Eclecticism of approach. We believe that language is so complex and the personalities of learners so different, that no single approach or method can possibly meet the needs of all learners at all times. For this reason, the pedagogical approach we have chosen is purposefully eclectic. This course is proficiency-oriented and situational in approach with a carefully ordered underlying grammatical foundation. We have borrowed freely from the audio-lingual, communicative, functional-notional, and grammar-translation approaches.

Maximum flexibility of use. Student and teacher needs and personalities vary widely, as do the types of programs in which Chinese is taught. We have tried to leave options open whenever possible. This is true, for example, in the question of how to teach pronunciation; whether to teach the spoken skills only or also the written skills; when to introduce reading and writing; whether to teach simplified or traditional characters or both; and which of the exercises to do and in which order to do them. There is detailed discussion of all these and other questions in the Instructor's Guide for *Basic Spoken Chinese* and *Basic Written Chinese*.

Attention to sociolinguistic and cultural features. Knowing how to say something with correct grammar and pronunciation is not sufficient for effective communication. Learners must know what to say and what not to say, when to say it, and how to adjust what they say for the occasion. How do the gender, age, and social position of the speaker and listener affect language? Finally, language does not exist apart from the culture of its speakers. What are the cultural assumptions of Chinese speakers? These are some of the matters to which we have tried to pay attention.

Extensive built-in review. In order to promote long-term retention of the material learned, a great effort has been made to recycle vocabulary and grammar periodically in later units in the textbook and *Practice Essentials* after they have been introduced. In addition, there is a review and study guide at the end of every unit.

Attention to the needs of learners with prior knowledge of Chinese. While the course is designed for beginners and assumes no prior knowledge of Chinese, it tries to take into account the special situation and needs of learners who possess some prior knowledge of the language acquired from home or residence overseas. Consequently, there are special notes on features of standard Mandarin pronunciation and usage that differ from the Cantonese or Taiwanese-influenced Mandarin to which some learners may have been exposed.

Organization and Use

The *Basic Spoken Chinese* materials introduce the Mandarin sound system, Hanyu Pinyin romanization, many of the major grammatical patterns of spoken Chinese, a core vocabulary of 931 high-frequency words, and the sociolinguistic and cultural information needed for learners to use these various linguistic components appropriately.

The textbook for *Basic Spoken Chinese* contains ten units, each of which is on a common daily life situation in which Americans typically find themselves interacting with Chinese. On the first page of each unit are listed the topic and communicative objectives for the unit. The communicative objectives reflect important language functions and give the learning a purpose. Learners should be sure to read through the objectives, since they will be more receptive to learning if they understand the purpose of the learning and have an idea of what to expect.

Every unit is divided into four parts, each of which includes the following sections:

Context: On the first page of each part you will see the title of the lesson, an image of the situation drawn from the on-location video, and a description of the situation. We always explain the sociolinguistic and cultural context, for example: where the conversation is taking place, who the speakers are, their positions in society, how well they know each other, their age, their gender, etc. It is important that learners study the image and read the description, so they have a clear idea of the context for the basic conversation they will be studying.

Basic Conversation: The basic conversations, which constitute the core of each lesson, normally consist of a conversation between one American and one (or occasionally more than one) Chinese speaker. The purpose of the conversations is to introduce high-frequency structural patterns, vocabulary, and cultural information that is relevant to learners' likely future needs in a situation-oriented format. To help make each conversation "come to life" and to show details of the sociolinguistic and cultural background, audio and video recordings of the basic conversations have been prepared, which should be used in conjunction with the textbook. The basic conversations are next presented in "Build Up" format, with each sentence of the basic conversation broken down into manageable chunks with pauses provided for repetition, so as to help learners gain fluency. In the textbook, the "Build Up" is presented in two columns: romanization, on the left; and English translation and word class, on the right. By working with the audio recordings and textbook, the student should thoroughly memorize the basic conversation so he or she can role play it (in class with the instructor and other students the next day, or, for independent learners, by using the software's conversation options) prior to beginning the drills and exercises. To a significant extent, the student has mastered the lesson to the degree that he or she has internalized the basic conversation. Of course, memorization of the basic conversation is only the first step in attaining communicative competence.

Supplementary Vocabulary: This section presents important supplementary vocabulary that, in many cases, is related in some way to the material introduced in the basic conversation. The supplementary vocabulary, which is included on the audio recordings after the basic conversation, is required for learning and may reoccur later in the course without further explanation.

Additional Vocabulary: This section, which exists only for some lessons, presents other useful words related to the content of the lesson for the learner's reference. The additional vocabulary, which is designed for students with extra time who desire to be challenged, is not required to be learned and will not reoccur in later lessons.

Grammatical and Cultural Notes: The major new grammatical structures in the basic conversation are here explained and exemplified from the point of view of the native English-speaking learner. There are also miscellaneous comments on the basic conversation, supplementary vocabulary, and additional vocabulary. A special effort has been made to incorporate important sociolinguistic and cultural information as well as practical advice for the learner of Chinese.

Review and Study Guide: At the end of every unit, there is a review and study guide consisting of: (1) the new vocabulary introduced in the basic conversation and supplementary vocabulary of the four parts of the unit, arranged according to word class; and (2) a list of the major new grammar patterns introduced in the unit, with an indication of where they first occurred.

An Overview of the Chinese Language

The primary emphasis of this course is on learning Chinese rather than learning about Chinese. Nevertheless, the Chinese language has so many special features about which there are so many common misconceptions, that it will help put your study of Chinese in better perspective to begin with a brief survey of the history and current status of the language.*

HISTORY

Chinese is a member of the Sino-Tibetan language family. This means it is related to languages such as Burmese and Tibetan, though too distantly to be apparent except to a specialist. To the best of our current knowledge, Chinese is unrelated to the Indo-European language family, to which English and most other European languages belong; nor is it genetically related to Japanese or Korean, even though its writing system and a portion of its vocabulary were borrowed and adapted by speakers of those languages.

By about 500 BCE, there had developed in the Yellow River Valley of North China a language now known as Old Chinese. This is the language which was spoken and written by Confucius and Mencius and which, more or less, was the ancestor of all the modern Chinese dialects. While spoken Old Chinese, like all languages, continued to evolve over the succeeding centuries, written Old Chinese—usually referred to as **Gǔwén** or "Classical Chinese"—became relatively fixed in form at an early date and changed little until the first few decades of the twentieth century.

With the overthrow of the Qing Dynasty in 1911, the twin issues of language standardization and language reform, which were considered essential for the building of a modern nation, attracted the attention of increasing numbers of intellectuals. In 1913 the Ministry of Education of the newly established Republic of China sponsored a Conference on the Unification of Pronunciation which, after protracted discussion, proclaimed the dialect of North China, known in English as Mandarin, as the **Guóyǔ** or "National Language" of China.

Several years later, in 1917, the American-educated philosopher and literary critic Hu Shih spearheaded a movement to replace Classical Chinese with written Mandarin, or **Báihuà**, as the standard written language. This movement, known as the **Xīn Wénxué Yùndòng** "New Literature Movement," gradually gained support during the 1920s and 1930s. After the founding of the People's Republic of China in 1949, the new government continued the previous government's policy of promoting Mandarin, to which it gave the new name **Pǔtōnghuà** "Common Speech." Beginning in the 1950s, a number of important reforms were implemented in China including standardization of variant characters, promotion of simplified characters, adoption of the horizontal style of writing, and creation of Hanyu Pinyin romanization.

Today, Mandarin Chinese is the native language of more people than any other language in the world; in fact, there are more native speakers of Mandarin than of English and Spanish, the languages in third and fourth place, combined (Hindi/Urdu is in second place). What is more, four of the twenty most widely spoken languages in the world are different dialects of Chinese. Chinese is also, after English and Spanish, the third most widely spoken language in the U.S.

In the same way that English is spoken as a native language in a number of different countries, Chinese is spoken in several different countries and societies. It is the national language of the People's Republic of China on the Chinese mainland, Hainan, and numerous smaller islands; it is also the national language of the Republic of China on Taiwan and several smaller island groups; and it is one of the official languages of the Republic of Singapore. In addition, Mandarin is spoken widely by the ethnic Chinese in Malaysia, who make up approximately one-fourth of the population. While different standards and usages exist among these various types of Chinese, they all represent slightly different forms of the same language and are, with few exceptions, mutually intelligible.

---

* The material in this section is adapted from a similar section, also written by the author, in the *NFLC Guide for Basic Chinese Language Programs*, 2nd rev. ed., National Foreign Language Resource Center, The Ohio State University, Columbus, 2006.

Figure 1

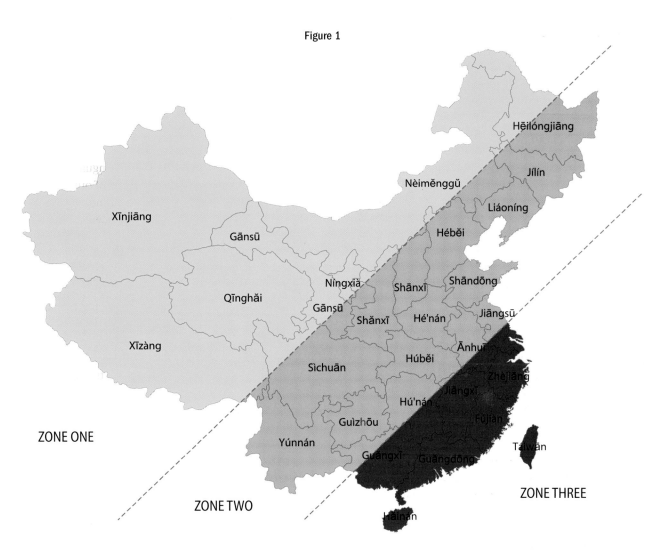

LANGUAGES AND DIALECTS

The languages of China are distributed over three large zones (see Figure 1). The first zone consists of the borderlands of North and West China, where non-Chinese languages such as Mongolian, Uighur, and Tibetan have traditionally been spoken. In the second zone, which stretches from Heilongjiang in the Northeast across most of northern and central China to Yunnan in the Southwest, four major varieties of Mandarin are the native language. The third zone extends from southern Jiangsu across southeastern China to southern Guangxi; here, six widely divergent Chinese dialects are the daily language of the people.

The four major varieties of Mandarin spoken in the second zone include: (1) **Běifāng Guānhuà** "Northern Mandarin," spoken in Beijing, Hebei, Henan, Shandong, Liaoning, Jilin, and Heilongjiang; (2) **Xīběi Guānhuà** "Northwestern Mandarin," spoken in Shanxi, Shaanxi, Ningxia, and Gansu; (3) **Xī'nán Guānhuà** "Southwestern Mandarin," spoken in Sichuan, Guizhou, Yunnan, and northern Guangxi; and (4) **Xiàjiāng Guānhuà** "Lower Yangtze Mandarin," spoken in Anhui and most of Hubei and Jiangsu. The differences among the four varieties of Mandarin are about as great as among American, Canadian, British, and Australian English.

The six major non-Mandarin dialects spoken in the third zone are: (1) **Wúyǔ** "Wu," spoken in Shanghai, Southern Jiangsu, and Zhejiang; (2) **Yuèyǔ** "Yue" or "Cantonese," spoken in Guangdong and most of Guangxi; (3) **Xiāngyǔ** "Xiang," spoken in Hunan; (4) **Mǐnyǔ** "Min," spoken in Fujian, Taiwan, Hainan, and part of Guangdong; (5) **Kèyǔ** "Hakka," spoken in parts of Guangdong, Jiangxi, Fujian, and Taiwan as well as in small concentrations in other provinces of China; and (6) **Gànyǔ** "Gan," which is spoken in Jiangxi. The relationship among Mandarin and the other six Chinese dialects is comparable to that among the Romance languages (e.g., French, Italian, Portuguese, and Spanish).

By purely linguistic criteria, Mandarin and the other six major Chinese dialects would be called languages rather than dialects, since they are all mutually unintelligible (i.e., speakers of one cannot understand speakers of another). For political and cultural reasons, however, they are usually termed dialects. The dialects differ most of all in pronunciation, to a lesser degree in vocabulary (more for everyday terms than for academic vocabulary), and least in grammar (though there are important differences there, too). Dialect speakers nowadays typically speak in their native dialect (and Mandarin, if they know it), but read and write in written Mandarin, which they have learned in school. The common claim that the various Chinese dialects are pronounced differently but are all written the same is not really true; if the dialects are written as they are spoken (which Cantonese and Taiwanese sometimes are), they are not fully comprehensible to readers from other parts of China.

Today, in both mainland China and Taiwan, dialect speakers—especially younger, urban residents—are likely to have some degree of proficiency in Mandarin, which they have studied in school and hear in the public media, but which they will most likely speak with a local accent. Should some of you already be familiar with a non-Mandarin dialect, this will be useful to you in learning Mandarin, though you will need to be attentive to the differences. By the same token, proficiency in Mandarin greatly reduces the amount of time required to learn a second Chinese dialect (or, to a lesser extent, Japanese, Korean, or Vietnamese).

PRONUNCIATION

One feature that distinguishes Mandarin from other Chinese dialects is its relative phonological simplicity, since of all the major dialects it has the smallest number of tones and the fewest final consonants. Compared to other languages, the sound system of Chinese is relatively simple. There are only about 400 basic syllables—far fewer than in English, which has several thousand. A Chinese syllable is traditionally divided into an initial sound, which some syllables lack, and a final sound, which is always present. The final sound normally includes a tone.

The initials, of which there are 23, are all single consonant sounds, there being no consonant clusters like [spl] or [nts] as in English *splints*. The finals, of which there are 34, all end in a vowel, **-r**, **-n**, or **-ng**. In addition, most Chinese syllables are pronounced with one of four tones. The same basic syllable pronounced with different tones is likely to have completely different meanings.

The tones of Chinese are one of the special characteristics of the language. Another is the fact that almost all Chinese syllables have distinct meanings of their own, even if they can't all be used independently in speech. For this reason, Chinese is often referred to as being "monosyllabic." But this should not be taken to mean that every Chinese word has only one syllable. Indeed, the majority of words in Chinese today have two syllables.

GRAMMAR

Many people, both Chinese and non-Chinese, have claimed that Chinese "has no grammar." What they usually mean by this is that the endings of Chinese words don't change depending on gender, case, number, person, or tense, as in many Western languages. For this reason, in typological classifications of languages, Chinese is often termed an "isolating" or "analytic" language. For the same reason, Chinese formerly had a reputation in the West as being a primitive language.

Actually, Chinese has its share of grammar rules, even if some of these are different kinds of rules than those of Western languages. In general, Chinese grammar depends heavily on word order, function words (independent particles that mark grammatical functions), and context. Some of the salient features of Chinese grammar include:

1. **Normal sentence order** is Subject-Verb-Object, as in English (though the subject and object are often omitted, and the object is sometimes placed at the beginning of the sentence).

2. **Topic/Comment** is often a more appropriate major division within a sentence than Subject/Predicate.

3. Adjectives (which are in this textbook termed stative verbs) can function as verbs when in verb position (e.g., **fángzi xiǎo** "the house smalls/the house is small").

4. Adjectives (or stative verbs) precede nouns, as in English (e.g., **xiǎo + fángzi** = "small" + "house").

5. Verbs have aspect rather than tense (e.g., is the action of the verb continuous or completed? Has it ever been experienced before?).

6. Measures, also termed classifiers, are used immediately before nouns when the nouns are modified by a number or specifier (e.g., **sānzhāng zhuōzi** "three flat-things tables").

7. Reduplication, i.e., repeating the same syllable twice, is frequently used to alter the meanings of words.

VOCABULARY

Chinese words may consist of one or more than one syllable, e.g., **shū** "book," **péngyou** "friend," **dǎzìjī** "typewriter." However, two-syllable words predominate. Words of two or more syllables are easily broken down into their constituent parts because each part usually has its own meaning and its own character, when written. The syllable is thus the basic building block of Chinese.

Because of the long and largely independent development of Chinese culture, there are few cognates between Chinese and English. Until quite recently, the cultural and social backgrounds of these two languages were almost totally different. The number of Chinese words, especially in literary and historical works, is enormous. During the last century, a fair number of words have been borrowed from English and other Western languages into Chinese and vice versa. In some cases, the sound of the Western word was borrowed into Chinese, as in the words **léidá** "radar" and **kělè** "cola." More typical, however, are loan translations such as **diànhuà** "electric speech—telephone" and **huǒchē** "fire cart—train," where the meaning of the foreign term is translated into Chinese.

Suggested Strategies for Learning Spoken Chinese

Chinese has for centuries had a reputation as being a language difficult or even impossible for Westerners to learn. It is quite true that for a native speaker of English to learn Chinese is a task of a whole different order than learning another Western language. The experience of the U.S. government language training agencies, for example, has shown that it takes about four times as long to train someone to a level where they can function professionally in Chinese as it takes in French or Spanish.

While it is important to realize the considerably greater investment of time and effort required to learn Chinese and to understand that, even after years of study, one is still not likely to approach the full range of skills of an educated native speaker, it is also true that the difficulty of Chinese tends to be overrated. Chinese is very learnable. The many Americans—including students, scholars, business people, and government personnel is—who have learned Chinese well are proof of this.

The basics of spoken Chinese, in particular, aren't really that hard at all. There are no verb conjugations or noun declensions to memorize, and the pronunciation system is limited to some four hundred-odd syllables. True, the Chinese characters present problems not encountered in an alphabetic writing system, and the sociolinguistic conventions and cultural background of Chinese are quite different from those of most Western languages. However, due to recent systematizations and simplifications in the Chinese language, advances in language pedagogy (better dictionaries, textbooks, and teaching methods), and the fact that Chinese and Western culture are moving ever closer together, the Chinese language is today considerably easier to learn than it used to be.

In studying Chinese, it's important not only to work hard but also to work smart. Listed below are some suggestions and strategies for learning Chinese that have helped others. Language learning is a personal thing and what works for one person will not necessarily work for another; nevertheless, you may wish to consider adopting some of these strategies for your own use.

GENERAL STRATEGIES

1. **Try to think in Chinese as much as possible.** Think in terms of images of things whenever you can and try to keep English out. In general, your approach should be to learn to speak and behave in as Chinese a manner as possible. At first it is natural to engage in a certain amount of translation, but you should make the effort to think directly in Chinese as soon as you can.

2. **Be aware** that there is more to language than the verbal signal and that the environment in which your mind best assimilates language is not a grammatical one but a communicative one. Learning to communicate in Chinese requires that you try to understand the whole web of expressions, gestures, actions, beliefs, and values of the Chinese people, i.e., the cultural assumptions that are part of being Chinese.

3. **Practice being a good observer** of members of Chinese culture—what Chinese people say, what they do as they speak, their gestures, expressions, etc. Also, be aware of your own behavior as it reflects your implicit attitude (or perceived attitude) toward Chinese culture. Try to be sensitive to those things in your conduct which members of Chinese society may find inappropriate. For example, putting your feet on a table or pointing at people with your forefinger would not be considered good manners. Similarly, you should not wear very casual clothes to class, wear a cap in class, or bring food to class if you're attending school in China or if your instructor or mentor is new to American culture.

TIME MANAGEMENT

1. **Learning Chinese takes a long time,** so smart use of time is important. If you are enrolled in a group class, then by all means attend every class session; frequent cutting equals certain disaster. Occasionally, a student who because of illness did not have time to prepare for class may decide to skip that class and instead use the time to catch up. Do not do this; though the intention is good, the result is that you will get further and further behind.

2. **Set aside a definite time for studying Chinese** each day and stick to it. A conscientiously observed daily schedule would be a good idea. Find the best time of day to do your studying; don't do it when you have other things on your mind or are exhausted, since your mind has to be receptive for effective learning to take place.

3. **An appropriate place for your studying is also important.** You should not choose a place (such as a shared dorm room) where you will frequently be interrupted or distracted. By providing a place specifically for oral language practice, a language learning center or language lab, if available, can help ensure concentration and efficient learning.

4. **For a college or university-level course** that meets an hour each day in class and covers one lesson per day (i.e., one part of the four parts of each unit) in both *Basic Spoken Chinese* and *Basic Written Chinese,* the average student will need to study two to three hours out of class on their own or in the language lab. Be flexible in arranging your study schedule. Instead of spending three straight hours all on Chinese, it would be more effective for most students to divide their study time into two or three separate study sessions.

IMPORTANCE OF ORAL PRACTICE

1. **The most important kind of class preparation** is working with the audio recordings that accompany the textbook. When working with the recordings, be active rather than passive. Always repeat after, or participate in, the drills on which you are working. Though it is fine to run through new material the first time with your book open, by the second or third time, your book should be closed (this is harder but more effective). When you are practicing, speak out loud—and as loud as possible! Experience has shown that people learn languages better when they practice out loud. You should never learn the spoken material primarily from studying the

romanized Chinese in your textbook; rather, you should learn from spoken models—your teachers and the voices on the audio recordings.

2. **Both in class and when listening to the audio recordings, force yourself to listen closely.** Always stay attentive to the meaning of what you hear. It is easy when doing a drill to, like a machine, mechanically spew forth the answer; but this is of much less benefit to you than also thinking of the meaning. The more active you are in your own learning process, the faster you will progress.

3. **Pay special attention to pronunciation.** A mispronounced initial, final, or tone will often make a word incomprehensible to a Chinese speaker. Accuracy of sentence rhythm and stress are also important in making your speech understandable. The pronunciation habits you establish during the first few weeks and months are likely to stay with you the remainder of your Chinese-speaking days, since it is difficult to correct bad habits later.

4. **Begin by focusing on accuracy, not speed.** Don't slur over words; there is no need to rush through a sentence. Speed will gradually develop over time. When you are practicing, say each phrase or sentence enough times so that you can render it with a reasonable degree of fluency.

5. **When the instructor calls on other students, avoid the temptation to tune out.** Listen carefully at all times and, to the extent possible, perform every classroom activity yourself. When the instructor asks another student a question, you also should prepare a response and answer silently yourself. Then listen as the teacher corrects the other student. This approach will help you get the most out of every class hour.

SPECIFIC TECHNIQUES

1. **Memorize each basic conversation thoroughly,** so you can perform it accurately and fluently in class. It is essential to internalize the new words and grammar patterns, so they will be available to you for your own creative use when needed. Doing this will greatly aid your fluency and naturalness of speaking. Memorization takes time and may not be the most interesting thing to do, but as an initial step in language learning, it is very effective.

2. **Students sometimes question the necessity of repetition, drill, and memorization.** Certainly, these are only the first steps leading to our ultimate goal of comunicative competence. However, they are very important steps, since they firmly establish in your brain the sounds and structures of the language for you to draw on later in your own creative speech. We hope that you understand the importance of these activities and ask that you work hard at them.

3. **One of the most effective ways of learning is to test yourself frequently.** For example, after you have worked with the audio recordings and studied the words and sentences on a page of the textbook, fold a sheet of paper down the long end, covering up the left-hand side of the page where the Chinese is, and see if you can reconstruct the Chinese by looking at the English. Flash cards are another useful learning device, since you can take them with you anywhere. Moreover, with flash cards it's easy to identify those cards that you frequently get wrong and remove them from the larger set for special attention.

4. **Learn phrases, sentences, and dialogs, not just individual vocabulary items.** By learning vocabulary in context (as part of phrases, sentences, and dialogs), you will be able to use it correctly in your own speech. Structural patterns are especially important, since grammar is the "glue" that holds all else together. Once you have internalized a pattern, it will be easy to substitute appropriate vocabulary items into it as necessary.

5. **If you don't know or forget the exact word for something, paraphrase.** For example, if you can't remember how to say "train station," then say "the place where trains stop" or "there are a lot of trains there."

6. **Work out a systematic personal review program.** A half hour daily or several hours on the weekend spent in thorough review of past material would be very useful. But be careful not to spend excessive time on

review. The material currently being worked on in class should always have priority.

7. **Use your Chinese outside of class as much as possible.** If you have a chance to listen to a lecture in Chinese or to see a Chinese film or television program, be sure to take advantage of the opportunity. If there are Chinese restaurants or other Chinese ethnic establishments where you live, patronize them and take advantage of the chance to further hone your language skills. You might also want to contact the representative offices of the various Chinese-speaking countries and societies to learn about activities in your area which they sponsor. In short, do all you can to take advantage of and create opportunities to use Chinese.

DEALING WITH ERRORS

1. **Don't be embarrassed or frustrated by your mistakes,** as they are a natural part of the language learning process. Try to develop what the Chinese call **kāi kǒude yǒngqì** "the courage to open your mouth." It may reassure you to know that, partially through natural politeness and partially because of the tremendous amount of dialectal variation in China, Chinese speakers are generally quite tolerant of mistakes in Chinese grammar and pronunciation and will usually be willing to communicate with you even if your Chinese is not correct.

2. **When the teacher corrects you, pay close attention.** Try to understand what was wrong and what the correct Chinese should be. Then make use of the corrected Chinese in your Chinese conversation later that day, so that you remember it. When you are corrected, be grateful to your instructor and make it clear to her or him that you appreciate the corrections.

3. **Many students find it useful to keep a notebook** of their most common errors with corrections. There is a famous saying in Sunzi's *Art of War*: **Zhī jǐ, zhī bǐ, bǎi zhàn bǎi shèng** "Know yourself and know your adversary, and in a hundred battles you will have a hundred victories." Understanding where your own weak points lie is often the first step toward eliminating them.

BE POSITIVE AND FLEXIBLE

1. **When you don't understand something, try to guess the meaning from the context.** Rather than focusing on the part you don't understand, listen to the message as a whole and see if you can make out the probable general meaning. Learn to treat uncertainty as part of the process of language learning.

2. **In your learning of Chinese, be aware of the difference between "fact"** (understanding how the language works) and "act" (being able to use the language). Both of these are important for adult language learners, with "fact" serving as an important enabling mechanism leading to and enhancing "act," but ultimately "act" is the more important. Personal learning styles differ, with some students learning best via a detailed understanding of the grammar followed by copious practice, and others learning best through practice alone. Some students prefer the oral mode, while others like to see the language as it is written. Each student must devise her or his own best method of learning, but the goal for everyone is the same—accurate, natural, effective control of the language. Seek to understand your own particular learning style and focus on your strengths, exploiting your personal learning style to your greatest advantage. At the same time, you should remain open to new possibilities and not be afraid to try out new language learning techniques or methods.

3. **You may find that after a period of obvious and satisfying progress,** you suddenly reach a "plateau" where learning seems to come to a standstill. This is a natural and frequently occurring phenomenon for language students. If this should happen to you, don't worry too much about it. First, you are probably still progressing, just not aware of it. Second, even if you really are on a plateau, things will probably seem better soon. If you have questions about your progress, you should feel free to speak with your instructor.

4. **Be patient and realistic.** Chinese is a difficult language and takes much time to learn. On the one hand, by the time you complete this course, you should be able to handle simple everyday conversation and "get

around" in China. On the other hand, due to the nature of the Chinese characters, it will take several years of hard work until you can read Chinese newspapers and books with any degree of fluency. But don't demand too much of yourself, either. Be proud of what you *do* know; don't always just berate yourself for what you *don't* know!

A NOTE FOR STUDENTS OF CHINESE HERITAGE

In recent years, a growing number of students of Chinese heritage have been entering basic Chinese language programs in the U.S. These learners may have spent part of their childhood in mainland China, Hong Kong, or Taiwan; or they may have been exposed to Chinese at home in the U.S.; or they may have studied Chinese in a Chinese heritage community language school. While some of these students have no practical Chinese language proficiency, others may possess a wide range of abilities ranging from simple listening comprehension to speaking to the ability to read and write but in a non-Mandarin dialect. Learners of Chinese heritage may also be familiar with aspects of Chinese culture and society.

This course is designed for students with no previous background in Chinese. If you do have some prior background, that will certainly be useful to you. At the same time, there are some aspects of Chinese language learning such as romanization, grammar, formal vocabulary, characters, and study skills that you will probably have to work at just as hard as everyone else. Also, note that this course teaches standard usage (basically, the dialect of Beijing), but many students of Chinese heritage in the U.S. speak with southern Chinese pronunciation and grammar. Where appropriate, we will refer to special problems faced by students of Chinese heritage, for example, as regards non-standard pronunciation and usage.

A NOTE FOR INTERNATIONAL STUDENTS

Whereas in the past, beginning Chinese language classes at American colleges and universities consisted largely of American students, that assumption can no longer be made, as many American institutions of higher learning are internationalizing. Now, there are not a few students from Europe or from Asian countries such as Japan, Korea, Thailand, Vietnam and elsewhere who choose to study Chinese in America. This is, of course, in many respects a welcome development; for example, students of diverse cultural backgrounds bring valuable assets to the language classroom, especially at the intermediate and advanced levels, since it is then often possible to conduct livelier and richer discussions when comparing the U.S., China, and other countries.

At the same time, it is also true that the most efficient way to teach adults a foreign language, especially at the basic level, is to group together students sharing the same native language and cultural background. This simplifies instruction, since those of the same background will typically face similar learning challenges and make similar mistakes. Moreover, in discussing pronunciation, grammar, and culture, the instructor can then point out similarities and differences between the "target" language and culture (Chinese) and the "base" language and culture (the English language and American culture).

For the reasons given in the preceding paragraph, this series of textbooks is designed first and foremost for American college and university students. If you should hail from another country, you can still put these materials to good use but occasionally there may be comments that do not apply to you or perhaps exercises that are too easy for you. In such cases, we ask for your patience and understanding. If you ever have questions about any aspect of Chinese language and culture that are not covered in the notes to each lesson, you should always feel free to ask your instructor.

A NOTE FOR INDEPENDENT LEARNERS

Though most learners of Chinese using *Basic Spoken Chinese* will be learning in a class with an instructor, these materials have been designed so that you may use them to learn Chinese on your own, if you so choose. Learning on your own actually has a number of advantages, including the freedom to learn at your own pace, and the flexibility to learn at a time and location of your convenience. However, to be a successful independent learner, you need to be disciplined, self-motivated, and willing to assume complete responsibility for your own language learning.

If you're an independent learner, then most of the strategies and comments discussed above apply to you also. Since you don't have access to an instructor, it's especially important for you to spend sufficient time working with the audio and video materials that accompany this textbook. You should also be sure to acquire and use to maximum advantage the accompanying *Basic Spoken Chinese Practice Essentials*, which was designed to provide lots of additional practice of the material introduced in the textbook.

As an independent learner, you should make a schedule as regards the amount of time to devote to language study and the rate of progress through the materials and then stick to it if at all possible. Ideal would be to spend an hour or two every day working with the audio, video, and print materials. If you can't spend an hour every day, then spend as much time as you can, but be aware that daily exposure to the language—even if for only twenty or thirty minutes a day—is more effective than a longer study period on the weekend. In the case of learners in a class, each part of each unit is designed for one hour of classroom instruction and two to three hours of self-study; so for an independent learner like you, four to five hours of self-study for each part should be about right. But if you find you can't do the various audio drills quickly enough in the pauses provided (without peeking at the text), or if you can't perform the role plays in the *Practice Essentials* fairly fluently, then that is probably a sign you aren't yet sufficiently familiar with the material, so you should review some more before moving on.

Now, an obvious disadvantage of learning on your own is that you don't have an instructor to interact with and guide you. To remedy this, you should try to find a native Chinese-speaking tutor or mentor who can meet with you once or twice a week to serve as your conversation partner, correct you, and answer questions that you may have. Perhaps a Chinese friend or Chinese foreign student in the area where you live could fill this role. Try to choose someone who has a clear voice and speaks standard Mandarin; since many Chinese speak Mandarin with an accent, you could perhaps ask other Chinese people if the person you are thinking of choosing as tutor speaks "good Chinese." Your tutor should be lively and outgoing; it's of less importance how good her or his English is. Do be sure to compensate your tutor in an appropriate manner—you could pay them by the hour, tutor them or their children in English in separate sessions, or help them in some other way.

To help your tutor conduct the tutorial sessions, you should obtain from the publisher of this book a copy of the Instructor's Guide for *Basic Chinese* to give your tutor. It contains detailed suggestions for using these materials as well as many questions and other exercises for each part that you and your tutor can work on during the tutorial sessions. If your tutor is not used to reading the Pinyin romanization in the *Basic Spoken Chinese* textbook, you may also wish to give her or him the *Basic Spoken Chinese* Character Transcription.

Assuming a one-hour tutorial session, we suggest that the first 40–45 minutes be conducted in Chinese only, with no English spoken by either the learner or the tutor. We recommend the following procedures:

1. **Learner and tutor role-play** the basic conversation in the textbook (the learner should be able to perform the conversation without reference to the text—in other words, have it memorized).

2. **Tutor asks learner the Chinese questions in the Instructor's Guide.**

3. **Tutor asks other questions in Chinese using the new vocabulary and grammar of the lesson.**

4. **Learner and tutor do the role play exercises in the *Practice Essentials*.**

5. **Learner and tutor go over the translation exercises in the *Practice Essentials*** (the learner should have prepared them in writing in advance).

6. **If there is time remaining, material introduced in earlier lessons can be reviewed.**

During the last 15–20 minutes of the tutorial session, either Chinese or English can be used. You can ask any questions you may have and your tutor can provide answers and offer any relevant comments or explanations. During the first few weeks, it would be best if you didn't ask how to say things that don't appear in the textbook. Even after several months, you shouldn't ask for too much "extra" vocabulary, as doing so tends to slow down your progress; it's generally best to stick with what is introduced in the textbook.

Pronunciation and Romanization

Getting Started

The first task facing you as you set about learning Chinese is to gain control over the sound system of the language. This is because sound is the medium through which the spoken language (and, in a more indirect way, the written language) is conveyed. Even if your main objective should be reading Chinese, this objective is most efficiently attained by starting with speaking and pronunciation. The reason for this is that to be able to read fluently, with full intellectual and emotional comprehension, one should know the spoken language in which a text was written. Gaining control over the sound system of Chinese will involve two different but related goals: (1) being able to recognize the sounds of Chinese when someone else produces them and (2) being able to produce the sounds of Chinese yourself.

Unlike some of your other tasks in learning Chinese, such as learning grammar, vocabulary, and characters—which will keep you busy for a fairly long time to come, the pronunciation system is closed-ended and, while there are some important differences from English, not so difficult to learn. Since the pronunciation you develop during your first few weeks of learning Chinese is likely to a large extent to stay with you for the rest of your Chinese-speaking days—and to a large degree will determine whether or not people understand you and what effect your speech has on them, it is crucial that you do all you can now to acquire the best pronunciation possible.

You will find that the investment in time and energy you make at the outset in acquiring a good pronunciation will be well worth your while later. Accuracy in pronunciation is even more important in Chinese than in most other languages. The reason for this is that the number of different basic syllables in Chinese is quite limited—only about 400, compared with many thousands in English. This means that every sound is important in distinguishing one word from another; the margin for error is much smaller than in other languages.

Transcription Systems for Chinese

As you no doubt are already aware, Chinese is ordinarily written in Chinese characters. However, as the characters take time to learn and do not provide information on pronunciation in a systematic manner, it is more efficient to begin the study of Chinese via a transcription system. Many transcription systems have been devised in the last few centuries in both China and the West. For example, the word for "China" is written as follows in several common transcriptions:

Wade-Giles romanization:	Chung[1]-kuo[2]
National Phonetic Alphabet:	ㄓㄨㄥ · ㄍㄨㄛ
National Romanization:	Jong.gwo
Yale romanization:	Jūnggwo
Hanyu Pinyin romanization:	Zhōngguo

Of the transcription systems above, Hanyu Pinyin romanization has come to be the most widely used. It is the official system of transcription for Chinese in China and Singapore, where it is used as a tool to teach Chinese characters to children, to indicate in dictionaries the pronunciations of characters which adult Chinese readers might not know, to spell Chinese words in Western-language publications, and to compile Chinese language textbooks for foreigners. The Pinyin system is the transcription system we will be using in this text.

The written symbols of Pinyin, which literally means "spell a sound," are basically the same as those of the Roman alphabet except that the letter **v** is not used. In referring to the letters of the Pinyin alphabet, the Chinese people use their own set of appellations, which are somewhat similar to French or German (e.g., **a b c** is pronounced something like "ah," "bay," "tsay"). However, it is not necessary to learn these since, when referring to the constituent components of written Chinese, you will be talking in terms of characters, not Pinyin. On the relatively rare occasions when you do need to refer to Pinyin letters, you can use the English names for the symbols.

Be aware that Pinyin, or for that matter any other transcription, does not and cannot record all the details of Chinese sounds. Pinyin is selective in what it indicates, recording only some sounds; other sounds are left out. Transcription can only be a rough reminder of the real sounds, which must exist in your heads, based on frequent hearing of live or recorded sounds. Thus, it is crucial that you practice in class with your instructor, and at home with the accompanying audio recordings, just as much as possible.

While learning to pronounce Pinyin correctly is very important, you should also learn how to write Pinyin. A considerable quantity of material is now published in China in Pinyin. Chinese street signs often contain some Pinyin, and Pinyin is being used increasingly to input Chinese characters on computers. Pinyin can also be useful for citing personal and place names when writing in English or for making a quick note of something you hear for which you don't know the characters, so that you can look them up in a dictionary later.

The Sounds of Mandarin

The basic unit of Mandarin pronunciation is the syllable. A typical Mandarin syllable is composed of three parts: an initial sound, a final sound, and a tone. For example, in the syllable **mà** "scold," **m** is the initial, **a** is the final, and the mark ` represents the tone. Some syllables lack an initial and some syllables, when they are unstressed, have no tone; but every syllable must have a final.

In Pinyin the same letter may have two or more different pronunciations depending on the environment in which it occurs (i.e., what letters come before or after). For example, the **i** in the syllable **xi** sounds different from the **i** in the syllable **zi**, or the **u** in **gu** sounds different from the **u** in **ju**. Therefore, it is best to learn Mandarin pronunciation via syllables rather than focusing on individual letters.

The initials and finals of Mandarin are listed below in the traditional order with instructions on how to produce them and a comparison with the closest English sounds.* There is also a pronunciation exercise for each initial and final, which includes several examples of syllables containing the sounds being practiced, almost all of them in Tone One. The pronunciation exercises are included on the accompanying audio recordings. Later, this section can serve as a reference if you should forget which Mandarin sound a Pinyin symbol stands for and don't have access to a native speaker or the audio recordings.

How to Learn Chinese Pronunciation

In class, listen attentively to your teachers, carefully observing their lip, tongue, and mouth movements. Mimic your instructors loudly and actively, trying to sound as "Chinese" as possible. Drill enthusiastically and be receptive to correction. You will want to work on both producing sounds correctly and recognizing them accurately.

For out-of-class study, read the descriptions of the sounds and the suggestions for producing them below. Work intensively with the audio recordings that accompany this section. Listen carefully, then repeat during the pause provided after each item. The first few times work with your book open, then practice with your book closed. Be sure to repeat out loud—and as loud (within reasonable limits, of course) as possible. The reasons for practicing in a loud voice are that, when speaking quietly, you are apt to be less precise in your pronunciation than when speaking aloud; and that speaking loudly helps build your confidence.

When reading Pinyin transcription, always remember that the symbols you see before you represent Chinese sounds—not English sounds. In the same way that French, German, and Spanish are written with the Roman alphabet but are not pronounced the same as English, Pinyin stands for Chinese sounds, many of which are very different from English. For example, what is spelled **hē cān diē** or **yòu likè a tiē** in Pinyin is pronounced quite differently and is completely unrelated in meaning to English *he can die* and *you like a tie*! So beware of the natural tendency to give English pronunciations to the Pinyin symbols. Trust your ears, not your eyes.

The pronunciation exercises were recorded in Beijing by native speakers in their early twenties who were born and raised in that city. While all of the examples are real words or parts of words, you do not need to learn the meanings at this point but should focus on learning the correct pronunciations and correct Pinyin spellings of the various sounds.

---

* The comparisons with English involve approximations, not exact equivalents. Our standard of comparison is American English as spoken on the U.S. West coast. Since few Chinese sounds are exactly like English, it is important to listen carefully to your instructor and the accompanying recordings.

Pronunciation Exercises, Part A: General Pronunciation

INITIALS

B   Like the **p** in English **spy** or **spa**. It differs from English **b** as in **by** in that English **b** is voiced (i.e., your Adam's apple is buzzing while you say it) while Mandarin **b** is voiceless. Hint: If you're having problems, first say **spa**, then hiss the **s** on **spa** like this: **sssspa**. Then, remove the **s**.

 Pronunciation Exercise A-1

1. bā "eight"	**3. bāo** "pack"	**5. bān** "move"	**7. bāng** "help"
2. bī "force"	**4. bēi** "cup of"	**6. bēn** "run"	**8. bīng** "soldier"

P   Like the **p** in English **pie** but with a stronger puff of breath. Similar to **p** plus the following **h** in English **hop high**.

Pronunciation Exercise A-2

1. pā "lie"	**3. pāi** "pat"	**5. Pān** (surname)	**7. piān** "essay"
2. pū "spread"	**4. piāo** "float"	**6. pēn** "squirt"	**8. pēng** "simmer" [BF]*

M   Like the **m** in English **my**.

Pronunciation Exercise A-3

1. mā "mom"	**3. māo** "cat"	**5. mōu** "moo"	**7. mēng** "cheat"
2. mō "grope"	**4. miāo** "meow"	**6. mēn** "stuffy"	

F   Like the **f** in English **fight**.

Pronunciation Exercise A-4

1. fā "issue"	**3. fēi** "fly"	**5. fēn** "divide"	**7. fēng** "wind"
2. fū "husband" [BF]	**4. fān** "overturn"	**6. fāng** "square"	

D   Like the **t** in English **steam**. It differs from English **d** as in **day** in that English **d** is voiced while Mandarin **d** is voiceless. Mandarin **d** is produced by most speakers with the tip of the tongue in a slightly more forward position than in English. Hiss the **s** on **stew** like this: **sssstew**. Then divide that into **ssss-tew**. Finally, omit the **sss-** altogether. The end result should be close to Mandarin **du**.

Pronunciation Exercise A-5

1. dā "get on"	**3. dāi** "stay"	**5. diē** "dad"	**7. duān** "hold"
2. dī "low"	**4. dāo** "knife"	**6. duō** "much"	**8. dēng** "lamp"

T   Like the **t** in **tea** but with a stronger puff of breath. Mandarin **t** is produced by most speakers with the tip of the tongue in a slightly more forward position than in English. Similar to the **t** plus the following **h** in English **can't he**.

 Pronunciation Exercise A-6

1. tā "she"	**3. tiē** "stick"	**5. tiān** "day"	**7. tāng** "soup"
2. tī "kick"	**4. tuī** "push"	**6. tūn** "swallow"	**8. tīng** "listen"

---

* The abbreviation [BF] after an example stands for Bound Form and indicates that the syllable in question is in normal speech always bound to another syllable or word. In other words, a syllable marked as [BF] can't ordinarily be said by itself.

N Like the **n** in English **neat**. Mandarin **n** is produced by most speakers with the tip of the tongue in a slightly more forward position than in English.

Pronunciation Exercise A-7

1. **Nā** (surname)   3. **niū** "girl" [BF]   5. **nāng** "murmur" [BF]
2. **niē** "pinch"   4. **niān** "pick up"

L Like the **l** in English **leaf** but tenser (like French, German, or Spanish l). Mandarin **l** is produced by most speakers with the tip of the tongue in a slightly more forward position than in English.

Pronunciation Exercise A-8

1. **lā** "pull"   3. **lēi** "tighten"   5. **lōu** "gather up"
2. **lāo** "fish for"   4. **liū** "sneak out"   6. **luō** "talkative" [BF]

G Like the **k** in English **sky**. It differs from English **g** as in **go** in that English **g** is voiced while Mandarin **g** is voiceless. First say **sky**, then hiss the **s** on **sky** like this: **sssssky**. Finally, remove the **s**. The end result should be close to Mandarin **gai**.

Pronunciation Exercise A-9

1. **gē** "brother"   3. **gāo** "tall"   5. **guō** "pot"   7. **gāng** "just"
2. **gāi** "should"   4. **guāi** "well-behaved"   6. **guān** "officer"   8. **gēng** "plough"

K Like the **k** in English **kite** but with a stronger puff of breath. Similar to the **ck** plus the following **h** in English **black hole**.

Pronunciation Exercise A-10

1. **kē** "harsh"   3. **kāi** "open"   5. **kuī** "lose"   7. **kuān** "wide"
2. **kū** "cry"   4. **kuā** "boast"   6. **kān** "print"   8. **kōng** "empty"

H Initial **h** sounds like the **h** in English **hand** but is pronounced with more friction so that it sounds rougher, like German **ch** in **Loch** "hole" or Spanish **j** in **mujer** "woman." There is some variation in the amount of friction depending on the speaker.

Pronunciation Exercise A-11

1. **Hā** (surname)   3. **hēi** "black"   5. **huī** "ashes"   7. **hēng** "hum"
2. **hē** "drink"   4. **huā** "flower"   6. **hūn** "faint"   8. **huāng** "panic"

J Like the **j** in English **jeep** but unvoiced and with the middle part of the tongue pressed tightly against the roof of the mouth. There is more friction in Mandarin than in English. Though the lips are always rounded in English, they are rounded in Mandarin only in front of **u**, being spread before the other vowels. Say the Biblical pronoun **ye**, then pronounce **j** as in **jeep** at the same time as **ye**, all the while pressing your tongue tightly against the roof of your mouth.

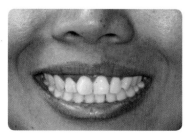

This shows the correct mouth position for the syllable **ji**, but the position of the lips and the teeth is the same for **qi**, **xi**, and **yi**.

Pronunciation Exercise A-12

1. **jī** "chicken"   2. **jū** "dwell"   3. **jiā** "home"

4. jiē "street"   **6. juān** "donate"   **8. jiāng** "ginger"
5. jiān "shoulder" [BF]   **7. jūn** "army" [BF]

Q   Like the **ch** in English **cheap** but with a stronger puff of breath and with the middle part of the tongue pressed tightly against the roof of the mouth. There is a greater amount of friction in Mandarin than in English, and while the lips are always rounded in English, they are rounded in Mandarin only in front of **u**, being spread before the other vowels. First say the Biblical pronoun **ye**, then pronounce **ch** as in **cheap** at the same time as **ye**, all the while pressing your tongue tightly against the roof of your mouth.

 Pronunciation Exercise A-13
   1. qī "seven"   **3. qiāo** "knock"   **5. quē** "lack"   **7. qiān** "thousand"
   2. qū "district"   **4. qiē** "slice"   **6. qīn** "kiss"   **8. qiāng** "rifle"

X   Between the **s** in English **see** and the **sh** in English **she**, with the middle part of the tongue pressed tightly against the roof of the mouth. There is a greater amount of friction in Mandarin than in English. While the lips are always rounded in English, they are rounded in Mandarin only in front of **u**, being spread in front of the other vowels. First say English **kiss Hugh**, then divide this into **ki-ssHugh**, finally dropping off the **ki** and **ugh** entirely. You should be left with a fairly authentic **x**.

 Pronunciation Exercise A-14
   1. xī "west"   **3. xiē** "some"   **5. xīn** "new"   **7. xīng** "putrid"
   2. xū "weak"   **4. xiā** "shrimp"   **6. xiān** "first"   **8. xiōng** "mean"

ZH   Like the **j** in English **jerk** but stronger, unvoiced, and with the tongue curled further back. Draw the tip of the tongue back and up to the roof of the mouth. While the lips are always rounded in English, they are rounded in Mandarin only in front of **u** and **o**, being spread before the other vowels. Mandarin **zh** does not sound like the **z** in English **azure**!

 Pronunciation Exercise A-15
   1. zhī "juice"   **3. zhuā** "catch"   **5. zhēn** "really"   **7. Zhāng** (surname)
   2. zhū "pig"   **4. zhuī** "chase"   **6. zhuān** "brick"   **8. zhōng** "clock"

CH   Like the **ch** in English **chirp** but with a stronger puff of breath and with the tongue curled further back. Draw the tip of the tongue back and up to the roof of the mouth. While the lips are always rounded in English, they are rounded in Mandarin only in front of **u** and **o**, being spread before the other vowels.

 Pronunciation Exercise A-16
   1. chē "car"   **3. chū** "out"   **5. chōu** "draw"   **7. chuān** "wear"
   2. chī "eat"   **4. chāo** "copy"   **6. chuī** "blow"   **8. chēng** "call"

SH   Like the **sh** in English **shrew** but with the tongue curled further back. Draw the tip of the tongue back and up to the roof of the mouth. There is a greater amount of friction in Mandarin than in English, and while the lips are always rounded in English, they are rounded in Mandarin only in front of **u** and **o**, being spread before the other vowels.

 Pronunciation Exercise A-17
   1. shā "kill"   **3. shāo** "burn"   **5. shān** "mountain" **7. shēng** "give birth"
   2. shū "book"   **4. shuā** "brush"   **6. shēn** "deep"   **8. shuāng** "frost"

R   Like the **r** in American English **shrew** but with the tongue tip curled a little further back and with more friction, so that it sounds almost like the **s** in English **measure** or the **z** in English **azure**. While English **r** is always accompanied by lip rounding, Mandarin **r** has lip rounding only when preceding **o** and **u**; in front of **a**, **e**, and **i** there is no lip rounding and the lips are spread. Never trill Mandarin **r** as in Italian or Spanish.

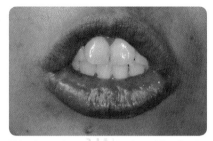

This shows the correct mouth position for the syllable **ri**, but the position of the lips and the teeth is the same for **zhi**, **chi**, and **shi**.

 Pronunciation Exercise A-18
1. rāng "shout"   **2. rēng** "throw"

Z   Like the **ds** in English **beds** but stronger and unvoiced. Mandarin **z** is produced by most speakers with the tongue tip in a slightly more forward position than in English. Say English **that zoo**, then divide this into **tha-tzoo**, and finally omit the **tha** entirely. The end result should be close to Mandarin **zu**. Mandarin **z** does not sound like the **z** in English **zoo**!

 Pronunciation Exercise A-19
1. zī "capital" [BF]   **3. zāo** "bad"   **5. zūn** "respect" [BF]   **7. zāng** "dirty"
2. zū "rent"   **4. Zōu** (surname)   **6. zuān** "bore"   **8. Zēng** (surname)

C   Like the **ts** in English **cats** but with a strong puff of breath immediately following. Mandarin **c** is produced by most speakers with the tip of the tongue in a slightly more forward position than in English. Say English **it's high** several times, then divide that into **i-tshigh**, and finally omit the **i-** entirely. The end result should be close to Mandarin **cai**.

 Pronunciation Exercise A-20
1. cā "wipe"   **3. cāi** "guess"   **5. cān** "meal" [BF]   **7. cāng** "cabin" [BF]
2. cū "coarse"   **4. cuī** "hurry"   **6. cūn** "village" [BF]   **8. cōng** "scallion"

S   Like the **s** in English **sigh** but stronger and more hissing. Mandarin **s** is produced by most speakers with the tip of the tongue in a slightly more forward position than in English. To attain the correct tongue position, pronounce **s** as in English **months**.

 Pronunciation Exercise A-21
1. sā "let go"   **3. sōu** "search" [BF]   **5. sān** "three"   **7. sēng** "monk"
2. Sū (surname)   **4. suī** "though" [BF]   **6. suān** "sour"   **8. sōng** "loose"

W   Like the **w** in English **wide**. The lips are not so tightly rounded as in English and are not pushed forward. When Mandarin **w** precedes **u**, it is often barely pronounced so that, as spoken by many people, **wu** sounds the same as **u**.[*]

 Pronunciation Exercise A-22
1. wā "dig"   **3. wāi** "crooked"   **5. wān** "bend"   **7. Wāng** (surname)
2. wū "room" [BF]   **4. wēi** "danger" [BF]   **6. wēn** "lukewarm"   **8. Wēng** (surname)

---

[*] In some analyses of Mandarin phonology, **w** is considered not as an initial but as part of several finals beginning with **u** with so-called "zero" initials. Whether **w** is analyzed as an initial or as part of the final is of no consequence to the speaker or learner of the language.

Y Initial **y** sounds like the **y** in English **yet**.* When initial **y** precedes **i** or **u**, it is often barely pronounced so that, as spoken by many people, **yi** sounds the same as **i**.

Pronunciation Exercise A-23

1. yī "one"	**3. yā** "press"	**5. yuē** "invite"	**7. yīng** "cherry" [BF]
2. yū "silt" [BF]	**4. yāo** "waist"	**6. yān** "smoke"	**8. yāng** "seedling" [BF]

FINALS

I (a) After **c, ch, r, s, sh, z**, and **zh**, **i** has no sound of its own but indicates the holding and voicing of the preceding consonant sound. These sounds should be pronounced without your tongue or lips changing position from the beginning to the end of the sound and with a good deal of tension in the throat.

(b) Everywhere else, **i** sounds like the **ee** of English **see**, but with the tongue tenser and with the lips spread flat. Mandarin **i** is a pure vowel, the tongue remaining steady throughout the production of the sound, not relaxing halfway through and adding a **y**-sound, as in English **see**.

Pronunciation Exercise A-24

(a) after **c, ch, r, s, sh, z**, and **zh**

1. cī "flaw" [BF]	**3. sī** "silk"	**5. zī** "money" [BF]
2. chī "eat"	**4. shī** "moist"	**6. zhī** (measure for pens)

(b) elsewhere

1. bī "press"	**3. jī** "chicken"	**5. qī** "seven"	**7. xī** "west"
2. dī "low"	**4. pī** "drape"	**6. tī** "kick"	**8. yī** "one"

U (a) After **j, q, x**, and **y**, the final **u** is pronounced like French **u** as in **tu** "you" or German **ü** as in **über** "over," made by rounding your lips while saying **ee** as in English **seat**. Say **eee** as in English **seat**. Without moving your tongue, move your lips from the spread position to a rounded, pursed position, then back to the spread position, giving the sequence **yi yu yi**. Then try to isolate the **yu** sound. Once you've learned how to make this sound, it won't be necessary to purse your lips quite so much—indeed, some speakers make this sound with only partly rounded lips.

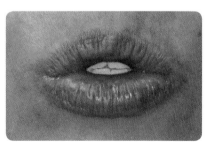

This shows the correct mouth position for the syllable **yu**, but the position of the lips and the teeth is the same for **ju, qu**, and **xu**.

(b) Everywhere else, **u** is pronounced like the **oo** of English **ooze** but tenser, with the lips rounded, and with the entire tongue higher and further back than in English. Mandarin **u** is a pure vowel, the tongue remaining absolutely steady throughout the production of the sound, not relaxing halfway through and moving toward a **w**-sound, as it does in English **shoe**.

Pronunciation Exercise A-25

(a) after **j, q, x**, and **y**

1. jū "arrest" [BF]	**3. xū** "weak"
2. qū "district"	**4. yū** "mud" [BF]

* In some analyses of Mandarin phonology, **y** is considered not as an initial but as part of several finals beginning with **i** or **ü** with so-called "zero" initials. Whether **y** is analyzed as an initial or as part of the final is of no consequence to the speaker or learner of the language.

(b) elsewhere

1. cū "coarse"   **3. kū** "cry"   **5. shū** "book"   **7. zū** "rent"
2. chū "go out"   **4. pū** "spread"   **6. wū** "room" [BF]   **8. zhū** "pig"

Ü   Like French **u** as in **tu** "you" or German **ü** as in **über** "over," made by rounding your lips while saying **ee** as in English **seat**. Say **eee** as in English **seat**. Without moving your tongue, move your lips from the spread position to a rounded, pursed position, then back to the spread position, giving the sequence **yi yu yi**. Then try to isolate the **yu** sound. Once you've learned how to make this sound, it won't be necessary to purse your lips quite so much—indeed, some speakers make this sound with only partly rounded lips. This final occurs only after **l** and **n**.*

Pronunciation Exercise A-26
1. lǜ "green"   **2. nǚ** "female" [BF]

A   Like the **a** in English **spa** but tenser, with the lower jaw well down and the mouth wide open.

Pronunciation Exercise A-27
1. bā "eight"   **3. fā** "issue"   **5. mā** "mom"   **7. tā** "he"
2. cā "rub"   **4. lā** "pull"   **6. shā** "kill"   **8. zhā** "sediment"

IA   Like the **ya** of English **yacht** but tenser.

Pronunciation Exercise A-28
1. jiā "home"   **2. qiā** "pinch"   **3. xiā** "shrimp"

UA   Like the **wa** of English **wash** but tenser and with the mouth open wider than in English. The emphasis is on the **a**-part of the final, with the **u**-part being quite short in duration.

Pronunciation Exercise A-29
1. guā "melon"   **3. kuā** "brag"   **5. zhuā** "catch"
2. huā "flower"   **4. shuā** "brush"

O   This final occurs after the initials **b**, **p**, **m**, and **f**, where it stands for the final **uo**.† The pronunciation of this final is between the **woe** of English **woe** and the **wa** of English **war**.

Pronunciation Exercise A-30
1. bō "dial"   **2. mō** "grope"   **3. pō** "slope"   **4. wō** "nest"

UO   Between the **woe** of English **woe** and the **wa** of English **war**. Begin with **u**, move to **o**, then end with the Mandarin **e**-sound without closing your lips again. Be very careful to distinguish the final **uo** from the final **ou**!

Pronunciation Exercise A-31
1. cuō "rub"   **3. duō** "much"   **5. suō** "shrink"   **7. tuō** "drag"
2. chuō "jab"   **4. guō** "pot"   **6. shuō** "speak"   **8. zhuō** "catch"

---

* Since the final **ü** does not occur in Tone One, examples in other tones have had to be chosen.
† In other words, **buo** is abbreviated as **bo**, **puo** as **po**, **muo** as **mo**, and **fuo** as **fo**.

E (a) After **y**, like the **e** in English **yet** but held longer. Be careful not to add a **y**-sound after the **e**.

(b) Everywhere else, somewhat like the **u** in English **bud**. The pronunciations of **u** in Southern American English **up**, or of **ir** in British English **bird**, are even closer. The back of the tongue is held high, then, as the vowel is pronounced, the tongue relaxes and moves down to a more central position. Say **oo** as in **wood**, but with your lips spread and your jaw lowered a little. Your mouth should be half open when making this sound, which should come from fairly deep down in your throat.

 Pronunciation Exercise A-32

(a) after **y**

1. yē "choke"

(b) elsewhere

1. chē "car"	**3. hē** "drink"	**5. shē** "extravagant" [BF]
2. gē "older brother"	**4. Kē** (surname)	**6. zhē** "cover"

IE Like the **ye** of English **yet** but held longer, or like saying rapidly the name of the English letter **E** plus **ye** as in **yet**. Be careful not to add a **y**-sound after the **ie**.

 Pronunciation Exercise A-33

1. biē "turtle"	**3. jiē** "street"	**5. piē** "cast away"	**7. tiē** "stick"
2. diē "dad"	**4. niē** "pinch"	**6. qiē** "cut"	**8. xiē** "some"

UE Like French **u** as in **tu** "you" or German **ü** as in **über** "over," followed immediately by **e** as in English **met**. The emphasis of the syllable is on the **e** rather than the **u**. First say **ee** as in English **keep** while rounding your lips, then open your lips very slightly to say **e** as in English **met**.

 Pronunciation Exercise A-34

1. juē "pout"	**2. quē** "lack"	**3. Xuē** (surname)	**4. yuē** "about"

ÜE Like French **u** as in **tu** "you" or German **ü** as in **über** "over", followed immediately by **e** as in English **met**. The emphasis of the syllable is on the **e** rather than the **u**. First say **ee** as in English **keep** while rounding your lips, then open your lips very slightly to say **e** as in English **met**. This final occurs only after **l** and **n**.[*]

 Pronunciation Exercise A-35

1. lüè "plunder"	**2. nüè** "malaria" [BF]

AI Like the **y** in English **my** but shorter and tenser. Unlike English, where the **a**-sound is emphasized over the **i**-sound, in Mandarin the **a** and **i** are given equal prominence. To produce this sound, repeat the names of the two English letters of the alphabet **I** and **E** rapidly, one immediately after the other.

 Pronunciation Exercise A-36

1. āi "be close"	**3. dāi** "foolish"	**5. kāi** "open"	**7. wāi** "crooked"
2. cāi "guess"	**4. gāi** "should"	**6. pāi** "pat"	**8. zhāi** "pick"

[*] Since the final that is spelled in Pinyin as **üe** does not occur in Tone One, examples in other tones have had to be chosen.

UAI   Like the **wy** in English **Wyoming**, but shorter and tenser. In Mandarin, unlike English, the **u**, **a**, and **i** are all given equal prominence. To make this sound, pronounce very rapidly English **oo-Y-E** (where **oo** sounds like the **oo** in **too** and **Y** and **E** are the names of the English letters of the alphabet).

 Pronunciation Exercise A-37

1. **guāi** "well-behaved"   2. **chuāi** "carry"   3. **shuāi** "fall"

EI   Like the **ei** in English **sleigh** but shorter and tenser. Unlike English, where the **e** is emphasized over the **i**, in Mandarin the **e** and **i** are given equal prominence. To produce this sound correctly, repeat the names of these two letters of the English alphabet rapidly, one immediately after the other: **A E**.

 Pronunciation Exercise A-38

1. **bēi** "cup of"   3. **hēi** "black"   5. **wēi** "danger" [BF]
2. **fēi** "fly"   4. **pēi** "embryo" [BF]

UI   For most speakers like the English word **way** but shorter and tenser. For some speakers, in syllables in tones one and two, this final sounds somewhere between English **way** and English **we**.

 Pronunciation Exercise A-39

1. **cuī** "hasten"   3. **duī** "heap"   5. **huī** "ashes"   7. **tuī** "push"
2. **chuī** "blow"   4. **guī** "return"   6. **kuī** "lack"   8. **zhuī** "chase"

AO   This sound falls midway between the **ow** of English **cow** and the **aw** of English **caw**. Unlike English, where the **a** is emphasized over the **o**, in Mandarin the **a** and **o** are given equal prominence.

 Pronunciation Exercise A-40

1. **āo** "concave"   3. **chāo** "copy"   5. **gāo** "high"   7. **māo** "cat"
2. **bāo** "wrap"   4. **dāo** "knife"   6. **lāo** "fish for"   8. **shāo** "burn"

IAO   Like the **yow** of English **yowl** but shorter and tenser. In Mandarin, unlike English, the **i**, **a**, and **o** are all given equal prominence.

 Pronunciation Exercise A-41

1. **biāo** "mark"   3. **jiāo** "hand over"   5. **piāo** "float"   7. **tiāo** "choose"
2. **Diāo** (surname)   4. **miāo** (cat's meow)   6. **qiāo** "knock"   8. **xiāo** "flute"

OU   Like the **o** in English **go** but shorter and tenser. Unlike English, where the **o**-sound is given prominence over the **u**-sound, in Mandarin the **o** and **u** are given equal prominence. Be careful to distinguish the final **ou** from the final **uo**!

 Pronunciation Exercise A-42

1. **chōu** "take"   3. **gōu** "hook"   5. **sōu** "search" [BF]   7. **tōu** "steal"
2. **dōu** "all"   4. **Ōu** "Europe" [BF]   6. **shōu** "receive"   8. **zhōu** "state"

IU   Starts out like English **yo** as in **yo-yo**, then ends up like the **oo** in English **too**. For some speakers, in syllables in tones one and two, this final sounds more like English **you**, while in syllables in tones three and four it sounds more like **yo** as in **yo-yo**.

Pronunciation Exercise A-43
1. diū "throw"
2. jiū "turtle dove" [BF]
3. liū "sneak out" [BF]
4. niū "maiden" [BF]
5. qiū "autumn" [BF]
6. xiū "rest" [BF]

AN   (a) After **y**, for most speakers, Mandarin **an** sounds like the **en** in English **Yen** (Japanese monetary unit) but shorter and tenser.

(b) Everywhere else, **an** sounds somewhat like the **awn** in English **pawn**, but shorter and tenser. Be careful not to pronounce **an** like English **an** in **pan**!

 Pronunciation Exercise A-44

(a) after **y**

1. yān "smoke"

(b) elsewhere

1. ān "at ease"
2. bān "class"
3. fān "overturn"
4. gān "dry"
5. sān "three"
6. shān "mountain"
7. tān "covet"
8. zhān "moisten"

IAN   Like the English word **Yen** (Japanese monetary unit) but shorter and tenser.

 Pronunciation Exercise A-45
1. biān "edge"
2. diān "bump"
3. jiān "sharp"
4. niān "pick"
5. piān "essay"
6. qiān "thousand"
7. tiān "day"
8. xiān "first"

UAN   (a) After **j, q, x,** and **y**, the final **uan** is pronounced by most speakers like French **u** as in **tu** "you" or German **ü** as in **über** "over," followed immediately by the **wen** of English **went**. The emphasis is on the **an**-part of the syllable.

(b) Everywhere else, **uan** is pronounced somewhat like the **wan** of English **want**, but shorter and tenser. Again, the emphasis is on the **an**-part of the syllable.

 Pronunciation Exercise A-46

(a) after **j, q, x,** and **y**

1. juān "donate"
2. quān "circle"
3. xuān "proclaim" [BF]
4. yuān "injustice" [BF]

(b) elsewhere

1. chuān "wear"
2. duān "carry"
3. guān "close"
4. kuān "wide"
5. suān "sour"
6. shuān "tie up"
7. zuān "bore"
8. zhuān "brick

EN   Somewhat like the **en** in English **chicken**.

 Pronunciation Exercise A-47
1. ēn "mercy" [BF]
2. fēn "divide"
3. gēn "and"
4. mēn "stuffy"
5. pēn "squirt"
6. shēn "deep"
7. wēn "warm"
8. zhēn "real"

IN   Between the **in** of English **sin** and the **een** of English **seen**, but tenser and with the lips spread more than in English.

 Pronunciation Exercise A-48
1. **bīn** "guest" [BF]   3. **pīn** "spell"   5. **xīn** "new"
2. **jīn** "catty"   4. **qīn** "kiss"   6. **yīn** "sound"

UN   (a) After **j**, **q**, **x**, and **y**, **un** is pronounced like French **u** as in **tu** "you" or German **ü** as in **über** "over," plus **win** as in English **win**.

(b) Everywhere else, **un** is pronounced somewhat like the **w** of English **won**, the **oo** of English **book**, plus the **n** of English **sun**.

 Pronunciation Exercise A-49

(a) after **j**, **q**, **x**, and **y**

1. **jūn** "army"   2. **qūn** "loiter" [BF]   3. **xūn** "smoke"   4. **yūn** "dizzy"

(b) elsewhere

1. **cūn** "village"   3. **dūn** "squat"   5. **kūn** "female" [BF]   7. **tūn** "swallow"
2. **chūn** "spring"   4. **hūn** "faint" [BF]   6. **Sūn** (surname)   8. **zūn** "statue"

ANG   Between the **ong** in English **song** and the **ung** in English **sung**. The tongue begins slightly further back and the vowel is longer than for **an**. The ng-sound should not be pronounced with too much force; it is lighter than in English. Do not pronounce Mandarin **ang** like English **ang** as in **sang**! Also, be careful to pronounce the **ng** as in English **hung** and not as in English **hunger**, where there is an additional **g**-sound.

 Pronunciation Exercise A-50
1. **bāng** "help"   3. **gāng** "just"   5. **tāng** "soup"   7. **zāng** "dirty"
2. **fāng** "square"   4. **rāng** "shout"   6. **Wāng** (surname)   8. **Zhāng** (surname)

IANG   Somewhat like the English word **young**. The ng-sound should not be pronounced with too much force; it is lighter than in English. Be careful not to pronounce the **ng** as in English **younger**, where there is an additional **g**-sound.

 Pronunciation Exercise A-51
1. **jiāng** "ginger"   2. **qiāng** "rifle"   3. **xiāng** "box of"

UANG   Somewhat like the **w** of English **won** plus the **ong** in English **song**, but shorter and tenser and with the mouth open wider. The emphasis should be on the **ang**-part of the syllable. Also, the **ng**-sound should not be pronounced with too much force; it is lighter than in English. Be careful to pronounce the **ng** as in English **long** and not as in English **longer**, where there is an additional **g**-sound.

 Pronunciation Exercise A-52
1. **chuāng** "window" [BF]   3. **huāng** "panic"   5. **shuāng** "frost"
2. **guāng** "only"   4. **kuāng** "basket" [BF]   6. **zhuāng** "pretend"

ENG Somewhat like the **ung** in English **lung**. The **ng**-sound should not be pronounced with too much force; it is lighter than in English. Be careful to pronounce the **ng** as in English **hung** and not as in English **hunger**, where there is an additional **g**-sound.

Pronunciation Exercise A-53

1. chēng "call"	**3. fēng** "wind"	**5. hēng** "hum"	**7. rēng** "throw"
2. dēng "lamp"	**4. gēng** "plough"	**6. kēng** "pit"	**8. shēng** "give birth"

ING Somewhat like the **ing** of English **sing**. The **ng**-sound should not be pronounced with too much force; it is lighter than in English. Consonants before the **i** are often pronounced with a slight **y**-sound after them, so that **bing** "soldier" sounds almost as if it were pronounced **bying**. Be careful to pronounce the **ng** as in English **sing** and not as in English **finger**, where there is an additional **g**-sound.

Pronunciation Exercise A-54

1. bīng "ice"	**3. jīng** "skillful"	**5. qīng** "light"	**7. xīng** "putrid"
2. dīng "nail"	**4. pīng** "ping-pong" [BF]	**6. tīng** "listen"	**8. yīng** "should" [BF]

ONG Somewhat like the **oo** of English book plus the **ng** of English **rung**. The **ng**-sound should not be pronounced with too much force but more lightly than in English. Be careful not to make this final rhyme with the **ong** in English **song**; and be careful to pronounce the **ng** as in English **sing** and not as in English **finger**, where there is an additional **g**-sound.

Pronunciation Exercise A-55

1. chōng "rush"	**3. gōng** "work"	**5. kōng** "empty"	**7. tōng** "penetrate"
2. dōng "east"	**4. hōng** "dry"	**6. sōng** "loose"	**8. zhōng** "middle" [BF]

IONG Somewhat like the **y** of English **you**, the **oo** of English **book**, plus the **ng** of English **rung**. The **ng**-sound should not be pronounced with too much force; it is lighter than in English. Be careful to pronounce the **ng** as in English **sing** and not as in English **finger**, where there is an additional **g**-sound.

Pronunciation Exercise A-56

1. jiōng "bolt"	**2. xiōng** "mean"

ER Between English **are** and **err**, but with the tongue curled even further back. For some speakers, the pronunciation may be different depending on the tone, sounding more like English **are** in tones two and four, and more like English **err** in Tone Three.*

Pronunciation Exercise A-57

1. ér "and"	**2. ěr** "ear" [BF]	**3. èr** "two"

There is a small number of additional initials and finals that do not fit into the framework above, for example, -**em** as in **shémme** "what," which is an assimilated form of -**en** through influence from the following **m**; -**am** as in **zámmen** "we," which is an assimilated form of -**an**, also through influence from the following **m**; and the interjections **m**, **ng**, and **o**. Note that not all initials can be combined with all finals. For information on the possible initial-final combinations, refer to Table 1 ("Basic Syllables of Mandarin") on the next pages.

* Since the final **er** happens not to occur in Tone One, examples in other tones have had to be chosen.

Tones

Every regularly stressed syllable in Mandarin is pronounced in one of four different tones. Actually, you have already been using one of these tones, Tone One, for most of the examples in the pronunciation exercises for the initials and finals above. Tone in Chinese refers to a characteristic pitch pattern which accompanies the pronunciation of the whole syllable. The tone of a Chinese syllable is as much a part of the syllable as are the consonants and vowels. Two syllables with the same initials and finals but with different tones are likely to have completely different meanings. For example, take the three verbs **wèn** "ask," **wén** "smell," and **wěn** "kiss." American students who mispronounce **Wǒ wèn nǐ** "I ask you" as **Wǒ wén nǐ** "I smell you" or **Wǒ wěn nǐ** "I kiss you" are apt to leave a rather curious impression on their Chinese interlocutors!

Sometimes American students who have trouble carrying a tune and believe themselves to be "tone deaf" wonder if they will be able to learn the Chinese tones. They should rest assured that there are also many "tone deaf" Chinese who may not be able to sing very well and yet speak Chinese completely normally. Actually, the same Americans who call themselves "tone deaf" with few exceptions use perfectly normal intonation when speaking English, so there really should not be a problem. The tone system of Mandarin consists not of fixed notes on a scale but rather of relationships between tones. The actual pitch of each of the four tones varies considerably depending on such factors as the speakers' voice range, sex, age, emotional state, and physical condition. What matters is relative pitch, i.e., the pitch of the four tones in relation to each other in the speech of a particular speaker.

Table 1: Basic Syllables of Mandarin

INITIALS											FINALS	
	-a	-ai	-an	-ang	-ao	-e	-ei	-en	-eng	-er	-i	-ia
(zero)	a	ai	an	ang	ao	e	ei	en		er		
b-	ba	bai	ban	bang	bao		bei	ben	beng		bi	
c-	ca	cai	can	cang	cao	ce		cen	ceng		ci	
ch-	cha	chai	chan	chang	chao	che		chen	cheng		chi	
d-	da	dai	dan	dang	dao	de	dei		deng		di	
f-	fa		fan	fang			fei	fen	feng			
g-	ga	gai	gan	gang	gao	ge	gei	gen	geng			
h-	ha	hai	han	hang	hao	he	hei	hen	heng			
j-											ji	jia
k-	ka	kai	kan	kang	kao	ke	kei	ken	keng			
l-	la	lai	lan	lang	lao	le	lei		leng		li	lia
m-	ma	mai	man	mang	mao	me	mei	men	meng		mi	
n-	na	nai	nan	nang	nao	ne	nei	nen	neng		ni	
p-	pa	pai	pan	pang	pao		pei	pen	peng		pi	
q-											qi	qia
r-			ran	rang	rao	re		ren	reng		ri	
s-	sa	sai	san	sang	sao	se		sen	seng		si	
sh-	sha	shai	shan	shang	shao	she	shei	shen	sheng		shi	
t-	ta	tai	tan	tang	tao	te			teng		ti	
w-	wa	wai	wan	wang			wei	wen	weng			
x-											xi	xia
y-	ya		yan	yang	yao	ye					yi	
z-	za	zai	zan	zang	zao	ze	zei	zen	zeng		zi	
zh-	zha	zhai	zhan	zhang	zhao	zhe	zhei	zhen	zheng		zhi	

Table 1: Basic Syllables of Mandarin (cont.)

INITIALS	-ian	-iang	-iao	-ie	-in	-ing	-iong	-iu	-o	-ong	-ou
(zero)									o		ou
b-	bian		biao	bie	bin	bing			bo		
c-										cong	cou
ch-										chong	chou
d-	dian		diao	die		ding		diu		dong	dou
f-									fo		fou
g-										gong	gou
h-										hong	hou
j-	jian	jiang	jiao	jie	jin	jing	jiong	jiu			
k-										kong	kou
l-	lian	liang	liao	lie	lin	ling		liu	lo	long	lou
m-	mian		miao	mie	min	ming		miu	mo		mou
n-	nian	niang	niao	nie	nin	ning		niu		nong	nou
p-	pian		piao	pie	pin	ping			po		pou
q-	qian	qiang	qiao	qie	qin	qing	qiong	qiu			
r-			rong	rou							
s-			song	sou							
sh-			shou								
t-	tian		tiao	tie		ting				tong	tou
w-									wo		
x-	xian	xiang	xiao	xie	xin	xing	xiong	xiu			
y-					yin	ying			yo	yong	you
z-										zong	zou
zh-										zhong	zhou

INITIALS	-u	-ua	-uai	-uan	-uang	-ue	-ui	-un	-uo	-ü	-üe
(zero)											
b-	bu										
c-	cu			cuan			cui	cun	cuo		
ch-	chu	chua	chuai	chuan	chuang		chui	chun	chuo		
d-	du			duan			dui	dun	duo		
f-	fu										
g-	gu	gua	guai	guan	guang		gui	gun	guo		
h-	hu	hua	huai	huan	huang		hui	hun	huo		
j-	ju			juan		jue		jun			
k-	ku	kua	kuai	kuan	kuang		kui	kun	kuo		
l-	lu			luan				lun	luo	lü	lüe
m-	mu										
n-	nu			nuan					nuo	nü	nüe
p-	pu										
q-	qu			quan		que		qun			
r-	ru			ruan			rui	run	ruo		
s-	su			suan			sui	sun	suo		
sh-	shu	shua	shuai	shuan	shuang		shui	shun	shuo		
t-	tu			tuan			tui	tun	tuo		
w-	wu										
x-	xu			xuan		xue		xun			
y-	yu			yuan		yue		yun			
z-	zu			zuan			zui	zun	zuo		
zh-	zhu	zhua	zhuai	zhuan	zhuang		zhui	zhun	zhuo		

In Hanyu Pinyin transcription, tones are indicated with diacritical marks which are written over the main vowel of a syllable, for example: **mā má mǎ mà**. The tone marks are iconic, meaning they are a "picture" of what they represent (since the high and level line ¯ represents the high and level Tone One, the high rising line ´ represents the high rising Tone Two, and so on). You need not learn this now but, for your future reference, the rules for determining on which vowel the tone mark is placed are as follows:

1. If there is only one vowel in a syllable, it is the main vowel and the tone mark is placed over it.

2. If there is more than one vowel, the first vowel in the syllable is considered the main vowel, except when **i**, **u**, or **ü** is the first vowel, in which case the second vowel is considered the main vowel.

3. When a tone mark is placed over the vowel **i**, the dot over the **i** is dropped. Examples: ī í ǐ ì

The four tones of Mandarin are described below and are illustrated in the diagrams in Figure 2 on the next page. Even though the tones have by convention been ordered in a certain way, from one to four, this may actually not be the best order in which to practice them. Therefore, students should carefully work their way through Contrastive Pronunciation Exercises B-1 to B-25, which have been designed so as to contrast various tones with each other. One general word of advice when it comes to tones: try to widen your voice range! You should try to make the highs higher, and the lows lower, than in your normal English voice range.

TONE ONE: HIGH LEVEL

Tone One has a steady high pitch and is average in length. It is pronounced at or near the top of your comfortable speaking voice range. Be sure to maintain the high level pitch from the beginning to the end of the syllable, without wavering until you are finished. Tone One is indicated by a straight line over the main vowel of the syllable: ¯. Be sure to make Tone One high enough, and be sure to keep it level. American students of Mandarin tend to relax and drop their voice at the end of this tone, making it sound similar to Tone Four.

 Pronunciation Exercise A-58

1. bāo "wrap"	**3. mā** "mother"	**5. qiān** "thousand"	**7. yī** "one"
2. gāng "just"	**4. Ōu** "Europe" [BF]	**6. shān** "mountain"	**8. Zhāng** (surname)

TONE TWO: HIGH RISING

Tone Two begins at about the middle of the voice range and rises rapidly to the top. It is average in length and increases in loudness as it rises. Tone Two is indicated by a rising mark on the main vowel of the syllable: ´. Don't start Tone Two too low, and be sure to emphasize the climb up.

 Pronunciation Exercise A-59

1. bái "white"	**3. máng** "busy"	**5. néng** "can"	**7. shí** "ten"
2. báo "thin"	**4. nán** "difficult"	**6. shéi** "who"	**8. wán** "finish"

TONE THREE: LOW DIPPING

Tone Three starts low, dips even lower to the bottom of the voice range, where it stays for a while, and then rises quickly above the middle of the pitch range. Speakers often omit the the final rise. The low part of this tone is emphasized, both in length and in pitch. Tone Three has greater than average length. Tone Three is indicated by a falling and rising mark over the main vowel of the syllable: ˇ. Be sure to make Tone Three low enough. Don't try too hard to produce the initial dip; just start as low as you can and the dip will take care of itself.

Figure 2: The Four Tones of Mandarin

TONE ONE: High Level	TONE TWO: High Rising	TONE THREE: Low Dipping	TONE FOUR: High Falling

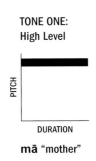
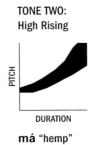
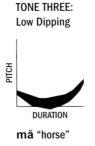
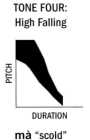

mā "mother"   má "hemp"   mǎ "horse"   mà "scold"

In these diagrams, the vertical dimension stands for pitch, with the top of each diagram slightly above the normal pitch range in English and the bottom slightly below. The horizontal dimension stands for duration, with the thickness of the tone curve representing loudness.

 Pronunciation Exercise A-60

1. gǒu "dog"   **3. jǐn** "tight"   **5. nǐ** "you"   **7. wǎn** "bowl"
2. hǎo "good"   **4. mǎ** "horse"   **6. qǐng** "invite"   **8. zhǎng** "grow"

TONE FOUR: HIGH FALLING

Tone Four starts at the top of the voice range and falls sharply to the bottom, diminishing in loudness as it falls. It has shorter than average length. Tone Four is indicated by a falling mark over the main vowel of the syllable: ` . Be sure to start Tone Four high enough and let it fall all the way down. In English, we often use this intonation in imperatives such as "Quick!" or when emphatically answering a ridiculous question with "No!".

 Pronunciation Exercise A-61

1. bào "newspaper"   **3. gèng** "even more"   **5. shì** "be"   **7. xìn** "letter"
2. èr "two"   **4. mà** "scold"   **6. wàn** "10,000"   **8. xìng** "surname"

NEUTRAL TONE

In normal Mandarin conversation, there is a fairly large number of unstressed syllables which are spoken in a weak and hurried manner and which have no discernible tone of their own. Such syllables, which bear no tone mark of any kind, are commonly referred to as being in the "neutral tone." Although you need not remember this, we will list here for your future reference the types of syllables which are typically in the neutral tone, along with some examples:

(1) sentence final particles (**a, ba, ne**)
(2) verb suffixes (**-guo, -le, -zhe**)
(3) noun and pronoun suffixes (**mùtou** "wood," **zhuōzi** "table," **wǒmen** "we")
(4) suffixes on question words and adverbs (**duōme** "how," **shémme** "what," **zèmme** "so")
(5) reduplicated syllables (**kànkan** "look")
(6) resultative complements (**dǎkai** "open," **jìnqu** "go in")
(7) infixed syllables (**shuōyishuō** "say," **tīngbudǒng** "can't understand")
(8) localizers (**dìshang** "on the ground," **jiāli** "at home")
(9) the second syllable of kinship terms (**dìdi** "younger brother," **jiějie** "older sister," **shūshu** "uncle")
(10) pronoun objects (**jiào ta huílai** "tell her to return")

In addition, there is a rather large number of common colloquial words in which the second syllable is neutral tone. In this text, all neutral tones will be so indicated. You should learn neutral tone syllables as you learn the words in which they occur.

Neutral tones are to some extent used in all dialects of Mandarin but are especially common in the speech of Beijing and other parts of North China. Speakers from southern China tend to use fewer neutral tones, especially as concerns the second syllable of two-syllable words. Use of neutral tones is also related to rate of speech and degree of formality. For example, more neutral tones would be used in an informal chat between close friends than in a formal lecture or when repeating something for someone who did not understand the first time. Or again, in the careful speech of a language teacher speaking to foreign students in the classroom, there would tend to be fewer neutral tones than when that same teacher returns to the office to chat with a Chinese colleague. Please bear this in mind if you notice discrepancies among the transcription, the audio recordings, and your instructor(s). While there are some cases where use of the neutral tone is mandatory (e.g., final particles), in many other cases it is optional. For your Chinese to sound fluent and natural, it is important for you to pay attention to and imitate the neutral tones in your instructor's speech and the speech on the accompanying recordings.

Although neutral tone syllables have no tone, they do have pitch. The pitch of neutral tone syllables is influenced mainly by the tone of the preceding syllable, so it is important to notice the pitch positions of neutral tone syllables relative to the preceding tone (cf. Figure 3 below).

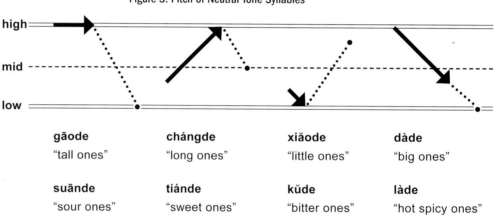

Figure 3: Pitch of Neutral Tone Syllables

| gāode | chángde | xiǎode | dàde |
| "tall ones" | "long ones" | "little ones" | "big ones" |

| suānde | tiánde | kǔde | làde |
| "sour ones" | "sweet ones" | "bitter ones" | "hot spicy ones" |

Generally speaking, after Tone One, Tone Two, and Tone Four, a neutral tone syllable drops to a fairly low pitch. After Tone Three, a neutral tone syllable jumps up to a fairly high pitch. Remember that, unlike syllables in one of the regular four tones, neutral tone syllables are never stressed and always spoken very lightly. The pitch of neutral tones is also affected to some degree by the tone of the syllable that follows, which may move the neutral tone in the direction of the start of the following tone.

In neutral tone syllables, the normally voiceless initials **b**, **d**, and **g** are sometimes voiced. For example, the **b** in **Zǒu ba** "Let's go!" may sound like an English voiced **b**. The vowels of neutral tone syllables are shorter, laxer, and more centralized than in syllables with tones.

Pronunciation Exercise A-62: Tone One + Neutral Tone
1. māma "mom"   **3. shuōzhe** "talking"   **5. wūzi** "room"
2. shūle "has lost"   **4. tāde** "hers"   **6. xiānsheng** "mister"

Pronunciation Exercise A-63: Tone Two + Neutral Tone
1. bízi "nose"   **3. niánji** "age"   **5. shéide** "whose?"
2. láile "has come"   **4. péngyou** "friend"   **6. Wáng jia** "the Wangs"

Pronunciation Exercise A-64: Tone Three + Neutral Tone
1. hǎode "O.K."   **3. liǎngge** "two of them"   **5. yǐzi** "chair"
2. hǎo ma "O.K.?"   **4. wǒmen** "we"   **6. zǒule** "has gone"

Pronunciation Exercise A-65: Tone Four + Neutral Tone
1. lèile "has become tired"   **3. qù ba** "let's go"   **5. shìde** "yes"
2. mèimei "younger sister"   **4. sìge** "four of them"   **6. zhànzhe** "standing"

TONE CHANGES

When certain tones occur directly before certain other tones, their tones change in fairly predictable ways. Although this may seem difficult and confusing at first, you will get used to these changes within a few weeks and they will soon become automatic for you. There are three major tone changes:

1. When a Tone Three syllable occurs directly before a syllable in Tone One, Tone Two, Tone Four or before most neutral tones, it loses its final rise and remains low throughout. The changed tone is then called a Half Tone Three. Note that in terms of overall frequency of occurrence, the Half Tone Three is actually more common than the unchanged, full Tone Three, which normally occurs only in isolation or at the end of a sentence or phrase followed by a pause. Thus it is very important that students pronounce Half Tone Three correctly.

 Pronunciation Exercise A-66: Half Tone Three
1. mǎi + shū = mǎi shū "buy books"
2. mǎi + xié = mǎi xié "buy shoes"
3. mǎi + cài = mǎi cài "buy groceries"
4. mǎi + le = mǎile "has bought"

2. When a Tone Three syllable occurs directly before another Tone Three syllable, the first Tone Three syllable changes to Tone Two. It is then called a Raised Tone Three.[*]

 Pronunciation Exercise A-67: Raised Tone Three
1. hěn + lǎo = hěn lǎo "very old"
2. gǎn + jǐn = gǎnjǐn "quickly"
3. mǎi + bǐ = mǎi bǐ "buy pens"
4. nǐ + hǎo = nǐ hǎo "how are you"

3. In the speech of many speakers, when two Tone Four syllables follow each other in close succession, the first receives lighter stress than the second. The tone of the first Tone Four syllable often does not fall all the way to the bottom of the pitch range but only to the middle. It is then called a Half Tone Four.

 Pronunciation Exercise A-68: Half Tone Four
1. dà + gài = dàgài "probably"
2. guì + xìng = guìxìng "what's your last name?"
3. tài + kuài = tài kuài "too fast"
4. zài + jiàn = zàijiàn "goodbye"

---

[*] When three or more Tone Three syllables come together in succession, the last syllable remains Tone Three, the next to last syllable changes to Tone Two, and the preceding Tone Three syllable(s) may either remain Tone Three or change to Tone Two depending on the speaker's preference and various grammatical and semantic factors. For example, **wǒ yě mǎi** "I'll also buy" could be either Tone Three + Tone Two + Tone Three or Tone Two + Tone Two + Tone Three. On the other hand, **lěng shuǐ zǎo** "cold water bath" can be only Tone Two + Tone Two + Tone Three, since it derives from **lěng shuǐ** "cold water."

The (r) Suffix

In the dialect of Beijing and many other Northern Chinese dialects, and to a lesser extent in standard Mandarin, some words end in a suffixed (**r**) which is attached to the ends of the finals listed previously. The (**r**) suffix may cause modifications in the vowels and consonants of those finals.

The (**r**) suffix sounds like the **-r** at the end of the Mandarin final **-er**, or much like the English word **are**. To pronounce the (**r**) suffix, draw back the tongue, at the same time turning the tip of the tongue upwards. The (**r**) suffix is always pronounced as part of the last syllable, not separately as a syllable of its own, even though in standard written Chinese it is written separately with its own character.*

The rules for pronouncing the (**r**) suffix finals are as follows:†

A. After **a**, **ao**, **e**, **ia**, **iao**, **iu**, **o**, **ou**, **ua**, **uo**, and **u** (except when **u** occurs after **j**, **q**, **x**, **y**): add **-r**.

Pronunciation Exercise A-69
1. **nà** "that" → **nàr** "there"
2. **xiǎodāo** → **xiǎodāor** "small knife"
3. **kàn yixia** → **kàn yixiar** "take a look"
4. **niǎo** → **niǎor** "bird"
5. **dǎqiú** → **dǎqiúr** "play ball"
6. **shānpō** → **shānpōr** "mountain slope"
7. **xiǎotōu** → **xiǎotōur** "thief"
8. **huà** "paint" → **huàr** "painting"
9. **xiǎoshuō** → **xiǎoshuōr** "novel"
10. **báitù** → **báitùr** "white rabbit"

B. After **u** (when **u** occurs after **j**, **q**, **x**, **y**) and after **i** (except when **i** occurs after **c**, **ch**, **s**, **sh**, **z**, **zh**): add **-er**.

Pronunciation Exercise A-70
1. **jīnjú** → **jīnjúr** "kumquat"
2. **yǒuqù** → **yǒuqùr** "interesting"
3. **yú** → **yúr** "fish"
4. **xiǎojī** → **xiǎojīr** "chick"
5. **xiǎomǐ** → **xiǎomǐr** "millet"
6. **pí** → **pír** "skin (of fruit)"

C. After **i** (when **i** occurs after **c**, **ch**, **s**, **sh**, **z**, **zh**): drop **i** and add **-er**.

Pronunciation Exercise A-71
1. **cì** → **cìr** "thorn"
2. **jùchǐ** → **jùchǐr** "tooth of a saw"
3. **ròusī** → **ròusīr** "meat shreds"
4. **méi shì** → **méi shìr** "never mind"
5. **guāzǐ** → **guāzǐr** "watermelon seed"
6. **guǒzhī** → **guǒzhīr** "fruit juice"

---

* There is some variation in the formation of the (**r**) suffix, depending on the subdialect of Mandarin spoken and the age of the speaker. Subtle differences in usage exist even from one district of Beijing to the next. For some speakers, there are differences depending on the tone of a syllable. However, these differences are all minor and relatively unimportant.

† The rules are given here for future reference. It is not necessary that you learn them; instead, learn words with the (**r**) suffix as they are introduced throughout the course. You will gradually develop a "feel" for how to form the **r**-suffix versions of the various basic syllables.

D. After **ai**, **uai**, **ei**, **ui**, **an**, **ian**, **en**, and **uan**: drop the final **i** or **n** and add **-r**.

Pronunciation Exercise A-72
1. **gài** "to cover" → **gàir** "a cover"
2. **yíkuài** "one dollar" → **yíkuàir** "together"
3. **xiāngwèi** → **xiāngwèir** "fragrant odor"
4. **qìshuǐ** → **qìshuǐr** "soda"
5. **duōbàn** → **duōbànr** "for the most part"
6. **yìdiǎn** → **yìdiǎnr** "a little"
7. **huāpén** → **huāpénr** "flower pot"
8. **fànguǎn** → **fànguǎnr** "restaurant"

E. After **in** and **un**: drop the **n** and add **-er**.

Pronunciation Exercise A-73
1. **méi jìn** → **méi jìnr** "have no energy"
2. **sòngxin** "deliver a letter" → **sòngxìnr** "deliver a message"
3. **huāqún** → **huāqúnr** "colored skirt"
4. **méi zhǔn** → **méi zhǔnr** "can't say for sure"

F. After **ng**: nasalize the vowel, drop the **ng**, and add **-r**.

Pronunciation Exercise A-74
1. **huāpíng** → **huāpíngr** "vase"
2. **xiàngyàng** → **xiàngyàngr** "decent"
3. **dàshēng** → **dàshēngr** "in a loud voice"
4. **yǒukòng** → **yǒukòngr** "have free time"

In listening to the accompanying audio recordings, you will have noted that the (**r**) suffix is simply added to some finals but absorbs, as it were, other finals. However, it is important to be aware that any phonetic changes caused by the addition of the (**r**) suffix are not indicated in the transcription. Words are spelled with the basic form of the final followed by an **-r**, regardless of whether or not the pronunciation of the final is modified by the **-r**. For example, we write **gēnr**, **shìr**, and **xiǎoháir**, even though these words are actually pronounced **gēr**, **shèr**, and **xiǎohár**. It will be clear from the above that it is not always possible to relate a word heard with an (**r**) suffix back to its non-suffixed form without already knowing the word. The syllable **war**, for example, could derive from **wa**, **wai**, or **wan**.

The (**r**) suffix is used most commonly with nouns, especially familiar colloquial terms. It sometimes connotes smallness (e.g., **xiǎojīr** "chick"), but this is not uniformly true. While it is attached most often to nouns, it does occur with a few verbs and in some kinds of adverbial constructions (e.g., **wánr** "have fun," **hǎohāorde shuō** "say it nicely"). The (**r**) suffix can sometimes make free forms out of bound ones (e.g., **zhuō** cannot be said while **zhuōr** "table" can). Although most words have the same meaning whether or not they have the suffix (e.g., **dìfang** and **dìfangr** both mean "place"), there are other words where presence or absence of the (**r**) affects the meaning (e.g., **zhè** "this" vs. **zhèr** "here"). In Beijing speech, there are some words which always have (**r**) (e.g., **yìhuǐr** "a little while"), some words with an optional (**r**) (e.g., **shíhour** "time"), and yet other words which never take the (**r**) suffix. You will need to learn whether a word takes, or can take, the **r**-suffix as you learn new vocabulary.*

Use or non-use of the (**r**) suffix is related to a number of rather complex sociolinguistic factors with which you should gradually try to become familiar:

---

* In this course, an optional (**r**) suffix is indicated by means of parentheses around the **r**, e.g., **shíhou(r)** "time." This means that this word can be pronounced as either **shíhou** or **shíhour**.

1. The (r) suffix is much more common in speech than in writing.

2. The (r) suffix is more common in informal conversation among family and friends than in formal speech such as in public lectures.

3. The (r) suffix is more common in Beijing and other parts of North China than in the rest of the country. Chinese from other parts of China often can't pronounce it correctly. The degree of **r**-ness may also vary depending on the dialect background of the speaker. Many speakers in the western and southern parts of China, including Taiwan, make little or no use of the (r) suffix.

4. In Beijing and environs, the (r) suffix is somewhat less common in the speech of intellectuals than among the less educated masses, especially those who come from the surrounding countryside.

At any point in a conversation, a speaker has the option of more or less use of the (r) suffix, which will have certain implications for the impression he or she makes upon listeners. Overuse of (r) may come across as expressing group solidarity with people from Beijing, as somewhat less intellectual and, in areas where (r) is not used, possibly as snobbish or effeminate. Modest use of (r) tends to give the impression that one speaks very standard Mandarin. Non-use of the suffix helps identify one as a regional dialect speaker.

ADVICE TO THE LEARNER

All you need to know for now is that the (r) suffix exists and how to pronounce it. Learn words with the (r) suffix as they come up during the course. Imitate the usage of your teacher and that of the speakers in the accompanying materials (don't worry if there are some discrepancies, this is to be expected). Do not add the (r) suffix to a word unless you have heard that word pronounced with the (r) suffix before.

Be aware that if you are in a part of China where the (r) suffix is seldom used, such as Taipei or Guangzhou, and you make excessive use of the (r) suffix, you may create distance between yourself and your interlocutors. While people will probably praise you for your excellent Beijing pronunciation, you may impress some of them as trying to "put on airs" or as a "Beijing chauvinist." If you are a male, you may also come across as somewhat effeminate to some listeners. On the other hand, when in Beijing and environs, frequent use of the (r) suffix will make your speech seem especially authentic and pleasing to the ears of those who hear you. So, try to adjust your speech to that of your interlocutors, either increasing or reducing your use of the (r) suffix depending on the circumstances and the impression you want to make.

If you have prior knowledge of Chinese acquired through contact with Chinese speakers from Western or Southern China including Taiwan and Hong Kong, then the (r) suffix may be new for you and may even sound "unnatural." On the one hand, you should be aware that this suffix is used with great frequency by northern Chinese and that it is considered characteristic of the most prestigious kind of spoken Chinese. Do learn how to pronounce it and become familiar with the sociolinguistic factors discussed above. On the other hand, it is also true that hundreds of millions of Mandarin speakers make minimal or no use of the (r) suffix and encounter no particular difficulties in communication. Therefore, if you feel very uncomfortable using (r) and don't mind being perceived as a "Southerner" or "Westerner" who speaks a regional variant of Mandarin, you needn't overly concern yourself with using this suffix in your own speech. You will, however, need to be able to understand it when others use it.

Transcriptional Conventions

The purpose of the following section is to explain transcriptional conventions employed in this course. As widespread use of Pinyin romanization is still relatively recent, there is not yet complete agreement about some of the details about how Pinyin is to be written. For our purposes, Pinyin is not a writing system for Chinese (only the characters are that) but rather a tool to help native English-speaking students learn spoken Chinese. With that in mind, the information below is for reference only; mastery of this material is not necessary to learn spoken Chinese well.

PUNCTUATION

In the Pinyin transcription, we follow the generally accepted rules of English punctuation. In standard written Chinese, as you will see in the accompanying volume *Basic Written Chinese*, punctuation is generally similar to English but differs in some details.

CAPITALIZATION

In the transcription, we follow the generally accepted rules for English capitalization, including the capitalization of personal and place names, titles, names of organizations, and the capitalization of the first letter of every sentence.

USE OF SPACE TO INDICATE WORD BOUNDARIES

As in standard English orthography, word boundaries in the transcription are generally indicated by space (as well as, in some cases, by punctuation and capitalization). However, what exactly constitutes a word is not so easy to define in Chinese. The standard Chinese writing system can offer us little help in this regard since, with few exceptions, it does not employ spacing to indicate word boundaries. This is why in China one sometimes encounters signs with romanizations like WENHUAYUJIAOYUJIE for what we would write in this book as **Wénhuà Yǔ Jiàoyù Jiē** "Culture and Education Street."

The principles we have followed in this text for determining word boundaries are as follows:

1. What must always be said together, or must be said together to retain the intended meaning, is written together; what can be said alone with the intended meaning is written apart. Take the word **lǎoshī** "teacher." One could never say in isolation the syllable **shī**. While one could say **lǎo** "old" alone, the meaning would be different. On the other hand, in the sentence **Tā shi lǎoshī** "She is the teacher," the words **tā** "she" and **shì** "to be" can be said alone and retain the intended meaning.

2. Verb-object compounds where the object consists of only one syllable and where verb and object combine to represent a generalized idea are written together (**chīfàn** "eat," **kànshū** "read"). When the object is more specific (**chī ròu** "eat meat," **kàn rén** "look at people") or when the verb and object are separated by other elements (**kàn hěn duō hǎokànde shū** "read a lot of good books"), the verb and object are written separately.

3. Two-syllable family names and two-syllable given names are written together (**Sīmǎ Qiān, Dèng Xiǎopíng**).

4. The particle **-de** is always written attached to the preceding syllable, even when it refers in part to previous elements of a phrase or sentence (**wǒde shū** "my books," **zuótiān wǎnshang bādiǎn zhōng láide nèige rén** "the person who came at 8:00 last night"). Writing **-de** attached to the previous syllable reflects the linguistic fact that in speech, **-de** is never said alone but is always attached to the previous syllable.

5. In borderline cases, we favor joining syllables together, since this speeds up writing or typing and saves space.

USE OF THE HYPHEN

In some set expressions from Classical Chinese, a hyphen is used between syllables to make the meaning more transparent, e.g., **dōng-nuǎn-xià-liáng** "warm in winter and cool in summer." A hyphen is also used between elements each of which is a one-syllable abbreviation, e.g., **Hàn-Yīng zìdiǎn** "Chinese-English dictionary," **Zhōng-Měi Màoyì Gōngsī** "Sino-American Trading Company." Finally, a hyphen is used in the case of years, e.g., **èr-líng-líng-jiǔ-nián** "the year 2009."

USE OF THE APOSTROPHE TO INDICATE SYLLABLE BOUNDARIES

In words of more than one syllable, there occasionally arise combinations of letters—typically involving vowels, the consonant **n**, or the combination **ng**—where the correct syllable division may not be clear. To clarify where one syllable ends and the next begins and to prevent mispronunciations or ambiguities, the apostrophe (') is employed in such cases to indicate the correct syllable boundaries. For example, contrast **fā'nàn** "rise in revolt" with **fān'àn** "reverse a verdict." Without the apostrophe, both of these words, which sound different and have different meanings, would be written as **fānàn** and it would be unclear how to pronounce the syllables or which of the two words was meant. Examples from this volume: **Jiā'nádà** "Canada," **sān'ge** "three (items)," **Xī'ān** (name of a city).

INDICATION OF TONE CHANGES

In general, tone changes are not indicated, since they are predictable and can be heard on the accompanying audio recordings. Thus, while the combination **hěn** "very" + **hǎo** "good" is in fact pronounced as **hén hǎo**, we write it with the basic, unchanged tones as **hěn hǎo**.

   The main exception involves Tone Three syllables that are followed by other Tone Three syllables which have become neutral tone. In such cases, in some words the first syllable changes to Tone Two but in other words it does not change. Since such tone changes are not predictable, we indicate them. For example, the word for "miss" is composed of the underlying Tone Three syllables **xiǎo** + **jiě**. Since in this word the first syllable changes to Tone Two after which the second syllable loses its tone to become neutral tone, we write the word as **xiáojie**. On the other hand, consider the word for "older sister," which is also composed of two underlying Tone Three syllables **jiě** + **jiě**. In this word the first syllable remains Tone Three while the second syllable becomes neutral tone, so we write the word as **jiějie**.

   Since they are word-specific rather than involving a whole class of tones, any tone changes involving the four words **yī** "one," **qī** "seven," **bā** "eight," and **bù** "not" are always indicated as actually pronounced; for example, we write **bù mǎi** "not buy" but **bú qù** "not go." This will be explained at the time we take up these words in the lessons.

Pronunciation Exercises, Part B: Contrastive Pronunciation

TONES

Pronunciation Exercise B-1: Tone One vs. Tone Three

Be sure to make Tone One high enough and Tone Three low enough. "Stretch" your voice so as to accommodate these two extremes.

1. bēi "cup", **běi** "north"   **3. gān** "dry", **gǎn** "dare"
2. dēng "light", **děng** "wait"   **4. wā** "dig", **wǎ** "tile"

Pronunciation Exercise B-2: Tone Two vs. Tone Four

Be sure to make Tone Two go up high enough, and be careful to start Tone Four on high enough a pitch before making it fall from high to low.

1. huáng "yellow", **huàng** "sway"   **3. tán** "discuss", **tàn** "sigh"
2. láo "firm", **lào** "bake"   **4. tú** "picture", **tù** "spit"

Pronunciation Exercise B-3: Tone One vs. Tone Four

Be sure Tone One is high enough, and be careful to make Tone Four fall down all the way.

1. cuī "hasten", **cuì** "crisp"   **3. sī** "silk", **sì** "four"
2. kān "care for", **kàn** "look"   **4. xīng** "putrid", **xìng** "surname"

Pronunciation Exercise B-4: Tone Three vs. Tone Four

Be sure to make Tone Three low enough and be sure to make Tone Four start high enough.

1. gǒu "dog", **gòu** "enough"
2. liǎn "face", **liàn** "practice"

3. liǎng "two", **liàng** "bright"
4. tǎ "pagoda", **tà** "tread"

 Pronunciation Exercise B-5: Tone One vs. Tone Two

Start Tone One high enough and keep it level; start Tone Two below the level of Tone One but then make it rapidly rise above it.

1. fēng "wind", **féng** "meet"
2. huā "flower", **huá** "slippery"

3. pī "comment", **pí** "leather"
4. shēn "deep", **shén** "god"

 Pronunciation Exercise B-6: Tone Two vs. Tone Three

Be sure to make Tone Two go up high enough and be careful to make Tone Three low enough.

1. bá "uproot", **bǎ** "take"
2. bái "white", **bǎi** "hundred"

3. tóng "same", **tǒng** "bucket"
4. yuán "round", **yuǎn** "far"

 Pronunciation Exercise B-7: Tones One, Two, Three, and Four

1. liū "sneak away", **liú** "keep", **liǔ** "willow" [BF], **liù** "six"
2. mā "mother", **má** "hemp", **mǎ** "horse", **mà** "scold"
3. suī "although", **suí** "follow", **suǐ** "marrow" [BF], **suì** "year of age"
4. tāng "soup", **táng** "sugar", **tǎng** "lie down", **tàng** "scalding"
5. wān "bend", **wán** "play", **wǎn** "bowl", **wàn** "10,000"
6. yāo "waist", **yáo** "shake", **yǎo** "bite", **yào** "want"
7. yōu "swing", **yóu** "oil", **yǒu** "have", **yòu** "again"

TONAL COMBINATIONS

For regularly stressed two-syllable words, there is a total of sixteen possible combinations of tones. Since the majority of Chinese words is composed of two syllables, mastery of the following sixteen tone patterns will greatly facilitate your correct pronunciation of the majority of the Chinese vocabulary.

 Pronunciation Exercise B-8: Tone One + Tone One

Be sure that Tone One is high enough, and keep it level.

1. dāochā "knife and fork"
2. gāozhōng "high school"

3. kāifā "developed"
4. kāiguān "control"

5. sānzhāng "three of them"
6. shūzhuō "desk"

 Pronunciation Exercise B-9: Tone One + Tone Two

Keep Tone One high and level, then push Tone Two up high enough.

1. bāngmáng "help"
2. fāmíng "invent"

3. huānyíng "welcome"
4. kāimén "open door"

5. tiāntáng "heaven"
6. Yīngwén "English"

Pronunciation Exercise B-10: Tone One + Tone Three

Be sure to make Tone One high enough, and be careful not to drop the pitch of Tone One as you get ready for Tone Three.

1. dōngběi "northeast"   **3. qiānbǐ** "pencil"   **5. tīngxiě** "dictation"
2. gānghǎo "just"   **4. shūfǎ** "calligraphy"   **6. Zhōng-Měi** "Sino-American"

 Pronunciation Exercise B-11: Tone One + Tone Four

Keep Tone One high and level, then let Tone Four fall its full length.

1. dōu yào "want all"   **3. sāncì** "three times"   **5. tīnghuà** "obey"
2. jīròu "chicken meat"   **4. tāngmiàn** "soup noodles" **6. zhēnzhèng** "real"

 Pronunciation Exercise B-12: Tone Two + Tone One

Push Tone Two up high enough to the level where you begin Tone One, being careful to keep Tone One high and level.

1. fángjiān "room"   **3. nánfāng** "south"   **5. shuí shuō** "who says?"
2. huíjiā "return home"   **4. pángtīng** "audit"   **6. shítiān** "ten days"

 Pronunciation Exercise B-13: Tone Two + Tone Two

Be sure to make both of the Tone Two syllables go high enough; and be careful to start the second Tone Two low enough.

1. chángcháng "often"   **3. míngnián** "next year"   **5. yínháng** "bank"
2. hái méi "not yet"   **4. shuí lái** "who's coming?" **6. yóutiáo** "cruller"

 Pronunciation Exercise B-14: Tone Two + Tone Three

Make Tone Two rise high enough, and make Tone Three low enough.

1. hái hǎo "O.K."   **3. máobǐ** "writing brush"   **5. shíběn** "ten volumes"
2. lián nǐ "even you"   **4. méi mǎi** "didn't buy it" **6. xuézhě** "scholar"

 Pronunciation Exercise B-15: Tone Two + Tone Four

Push Tone Two all the way to the top, then let Tone Four come crashing down.

1. báicài "cabbage"   **3. shuí yào** "who wants it?" **5. tóngyì** "agree"
2. bú zài "not present"   **4. táonàn** "flee"   **6. xuéhuì** "learn"

 Pronunciation Exercise B-16: Tone Three + Tone One

Drop all the way down on Tone Three without rising; then start high enough for Tone One and keep it level.

1. hǎochī "good-tasting"   **3. jiǎndān** "simple"   **5. měitiān** "every day"
2. hěn jiān "very sharp"   **4. mǎi shū** "buy books"   **6. wǎn'ān** "good evening"

 Pronunciation Exercise B-17: Tone Three + Tone Two

Make sure Tone Three dips all the way down before beginning the upward climb of Tone Two.

1. dǎ rén "hit someone"   **3. hǎowánr** "be fun"   **5. wǎngqiú** "tennis"
2. gěi shuí "give whom?"   **4. liǎngnián** "two years"   **6. yǒuqián** "rich"

Pronunciation Exercise B-18: Tone Three + Tone Three

Keep in mind that Tone Three changes to Tone Two before another Tone Three syllable.

1. dǎdǎo "knock down"   **3. lǎo mǎ** "old horses"   **5. shǒubiǎo** "watch"
2. hěn zǎo "very early"   **4. lěng shuǐ** "cold water"   **6. yǒnggǎn** "brave"

 Pronunciation Exercise B-19: Tone Three + Tone Four

Dip all the way down for Tone Three without rising. Then start at the top of your pitch range for Tone Four and come crashing down.

1. hǎokàn "good-looking"   **3. lǐbài** "week"   **5. mǎshàng** "immediately"
2. hěn huài "very bad"   **4. mǎlù** "paved road"   **6. zǎofàn** "breakfast"

 Pronunciation Exercise B-20: Tone Four + Tone One

After the drop of Tone Four, be sure to make Tone One high and level.

1. dìyī "number one"   **3. qìchē** "car"   **5. zài jiā** "at home"
2. kànshū "read"   **4. tài hēi** "too black"   **6. zuì gāo** "tallest"

 Pronunciation Exercise B-21: Tone Four + Tone Two

Let Tone Four drop all the way down before beginning the upward rise of Tone Two (don't let Tone Four sound like Tone One!). Also, be sure Tone Two goes up high enough, lest it be confused with Tone Three.

1. fànhér "lunch box"   **3. pèihé** "coordinate"   **5. xiàngyá** "ivory"
2. kuài lái "come quick"   **4. tài tián** "too sweet"   **6. zuì máng** "busiest"

 Pronunciation Exercise B-22: Tone Four + Tone Three

Let Tone Four come crashing down, then concentrate on the low part of Tone Three, concluding with a slight rise.

1. dàxiǎo "size"   **3. ròubǐng** "meat pancake"   **5. xiàxuě** "snow"
2. fùmǔ "parents"   **4. tài zǎo** "too early"   **6. zhìshǎo** "at least"

 Pronunciation Exercise B-23: Tone Four + Tone Four

Remember that when two Tone Four syllables are pronounced in succession, the first one falls only about halfway down. But be careful not to make the first Tone Four sound like Tone One.

1. bànshì "do things" **3. tài lèi** "too tired"   **5. zhùzhòng** "emphasize"
2. diànhuà "phone"   **4. zàijiàn** "goodbye"   **6. zuìhòu** "in the end"

 Pronunciation Exercise B-24: Some Common Phrases Containing the Four Tones
   1. fānqié chǎodàn "fried eggs with tomatoes"
   2. duō dú jǐbiàn "read a few more times"
   3. fēiqínzǒushòu "birds and beasts"
   4. pīpíng tǎolùn "criticize and discuss"
   5. Sān Huáng Wǔ Dì "The Three Emperors and Five Rulers"
   6. Sān Mín Zhǔyì "The Three People's Principles"
   7. shēnmóuyuǎnlǜ "circumspect and farsighted"
   8. xīqí gǔguài "strange and curious"
   9. xīnqíng kǔmèn "in a depressed mood"
10. xīnzhíkǒukuài "blunt and outspoken"

11. **yīliáo bǎojiàn** "medical health care"
12. **yīngxióng hǎohàn** "heroes and other brave people"
13. **zāiqíng cǎnzhòng** "a terrible disaster"

Pronunciation Exercise B-25: Some Examples of Tone Contrasts
1. **bú duì** "not correct", **bùduì** "troops"
2. **bǔkǎo** "make up an exam", **bù kǎo** "not take an exam"
3. **dàishǔ** "kangaroo", **dàishù** "algebra"
4. **Dōngjīng** "Tokyo", **dòngjìng** "movement"
5. **fánghuǒ** "prevent fire", **fànghuǒ** "set on fire"
6. **gānbēi** "cheers!", **gānbèi** "scallop"
7. **gūlì** "isolate", **gǔlì** "encourage"
8. **Gǔwén** "Classical Chinese", **gùwèn** "adviser"
9. **hǎidǎo** "island", **hǎidào** "pirate"
10. **Hányǔ** "Korean language", **Hànyǔ** "Chinese language"
11. **huǒchē** "train", **huòchē** "freight train"
12. **huīzhāng** "insignia", **huìzhǎng** "club president"
13. **jiēfang** "neighbor", **jiěfàng** "liberate"
14. **júzi** "tangerine", **jùzi** "sentence"
15. **kǎnshù** "cut down trees", **kànshū** "read"
16. **kěqì** "annoying", **kèqi** "polite"
17. **liánxì** "contact", **liànxí** "exercise"
18. **lòushuǐ** "leak", **lòushuì** "evade taxes"
19. **núlì** "slave", **nǔlì** "exert effort"
20. **qíchē** "ride a bicycle", **qìchē** "car"
21. **Shāndōng** (name of a province), **shāndòng** "cave"
22. **Shānxī** (name of a province), **Shǎnxī** (name of another province)
23. **shōupiàoyuán** "ticket collector", **shòupiàoyuán** "ticket seller"
24. **sīrén** "private", **sǐrén** "dead person"
25. **sōngshǔ** "squirrel", **sōngshù** "pine tree"
26. **tōngzhī** "notify", **tóngzhì** "comrade"
27. **xiāngjiāo** "banana", **xiàngjiāo** "rubber"
28. **zhíyuán** "employee", **zhìyuàn** "wish"
29. **zìmǔ** "letter of the alphabet", **zìmù** "subtitle"
30. **zhōngshí** "faithful", **zhòngshì** "attach importance to"
31. **Zhōngyào** "Chinese medicine", **zhòngyào** "important"

Pronunciation Exercise B-26: Full Tone vs. Neutral Tone
1. **dōngxī** "east and west", **dōngxi** "thing"
2. **jìnqū** "prohibited area", **jìnqu** "enter"
3. **lìhài** "advantage and disadvantage", **lìhai** "terrible"
4. **mùdì** "cemetery", **mùdi** "purpose"
5. **shétóu** "snake's head", **shétou** "tongue"
6. **shìlì** "vision", **shìli** "force"
7. **wénzì** "written symbols", **wénzi** "mosquito"
8. **xínglǐ** "salute", **xíngli** "luggage"
9. **yǎnjìng** "glasses", **yǎnjing** "eyes"
10. **tízì** "inscribe characters", **tízi** "hoof"

INITIALS

 Pronunciation Exercise B-27: **b** vs. **p**

Be sure to pronounce the **b** without voicing, and be sure to pronounce the **p** with a strong puff of breath.

1. **bà** "dad", **pà** "fear"
2. **bāo** "wrap", **pāo** "throw"
3. **bèi** "back", **pèi** "match"
4. **bèng** "hop", **pèng** "bump"
5. **bàwáng** "despot", **pà wáng** "fear the king"
6. **bǎole** "has eaten to her/his fill", **pǎole** "has run away"
7. **bízi** "nose", **pízi** "leather"

 Pronunciation Exercise B-28: **d** vs. **t**

Be sure to pronounce the **d** without voicing, and be sure to pronounce the **t** with a strong puff of breath.

1. **dà** "big", **tà** "couch"
2. **dào** "arrive", **tào** "set"
3. **dīng** "drive a nail", **tīng** "listen"
4. **dòng** "move", **tòng** "hurt"
5. **dízi** "flute", **tízi** "hoof"
6. **dùzi** "tummy", **tùzi** "rabbit"
7. **dúshū** "study", **túshū** "books"
8. **duìkuǎn** "exchange money", **tuìkuǎn** "return money"

 Pronunciation Exercise B-29: **g** vs. **k**

Be sure to pronounce the **g** without voicing, and be sure to pronounce the **k** with a strong puff of breath.

1. **gǎo** "do", **kǎo** "bake"
2. **gàn** "do", **kàn** "look"
3. **gè** "each", **kè** "engrave"
4. **gēng** "plough", **kēng** "pit"
5. **guài** "strange", **kuài** "fast"
6. **guò** "pass", **kuò** "rich"
7. **gǎizì** "correct characters", **kǎizì** "standard characters"
8. **bù gāi** "should not", **bù kāi** "not open"

 Pronunciation Exercise B-30: **j** vs. **q**

Be sure to pronounce the **j** without voicing, and be sure to pronounce the **q** with a strong puff of breath.

1. **jī** "chicken", **qī** "seven"
2. **jiān** "pointed", **qiān** "thousand"
3. **jiāng** "will", **qiāng** "rifle"
4. **jiáo** "chew", **qiáo** "bridge"
5. **jù** "phrase", **qù** "go"
6. **juān** "donate", **quān** "circle"

 Pronunciation Exercise B-31: **z** vs. **c**

Be sure to pronounce the **z** without voicing, and be sure to pronounce the **c** with a strong puff of breath.

1. **zǎn** "save", **cǎn** "tragic"

2. zǎo "early", **cǎo** "grass"

3. zài "again", **cài** "dish of food"

4. zì "character", **cì** "thorn"

5. zū "rent", **cū** "coarse"

6. zuì "drunk", **cuì** "brittle"

7. zìwèi "defend oneself", **cìwèi** "hedgehog"

 Pronunciation Exercise B-32: **zh** vs. **ch**

Be sure to pronounce the **zh** without voicing, and be sure to pronounce the **ch** with a strong puff of breath.

1. zhǎo "look for", **chǎo** "noisy"

2. zhàng "account", **chàng** "sing"

3. zhē "cover", **chē** "car"

4. zhū "pig", **chū** "out"

5. zhuō "grasp", **chuō** "stab"

6. zhuī "chase", **chuī** "blow"

7. zhǔn "accurate", **chǔn** "stupid"

 Pronunciation Exercise B-33: **s** vs. **sh**

1. sā "let go", **shā** "kill"

2. sǎo "sweep", **shǎo** "few"

3. sān "three", **shān** "mountain"

4. sāng "mulberry" [BF], **shāng** "wound"

5. sēn "forest" [BF], **shēn** "deep"

6. sēng "monk", **shēng** "give birth to"

7. sānjiǎo "triangle", **shānjiǎo** "foot of a mountain"

8. sīrén "private individual", **shīrén** "poet"

 Pronunciation Exercise B-34: **z** vs. **zh**

1. zǎo "early", **zhǎo** "look for"

2. zài "be present", **zhài** "debt"

3. zāng "dirty", **Zhāng** (surname)

4. zé "then", **zhé** "break"

5. zōng "ancestor" [BF], **zhōng** "middle"

6. zū "rent", **zhū** "pig"

7. zuàn "bore", **zhuàn** "earn"

8. zìxù "self-introduction", **zhìxù** "order"

 Pronunciation Exercise B-35: **c** vs. **ch**

1. cā "rub", **chā** "insert"

2. cāi "guess", **chāi** "take apart"

3. cáng "hide", **cháng** "often"

4. céng "level", **chéng** "city"

5. cū "coarse", **chū** "go out"

6. cuī "hasten", **chuī** "blow"

7. cūn "village" [BF], **chūn** "spring" [BF]

8. mùcái "lumber", **mùchái** "firewood"

9. tuīcí "decline", **tuīchí** "postpone"

Pronunciation Exercise B-36: **zh** vs. **j**
1. **zhào** "according to", **jiào** "shout"
2. **zhān** "glue", **jiān** "sharp"
3. **Zhāng** (surname), **jiāng** "stiff"
4. **zhǐ** "paper", **jǐ** "squeeze"
5. **zhòu** "wrinkled", **jiù** "then"
6. **zhù** "live", **jù** "phrase"
7. **zhìxù** "order", **jìxù** "continue"
8. **jīngzhì** "exquisite", **jīngjì** "economy"
9. **zázhì** "magazine", **zájì** "acrobatics"

 Pronunciation Exercise B-37: **ch** vs. **q**
1. **chǎo** "noisy", **qiǎo** "coincidental"
2. **cháng** "long", **qiáng** "wall"
3. **chī** "eat", **qī** "seven"
4. **chízi** "pool", **qízi** "flag"
5. **chū** "go out", **qū** "maggot"
6. **chuán** "boat", **quán** "whole"
7. **báichī** "idiot", **báiqī** "white paint"
8. **bù chí** "not late", **bù qí** "not in unison"
9. **fāchóu** "worry", **fāqiú** "serve a ball"

 Pronunciation Exercise B-38: **z** vs. **j**
1. **zā** "tie", **jiā** "add"
2. **zǎn** "save", **jiǎn** "pick up"
3. **zāng** "dirty", **jiāng** "stiff"
4. **zǎo** "early", **jiǎo** "foot"
5. **zé** "then", **jié** "holiday"
6. **zì** "character", **jì** "record"
7. **zǒu** "walk", **jiǔ** "nine"
8. **zuàn** "bore", **juàn** "volume"
9. **bù zū** "doesn't rent", **bù jū** "not limited"

 Pronunciation Exercise B-39: **sh** vs. **x**
1. **shā** "kill", **xiā** "shrimp"
2. **shān** "mountain", **xiān** "first"
3. **shāng** "injure", **xiāng** "fragrant"
4. **shǎo** "few", **xiǎo** "small"
5. **shōu** "receive", **xiū** "repair"
6. **shū** "book", **xū** "weak"
7. **shīwàng** "despair", **xīwàng** "hope"
8. **shòuzi** "skinny-bones", **xiùzi** "sleeve"
9. **bù shī** "not moist", **bù xī** "not inhale"
10. **dàshǐ** "ambassador", **dàxǐ** "great happiness"

 Pronunciation Exercise B-40: **t** vs. **q**
1. **tī** "kick", **qī** "seven"
2. **tiān** "day", **qiān** "lead"
3. **tián** "fill out", **qián** "money"
4. **tiáo** "adjust", **qiáo** "bridge"

5. **tiē** "stick", **qiē** "slice"

6. **tǐng** "very", **qǐng** "invite"

7. **tóu** "head", **qiú** "ball"

 Pronunciation Exercise B-41: **t** vs. **c**

1. **tā** "she", **cā** "rub"

2. **tài** "too", **cài** "dish of food"

3. **tān** "greedy", **cān** "food" [BF]

4. **táng** "candy", **cáng** "hide"

5. **tǎo** "marry (a woman)", **cǎo** "grass"

6. **tōng** "open", **cōng** "scallion"

7. **tòu** "penetrate", **còu** "gather"

8. **tuō** "drag", **cuō** "rub the hands"

 Pronunciation Exercise B-42: **s** vs. **c**

1. **sā** "let go", **cā** "rub"

2. **sǎo** "sweep", **cǎo** "grass"

3. **sāi** "stuff", **cāi** "guess"

4. **sān** "three", **cān** "food" [BF]

5. **sāng** "funeral" [BF], **cāng** "cabin" [BF]

6. **sè** "astringent", **cè** "volume"

7. **sì** "four", **cì** "time"

8. **sù** "vegetables", **cù** "vinegar"

9. **suì** "year of age", **cuì** "crispy"

 Pronunciation Exercise B-43: **c** vs. **q**

1. **cā** "rub", **qiā** "pinch"

2. **cān** "food" [BF], **qiān** "thousand"

3. **cǎo** "grass", **qiǎo** "coincidental"

4. **cāng** "cabin" [BF], **qiāng** "rifle"

5. **cì** "thorn", **qì** "air"

6. **cóng** "from", **qióng** "poor"

7. **cū** "coarse", **Qiū** (surname)

8. **cún** "store", **qún** "flock"

9. **cuàn** "scurry", **quàn** "urge"

 Pronunciation Exercise B-44: **s** vs. **x**

1. **sā** "three", **xiā** "shrimp"

2. **sǎo** "sweep", **xiǎo** "small"

3. **sān** "three", **xiān** "first"

4. **sāng** "mulberry" [BF], **xiāng** "fragrant"

5. **sì** "four", **xì** "fine"

6. **sōng** "loose", **xiōng** "mean"

7. **Sūn** (surname), **xūn** "smoke"

 Pronunciation Exercise B-45: **r** vs. **zh**

1. **rǎn** "dye", **Zhǎn** (surname)

2. **rǎng** "shout", **zhǎng** "grow"

3. **rào** "wind", **zhào** "according to"

4. **rēng** "throw", **zhēng** "argue"

5. rì "day" [BF], **zhì** "treat"
6. rù "enter", **zhù** "live"

 Pronunciation Exercise B-46: **w** vs. **hu**

In English many speakers drop the **h**-sound in **wh**, so that **where** sounds like **wear** and **which** sounds like **witch**. In Chinese, **h** must never be dropped! Be careful to distinguish Chinese **w** from Chinese **hu**, and be sure to make the **h** rough enough.

1. wā "dig", **huā** "flower"
2. wàn "10,000", **huàn** "change"
3. Wáng (surname), **Huáng** (surname)
4. wài "outside", **huài** "bad"
5. wèi "feed", **huì** "can"
6. wǒ "I", **huǒ** "fire"
7. lǎowǔ "child number five", **lǎohǔ** "tiger"
8. xīwàng "hope", **xǐhuan** "like"

FINALS

 Pronunciation Exercise B-47: **i** vs. **e**
1. cì "time", **cè** "volume"
2. chī "eat", **chē** "car"
3. rì "day" [BF], **rè** "hot"
4. sì "four", **sè** "astringent"
5. shì "be", **shè** "shoot"
6. zhì "cure", **zhè** "this"
7. shítou "stone", **shétou** "tongue"
8. báichī "idiot", **bái chē** "white car"
9. yícì "one time", **yícè** "one volume"

 Pronunciation Exercise B-48: **i** vs. **u/ü**
1. jì "send", **jù** "gather together"
2. nǐ "you", **nǚ** "woman" [BF]
3. qī "seven", **qū** "district"
4. xǐ "wash", **xǔ** "allow"
5. bànlǐ "arrange", **bànlǚ** "partner"
6. dàyí "sister-in-law", **dà yú** "big fish"
7. liánxì "contact", **liánxù** "continued"
8. míngyì "capacity", **míngyù** "honor"
9. shūjí "books", **shūjú** "book store"
10. yìjiàn "opinion", **yùjiàn** "foresee"

 Pronunciation Exercise B-49: **u** vs. **u/ü**
1. chū "out", **qū** "district"
2. lù "road", **lǜ** "green"
3. nǔ "make efforts" [BF], **nǚ** "woman" [BF]
4. sù "vegetables", **xù** "foreword"
5. wù "fog", **yù** "jade"
6. zhù "live", **jù** "phrase"

Pronunciation Exercise B-50: **e** vs. **ye/ie**
1. **è** "hungry", **yè** "night"
2. **dé** "obtain", **dié** "fold"
3. **lè** "happy", **liè** "intense"
4. **sè** "color", **xiè** "thank"
5. **zhé** "fold", **jié** "festival"

 Pronunciation Exercise B-51: **e** vs. **wo/uo**
1. **chē** "vehicle", **chuō** "stab"
2. **è** "hungry", **wò** "sleep" [BF]
3. **hé** "and", **huó** "alive"
4. **gē** "song", **guō** "pot"
5. **lè** "happy", **luò** "fall"
6. **rè** "hot", **ruò** "weak"
7. **shè** "shoot", **shuò** "large" [BF]
8. **tè** "especially", **tuò** "open up" [BF]
9. **zhé** "break", **zhuó** "peck"

 Pronunciation Exercise B-52: **ei** vs. **ie**
1. **bēi** "cup", **biē** "suppress"
2. **pēi** "embryo", **piē** "cast aside"
3. **zhèi** "this", **jiè** "borrow"

 Pronunciation Exercise B-53: **er** vs. **ri**
1. **èr** "two", **rì** "day" [BF]
2. **dì'èrshi'èrběn** "volume number 22"
3. **dì'èr shi Rìběn** "number 2 is Japan"

 Pronunciation Exercise B-54: **ai** vs. **ei**
1. **bǎi** "hundred", **běi** "north"
2. **gǎi** "correct", **gěi** "give"
3. **lái** "come", **léi** "thunder"
4. **mái** "bury", **méi** "coal"
5. **nài** "patience" [BF], **nèi** "within" [BF]
6. **pài** "dispatch", **pèi** "match"
7. **zhài** "debt", **zhèi** "this"
8. **bù mǎi** "not buy", **bù měi** "not beautiful"
9. **xiǎomài** "wheat", **xiǎomèi** "little sister"

 Pronunciation Exercise B-55: **ie** vs. **ue/üe**
1. **jié** "festival", **jué** "funny"
2. **liè** "hunt" [BF], **lüè** "slightly"
3. **qiē** "slice", **quē** "lack"
4. **xiě** "write", **xuě** "snow"
5. **xié** "shoe", **xué** "learn"
6. **yè** "night", **yuè** "month"
7. **jiēzhe** "and then", **juēzhe** "pouting"
8. **qièshí** "practical", **quèshí** "actually"
9. **xiēzi** "scorpion", **xuēzi** "boot"

Pronunciation Exercise B-56: **ou/iu** vs. **u/ü**
1. jiù "rescue", jù "phrase"
2. liù "six", lǜ "green"
3. niǔ "twist", nǚ "woman" [BF]
4. Qiū (surname), qū "maggot"
5. xiù "sleeve" [BF], xù "foreword"
6. yóu "oil", yú "fish"

 Pronunciation Exercise B-57: Absence vs. presence of **i**
1. dōu "all", diū "throw"
2. láng "wolf", liáng "measure"
3. lóu "building", liú "keep"
4. nào "be noisy", niào "urine"
5. pào "immerse", piào "ticket"
6. tāo "take out", tiāo "select"

 Pronunciation Exercise B-58: **ui** vs. **uai**
1. huì "know how to", huài "bad"
2. guì "expensive", guài "strange"
3. shuì "sleep", shuài "handsome"

 Pronunciation Exercise B-59: **wa/ua** vs. **wo/uo**
1. guā "melon", guō "pot"
2. huà "speech", huò "goods"
3. kuà "step", kuò "rich"
4. shuā "brush", shuō "say"
5. wǎ "tile", wǒ "I"
6. zhuā "grab", zhuō "catch"

 Pronunciation Exercise B-60: **ou** vs. **uo**

Be very careful to distinguish the final **ou** from the final **uo**. Pay special attention to the pair of words in number 1 and number 9. Many learners of Chinese mix these up!

1. dōu "all", duō "many"
2. dǒu "steep", duǒ "hide"
3. gòu "enough", guò "pass"
4. hòu "thick", huò "or"
5. ròu "meat", ruò "weak"
6. shōu "receive", shuō "speak"
7. tōu "steal", tuō "drag"
8. Zhōu (surname), zhuō "table" [BF]
9. zǒu "walk", zuǒ "left"
10. zòu "perform", zuò "do"

 Pronunciation Exercise B-61: Absence vs. presence of **u**
1. gāi "should", guāi "well-behaved"
2. gāng "just", guāng "only"
3. gěi "give", guǐ "devil"
4. hài "harm", huài "bad"
5. hēi "black", huī "grey"

6. **kān** "watch over", **kuān** "wide"
7. **lǎn** "lazy", **luǎn** "ovum"
8. **rǎn** "dye", **ruǎn** "soft"
9. **shā** "kill", **shuā** "brush"
10. **zhā** "prick", **zhuā** "catch"

 Pronunciation Exercise B-62: **an** vs. **en**
1. **bàn** "half", **bèn** "stupid"
2. **fān** "leaf through", **fēn** "divide"
3. **hǎn** "shout", **hěn** "very"
4. **kǎn** "chop down", **kěn** "be willing"
5. **màn** "slow", **mèn** "stifling"
6. **shān** "mountain", **shēn** "deep"
7. **wàn** "10,000", **wèn** "ask"
8. **zhān** "stick to", **zhēn** "real"
9. **bǎnzi** "board", **běnzi** "notebook"
10. **pánzi** "plate", **pénzi** "basin"

 Pronunciation Exercise B-63: **an** vs. **yan/ian**
1. **àn** "press", **yàn** "examine"
2. **bàn** "arrange", **biàn** "argue"
3. **cān** "meal" [BF], **qiān** "thousand"
4. **lǎn** "lazy", **liǎn** "face"
5. **màn** "slow", **miàn** "noodles"
6. **nán** "difficult", **nián** "sticky"
7. **pàn** "sentence", **piàn** "slice"
8. **zhàn** "stand", **jiàn** "see"

 Pronunciation Exercise B-64: **yan/ian** vs. **yuan/uan**
1. **jiǎn** "pick up", **juǎn** "roll up"
2. **qiān** "sign", **quān** "circle"
3. **yán** "salt", **yuán** "round"
4. **píjiàn** "leather clothes", **píjuàn** "exhausted"
5. **qiántou** "front", **quántou** "fist"
6. **yìqiān** "one thousand", **yìquān** "circle"
7. **yǒuqián** "rich", **yǒuquán** "powerful"
8. **xiánzhe** "being idle", **xuánzhe** "hanging"
9. **yànzi** "swallow", **yuànzi** "courtyard"

 Pronunciation Exercise B-65: **en** vs. **un**
1. **Chén** (surname), **chún** "pure"
2. **hèn** "hate", **hùn** "confuse"
3. **kěn** "be willing", **kǔn** "bundle"
4. **rèn** "recognize", **rùn** "moist"
5. **sēn** "forest" [BF], **Sūn** (surname)
6. **shèn** "kidney", **shùn** "smooth"
7. **zhěn** "examine" [BF], **zhǔn** "accurate"

 Pronunciation Exercise B-66: **un** vs. **(y)un**
1. **chún** "pure", **qún** "flock"

2. shùn "smooth", **xùn** "train"

3. zhūn "earnest" [BF], **jūn** "army" [BF]

 Pronunciation Exercise B-67: **in** vs. **(y)un**

1. jīn "catty", **jūn** "army" [BF]

2. qín "Chinese zither", **qún** "flock"

3. xìn "letter", **xùn** "train"

4. báiyín "silver", **báiyún** "white cloud"

5. yìnshū "print books", **yùnshū** "transportation"

 Pronunciation Exercise B-68: **an** vs. **ang**

1. bān "move", **bāng** "clique"

2. chuán "ship", **chuáng** "bed"

3. lán "blue", **láng** "wolf"

4. mán "deceive", **máng** "busy"

5. wán "play", **wáng** "king"

6. chǎnzi "shovel", **chǎngzi** "factory"

7. dānxīn "worry", **dāngxīn** "be careful"

8. fǎnwèn "ask a question in reply", **fǎngwèn** "visit"

9. gānzi "bamboo pole", **gāngzi** "bowl"

10. kāifàn "start eating", **kāifàng** "open"

 Pronunciation Exercise B-69: **ian** vs. **iang**

1. jiǎn "minus", **jiǎng** "speak"

2. lián "even", **liáng** "cool"

3. nián "year", **niáng** "mom"

4. jiǎnhuà "simplify", **jiǎnghuà** "speak"

5. jiǎnlì "short resume", **jiǎnglì** "reward"

6. jiānyìng "hard", **jiāngyìng** "stiff"

7. lǎonián "later years", **lǎo niáng** "old mother"

8. shìyàn "test", **shìyàng** "style"

9. yànzi "swallow", **yàngzi** "kind"

 Pronunciation Exercise B-70: **en** vs. **eng**

1. bēn "run", **bēng** "jump"

2. Chén (surname), **chéng** "city"

3. fēn "minute", **fēng** "wind"

4. mèn "depressed", **mèng** "dream"

5. shēn "deep", **shēng** "give birth to"

6. zhèn "town", **zhèng** "just"

7. chénjiù "obsolete", **chéngjiù** "achievement"

8. guāfēn "partition", **guāfēng** "wind blows"

9. mùpén "wooden bowl", **mùpéng** "wooden shack"

10. rénshēn "ginseng", **rénshēng** "human life"

 Pronunciation Exercise B-71: **in** vs. **ing**

1. bīn "guest" [BF], **bīng** "soldier"

2. jīn "gold", **jīng** "perfect"

3. Lín (surname), **líng** "zero"

4. qīn "close", **qīng** "light"

5. xìn "letter", **xìng** "surname"

6. yìn "print", **yìng** "hard"

7. bú xìn "not believe", **bú xìng** "unfortunate"

8. hěn jìn "very close", **hěn jìng** "very still"

9. pínfán "frequent", **píngfán** "ordinary"

10. rénmín "people", **rénmíng** "person's name"

 Pronunciation Exercise B-72: **ang** vs. **eng**

1. bàng "great", **bèng** "jump"

2. fàng "put", **fèng** "crack"

3. mǎng "python" [BF], **Měng** "Mongolian" [BF]

4. pàng "fat", **pèng** "bump"

5. rāng "shout", **rēng** "throw away"

6. dōngfāng "the east", **dōngfēng** "east wind"

7. mángzhe "being busy", **méngzhe** "covering"

 Pronunciation Exercise B-73: **ang** vs. **eng** vs. **ong**

1. cáng "hide", **céng** "level", **cóng** "from"

2. cháng "long", **chéng** "O.K.", **chóng** "bug"

3. dǎng "party", **děng** "wait", **dǒng** "understand"

4. gāng "just", **gēng** "plough" [BF], **gōng** "supply"

5. háng "line", **héng** "horizontal", **hóng** "red"

6. kāng "health" [BF], **kēng** "pit", **kōng** "empty"

7. láng "wolf", **léng** "edge" [BF], **lóng** "cage" [BF]

8. táng "sugar", **téng** "hurt", **tóng** "same"

Pronunciation Exercises, Part C: English-Chinese Contrastive Pronunciation

There are a number of Chinese sounds which students often confuse with certain English sounds that, to the non-Chinese ear, may sound somewhat similar. It is important to be aware of the differences between the Chinese and English sounds and to pronounce the Chinese sounds as accurately as possible. The exercises in this section will give you practice in contrasting some of these frequently confused sounds. In the exercises below, English words will be enclosed in quotation marks with Chinese words or syllables, as before, in bold print.

 Pronunciation Exercise C-1: English "b" vs. Chinese **b**

Remember that Chinese **b** is voiceless while English initial "b" is voiced.

1. "bay", bèi "by"

2. "bin", bīn "guest" [BF]

3. "boo", bù "not"

4. "bow", bào "embrace"

5. "bye", bài "defeat" [BF]

 Pronunciation Exercise C-2: English "d" vs. Chinese **d**

Remember that Chinese **d** is voiceless while English initial "d" is voiced.

1. "D", dì "give"

2. "day", děi "must"

3. "dew", Dù (surname)

4. "die", dài "take"
5. "doe", dòu "tease"

 Pronunciation Exercise C-3: English "g" vs. Chinese **g**

Remember that Chinese **g** is voiceless while English initial "g" is voiced.

1. "gay", gěi "give"
2. "go", gòu "enough"
3. "gone", gàn "do"
4. "goo", Gù (surname)
5. "guy", gài "cover"

 Pronunciation Exercise C-4: English "p" vs. Chinese **p**

Remember that Chinese **p** has a stronger puff of breath following it than does English "p."

1. "paw", pà "fear"
2. "pay", pèi "match"
3. "pea", pì "fart"
4. "pie", pài "dispatch"
5. "pin", pìn "hire"

 Pronunciation Exercise C-5: English "t" vs. Chinese **t**

Remember that Chinese **t** has a stronger puff of breath following it than does English "t."

1. "tan", tàn "sigh"
2. "tea", tì "on behalf of"
3. "tie", tài "excessively"
4. "tow", tòu "penetrate"
5. "two", tǔ "vomit"

 Pronunciation Exercise C-6: English "k" vs. Chinese **k**

Remember that Chinese **k** has a stronger puff of breath following it than does English "k" (which is often spelled "c").

1. "can", kàn "look"
2. "coo", kù "pants" [BF]
3. "core", kǒur "opening"
4. "cow", kào "depend on"
5. "Ken", kěn "be willing to"

 Pronunciation Exercise C-7: English "j" vs. Chinese **zh**

Remember that Chinese **zh** is voiceless with the tongue curled further back, while English "j" is voiced with the tongue further forward.

1. "jaw", zhà "explode"
2. "Jay", zhèi "this"
3. "Jew", Zhù (surname)
4. "Joe", zhòu "wrinkle"
5. "John", zhàn "occupy"

Pronunciation Exercise C-8: English "j/g" vs. Chinese **j**

Remember that Chinese **j** is voiceless and is pronounced with the lips spread (except when before **u**), while English "j" or "g" is voiced and pronounced with rounded lips.

1. **"gee", jì** "send"
2. **"gin", jìn** "close"
3. **"Jay", jiè** "borrow"
4. **"Jew", jù** "phrase"
5. **"Joe", jiù** "old"

 Pronunciation Exercise C-9: English "sh" vs. Chinese **sh**

Remember that Chinese **sh** is pronounced with the tongue curled further back than in English. While English "sh" is always followed by rounding of the lips, Chinese **sh** has lip rounding only before **u** and **o**.

1. **"Sean", shàn** "fan" [BF]
2. **"shoe", shù** "tree"
3. **"show", shòu** "skinny"
4. **"shun", shùn** "smoothly"
5. **"shy", shài** "put something in the sun"

 Pronunciation Exercise C-10: English "h" vs. Chinese **h**

Remember that Chinese **h** is pronounced with more friction and sounds rougher than English "h."

1. **"hay", hēi** "black"
2. **"high", hài** "harm"
3. **"hoe", hòu** "thick"
4. **"how", hào** "number"
5. **"Hun", hàn** "sweat"
6. **"whey", huì** "be able"
7. **"who", hù** "household"
8. **"why", huài** "bad"

 Pronunciation Exercise C-11: English "l" vs. Chinese **l**

Remember that Chinese **l** is tenser and pronounced with the tip of the tongue in a more forward position than English "l."

1. **"lay", lèi** "tired"
2. **"Lee", lì** "sharp"
3. **"lie", lài** "rely on"
4. **"Lou", lù** "road"
5. **"low", lòu** "leak"

 Pronunciation Exercise C-12: English "r" vs. Chinese **r**

Remember that Chinese **r** is pronounced with the tongue tip curled further back than English "r." While English "r" is always accompanied by lip rounding, Chinese **r** is rounded only in front of **o** and **u**.

1. **"ran", rán** "ignite"
2. **"row", ròu** "meat"
3. **"rue", rù** "enter" [BF]
4. **"rung", ràng** "let"
5. **"wren", rèn** "appoint"

Pronunciation Exercise C-13: English "i" vs. Chinese (**y**)**u**

Remember that, while both of these sounds are pronounced with the tongue in a high position, Chinese (**y**)**u** is pronounced with rounded lips while English "i" is pronounced with spread lips.

1. **"E", yù** "jade"
2. **"G", jù** "phrase"
3. **"knee", nǚ** "woman" [BF]
4. **"Lee", lǜ** "green"
5. **"she", xù** "continue" [BF]

 Pronunciation Exercise C-14: English "u" vs. Chinese (**y**)**u**

Remember that, while both of these sounds are pronounced with rounded lips, Chinese (**y**)**u** is pronounced with the tongue in a high position while English "u" is pronounced with the tongue in a low position.

1. **"chew", qù** "go"
2. **"Lou", lǜ** "green"
3. **"new", nǚ** "woman" [BF]
4. **"shoe", xù** "continue" [BF]
5. **"you", yù** "jade"

 Pronunciation Exercise C-15: English "o" vs. Chinese (**u**)**o**

Remember that Chinese (**u**)**o** starts with a "w"-sound, while English "o" has no "w"-sound at the beginning but ends in a "w"-glide.

1. **"foe", Fó** "Buddha"
2. **"go", guò** "pass"
3. **"low", luò** "fall"
4. **"no", nuò** "promise" [BF]
5. **"woe", wò** "sleep" [BF]

 Pronunciation Exercise C-16: English "un" vs. Chinese **en**
1. **"bun", bèn** "stupid"
2. **"fun", fèn** "copy"
3. **"gun", gēn** "with"
4. **"pun", pēn** "squirt"
5. **"shun", shèn** "kidney"

 Pronunciation Exercise C-17: English glide vs. Chinese no glide

Remember that Chinese vowels are pronounced "purely," while English vowels are often part of a diphthong, with a following "y"-glide or "w"-glide.

1. **"B", Bì** (surname)
2. **"C", xì** "fine"
3. **"chew", chù** "place" [BF]
4. **"D", dì** "number so-and-so"
5. **"E", yì** "easy" [BF]
6. **"new", nù** "anger" [BF]
7. **"P", pì** "fart"
8. **"Sue", sù** "element" [BF]
9. **"T", tì** "on behalf of"
10. **"too", tù** "vomit"

Pronunciation Exercises, Part D: Content-based Pronunciation

The following exercises consist of words the meanings of which are already known, or easily learnable, by beginning American students. The purpose of including such content-based material is to make these pronunciation exercises more meaningful, more interesting, and—hopefully—have them make a deeper impression on the student.

 Pronunciation Exercise D-1: American City Names
1. **Bōshìdùn** "Boston"
2. **Huáshèngdùn** "Washington"
3. **Luòshānjī** "Los Angeles"
4. **Mài'āmì** "Miami"
5. **Niǔyuē** "New York"
6. **Xīyǎtú** "Seattle"
7. **Yàtèlándà** "Atlanta"
8. **Zhījiāgē** "Chicago"

 Pronunciation Exercise D-2: Chinese City Names
1. **Běijīng** "Beijing"
2. **Chóngqìng** "Chongqing"
3. **Gāoxióng** "Kaohsiung"
4. **Guǎngzhōu** "Guangzhou"
5. **Nánjīng** "Nanjing"
6. **Shànghǎi** "Shanghai"
7. **Shěnyáng** "Shenyang"
8. **Táiběi** "Taipei"
9. **Tiānjīn** "Tianjin"
10. **Xiānggǎng** "Hong Kong"

 Pronunciation Exercise D-3: American State Names
1. **Ālābāmǎ** "Alabama"
2. **Ālāsījiā** "Alaska"
3. **Éhài'é** "Ohio"
4. **Fóméngtè** "Vermont"
5. **Kānsàsī** "Kansas"
6. **Kēluólāduō** "Colorado"
7. **Mìxīxībǐ** "Mississippi"
8. **Tiánnàxī** "Tennessee"
9. **Wēisīkāngxīn** "Wisconsin"
10. **Yóutā** "Utah"

 Pronunciation Exercise D-4: Names of Chinese Provinces and Regions
1. **Fújiàn** "Fujian"
2. **Guǎngdōng** "Guangdong"
3. **Hǎinán** "Hainan"
4. **Húběi** "Hubei"
5. **Hú'nán** "Hunan"
6. **Shāndōng** "Shandong"
7. **Sìchuān** "Sichuan"
8. **Táiwān** "Taiwan"
9. **Xīnjiāng** "Xinjiang"
10. **Zhèjiāng** "Zhejiang"

Pronunciation Exercise D-5: Other Countries
   1. **Ài'ěrlán** "Ireland"
   2. **Bā'námǎ** "Panama"
   3. **Fēnlán** "Finland"
   4. **Gǔbā** "Cuba"
   5. **Hǎidì** "Haiti"
   6. **Mǎlǐ** "Mali"
   7. **Nuówēi** "Norway"
   8. **Tǎnsāngníyà** "Tanzania"
   9. **Yěmén** "Yemen"
   10. **Yìdàlì** "Italy"

 Pronunciation Exercise D-6: Famous Chinese
   1. **Dèng Xiǎopíng** "Deng Xiaoping"
   2. **Jiǎng Jièshí** "Chiang Kai-shek"
   3. **Jiǎng Jīngguó** "Chiang Ching-kuo"
   4. **Jiāng Qīng** "Jiang Qing"
   5. **Kǒngfūzǐ** "Confucius"
   6. **Lǎozǐ** "Lao-tse"
   7. **Liú Shàoqí** "Liu Shaoqi"
   8. **Máo Zédōng** "Mao Zedong"
   9. **Sūn Zhōngshān** "Sun Yat-sen"
   10. **Yáo Míng** "Yao Ming"

 Pronunciation Exercise D-7: Famous Americans
   1. **Àidíshēng** "Edison"
   2. **Kěnnídí** "Kennedy"
   3. **Jīxīn'gé** "Kissinger"
   4. **Hǎilún Kǎilè** "Helen Keller"
   5. **Lǐ Xiǎolóng** "Bruce Lee"
   6. **Línkěn** "Lincoln"
   7. **Mǎdīng Lùdé Jīn** "Martin Luther King"
   8. **Níkèsōng** "Nixon"
   9. **Àobāmǎ** "Obama"
   10. **Luósīfú** "Roosevelt"

 Pronunciation Exercise D-8: Similar-sounding Chinese Surnames Contrasted
Be careful to keep the similar-sounding surnames below apart. Nobody likes for their name to be mispronounced or, even worse, to be confused with someone else's!

   1. **Bān, Pān**
   2. **Bāo, Bào**
   3. **Chén, Chéng**
   4. **Dèng, Zhèng**
   5. **Gū, Gǔ, Gù**
   6. **Hé, Hè, Hóu**
   7. **Huáng, Wáng**
   8. **Hú, Wú, Wǔ**
   9. **Jiāng, Jiǎng**
   10. **Lí, Lǐ, Lǚ**

11. Lín, Líng
12. Lú, Lǔ, Lù, Lǚ
13. Sī, Shī, Shí, Shǐ
14. Sūn, Sòng
15. Tán, Táng, Tāng
16. Tián, Qián
17. Wāng, Wáng
18. Wēn, Wén
19. Xú, Xǔ
20. Yán, Yuán
21. Zāng, Zhāng, Zhuāng
22. Zhān, Zhǎn
23. Zhū, Zhù
24. Zōng, Zhōng
25. Zōu, Zhōu

 Pronunciation Exercise D-9: English Borrowings from Chinese
1. **gōngfu** "kungfu"
2. **gònghé** "gung ho"
3. **kòutóu** "kowtow"
4. **lìzhī** "lichee"
5. **májiàng** "mahjongg"
6. **qiézhī** "ketchup"
7. **rénshēn** "ginseng"
8. **sī** "silk"
9. **táifēng** "typhoon"
10. **tàijíquán** "Chinese shadow boxing, taiji"

 Pronunciation Exercise D-10: Chinese Borrowings from English
1. **hànbǎo** "hamburger"
2. **kāngnǎixīn** "carnation"
3. **kělè** "cola"
4. **Kěndéjī** "Kentucky Fried Chicken®"
5. **léidá** "radar"
6. **màikèfēng** "microphone"
7. **mǐ** "meter"
8. **pīngpāngqiú** "Ping Pong"
9. **qiǎokèlì** "chocolate"
10. **sānmíngzhì** "sandwich"

Pronunciation Supplements

A. SOME COMMON CHINESE TONGUE TWISTERS

Below are five well-known Chinese tongue twisters, called **ràokǒulìng** in Chinese. First, listen to your instructor or the audio recording and practice saying each of them several times slowly, syllable by syllable. Then say each one as fast as you can. You may wish to memorize one or more of the tongue twisters to further practice your pronunciation, absorb a bit of Chinese popular culture, and perhaps impress your family and friends!

1. **Māma qí mǎ, mǎ màn, māma mà mǎ.**
   Mother rides a horse, the horse is slow, mother scolds the horse.

2. **Sìshisìzhī sǐ shí shīzi**
   Forty-four dead stone lions

3. **Sìshisìzhī xǐquè zuòzai sìshisìkē shìzi shùshang.**
   Forty-four magpies sit on forty-four persimmon trees.

4. **Yìzhī dà huā wǎn kòuzhe yìzhī dà huā huó háma.**
   A big colored bowl has been placed over a big colored live toad.

5. **Chī pútao bù tǔ pútao pír, bù chī pútao dào tǔ pútao pír.**
   When eating grapes, (he/she) doesn't spit out grape skins, when not eating grapes, on the contrary, (he/she) spits out grape skins.

B. A FAMOUS TANG DYNASTY POEM

The following poem, entitled **Jìng Yè Sī** "Calm Night Thoughts," was written by the famous Tang Dynasty poet Li Bai (701–762) and is memorized by most Chinese children. To practice your pronunciation and learn some Chinese culture, try repeating it after your teacher or the recording. If you want to impress your Chinese friends, memorize it.

Chuáng qián míng yuè guāng,
In front of the bed (there is) the bright moon's light,

Yí shì dì shàng shuāng.
(I) suspect that (on) this ground there has appeared frost.

Jǔ tóu wàng míng yuè,
(I) raise (my) head and look at the bright moon,

Dī tóu sī gù xiāng.
(I) lower (my) head and think of (my) old home.

C. SEVERAL SAYINGS FROM CONFUCIUS

The following well-known sayings, which are in Classical Chinese, are by **Kǒngzǐ** or Confucius (551–479 BCE), as collected by his disciples in the famous volume entitled **Lúnyǔ**, *The Analects*.

Zǐ yuē: "Sì hǎi zhī nèi jiē xiōngdì yě."
The master says: "Within the four seas we are all brothers."

Zǐ yuē: "Jǐ suǒ bú yù, wù shī yú rén."
The master says: "What you yourself do not want, do not do it unto others."

Zǐ yuē: "Yǒu péng zì yuǎn fāng lái, bú yì lè hū?"
The master says: "If there is a friend who comes from afar, is this not also a happy thing?"

Zǐ yuē: "Xué ér shí xí zhī, bú yì yuè hū?"
The master says: "To learn something and often practice it, is this not also a happy thing?"

Classroom Expressions

To help you learn Chinese as efficiently as possible, it's important to immerse yourself in as "Chinese" an atmosphere as you can. Therefore, as much as possible of each class should be conducted in Chinese only. To facilitate this, your instructors will frequently be using the Chinese classroom expressions below. While it will be helpful for you to repeat each one several times after your instructor and after the accompanying audio recordings, for now your primary task is to learn to understand these expressions when you hear them; you needn't learn how to use them yourself just yet. Although the individual words and grammatical structures in the classroom expressions are explained for those who are curious in the notes that follow, don't worry too much about what the individual words mean but rather try to understand the meaning of each expression as a whole.

 Group One

| 1. **zǎo** | be early |
| Zǎo! | Good morning! |

2. **nǐ**	you (singular)
hǎo	be good, be all right
Nǐ hǎo!	How are you?

| 3. **nǐmen** | you (plural) |
| Nǐmen hǎo! | How are you? |

4. **wǒmen**	we, us
shàngkè	have class
ba	(indicates suggestions)
Wǒmen shàngkè ba.	Let's begin class.

 Group Two

5. **tīng**	listen
wǒ	I, me
shuō	speak, say
Nǐmen tīng wǒ shuō.	You all listen to me say it.

| 6. **gēn** | follow |
| Nǐmen gēn wǒ shuō. | You all repeat after me. |

7. **xiàkè**	end class; get out of class
le	(indicates changed status)
Hǎo, wǒmen xiàkèle.	All right, we end class now.

 Group Three

| 8. Hǎo. | Good. |

| 9. **hěn** | very |
| Hěn hǎo. | Very good. |

10. **qǐng**	please
zài	again
yíbiàn	one time
Qǐng nǐ zài shuō yíbiàn.	Please say it again.

11. **míngtiān**	tomorrow
jiàn	see
Míngtiān jiàn.	See you tomorrow.

| 12. Zàijiàn. | Goodbye. |

Group Four

13. **dì-**	(forms ordinal numbers)
jǐ-	how many
shēng	tone
Dìjǐshēng?	Which tone?

| 14. **yī** | one |
| **Dìyīshēng.** | First tone. |

| 15. **èr** | two |
| **Dì'èrshēng.** | Second tone. |

| 16. **sān** | three |
| **Dìsānshēng.** | Third tone. |

| 17. **sì** | four |
| **Dìsìshēng.** | Fourth tone. |

| 18. **qīng** | be light (not heavy) |
| **Qīngshēng.** | Neutral tone. |

19. **zhùyì**	pay attention to
nǐde	your
shēngdiào	tone(s)
Qǐng zhùyì nǐde shēngdiào.	Please pay attention to your tones.

Group Five

| 20. Duì. | Correct. |

| 21. Bú duì. | Not correct. |

22. **dà**	be big, large
dà shēng	in a big voice, loud
yìdiǎnr	a little
Qǐng nǐ dà shēng yidianr.	Please a little louder.

| 23. **kuài** | be fast |
| **Qǐng nǐ kuài yidianr.** | Please a little faster. |

24. màn	be slow
Qǐng nǐ màn yidianr.	Please a little slower.
25. wèn	ask
tā	he, she; her, him
Qǐng nǐ wèn tā.	Please you ask her/him.

 Group Six

26. huídá	answer
wèntí	question(s)
Qǐng huídá wǒde wèntí.	Please answer my question(s).
27. xiànzài	now
tīngxiě	take a dictation quiz
Wǒmen xiànzài tīngxiě.	We'll now take a dictation quiz.
28. kǎoshì	take a test
Wǒmen xiànzài kǎoshì.	We'll now take a test.
29. míngtiān	tomorrow
Wǒmen míngtiān kǎoshì.	We'll take a test tomorrow.

 Group Seven

30. bǎ	take
gōngkè	homework
gěi	give
Qǐng nǐmen bǎ gōngkè gěi wǒ.	Please you all give me your homework.
31. kǎojuàn	test paper(s)
Qǐng nǐmen bǎ kǎojuàn gěi wǒ.	Please you all give me your test papers.
32. Zhōngwén	Chinese language
bié	don't
Yīngwén	English language
Qǐng nǐmen shuō Zhōngwén, bié shuō Yīngwén!	Please you all speak Chinese, don't speak English!

Notes on the Classroom Expressions

The numbers of the notes below correspond to the numbers of the Classroom Expressions above.

1. **Zǎo** is actually a stative verb meaning "be early." Thus, when someone says this to you, they are literally saying "It's early." **Zǎo** has become a conventionalized greeting which can be used on first seeing someone in the morning any time until about 10:00 A.M. If someone says **Zǎo!** to you, you would typically reply in the same way. So a conversational exchange repeated countless times every morning in China is:

    Speaker A: **Zǎo!**

    Speaker B: **Zǎo!**

2–3. The basic structure of classroom expressions 2 and 3 is "You are good." Presumably, a preceding verbal expression meaning something like "I hope that..." has been deleted. In any case, the functional meaning is that of a greeting, similar to English "How are you?" Note that in Chinese, **hǎo** is a stative verb meaning "be good" or "be all right," and observe how **hǎo** is used in classroom expressions 7, 8, and 9 below.

5. This sentence literally means "You (plural) listen (to) me say (something)." Notice that some verbs that require an object (like "it") in English don't require an object in Chinese.

6. **Gēn** is a verb with the basic meaning "follow," so this sentence literally means "You (plural) follow me (in) saying."

7. **Hǎo** here means "it is all right." **Xiàkè** is a verb that can be translated "get out of class," "finish class," "end class," or "adjourn class." The **le** at the end of this sentence is a final particle indicating that there has been a change of status (i.e., "before we were in class but now class is over").

8–9. In these two expressions, **hǎo** has its basic meaning of "be good" or "it is good" or simply "good."

10. **Qǐng** literally means "request politely." It commonly occurs at the beginning of sentences indicating requests, much like English "please." **Nǐ** means "you" (singular). **Zài shuō yíbiàn**, which can be used alone to mean "say it again," literally means "again say one time."

12. **Zàijiàn** "goodbye" literally means "again see" (cf. **zài** "again" in classroom expression 10 and **jiàn** "see" in classroom expression 11). Compare this to French **au revoir** and German **auf Wiedersehen**, both of which mean "again see."

13. **Dìjǐshēng?** literally means "number what tone?"

13–17. Some speakers say these without the initial syllable **dì-**.

16. **Qīng** literally means "be light (not heavy)," and refers to the very light stress given neutral tone syllables.

18. Both **shēngdiào** and **shēng**, which was introduced in line 13, mean "tone," but while **shēngdiào** can be said by itself, **shēng** is usually said only in combination with other syllables.

22–24. The basic structure of all these sentences is **Qǐng nǐ...yidianr** "(I) request that you a little more...." Instead of classroom expression 22, **Qǐng nǐ dà shēng yidianr**, there are also some speakers who prefer **Qǐng nǐ dà yidianr shēng**.

25. **Tā** is the third person singular pronoun, meaning "he," "she." "her," "him" (and occasionally "it"). You have by now encountered the following personal pronouns:

wǒ "I, me"	**wǒmen** "we, us"
nǐ "you" (singular)	**nǐmen** "you" (plural)
tā "he, she; her, him"	

Observe how the pluralizing suffix **-men** converts pronouns from singular to plural. How do you think one would say "they" in Chinese? (Answer: **tāmen**.)

30. **Qǐng nǐmen bǎ gōngkè gěi wǒ** literally means "Please you all take (the) homework (and) give (it to) me."

31. **Qǐng nǐmen bǎ kǎojuàn gěi wǒ** literally means "Please you all take (the) test paper (and) give (it to) me."

Abbreviations

Word Classes*

[A]	Adverb
[AT]	Attributive
[AV]	Auxiliary Verb
[BF]	Bound Form
[CJ]	Conjunction
[CV]	Coverb
[EV]	Equative Verb
[EX]	Expression
[I]	Interjection
[IE]	Idiomatic Expression
[L]	Localizer
[M]	Measure
[MA]	Moveable Adverb
[N]	Noun
[NU]	Number
[P]	Particle
[PH]	Phrase
[PR]	Pronoun
[PT]	Pattern
[PV]	Postverb
[PW]	Place Word
[QW]	Question Word
[RC]	Resultative Compound
[RE]	Resultative Ending
[SN]	Surname
[SP]	Specifier
[SV]	Stative Verb
[TW]	Time Word
[V]	Verb
[VO]	Verb-Object Compound

Other Abbreviations and Symbols

(B)	Beijing
(T)	Taipei
lit.	literally
SV	Supplementary Vocabulary
AV	Additional Vocabulary
*	(indicates that what follows is incorrect)
/	(separates alternate forms)

* For explanations of the word classes, see the section on "Word Classes of Spoken Chinese" at the end of this volume.

Greetings and Useful Phrases

COMMUNICATIVE OBJECTIVES

Once you have mastered this unit, you will be able to use Chinese to:

1. Greet Chinese people you meet and respond to their greetings.

2. Inquire about how someone is and reply to questions about how you are.

3. Ask about how the members of someone's family are and answer questions about how your own family is.

4. Ask where someone is going and answer questions about where you are going.

5. Ask about someone's work or studies and answer questions about your own work or studies.

6. Visit someone at their home, employing typical courtesy language and appropriate accompanying behavior.

"Where Are You Going?"

Wang Jingsheng, a Chinese student who is studying economics, and Alex Crane, an American student who is studying Chinese language, pass each other on the campus of Capital University of Economics and Business in Beijing. The two young men have come to know each other fairly well over the past few months.

Basic Conversation 1-1

1.	WANG	**Kē Léi'ēn, nǐ hǎo!**
		Hi, Alex!
2.	CRANE	**Wáng Jīngshēng, nǐ hǎo!**
		Hi, Jingsheng!
3.	WANG	**Nǐ dào nǎr qù a?**
		Where are you going?
4.	CRANE	**Wǒ qù túshūguǎn. Nǐ ne?**
		I'm going to the library. How about you?
5.	WANG	**Wǒ huí sùshè.**
		I'm going back to the dorm.

Build Up

Throughout the book, if an item in the Basic Conversation or Supplementary Vocabulary section shows a word class abbreviation after the English translation [in brackets], this indicates that the item occurs at that point for the *first time* in the course. It should be given special attention for learning, since knowledge of it will be assumed in the rest of the course.

....

1. Wang

Kē	Ke [SN]
Kē Léi'ēn	(Chinese for "Crane")
nǐ	you [PR]
nǐ hǎo	"how are you?," "hi" [IE]
Kē Léi'ēn, nǐ hǎo!	Hi, Alex!

....

2. Crane

Wáng	Wang [SN]

| **Jingsheng** | Jingsheng (given name) |
| Wáng Jīngshēng, nǐ hǎo! | Hi, Jingsheng! |

3. Wang

dào	to [CV]
nǎr	where [QW]
qù	go, go to [V]
dào nǎr qù	go where
a	(softens the sentence) [P]
Nǐ dào nǎr qù a?	Where are you going?

4. Crane

wǒ	I, me [PR]
túshūguǎn	library [PW]
qù túshūguǎn	go to the library
wǒ qù túshūguǎn	I go to the library
ne	and how about, what about [P]
nǐ ne	and what about you
Wǒ qù túshūguǎn. Nǐ ne?	I'm going to the library. How about you?

5. Wang

huí	go back to [V]
sùshè	dormitory [PW]
huí sùshè	go back to the dormitory
Wǒ huí sùshè.	I'm going back to the dorm.

 ## Supplementary Vocabulary

The Supplementary Vocabulary of each lesson is required for learning and may reoccur later in the course without additional explanation.

| **1. shítáng** | cafeteria, dining hall [PW] |
| Wǒ qù shítáng. | I'm going to the cafeteria. |

2. bàn	take care of, do [V]
yìdiǎn(r)	a little, some [NU+M]
shì(r)	matter, thing (abstract) [N]
yìdiǎnr shìr	some things
bàn yìdiǎnr shìr	take care of some things
Wǒ qù bàn yìdiǎnr shìr.	I'm going to take care of some things.

3. yě	also, too [A]
yě qù bàn yìdiǎnr shìr	also go take care of some things
Wáng Jīngshēng yě qù bàn yìdiǎnr shìr.	Wang Jingsheng is also going to take care of some things.

Grammatical and Cultural Notes

A NOTE ON THE NOTES

For most adults learning a foreign language, explicit knowledge of how the grammar of a language works and an understanding of the cultural and social background are beneficial in attaining proficiency better and faster. That is the main rationale for the Grammatical and Cultural Notes provided for every lesson. At the beginning, precisely because it is the beginning, there are fairly many notes for you to read and study; later, as you will see in Volume Two, they gradually peter out. The good news is that by the time you finish this basic

Students walking to class at Beijing Language and Culture University

course, you will have encountered the majority of everyday spoken Chinese grammar. As you finish a unit, you should also review the section entitled "Major New Grammar Patterns" in the Review and Study Guide at the end of each unit.

Here and in subsequent lessons, **the numbers of the notes** correspond to the numbers of the utterances in the basic conversation. **SV** followed by a number refers to "Supplementary Vocabulary" while **AV** followed by a number refers to "Additional Vocabulary."

WORD CLASSES

The words of any language can be divided into word classes so that all the words of any one class share certain characteristics that set them apart from words in other classes. For example, the word classes of English include nouns, adjectives, and prepositions. To be able to use a Chinese word correctly, you need to know to which word class it belongs. Be careful not to assume that the word classes of Chinese are necessarily the same as in English (e.g., Chinese has nouns and pronouns but not adjectives or prepositions). The first word in this first basic conversation, **Kē**, belongs to the word class *surname*, which will be abbreviated [SN]. For a list of word class abbreviations, see p. 70; for a detailed explanation of those word classes, see "Word Classes of Spoken Chinese" on page 354.

1A.   Name + Greeting. The pattern **Name + Greeting** is very common in Chinese. Example:

Name	+	Greeting
Kē Léi'ēn,		**nǐ hǎo!**

"Ke Lei'en, how are you?"

Sometimes speakers will reverse the order, first giving the greeting and then saying the person's name, which is also acceptable. For example:

Nǐ hǎo, Wáng Jīngshēng!

"How are you, Wang Jingsheng?"

A greeting may also simply consist of a person's name:

Wáng Jīngshēng!

"Wang Jingsheng!"

A common response to the pattern **Name + Greeting** is to say the name of the other person followed by the same greeting (cf. lines 1 and 2 of this conversation). Compare English "Hi, Sally, how are you?" followed by the other speaker's "Hi, Sylvia, how are *you*?"

1B.   **Kē Léi'ēn** is a transliteration of the English surname Crane. Since in Chinese the surname comes first, **Kē** would be analyzed as the surname and **Léi'ēn** as the given name. Among students, it is common to address each other by the full name. Within families or among close friends, the surname is usually omitted, so that one would then say only **Léi'ēn**. Note that a one-syllable given name cannot be said alone; thus, someone by the name of **Wāng Yáng** could be called only **Wāng Yáng**, never **Yáng**.

1C.   The **nǐ** in **nǐ hǎo** literally means "you" while the **hǎo** means "be good." The whole greeting literally means something like "(I hope that) you are well." **Nǐ hǎo** has become a conventionalized greeting similar to English "How are you?," "Hello," or "Hi." It can be used with people you know or with people you don't know at any time of the day. As in English, when someone greets you with **Nǐ hǎo**, an acceptable way to respond is simply to say the same thing. Thus, a frequent exchange in China is:

Speaker A: **Nǐ hǎo!**

Speaker B: **Nǐ hǎo!**

1D.   Greeting People. When greeting someone in China, it is customary to smile and nod your head slightly. Shaking hands with others is not part of traditional Chinese culture. In traditional China, people would sometimes shake hands with themselves, raising their hands in front of their chest, but this is no longer done. Due to Western influence, Chinese people now sometimes do shake hands with others, especially when they interact with non-Chinese, since they assume that this is expected. Though handshakes are now acceptable, they are still less common than in Europe or America. They are more common among urban than rural residents, and more common between men than between women (and not very common between men and women). In general, it is not necessary to shake hands unless someone offers their hand to you first. Follow the lead of the more senior person; if they don't reach out their hand, you don't have to either. In any case, you should avoid bone-crunching handshakes, vigorous slaps on the back, bear-hug greetings, or kissing of people you have just met; more than one business deal has been lost this way! Though handshakes are gaining in popularity, it is almost always appropriate to smile and nod the head slightly when greeting someone or parting with someone (there is no need for a deep bow from the waist, as in Japanese culture).

> **Avoid bone-crunching handshakes, vigorous slaps on the back, bear-hug greetings, or kissing of people you have just met; more than one business deal has been lost this way!**

2.   Chinese Personal Names. **Wáng Jīngshēng** is a typical Chinese name. **Wáng** is the surname, which in Chinese always comes first, while **Jīngshēng** is the given name, which in Chinese always comes after the surname. To the Chinese way of thinking, the larger category (the name of the family) comes first, followed by the name of the individual who is a member of that larger category. This order is, of course, the opposite from English. To summarize, the pattern for names in Chinese is:

Surname	+	Given Name
Wáng		**Jīngshēng**

"Jingsheng Wang"

3A.   **DÀO** "to, toward" is a coverb. Coverbs function much like prepositions in English, but they are classified as verbs in Chinese. We will discuss coverbs in more detail later.

3B.   **DÀO...QÙ.** The pattern **dào...qù** "go to…" is commonly used for asking or stating where someone is going. **Dào** literally means "arrive" or "to," while **qù** literally means "go." Between the **dào** and the **qù** is placed a question word indicating place, such as **nǎr** "where," or a place word such as **túshūguǎn** "library." The basic pattern is:

Subject	+	DÀO	+	Place	+	QÙ
Wáng Jīngshēng		**dào**		**nǎr**		**qù?**

"Where is Jingsheng Wang going?" (lit. "Wang Jingsheng to where goes?")

Another example of this pattern as a statement:

Wǒ dào túshūguǎn qù.

"I'm going to the library." (lit. "I to library go.")

Notice that, unlike in English, in Chinese the word order of the question and the statement are the same.

3C.   Question Word Questions. One common way of forming a question in Chinese is by using a question word such as **nǎr** "where." Examples:

Nǐ dào nǎr qù?

"Where are you going?" (lit. "You to where go?")

Kē Léi'ēn dào nǎr qù?

"Where is Crane going?" (lit. "Crane to where go?")

As we noted in 3B, above, the word order of a Chinese question is the same as in the corresponding statement, not inverted as in an English question. That is, in English we say, with differing word orders:

Statement: Crane is going to the library.

Question: Where is Crane going?

In Chinese, however, the word order remains exactly the same:

Statement: **Kē Léi'ēn dào túshūguǎn qù.**

Question: **Kē Léi'ēn dào nǎr qù?**

3D.   **A** as final particle to soften questions, greetings, and exclamations. **A** is our first example of a sentence-final particle. A sentence-final particle does not have any substantive meaning itself but renders a certain "flavor" to the whole sentence in which it occurs. Particles often serve as the carriers of various final intonation contours which can affect meaning. The particle **a** at the end of a question, greeting, or exclamation functions to make the utterance it is in softer, less abrupt, and more conversational. The difference between **Nǐ dào nǎr qù?** and **Nǐ dào nǎr qù a?** might be compared to English "Where are you going?" (as in an interrogation) vs. "And where might you be going?" (as in a casual conversation among good friends). To give another example, while **Nǐ hǎo!** is fine as a greeting, if one adds a sentence-final particle **a** at the end and says **Nǐ hǎo a!**, this sounds a little more casual and more colloquial. The exact phonetic realization of the particle **a** depends on the sound immediately preceding it. After a preceding **-a, -e, -i, -o, -ü, yu, ju, qu,** or **xu,** the particle **a** is often pronounced as **ya**. In other environments, it may be pronounced **na, nga, ra,** or **wa**. Don't worry about these phonetic changes for now; just try to mimic your instructors and the audio recordings, and these adjustments in pronunciation will gradually become automatic.

3E.   Inquiring where another person is going is one common type of greeting in Chinese. Some Americans might view this as a personal question which they would consider none of the other person's business. To a Chinese, however, this is usually just a way of making casual conversation, indicating that communication lines are open, and indicating interest and concern for the other person. A precise reply to such a question is not necessary, in the same way that English "How are you?" does not require a detailed answer. If you don't wish to tell the questioner where you are going, you could respond as in the second sentence in the supplementary vocabulary for this lesson:

Wǒ qù bàn yìdiǎnr shìr.

"I'm going to take care of a little something."

4A.   The pronoun **wǒ** can mean "me" as well as "I." When they wish to indicate themselves ("You mean me?"), many Chinese touch the tip of their nose with their index finger rather than placing their palm on their chest, as many Americans do.

4B.   **QÙ** + Place Word to indicate "go to a certain place." One common way to state where one is going is simply to use the verb **qù** "go" followed immediately by a place word, such as **túshūguǎn** "library" or **shítáng** "cafeteria." The pattern is:

Subject	+	QÙ	+	Place Word
Wǒ		qù		túshūguǎn.

"I'm going to the library."

Review note 3B above on **dào...qù** "go to...." Instead of **Wǒ qù túshūguǎn**, one could also say **Wǒ dào túshūguǎn qù** "I'm going to the library"; and instead of **Nǐ dào nǎr qù?** one could also ask **Nǐ qù nǎr?** "Where are you going?"

4C.   Although the English translation of this sentence includes the word "the" ("I'm going to the library"), the Chinese original has no word for "the." The English articles "a," "an," and "the" must sometimes be supplied when translating Chinese into English.

4D.   **NE** as final particle to abbreviate questions. One function of the final particle **ne** is to abbreviate questions when a question which has previously been asked is repeated with a new subject or topic, but the rest of the question remains the same. Compare examples 1 and 2 below:

1. Speaker A: **Nǐ dào nǎr qù?**

"Where are you going?"

Speaker B: **Wǒ qù túshūguǎn. Nǐ dào nǎr qù?**

"I'm going to the library. Where are you going?"

2. Speaker A: **Nǐ dào nǎr qù?**

"Where are you going?"

Speaker B: **Wǒ qù túshūguǎn. Nǐ ne?**

"I'm going to the library. And you?"

While example 1 is possible, most Chinese speakers would consider the second **dào nǎr qù** in example 1 as repetitive and instead use **ne** to stand for **dào nǎr qù**, as in Speaker B's question in example 2. The effect of the particle **ne** here is somewhat like English "and" as in "And you?" or like English "what about" in "What about you?"

5A. Unlike the verb **qù** "go," which can occur alone or be followed by other words, the verb **huí** "go back to" cannot occur alone but must be followed directly by a place word or other words. Note that the English "to" does not need to be expressed, as it is "built into" the verb **huí**. Examples:

Tā huí sùshè.

"She's going back to the dorm."

Wǒ huí túshūguǎn.

"I'm going back to the library."

5B. Besides referring to dormitories for students, the Chinese noun **sùshè** can also indicate housing supplied by an institution for its employees. For example, college housing for faculty members would also be called **sùshè**, as would housing for factory workers that is supplied by the factory. Such arrangements are very common in China.

SV1. The word **shítáng** means "cafeteria, dining hall, mess hall, canteen," as in a school or factory. Remember that the syllable **shí** is pronounced somewhat like English "sher" in "fisherman" and NEVER like English "she" or "shy"! Be careful not to let English spelling influence you when you see Chinese syllables that are spelled **shi**.

SV2A. Remember that an (**r**) in parentheses at the end of a word—as in **yìdiǎn(r)** "a little, some" and **shì(r)** "matter, thing"—indicates that the word can be pronounced with or without a final (**r**) suffix. On the accompanying audio recordings, words with optional (**r**) suffixes are always pronounced twice, first without the (**r**), then with the (**r**). For information on the (**r**) suffix, cf. pages 40-42 in the Pronunciation and Romanization section.

SV2B. **Shì(r)** "matter, thing." This word is used only for abstract things (e.g., things one is doing, matters one is involved in), never for concrete physical objects, for which there is an entirely different word.

SV2C. **QÙ** + Verb to indicate purpose. The verb **qù** "go" can be followed directly by another verb to indicate the purpose for which one is going to a certain place. A place word can optionally be inserted between **qù** and the second verb to indicate where it is that one is going. The pattern is:

Subject +	**QÙ** +	**(Place Word)** +	**Verb Phrase**
Wǒ	qù	(túshūguǎn)	bàn yìdiǎnr shì.

"I'm going (to the library) to take care of a little something."

Here, **qù** indicates purpose ("I'm going in order to take care of something"). This is somewhat different from a sentence like **Wǒ qù túshūguǎn** "I'm going to the library," which merely indicates that you are going to a certain place.

There are a few other Chinese verbs indicating movement in a certain direction that can also indicate purpose. One that appears in this lesson is **huí** "go back to." Example:

> **Wǒ huí sùshè bàn yìdiǎnr shì.**
>
> "I'm going back to my dorm to take care of something."

SV2D. A vague response like **Wǒ qù bàn yìdiǎnr shì** "I'm going to take care of some things" is a common reply to a question like **Nǐ dào nǎr qù a?**, when one for whatever reason does not wish to give a specific or detailed reply to the question.

SV2E. In rapid speech, the **yì** of **yìdiǎnr** is often omitted, so that the sentence then becomes **Wǒ qù bàn diǎnr shì**. Either way, with or without the **yì**, is correct.

SV3. **Yě** "also, too" is an adverb, abbreviated as [A]. Chinese adverbs can occur only before verbs or before other adverbs (unless they are members of a separate word class called "moveable adverbs" which we will take up later). **Yě** cannot move around in a sentence as can English "also" or "too" and, in particular, it can never occur at the beginning of a sentence. So in Chinese you could say **Wǒ yě qù** "I'm also going" but you could NEVER say ***Yě wǒ qù** "Also, I'm going" or ***Wǒ qù yě** "I'm going also."* Moreover, in Chinese, adverbs can't occur without the presence of a verb. So, while in English a noun or pronoun and an adverb may occur together (e.g., "Me too"), this is not possible in Chinese. Thus, if someone says to you in Chinese **Wǒ qù shítáng** "I'm going to the dining hall," you could NEVER respond ***Wǒ yě** "Me too." Instead, you would reply **Wǒ yě qù shítáng** "I'm also going to the dining hall" or, if you wished to use a shorter form, you could say **Wǒ yě qù** "I'm also going."

---

* The asterisk (*) indicates that what follows is incorrect and should never be said. Cf. the List of Abbreviations on p. 70.

Library of Beijing Language and Culture University

"Long Time No See!"

Michael Smith, an American who works for an international bank, meets his Chinese friend Zhao Guocai on the street in Beijing one morning. The two men, both in their early 30s, have been acquainted for years, but they haven't seen each other for a while. Smith is in a bit of a hurry, as he has an appointment in a few minutes.

Basic Conversation 1-2

1. SMITH **Zhào Guócái, nǐ hǎo a!**
Zhao Guocai, how are you?

2. ZHAO **Nǐ hǎo! Hǎo jiǔ bú jiànle. Zěmmeyàng a?**
How are you? Haven't seen you for a long time. How have you been?

3. SMITH **Hái xíng. Nǐ àirén, háizi dōu hǎo ma?**
Pretty good. Are your wife and child both well?

4. ZHAO **Tāmen dōu hěn hǎo, xièxie.**
They're both fine, thanks.

5. SMITH **Wǒ yǒu yìdiǎnr shìr, xiān zǒule. Zàijiàn!**
I have something I have to do, I'll be going now. Goodbye!

6. ZHAO **Zàijiàn!**
Bye!

Build Up

1. Smith
Zhào	Zhao [SN]
Guócái	Guocai (given name)
Zhào Guócái, nǐ hǎo a!	Zhao Guocai, how are you?

2. Zhao
hǎo jiǔ bú jiànle	"long time no see" [IE]
zěmmeyàng	how, in what way [QW]
zěmmeyàng a	and how have you been
Nǐ hǎo! Hǎo jiǔ bú jiànle.	How are you? Haven't seen you for a long time.
Zěmmeyàng a?	How have you been?

3. Smith

hái	still [A]
xíng	be all right, O.K. [V]
hái xíng	still O.K., pretty good
àirén (B)*	spouse, husband, wife [N]
nǐ àirén	your spouse
háizi	child, children [N]
nǐ àirén, háizi	your spouse and children
dōu	all, both [A]
hǎo	be good [SV]
ma	(indicates questions) [P]
dōu hǎo ma	are they all/both O.K.
Hái xíng. Nǐ àirén, háizi dōu hǎo ma?	Pretty good. Are your wife and child both well?

4. Zhao

tāmen	they, them [PR]
hěn	very [A]
hěn hǎo	very good
tāmen dōu hěn hǎo	they are all/both well
xièxie	"thank you" [IE]
Tāmen dōu hěn hǎo, xièxie.	They're both fine, thanks.

5. Smith

yǒu	have [V]
wǒ yǒu yìdiǎnr shìr	I have a little matter
xiān	first, before someone else [A]
zǒu	leave, depart [V]
le	(indicates changed status) [P]
xiān zǒule	(I'll) leave first
zàijiàn	"goodbye" [IE]
Wǒ yǒu yìdiǎnr shìr, xiān zǒule.	I have something I have to do, I'll be going now.
Zàijiàn!	Goodbye!

6. Zhao

Zàijiàn!	Bye!

 ## Supplementary Vocabulary

1.
bàba	dad [N]
māma	mom [N]
bàba māma	dad and mom
máng	be busy [SV]
dōu hěn máng	(they) are both busy
Wǒ bàba, māma dōu hěn máng.	My dad and mom are both busy.

2.
tā	he, she; him, her [PR]
tā hěn hǎo	she is well
Tā hěn hǎo, xièxie.	She's fine, thanks.

3.
lèi	be tired, fatigued [SV]
wǒ hěn lèi	I'm tired
tā yě hěn lèi	he is also tired
Wǒ hěn lèi, tā yě hěn lèi.	I'm tired and he's also tired.

---

* Remember that, as indicated on the list of abbreviations on page 70, (B) indicates that a vocabulary item is used mainly in Beijing or mainland China.

Grammatical & Cultural Notes

2A.   **Hǎo jiǔ bú jiànle** is an idiomatic expression that is used when one has not seen someone else for a long time. It is best learned as a chunk. If you are curious about the meaning of the individual parts, the first four syllables literally mean "very long not see" and are probably the source of the English expression "long time no see." The particle **le** at the end indicates that the situation of not having seen someone has been continuing for a period of time right up to the present. Don't worry about the **le** for now; it will be explained more fully later.

2B.   In standard Chinese orthography, **zěmmeyàng** "how" is written with three characters that are individually pronounced and spelled as **zěn me yàng**. For this reason, in dictionaries and in many other textbooks, the word is usually spelled **zěnmeyàng**. However, when it is pronounced, because of assimilation with the following **m**, the **n** actually changes to an **m**. Therefore, in this course we spell the word as it is actually pronounced, as **zěmmeyàng**.

2C.   **Zěmmeyàng** is your second example of a question word. It can be used by itself or, as here, with the final particle **a** to form a Question Word Question. You should be aware that **Zěmmeyàng a?** "How are you?" or "How have you been?" is quite informal (in flavor it is actually a little like English "How are ya?"). It would be appropriate to say this to someone of equal or lower status with whom you are well acquainted, such as a good friend, a classmate, or a child. However, while it would be fine for instructors to use this when speaking to students (since instructors are of higher status than students), it would not be considered good manners for students to say **Zěmmeyàng a?** to their instructors, as it is too informal.

2D.   You will have noticed that there is no word in the Chinese question **Zěmmeyàng a?** "How have you been?" corresponding to English "you." It is very common and quite normal in Chinese to have subjectless sentences, if the subject or topic is clear from the context. It would, however, also be fine to add a subject **nǐ**, if you wanted to. Here are several possible formulations of this question, all with approximately the same meaning:

> **Zěmmeyàng?** "How are you?"
>
> **Zěmmeyàng a?** "How are you?"
>
> **Nǐ zěmmeyàng?** "How are you?"
>
> **Nǐ zěmmeyàng a?** "How are you?"

Notice that the subject, if present, always precedes; you could not say ****Zěmmeyàng Zhào Guócái?** to mean "How is Zhao Guocai?" Instead, you would have to say **Zhào Guócái zěmmeyàng?**

3A.   The expression **hái xíng**, literally "still goes," could be translated in a number of ways: "it is still all right," "not too bad," "pretty good," "so-so," "O.K." This is an informal expression which would be used with people whom you know well. It is especially common in Beijing and is not often used in Southern China or Taiwan.

3B.   You have learned **nǐ** as the pronoun "you." Now consider **nǐ àirén** "your spouse." When pronouns like **wǒ**, **nǐ**, and **tā** occur before words that are closely related to the person being referred to by the pronoun (like family members, for instance), the pronouns can acquire a possessive meaning. Examples:

> **wǒ àirén** "my wife"
>
> **nǐ bàba** "your dad"
>
> **tā māma** "her mom"

3C.   The term **àirén** "spouse" is used in that sense only in China and can be offensive when used with Chinese speakers from Taiwan or Hong Kong. The reason is that the original meaning of the word is "(illicit) lover," a meaning it has retained outside of China. The reasons why the term **àirén** was promoted in China included that it is egalitarian, since it doesn't distinguish between "husband" and "wife," and that the traditional words for "husband" and "wife" were considered feudalistic and representative of the "old society," which the Communist revolutionaries were trying to change. The traditional words for "husband" and "wife" which are usually used in Taiwan and Hong Kong—and which have in recent years been making a comeback in China—will be introduced later.

3D.   Unmarked Coordination. In **nǐ àirén, háizi** "your wife and child" there is no word in the Chinese corresponding to English "and." In Chinese, items in a series are often said in succession without any word for "and." This is called unmarked coordination. Of course, Chinese also has explicit words for "and" that we will take up later. Here are some more examples of unmarked coordination:

wǒ bàba, māma	"my mom and dad"
Wáng Jīngshēng, Zhào Guócái	"Wang Jingsheng and Zhao Guocai"

3E.   Chinese nouns are normally not marked for number, i.e., whether they are singular or plural. Thus, **háizi** in this sentence could be either singular or plural, depending on the context. If the speaker feels the context may not be known to the hearer and that it is important to make the number clear, one common strategy is to add a preceding number, as in "two children" or "three children."

3F.   **Dōu** can be translated into English as "all" or "both"; the context usually makes the meaning clear. In China today, most families have only one child, so the most likely translation of the question **Nǐ àirén, háizi dōu hǎo ma?** in the Chinese context would be "Are your wife and child both well?"

3G.   Since **dōu** is an adverb, it must always precede a verb or other adverb and can never precede a noun like English "all." So while **Háizi dōu hěn hǎo** "The children are all (or both) fine" is good Chinese, you could NEVER say *__Dōu háizi hěn hǎo__ to mean "All the children are very good."

3H.   **MA** to Transform Statements into Questions. One of the most common ways of forming a question in Chinese is by adding the sentence-final particle **ma** to the end of a statement. For example, take the statement **Tāmen qù shítáng** "They are going to the dining hall." By adding ma to the end of that statement, we can transform the statement into a question: **Tāmen qù shítáng ma?** "Are they going to the dining hall?" Notice that the order of the elements in the question is the same as in the statement, the only difference being the addition of **ma** at the end (in addition, in the case of **ma** questions, the whole sentence has a higher, rising intonation). To summarize, the pattern for forming questions with **ma** is:

Statement	MA
Tāmen qù shítáng	**ma?**

"Are they going to the dining hall?"

In northern China, the question particle **ma** is often pronounced very lightly, with weak stress, so that it sometimes sounds almost like **me**. Here are some more examples of questions formed with the question particle **ma**:

Statement:	**Tā bàba hěn máng.**	"Her dad is busy."
Question with **ma**:	**Tā bàba hěn máng ma?**	"Is her dad busy?"
Statement:	**Tā qù túshūguǎn.**	"She's going to the library."
Question with **ma**:	**Tā qù túshūguǎn ma?**	"Is she going to the library?"

Be careful not to confuse **Ma** Questions with Question Word Questions. If a question already contains a question word such as **nǎr** or **zěmmeyàng**, then **ma** is NOT added. Thus, one would NEVER say *__Nǐ dào nǎr qù ma?__ to mean "Where are you going?" The correct way to ask this would be: **Nǐ dào nǎr qù?**

4A.   The adverb **hěn** "very" is a very important adverb in Chinese. In English, if we want to stress the "very," we often give it a high or high falling intonation ("Be careful, this plate is very hot!"). But this must not be done with **hěn** when speaking Chinese, since **hěn** is a Tone Three word, which is spoken with a low tone (unless, before another Tone Three syllable, it changes to Tone Two, which is said with a rising tone). To stress **hěn**, draw it out and say it more loudly, but be sure not to give it a high tone!

4B.   You have now been introduced to several different adverbs: **dōu** "all, both," **hěn** "very," and **yě** "also." Remember that adverbs can occur only before verbs or before other adverbs. When two or more of these adverbs occur together, the normal order is: first **yě**, then **dōu**, and finally **hěn**. To help you remember the correct order, memorize this sentence:

Tāmen yě dōu hěn hǎo.

"They also are all very well."

4C. Stative Verb Sentences. Disregarding for the moment the optional **dōu** and final **xièxie** from line 4, we are left with the sentence: **Tāmen hěn hǎo**, meaning "They are very good." This is an example of a Stative Verb Sentence, a very important type of sentence in Chinese. Stative Verb Sentences consist of a subject or topic, an adverb like **hěn** (optional but very common), and a stative verb like **hǎo** "be good." The pattern is:

Subject	Adverb	Stative Verb
Tāmen	hěn	hǎo.

"They are very good." or "They're fine." (lit. "They very be-good.")

Here are some more examples of Stative Verb Sentences:

Wǒ hěn lèi.

"I am very tired." or "I'm tired." (lit. "I very be-tired.")

Wǒ àirén hěn máng.

"My spouse is very busy." (lit. "My spouse very be-busy.")

Wǒ bàba, māma dōu hěn hǎo.

"My mom and dad are both very good." or "My mom and dad are both fine." (lit. "My dad and mom both very be-good.")

Unless it is stressed, the adverb **hěn** in Stative Verb Sentences often contributes little to the meaning, so that the best translation of a sentence like **Tāmen hěn hǎo** would often be "They're fine" rather than "They are very fine" (which would, however, not be incorrect). If you say only **Tāmen hǎo**, without the **hěn**, this is may imply comparison or contrast, e.g., "They're fine (but somebody else is not)." Example: **Nǐ hǎo, wǒ bù hǎo** "You're fine, but I'm not." However, if **hěn** is stressed (as in **Tāmen hěn hǎo**), it retains its basic meaning of "very" and the sentence would be translated as "They are very good." Keep in mind that Chinese stative verbs correspond to English adjectives plus the verb "to be." Thus, when using a Chinese stative verb, there is no need to add an extra verb "to be," since the "to be" is built into the Chinese stative verb.

Students talking at Beijing University

4D. Use of **XIÈXIE**. **Xièxie** "thank you" can be used to thank someone for their concern, as here, or to thank someone for a favor or a present. In traditional Chinese society, **xièxie** was seldom used to thank someone for a compliment, but in urban culture this is changing due to Western influence. Although **xièxie** is used frequently in formal situations, it is used less often than in America in informal situations among intimates (e.g., husbands and wives, parents and children, or close friends). Chinese people are sometimes surprised when they hear Americans in the movies say to their spouse "Thanks, honey"; in Chinese society, it is expected that spouses help each other, no word for "thanks" needing to be expressed. If you become close friends with a Chinese person and speak to them in Chinese, be careful about overusing **xièxie**. Overuse of **xièxie** can sound hypocritical and insincere and make the other person think you are purposely trying to create distance. Chinese people tend to express appreciation in more tangible ways, such as through gifts or by doing (or returning) favors; in Chinese society, it is considered more sincere to demonstrate gratitude rather than to express it verbally.

5A.   If the sentence **Wǒ yǒu yìdiǎnr shìr** is said quickly, the **yì** of **yìdiǎnr** often drops out, so that the sentence then sounds like **Wǒ yǒu diǎnr shìr**. We don't recommend that you speak this way at this initial stage of your study of Chinese, but you should be able to understand this if you hear it.

5B.   **Wǒ yǒu yìdiǎnr shìr** "I have a little matter (to do)" can also be said as **Wǒ yǒu yìdiǎn shì**, without an **-r** on **yìdiǎnr** and **shìr**. With the two **-r**, the sentence has a distinctly "Northern Chinese" flavor.

5C.   If someone tells you **Wǒ yǒu yìdiǎnr shìr** "I have a little something I have to do," it's better not to ask what it is that they must do. This is often just a conventional excuse for departing; maybe the person really has something they have to do, or maybe they don't.

5D.   Be careful to distinguish **zǒu** "leave, depart, go away" from **qù** "go, go to," to which you were introduced in 1-1.

5E.   **Xiān zǒule** means "I'll be leaving now (first, before you)." Since the ideal is normally for two friends to leave together, if one person has to leave first, some sort of explanation is expected. This phrase is very common and useful. You could use it, for example, when you are eating a meal in a college cafeteria with several classmates but need to get up to leave before they do. The **le** in this phrase indicates a changed situation (i.e., before you didn't have to leave, but now you do). Don't worry about **le** for now; it will be explained more fully later.

5F.   The expression **zàijiàn** "goodbye" is composed of the words **zài** "again" plus **jiàn** "see" (compare French **au revoir** or German **auf Wiedersehen**). It would be wise to keep the literal meaning of "see you again" in mind, as some Chinese people think one shouldn't say **zàijiàn** in inauspicious places like doctors' offices, hospitals, at funerals, or at the scenes of accidents. In those places, there is another expression that can be used: **bǎozhòng** "take care."

SV1.   The words **bàba** "dad" and **māma** "mom" can be used to talk about your own or other people's parents, or they can be used to address your own mother and father. Note that **bàba māma** "mom and dad" literally means "dad and mom." There are in Chinese set orders for mentioning the elements of certain groups of related words. If **bàba** and **māma** are said together, **bàba** must be said first. It would sound strange if one said the words in the common English order as *****māma bàba**.

SV2.   Review the pronouns that have been introduced so far:

wǒ	"I/me"
nǐ	"you" (singular)
tā	"he/him," "she/her"
tāmen	"they/them"

Compare **tā** and **tāmen**. How do they differ? What do you think the function of the suffix **-men** is? (The answer: **-men** is a suffix that can form the plural of pronouns.)

Chance Encounter on the Street

Brian Kao, a Chinese-American college student who is studying martial arts in Beijing, runs into his Chinese friend, He Zhiming, an employee at a local trading firm, on the street in Beijing one morning. Kao, who is in his early twenties, and He, who is in his mid-thirties, have become good friends over the past year.

Basic Conversation 1-3

1.	KAO	**Èi, Lǎo Hé!**
		Hey, Old He!
2.	HE	**Xiǎo Gāo!**
		Little Gao!
3.	KAO	**Zuìjìn zěmmeyàng a?**
		How've you been lately?
4.	HE	**Hái kéyi. Nǐ ne?**
		Pretty good. How about you?
5.	KAO	**Hái shi lǎo yàngzi. Nǐ gōngzuò máng bu máng?**
		Still the same as before. Is your work keeping you busy?
6.	HE	**Bú tài máng. Nǐ xuéxí zěmmeyàng?**
		Not too busy. How are your studies going?
7.	KAO	**Tǐng jǐnzhāngde.**
		Very intense.

 ## Build Up

1. Kao

èi	"hey, hi" [I]
lǎo	be old (of people) [SV]
Hé	He [SN]
Lǎo Hé	Old He
Èi, Lǎo Hé!	Hey, Old He!

2. He

xiǎo	be small, little, young [SV]
Gāo	Gao (lit. "tall") [SN]
Xiǎo Gāo	Little Gao
Xiǎo Gāo!	Little Gao!

3. Kao

zuìjìn	recently [MA]
Zuìjìn zěmmeyàng a?	How've you been lately?

4. He

kéyi	be O.K. [SV]
hái kéyi	still be O.K.
Hái kéyi. Nǐ ne?	Pretty good. How about you?

5. Kao

shì	be [EV]
hái shi	still is
yàngzi	way, appearance [N]
lǎo yàngzi	old way, as before
hái shi lǎo yàngzi	still is the old way
gōngzuò	work [N]
bù	not [A]
máng bu máng	busy or not busy
gōngzuò máng bu máng	work is busy or not busy
Hái shi lǎo yàngzi. Nǐ gōngzuò máng bu máng?	Still the same as before. Is your work keeping you busy?

6. He

tài	too, excessively [A]
tài máng	too busy
bú tài máng	not too busy
xuéxí (B)	study, studies [N]
xuéxí zěmmeyàng	studies have been how
Bú tài máng. Nǐ xuéxí zěmmeyàng?	Not too busy. How are your studies going?

7. Kao

tǐng	quite, very [A]
jǐnzhāng	be intense, nervous [SV]
-de	(in **tǐng ... -de** pattern) [P]
Tǐng jǐnzhāngde.	Very intense.

 ## Supplementary Vocabulary

1. **Zhōngwén**	written Chinese, Chinese [N]
nán	be difficult, hard [SV]
nán bu nán	hard or not hard
Zhōngwén nán bu nán?	Is Chinese difficult?

2. **bù nán**	not hard
Zhōngwén bù nán	Chinese is not hard
róngyi	be easy [SV]
Zhōngwén bù nán, hěn róngyi.	Chinese is not hard, it's easy.

3. **kùn**	be sleepy [SV]
bú kùn	not sleepy
nǐ bú kùn ma	you are not sleepy?
wǒ hěn kùn	I'm sleepy
Nǐ bú kùn ma? Wǒ hěn kùn.	You aren't sleepy? I'm very sleepy.
4. **gāo**	be tall, high [SV]
Xiǎo Gāo bù gāo	Little Gao is not tall
ǎi	be short (not tall) [SV]
tā hěn ǎi	he is short
Xiǎo Gāo bù gāo, tā hěn ǎi.	Little Gao is not tall, he's very short.

Grammatical and Cultural Notes

1A.   **LǍO** and **XIǍO** Before Monosyllabic Surnames. **Lǎo** is a stative verb meaning "be old" (of people, not things). Unlike English "old," **lǎo** usually has favorable connotations, indicating wisdom and experience. **Xiǎo** is also a stative verb; it means "be small, little, young." **Lǎo** and **Xiǎo** followed by a monosyllabic surname are commonly used together in informal, colloquial conversation to address people or to refer to them. The patterns are:

LǍO	Surname
Lǎo	Lǐ
"Old Li"	

XIǍO	Surname
Xiǎo	Gāo
"Little Gao"	

Lǎo is used for people who are older than oneself while **Xiǎo** is used for people who are younger than or about the same age as oneself. These terms are especially common in China, where they are used for women as well as men; in other Chinese-speaking areas they are used less often, and usually for men only. It is best for non-native speakers not to use these terms until invited to do so by a Chinese. In this text, we will translate **Lǎo** as "Old" and **Xiǎo** as "Little," though in English the best translation of **Lǎo** or **Xiǎo** plus surname would often be the given name of the person. Once two people have gotten into the habit of calling each other **Lǎo...** or **Xiǎo...**, that habit usually stays with them, regardless of their getting older as the years pass. So if a twenty-five-year-old man and his twenty-year-old friend refer to each other as **Lǎo Wáng** and **Xiǎo Zhào**, they will probably still refer to each other that way when they are eighty-five and eighty, respectively. Also, note that the same person will typically be called **Lǎo** by some of his or her friends and **Xiǎo** by others, depending on the ages of the people involved and their particular relationships. Here is a list of all the possible combinations, based on the surnames that have appeared so far:

Lǎo Wáng	"Old Wang"
Xiǎo Wáng	"Little Wang"
Lǎo Zhào	"Old Zhao"
Xiǎo Zhào	"Little Zhao"
Lǎo Kē	"Old Ke"
Xiǎo Kē	"Little Ke"
Lǎo Gāo	"Old Gao"
Xiǎo Gāo	"Little Gao"
Lǎo Hé	"Old He"
Xiǎo Hé	"Little He"

Lǎo and **Xiǎo** are not used with bisyllabic surnames like **Duānmù**, **Ōuyáng**, or **Sītú**. Unlike the monosyllabic surnames, which are not normally said alone, the bisyllabic ones can be called out directly (e.g., **Ōuyáng, nǐ dào nǎr qù a?**), very much like "Smith!" or "Jones!" in English.

1B.   Vocative Expressions.In Chinese, just as in English, the given name, full name, name and title, or family relationship of a person can be called out by itself as a greeting or to attract the listener's attention. Such expressions are called vocative expressions. Examples:

Jīnghuá!	"Jinghua!"
Zhào Guócái!	"Zhao Guocai!"
Xiǎo Liú!	"Little Liu!"
Lǎo Wáng a!	"Old Wang!"
Bàba!	"Dad!"
Māma!	"Mom!"
Háizi!	"Child!"

2.   Notice that in this line, the Chinese-American student's surname is spelled according to the rules of Pinyin romanization as Gao, but in the description next to the image at the beginning of this lesson, his surname is spelled Kao. This is because other romanization systems (in this case, Wade-Giles romanization) were in common use in America until about the 1980s. Those Chinese who immigrated to the U.S. before then romanized their surnames in different ways.

3A.   **Zuìjìn zěmmeyàng a?** "How've you been lately?" This is a very common but quite informal question. It is often used among people of approximately equal status, such as classmates or colleagues, but would not be used by an inferior to a superior. So you should not say this to your teacher or to a Chinese person who is older than you are.

3B.   **Zuìjìn zěmmeyàng a?** is a subject-less sentence. The subject, **nǐ** "you," has been omitted, since it is clear from the context who is meant.

3C.   **Zuìjìn** is a moveable adverb, meaning that it may occur before or after the subject of the sentence. So one could say either of the following:

Zuìjìn wǒ hěn máng.

"Recently I've been very busy."

Wǒ zuìjìn hěn máng.

"I've recently been very busy."

Zuìjin, usually translated into English as "recently," actually means "in the recent past or in the near future," that is, very close to the current point in time (this expression literally means "most close"). English translations can be misleading! Though this term is usually used for the recent past, it could be used for the future, as in this example:

Ni zuìjìn qù túshūguǎn ma?

"Are you going to the library any time soon?"

4.   The expression **hái kéyi** "pretty good" means about the same as **hái xíng**, which you learned in 1-2. The difference is that **hái xíng** is used mostly in northern China, while **hái kéyi** can be used anywhere Chinese is spoken.

5A.   Stative Verbs Before Nouns as Adjectives.One-syllable stative verbs can stand directly before nouns to describe them. In this sentence, the stative verb **lǎo** "be old" stands before the noun **yàngzi** "way" to describe it, creating the phrase **lǎo yàngzi** "old way." The pattern is:

Stative Verb	Noun
lǎo	yàngzi
"old way"	

Some more examples of stative verbs before nouns functioning as adjectives:

hǎo bàba	"good father"
hǎo māma	"good mother"
hǎo háizi	"good child"
hǎo gōngzuò	"good job"
xiǎo shìr	"small matter"

Entrance to the panda exhibit at Beijing Zoo

The stative verb and noun can then be inserted together into a sentence, as in **Tā shi hǎo māma** "She is a good mother." Be careful to distinguish stative verb + noun constructions like **hǎo māma** "good mother" from noun + stative verb constructions like **Māma hěn hǎo** "Mom is good."

5B. **Hái shi lǎo yàngzi** literally means "(It) is still the old way," i.e., "still the same way as before." Note the very important equative verb **shì** "to be," which will be taken up in more detail in 2-1. The verb **shì** usually loses its fourth tone and becomes neutral tone **shi** when it is in the middle of a sentence.

5C. Note the the **-zi** at the end of **yàngzi**. This is a very common noun suffix. You have seen it previously in **háizi** "child" (1-2).

5D. **BÙ** to Negate Verbs. With the exception of the verb **yǒu** "have," all other verbs in Chinese are negated by placing the adverb **bù** "not" before the verb. The pattern is:

BÙ	Verb
bù	máng
"not be busy"	

Here are the affirmative and negative forms of several other verbs you have already had for you to compare:

Affirmative	Negative
hǎo	bù hǎo
"be good"	"not be good"
xíng	bù xíng
"be O.K."	"not be O.K."
zǒu	bù zǒu
"leave"	"not leave"
huí sùshè	bù huí sùshè
"go back to the dormitory"	"not go back to the dormitory"

5E. Affirmative-Negative Questions. One of the most common ways of creating a question in Chinese is to give the affirmative and negative forms of the verb, one after another, and let the person who is asked choose one of the two alternatives as the answer. The pattern for Affirmative-Negative Questions is:

Subject/Topic	Affirmative	Negative
Nǐ	gōngzuò	bu gōngzuò?
"Do you work?" (lit. "You work not work?")		

Notice that in affirmative-negative questions, the **bù** is often pronounced in the neutral tone as **bu**. The answer to the above question would be either (**Wǒ**) **gōngzuò** "I work" or (**Wǒ**) **bù gōngzuò** "I don't work" (the pronoun **wǒ** being optional). Here are some more examples of affirmative-negative questions:

Nǐ máng bu máng?

"Are you busy?"

Zhōngwén nán bu nán?

"Is Chinese hard?"

Nǐ māma hǎo bu hǎo?

"Is your mom well?"

Xiǎo Wáng qù bu qù?

"Is Little Wang going?"

One could, of course, have created all the above questions with **ma**. There is, however, a slight difference in meaning between Affirmative-Negative Questions and **Ma** Questions. In the case of **Ma** Questions, there is sometimes a slight presumption that matters are as the statement form of the question describes (in other words, if you ask **Nǐ māma hǎo ma?**, there may be a slight presumption that your mother is indeed well). With Affirmative-Negative Questions (as in **Nǐ māma hǎo bu hǎo?**), there is no presumption at all, either positive or negative.

Note that adverbs like **dōu** "all, both," **yě** "also," or **hěn** "very" are not compatible with Affirmative-Negative Questions. So one could NEVER ask a question like *Tāmen dōu qù bu qù? to mean "Are they all going?" Instead, one would just say **Tāmen qù bu qù?** "Are they going?" If the speaker felt it were important to keep the sense of **dōu**, then one could use a **Ma** question and ask **Tāmen dōu qù ma?** "Are they all going?" Another alternative would be to express this with **shì bu shì: Tāmen shì bu shì dōu qù?** "Is it or is it not the case that they are all going – are they all going?"

To review, you have now been introduced to three basic question types of Chinese, which you should be sure to distinguish carefully:

1. Question Word Questions: **Nǐ dào nǎr qù?**

2. **Ma** Questions: **Nǐ àirén, háizi dōu hǎo ma?**

3. Affirmative-Negative Questions: **Nǐ gōngzuò máng bu máng?**

5F.   Topic-Comment Construction. The second sentence in utterance 5, **Nǐ gōngzuò máng bu máng?**, is an example of a Topic-Comment construction, a very common sentence type in Chinese. The topic is **nǐ** "you" and the comment is **gōngzuò máng bu máng** "work is busy or not busy?." The pattern is as follows:

Topic	Comment
Nǐ	gōngzuò máng bu máng?

"Are you busy with your work?"

A literal translation of this sentence would be like this: "As far as you are concerned, is (your) work busy or not busy?" The word **gōngzuò** can be analyzed either as the subject of the sentence or, alternatively, as a second topic embedded within the first comment. In that case, a literal rendering of the whole sentence might be: "As far as you are concerned (topic number one), regarding your work (topic number two), is it busy or not busy?"

6A.   Tone Change of **BÙ** To **BÚ** Before Tone Four Syllables. Look carefully at the sentence **Bú tài máng** "Not too busy." The adverb **bù** "not" is normally a Tone Four syllable. However, when it stands directly before another Tone Four syllable, as here, **bù** changes from Tone Four to Tone Two. That is to say, **bù + tài** > **bú tài** "not very." Here are some more examples of the tone change of **bù** to **bú** before Tone Four syllables:

bù + qù	→	**bú qù**	"not go"
bù + lèi	→	**bú lèi**	"not be tired"
bù + bàn	→	**bú bàn**	"not take care of"
bù + tài + hǎo	→	**bú tài hǎo**	"not too good"
bù + tài + gāo	→	**bú tài gāo**	"not too tall"

6B. **BÚ TÀI MÁNG** "not too busy, not very busy." In general, Chinese speakers often tend to avoid directness and may be reluctant to pin themselves down too exactly. They often prefer more indirect ways of speaking. The combination **bú tài** + stative verb "not very..." is very common in Chinese. As another example, in English we might say something is "pretty bad," but the normal Chinese way to say this would be **bú tài hǎo** "not too good."

6C. **Nǐ xuéxí zěmmeyàng?** is another example of a Topic-Comment Construction, which can be analyzed as in 5f above. A literal translation of this question would be "As for you, how have your studies been going?" or "As for you, regarding your studies, how have they been going?"

6D. Notice that, in the Build Up, the noun **xuéxí** is followed by an indication (B); this means that this word is used in Beijing and elsewhere in China, but not often, in this sense, in Taipei. Even though Mandarin is the national language in both China and Taiwan, there are some vocabulary differences, like American English "elevator" but British English "lift."

7A. **TǏNG...-DE.** The pattern **tǐng...-de** can surround stative verbs to indicate "quite, very." The pattern is:

TǏNG	Stative Verb	DE
tǐng	jǐnzhāng	-de
"quite intense"		

Tǐng...-de has about the same meaning as **hěn** "very" but is more colloquial and less formal. **Tǐng** is also sometimes used alone without a following **-de** with the same meaning, so one could simply say **tǐng jǐnzhāng** "very intense." Some more examples with the **tǐng...-de** pattern:

tǐng hǎode	"quite good"
tǐng lèide	"quite tired"
tǐng mángde	"very busy"
tǐng róngyide	"very easy"

7B. **Jǐnzhāng** has two somewhat different meanings. It can mean "be intense, busy" of work, study, or other activities; and it can also mean "be tense, nervous" of people. So you can say both **Wǒ xuéxí hěn jǐnzhāng** "My studies are intense" and **Wǒ hěn jǐnzhāng** "I'm nervous." When referring to housing or other commodities, **jǐnzhāng** can also mean "in tight supply."

SV1. Strictly speaking, **Zhōngwén** means "written Chinese." However, many Chinese people use it to refer to the Chinese language, written and/or spoken.

SV3. Be careful to distinguish **kùn** from **lèi**, which was introduced in 1-2. **Kùn** means "be tired" in the sense of "be sleepy," while **lèi** means "be tired" in the sense of "be physically exhausted."

SV4. **Ǎi** means "be short" in the sense that someone or something is "not tall." To indicate "short, not long," you would use a different word, which will be introduced later.

P
A
R
T

4

Visiting an Acquaintance at Her Home

Jean Smith visits Li Xianfen at her home in downtown Taipei. Mrs. Smith and Mrs. Li, both of whom are in their forties, met recently at a reception, so they do not yet know each other very well.

Basic Conversation 1-4

1. MRS. LI **Xiè Tàitai, huānyíng, huānyíng!**
Mrs. Smith, welcome!

   Qǐng jìn, qǐng jìn.
   Please come in.

2. MRS. SMITH *(removes her shoes)* **Xièxie.**
Thank you.

3. MRS. LI **Qǐng zuò, qǐng zuò.**
Please sit down.

4. MRS. SMITH **Xièxie.**
Thank you.

   (after a while)

   Lǐ Tàitai, wǒ yǒu yìdiǎn shì,
   Mrs. Li, I have something I need to do,

   děi zǒule.
   I must be going now.

   (as she leaves the apartment)

   Lǐ Tàitai, xièxie nín le.
   Mrs. Li, thank you.

5. MRS. LI **Bú kèqi. Màn zǒu a!**
You're welcome. Take care!

6. MRS. SMITH **Zàijiàn, zàijiàn!**
Goodbye!

Build Up

1. Mrs. Li

Xiè	Xie (lit. "thank") [SN]
tàitai	Mrs. (as a title) [N]
Xiè Tàitai	Mrs. Xie
huānyíng	"welcome" [IE]
qǐng	"please" [IE]
jìn	enter [V]
qǐng jìn	"please come in" [IE]
Xiè Tàitai, huānyíng, huānyíng!	Mrs. Smith, welcome!
Qǐng jìn, qǐng jìn.	Please come in.

2. Mrs. Smith

Xièxie.	Thank you.

3. Mrs. Li

zuò	sit [V]
qǐng zuò	"please sit down" [IE]
Qǐng zuò, qǐng zuò.	Please sit down.

4. Mrs. Smith

Xièxie.	Thank you.

(after a while)

Lǐ	Li [SN]
Lǐ Tàitai	Mrs. Li
děi	must [AV]
děi zǒule	(I) must go now
Lǐ Tàitai, wǒ yǒu yìdiǎn shì,	Mrs. Li, I have something I need to do,
děi zǒule.	I must be going now.

(as she leaves the apartment)

xièxie	thank [V]
nín	you (singular, polite) [PR]
xièxie nín le	(I) thank you
Lǐ Tàitai, xièxie nín le.	Mrs. Li, thank you.

5. Mrs. Li

bú kèqi	"you're welcome" [IE]
màn zǒu	"take care" [IE]
Bú kèqi. Màn zǒu a!	You're welcome. Take care!

6. Mrs. Smith

Zàijiàn, zàijiàn!	Goodbye!

Supplementary Vocabulary

1. **Lín**

Lín	Lin [SN]
lǎoshī	teacher [N]
Lín Lǎoshī	Teacher Lin
Lín Lǎoshī, qǐng jìn!	Teacher Lin, please come in!

2. xiáojie   Miss, Ms. (as a title) [N]
   Kē Xiáojie   Ms. Ke
  Kē Xiáojie, qǐng zuò.   Ms. Ke, please sit down.

3. xiānsheng   Mr. (as a title) [N]
   Wáng Xiānsheng   Mr. Wang
   wǒmen   we, us [PR]
 Wáng Xiānsheng, wǒmen yǒu yìdiǎn shì, děi zǒule.   Mr. Wang, we have something we have to take care of, we must be going now.

4. yǒu yìsi   be interesting [PH]
  hěn yǒu yìsi   is very interesting
 Zhōngwén hěn yǒu yìsi.   Chinese is very interesting.

5. méi yìsi   not be interesting [PH]
 Zhōngwén méi yìsi.   Chinese is not interesting.

6. nǐmen   you (plural) [PR]
 Nǐmen qù bu qù túshūguǎn?   Are you going to the library?

Grammatical and Cultural Notes

1A.   This entire conversation is in formal style and therefore includes a good deal of polite language.

1B.   **Xiè** is here the Chinese rendering of the English surname Smith; it was chosen because it is a common Chinese surname and sounds a little like Smith.

1C.   Titles. **Tàitai** "Mrs." is an example of a title, as are the words **xiānsheng** "Mr.," **xiáojie** "Miss, Ms.," and **Lǎoshī** "Teacher" in the Supplementary Vocabulary for this lesson. Chinese titles, all of which function as nouns, stand in apposition after a person's surname—the opposite order from English. The pattern is:

Surname	Title
Wáng	**Xiānsheng**

"Mr. Wang" (lit. "Wang Mr.")

Be careful always to say the surname first and then the title; it would be totally incorrect to say ***Xiānsheng Wáng**, in the English order. Also, be sure to distinguish the position of titles (after the surname) from the position of **Lǎo** and **Xiǎo** (before the surname, cf. 1-3: 1A). Here are some examples of Chinese surnames followed by titles:

Xiè Xiānsheng	"Mr. Xie" (lit. "Xie Mr.")
Lǐ Tàitai	"Mrs. Li" (lit. "Li Mrs.")
Wáng Xiáojie	"Miss Wang, Ms. Wang" (lit. "Wang Ms.")
Lín Lǎoshī	"Teacher Lin" (lit. "Lin Teacher")

The terms **tàitai** and **xiáojie** are not often used by Chinese in China when talking among themselves, though their use has been increasing in recent years. These terms are, however, used commonly elsewhere in the Chinese-speaking world and are sometimes used in China when addressing overseas Chinese and non-Chinese.

Titles are also sometimes used alone, without any surname, like English "Miss" in "Excuse me, Miss." In Chinese, such usage is considered especially respectful. Examples:

   Lǎoshī, qǐng jìn!

   "Teacher, please come in!"

   Xiáojie qǐng zuò.

   "Please sit down, Miss."

> **Xiānsheng dào năr qù a?**
>
> "Where are you going, sir?"

1D.   **Tàitai** "Mrs." The second syllable of this word is always neutral tone. After surnames ending in Tone One, Tone Two, and Tone Four, the first syllable of **Tàitai** is also often neutral tone. After surnames in Tone Three, however, the first syllable of **Tàitai** carries a full tone. The same is true of the titles **Xiáojie** "Miss, Ms." and **Xiānsheng** "Mr." Thus, one would usually pronounce these words as follows:

> **Gāo Xiansheng, Gāo Taitai, Gāo Xiaojie**
>
> **Wáng Xiansheng, Wáng Taitai, Wáng Xiaojie**
>
> **Xiè Xiansheng, Xiè Taitai, Xiè Xiaojie**

but

> **Lǐ Xiānsheng, Lǐ Tàitai, Lǐ Xiáojie**

1E.   **Huānyíng** "welcome" can be used as a greeting, in introductions, or as an invitation for the future.

1F.   Notice the repetition in **huānyíng, huānyíng** and **qǐng jìn, qǐng jìn**. It is quite common to repeat common greetings and other courtesy expressions in this way (cf. also lines 3 and 6, where **qǐng zuò** and **zàijiàn** are repeated). It would not be incorrect to say these phrases only once, but it would sound more abrupt, a little less warm, and a little less polite.

1G.   Imperatives. One common way of forming imperatives (i.e., expressions that tell someone to do something) is with **qǐng** "please" followed by a verb. This conversation contains two very common examples of imperatives that begin with **qǐng: Qǐng jin** "Please come in" in line 1, and **Qǐng zuò** "Please sit down" in line 3. In English, subjects are not ordinarily used with imperatives (i.e., we usually say "Please come in" rather than "Please you come in"), but Chinese imperatives frequently do include the subject, so one can say either **Qǐng qù** "Please go" or, even more commonly, **Qǐng nǐ qù** "Please (you) go." If one wishes to be especially polite, one can use the polite form **nín** "you" and say **Qǐng nín qù** "Please go." If one is asking several people do something, one can use the plural pronoun **nǐmen** "you" and say **Qǐng nǐmen qù** "Please you all go." If one does not wish to be particularly polite, it is also possible to omit the **qǐng** entirely and say **Nǐ qù** "You go" or **Nǐmen qù** "You guys go" or even just **Qù** "Go!" But the most common pattern, which is what we recommend you learn for active use, is with **qǐng** followed by a pronoun and a verb:

QǏNG	Pronoun	Verb
Qǐng	nǐ	qù.

"Please go."

Here are some more examples of imperatives formed with verbs you have learned:

Qǐng nǐ huí sùshè.	"Please return to the dorm."
Qǐng nǐmen xièxie tā.	"Please you all thank her."
Qǐng nín dào túshūguǎn qù.	"Please go to the library." (polite)

1H.   **Qǐng** can also be used alone as a very polite invitation for someone to go ahead or to do something, as in **Nín xiān qǐng** "You first, please," which might be said when you are inviting someone to enter or exit a room or an elevator before you.

2.   It is the custom when entering many private homes in Taiwan to remove one's shoes and put on slippers, which are often provided for this purpose. In China, some families also follow this custom while many others do not; it's always important for you, as a nonnative, to be a good observer and follow local practice. Sometimes the host will say **Bú yòng tuōxié** "(You) don't need to take off (your) shoes," in which case it is acceptable to leave your shoes on, though it would be considered especially considerate to take them off anyway. It is also customary, when visiting someone's home, to bring a gift such as fruit.

3.   After a guest is seated, the host will normally offer a refreshment, typically tea.

4A.   **Děi** "must" is the first auxiliary verb you have learned. Chinese auxiliary verbs are similar to English so-called "helping verbs" like "can," "may," or "must." Auxiliary verbs always cooccur with a main verb; they precede the main verb and serve to modify the meaning of the main verb in various ways. Note that **děi** is unusual in that it can never be said with **bù** as *bùděi; instead, **bú yòng** "don't need to" (cf. 9-1) or **búbì** "don't need to" (cf. 9-2) are used.

4B.   The phrase **děi zǒule** has no explicit subject. As we have seen before, subjectless sentences are common when the subject is clear from the context. Here, the understood subject is **wǒ**, which was mentioned in the previous sentence. While it would not be incorrect to add a second **wǒ**, it would sound redundant. Overuse of the pronoun **wǒ**, to which American speakers of Chinese are prone, strikes some Chinese as arrogant and egocentric.

4C.   **LE** to Indicate a Changed Situation. In Lesson 1-2, we learned the phrase **Xiān zǒule** "I'll be leaving now" with the particle **le**. We now encounter another sentence with a **le** at the end: **(Wǒ) děi zǒule** "I must be leaving now" or "I'll have to be going now." The particle **le** attached to the end of a sentence can express a changed situation; either the situation described is new, or the speaker has made a new discovery of an existing situation. The pattern is:

Sentence	LE
Wǒ děi zǒu	**le.**
"I must be leaving now."	

The sentence **Wǒ děi zǒu**, without a **le** at the end, is also correct but would simply mean "I must leave." In contrast with that, **Wǒ děi zǒule** means "I must be leaving now," i.e., "An hour ago I didn't yet have to leave, but now the situation has changed and now I do have to be leaving." After an affirmative verb, **le** can often best be translated with "now," to indicate the change in the situation. **Le** can also sometimes be translated as "become" or "get," as in **Wǒ kùnle** "I've become tired" or "I've gotten tired." Here are some more examples of **le** to indicate a changed situation:

Hǎole.	"It's O.K. now." (e.g., a little while back the TV was malfunctioning but now it has been fixed)
Wǒ zǒule.	"I'll be leaving now."
Tā lèile.	"She has become tired."

In the case of **Ma** Questions, **le** is added right after the verb, with **ma** placed after the **le**. Examples:

Nǐ māma hǎole ma?	"Has your mom gotten well?" (e.g., I know she was ill, but I've heard there's been a change for the better)
Nǐ lèile ma?	"Have you become tired?"
Nǐ jǐnzhāngle ma?	"Have you gotten nervous?"

With a negative verb, **le** can often be translated as "no longer" or "not...anymore." Examples:

Wǒ bú qùle.	"I'm no longer going." (lit. "I do not go now" or "I am not going now.")
Wǒ bù shuōle.	"I'm not going to say anything anymore." (lit. "I do not speak now" or "I am not going to speak now.")
Tā bù mángle.	"She's no longer busy." (lit. "She is not busy now" or "She is not busy anymore.")

4D.   At this point, let's briefly review the various verb forms that have come up so far. It's important that you be clear about what they mean and how to use them:

	STATIVE VERBS	OTHER VERBS
Affirmative Statement	Tā hěn máng.	Tā qù.
	"She is busy."	"She goes."

	STATIVE VERBS	OTHER VERBS
Negative Statement	Tā bù máng.	Tā bú qù.
	"She is not busy."	"She doesn't go."
	STATIVE VERBS	**OTHER VERBS**
ma Question	Tā máng ma?	Tā qù ma?
	"Is she busy?"	"Does she go?"
Affirmative-Negative Question	Tā máng bu máng?	Tā qù bu qu?
	"Is she busy?"	"Does she go?"
le to Indicate Changed Situation (affirmative)	Tā mángle.	Tā qùle.
	"She has become busy."	"She went."
le to Indicate Changed Situation (negative)	Tā bù mángle.	Tā bú qùle.
	"She's not busy anymore."	"She's not going anymore."

4E.   In lesson 1-2, we learned **xièxie** as an idiomatic expression meaning "thank you." Here, in the sentence **Lǐ Tài-tai, xièxie nín le** "Mrs. Li, (I) thank you," the word **xièxie** is a verb meaning "to thank" that can take an object. Thus, we can have sentences such as **Wǒ xièxie nǐ** "I thank you," **Tāmen xièxie wǒmen** "They thank us," etc.

4F.   Here we also see for the first time the second person pronoun **nín** "you," which is the polite form for **nǐ**. **Nín** would be used by students when addressing their teachers, by younger people when addressing older people, or by adults in polite society when addressing other adults whom they do not know well. **Nín** is more common in northern China, especially in Beijing and environs, than in southern China and Taiwan; in fact, some people in the the South rarely or never use **nín**. We recommend you use **nín** to your teachers and to others who are senior to you, but accidentally using **nǐ** instead of **nín** is not as serious a faux pas as, for example, using **tu** instead of **vous** would be in French.

4G.   The **le** at the end of the sentence **Lǐ Tàitai, xièxie nín le** is optional. It would also be correct to say **Lǐ Tàitai, xièxie nín**. If **le** is used, it expresses a changed situation (cf. 4C, above). The exact nature of the change is a bit vague, but the feeling in the speaker's mind is something like "before, I hadn't yet thanked you, but now the situation has changed, I'm about to leave, so now I'm going to thank you, indeed, now I have thanked you." Don't be concerned if you find this hard to understand; just repeat, memorize, and remember that one key function of **le** is to indicate a changed situation. With more exposure and more practice, this will start to sound right and come naturally.

4H.   It is customary for the host to escort the guest part of the way home. Here, the host has escorted the guest to the elevator on her floor of the apartment building. In other situations, one might escort one's guest to their car or taxi.

5A.   The idiomatic expression **màn zǒu** "take care, take it easy" is composed of the stative verb **màn** "be slow" followed by the verb **zǒu** "leave, depart," so this expression literally means "slowly leave." This is friendly advice by the host to the guest not to rush away but to be careful and keep safe when departing the host's home. **Màn zǒu** would not be used if two people met on campus and each went their separate ways.

5B.   Be very careful to distinguish the pronunciation of **zǒu** "leave, depart" (as in **màn zǒu** in this line) from **zuò** "sit" (as in **qǐng zuò** "please sit down" in line 3). In fact, we could even make up two somewhat similar sentences with dramatically different meanings as follows:

Qǐng nǐ zuò!   "Please sit down!"

Qǐng nǐ zǒu!   "Please leave!"

SV1A.   Be careful about the pronunciation of **lǎoshī** "teacher" and be sure not to make it sound like **lǎoshǔ**, which is the word for "mouse"! **Lǎoshī** is both the word for "teacher" and the title for someone who is a teacher. In English, when speaking to a teacher named Li, we would ordinarily say "Mr./Mrs./Ms. Li, how are you?"; in Chinese, one would say **Lǐ Lǎoshī, nín hǎo!** "Teacher Li, how are you?" Furthermore, if only one teacher is present, it is considered more respectful to use the title without the surname: **Lǎoshī, nín hǎo!** "Teacher, how are you?" Teachers refer to each other as **lǎoshī**, and the school principal usually also refers to them as **lǎoshī**. In fact, when talking to their students, teachers will sometimes refer to themselves as **lǎoshī**, instead of using the pronoun **wǒ** "I" (much as American mothers may tell their small children "Mommy wants you to take a bath right now").

SV1B. The Concept of Teacher in Chinese Society. The position of teachers in Chinese society is much higher than in American society. In China, teachers are treated with more respect by students and parents alike. For example, in China students would not ask their teachers questions that might embarrass them or make them lose face. Always be respectful to your Chinese teachers. Be deferential and address them as **lǎoshī** or **nín**. Don't use the pronoun **nǐ** and never address them by their given name.

In China, it is the custom for students to erase the blackboard for their teachers at the end of class. You could consider doing this if you have time and don't need to rush off to your next class. In China, a teacher takes a strong interest in the development of each student as a whole person and is concerned about all aspects of her or his students' lives. So if it's cold outside, a Chinese instructor may tell you to wear more clothes; if you are ill, they may give you medicine or even go visit you in your dorm. This doesn't mean your teacher is coming to check up on you but merely shows concern for you as a student.

Always attend classes, since cutting class or being late for class is a sign of disrespect. Don't wear overly casual clothes, put your feet on tables or chairs, tilt your chair back, or adopt an overly casual posture, all of which convey disrespect. Don't drink or (especially) eat in class. Also, don't underestimate the effect that your preparation for class and enthusiastic participation in class activities has on the morale of those teaching you. When your instructor corrects you, accept the correction gracefully with appreciation. If the expression on your face when you are corrected indicates embarrassment or annoyance, then the instructor may think you are not serious about learning and may not correct you so carefully the next time. Never criticize a Chinese teacher directly, especially in front of others. If you have problems with a class, first be patient and give it a few more days. If the problem still exists, you could then politely explain that you are very interested in Chinese and are working hard, but you are having problems learning something for a certain reason and wish to ask the instructor what he or she suggests you do.

In China, social relationships, once established, are less fluid than in the U.S. If a person was once your **lǎoshī**, they will forever be your **lǎoshī**. So in China, it would not be at all unusual for a sixty-year-old professor to still call his eighty-year-old retired teacher (whether from elementary school or college) **lǎoshī** and treat him accordingly.

SV2.   The term **xiáojie** "Miss, Ms." is commonly used in Taiwan and Hong Kong as a term of address, either following a surname or by itself. Because **xiáojie** used to have bourgeois connotations, this title was for political reasons seldom used in China from 1949 until the 1980s. Now it is once again common in larger Chinese cities, particularly Guangzhou and Shanghai. However, in some parts of China, it sometimes is used to refer to prostitutes. Therefore, observe how your Chinese interlocutors use the term and, of course, cease using it if they indicate that it is objectionable. In Taiwan and Hong Kong, **xiáojie** doesn't necessarily refer only to unmarried women; it is often used for professional women. Americans are sometimes surprised when a Miss Wang invites them to her home to meet her husband.

SV6.   Pronouns. With the addition here of **nǐmen** "you (plural)," you have now learned all of the common personal pronouns.* Be sure you are thoroughly familiar with them. To recapitulate:

SINGULAR	PLURAL
wǒ "I/me"	**wǒmen** "we/us"
nǐ "you"	**nǐmen** "you" (plural)
nín "you" (polite)	
tā "he/him, she/her"	**tāmen** "they/them"

* There is one additional pronoun, **zámmen**, which is used in northern China only to indicate inclusive "we." It will be introduced later.

Unit 1: Review and Study Guide

New Vocabulary

The new vocabulary of the unit, which is arranged by word class and then alphabetically within each word class, includes all items that were introduced in the Basic Conversation and Supplementary Vocabulary of each lesson. The English glosses after the Chinese are in many cases incomplete and are meant only to jog your memory. Do not learn new vocabulary from these lists. If you are unsure of the meaning or usage of an item, go back to the section in the textbook where the item first occurred and study the information included there, paying particular attention to how the item occurs in the context of the Basic Conversation.

ADVERBS

bù	not
dōu	all
hái	still
hěn	very
tài	too, excessively
tǐng	quite
xiān	first
yě	also

AUXILIARY VERBS

děi	must

COVERBS

dào	to

EQUATIVE VERBS

shì	be

IDIOMATIC EXPRESSIONS

bú kèqi	you're welcome
hǎo jiǔ bú jiànle	long time no see
huānyíng	welcome
màn zǒu	take care
nǐ hǎo	how are you?
qǐng	please
qǐng jìn	please come in
qǐng zuò	please sit down
xièxie	thank you
zàijiàn	goodbye

INTERJECTIONS

èi	hey, hi

NOUNS

àirén	spouse
bàba	dad
gōngzuò	work
háizi	child
lǎoshī	teacher
māma	mom
shì(r)	matter
tàitai	Mrs.
xiānsheng	Mr.
xiáojie	Miss
xuéxí	study, studies
yàngzi	way
yìdiǎn(r)	a little
Zhōngwén	Chinese language

PARTICLES

a	(softens sentence)
-de	(in tǐng…-de "quite, very")
le	(changed situation)
ma	(questions)
ne	and how about

PHRASES

méi yìsi	not be interesting
yǒu yìsi	be interesting

PLACE WORDS

shítáng	cafeteria
sùshè	dormitory
túshūguǎn	library

PRONOUNS

nǐ	you
nǐmen	you (plural)
nín	you (polite)
tā	he, she
tāmen	they
wǒ	I
wǒmen	we

QUESTION WORDS

nǎr	where
zěmmeyàng	how

STATIVE VERBS

ǎi	be short
gāo	be tall
hǎo	be good
jǐnzhāng	be intense
kéyi	be O.K.
kùn	be sleepy
lǎo	be old
lèi	be tired
máng	be busy
nán	be difficult
róngyi	be easy
xiǎo	be small

SURNAMES

Gāo	Gao
Hé	He
Kē	Ke
Lǐ	Li
Lín	Lin
Wáng	Wang
Xiè	Xie
Zhào	Zhao

TIME WORDS

zuìjìn	recently

VERBS

bàn	take care of
huí	go back to
jìn	enter
qù	go
xièxie	thank
xíng	be O.K.
yǒu	have
zǒu	depart
zuò	sit

Major New Grammar Patterns

Names: Wáng Jīngshēng "Jing-sheng Wang" (1-1)

Name + Greeting: Wáng Jīngshēng, nǐ hǎo! "Jingsheng Wang, how are you?" (1-1)

DÀO...QÙ "go to...": Wáng Jīngshēng dào nǎr qù? "Where is Jingsheng Wang going?" (1-1)

Question Word Questions: Nǐ dào nǎr qù? "Where are you going?" (1-1)

A as final particle to soften questions, greetings, and exclamations: Nǐ dào nǎr qù a? "And where might you be going?" (1-1)

QÙ + Place Word to indicate "Go to a certain place": Wǒ qù túshūguǎn. "I'm going to the library." (1-1)

NE as final particle to abbreviate questions: Wǒ qù shítáng. Nǐ ne? "I'm going to the dining hall. And what about you?" (1-1)

QÙ + Verb to indicate purpose: Wǒ qù túshūguǎn bàn yìdiǎnr shì. "I'm going to the library to take care of something." (1-1)

Unmarked coordination: nǐ àirén, háizi "your wife and children" (1-2)

MA to transform statements into questions: Tāmen yě qù shítáng ma? "Are they going to the dining hall, too?" (1-2)

Stative Verb sentences: Wǒ hěn lèi. "I'm tired." (1-2)

LĂO and XIĂO before monosyllabic surnames: Lǎo Gāo "Old Gao," Xiǎo Wáng "Little Wang" (1-3)

Vocative expressions: Xiǎo Liú! "Little Liu!," **Bàba!** "Dad!" (1-3)

Stative verbs before nouns as adjectives: lǎo yàngzi "old way," **hǎo háizi** "good child," **xiǎo shìr** "small matter" (1-3)

BÙ to negate verbs: bù máng "not be busy," **bù huí sùshè** "not go back to the dormitory" (1-3)

Affirmative-negative questions:

Zhōngwén nán bu nán? "Is Chinese hard?" (1-3)

Topic-comment construction: Nǐ gōngzuò máng bu máng? "Is your work busy or not busy?" (1-3)

Tone change of BÙ to BÚ before tone four syllables: bù + qù → bú qù (1-3)

TĬNG...-DE: tǐng jǐnzhāngde "quite intense," **tǐng róngyide** "quite easy" (1-3)

Titles: Wáng Xiānsheng "Mr. Wang," **Lǐ Tàitai** "Mrs. Li," **Wáng Xiáojie** "Miss/Ms. Wang" **Lín Lǎoshī** "Teacher Lin" (1-4)

Imperatives: Qǐng nín dào túshūguǎn qù. "Please go to the library." (1-4)

LE to indicate a changed situation: Nǐ māma hǎole ma? "Has your mom gotten well?," **Wǒ bú qùle.** "I'm no longer going." (1-4)

Pronouns: wǒ, nǐ, nín, tā, wǒmen, nǐmen, tāmen (1-4)

Introductions

COMMUNICATIVE OBJECTIVES

Once you have mastered this unit, you will be able to use Chinese to:

1. Introduce yourself to someone—both formally and informally—and introduce someone else to a third party.

2. Ask, on both formal and informal occasions, what someone's name is and answer what your own name is when you are asked.

3. Ask others how you should address them and tell others how they should address you.

4. Ask what country someone is from and answer questions about what country you are from.

5. Present someone with your name card or apologize if you didn't bring your name card.

6. Welcome someone to a certain place.

7. Ask questions about where someone works or studies and answer questions about where you or others work or study.

8. Apologize for having made a mistake and explain to someone who has apologized to you that it's O.K.

Asking About Name and Nationality

It's registration day at the Mandarin Training Center at National Taiwan Normal University in Taipei. American student Jerry Parsons is waiting in line to register when a Taiwanese student asks him where he's from.

 Basic Conversation 2-1

1. TAIWANESE STUDENT   **Qǐng wèn, nǐ shi něiguó rén?**
                         Excuse me, what country are you from?

2. PARSONS   **Wǒ shi Měiguo rén.**
                         I'm an American.

3. TAIWANESE STUDENT   **Nǐ jiào shémme míngzi?**
                         What's your name?

4. PARSONS   **Wǒ jiào Bái Jiéruì.**
                         My name is Jerry Parsons.

5. TAIWANESE STUDENT   **Nǐmen dōu shi Měiguo rén ma?**
                         Are all of you Americans?

6. PARSONS   **Wǒmen bù dōu shi Měiguo rén. Zhèiwèi tóngxué yě shi Měiguo rén, kěshi nèi-wèi tóngxué shi Jiā'nádà rén.**
                         Not all of us are Americans. This classmate is also American, but that classmate is Canadian.

 Build Up

1. Taiwanese student

wèn	ask [V]
qǐng wèn	"excuse me," "may I ask" [IE]
něi-	which [QW]
něiguó	which country [QW]
rén	person [N]
něiguó rén	a native of what country
nǐ shi něiguó rén	you are a native of what country
Qǐng wèn, nǐ shi něiguó rén?	Excuse me, what country are you from?

2. Parsons

Měiguo	America [PW]
Měiguo rén	American, native of America
Wǒ shi Měiguo rén.	I'm an American.

3. Taiwanese student

jiào	be called or named [EV]
shémme	what [QW]
míngzi	name [N]
jiào shémme míngzi	be called what name
Nǐ jiào shémme míngzi?	What's your name?

4. Parsons

Bái	Bai (lit. "white") [SN]
Jiéruì	(Chinese for "Jerry")
Wǒ jiào Bái Jiéruì.	My name is Jerry Parsons.

5. Taiwanese student

Nǐmen dōu shi Měiguo rén ma?	Are all of you Americans?

6. Parsons

bù dōu	not all
wǒmen bù dōu shi Měiguo rén	we are not all Americans
zhèi-	this [SP]
wèi	(polite measure for people) [M]
zhèiwèi	this (person, polite)
tóngxué	classmate [N]
zhèiwèi tóngxué	this classmate (polite)
kěshi	but [MA]
nèi-	that [SP]
nèiwèi	that (person, polite)
nèiwèi tóngxué	that classmate (polite)
Jiā'nádà	Canada [PW]
Jiā'nádà rén	Canadian
Wǒmen bù dōu shi Měiguo rén. Zhèiwèi tóngxué yě shi Měiguo rén, kěshi nèiwèi tóngxué shi Jiā'nádà rén.	Not all of us are Americans. This classmate is also American, but that classmate is Canadian.

Supplementary Vocabulary

1.
něiwèi	which, which one (of people; polite)
něiwèi tóngxué	which classmate (polite)
Xībānyá	Spain [PW]
Xībānyá rén	Spaniard, Spanish person
Něiwèi tóngxué shi Xībānyá rén?	Which classmate is Spanish?

2.
Mǎ	Ma (lit. "horse") [SN]
Mǎ Xiānsheng	Mr. Ma
Zhōngguo	China [PW]
Zhōngguo rén	Chinese person, native of China
bú shi	is not, are not
Rìběn	Japan [PW]
Rìběn rén	Japanese, native of Japan
bú shi Rìběn rén	is not Japanese
Mǎ Xiānsheng shi Zhōngguo rén, bú shi Rìběn rén!	Mr. Ma is Chinese, not Japanese!

3. **Chén**   Chen [SN]
   Chén Xiáojie   Ms. Chen
   Táiwān   Taiwan [PW]
   Táiwān rén   Taiwanese, native of Taiwan
   Xīnjiāpō   Singapore [PW]
   Xīnjiāpō rén   Singaporean, native of Singapore
   Măláixīyà   Malaysia [PW]
   Măláixīyà rén   Malaysian, native of Malaysia
Chén Xiáojie bú shi Táiwān rén,   Ms. Chen is not Taiwanese,
yě bú shi Xīnjiāpō rén, tā shi Măláixīyà rén.   and she also isn't Singaporean; she's Malaysian.

4. **Huáyì**   person of Chinese descent [N]
   Huáyì Měiguo rén   Chinese-American [PH]
Tā shi Huáyì Měiguo rén.   She's a Chinese-American.

Additional Vocabulary: More American Ethnicities*

1. **Fēizhōuyì Měiguo rén**   African-American [PH]
2. **Ālābóyì Měiguo rén**   Arab-American [PH]
3. **Yàyì Měiguo rén (B)**   Asian-American [PH]
4. **Ōuzhōuyì Měiguo rén**   European-American [PH]
5. **Xībānyáyì Měiguo rén**   Hispanic, Latino, Spanish-American [PH]
6. **Yóutàiyì Měiguo rén**   Jewish-American [PH]
7. **Hánguoyì Měiguo rén**   Korean-American [PH]
8. **Měiguode Yuánzhùmín**   Native-American [PH]
9. **Yuènányì Měiguo rén**   Vietnamese-American [PH]

Grammatical and Cultural Notes

1A. The idiomatic expression **qǐng wèn** literally means "please may I ask (the following question)." It is commonly used in polite conversation to introduce questions. It's fine to translate this expression as "excuse me," but be careful to use it only when asking questions, not to apologize. For example, you could NOT use **qǐng wèn** to say "Excuse me, I have to be going now," since that is not a question. Also, since **qǐng wèn** is a polite expression, you would not use it with people with whom you have gotten to be close. For example, if you are an American student who is living in a dorm with Chinese students, you could use **qǐng wèn** with your Chinese roommates the first few days, when you don't yet know them very well; but if you were still using it with them several months later, they would probably consider this as excessively polite and it could create distance between you and them.

1B. **SHÌ** In Equative Verb Sentences. The equative verb **shì** "be" is one of the most frequently used verbs in the Chinese language. It indicates that the topic or subject of the sentence is the same as or "equals" the predicate (the part of the sentence after the verb). This is why it is called an "equative" verb. Sentences containing the equative verb **shì** are called Equative Verb Sentences. The pattern is:

Subject	SHÌ	Predicate
Wŏ	shi	**Měiguo rén.**

"I am (an) American."

The verb **shì** is ordinarily pronounced in the neutral tone (**shi**) unless it is stressed. The negative of **shì** is **bú shi**. Some more examples:

Zhèiwèi tóngxué shi Jiā'nádà rén.

"This classmate is Canadian." (lit. "This-polite classmate is Canada person.")

Tā shi wŏ bàba.

"He's my dad."

* The Additional Vocabulary sections included in some of the lessons present useful words related to the content of the lesson for learners' reference. Meant for students and classes with extra time who desire to be challenged, the additional vocabulary is not required for learning.

Tāmen bú shi Zhōngguo rén.

"They're not Chinese."

The equative verb **shì** can be used with all three types of questions you have learned. Compare:

Question Word Question: **Nǐ shi něiguó rén?**

"What country are you from?"

ma Question: **Nǐ shi Zhōngguo rén ma?**

"Are you Chinese?"

Affirmative-Negative Question: **Nǐ shì bu shi Zhōngguo rén?**

"Are you Chinese?"

Be careful not to confuse Equative Verb Sentences with Stative Verb Sentences. Compare the following two sentences, which have the same English structure with the verb "to be" (here in the form "is"), but have very different Chinese structures:

Equative Verb Sentence: **Tā shi Zhōngguo rén.**

"She is Chinese."

Stative Verb Sentence: **Tā hěn máng.**

"She is busy."

With stative verbs, remember that "to be" is built into the meaning of the stative verb; no **shì** is added. Simply put, if the predicate equals the subject, use **shì**; if the predicate describes the subject, use a stative verb. So you could NEVER say a sentence like **Tā shi máng** to mean "She is busy."*

1C.   Because of the question word **něiguó** "which country?," this whole sentence is a Question Word Question. Remember that, in the case of a Question Word Question, there is no **ma** at the end.

1D.   Instead of **něiguó**, which is the form we recommend you learn, some people say **nǎguó** or **nǎyìguó**, which are also correct.

2A.   Names of Countries. The everyday names for many countries consist of a two-syllable word ending in **-guó** "country," with the first syllable being a phonetic approximation of the pronunciation of the name of the country in the native language. For example, the syllable **měi** in **Měiguo** "America" represents the syllable **me** in the English word "America." Many Chinese speakers pronounce the syllable **guó** at the end of these words for countries with a neutral tone as **guo**.

2B.   Nationalities. Nationalities are expressed by saying first the name of the country and then adding **rén** "person." Consider:

Name of Country	+	RÉN	=	Nationality
Měiguo "America"	+	rén "person"	=	**Měiguo rén** "American"
Zhōngguo "China"	+	rén "person"	=	**Zhōngguo rén** "Chinese"
Jiā'nádà "Canada"	+	rén "person"	=	**Jiā'nádà rén** "Canadian"

---

* The only exception is in cases of unusual stress. For example, if someone had just told you that a certain woman is not at all busy but you wanted to contradict them and emphasize that she indeed is busy, then you could say **Tā shì hěn máng!** "She is busy!" Note that here, the verb **shì** has its full fourth tone because of the emphasis.

2C. Be careful to distinguish the pronunciation and meaning of **něiguó rén** "a person from which country?" as contrasted with **Měiguo rén** "American." Not a few beginning American students of Chinese misunderstand the question **Nǐ shi něiguó rén?** "What country are you from?" and interpret it instead as **Nǐ shi Měiguo rén** "You are American."

2D. If you are a dual national or just want to say that you consider yourself both American and some other nationality, you can use the adverb **yě** "also" in the following way:

> **Wǒ shi Měiguo rén yě shi Jiā'nádà rén.**
>
> "I'm American and I'm also Canadian."

> **Wǒ shi Měiguo rén yě shi Zhōngguo rén.**
>
> "I'm American and I'm also Chinese."

3A.   JIÀO In Equative Verb Sentences.

Jiào "be called, be named" is another common equative verb. The pattern for saying that someone is called a certain surname plus a certain given name, or that someone is called a certain given name, is:

Subject	JIÀO	(Surname +) Given Name
Wǒ	jiào	(Bái) Jiéruì.

"My name is (Bai) Jierui." (lit. "I am called [Bai] Jierui.")

As we saw earlier, equative sentences derive their name from the fact that, in them, the subject of the sentence "equals" the predicate. The equative verb **jiào** here has a passive sense of "be named" or "be called"; it is often best translated as "(someone's) name is...." As the diagram above makes clear, it is possible to use this pattern to indicate what someone's whole name is (i.e., surname and given name) or to indicate the given name only. However, it is NOT possible to give only the surname when using **jiào**. Some more examples of **jiào** in Equative Verb Sentences:

> **Wǒ jiào Zhāng Míng'ēn.**
>
> "My name is Zhang Ming'en." (lit. "I am called Zhang Ming'en.")

> **Wǒ jiào Míng'ēn.**
>
> "My name is Ming'en." (lit. "I am called Ming'en.)

> **Wǒ māma jiào Guō Zhìlíng.**
>
> "My mom's name is Guo Zhiling." (lit. "My mom is called Guo Zhiling.")

> **Nǐ jiào shémme?**
>
> "What's your name?" (lit. "You are called what?")

> **Nǐ jiào shémme míngzi?**
>
> "What's your name?" (lit. "You are called what name?")

> **Tā jiào Wáng Ruìlíng.**
>
> "Her name is Wang Ruiling." (lit. "She is called Wang Ruiling.")

3B.   Shémme "what" is another example of a question word. It makes this sentence into a Question Word Question. You have now had three question words: **zěmmeyàng**, **něiguó**, and **shémme**. Remember that there is no need for a **ma** at the end of questions containing question words like **shémme** because such sentences are already questions. Note that **shémme** can be used either to modify a following noun (as in **Shémme míngzi?** "What name?," **Shémme gōngzuò?** "What work?"), or by itself (as in **Nǐ jiào shémme?** "You are called what?"

or "What is your name?"). In Chinese questions, the word order is the same as in statements, but in English questions, we switch the word order. So, for "What are you called?," in Chinese you can say only **Nǐ jiào shémme?** (lit. "You are called what?"). You could NEVER say ***Shémme nǐ jiào?**

3C.   In standard Chinese orthography, **shémme** "what" is written with two characters that are individually pronounced and spelled as **shén me**. For this reason, in dictionaries and in many other textbooks, the word is usually spelled **shénme**. However, when it is pronounced, because of assimilation with the following **m**, the **n** actually changes to an **m**. Therefore, in this course we spell the word as it is actually pronounced, as **shémme**.

3D.   In rapid conversation, before another word which begins with a consonant sound, **shémme** is sometimes pronounced as if it were spelled **shém**, i.e., **shémme míngzi → shém míngzi** "what name," or **shémme gōngzuò → shém gōngzuò** "what job." You should try to understand such usage if you hear it, but when you yourself speak, it would be best for you to use the full forms.

3E.   Just like the English word "name," Chinese **míngzi** can refer to a person's given name only, or to his or her surname and given name. In a sentence like the one here, the full name (surname and given name) would clearly be meant. Note that **míngzi** is another example of a noun ending in the noun suffix **-zi**, like **háizi** and **yàngzi**.

5.   The affirmative response to the question **Nǐmen dōu shi Měiguo rén ma?** would be **Shì, wǒmen dōu shi Měiguo rén** "Yes, we are all Americans" (note the full tone on **Shì**, since the word is here being emphasized). An abbreviated response to the same question would be just **Shì** "Yes" (lit. "[It] is [so]").

6A.   **BÙ DŌU** vs. **DŌU BÙ**. **Bù dōu** means "not all" while **dōu bù** means "all not." It is easy to confuse the two. Sentences with **bù dōu** state that the members of a class are not all something, implying that some members of the class are something and that other members of the class are not. Sentences with **dōu bù**, on the other hand, state that all members of a class are not something. Carefully contrast the different orders of **bù** and **dōu** and the corresponding differences in meaning in the following pair of sentences:

> **Wǒmen bù dōu shi Měiguo rén.**
>
> "We are not all Americans." or "Not all of us are Americans."

> **Wǒmen dōu bú shi Měiguo rén.**
>
> "All of us are not Americans." or "None of us is American."

The Mandarin Training Center

Remember that because of the tone change rule involving **bù** (1-3: 6A), **dōu bù** becomes **dōu bú** before a syllable in Tone Four (even if, as in the case of **shì**, the syllable has a basic tone of Tone Four but lost its tone to become neutral tone).

Also, while in English we could say "Not all" as a brief response to a question ("Are they all going?" "No, not all."), in Chinese **bù dōu** can never end a sentence or be said by itself, but must always be followed by some kind of verb. The briefest possible negative response to the question **Nǐmen dōu shì Měiguo rén ma?** would be **Bù dōu shì** "Not all." Finally, everywhere above where we have translated **dōu** as "all" it could, of course, also be translated as "both."

6B.   **ZHÈI-** and **NÈI-** as Specifiers. **Zhèi-** "this" and **nèi-** "that" are examples of a word class we will call specifiers. Specifiers are adjectival expressions that point to or "specify" a definite person or persons, animal or animals, or thing or things. Specifiers never occur by themselves but are always connected to other words as part of a noun phrase. The basic order is specifier + measure + noun or noun phrase, e.g., **zhèiwèi tóngxué** "this classmate." To summarize:

Specifier	Measure	Noun
zhèi	**wèi**	**tóngxué**

"this classmate"

nèi	**wèi**	**lǎoshī**

"that teacher"

Some more examples of the Specifier + Measure + Noun or noun phrase pattern:

zhèiwèi lǎoshī	"this teacher"
nèiwèi tóngxué	"that classmate"
nèiwèi Měiguo lǎoshī	"that American teacher"
nèiwèi Zhōngguo tóngxué	"that Chinese classmate"
nèiwèi Xiè Xiānsheng	"that Mr. Xie"

If the noun is understood from the context, it can be deleted; for example, if you have been talking about teachers, then **zhèiwèi** by itself could mean "this one" and **nèiwèi** by itself could mean "that one."

In line 1 of this conversation, you already saw **něi-** "which?" (as in **něiguó rén** "a person from which country?"). **Něi-** is both a question word and a specifier. Here are some more examples with **něi-**:

Něiwèi tóngxué?	"Which classmate?"
Něiwèi lǎoshī?	"Which teacher?"
Něiwèi Wáng Xiáojie?	"Which Miss Wang?"
Xiè Xiānsheng shi něiguó rén?	"What country is Mr. Xie from?"

6C.   Measures. Unlike English, where we count or specify most nouns directly ("one classmate," "this classmate"), in Chinese a so-called measure word must be used before a noun if it is counted or specified. Chinese specifiers like **zhèi-** "this" and **nèi-** "that" cannot ordinarily occur directly before the noun they modify (you could NEVER say *zhèi tóngxué to mean "this classmate"). Instead, a measure must occur between the specifier and the noun. Your first example of a measure is **wèi**, which is the polite measure for people. To say "this classmate" in Chinese, you have to say: **zhèi** "this" + **wèi** (polite measure for people) + **tóngxué** "classmate" = **zhèiwèi tóngxué** "this classmate." Another example would be **nèiwèi lǎoshī** "that teacher." But note that **wèi** is too respectful to be used with an ordinary noun like **rén**, so you could never say *zhèiwèi rén (you would use another, general measure instead). We will study measures in greater detail later.

6D.   The Concept of **TÓNGXUÉ** in Chinese Society. **Tóngxué** "classmate, schoolmate, fellow student" refers to students who are (or at some point in the past were) in the same class or school as you. This term can also be used by a principal, teacher, or guest speaker when addressing students—even though the students are, of course, not classmates of the teacher. **Tóngxué** can also be used as a title, e.g., **Bái Jiérùi Tóngxué** "Classmate Bai Jierui" or **Wáng Tóngxué** "Classmate Wang." The concept of **tóngxué** is very important in Chinese society. If two people have at one time been **tóngxué**, even if it was a very long time ago, then there exists an important and potentially useful relationship between them involving both privileges and responsibilities.

6E.   The place word **Jiā'nádà** "Canada" is a phonetic borrowing from the English.

6F.   In the Basic Conversation, Parsons indicates his fellow American classmate with his index finger. But you should never point this way to Chinese people, as it's considered impolite; instead, use your open hand.

SV1.   The place word **Xībānyá** "Spain" is a phonetic borrowing from the Spanish word **España** "Spain."

SV2.   In the place word **Zhōngguo** "China," **zhōng** is a bound form meaning "middle" or "center," while **guó** means "country." This is the origin of the expression "the Middle Kingdom." The ancient Chinese considered their country as the only civilized country in the whole world, which was surrounded on all sides by barbarians. In the same way that the ancient Chinese believed they were in the middle of the world, so did the ancient

Romans; consider the name of the sea surrounding Italy, the Mediterranean, composed of the Latin roots medi and terra, "in the middle of the earth."

SV3.   **TÁIWĀN RÉN** "Taiwanese." Some of the twenty-four million citizens of Taiwan consider themselves as Chinese, others as both Chinese and Taiwanese, and yet others as only Taiwanese. Although this question can now be openly discussed in Taiwan, it is still sensitive, so it would be best not to ask anyone point-blank what they consider themselves to be, unless you have gotten to know them rather well.

SV4.   Chinese-Americans. **Huáyì Měiguo rén** "Chinese-American" is an expression that represents an American, not a Chinese, point of view. While the expression is perfectly correct, it is not often used in China. To the Chinese, Chinese-Americans are basically Chinese who happen to be living overseas. Therefore, they use other expressions such as **Měijí Huárén** "Chinese with U.S. citizenship" or **Měiguo Huáqiáo** "American overseas Chinese." In China, there is a bit of a double standard when it comes to Chinese-Americans; native Chinese don't expect African-Americans or European-Americans to speak Chinese well or use chopsticks perfectly, but they often do expect these things from Chinese-Americans. Even more unfairly, when Chinese people hire private English tutors, they sometimes say they want to learn from a "real" American, not from a Chinese-American. On the other hand, to some extent, Chinese-Americans are considered by native Chinese as "bridges" between Chinese and American culture, i.e., they are at the same time both foreign and familiar. This in part may account for the appeal of Chinese-American pop music stars.

AV1-9.   These common American ethnicities are arranged in alphabetical order of the English equivalents.

AV3.   Alternate Pronunciations. Like English and Spanish, which are also spoken by large populations in several countries, the Chinese language exhibits a fair amount of variation from place to place. There are multiple standards (China, Taiwan, Singapore) as well as regional and dialectal differences. For a limited number of words, there are different official pronunciations in China, Taiwan, and Singapore. Your first example of such alternate pronunciations is the syllable **Yà** in **Yàyì Měiguo rén** "Asian-American." In Taiwan and occasionally elsewhere, this syllable is pronounced as **Yǎ**, resulting in **Yǎyì Měiguo rén**. The transcriptions in the Basic Conversations have been regularized to reflect standard Beijing pronunciation. In case of common alternate usages, notes have been added. But regardless of the official pronunciation, there are typically speakers in Taiwan who will use the "mainland pronunciation" and some in China who will use the "Taiwan pronunciation." It is recommended that you learn for your own active use the pronunciation of the speakers (i.e., China or Taiwan) with whom you expect

A student pays for his dinner in the dining hall at National Taiwan Normal University

to spend the majority of your time, but that you be able to understand the alternate form when you hear it. If you're not sure where you'll spend the majority of your time, then we suggest you learn the mainland Chinese pronunciation, simply because of the much larger population of speakers. In any case, either pronunciation is "correct"; don't be overly concerned about this kind of variation at this point.

Introducing a Roommate

In the women's dormitory at Beijing Normal University, a Chinese student (Ma Yulan, seated) has introduced her new roommate, a Chinese-American woman from New Jersey named Ivey Wang (at left), to a Chinese classmate of hers (Chen Li, standing in the middle).

 Basic Conversation 2-2

1. **FIRST CHINESE**   *(hears knock at door)*

   Qǐng jìn!
   Come in!

2. **SECOND CHINESE**   *(enters and greets Chinese classmate, then notices American student)*

   Èi, Xiǎo Mǎ. Ò.
   Hi, Little Ma. Oh.

3. **FIRST CHINESE**   **Ò, Xiǎo Chén, wǒ gěi nǐ jièshao yixiar. Zhè shi wǒde xīn tóngwū, tā jiào Wáng Àihuá. Wáng Àihuá, zhè shi wǒde lǎo tóngxué, Xiǎo Chén.**
   Oh, Little Chen, let me introduce you. This is my new roommate, her name is Ivy Wang. Ivy, this is my old classmate, Little Chen.

4. **SECOND CHINESE**   **Ò, huānyíng nǐ dào Zhōngguo lái!**
   Oh, welcome to China!

5. **AMERICAN**   **Hěn gāoxìng rènshi nǐ, Chén Xiáojie!**
   Happy to meet you, Miss Chen!

6. **SECOND CHINESE**   **Ò, bié zhèmme chēnghu wǒ. Hái shi jiào wǒ Xiǎo Chén hǎole.**
   Oh, don't address me like this. It's better if you call me Little Chen.

7. **AMERICAN**   **Xíng. Nà, nǐ yě jiào wǒ Xiǎo Wáng hǎole.**
   O.K. In that case, why don't you also call me Little Wang.

8. **SECOND CHINESE**   **Hǎo.**
   O.K.

Build Up

1. First Chinese

Qǐng jìn!   Come in!

---

2. Second Chinese

ò   "oh" [I]

Èi, Xiǎo Mǎ. Ò.   Hi, Little Ma. Oh.

---

3. First Chinese

gěi   for [CV]

jièshao   introduce [V]

wǒ gěi nǐ jièshao   I introduce (someone) for/to you

yíxià(r)   (softens the verb) [NU+M]

jièshao yixiar   introduce

zhè   this [PR]

-de   (indicates possession) [P]

wǒde   my

xīn   be new [SV]

tóngwū(r)   roommate [N]

wǒde xīn tóngwū   my new roommate

zhè shi wǒde xīn tóngwū   this is my new roommate

Wáng Àihuá   Wang Aihua (Chinese name)

lǎo tóngxué   old classmate

zhè shi wǒde lǎo tóngxué   this is my old classmate

Ò, Xiǎo Chén, wǒ gěi nǐ jièshao yixiar.   Oh, Little Chen, let me introduce you.

Zhè shi wǒde xīn tóngwū, tā jiào Wáng Àihuá.   This is my new roommate, her name is Ivy Wang.

Wáng Àihuá, zhè shi wǒde lǎo tóngxué, Xiǎo Chén.   Ivy, this is my old classmate, Little Chen.

---

4. Second Chinese

huānyíng   welcome [V]

huānyíng nǐ   (I) welcome you

lái   come [V]

dào Zhōngguo lái   come to China

Ò, huānyíng nǐ dào Zhōngguo lái!   Oh, welcome to China!

---

5. American

gāoxìng   be happy [SV]

rènshi   be acquainted with, know [V]

hěn gāoxìng rènshi nǐ   (I) am happy to meet you

Hěn gāoxìng rènshi nǐ, Chén Xiáojie!   Happy to meet you, Miss Chen!

---

6. Second Chinese

bié   don't [AV]

zhèmme   like this, in this way, so [A]

chēnghu   address [V]

bié zhèmme chēnghu wǒ   don't in this way address me

jiào   call (someone a name) [V]

jiào wǒ Xiǎo Chén   call me Little Chen

hái shi jiào wǒ Xiǎo Chén hǎole   it would still be better if you called me Little Chen

Ò, bié zhèmme chēnghu wǒ.   Oh, don't address me like this.

Hái shi jiào wǒ Xiǎo Chén hǎole.   It's better if you call me Little Chen.

7. American

nà	in that case, so [CJ]
nǐ yě jiào wǒ Xiǎo Wáng hǎole	it would be better if you also called me Little Wang
Xíng. Nà, nǐ yě jiào wǒ Xiǎo Wáng hǎole.	O.K. In that case, why don't you also call me Little Wang.

8. Second Chinese

hǎo	"all right," "O.K." [IE]
Hǎo.	O.K.

Supplementary Vocabulary

1. **nà**	that [PR]
shéi	who, whom [QW]
Nà shi shéi a?	Who is that?
2. **búyào**	don't [AV]
búyào zǒu	don't leave
Nǐ búyào zǒu.	Don't leave.
3. **yīnggāi**	should [AV]
zěmme	how [QW]
Wǒ yīnggāi zěmme chēnghu nín?	How should I address you?

Grammatical and Cultural Notes

3A. In the phrase **wǒ gěi nǐ jièshao yixiar**, the coverb **gěi** literally means "for." The whole phrase literally means "I introduce (someone) for you."

3B. The Chinese verb **jièshao** "introduce" has a broader range of use than English "introduce." Besides introducing people, one can also use **jièshao** to "introduce" places, books, or subject matter to people.

3C. **YÍXIÀ(R)** after Verbs to Make Them Less Abrupt. Note the grammatical construction **jièshao yixiar** "introduce." **Yíxià(r)**, literally "a bit," is often added after certain verbs to soften them and make them sound less abrupt. Sometimes **yíxià(r)** also indicates that an action lasts for only a short period of time. After a verb, **yíxià(r)** is often in the neutral tone. Here are some more examples of **yíxià(r)** with verbs you have had:

lái yixia	"come"
qù yixia	"go"
tīng yixia	"listen"
wèn yixia	"ask"
zuò yixia	"sit"

3D. **ZHÈ** "This" and **NÀ** "That" as Pronoun Subjects. In the previous lesson (2-1: 6B), you were introduced to **zhèi-** "this" and **nèi-** "that" as specifiers, e.g., **zhèiwèi tóngxué** "this classmate" and **nèiwèi tóngxué** "that classmate." Note carefully that **zhèi-** and **nèi-** never occur by themselves, but that there is always a measure word, or number plus measure word, after them. Now, in this lesson, you are introduced to the related—but different!—words **zhè** "this" and **nà** "that," which are pronouns that occur by themselves as the subjects of sentences. For example, a common formula for making introductions is **Zhè shi A, zhè shi B** "This is A, this is B," as in **Zhè shi Wáng Àihuá, zhè shi Chén Lì** "This is Wang Aihua, this is Chen Li." Here are the basic patterns with **zhè** and **nà** as pronoun subjects:

ZHÈ	Verb	Noun Phrase
Zhè	shi	wǒde tóngxué.

"This is my classmate."

NÀ	Verb	Noun Phrase
Nà	shi	wǒde lǎoshī.

"That is my teacher."

Some more examples with **zhè** "this" and **nà** "that" as pronoun subjects:

Zhè shi shémme?	"What is this?" (lit. "This is what?")
Zhè shi wǒde sùshè.	"This is my dorm."
Nà shi shéi?	"Who is that?" (lit. "That is who?")
Nà shi wǒde tóngwū.	"That is my roommate."

With **zhè** and **nà**, reference is usually to singular number but can sometimes be to plural. For example, if two people were trying to make out unclear images on a painting, one of them might ask: **Nà shi shémme?** "What are those?" And the other person might answer: **Nà shi rén** "Those are people." Finally, be sure to keep in mind that **zhè** and **nà** can occur only as subjects, not as objects, so you could NEVER say something like ***Wǒ yǒu nà** to mean "I have that."

A section of the Great Wall at Badaling

3E.   **-DE** to Indicate Possession. Examine the particle **-de** in the phrase **wǒde xīn tóngwū** "my new roommate." One important function of **-de** is to indicate possession. In the phrase **wǒde xīn tóngwū**, **wǒde** means "my." Typically, a noun or pronoun will stand before the **-de** and another noun will stand after the **-de**. The meaning is that the second noun is possessed by the first noun or pronoun. The pattern is:

Noun1 or Pronoun	-DE	Noun2
wǒ	de	tóngwū

"my roommate"

Nouns or stative verbs that are functioning as adjectives can be added after the **-de** and before the second noun, for example, **wǒde xīn tóngwū** "my new roommate." Here are some more examples of **-de** indicating possession:

wǒde gōngzuò	"my work"
wǒmende túshūguǎn	"our library"
wǒde Zhōngwén lǎoshī	"my Chinese language teacher"
nǐde xīn tóngxué	"your new classmate"
tāmende lǎo tóngxué	"their old classmate"
Wáng Xiānshengde àirén	"Mr. Wang's wife"
nèiwèi lǎoshīde sùshè	"that teacher's dormitory"

You will probably have noticed that the function of **-de** to indicate possession is often similar to the use of "apostrophe s" ('s) in English to indicate possession. When one noun precedes the **-de** and another noun follows the **-de**, you should be careful not to become confused about what describes what. Contrast the following:

wǒ māmade bàba	"my mom's dad"
wǒ bàbade māma	"my dad's mom"

Note that **-de** can be omitted when the possessor is a pronoun and the possessed is a person that the possessor is very close to, such as one's relatives. Examples:

wǒde māma	→	**wǒ māma**	"my mom"
tāde bàba	→	**tā bàba**	"my dad"

3F.   Here the speaker chose to introduce her classmate as **Xiǎo Chén** "Little Chen." However, she could have just as well introduced her classmate by using her full name, e.g., **Zhè shi wǒde lǎo tóngxué, Chén Lì** "This is my old classmate, Chen Li."

4A.   You learned **huānyíng** in 1-4 as an idiomatic expression meaning "welcome." Now you see it as a verb meaning "to welcome." As a verb, **huānyíng** can sometimes, as here, be used without a subject (**wǒ** "I" being understood from the context). In this sentence, **huānyíng** takes as its object an entire sentence (**nǐ dào Zhōngguo lái**).

4B.   **DÀO...LÁI**. In 1-1:3B, you were introduced to the pattern **dào...qù** "go to...." Now, in this sentence, we see the closely related pattern **dào...lái** "come to...," which expresses where someone is coming. **Dào** literally means "arrive" or "to" and **lái** literally means "come." A place word occurs between the **dào** and the **lái**. The basic pattern is:

Subject	DÀO	Place Word	LÁI
Wáng Jīngshēng	dào	Měiguo	lái.

"Wang Jingsheng is coming to America."

Some more examples:

Huānyíng nǐmen dào Měiguo lái!	"Welcome to America!" (lit. "Welcome you to come to America!")
Qǐng nǐ dào túshūguǎn lái.	"Please come to the library."
Qǐng tā dào shítáng lái.	"Ask him to come to the cafeteria."

5A.   **Gāoxìng** "be happy" can take a clause like **rènshi nǐ** "become acquainted with you" as its object. The sentence **Hěn gāoxìng rènshi nǐ** literally means "(I'm) happy to become acquainted with you." Some older Chinese might find this sentence slightly foreign in style, and it is true that it probably originated in translation from English. However, such usage has become widespread among educated, urban Chinese. An alternate ordering of the sentence, with exactly the same meaning, is **Rènshi nǐ hěn gāoxìng**.

5B.   **Gāoxìng** "be happy" is a very common and useful stative verb. **Gāo** literally means "high" and the bound form **xìng** means "mood" (cf. English "in high spirits"). Be sure to give the **gāo in gāoxìng** a nice "high" Tone One. Here are some things you could say using **gāoxìng**:

Wǒ hěn gāoxìng.	"I'm happy."
Wǒmen dōu hěn gāoxìng.	"We're all happy."
Nǐ yě gāoxìng ma?	"Are you happy, too?"

Be aware that the negative form **bù gāoxìng** "unhappy" often indicates anger (Chinese people often tend not to say things directly and are fond of understatement). So if someone says to you **Wǒ bú tài gāoxìng** "I'm not too happy," you had better look out; they probably mean that they are angry. An even stronger expression is **hěn bù gāoxìng** "very unhappy," as in **Tā hěn bù gāoxìng** "He's really mad."

6A.   **BIÉ** or **BÚYÀO** to Indicate Negative Imperative. The negative imperative (i.e., "don't do such-and-such") is formed by using the auxiliary verb **bié** "don't" plus a verb phrase indicating what it is that one doesn't want someone else to do. The use of a second person pronoun like **nǐ**, **nín**, or **nǐmen** is common but optional. Adding **qǐng** makes the request more polite. The pattern is:

(QǏNG)	(Pronoun)	BIÉ	Verb Phrase
Qǐng	nǐ	bié	qù!

"Please don't go!" (lit. "Please you don't go!")

Búyào "don't" is a synonym of **bié** (cf. SV2 in this lesson). Some more examples with **bié** and **búyào**:

Bié zǒu!	"Don't leave!"
Nǐmen bié jiào wǒ Lǎo Wáng!	"You guys don't call me Old Wang!"

| **Qǐng nǐ búyào zhèmme jǐnzhāng.** | "Please don't be so nervous." |
| **Qǐng nín bié qù shítáng!** | "Please don't go to the dining hall!" |

6B.   The word **zhèmme** "like this, in this way" has an alternate pronunciation **zèmme**.

6C.   In 2-1 you learned **jiào** as an equative verb meaning "be called or named." Here **jiào** is a regular verb meaning "call (someone else a certain name)." In general, Chinese verbs are more "flexible" than English verbs; depending on the context, many Chinese verbs can be interpreted in an active or a passive sense.

6D.   ...**HǍOLE**. Examine the second sentences in utterances 6 and 7 and notice the **hǎole** at the end of both of them. You will remember that **hǎo** alone means "be good." A sentence followed by **hǎole** (which consists of **hǎo** plus the **le** indicating a changed situation, cf. 1-4: 4C) means "if so-and-so, then it would be good" or "it would be better if so-and-so" or "doing such-and-such would be best." A pronoun subject is common (but not required) at the beginning of the sentence. It is also common (but not required) to add the words **hái shi**, literally "still is," before the main verb of the sentence. The **hái shi** indicates a preference after consideration of the alternatives; a literal translation might be: "After considering all the alternatives, it still is the case that..." To sum up, the pattern is:

(Subject)	+	(hái shi)	+	Sentence	HǍOLE
Nǐ		hái shi		jiào wǒ Xiǎo Chén	hǎole.

"It would be better if you called me Little Chen." (lit. "After considering all the alternatives, it is still the case that it would be better if you called me Little Chen.")

Examples:

Hái shi qù chīfàn hǎole.	"It would, on consideration, be best if we went to eat."
Hái shi shuō hǎole.	"It would, after all, be better if you said it." (e.g., something unpleasant that nonetheless should be said)
Wǒmen qù Jiā'nádà hǎole.	"Let's go to Canada." (i.e., "If we went to Canada, then it would be good.")

7.   The conjunction **nà** "in that case" connects the preceding part of a conversation with what follows and draws a conclusion. **Nà** is most commonly used in turn-taking between speakers, but it could also occur within the same speaker's speech, e.g., if he or she is asking and then answering a rhetorical question. Appropriate use of **nà** will make your Chinese seem more fluent as well as give you a bit of extra time to think of how to phrase what you want to say next.

> Appropriate use of the conjunction **nà** "in that case" will make your Chinese seem more fluent, and will give you a bit of extra time to think of how to phrase what you want to say next.

8.   **Hǎo** "all right," "O.K." derives from the stative verb **hǎo** "be good." The meaning here is something like "your suggestion that I call you Little Wang is good, I agree to it." **Hǎo** has an important discourse function in that, like English "O.K.," it can simultaneously describe the outcome of a discussion and end it.

SV1A.   Contrast carefully the pronoun **nà** "that" (as in **Nà shi wǒ àirén** "That is my husband") with the specifier **nèi-** "that" (as in **Nèiwèi lǎoshī hěn hǎo** "That teacher is good"). **Nà** can occur alone while **nèi-** must be followed by a measure or number (reread note 3D in this lesson).

SV1B.   The question word and pronoun **shéi** "who/whom" is important to know. Remember that since **shéi** is a question word, the word order in Question Word Questions containing **shéi** is the same as in the corresponding statements. So while in English we say "Who is that?," in Chinese one asks **Nà shi shéi** (NOT *Shéi shi nà?). Also, it is grammatically correct but rude (just as in English) to ask someone **Nǐ shi shéi a?** "Who are you?" It is also considered rude to use **shéi** in the presence of the person referred to, so don't ask **Tā shi shéi?** if the person being referred to as **tā** is within hearing distance. Instead, you should ask **Qǐng wèn, nèiwèi shi shéi?**

SV1C.   Some speakers, especially in the Beijing area, pronounce **shéi** as **shuí**.

SV2. **Búyào** "don't" is a synonym of **bié**. The difference is that while **bié** is used primarily in northern China, **búyào** is used everywhere Chinese is spoken. **Búyào**, which literally means "should not," is composed of **bù/bú** "not" + **yào** "should." Actually, **bié** is a shortened form of **búyào**.

SV3A. **Wǒ yīnggāi zěmme chēnghu nín?** "How should I address you?" This question can come in handy when you are in doubt about how to address someone.

Downtown Beijing near Tiananmen

SV3B. In standard Chinese orthography, **zěmme** "how" is written with two characters that are individually pronounced and spelled as **zěn me**. For this reason, in dictionaries and in many other textbooks, the word is usually spelled **zěnme**. However, when it is pronounced, because of assimilation with the following **m**, the **n** actually changes to an **m**. Therefore, in this course we spell the word as it is actually pronounced, as **zěmme**.

SV3C. Introductions. The topic of this unit and, in particular, of this lesson is introductions. Be aware that introductions have special importance in Chinese culture. According to the rules of Chinese etiquette, when introducing someone to a third party, you are not only being polite but actually passing on to them your network of social connections (called **guānxiwǎng** in Chinese). In Chinese culture, the introducer serves as a kind of guarantor for the person who has been introduced. Therefore, you should be aware that if a Chinese friend introduces you to one of their acquaintances and you subsequently create problems for that acquaintance, you may cause loss of face for your friend, since the introducer will to some degree be considered responsible for whatever transpires in the future between the individuals introduced.

When a Chinese person first meets someone with whom a continued relationship may be desirable, the initial conversation is devoted primarily to collecting potentially useful biographical information about the new acquaintance. There is, as it were, a mutual biographical probing between the two persons involved. The individuals must be identified socially and economically and the potential value of each individual to the other's social network must be determined. One mistake that American business people and diplomats working in China sometimes make is to rush too quickly to the business at hand, not realizing the importance of this introductory "small talk" for building a relationship.

There is often a litany of tedious questions, always about the same, of which the "infamous top 20" are:

1. What is your name?

2. Who gave you your name?

3. What country are you from?

4. What is your hometown?

5. Is this your first time in China?

6. How long have you been in China?

7. What cities in China have you visited?

8. Do you like China?

9. Do you like Chinese food?

10. What do you like better, China or America?

11. Do you speak Chinese? [This sometimes after the preceding questions were all in Chinese!]

12. Is Chinese hard?

13. How old are you?

14. Are you married? (If not, why not?)

15. Do you have children? (If not, why not?)

16. Where do you work?

17. How much do you earn per month?

18. Please introduce your hobbies.

19. What's the best way to learn English conversation? Can you teach me?

20. My children want to go to the U.S. to study. Can you help them?

Other topics Chinese people sometimes discuss include blood type (**Nǐ shi shémme xuěxíng? —Wǒ shi O-xíng**), since many Chinese people believe that one's blood type influences one's personality.

Though having so many people ask you the same questions may become stale after a while, it is best to grin and bear it and not resist, since if you answer the questions, your interlocutors will eventually move on to more interesting topics. If you don't want to answer some of the questions, humor is often a good strategy, or else you can give a vague, general answer; there is certainly no need to answer every question in detail. However, you should resist the temptation to be "smart" or "funny" in your answers, since this can easily lead to misunderstandings. It is best to consider this as useful language practice and try to understand your interlocutors' need to know where you "fit in." Obviously, the smart thing for a Chinese language learner to do is to anticipate the "infamous top 20 questions" and prepare for them—and that is precisely what we shall be doing in the lessons to come.

Stand selling apples outside the railroad station in Tianjin

Inquiring Formally as to Name and Place of Work

Suzanne Wood, a foreign service officer in the Political Section at the U.S. Embassy in Beijing, is attending a reception at the Shangrila Hotel in Beijing. Accompanying her is her colleague, Ron Myers, from the embassy's Economic Section. Wood notices a Chinese guest and decides to engage him in conversation.

 Basic Conversation 2-3

1. AMERICAN **Nín guìxìng?**
What's your last name?

2. CHINESE **Wǒ xìng Gāo. Nín guìxìng?**
My last name is Gao. What's your last name?

3. AMERICAN **Wǒ xìng Wú, Wú Sùshān. Gāo Xiānsheng, nín zài něige dānwèi gōngzuò?**
My last name is Wood, Suzanne Wood. Mr. Gao, at which organization do you work?

4. CHINESE **Wǒ zài Wàijiāobù gōngzuò. Nín ne?**
I work at the Foreign Ministry. And you?

5. AMERICAN **Wǒ zài Měiguo Dàshǐguǎn gōngzuò.**
I work at the U.S. Embassy.

6. CHINESE **Nèiwèi shi nínde xiānsheng ba?**
I suppose that must be your husband?

7. AMERICAN **Bú shì, bú shì! Tā shi wǒde tóngshì.**
No, no! He's my colleague.

8. CHINESE *(after a while)* **Ò, Wú Nǚshì, duìbuqǐ. Wǒ yǒu yìdiǎnr shìr, xiān zǒule. Zàijiàn!**
Oh, Madam Wood, excuse me. I have something I have to do, I have to be going now. Goodbye!

9. AMERICAN **Zàijiàn!**
Goodbye!

 Build Up

1. American
 guìxìng "what's your honorable surname?" [IE]
Nín guìxìng? What's your last name?

2. **Chinese**

xìng	be surnamed [EV]
wǒ xìng Gāo	my surname is Gao
Wǒ xìng Gāo. Nín guìxìng?	My last name is Gao. What's your last name?

3. **American**

Wú	Wu [SN]
Sùshān	(Chinese for "Suzanne")
zài	be located at, at [CV]
ge	(general measure) [M]
něige	which one, which
dānwèi	work unit, organization [PW]
něige dānwèi	which organization
zài něige dānwèi	at which organization
gōngzuò	work [V]
zài něige dānwèi gōngzuò	work at which organization
Wǒ xìng Wú, Wú Sùshān.	My last name is Wood, Suzanne Wood.
Gāo Xiānsheng, nín zài něige dānwèi gōngzuò?	Mr. Gao, at which organization do you work?

4. **Chinese**

wàijiāobù	foreign ministry [PW]
zài Wàijiāobù gōngzuò	work at the Foreign Ministry
Wǒ zài Wàijiāobù gōngzuò. Nín ne?	I work at the Foreign Ministry. And you?

5. **American**

dàshǐguǎn	embassy [PW]
Měiguo Dàshǐguǎn	American Embassy
Wǒ zài Měiguo Dàshǐguǎn gōngzuò.	I work at the U.S. Embassy.

6. **Chinese**

nèiwèi	that (person, polite)
xiānsheng	husband [N]
nínde xiānsheng	your (polite) husband
nèiwèi shi nínde xiānsheng	that is your husband
ba	(indicates supposition) [P]
Nèiwèi shi nínde xiānsheng ba?	I suppose that must be your husband?

7. **American**

bú shì	it is not so
tóngshì	colleague [N]
wǒde tóngshì	my colleague
tā shi wǒde tóngshì	he is my colleague
Bú shì, bú shì! Tā shi wǒde tóngshì.	No, no! He's my colleague.

8. **Chinese**

nǚshì	madam, lady [N]
Wú Nǚshì	Madam Wu
duìbuqǐ	"excuse me," "sorry" [IE]
Ò, Wú Nǚshì, duìbuqǐ.	Oh, Madam Wood, excuse me.
Wǒ yǒu yìdiǎnr shìr, xiān zǒule. Zàijiàn!	I have something I have to do, I have to be going now. Goodbye!

9. **American**

Zàijiàn!	Goodbye!

Supplementary Vocabulary

1. **tàitai**   wife [N]
   Zhè shi wǒ tàitai.   This is my wife.

2. **yī**   one, a [NU]
   jiā   (for companies, factories) [M]
   yìjiā   a (company, factory)
   gōngsī   company, firm [PW]
   yìjiā gōngsī   a company
   zài yìjiā gōngsī gōngzuò   work at a company
   Wǒ bàba zài yìjiā gōngsī gōngzuò.   My dad works at a company.

3. **xuéxí (B)**   learn, study [V]
   Nǐ zài nǎr xuéxí?   Where do you study?

4. **dàxué**   university, college [PW]
   Xiānggǎng   Hong Kong [PW]
   Xiānggǎng Zhōngwén Dàxué   Chinese University of Hong Kong [PW]
   Wǒ zài Xiānggǎng Zhōngwén Dàxué xuéxí.   I study at the Chinese University of Hong Kong.

5. **xiàozhǎng**   head of a school [N]
   xìng shémme   be surnamed what
   Nǐmende xiàozhǎng xìng shémme?   What's the last name of your principal?

Grammatical and Cultural Notes

1A.   **Guì-**, which literally means "be expensive, precious, honorable," is an honorific prefix which indicates respect by the person speaking for the person spoken to. By far the most common use of **guì-** is in the following question:

> **Nín guìxìng?**
>
> "What is your last name?" (lit. "Your honorable surname?")

If someone asks you **Nín guìxìng?**, you would answer **Wǒ xìng...** followed by your Chinese surname. You could NEVER answer **Wǒ guìxìng...*, because **guì-** is an honorific and can only be used to refer to others, never to yourself.

The question **Nín guìxìng?** can be extended to **Qǐng wèn, nín guìxìng?** "Excuse me, what is your honorable surname?" or it can be shortened to simply **Guìxìng?** "Your honorable last name?" Somewhat more formal would be to avoid **nín** and give the title of the person followed by **guìxìng** as in:

> **Xiānshēng guìxìng?**
>
> "Sir, what is your honorable last name?"

> **Xiáojie guìxìng?**
>
> "Miss, what is your honorable last name?"

These expressions with **guìxìng** are commonly used by educated adults on formal occasions when meeting someone for the first time, but would not be used in informal situations such as among students at a university. Students or working class people would usually ask each other **Nǐ xìng shémme?** "What is your last name?" or **Nǐ jiào shémme míngzi?** "What is your name?" Also, you should note that the questions with **Guìxìng?** are used only for a person directly addressed; if discussing a third party, one would say **Tā xìng shémme?** "What is her/his last name?" The honorific prefix **guì-** is also occasionally attached to other nouns such as **guó** "country" (e.g., **Nín guìguó shi něiguó?** "What is your honorable country?") but such usage is considered very formal.

1B. Be careful to distinguish the pronunciation of **Guìxìng?** "What is your honorable surname?" from the stative verb **gāoxìng** "be happy" that we learned in 2-2.

1C. Intonation Questions. Besides the question types we have already taken up, there is a fourth question type, the Intonation Question. In intonation questions, the pitch of the whole sentence is slightly higher than normal. **Nín guìxìng?**, literally "Your honorable surname?," is your first example of an Intonation Question.

2. **XÌNG** in Equative Verb Sentences. **Xìng** is an equative verb meaning "be surnamed." As we have seen before in the cases of **shì** and **jiào** (cf. 2-1: 1B and 2-1: 3A), in Equative Verb Sentences the subject "equals" the object. The pattern for indicating that one has a certain surname is:

Subject	XÌNG	Surname
Wǒ	xìng	Gāo.

"My last name is Gao." (lit. "I am surnamed Gao.")

For smoother English, equative sentences with **xìng** can be translated as "(subject's) family name is…" or "(subject's) last name is…." Now, some more examples of **xìng** in Equative Verb Sentences:

Wǒ xìng Zhāng.	"My last name is Zhang."
Tā yě xìng Zhāng.	"Her last name is Zhang, too."
Nǐ xìng shémme?	"What's your last name?"

If someone asks you **Nín guìxìng?**, it is common (but not required) to answer by first saying **Wǒ xìng…** plus your surname, and then to follow that by saying your whole name. This is what Suzanne Wood does in the next line of this conversation, where she says:

Wǒ xìng Wú, Wú Sùshān.	"My last name is Wood, Suzanne Wood."

An even more complete reply would have been **Wǒ xìng Wú, (wǒ) jiào Wú Sùshān** "My last name is Wu, my whole name is Wu Sushan."

At this point, let us briefly review the various ways to ask and answer questions about people's names. Let's say you want to ask a man what his name is and the man happens to be named **Wáng Dàmíng** (except you don't know that yet!). Here is what you would ask and what Mr. Wang would answer:

TO ASK ABOUT HIS:	YOU ASK:	HE ANSWERS:
Surname only (ordinary style)	**Nǐ xìng shémme?**	**Wǒ xìng Wáng.**
Surname only (polite style)	**Nín guìxìng?**	**Wǒ xìng Wáng.**
Surname and given name	**Nǐ jiào shémme míngzi?**	**Wǒ jiào Wáng Dàmíng.**
Given name only	**Nǐ jiào shémme míngzi?**	**Wǒ jiào Dàmíng.**

Study carefully the chart above of what you SHOULD say. Now, below, are some things you SHOULD NOT say. Let's assume your name is **Wú Sùshān** and a Chinese person has just asked you what your name is. The following responses would be INCORRECT:

  *****Wú.** (unlike English, you can't answer with your last name only; say **Wǒ xìng Wú.**)

  *****Sùshān.** (unlike English, you can't answer with your first name only; say **Wǒ jiào Sùshān.**)

  *****Wú Sùshān.** (unlike English, you can't answer with your whole name only; say **Wǒ jiào Wú Sùshān.**)

  *****Wǒ guìxìng Wú.** (guì- is an honorific used only in polite reference to others; say **Wǒ xìng Wú.**)

  *****Wǒ xìng Wú Xiáojie.** (you can't use a title with your own name; say **Wǒ xìng Wú.**)

  *****Wǒ guìxìng Wú Xiáojie.** (you can't use guì- and a title for yourself; say **Wǒ xìng Wú.**)

  *****Wǒ xìng Sùshān.** (xìng must be followed by a surname only; say **Wǒ jiào Sùshān.**)

*Wǒ xìng Wú Sùshān. (xìng must be followed by a surname only; say Wǒ jiào Wú Sùshān.)

*Tā shi xìng Wú. (the verb "to be" is "built in" to the verb xìng; say Tā xìng Wú.)

3A. Note in this sentence the use of the coverb **zài** "be located at, in, on" together with the main verb **gōngzuò** "work." The literal meaning of the question **Nín zài nĕige dānwèi gōngzuò?** is "You located at which organization work?," in other words, "Which organization do you work in?" We will take up **zài** in more detail in a later lesson. For now, just learn how to ask where someone works or goes to school and be able to answer when you are asked. Here are some more examples with **zài** as coverb plus another main verb:

Nĭ zài năr gōngzuò?	"Where do you work?"
Wŏ zài yìjiā gōngsī gōngzuò.	"I work at a company."
Nĭ zài năr xuéxí?	"Where do you study?"
Wŏ zài Bĕijīng Dàxué xuéxí.	"I study at Peking University."

3B. You have previously seen the question word/specifier **nĕi-** "which?" in **nĕiguó rén** "a person from which country?" and in **nĕiwèi** "which? (of people, polite)" as in **Nĕiwèi tóngxué?** "Which classmate?" Now you are introduced to the very common expression **nĕige** "which one?" or "which?," composed of **nĕi-** and the general measure **ge** "item, unit." Study these three hugely important words:

zhèige "this one," "this"

nèige "that one," "that"

nĕige "which one?," "which?"

3C. Notice that there is no question particle **ma** at the end of the question **Nín zài nĕige dānwèi gōngzuò?** Do you remember the reason why? Answer: If there is already a question word in a sentence (here the question word is **nĕige**), there is ordinarily no **ma** at the end of the sentence.

3D. The Concept of the **DĀNWÈI** In PRC Chinese Society. The **dānwèi** or "work unit," which refers to a person's place of employment, was long one of the basic socio-political structures of society in the People's Republic of China. **Dānwèi** is the general term for the organization where one works, be it a factory, company, school, hospital, government office, or other organization. Most Chinese people belong to a **dānwèi**: it assigns work duties, pays one's salary, and may arrange housing and other benefits. If there are political instructions from higher levels, it is usually through the **dānwèi** that they are transmitted. Until only a few years ago, if one wished to move, change jobs, travel abroad, get married, get divorced, or have a child, one had to apply for permission from one's **dānwèi**. Foreigners who work or study in China also have a **dānwèi**. If you're a student, your school is your **dānwèi** and you have obligations to it; it will be held responsible for any mistakes you make. In the past, most people were assigned to a **dānwèi** on graduation from school and tended to remain in the same **dānwèi** through retirement. In recent years, as China's economy has liberalized, the influence of the **dānwèi** in daily life has lessened and there has begun to be more job mobility than before. The term **dānwèi** is also used by Chinese people outside of China to refer generally to organizations.

3E. In 1-3 you learned **gōngzuò** as a noun meaning "work." Now, you learn it as a verb meaning "to work." There are many words in Chinese which belong to more than one word class. Another is **xuéxí** in the Supplementary Vocabulary of this lesson, which functions both as a noun meaning "studies" and as a verb meaning "to study, to learn."

3F. Instead of **Nín zài nĕige dānwèi gōngzuò?** "At which organization do you work?," the speaker could just as well have asked **Nín zài năr gōngzuò?** "Where do you work?."

5. The place word **dàshĭguăn** "embassy" is composed of the noun **dàshĭ** "ambassador" plus the noun suffix **-guăn** "large building, establishment." You have seen **-guăn** before in the word **túshūguăn** "library."

6A. You have previously seen **xiānsheng** used as a title similar to English "Mr." This same word can also be used, as here, to mean "husband."

6B.   **BA to Indicate Supposition.** The sentence-final particle **ba** can be added to the end of a statement to indicate that the speaker supposes that what he or she has said must be so. For example, take the statement **Tā shi Yīngguo rén** "She's English." By adding **ba** to the end of this statement, we transform the statement into a supposition: **Tā shi Yīngguo rén ba** "I suppose she's English." The pattern is:

Statement	BA
Tā shi Yīngguo rén	**ba.**
"I suppose she's English."	

The pattern with **ba** indicating supposition is very common in spoken Chinese. Frequent, appropriate use of **ba** will make your Chinese sound fluent and natural. Common English translations of this **ba** include "I suppose that...," "I guess...," and "...must be...." Here are additional examples with **ba** to indicate supposition:

Tāmen yě shi Yīngguo rén ba?	"I suppose they must be English, too."
Tā bú shi nǐde tóngxué ba?	"She's not your classmate, is she?"
Zhèiwèi shi nín tàitai ba?	"I suppose this must be your wife?"
Nǐde gōngzuò hěn máng ba?	"Your work must be pretty busy?"
Nǐ lèile ba?	"I suppose you must be tired?"

(This last expression is particularly useful. It might be said to express your sincere concern for a person when meeting them at the airport or train station after a long trip, much as in English we would say "How are you?" Less sincerely, this is also a useful expression when you are with someone and it is getting late and you wish to go home; in this case you can say to the other person **Nǐ lèile ba?**, which on the surface would seem to mean that you are concerned that they may be tired, but actually it can also indicate to the other person that it is you who is getting tired and needs to go home.)

Try to avoid saying **ba** after syllables ending in **wáng** or **jī**, because in the former case it creates an epithet meaning "tortoise," and in the latter case it creates a vulgar word for male sexual organ.

> If it's getting late and you wish to go home, you can say **Nǐ lèile ba?** "You must be tired?", which actually can indicate it's *you* who's getting tired and needs to go home.

7.   There are three things to note about **Bú shì, bú shì!** "No, no!" First, in **bú shì** "it is not (thus)," the **bù** "not" has changed to Tone Two (**bú**) because the following syllable (**shì** "be") is Tone Four. You may wish to review the rule about the tone change of **bù** to **bú** before Tone Four syllables (cf. 1-3: 6A). Second, **shì** is here pronounced with a full Tone Four rather than neutral tone because of emphasis. And third, **Bú shì** is repeated for additional emphasis and also because of the Chinese predilection for repeating short phrases, as we saw in lesson 1-4.

8A.   **Nǚshì** "madam, lady" is a formal, polite title for a married or unmarried woman. It can be used alone (e.g., **Nèiwèi nǚshì shi shéi?** "Who is that lady?") or after a woman's own surname (e.g., **Wú Nǚshì** "Madam Wood," **Lǐ Nǚshì** "Madam Li").

8B.   **Duìbuqǐ** "I'm sorry, excuse me" literally means "I can't face you (because of my shame at the terrible mistake that I have made)." You cannot use this if something is obviously not your fault. There is a story about a foreigner who, on hearing that a Chinese friend's grandmother had died, said to his friend **Duìbuqǐ** "I'm sorry." But unlike English "I'm sorry" (which expresses general regret, either about things one has done oneself or about things that have happened which are out of one's control), Chinese **duìbuqǐ** implies that the speaker has done something wrong. In other words, it sounded as though the speaker had had a hand in the death of his friend's grandmother! So if you accidentally step on someone's foot on a crowded bus, by all means say **duìbuqǐ**. But if someone says to you they don't feel well, you should not say **duìbuqǐ** to them. Also, be sure to contrast **duìbuqǐ** with **qǐng wèn** "excuse me (I would like to ask a question)" that you had in 2-1.

SV1.   You have seen the word **tàitai** previously as a title meaning "Mrs.," for example, in **Wáng Tàitai** "Mrs. Wang." In this lesson, **tàitai** is introduced as the word for "wife" or "married lady," as in **Tā shi wǒ tàitai** "She is my wife." The word **tàitai** is very common in Taiwan, Hong Kong, Singapore, and overseas Chinese communities. But you should be aware that, from 1949 until the 1980s, **tàitai** was not used in China, since it carried connotations of the old, pre-Communist society; in its place, the term **àirén** came to be used, as it still is today (of course, **àirén** can also mean "husband"). However, in the larger Chinese cities, especially in conversation with foreigners and overseas Chinese, **tàitai** can now again be used.

SV2.   Tone Changes Involving **YĪ**. By itself, as in counting, the number **yī** "one" or "a" is pronounced in Tone One as **yī**. However, **yī** changes to Tone Four **yì** before syllables in Tones One, Two, and Three. Examples:

Before Tone One:	**yī + jiā** →	**yìjiā** (e.g., **yìjiā gōngsī** "a company")
Before Tone Two:	**yī + nián** →	**yìnián** "one year"
Before Tone Three:	**yī + diǎnr** →	**yìdiǎnr** "a little"

In addition, before syllables in Tone Four, **yī** changes to Tone Two **yí**. Example:

Before Tone Four: **yī + wèi → yíwèi** (e.g., **yíwèi xiáojie** "a young lady")

SV3.   You previously learned **xuéxí** as a noun meaning "studies." Now you learn it as a verb meaning "to study, to learn." When used without a following object, **xuéxí** often means "study." Examples:

Tā zài Běijīng Dàxué xuéxí.	"She is studying at Peking University."
Tā zài túshūguǎn xuéxí.	"She is studying in the library."

Xuéxí can also be used with an object, in which case it can mean "study" or "learn." Examples:

Nǐ zài nǎr xuéxí Zhōngwén?	"Where are you learning Chinese?"
Wǒ zài Wēilián Dàxué xuéxí Zhōngwén.	"I'm studying Chinese at Williams College."

The verb **xuéxí** is a new term in spoken Chinese that is used principally in China. In other Chinese-speaking regions of the world, more traditional expressions that we will take up later are usually used.

SV5A.   Translation from Chinese into English, or from English into Chinese, can be tricky. Always be on your guard about making unwarranted assumptions about equivalences between the two languages. In the context of colleges and universities, the noun **xiàozhǎng** "head of a school" is often translated into English as "president," but **xiàozhǎng** could never be used to refer to the president of a country. In the context of elementary and secondary schools, the best translation of **xiàozhǎng** would actually be "principal."

SV5B.   Unless several school presidents or principals are present and you need to distinguish between them, the most respectful way to address a school president or principal is just to call out the title **Xiàozhǎng**, since saying this without a preceding surname implies that he or she is the "one and only" **xiàozhǎng** present. The same principle applies to many other titles. Of course, if there is a meeting of the county education bureau with numerous school principals in attendance, then you would have to address them as **Wáng Xiàozhǎng, Lǐ Xiàozhǎng**, and so forth.

SV5C.   Distinguish the pronunciation of the following two terms of address: **Xiàozhǎng** "School President" versus **Xiǎo Zhāng** "Little Zhang."

SV5D.   Look at the question **Nǐmende xiàozhǎng xìng shémme?** "What is the last name of your principal?" According to dictionaries, the question word **shémme** "what?" should be pronounced with Tone Two on the first syllable, and this is how we recommend you pronounce it. However, the fact is that many speakers pronounce this word with Tone Three on the first syllable, so that **xìng shémme** is pronounced as **xìng shěmme**.

The U.S. Embassy in Beijing

SV5E. More On Chinese Personal Names. One of the commonest types of words you will encounter in using Chinese is personal names. Like English names, Chinese names consist of a surname (**xìng**) and a given name (**míngzi**). Unlike English, in Chinese the surname always comes first, followed by the given name. This is in accordance with a general tendency in Chinese to proceed from the larger or more general category to the smaller or more specific one, which is the reverse of English. Thus, the Chinese say "Doe Jane," i.e., "of the larger class Doe, we are talking about the individual named Jane," while in English we say "Jane Doe," i.e., "the individual named Jane who is a member of the larger class named Doe."

Traditionally, the commonest pattern for Chinese names consists of a one-syllable surname followed by a two-syllable given name, for example, **Máo Zédōng**, where **Máo** is the surname and **Zédōng** the given name. Other examples of this pattern are **Jiǎng Jièshí** and **Zhōu Ēnlái**. In such cases, even though we are in fact dealing with a two-syllable given name, when romanizing it (i.e., writing it in English), some Chinese prefer to write each syllable separately. Thus, a name like **Lǐ Zhènjié** might be written in English by some Chinese as Li Zhen Jie. This is a little like writing the English given name "Maryanne" as "Mary Anne."

Another common pattern for Chinese names is a one-syllable surname followed by a one-syllable given name, for example, **Huáng Huá** and **Hú Shì**, where **Huáng** and **Hú** are the surnames and **Huá** and **Shì** are the given names. This type of name was very popular in mainland China during the second half of the 20th century. A much less frequent pattern, but one still encountered from time to time, consists of a two-syllable surname with either a one-syllable or a two-syllable given name, for example, **Sīmǎ Xiàngrú** and **Sītú Fú**, where **Sīmǎ** and **Sītú** are the surnames and **Xiàngrú** and **Fú** are the given names.

The different possibilities may be summed up in the following table:

EXAMPLE	SURNAME	GIVEN NAME
Máo Zédōng	**Máo** (1 syllable)	**Zédōng** (2 syllables)
Hú Shì	**Hú** (1 syllable)	**Shì** (1 syllable)
Ōuyáng Xiū	**Ōuyáng** (2 syllables)	**Xiū** (1 syllable)
Sīmǎ Xiàngrú	**Sīmǎ** (2 syllables)	**Xiàngrú** (2 syllables)

Although over three thousand surnames exist, only about 150 are commonly used, with the most frequent twenty surnames representing over 95% of the Chinese population. Literally tens of millions of people have the three most common surnames: **Wáng**, **Zhāng**, and **Lǐ**, making these three names the most common in the world.

The twenty most common surnames, with which you should gradually familiarize yourself, are:

Bái	**Hé**	**Wáng**	**Yáng**
Cài	**Huáng**	**Wú**	**Yè**
Chén	**Lǐ**	**Xiè**	**Zhāng**
Gāo	**Liú**	**Xǔ**	**Zhào**
Guō	**Lín**	**Xú**	**Zhōu**

As in the case of English surnames, Chinese surnames originally had meanings, for example, **Bái** "White" and **Wáng** "King"; but in the same way that the English surnames "White" and "King" are now not usually associated with the meanings of those words, so in Chinese if one speaks of **Bái Xiānsheng** "Mr. Bai" or **Wáng Xiáojie** "Ms. Wang," one does not usually think of the original meaning of those words. There are a few common, single-syllable surnames that sound exactly alike (e.g., 江 **Jiāng** and 姜 **Jiāng**), even though they are written differently. This is a little like English "Johnson" and "Johnston."

Unlike Chinese surnames, which are limited in number, there is no end to the number of given names in Chinese. Thus, the Chinese situation—with relatively few surnames but many given names—is the opposite

National Centre for the Performing Arts, Beijing

of English, where there exists an endless variety of different surnames but a fairly limited number of given names.

A child's given name is usually made up by the parents or other relatives, often with the help of a fortune teller, by combining characters that have a pleasant or auspicious meaning or that express some sentiment or aspiration of the family. Sometimes characters are chosen from a famous poem or literary work, or characters are chosen to describe a historical or current event. Thus, many Chinese born in the People's Republic of China in the 1950s through the 1970s have names related to modern Chinese history, such as **Jiànjūn** "establish the army," **Yǒnghóng** "forever red," or **Wèidōng** "safeguard Mao Zedong." Many Chinese believe that the kind of name a person has may influence their future, i.e., the combination of characters expresses the parents' hopes for their child's future, or may be a description of the qualities they wish for their child to possess.

In tradition-oriented families of the upper classes, each generation in the male line, and sometimes in the female line, carries a common generation name as one of the syllables of a two-syllable given name. As examples, take the daughters and sons of the famous Song family: **Sòng Qìnglíng** (Madam Sun Yat-sen), **Sòng Měilíng** (Madam Chiang Kai-shek), **Sòng Àilíng** (Madam H. H. Gong); and their brothers **Sòng Zǐwén**, **Sòng Zǐliáng**, and **Sòng Zǐ'ān**.

One can usually, though not always, distinguish masculine from feminine given names based on the meanings of the characters. Names chosen for men typically suggest attributes of strength, bravery, or scholarliness while those for women often connote delicacy, beauty, and virtuousness. Examples:

(Men's Names)

Zhāng Lìxiàn	"establish-the-constitution Zhang"
Lǐ Qúnhǔ	"pack-of-tigers Li"
Gù Guóguāng	"country brightness Gu"

(Women's Names)

Huáng Měiyù	"beautiful-jade Huang"
Léi Tíngtíng	"slim-and-graceful Lei"
Zhāng Lìróng	"jasmine-hibiscus Zhang"

Married women retain their own names after marriage and are known by them where they work. In Taiwan, their formal name would be the surname of the husband plus their whole maiden name. For example, **Jiǎng Sòng Měilíng**. Children ordinarily receive the surnames of their fathers, though sometimes if on the mother's side there is no male heir to carry on the family line, a son may take the mother's name. In some families, one child may have the father's surname and the other child the mother's surname.

While Pinyin is now the standard for spelling Chinese names in English, in the past there was a proliferation of different romanization systems. Consider the following commonly seen spellings and their Pinyin equivalents:

COMMON SPELLING	STANDARD PINYIN
Confucius	**Kǒngzǐ**
Chiang Kai-shek	**Jiǎng Jièshí**
Mao Tse-tung	**Máo Zédōng**
Peking	**Běijīng**
Nanking	**Nánjīng**
Chungking	**Chóngqìng**
Hongkong	**Xiānggǎng**

As you might guess, the same Chinese name is frequently romanized in more than one way. Here are some of the ways the common surname **Chén** is romanized: Chen, Ch'en, Chan, Tan, and Tam. Or take the various romanizations of the surname **Huáng**: Huang, Hwang, Whang, Wang, Wong, Ong, Oey, Oei, Oeij, Ooi, Oij, Woei, Wee, Uy, Ng, Go, Ang, Eung, Hang, and Ueng!

The reasons for this proliferation of spellings, which can make consular work for American visa officers very difficult, include the different dialects spoken by the persons involved, different romanization systems used, different local traditions in the various overseas Chinese communities, and—not infrequently—mistakes by the original transliterator. Obviously, as in the case when both **Huáng** and **Wáng** are romanized Wong (because that is how both are pronounced in Cantonese), it can sometimes be difficult to determine what the original character for a name was.

Be aware that some Chinese names are the same or similar to some Korean names (e.g., Chang, Han, Lee, Song) or to certain Vietnamese names (e.g., Cao, Ho, Hoang, Li). And then, some Chinese have chosen native English surnames like Dew (from **Dù**), King (from **Wáng** "king"), Lee (from **Lǐ**), or Lowe (from **Liú**). So it is best to be careful about making assumptions about people's ethnic backgrounds from the spelling of their surnames.

Above, we have been discussing traditional naming patterns for the Han majority of China, which constitutes some 94% of the total Chinese population. Names for members of the over fifty ethnic minorities may be quite different in structure. Regarding the transliteration of non-Chinese names, in the case of foreigners who are not particularly closely associated with China, such as foreign newsmakers who are mentioned in the Chinese press, their names are transliterated according to the Chinese translator's best rendition of the Western language sound.

Bicultural wedding celebrated in traditional style in Beijing

Thus, Alexander Haig would be transliterated as **Yàlǐshāndá Hēigé**, which would be a give-away as a non-Chinese person's name. However, most foreigners in frequent direct contact with Chinese society choose names for themselves that, while based roughly on the sounds of their Western name, are more in accord with the Chinese pattern of a one-syllable surname and a one or two-syllable given name.

A Self-introduction

Jan Rogers, an American working for an English trading firm in Taipei, is attending a reception hosted by her firm. She sees a Taiwanese guest whom she does not recognize, so she walks up to the guest and introduces herself. Standing not far away is Lester Holbrooke, general manager of the trading firm, who is also American.

 Basic Conversation 2-4

1.	ROGERS	**Nǐ hǎo! Wǒ jiào Luó Jiésī. Qǐng duō zhǐjiào.** How do you do? My name is Rogers. *(taking out her name card)* Please give me much advice
2.	TAIWANESE GUEST	**Wǒ xìng Shī. Duìbuqǐ, wǒ méi dài míngpiàn.** **Wǒ zài Zhōng-Měi Màoyì Gōngsī gōngzuò.** My name is Shi. Sorry, I didn't bring name cards. I work at Sino-American Trading Company.
3.	ROGERS	*(introduces Shi to Holbrooke)* **Zǒngjīnglǐ, zhè shi Zhōng-Měi** **Màoyì Gōngsīde Shī Xiáojie.** Mr. Holbrooke, this is Ms. Shi from Sino-American Trading Company.
4.	HOLBROOKE	*(Gives Shi his name card)* **À, huānyíng, huānyíng! Wǒ xìng Hóu.** Oh, welcome! My name is Hou.
5.	TAIWANESE GUEST	**Xièxie. Zǒngjīnglǐ yě shi Yīngguo rén ba?** Thank you. Mr. Holbrooke, I suppose you also must be English?
6.	HOLBROOKE	**Bù, wǒ gēn Luó Xiáojie dōu bú shi Yīngguo rén.** **Wǒmen shi Měiguo rén.** No, neither Ms. Rogers nor I are English. We're American.
7.	TAIWANESE GUEST	**Ò, duìbuqǐ, wǒ gǎocuòle.** Oh, sorry, I got it wrong.
8.	HOLBROOKE	**Méi guānxi.** That's all right.

Build Up

1. Rogers (taking out her name card)

Luó	Luo [SN]
Luó Jiésī	(Chinese for "Rogers")
Nǐ hǎo! Wǒ jiào Luó Jiésī.	How do you do? My name is Rogers.
qǐng duō zhǐjiào	"please instruct (me)"
Qǐng duō zhǐjiào.	Please give me much advice.

2. Taiwanese guest

Shī	Shi [SN]
méi	(indicates past negative of action verbs) [AV]
dài	take along, bring [V]
méi dài	didn't bring
míngpiàn	name card, business card [N]
wǒ méi dài míngpiàn	I didn't bring name cards
Zhōng-Měi	Sino-American [AT]
màoyì	trade [N]
màoyì gōngsī	trading company [PH]
Zhōng-Měi Màoyì Gōngsī	Sino-American Trading Company
Wǒ xìng Shī. Duìbuqǐ, wǒ méi dài míngpiàn.	My name is Shi. Sorry, I didn't bring name cards.
Wǒ zài Zhōng-Měi Màoyì Gōngsī gōngzuò.	I work at Sino-American Trading Company.

3. Rogers (introduces Shi to Holbrooke)

jīnglǐ	manager [N]
zǒngjīnglǐ	general manager [N]
-de	(indicates that what precedes describes what follows)
Zhōng-Měi Màoyì Gōngsīde Shī Xiáojie	Sino-American Trading Company's Ms. Shi
Zǒngjīnglǐ, zhè shi Zhōng-Měi Màoyì Gōngsīde Shī Xiáojie.	Mr. Holbrooke, this is Ms. Shi from Sino-American Trading Company

4. Holbrooke

à	"oh" [I]
Hóu	Hou [SN]
À, huānyíng, huānyíng! Wǒ xìng Hóu.	Oh, welcome! My name is Hou.

5. Taiwanese guest

Yīngguo	England [PW]
Yīngguo rén	native of England
yě shi Yīngguo rén ba	must probably also be from England
Xièxie. Zǒngjīnglǐ yě shi Yīngguo rén ba?	Thank you. Mr. Holbrooke, I suppose you also must be English?

6. Holbrooke

gēn	and [CJ]
wǒ gēn Luó Xiáojie	I and Ms. Luo
dōu bù	all not, none, neither
dōu bú shi Yīngguo rén	are both not English
Bù, wǒ gēn Luó Xiáojie dōu bú shi Yīngguo rén. Wǒmen shi Měiguo rén.	No, neither Ms. Rogers nor I are English. We're American.

7. Taiwanese guest

gǎo	get, do [V]
cuò	be wrong [SV]
-cuò	wrong [RE]
gǎocuò	get or do something wrong [RC]
-le	(indicates completed action) [P]
gǎocuòle	did something wrong
Ò, duìbuqǐ, wǒ gǎocuòle.	Oh, sorry, I got it wrong.

8. Holbrooke

méi guānxi	"never mind," "it doesn't matter" [IE]
Méi guānxi.	That's all right.

Supplementary Vocabulary

1. xiānsheng	gentleman [N]
nèiwèi xiānsheng	that gentleman (polite)
Nèiwèi xiānsheng shi shéi?	Who is that gentleman?
2. tàitai	married woman, lady [N]
nèiwèi tàitai	that lady (polite)
Nǐ rènshi nèiwèi tàitai ma?	Do you know that lady?
3. xiǎojie	young lady [N]
zhèiwèi xiǎojie	this young lady (polite)
Zhèiwèi xiǎojie xìng Bái.	This young lady's last name is Bai.

Grammatical and Cultural Notes

1A. Business Cards. While it is in general better to be introduced by a third party, it is also acceptable to introduce oneself, as here. Exchanging business cards or name cards at the time of introduction is very common among professional people; Chinese students don't do this, though it could be useful for American graduate students in China to have name cards printed. Chinese people who frequently travel abroad or often have contact with foreigners typically have business cards printed in Chinese on one side and in English on the other; you should do this also when the time comes that you have name cards printed. Included on such a card are the person's name, **dānwèi** or employer, position, possibly their highest academic degree and field, office (and possibly home) address, landline and cellphone numbers, e-mail address, and possibly fax or website. Some even put a mini version of their CV on their card. While most cards are printed on white card stock, the author has received business cards that were printed on bamboo or even 24K gold foil! Business cards fulfill a vital function in Chinese society in that they make instantly clear, and serve as a convenient record of, a person's position and "pecking order" in Chinese society. Business cards help to establish credentials and are a convenient way of providing information about oneself to others. When someone else gives you their business card, you should study it with interest before pocketing it. Chinese people often collect the business cards they have received in special albums which they refer to as needed, for example, at Chinese New Year's when it is time to send holiday cards. At a banquet or business meeting, it can be helpful to place the business cards you have received in front of you to help keep people's names straight. Always give a card if you have received one; it's expected that professionals always carry business cards, so not having cards on one calls for an apology, as occurs in this lesson's Basic Conversation. When giving someone your business card, hold it with the thumb and forefingers of both hands (which is a sign of respect) with the Chinese side up, so the recipient may read your name as the card is handed to them, and nod slightly as you present it. If you are seated, get up to present your

Business cards fulfill a vital function in that they make instantly clear a person's position and "pecking order" in Chinese society.

business card, unless it is a person sitting close to you; never throw your card across the table.

1B.   **Qǐng duō zhǐjiào** is a polite phrase that literally means "Please more instruct me" or "Please give me much advice." It is functionally equivalent to English "Pleased to meet you." This is merely a polite phrase; the person saying it does not necessarily mean that he or she really desires advice. Be careful to keep **duō** "much, more" from sounding like the very different word **dōu** "all, both." And notice that here, as always, the adverb (**duō**) occurs before the verb (**zhǐjiào**).

A well-to-do couple at dinner in their home in Taipei

2A.   **MÉI** to Indicate Past Negative of Action Verbs. The auxiliary verb **méi** in front of an action verb indicates the past negative of the verb (i.e., that the action of the verb did not take place). In this utterance, **méi dài** means "didn't bring" or "haven't brought" and **wǒ méi dài míngpiàn** means "I didn't bring name cards" or "I haven't brought name cards." We will take up in note 7B in this lesson how to express completed action (i.e., that an action did take place). The pattern with **méi** indicating past negative of action verbs is:

Subject	MÉI	Action Verb
Tāmen	méi	lái.

"They didn't come." or "They haven't come."

Here are some more examples with **méi** indicating the past negative of action verbs:

méi qù	"didn't go," "hasn't gone"
méi wèn	"didn't ask," "hasn't asked"
méi zǒu	"didn't leave," "hasn't left"
méi gōngzuò	"didn't work," "hasn't worked"
méi gǎocuò	"didn't get it wrong," "hasn't got it wrong"
méi huí sùshè	"didn't go back to their dorm," "haven't gone back to their dorm"

It is possible to add question particle **ma** to a sentence containing méi plus action verb. For example:

Nǐ méi qù ma?   "You didn't go?"

2B.   **BÙ, BIÉ, BÚYÀO**, and **MÉI** Contrasted. You have now learned four negatives—**bù, bié, búyào**, and **méi**—that tend to be confused by beginning learners of Chinese. Perhaps the following chart will be useful in contrasting and reviewing these four negatives:

NEGATIVE	BASIC MEANING	EXAMPLE	ENGLISH
bù	not	Tā bù gōngzuò.	He doesn't work.
bié	do not!	Nǐ bié gōngzuò!	Don't work!
búyào	do not!	Nǐ búyào gōngzuò!	Don't work!
méi	did not	Tā méi gōngzuò.	He didn't work.

3A.   As we have mentioned before, it is common in Chinese society to address one's interlocutor by her or his title rather than by their name or by the pronouns **nǐ** or **nín** "you." One would frequently address the general manager of a firm as "General Manager" or one's school president as "President" or one's teacher as "Teacher." Using the title alone is considered politer than using the person's name and title, or pronouns. Of course, if several general managers were present, then one would have to use surnames, e.g., **Hóu Zǒngjīnglǐ** "General Manager Hou," **Wáng Zǒngjīnglǐ** "General Manager Wang," etc. (notice that with **Zǒngjīnglǐ**, if a surname is included, the surname is placed BEFORE the title, as with all titles).

3B. **-DE** to Indicate That What Precedes Describes What Follows. Notice the particle **-de** in **Zhōng-Měi Màoyì Gōngsīde Shī Xiáojie** "Ms. Shi from Sino-American Trading Company." The **-de** indicates that what precedes it describes or modifies what follows it. This pattern of descriptive phrase + **-de** + noun phrase is frequently used to indicate the affiliation of a person with a company or an institution. The pattern is:

Preceding Descriptive Phrase	-DE	Following Noun Phrase
Zhōng-Měi Màoyì Gōngsī	de	**Shī Xiáojie**

"Sino-American Trading Company's Ms. Shi" or "Ms. Shi from Sino-American Trading Company"

Note that this **-de** is closely related to the **-de** you learned earlier that indicates possession, as in **wǒde tóngwū** "my roommate" (cf. 2-2: 3E). Now, here are some examples of complete sentences containing **-de** to indicate that what precedes describes what follows:

Zhèiwèi shi Zhōngguo Wàijiāobùde Mǎ Xiānsheng.

"This is Mr. Ma from the Chinese Foreign Ministry."

(lit. "This honorable-one is China Foreign Ministry's Ma Mr.")

Wǒmen huānyíng Yīngguo Dàshǐguǎnde Xiè Nǚshì!

"Let us welcome Madam Smith from the British Embassy!"

(lit. "We welcome England Embassy's Smith Madam.")

Nà shì bu shi Xiānggǎng Zhōngwén Dàxuéde Bái Yùhuì Lǎoshī?

"Is that Professor Bai Yuhui from Chinese University of Hong Kong?"

(lit. "That is not is Hong Kong Chinese University's Bai Yuhui Teacher?")

6A. Notice that **bù** can be used alone to mean "no." A fuller form of this would be **bú shì**. We recommend that for now you use the fuller form **bú shì**.

Mazu Temple in Magong, Penghu Archipelago

6B. Gēn can ordinarily be used only to connect nouns and pronouns, not to connect verbs or phrases. So you can say **nǐ gēn tā** "you and she" or **Běijīng gēn Táiběi** "Beijing and Taipei," but you could NEVER say ****Tā xuéxí gēn gōngzuò** to mean "She studies and works." Instead, you would have to use **yě** "also" and say: **Tā xuéxí, yě gōngzuò**, literally "She studies, also works."

6C. The literal meaning of **Wǒ gēn Luó Xiáojie** is "I and Ms. Rogers." In polite English, when talking about oneself and another person, it is customary to say the name of the other person first, for example, "Ms. Rogers and I." This custom does not exist in Chinese. In Chinese one would say **wǒ gēn nǐ** "you and I," **wǒ gēn tā** "she and I," etc.

6D. BÙ DŌU vs. **DŌU BÙ**, and **MÉI DŌU** vs. **DŌU MÉI**. In the Basic Conversation for lesson 2-1, we encountered the expression **bù dōu** in the sentence:

Wǒmen bù dōu shi Měiguo rén.

"Not all of us are Americans." (lit. "We not all are American people.")

Now, in the Basic Conversation for this lesson, we see the following sentence with **dōu bù**:

Wǒ gēn Luó Xiáojie dōu bú shi Yīngguo rén.

"Neither Ms. Rogers nor I are English." (lit. "I and Ms. Luo both not are English people.")

As we noted previously (2-1: 6A), it is important to distinguish between **bù dōu** "not all" and **dōu bù** "all not, none of." Sentences with **bù dōu** state that the members of a class are not all something, implying that some members of the class are something and that other members of the class are not. Sentences with **dōu bù**, on the other hand, state that all members of a class are not something. Compare these two sentences:

Wǒmen bù dōu shi Měiguo rén.   "Not all of us are American."

Wǒmen dōu bú shi Měiguo rén.   "None of us is American."

In this lesson, we also introduced **méi** for the past negative of action verbs. The combinations **méi dōu** "did not all" and **dōu méi** "all did not" are both possible and operate in parallel ways to **bù dōu** and **dōu bù**. Contrast the following two sentences with **méi**:

Tāmen méi dōu qù.   "They didn't all go." (i.e., some of them went but others didn't)

Tāmen dōu méi qù.   "None of them went." (i.e., all of them didn't go)

Like **bù dōu** and **dōu bù**, **méi dōu** and **dōu méi** cannot be said alone but must always be followed by a verb. In English, if someone asks "Did they all go?," we could answer "Not all"; but in Chinese, one could not answer *Méi dōu but would have to say, as the briefest possible response, **Méi dōu qù**, literally "Didn't all go."

7A. **Gǎocuò** is an example of a resultative compound verb. It is composed of the action verb **gǎo** "get, do" and the resultative verb ending **-cuò** "wrong," which indicates the result of the action. The literal meaning of the two constituents when compounded together is "get or do something with the result that it is wrong," i.e., "get wrong." Resultative verbs, which are very common in Chinese, will be discussed in more detail later.

7B. **-LE to Indicate Completed Action.** The verb suffix **-le** attached to an action verb like **gǎocuò** "get something wrong" indicates completed action. Thus, **Wǒ gǎocuòle** means "I got it wrong" or "I made a mistake." The pattern is:

Subject	Action Verb	-LE
Tāmen	lái	le.

"They came." or "They have come."

It is possible to add question particle **ma** to a sentence ending in **-le**. For example:

Tāmen láile ma?   "Did they come?" or "Have they come?"

If **-le** occurs attached to an action verb at the end of a sentence, it actually represents both the **-le** that indicates completed action and the **le** that indicates a changed situation (1-4: 4C); in other words, in such a case the two **le** combine into one **le**. Non-action verbs like **shì** "be" never take **-le** to indicate completed action; with non-action verbs, the context or additional adverbs of time would make it clear when past time was meant. Here, now, are some more examples of **-le** indicating completed action:

Tā dàile.	"She brought them."
Wǒ qùle.	"I went."
Shìr wǒ dōu bànle.	"I took care of all the things."
Lǎo Gāo, Xiǎo Lǐ dōu zǒule.	"Old Gao and Little Li have both left."
Xīn tóngxué nǐ dōu jièshaole ma?	"Have you introduced all the new classmates?"

The negative form of a sentence containing completed action **-le** is **méi** plus the verb (cf. note 2A above). There is no **-le** in such sentences because the **-le** is cancelled out by the presence of the **méi**, so you could never say ***Wǒ méi qùle** for "I didn't go." The following chart will be helpful for reviewing the positive and negative forms of action verbs:

POSITIVE		NEGATIVE	
(an action has been completed; completed action **-le** *after verb)*		*(an action did not take place;* **méi** *in front of verb, no completed action* **-le**)	
Wǒ qùle.	"I went."	**Wǒ méi qù.**	"I didn't go."
Tā gǎocuòle.	"She got it wrong."	**Tā méi gǎocuò.**	"She didn't get it wrong."

8.   In this line note the very common and useful idiomatic expression **méi guānxi** "never mind" or "it doesn't matter" or "it's O.K." This phrase literally means "it doesn't have relevance."

SV1-3. Review the different English meanings of **xiānsheng**, **tàitai**, and **xiáojie** which you have encountered in this and the last several lessons:

CHINESE TERM	AS TITLE	INDICATING FAMILY RELATIONSHIP	AS ORDINARY NOUN
xiānsheng	Mr., Sir	husband	gentleman
tàitai	Mrs., Ma'am	wife	(married) lady
xiáojie	Miss, Ms.	—	(unmarried) lady

A few examples with **xiānsheng** will further clarify this:

Lǐ Xiānsheng shi Jiā'nádà rén.	"Mr. Li is Canadian."
Xiānsheng, qǐng nín bié qù!	"Sir, please don't go!"
Tā shi nǐde xiānsheng ma?	"Is he your husband?"
Nèiwèi xiānsheng xìng shémme?	"What is that gentleman's last name?"

SV3.   While **xiáojie** normally means "unmarried lady," in Taiwan it can sometimes also refer to married ladies when used with their maiden names. Therefore, a married lady whose maiden name is **Wáng** and whose husband's name is **Lǐ** might be known at work as **Wáng Xiáojie**, but might be addressed by her husband's friends as **Lǐ Tàitai**.

Unit 2: Review and Study Guide

ADVERBS
zhèmme — like this, in this way, so

ATTRIBUTIVES
Zhōng-Měi — Sino-American

AUXILIARY VERBS
bié — don't
búyào — don't
méi — (indicates past negative of action verbs)
yīnggāi — should

CONJUNCTIONS
gēn — and
nà — in that case

COVERBS
gěi — for
zài — be located at, at

EQUATIVE VERBS
jiào — be called or named
xìng — be surnamed

IDIOMATIC EXPRESSIONS
hǎo — "all right," "O.K."
guìxìng — "what's your honorable surname?"
méi guānxi — "never mind"
qǐng wèn — "excuse me," "may I ask"

INTERJECTIONS
à — "oh"
ò — "oh"

MEASURES
ge — (general measure)
jiā — (for companies, factories)
wèi — (polite measure for people)

MOVEABLE ADVERBS
kěshi — but

NOUNS
Huáyì — person of Chinese descent
jīnglǐ — manager
màoyì — trade
míngpiàn — name card, business card
míngzi — name
nǚshì — madam, lady
rén — person
tàitai — married woman, lady; wife
tóngshì — colleague
tóngwū(r) — roommate
tóngxué — classmate
xiānsheng — husband; gentleman
xiáojie — young lady
xiàozhǎng — head of a school
zǒngjīnglǐ — general manager

NUMBERS
yī — one, a

PARTICLES
-de — (indicates possession)
-de — (indicates that what precedes describes what follows)
ba — (indicates supposition)
-le — (indicates completed action)

PHRASES
Huáyì Měiguo rén — Chinese-American
màoyì gōngsī — trading company

PLACE WORDS
dānwèi — work unit, organization
dàshǐguǎn — embassy
dàxué — university, college
gōngsī — company, firm
Jiā'nádà — Canada
Mǎláixīyà — Malaysia
Měiguo — America
Rìběn — Japan
Táiwān — Taiwan
wàijiāobù — foreign ministry
Xībānyá — Spain
Xiānggǎng — Hong Kong
Xīnjiāpō — Singapore
Yīngguo — England
Zhōngguo — China

PRONOUNS
nà — that
zhè — this

QUESTION WORDS
něi- — which
něiguó — which country
shéi — who, whom
shémme — what
zěmme — how

RESULTATIVE COMPOUNDS
gǎocuò — get or do something wrong

RESULTATIVE ENDINGS
-cuò — wrong

SPECIFIERS
nèi- — that
zhèi- — this

STATIVE VERBS
cuò — be wrong
gāoxìng — be happy
xīn — be new

SURNAMES
Bái — Bai (lit. "white")
Chén — Chen
Hóu — Hou
Luó — Luo
Mǎ — Ma (lit. "horse")
Shī — Shi
Wú — Wu

VERBS
chēnghu — address
dài — take along, bring
gǎo — get, do
gōngzuò — work
huānyíng — welcome
jiào — call (someone a name)
jièshao — introduce
lái — come
rènshi — be acquainted with, know
wèn — ask
xuéxí — learn, study

Major New Grammar Patterns

SHÌ in equative verb sentences: **Wǒ shi Měiguo rén.** "I am (an) American." (2-1)

Nationalities: Měiguo rén "American," **Zhōngguo rén** "Chinese," etc. (2-1)

JIÀO in equative verb sentences: Wǒ jiào Bái Jiéruì. "My name is Bai Jierui." **Nǐ jiào shémme míngzi?** "What's your name?" (2-1)

BÙ DŌU vs. DŌU BÙ: Wǒmen bù dōu shi Měiguo rén. "We are not all Americans." **Wǒmen dōu bú shi Měiguo rén.** "None of us is American." (2-1, 2-4)

ZHÈI- and NÈI- as specifiers with the polite measure WÈI: **zhèiwèi lǎoshī** "this teacher," **nèiwèi tóngxué** "that classmate" (2-1)

YÍXIÀ(R) after verbs to make them less abrupt: jièshao yixiar "introduce," **lái yixia** "come," **wèn yixia** "ask" (2-2)

ZHÈ "this" and NÀ "that" as pronoun subjects: Zhè shi Wáng Àihuá, zhè shi Chén Lì "This is Wang Aihua, this is Chen Li," **Nà shi shéi?** "Who is that?" (2-2)

-DE to indicate possession: wǒde gōngzuò "my work," **nǐde xīn tóngxué** "your new classmate" (2-2)

DÀO...LÁI: Qǐng nǐ dào túshūguǎn lái. "Please come to the library." (2-2)

BIÉ or BÚYÀO to indicate negative imperative: Qǐng nǐ bié qù! "Please don't go!" **Búyào jiào wǒ Lǎo Wáng!** "Don't call me old Wang!" (2-2)

...HǍOLE: Nǐ hái shi jiào wǒ Xiǎo Chén hǎole. "It would be better if you called me Little Chen." (2-2)

XÌNG in equative verb sentences: Wǒ xìng Zhāng. "My last name is Zhang." **Nǐ xìng shémme?** "What's your last name?" (2-3)

BA to indicate supposition: Tā shi Yīngguo rén ba "I suppose she's English." **Nǐ lèile ba?** "You must be tired?" (2-3)

MÉI to indicate past negative of action verbs: Tāmen méi lái. "They didn't come." (2-4)

-DE to indicate that what precedes describes what follows: Zhōng-Měi Màoyì Gōngsīde Shī Xiáojie "Ms. Shi from Sino-American Trading Company" (2-4)

MÉI DŌU vs. DŌU MÉI: Tāmen méi dōu qù. "They didn't all go." **Tāmen dōu méi qù.** "None of them went." (2-4)

-LE to indicate completed action: Wǒ gǎocuòle. "I got it wrong." (2-4)

Numbers, Dates, Time, and Money (I)

COMMUNICATIVE OBJECTIVES

Once you have mastered this unit, you will be able to use Chinese to:

1. Introduce yourself to someone. Count from 0 to 9,999.

2. Discuss a Chinese class: how many students and teachers, how many males and females, their nationalities, etc.

3. Ask how old someone is and answer when you are asked.

4. Ask what time it is and answer when you are asked.

5. Ask how long it takes to get to a certain place and answer when you are asked.

6. Make simple purchases: ask if you can look at something, inquire how much something costs, indicate whether you think something is cheap or expensive, discuss prices from one fen or cent up to 9,999 yuan or dollars.

7. Talk simply about the members of your family: father, mother, older and younger brothers, older and younger sisters.

"How Many Students in Your Class?"

Zhang Xiaohui, an English major at Beijing Foreign Studies University, asks her American friend, Jerry Freeman, about the Chinese class he is taking at the university's Chinese language training center.

Basic Conversation 3-1

1. CHINESE Nǐmen bānshang yǒu jǐwèi tóngxué?
   How many students are there in your class?

2. AMERICAN Yǒu shíwèi.
   There are ten.

3. CHINESE Dōu shi Měiguo rén ma?
   Are they all Americans?

4. AMERICAN Bù dōu shi Měiguo rén. Yǒu qíge Měiguo rén, liǎngge Déguo rén gēn yíge Fǎguo rén.
   They're not all Americans. There are seven Americans, two Germans and one Frenchman.

5. CHINESE Jǐge nánshēng, jǐge nǚshēng?
   How many male students and how many female students?

6. AMERICAN Yíbànr yíbànr. Wǔge nánde, wǔge nǚde.
   Half and half. Five men and five women.

7. CHINESE Nà, nǐmen yǒu jǐwèi lǎoshī ne?
   So, how many teachers do you have?

8. AMERICAN Yígòng yǒu sānwèi. Liǎngwèi shi nǚlǎoshī, yíwèi shi nánlǎoshī.
   There are three in all. Two are female teachers, and one is a male teacher.

Build Up

1. Chinese

bān	class [N]
bānshang	in a class [N+L]
nǐmen bānshang	in your class
yǒu	there is, there are [V]

jǐ-	how many [QW]
jǐwèi	how many (people, polite)
jǐwèi tóngxué	how many classmates (polite)
yǒu jǐwèi tóngxué	how many classmates are there
Nǐmen bānshang yǒu jǐwèi tóngxué?	How many students are there in your class?

2. American

shí	ten [NU]
shíwèi	ten (people, polite)
Yǒu shíwèi.	There are ten.

3. Chinese

| Dōu shi Měiguo rén ma? | Are they all Americans? |

4. American

qī	seven [NU]
qíge	seven (people or things)
yǒu qíge Měiguo rén	there are seven Americans
liǎng-	two [NU]
liǎngge	two (people or things)
Déguo	Germany [PW]
Déguo rén	German, native of Germany
liǎngge Déguo rén	two Germans
yíge	one, a
Fǎguo	France [PW]
Fǎguo rén	native of France
yíge Fǎguo rén	one Frenchman
Bù dōu shi Měiguo rén. Yǒu qíge Měiguo rén, liǎngge Déguo rén gēn yíge Fǎguo rén.	They're not all Americans. There are seven Americans, two Germans and one Frenchman.

5. Chinese

jǐge	how many [QW+M]
nánshēng	male student [N]
nǚshēng	female student [N]
Jǐge nánshēng, jǐge nǚshēng?	How many male students and how many female students?

6. American

bàn(r)	half [NU]
yíbàn(r)	one-half
yíbànr yíbànr	half and half
wǔ	five [NU]
wǔge	five (people or things)
nánde	man, male [N]
nǚde	woman, female [N]
Yíbànr yíbànr. Wǔge nánde, wǔge nǚde.	Half and half. Five men and five women.

7. Chinese

| jǐwèi lǎoshī | how many teachers (polite) |
| Nà, nǐmen yǒu jǐwèi lǎoshī ne? | So, how many teachers do you have? |

8. American

yígòng	in all [A]
sān	three [NU]
sānwèi	three (persons, polite)

yígòng yǒu sānwèi	in all there are three of them
liǎngwèi	two (persons, polite)
nǚlǎoshī	female teacher [N]
liǎngwèi shi nǚlǎoshi	two of them are female teachers
yíwèi	one (person, polite)
nánlǎoshī	male teacher [N]
yíwèi shi nánlǎoshī	one of them is a male teacher
Yígòng yǒu sānwèi. Liǎngwèi shi nǚlǎoshī, yíwèi shi nánlǎoshī.	There are three in all. Two are female teachers, and one is a male teacher.

Supplementary Vocabulary: The Numbers from 1–10

1. **yī**	one [NU]
2. **èr**	two [NU]
3. **sān**	three [NU]
4. **sì**	four [NU]
5. **wǔ**	five [NU]
6. **liù**	six [NU]
7. **qī**	seven [NU]
8. **bā**	eight [NU]
9. **jiǔ**	nine [NU]
10. **shí**	ten [NU]

Additional Vocabulary: More Countries

1. **Āfùhàn**	Afghanistan* [PW]
2. **Bùdān**	Bhutan* [PW]
3. **Āijí**	Egypt [PW]
4. **Yìndù**	India* [PW]
5. **Yìndùníxīyà (B)**	Indonesia [PW]
6. **Yǐsèliè**	Israel [PW]
7. **Yìdàlì**	Italy [PW]
8. **Hāsàkèsītǎn**	Kazakhstan* [PW]
9. **Jí'ěrjísīsītǎn**	Kyrgyzstan* [PW]
10. **Lǎowō**	Laos* [PW]
11. **Mòxīgē**	Mexico [PW]
12. **Měnggǔ**	Mongolia* [PW]
13. **Miǎndiàn**	Myanmar, Burma* [PW]
14. **Níbó'ěr**	Nepal* [PW]
15. **Cháoxiǎn (B)**	(North) Korea* [PW]
16. **Bājīsītǎn**	Pakistan* [PW]
17. **Fēilǜbīn**	Philippines [PW]
18. **Éguo (B)**	Russia* [PW]
19. **Nánfēi**	South Africa [PW]
20. **Hánguo**	(South) Korea [PW]
21. **Tǎjíkèsītǎn**	Tajikistan* [PW]
22. **Tàiguo**	Thailand [PW]
23. **Yuènán**	Vietnam* [PW]

Grammatical and Cultural Notes

1A.   The expression **bānshang** "in the class" is composed of the noun **bān** "class" and the localizer **-shang** "in." Localizers, which are word elements that indicate location, will be taken up in more detail later. **Bān** could also be used alone without the **-shang** in a question such as the following:

* Denotes a country that borders China.

Zhèige bān yǒu jǐge tóngxué?

"How many students does this class have?" or "How many students are there in this class?"

1B.   Place Word + **YǑU** + Noun Phrase to Indicate Existence.

Besides indicating possession ("have," cf. 1-2), the verb **yǒu** can also indicate existence ("there is, there are"). The pattern for indicating the existence of something in a certain place is:

Place Word	YǑU	Noun Phrase
Bānshang	**yǒu**	**qíge tóngxué.**

"In the class there are seven classmates."

Some more examples of this usage:

Túshūguǎn yǒu jǐge rén?	"How many people are there in the library?"
Shítáng xiànzài yǒu shíge rén.	"Right now in the dining hall there are ten people."
Gōngsī yǒu yíwèi Yīngguo tóngshì.	"In the company there is an English colleague."
Zhōngguo yǒu hěn hǎode dàxué!	"In China there are very fine universities!"

Yǒu can also be used at the beginning of a sentence, or preceded by an adverb, to mean "there is, there are." Examples:

Yǒu liǎngwèi Zhōngguo lǎoshī gēn yíwèi Měiguo lǎoshī.

"There are/were two Chinese teachers and one American teacher."

Míngtiān yǒu gōngkè ma?

"Is there homework (for) tomorrow?"

In general, if the subject of a sentence containing **yǒu** is a noun or pronoun denoting a person or animal, **yǒu** means "possess, have." On the other hand, if the subject is a word denoting a place or time, **yǒu** usually means "there is, there are." To Chinese native speakers, however, there is no real difference; a sentence like **Wǒ yǒu yíge háizi** "I have one child" could also be analyzed as meaning "As for me, there exists one child" and **Zhōngwén yǒu shēngdiào** "Chinese has tones" could also be analyzed as "Regarding the Chinese language, there are tones."

1C.   **Jǐ-** attached to a measure word (such as **ge** or **wèi**) means "how many." It is generally used when the number is expected to be ten or fewer.

1D.   **Jǐwèi** is a polite expression meaning "how many (people)?" It is composed of the question word **jǐ-** and the polite measure for people **wèi**. **Jǐwèi** can be used, as here, before a noun referring to people, or it can be used by itself as a question: **Jǐwèi?** "How many?" A waiter in a restaurant might ask this when greeting a new group of guests. Some more examples of **jǐ-** attached to the measures **wèi** and **ge**:

JǏ- + MEASURE + NOUN	JǏ- + MEASURE (NOUN OMITTED BUT UNDERSTOOD)
Jǐwèi xiānsheng? "How many gentlemen?"	**Jǐwèi?** "How many?"
Jǐwèi lǎoshī? "How many teachers?"	**Jǐwèi?** "How many?"
Jǐge rén? "How many people?"	**Jǐge?** "How many?"
Jǐge tóngxué? "How many classmates?"	**Jǐge?** "How many?"

2.   In answering the question "How many students do you have in your class?," one could in Chinese NEVER say just *shí to mean "ten." In Chinese, one must always add a measure such as **wèi** or **ge** after a number when it describes how many people or how many of something, so for "ten (students)" one would have to say **shíwèi** "ten polite units of people." If one didn't wish to be particularly polite, one could also say **shíge** "ten."

4A.   **Qíge** "Seven (Persons)." In the speech of many Chinese, the number **qī** "seven," which is normally Tone One, changes to Tone Two when standing directly before a syllable in Tone Four. The same is true of the number **bā** "eight." In other words:

qī + ge   →   qíge
bā + ge   →   báge

These are considered optional tone changes, since not everyone makes them. It is not incorrect to say **qīge** and **bāge** without the tone change.

4B.   Be careful to distinguish the pronunciations of **jǐge** "how many?" and **qíge** "seven." The **q** of **qíge** has a strong puff of breath, while the **j** of **jǐge** does not. The same applies to **jǐwèi** "how many (polite)?" vs. **qíwèi** "seven (polite)." Of course, the tones of the first syllable are also different.

4C.   Here, the speaker changes from using the polite measure **wèi** to the more general **ge**. There are two reasons for this. First, **wèi** is not usually used before the noun **rén**, since **rén** is considered too general. Second, while it is appropriate for a person asking a question to be polite when referring to the students in someone else's class, it is not necessary to be so polite when referring to the students in one's own class.

4D.   **Liǎngge** or **liǎng-** plus some other measure is what you say when you wish to refer to two of almost anything. In counting off numbers or giving addresses and phone numbers, another word for "two" is used: **èr** (cf. SV2 in this lesson). However, you could NEVER say ***èrge rén** to mean "two people." Here are some examples of **liǎng-** plus a measure:

liǎngge rén	"two people"
liǎngge míngzi	"two names"
liǎngwèi xiáojie	"two young ladies"
liǎngjiā màoyì gōngsī	"two trade companies"

4E.   Remember that **gēn** "and," which you had in 2-4, can ordinarily be used only to connect nouns, not to connect verbs or clauses.

4F.   **Yíge** "one (person)" is composed of the number **yī** "one" plus the general measure **ge** (which is pronounced **gè** when it has a full tone). As we saw in note 2-3: SV2, when **yī** stands directly before a syllable in Tone Four, it usually changes to Tone Two. Another example of this tone change is **yíwèi** "one (person)."

4G.   An alternate pronunciation of **Fǎguo** "France" that you will hear in Taiwan and occasionally elsewhere is **Fàguo**.

5A.   **Jǐge** "how many (up to ten)" can be used alone or before a noun. Examples:

Yǒu jǐge?	"How many are there?"
Nǐ yǒu jǐge tóngxué?	"How many classmates do you have?"

5B.   **Jǐge nánshēng, jǐge nǔshēng?** "How many male students and how many female students?" Note that there is no word for "and" in the Chinese. In note 1-2: 3D, we learned about unmarked coordination. If there are two balanced parts of a question or statement, the word for "and" is often omitted in Chinese. The same is true of the second sentence of utterance 6 below: **Wǔge nánde, wǔge nǔde** "Five men and five women."

6.   In Beijing and other parts of northern China, one says **yíbànr yíbànr**. In most other Chinese speech areas, one would say **yíbàn yíbàn**.

7A.   The word **nà** "in that case," which we first saw in 2-2, often functions to indicate that the speaker wishes to introduce some change in the topic of discussion. Here, the Chinese speaker had been asking about numbers of students but now uses **nà** to indicate the transition to talking about numbers of teachers. **Nà** is thus somewhat similar to English "So...," "Well, then...," "Now,...," or "And...." Some Chinese speakers begin many of their utterances with **Nà**.

7B. It is very common to add a **ne** at the end of a question part of which is a continuation of a previous question and part of which is new. The previous question, in line 1, was **Nǐmen yǒu jǐwèi tóngxué?** "How many classmates do you have?" Now, the Chinese student changes the focus of her question from **tóngxué** to **lǎoshī** and asks: **Nà, nǐmen yǒu jǐwèi lǎoshī ne?** "Well, and how many teachers do you have?"

8A. Notice in line 5 **nánshēng** "male student" and **nǚshēng** "female student." Notice in line 6 **nánde** "man, male" and **nǚde** "woman, female." Now in line 8 notice **nánlǎoshī** "male teacher" and **nǚlǎoshi** "female teacher." It should be obvious by now that the bound forms **nán-** and **nǚ-** mean "male" and female." These bound forms occur as parts of many other words. Try to get into the habit of paying attention to parts of words in this way.

Ming Dynasty imperial tombs near Beijing

SV1–10. Numbers from One to Ten. Be sure to memorize the numbers from 1–10 thoroughly. The basic forms of the numbers, as given here, are used for counting and citing telephone numbers, addresses, and years. To count nouns with numbers, in other words, to indicate how many of something, a measure such as **ge** or **wèi** has to be added. Keep in mind that **èr** changes to **liǎng-** when a measure follows (e.g., **liǎngge** or **liǎngwèi**; you could NEVER say *èrge). Also, remember that **yī**, **qī**, and **bā** usually change to Tone Two before Tone Four syllables (e.g., **yíge**, **qíge**, **báge**); and that, in addition, **yī** changes to **yì** before syllables in Tone One, Tone Two, and Tone Three. This may seem difficult and confusing at first, but you will get used to it as you hear and speak Chinese more in the weeks and months to come.

SV6. In pronouncing the number **liù** "six," remember that the syllable which is spelled as **liu** in Pinyin is pronounced as if it were written **liou** (so that it rhymes with English "low" but not with the name "Lou").

AV1–23. The names of these countries are arranged in alphabetical order of the English equivalents. The fourteen countries that border China are indicated with an asterisk (*).

AV5. An alternate pronunciation (actually an abbreviation) of **Yìndùníxīyà** "Indonesia" that you will hear in Taiwan and occasionally elsewhere is **Yìnní**.

AV15. An alternate pronunciation of **Cháoxiān** "Korea" that you will hear occasionally is **Cháoxiǎn**.

AV18. An alternate pronunciation of **Éguo** "Russia" that you will hear in Taiwan and occasionally elsewhere is **Èguo**.

AV20. In China, **Hánguo** usually refers to South Korea while **Cháoxiān** (or **Cháoxiǎn**) usually refers to "North Korea." In Taiwan, **Hánguo** is the word for "Korea," with **Nánhán** used for "South Korea" and **Běihán** used for "North Korea."

Inquiring About Age

Sylvia Thompson, an American undergraduate who is enrolled in a study abroad program in Beijing, is showing photographs of her family to one of her teachers.

Basic Conversation 3-2

1. TEACHER *(looking at a photograph)*
Zhè shi nǐ fùqin ma? Tā duō dà niánji le?
Is this your father? How old is he?

2. THOMPSON
Wǒ xiángxiang kàn. Tā jīnnián
wǔshisānsuì le—bù, wǔshisìsuì le.
Let me try to think. He's fifty-three this year—no, fifty-four.

3. TEACHER
Ò. Nà, zhèiwèi shi nǐ mǔqin ba?
Oh. So I suppose this must be your mother?

4. THOMPSON
Duì, tā jīnnián sìshibāsuì le.
Right, she's forty-eight this year.

5. TEACHER
Zhè shi nǐ mèimei, duì bu dui? Tā hěn kě'ài! Tā jǐsuì le?
This is your younger sister, right? She's cute! How old is she?

6. THOMPSON
Tā bāsuì. Xiàge yuè jiù jiǔsuì le.
She's eight years old. She'll be nine next month.

Build Up

1. Teacher

fùqin	father [N]
nǐ fùqin	your father
duō	how [QW]
dà	be big; old (of people) [SV]
duō dà	how old
niánji	age [N]

duō dà niánji	how many years old
tā duō dà niánji le	how old is he
Zhè shi nǐ fùqin ma? Tā duō dà niánji le?	Is this your father? How old is he?

2. Thompson

xiǎng	think [V]
kàn	look, see [V]
xiángxiang kàn	try to think
wǒ xiángxiang kàn	I will try to think
jīnnián	this year [TW]
suì	year of age [M]
wǔshisānsuì	fifty-three years old
tā jīnnián wǔshisānsuì le	he this year is 53 years old
wǔshisìsuì	fifty-four years old
Wǒ xiángxiang kàn. Tā jīnnián	Let me try to think. He's
wǔshisānsuì le—bù, wǔshisìsuì le.	fifty-three this year—no, fifty-four.

3. Teacher

mǔqin	mother [N]
Ò. Nà, zhèiwèi shi nǐ mǔqin ba?	Oh. So I suppose this must be your mother?

4. Thompson

duì	be correct [SV]
sìshibāsuì	forty-eight years old
Duì, tā jīnnián sìshibāsuì le.	Right, she's forty-eight this year.

5. Teacher

mèimei	younger sister [N]
zhè shi nǐ mèimei	this is your younger sister
duì bu dui	correct or not correct, "right?"
ài	love; like [V/AV]
kě'ài	be loveable, cute [SV]
tā hěn kě'ài	she is cute
jǐsuì	how many years old (of a child)
tā jǐsuì le	how old is she
Zhè shi nǐ mèimei, duì bu dui?	This is your younger sister, right?
Tā hěn kě'ài! Tā jǐsuì le?	She's cute! How old is she?

6. Thompson

tā bāsuì	she is eight years old
xià-	next [SP]
xiàge	next
yuè	month [N]
xiàge yuè	next month
jiù	then [A]
xiàge yuè jiù jiǔsuì le	next month then will be nine years old
Tā bāsuì. Xiàge yuè jiù jiǔsuì le.	She's eight years old. She'll be nine next month.

Supplementary Vocabulary

1. dìdi	younger brother [N]
shàng-	last [SP]
shàngge	last
shàngge yuè	last month
Wǒ dìdi shàngge yuè hěn máng.	My younger brother was busy last month.

2. méiyou	not have; there is/are not [V]
gēge	older brother [N]
wǒ méiyou gēge	I don't have an older brother
jiějie	older sister [N]
yě méiyou jiějie	also don't have an older sister
Wǒ méiyou gēge, yě méiyou jiějie.	I have neither older brothers nor older sisters.

3. cāi	guess [V]
cāicai kàn	try to guess
Nǐ cāicai kàn!	You try to guess!

Grammatical and Cultural Notes

1A.   Age.

a.   The most common way to ask someone's age is: **Nǐ duō dà niánji le?** "How old are you?" (lit. "You are how big of age?"). The reason why **le** often occurs at the end of this question is that, in the mind of Chinese speakers, age is considered as something ever changing. The actual meaning of the Chinese is really closer to "How old have you become?" or "How old are you now?"

b.   A shorter and somewhat less formal way of asking someone's age is to drop **niánji** "age" and ask simply: **Nǐ duō dà le?** "How old are you?" (lit. "You are how big?").

c.   A more formal and more polite way to ask someone's age is: **Nín duō dà suìshu le?** "How old are you?" (lit. "You are how big of age?"; the noun **suìshu** means "age"). This would be appropriate when asking someone who is considerably older than you or clearly senior to you.

d.   To ask the age of children ten years old and under, **Nǐ jǐsuì le?** is commonly used (cf. line 5 of this conversation). Some speakers, especially in Taiwan, use **Nǐ jǐsuì le?** even for somewhat older people, e.g., teenagers and college students. Most Chinese would consider it rude, however, for a younger person to ask an older person her or his age with **Nǐ jǐsuì le?**

e.   The pattern for saying how old you are is:

Subject	Time Word	Number	SUÌ	LE
Wǒ	jīnnián	shíbā	suì	le.

"I'm eighteen years old."

The measure **suì** means "year of age" (cf. lines 2, 4, 5, and 6 of the conversation); **suì** cannot mean simply "year" as in "I want to go to Beijing for a year." Unlike most measures, no noun follows **suì**. To say "two years of age," say **liǎngsuì**, NOT *èrsuì. However, to express "two" everywhere else, use **èr**: e.g., "twenty-two years of age" would be **èrshi'èrsuì** and "forty-two years of age" would be **sìshi'èrsuì**. It is always acceptable to use the term **suì**; in informal conversation, when the age is eleven or greater, it is possible to omit **suì**, so that **Tā jīnnián sìshibā le** would mean "She's forty-eight this year." The effect of omitting the **suì** is slightly less formal and more colloquial. However, we recommend that, at least at this stage in your Chinese learning career, you always add the measure **suì**. In any case, for ages from one to ten years, **suì** is required. To say "an elderly gentleman of over eighty years of age" say **yíwèi bāshi duō suìde lǎo xiānsheng**.

f. To say "(a certain age and) a half" one would use **bàn** "half"; for example, **sānsuì bàn** "three and a half years old."

g. To negate sentences about age with **suì**, use **méiyou** "have not" (cf. SV2A); for example, "I'm not eighteen years old" would be **Wǒ méiyou shíbāsuì**.

h. To ask a question about age with **suì**, use the affirmative-negative verb construction **yǒu méiyou** "have/not have"; e.g., **Nǐ xiǎng tā yǒu méiyou liùshisuì? –Yǒu, tā yǒu!** "Do you think she's 60 years old? –Yes, she is!"

i. In China, asking people's ages—even of women—is not considered impolite, as it often is in American society. In fact, Chinese will frequently ask one's age relatively early on in a relationship to ascertain where the person fits in in the social hierarchy, since age matters more in China than in America. (Compare the use, in informal conversation, of **Lǎo** for people older than you and **Xiǎo** for those younger than you.) Do not be offended if you are suddenly asked how old you are. If you really don't wish to answer, you can always say **Nǐ cāicai kàn!** "Try to guess!" and then respond to your interlocutor's guess with a smile, or say **Chàbuduō ba** "I suppose that's about right" if their guess is within your "acceptable" range; or you could say **Fǎnzhèng bǐ nǐ dà!** "In any case, older than you!" or **Fǎnzhèng bǐ nǐ xiǎo!** "In any case, younger than you!," depending on the situation. Far from being stigmatized as in America, old age is much respected in China.

If you want to ask how old someone is, you should nevertheless exercise caution, because educated Chinese have heard that in America you're not supposed to ask, so they may find it strange if you then do the unexpected. You could guess and make them extra young, in which case, more often than not, they'll correct you and tell you their actual age. Or you could ask, a little less directly, **Nǐ shi něinián shēngde?** "What year were you born in?" or, even more discreetly, **Nǐ shǔ shémme?** "You belong to what (animal year of the Chinese zodiac)?" This refers to the twelve animals of the Chinese zodiac, each of which represents one year in a twelve-year cycle. The twelve animals, in the correct order (with Western calendar equivalents), are:

1. **lǎoshǔ** "rat" (1900, 1912, 1924, 1936, 1948, 1960, 1972, 1984, 1996, 2008, 2020)

2. **niú** "ox" (1901, 1913, 1925, 1937, 1949, 1961, 1973, 1985, 1997, 2009, 2021)

3. **hǔ** "tiger" (1902, 1914, 1926, 1938, 1950, 1962, 1974, 1986, 1998, 2010, 2022)

4. **tù** "rabbit" (1903, 1915, 1927, 1939, 1951, 1963, 1975, 1987, 1999, 2011, 2023)

5. **lóng** "dragon" (1904, 1916, 1928, 1940, 1952, 1964, 1976, 1988, 2000, 2012, 2024)

6. **shé** "snake" (1905, 1917, 1929, 1941, 1953, 1965, 1977, 1989, 2001, 2013, 2025)

7. **mǎ** "horse" (1906, 1918, 1930, 1942, 1954, 1966, 1978, 1990, 2002, 2014, 2026)

8. **yáng** "goat" (1907, 1919, 1931, 1943, 1955, 1967, 1979, 1991, 2003, 2015, 2027)

9. **hóu** "monkey" (1908, 1920, 1932, 1944, 1956, 1968, 1980, 1992, 2004, 2016, 2028)

10. **jī** "rooster" (1909, 1921, 1933, 1945, 1957, 1969, 1981, 1993, 2005, 2017, 2029)

11. **gǒu** "dog" (1910, 1922, 1934, 1946, 1958, 1970, 1982, 1994, 2006, 2018, 2030)

12. **zhū** "pig" (1911, 1923, 1935, 1947, 1959, 1971, 1983, 1995, 2007, 2019, 2031)

Of course, the cycle starts over again every twelve years, but normally you can tell whether a person is 12, 24, 36, or 48.

(In the Western year equivalents above, note that a certain Western year applies beginning after the Chinese New Year in that year; so some January and even February dates actually fall under the animal of the preceding year.)

j. According to the traditional Chinese system of calculating ages, a person is one **suì** old at birth and another **suì** old on the first Chinese New Year's following their birth. So if the first day of the Chinese New Year fell on

February 6, a child born February 5 would be two years old (**liǎngsuì**) when it is two days old. A person's age calculated by the traditional system is called their **xūsuì**. However, in the cities, many Chinese now use the Western method of calculating ages, which is called **shísuì**. In practice, one can never be quite sure of people's ages in casual conversation, unless one asks specifically if it is their **xūsuì** or their **shísuì**.

1B. In the questions **Tā duō dà niánji le?** and **Tā duō dàle?**, both of which mean "How old is s/he?," **duō** is a question word meaning "how?" or "to what extent?" **Duō** and the stative verb **dà** "be big" go together to mean "how big?" or "how old?." **Duō** can also precede other stative verbs, for example:

Duō nán?	"How difficult?"
Duō hǎo?	"How good?"
Nǐ duō gāo?	"How tall are you?"

The reason that there is no question particle **ma** at the ends of these questions is that **duō** is itself a question word; remember that if there is already a question word in a sentence, **ma** is not added at the end. Note also that **duō** in the sense of "how" has an alternate pronunciation **duó** that you will hear in Taiwan and occasionally elsewhere.

2A. In this line you learn the common and useful verb **xiǎng** "think." Just like in English, in Chinese this verb can take a sentence object, as in **Wǒ xiǎng tā shi Déguo rén** "I think she's German." But note that the verb **xiǎng** cannot be negated with **bù** in the sense of "I don't think that...." If you wish to say "I don't think that...," then in Chinese you must say **Wǒ xiǎng...bù...** For example, to say "I don't think she's German," you could NOT say *Wǒ bù xiǎng tā shi Déguo rén** but instead you would have to say **Wǒ xiǎng tā bú shi Déguo rén**.

2B. Reduplicated Monosyllabic Verbs + **KÀN**. Note the phrase **xiángxiang kàn** "try and think." A reduplicated (i.e., repeated) single-syllable verb followed by **kàn** (lit. "see") has the meaning "try and..." or "try to..." plus the meaning of the single-syllable verb. The second syllable of the reduplicated verb is often in the neutral tone. The pattern is:

Reduplicated Monosyllabic Verb	KÀN
xiángxiang	**kàn**
"try and think"	

Some more examples:

Zuòzuo kàn.	"Try and sit on it." (e.g., a chair at a furniture store)
Shuōshuo kàn.	"Try saying it." (e.g., a difficult tongue-twister)
Tīngting kàn.	"Try listening to it." (e.g., a new kind of music)

2C. Numbers from 11 to 99 with SHÍ. To create the numbers between 11 and 19, say **shí** "ten" followed immediately by the additional number:

shíyī	"11"	**shísì**	"14"	**shíqī**	"17"
shí'èr	"12"	**shíwǔ**	"15"	**shíbā**	"18"
shísān	"13"	**shíliù**	"16"	**shíjiǔ**	"19"

To create multiples of ten, say the number of times you want to multiply, followed immediately by **shí** "ten ":

èrshí	"20"	**wǔshí**	"50"	**bāshí**	"80"
sānshí	"30"	**liùshí**	"60"	**jiǔshí**	"90"
sìshí	"40"	**qīshí**	"70"		

To create the numbers between one multiple of ten and the next, say the multiple of ten, then say **shí**, and then say the additional number. Examples: **èrshiyī** "21," **liùshisān** "63," **jiǔshijiǔ** "99." When **shí** is the middle syllable in a three-syllable number, it usually loses its tone.

2D. **Tā jīnnián wǔshisānsuì le** "He's 53 this year" (lit. "He has gotten to be 53 years old this year"). It is very common to add a **jīnnián** "this year" in Chinese questions and answers about age (in English we would often just say "He's 53"). Note that there is no **shi** "to be" added (one would normally NOT say *Tā jīnnián shi wǔshisānsuì le).

Guardian animal from Ming tombs near Beijing

3. You have now been introduced to **fùqin** "father" (in line 1) and **mǔqin** "mother" (in this line). These words are somewhat more formal terms than **bàba** "dad" and **māma** "mom" that you learned in 1-2. On most occasions, you can use either set to talk about your own parents, but it's usually better to use **fùqin mǔqin** when talking about someone else's parents. On the other hand, only **bàba māma** can be used to address one's own parents. There is no question that there is sexism in the ordering of numerous terms referring to female and male, even more so than in English. Thus, one must say **fùqin mǔqin** "father and mother" or **bàba māma** "dad and mom." It would sound very strange to reverse the order.

4A. There is no all-purpose word for "yes" in Chinese. **Duì** "be correct, right, yes, yeah" is one common equivalent. Another is **shì** "be (so)." But be careful in the negative: while **bú duì** "not correct, wrong, no" is correct Chinese (especially in response to the question **Duì bu duì?**), it is considered somewhat abrupt and impolite and would only be used by people who know each other well, or by superiors to subordinates. A student would not normally say **bú duì** to a teacher, though a teacher might frequently say this to a student. A safer alternative for saying "no" is to use **bú shì** "it is not so."

4B. In pronouncing **duì** "be correct, right," remember that the syllable which is spelled as **dui** in Pinyin is pronounced as if it were written **duei** (so that it rhymes with English "lay" but not with "Louie").

5A. Since in Chinese society age matters—not only across generations but also in the same generation, the Chinese terms for siblings are distinguished not only by sex, as in English (i.e., "brother" vs. "sister"), but also by age relative to the speaker (i.e., "older brother/sister" vs. "younger brother/sister").

5B. Tag Questions. Look at the first sentence in line 5: **Zhè shi nǐ mèimei, duì bu duì?** "This is your younger sister, right?" One could also ask **Zhè shi nǐ mèimei, shì bu shì?** or **Zhè shi nǐ mèimei, shì ma?** "This is your younger sister, isn't it?" Questions such as this, where an affirmative-negative question or a **ma** question has been "tagged on" at the end of a statement to transform the statement into a question, are very common in Chinese and will be termed tag questions. The tag question pattern will be useful to you in confirming your understanding of various matters or in making polite suggestions, and will help you sound more natural and gain fluency in speaking Chinese. Some more examples of tag questions:

Tā shi nǐ àirén, duì bu duì?	"She's your wife, right?"
Bānshang yǒu liǎngge Jiā'nádà rén, duì ma?	"There are two Canadians in the class, right?"
Nǐ shi Zhào Xiansheng, shì bu shì?	"You're Mr. Zhao, aren't you?"
Wǒmen qù shítáng, hǎo bu hao?	"Let's go to the cafeteria, O.K.?"
Wǒmen jīnnián bú qù, hǎo ma?	"Let's not go this year, O.K.?"

6A. Some speakers say **bāsuì** "eight years of age" (without a tone change on **bā**) while others would say **básuì** (with the tone change, because of the following Tone Four word **suì**).

6B. Learn **xiàge** "next" and, in SV1 in this lesson, **shàngge** "last." These two words may be used with **yuè** "month" or with the days of the week, which you will learn in 4-1. Examples:

shàngge yuè	"last month"
xiàge yuè	"next month"

6C.   The adverb **jiù** means "then" in the sense of "as early as then" or "as quickly as then."

6D.   **LE** to Indicate Anticipated Change in a Situation. Consider the sentence **Xiàge yuè jiù jiǔsuì le** "Next month (my little sister) will be nine years old." The **le** at the end of this sentence indicates a changed situation, even though that change (the little sister's becoming nine years old) has not yet occurred and is anticipated in the future. In other words, if in the mind of a speaker a change of status is anticipated in the future, **le** can be used just as readily as if change had already taken place in the past. The pattern for this **le** that indicates anticipated change in a situation is:

Sentence	LE
Tā xiàge yuè jiù jiǔsuì	**le.**
"Next month she will be nine years old."	

The use of **le** to indicate anticipated change in a situation is really only an extension of **le** to indicate a changed situation (cf. 1-4: 4C).

SV2A.   **MÉIYOU** as the Negative of **YǑU**. **Méiyou** "not have; there is not/there are not" is the negative form of the verb **yǒu**. This negative form is extremely common in Chinese, so be sure to learn it thoroughly. Attention: Never say *bù yǒu as the negative of **yǒu**. Though the negative forms of all other verbs are formed with **bù**, the negative of **yǒu** is **méiyou**. Contrast:

AFFIRMATIVE		NEGATIVE	
qù	"go"	**bú qù**	"not go"
yào	"want"	**bú yào**	"not want"
yǒu	"have"	**méiyou**	"not have"

The question form **yǒu méiyou** "have or not have" is extremely common. For example:

Nǐ yǒu méiyou gēge? "Do you have older brothers?"

As we have pointed out above, **bù** and **yǒu** are never said together but instead become **méiyou**. However, if another word intervenes between the **bù** and the **yǒu**, then the negative is still with **bù**. So, for example, you would say **Yǒu yìsi** "It's interesting" and **Méiyou yìsi** "It's not interesting'; but if you add the adverb **tài** "too," then you would say **Bú tài yǒu yìsi** "It's not very interesting."

SV2B.   At this point, it would be good for you to review the following negatives that have been introduced up to this point, making certain that you can distinguish among them:

NEGATIVE	BASIC MEANING	EXAMPLE	ENGLISH
bù	not	**Tā bù gōngzuò.**	He doesn't work.
bié	do not!	**Nǐ bié gōngzuò!**	Don't work!
búyào	do not!	**Nǐ búyào gōngzuò!**	Don't work!
méi	did not	**Tā méi gōngzuò.**	He didn't work.
méiyou	not have;	**Wǒ méiyou jiějie.**	I don't have an older sister.
	there is not/are not	**Míngtiān méiyou gōngkè!**	There is no homework tomorrow!

Purchasing a Tea Cup

P A R T 3

Jonathan Little, an American student who is spending six months as an intern in a law firm in Beijing, passes a store selling clothing and kitchenware. He first asks the salesman how much one of the coats on display costs, then asks how much a tea cup costs.

 Basic Conversation 3-3

1.	LITTLE *(looking at a coat)*	**Qǐng wèn, zhèige duōshǎo qián?** Excuse me, how much is this?
2.	SALESMAN	**Yìbǎi jiǔshíbākuài.** One hundred and ninety-eight dollars.
3.	LITTLE	**Yò, tài guìle!** Gosh, that's too expensive!
	(pointing at a cup)	**Zhèige bēizi duōshǎo qián?** How much is this cup?
4.	SALESMAN	**Nèige zhǐ yào sānkuài wǔ.** That only costs three dollars and fifty cents.
5.	LITTLE	**Wǒ kànkan, xíng bu xíng?** Would it be all right if I took a look at it?
6.	SALESMAN	**Xíng, nín kàn ba.** Sure, take a look.
7.	LITTLE *(looking at the cup)*	**Hǎo, wǒ mǎi liǎngge.** O.K., I'll buy two.

Build Up

1. Little

zhèige	this one, this
duōshǎo	how much, how many [QW]
qián	money [N]
duōshǎo qián	how much money
Qǐng wèn, zhèige duōshǎo qián?	Excuse me, how much is this?

2. Salesman

-bǎi	hundred [NU]
yìbǎi	one hundred
kuài	dollar (monetary unit) [M]
jiǔshibākuài	ninety-eight dollars
Yìbǎi jiǔshibākuài.	One hundred and ninety-eight dollars.

3. Little

yò	"gosh," "wow" [I]
guì	be expensive [SV]
tài guìle	too expensive
Yò, tài guìle!	Gosh, that's too expensive!
bēizi	cup [N]
zhèige bēizi	this cup
Zhèige bēizi duōshǎo qián?	How much is this cup?

4. Salesman

nèige	that one, that
zhǐ	only [A]
yào	want, need, cost, take [V]
zhǐ yào	only costs
sānkuài wǔ	three fifty, 3.50
Nèige zhǐ yào sānkuài wǔ.	That only costs three dollars and fifty cents.

5. Little

kànkan	take a look
wǒ kànkan	I take a look
xíng bu xíng	is it O.K. or is it not O.K.
Wǒ kànkan, xíng bu xíng?	Would it be all right if I took a look at it?

6. Salesman

ba	(indicates suggestions) [P]
nín kàn ba	why don't you look
Xíng, nín kàn ba.	Sure, take a look.

7. Little

mǎi	buy [V]
wǒ mǎi liǎngge	I buy two of them
Hǎo, wǒ mǎi liǎngge.	O.K., I'll buy two.

 ## Supplementary Vocabulary

1. máo — ten cents, dime [M]
    wǔmáo — fifty cents
    fēn — fen, cent [M]
    jiǔfēn — nine cents
sānkuài wǔmáo jiǔfēn qián — three dollars and fifty-nine cents

2. líng — zero [NU]
yìbǎi líng yī — one hundred and one

3. gōngshìbāo — briefcase, attaché case [N]
    nèige gōngshìbāo — that briefcase
    -qiān — thousand [NU]
    yìqiān — one thousand

yìqiānkuài	one thousand dollars
yào yìqiānkuài	costs one thousand dollars
Yò, nèige gōngshìbāo yào yìqiānkuài!	Wow, that attache case costs $1,000!

4. mài — sell [V]
bēibāo	knapsack, backpack [N]
tāmen màide bēibāo	the backpacks that they sell
dàizi	bag [N]
bēibāo gēn dàizi	backpacks and bags
piányi	be cheap [SV]
dōu tǐng piányide	are all quite cheap
Tāmen màide bēibāo gēn dàizi dōu tǐng piányide.	The backpacks and bags they sell are all quite cheap.

5. jiā — add; plus [V]
Qīshí jiā èrshí shi duōshǎo?	Seventy plus twenty is how much?

6. jiǎn — subtract; minus [V]
Jiǔshí jiǎn liùshí shi sānshí.	Ninety minus sixty is thirty.

Additional Vocabulary

1. **Rénmínbì**	RMB, Chinese currency [N]
2. **Táibì**	NT, Taiwan currency [N]
3. **Gǎngbì**	Hong Kong dollar, Hong Kong currency [N]
4. **Xīnbì**	Singapore dollar, Singapore currency [N]
5. **Měiyuán**	U.S. dollar [N]
6. **Ōuyuán**	Euro [N]
7. **Yīngbàng**	British pound [N]

Grammatical and Cultural Notes

1A. **ZHÈIGE** and **NÈIGE.** Note **zhèige** "this one" in line 1, **zhèige bēizi** "this cup" in line 3, **nèige** "that one" in line 4, and **nèige gōngshìbāo** "that attache case" in SV3. The words **zhèige** and **nèige** are both composed of a specifier (**zhèi-** or **nèi-**) plus the general measure **ge**. The pattern is:

Specifier	Measure	English
zhèi-	ge	"this"
nèi-	ge	"that"

Zhèige and **nèige** can function either as demonstrative adjectives that describe a following noun (e.g., **Wǒ mǎi zhèige bēizi** "I'll buy this cup") or as pronouns, in which case the noun that would ordinarily follow them has been omitted or must be assumed (e.g., **Wǒ mǎi zhèige** "I'll buy this one"). The literal meaning of **zhèige bēizi** is something like "this (item of) cup." Some more examples with **zhèige** and **nèige**:

zhèige bān	"this class"
zhèige yuè	"this month"
zhèige niánji	"this age"
zhèige nǚshēng	"this female student"
nèige nánde	"that guy"
nèige bēibāo	"that backpack"
nèige dānwèi	"that organization"
nèige Fǎguo rén	"that French person"
Zhèige, bú shi nèige!	"This one, not that one!"

Be sure to contrast carefully with the above expressions the corresponding question word **něige** "which one?." **Něige** "which one?" and **nèige** "that one" are especially easy to confuse. Study the following conversational exchanges:

Speaker A:	**Něige rén?**
	"Which person?"
Speaker B:	**Nèige rén!**
	"That person!"
Speaker A:	**Něige?**
	"Which one?"
Speaker B:	**Nèige!**
	"That one!"

Finally, be aware that some speakers say **zhège**, **nàge**, and **năge** instead of **zhèige**, **nèige**, and **něige**.

1B.   The question word **duōshǎo** "how much, how many" is used where the number is known or expected to be 10 or more. As we learned previously, the question word **jǐ-**, followed by an appropriate measure, is used when the number is under 10. Study carefully the following examples:

Nǐ yǒu duōshǎo qián?	"How much money do you have?"
Nǐ yǒu jǐkuài qián?	"How many dollars do you have?" (assumption is under 10)
Yígòng yǒu duōshǎo rén?	"How many people are there in all?"
Yígòng yǒu jǐge rén?	"How many people are there in all?" (assumption is under 10)

2A.   Numbers from 100 to 999 with **-BǍI**. To form the words for "hundreds," say the multiplier times **-bǎi** "hundred." The multiples of a hundred are:

yībǎi	"100"	**sìbǎi**	"400"	**qībǎi**	"700"
liǎngbǎi	"200"	**wǔbǎi**	"500"	**bābǎi**	"800"
sānbǎi	"300"	**liùbǎi**	"600"	**jiǔbǎi**	"900"

For "one hundred," either **yībǎi** or **yìbǎi** (with a tone change on the **yī**) is possible. For "two hundred," most speakers say **liǎngbǎi**, which we recommend you use, while other speakers may say **èrbǎi**. To create numbers that fall between two multiples of a hundred (such as "358"), simply say the multiple of a hundred ("300" or **sānbǎi** in this case) followed directly by the word for the number under one hundred ("58" or **wǔshibā**), resulting in **sānbǎi wǔshibā** "358."

3.   LE after TÀI in Affirmative Sentences. Notice that in the sentence **Yò, tài guìle** "Gosh, that's too expensive," there is a **le** after the stative verb **guì** "be expensive." When stative verbs (and, less commonly, some auxiliary verbs) are preceded by a **tài** "too" in affirmative sentences, they are often followed by a **le**. The pattern is:

Subject	TÀI	Verb	LE
Nèige	tài	guì	le.

"That one is too expensive."

Actually, this **le** is none other than the **le** that indicates a changed situation that we took up in 1-4: 4C. In a sentence like **Nèige tài guìle**, in the mind of the speaker there has been a change in the degree of expensiveness of the item in question. That is, the speaker had assumed previously that it was not so expensive but has now learned that it is more expensive than he or she had imagined. In negative sentences, there usually is no **le** after **tài**, so one normally would just say **Bú tài guì** rather than *Bú tài guìle. Some more examples of **le** after **tài** in affirmative sentences:

Tài hǎole!	"That's great!"
Nǐ tài jǐnzhāngle!	"You're too nervous!"
Zhèige bēizi tài dàle.	"This cup is too big."
Nèige háizi tài kě'àile!	"That kid is so cute!" (lit. "That child is too cute!")

4A.   **YÀO** to Indicate Price. You have seen the word **yào** "want, need, cost" before in the expression **búyào** "don't" in 2-2. **Búyào** literally means "(you) don't want to." The pattern in Chinese for indicating the price of something is:

Item	YÀO	Price
Nèige bēizi	**yào**	**sānkuài wǔ.**

"That cup costs three fifty." (lit. "That cup wants three fifty.")

Examples:

Zhèige yào shíkuài.	"This one costs ten dollars."
Nèige yào duōshǎo qián?	"How much does that one cost?"
Nèige gōngshìbāo yào yìbǎikuài.	"That briefcase sells for one hundred dollars."

Be careful to distinguish the pronunciation of **yào** from **yǒu** "have." Also, note that in place of **yào**, the verbs **mài** "sell for" and **děi** "must" (i.e., "you must pay") are also sometimes used to indicate price. Finally, it is also possible to drop **yào** and have no verb between the item and the price.

4B.   **Sānkuài wǔ** is a short form of **sānkuài wǔmáo**, which is itself a shorter form of **sānkuài wǔmáo qián** (cf. SV1).

5A.   REDUPLICATION OF VERBS. Some verbs are frequently reduplicated (i.e., repeated) so as to give a relaxed, casual sense to the verb and make the sentence they occur in sound smoother and less abrupt. The basic meaning is the same as when they are not reduplicated. For example, the verb **kàn** "look" is often reduplicated into the form **kànkan** "take a look." The second iteration of the verb is often in the neutral tone. The pattern is:

Verb	→	Verb Verb
kàn	→	**kànkan**

"take a look"

Some other verbs you have had besides **kàn** that can be reduplicated in this manner include:

shuō	"say"	→	**shuōshuo**
tīng	"listen"	→	**tīngting**
wèn	"ask"	→	**wènwen**
zuò	"sit"	→	**zuòzuo**
xiǎng	"think"	→	**xiángxiang**
cāi	"guess"	→	**cāicai**
jièshao	"introduce"	→	**jièshao jieshao**
rènshi	"get to know"	→	**rènshi renshi**
xuéxí	"learn"	→	**xuéxí xuexi**

Semantically and gramatically, such reduplication is similar to the use of **yíxià(r)** after a verb, as in **jièshao yixiar** "introduce," which you saw in 2-2. In fact, one could say **Wǒ kàn yixia** instead of **Wǒ kànkan**.

5B.   **Xíng bu xíng** "is it O.K.?" is another example of a Tag Question (cf. note 5B in 3-2, where we introduced **duì bu dui**). **Xíng bu xíng** is especially common in north China.

6.   **BA** to Indicate Suggestions. In 2-3: 6B we introduced the sentence-final particle **ba** as having the function of indicating supposition, as in **Nǐ bú shi Zhōngguo rén ba?** "I suppose you're not Chinese?" The particle **ba** can also be added to the end of a statement to indicate a suggestion, as in **Nín kàn ba** "Why don't you take a look?" Common English translations of this new **ba** that indicates suggestions include "why don't you," "how about," "let's," or simply the imperative form of the verb. The pattern is:

Statement	BA
Nín kàn	**ba.**

"Why don't you take a look?"

Study the following examples of **ba** used to indicate suggestions:

Zuò ba!	"Sit down!"
Nǐ qù ba.	"Why don't you go?"
Nǐ yě mǎi yíge ba.	"Why don't you buy one, too?"
Wǒmen zǒu ba.	"Let's leave."

7A.   Notice that the first four syllables of the utterance **Hǎo, wǒ mǎi liǎngge** are all Tone Three. You've learned about tone changes in the case of two Tone Three syllables in succession; but what happens in a case like this, where there are four Tone Three syllables? First, if there is a pause, nothing changes, so **hǎo** remains Tone Three. As regards the remaining syllables, the **liǎng-** of **liǎngge** also does not change, since it is the last Tone Three syllable of this group. Regarding **wǒ** and **mǎi**, some speakers would change both to Tone Two whereas other speakers would change only **mǎi** to Tone Two. In other words, one can say either (with the tone changes spelled in) **wó mái liǎngge** or **wǒ mái liǎngge**.

Bears and spectators at Beijing Zoo

7B. Of course we can say that the **hǎo** in **Hǎo, wǒ mǎi liǎngge** means "good" or "O.K." but, just as in English, this **hǎo** also has the function of indicating the end of a discourse. That is, it signals that the period of negotiation and reflection is over and that a decision has been reached.

SV1. Monetary System. The basic currency unit of China is the yuan (pronounced **yuán**), which means "dollar." It is also referred to in English as the RMB, an acronym for **Rénmínbì** "the people's currency," which is the official term for the currency circulated in China after the establishment of the People's Republic in 1949.

The basic currency unit of Taiwan is also called the **yuán**, which is referred to in English as the NT (from "New Taiwan dollar"), from **Xīn Táibì** "new Taiwan currency," which is the official term for Taiwanese currency.

In both China and Taiwan, the **yuán** is divided into ten **jiǎo** "dimes," with each **jiǎo** being further divided into ten **fēn** "cents" (however, with the rise in prices in the last few decades, **jiǎo** and **fēn** are now seldom used). **Yuán** and **jiǎo** are formal written terms, which some people also use in speech. The colloquial terms **kuài** "dollar" and **máo** "dime" are often substituted for **yuán** and **jiǎo** in speech. To sum up:

FORMAL TERM	COLLOQUIAL TERM	ENGLISH
yuán	**kuài**	dollar
jiǎo	**máo**	dime
fēn	**fēn**	cent

Be careful not to mix the formal and colloquial terms in the same phrase.

Other comments on money:

a. Use of **máo**: In Chinese you can NEVER say *ershiwǔfēn** for "twenty-five cents"; instead, you should say **liǎngmáo wǔfēn**, which literally means "two dimes and five cents." Also, though we recommend you use **liǎng** with **máo**, you should be aware that some speakers use **èr**; so, to say "twenty cents," either **liǎngmáo** or **èrmáo** would be correct. In fact, some speakers mix the two up in the same expression, for example, **liǎngkuài èrmáo wǔ** "two dollars and twenty cents." Finally, only **èr** can occur at the end of a money expression, never **liǎng**; thus, one could say the abbreviated form **liǎngkuài èr** "$2.20" but could NEVER say *liǎngkuài liǎng** (see next section on abbreviations).

Basketball game at Beijing Language and Culture University

b. Consider English money expressions like "two seventy-five" (abbreviated from "two dollars and seventy-five cents") or "a dollar fifty" (from "a dollar and fifty cents"). Here, words that are easily understood from the context are dropped. Similar abbreviations exist in Chinese, e.g., **yìmáo** (from **yìmáo qián**), **liǎngmáo wǔ** (from **liǎngmáo wǔfēn qián**), **sānbǎikuài** (from **sānbǎikuài qián**). If **fēn** or **máo** are the final denomination of currency in a compound money phrase, they are commonly dropped in conversation. For example, **liǎngmáo wǔfēn** becomes **liǎngmáo wǔ** and **sānkuài wǔmáo** becomes **sānkuài wǔ**. However, if the money phrase has only one denomination, the word for that denomination cannot be dropped (i.e., you could not abbreviate **sānkuài** to **sān**). From the point of view of listening comprehension, if you hear a money amount with a number in the final position and no final denomination is given, assume it is the next lower denomination after the denomination that was just mentioned.

c. After sums consisting of a single denomination, the word **qián** "money" is commonly added. Examples: **qīkuài qián** "$7.00," **jiǔmáo qián** "ninety cents," **sānfēn qián** "three cents." But there must always be a measure before the **qián**, so you could NEVER say *sānbǎi èrshiwǔ qián**; this would have to be said as **sānbǎi èrshiwǔ kuài qián**.

d. **Bàn** "half" can also be used with amounts of money. To express "$3.50," one could say either **sānkuài wǔ** or **sānkuài bàn**. Note that **bàn** is placed after the measure **kuài**.

To summarize the most important points above, we can say that the basic pattern for giving money amounts, in its full form, is:

Number	KUÀI	Number	MÁO	Number	FĒN	QIÁN
liù	kuài	wǔ	máo	jiǔ	fēn	qián

"six dollars and fifty-nine cents"

SV2. The word **líng** "zero" must be inserted if there are one or more zeros within a number; it is spoken only once, no matter how many zeros are in the number. Examples:

yìbǎi líng yī   "101"

yìqiān líng yī   "1,001"

This rule holds true for money amounts as well: **shíkuài líng wǔfēn** "$10.05." However, if numbers are simply being read off digit by digit, as in English "one zero zero one" for "1-0-0-1" (instead of "one thousand and one"), then every **líng** in the number must be spoken: **yī líng líng yī** "1-0-0-1."

SV3.   Numbers from 1,000 to 9,999 with **-QIĀN**. The pattern for forming the words for thousands is multiplier times **-qiān** "thousand." The multiples of a thousand are:

yìqiān	"1000"	**sìqiān**	"4000"	**qīqiān**	"7000"
liǎngqiān	"2000"	**wǔqiān**	"5000"	**bāqiān**	"8000"
sānqiān	"3000"	**liùqiān**	"6000"	**jiǔqiān**	"9000"

Note that **-qiān**, like **-bǎi**, cannot be said alone. "Nine thousand nine hundred and ninety-nine" would be **jiǔqiān jiǔbǎi jiǔshíjiǔ**.

SV4A.   Distinguish carefully between **mǎi** "buy" and **mài** "sell."

SV4B.   Distinguish carefully between **piányi** "be cheap" and **róngyi** "be easy."

SV4C.   Note that the **-n** in **piányi** is not pronounced like a normal **-n** but is nasalized. This is because if a syllable ending in **-n** is followed immediately by a syllable beginning with **y-**, **w-**, **h-**, or a vowel, the **-n** of the first syllable is often not fully pronounced. In this case, the tongue does not quite reach the roof of the mouth, and the vowel in the first syllable ends up being nasalized.

SV4D.   In **tāmen màide bēibāo gēn dàizi** "the backpacks and bags that they sell," the **-de** indicates that what precedes it (**tāmen mài** "they sell") describes what follows it (**bēibāo gēn dàizi** "backpacks and bags"). A literal translation might be: "the they-sell backpacks and bags." The grammatical structure is the same as in **wǒde tóngwū** "my roommate" or **Zhōng-Měi Màoyì Gōngsīde Shī Xiáojie** "Ms. Shi from Sino-American Trading Company" (cf. 2-4: 3B).

The famous **Gǒu Bu Lǐ Bāozi** ("Steamed Filled Bun") Restaurant in Tianjin

Buying a Train Ticket

Paige Haynes, who is in China on a two-year assignment teaching English at a language institute, walks up to a ticket window at Beijing West Railway Station to purchase a ticket to Tianjin.

Basic Conversation 3-4

1. **HAYNES**
Qǐng wèn, xiàyítàng dào Tiānjīnde huǒchē jǐdiǎn kāi?
Excuse me, when does the next train to Tianjin depart?

2. **TICKET AGENT**
Jiǔdiǎn èrshí. Kěshi xiànzài yǐjīng jiǔdiǎn yíkè le, kǒngpà nín láibujíle.
Nine twenty. But it's now already a quarter past nine, I'm afraid you're not going to make it.

3. **HAYNES**
Nèmme, zài xiàyítàng ne?
Well, what about the one after that?

4. **TICKET AGENT**
Wǒ kànkan. Zài xiàyítàng shi shídiǎn bàn.
Let me see. The one after that is at 10:30.

5. **HAYNES**
Hǎo. Nà, wǒ jiù zuò shídiǎn bànde. Duōshǎo qián?
O.K. In that case, I'll take the ten-thirty one. How much is it?

6. **TICKET AGENT**
Shíyīkuài wǔ.
Eleven dollars and fifty cents.

7. **HAYNES**
Dào Tiānjīn yào duō cháng shíjiān?
How long does it take to get to Tianjin?

8. **TICKET AGENT**
Chàbuduō yào liǎngge bàn zhōngtóu.
It takes about two and a half hours.

9. **HAYNES**
Hǎo, xièxie nín.
O.K., thanks.

Build Up

1. Haynes

tàng	(for runs by trains, buses) [M]
xiàyítàng	the next (trip of a train or bus)
dào	arrive, reach [V]
Tiānjīn	Tianjin [PW]
huǒ	fire [N]
chē	vehicle (car, cab, bus, bicycle) [N]
huǒchē	train [N]
dào Tiānjīnde huǒchē	a train which goes to Tianjin
xiàyítàng dào Tiānjīnde huǒchē	the next train to Tianjin
diǎn	o'clock, hour [M]
jǐdiǎn	what time
kāi	depart (of a train, bus, ship) [V]
jǐdiǎn kāi	what time does it depart
Qǐng wèn, xiàyítàng dào Tiānjīnde huǒchē jǐdiǎn kāi?	Excuse me, when does the next train to Tianjin depart?

2. Ticket agent

jiǔdiǎn	nine o'clock
jiǔdiǎn èrshí	nine twenty
xiànzài	now [TW]
yǐjīng	already [A]
kè	quarter of an hour [M]
yíkè	a quarter of an hour
jiǔdiǎn yíkè	a quarter past nine
xiànzài yǐjīng jiǔdiǎn yíkè	now it's already a quarter past nine
kǒngpà	"I'm afraid that"; probably [MA]
-jí	reach a goal in time [RE]
láibují	not have enough time [RC]
kǒngpà nín láibujíle	afraid you won't have enough time
Jiǔdiǎn èrshí. Kěshi xiànzài yǐjīng jiǔdiǎn yíkè le, kǒngpà nín láibujíle.	Nine twenty. But it's now already a quarter past nine, I'm afraid you're not going to make it.

3. Haynes

nèmme	then, in that case, well [CJ]
zài	again [A]
zài xiàyítàng	the (train) after the next one
Nèmme, zài xiàyítàng ne?	Well, what about the one after that?

4. Ticket agent

shídiǎn bàn	half past ten, 10:30
Wǒ kànkan. Zài xiàyítàng shi shídiǎn bàn.	Let me see. The one after that is at 10:30.

5. Haynes

zuò	travel by, take [V]
shídiǎn bànde	the ten thirty one
wǒ jiù zuò shídiǎn bànde	I then take the ten thirty one
Hǎo. Nà, wǒ jiù zuò shídiǎn bànde.	O.K. In that case, I'll take the ten thirty one.
Duōshǎo qián?	How much is it?

6. Ticket agent

Shíyīkuài wǔ.	Eleven dollars and fifty cents.

7. Haynes

cháng	be long [SV]
duō cháng	how long
shíjiān	time [N]
duō cháng shíjiān	how long a time, how long
Dào Tiānjīn yào duō cháng shíjiān?	How long does it take to get to Tianjin?

8. Ticket agent

chàbuduō	almost, about [A]
zhōngtóu	hour [N]
liǎngge bàn zhōngtóu	two and a half hours
Chàbuduō yào liǎngge bàn zhōngtóu.	It takes about two and a half hours.

9. Haynes

Hǎo, xièxie nín.	O.K., thanks.

Supplementary Vocabulary: Talking About Time

1. zhōng — clock, o'clock; bell [N]
Yǐjīng shídiǎn zhōng le, wǒ děi zǒule. — It's already ten o'clock, I must be going.

2. fēn — minute [M]
shífēn — ten minutes
shífēn zhōng — ten minutes (of the clock)
Zhǐ yào shífēn zhōng. — It will only take ten minutes.

3. chà — lack [V]
chà yíkè — lacking a quarter of an hour
chà yíkè bādiǎn — a quarter to eight
Xiànzài chà yíkè bādiǎn. — It's now a quarter to eight.

4. sānkè — three quarters of an hour
sāndiǎn sānkè — three forty-five
Yǐjīng sāndiǎn sānkè le. — It's already three forty-five.

Grammatical and Cultural Notes

1A. The noun **huǒchē** means "train." This word, which literally means "fire vehicle," is composed of the two nouns **huǒ** "fire" and **chē** "vehicle," since (traditionally) a train is a vehicle involving the burning of some fuel. There are many two-syllable words like this in Chinese that are composed of two nouns, the first one describing the second.

1B. Chinese trains are convenient and relatively inexpensive. Traveling on trains is an excellent way to meet people and talk to them. In general, Chinese people are especially open to conversation with foreigners on trains.

1C. To indicate a scheduled run of a train from one place to another, one says **yítàng huǒchē**, literally "a trip of a train." The word **tàng** is a so-called measure; it measures the number of trips, or runs, of trains and other vehicles. **Xiàyítàng** means "the next scheduled trip of a train."

1D. **-DE** Following Long Phrases to Indicate Modification. As we already saw in 2-4: 3B, the particle **-de** can indicate that what precedes it describes what follows it. This holds true whether the descriptive phrase with **-de** consists of one word or a phrase containing many words. In **xiàyítàng dào Tiānjīnde huǒchē**, the **-de** indicates that the part before it (**xiàyítàng dào Tiānjīn** "the next trip of it goes to Tianjin") describes the part after it (**huǒchē** "train"), resulting in the meaning "the next train which goes to Tianjin." The pattern is:

Long Phrase	-DE	Noun
xiàyítàng dào Tiānjīn	**-de**	**huǒchē**

"the next train that goes to Tianjin"

Here are some other examples of nouns modified by long phrases ending in **-de**:

wǒ yào mǎide bēizi	"the cup that I want to buy"
zài Měiguo gōngzuòde nèige Zhōngguo nánshēng	"that male Chinese student who works in America"
sāndiǎn zhōng zuò huǒchē dào Běijīng qùde nèiwèi Měiguo xiáojie	"that young American woman who took the train at three o'clock to go to Beijing"

1E.   Time When Before the Verb. Time expressions indicating the point in time when something happens, happened, or will happen are placed immediately after the subject and before the verb. Note that this order is different from English, since in English time when is indicated after the verb. The same rule applies to question words like **jǐdiǎn** "at what o'clock, when." We shall call all such expressions "time when" expressions. The pattern is:

Subject	Time When	Verb
Wǒ	**bādiǎn zhōng**	**qù.**

"I go at eight o'clock." (lit. "I at eight o'clock go.")

"Time when" is always before the verb and usually immediately before the verb; but if an adverb such as **hěn** "very" or **jiù** "then" or **yǐjīng** "already" is present, then the order is subject + time when + adverb + verb.

Some more examples of "time when" before the verb:

Huǒchē jǐdiǎn lái?	"When is the train coming?"
Huǒchē jiǔdiǎn èrshí lái.	"The train is coming at 9:20."
Wǒ míngtiān hěn máng.	"I'm busy tomorrow."

As regards the last example above, note that in Chinese you could NEVER say a sentence such as ***Wǒ hěn máng míngtiān** "I'm busy tomorrow" where the "time when" expression occurs after the verb as in English.

2A.   Clock Times.

a.   All of China, Hong Kong, Macao, and Taiwan are in the same time zone. The time in China is twelve hours ahead of Eastern Standard Time in the U.S. when the U.S. is not on daylight saving time; otherwise, China is thirteen hours ahead (there is no daylight saving time in China).

b.   The pattern for creating clock times that involve whole hours is: number of the hour + **diǎn** + **zhōng** "o'clock." The **diǎn**, literally "dot," corresponds to the English colon (:) in clock times (e.g., **yìdiǎn zhōng** "1:00"). In the same way that in English the "o'clock" can be omitted, in Chinese the **zhōng** may be omitted, so one could say either the full form **yìdiǎn zhōng** or just **yìdiǎn**; however, for now we recommend you use the full form. Be sure to use **liǎngdiǎn** for "2:00," NEVER ***èrdiǎn**. More examples:

sāndiǎn zhōng or **sāndiǎn**	"3:00"
wǔdiǎn zhōng or **wǔdiǎn**	"5:00"
shíyīdiǎn zhōng or **shíyīdiǎn**	"11:00"

c.   If the number of minutes is to be indicated, this is done by adding after **diǎn** the number of minutes + **fēn** "minute." **Zhōng** is usually omitted. **Fēn** may be omitted after numbers that are multiples of ten. Examples:

sāndiǎn líng sānfēn	"3:03"
sāndiǎn èrshisānfēn	"3:23"
sāndiǎn èrshí	"3:20"

d. **Yíkè** "quarter after," **bàn** "thirty," and **sānkè** "three quarters after" are used with times involving 15, 30, and 45 minutes after the hour. Examples:

liùdiǎn yíkè	"6:15"
qīdiǎn bàn	"7:30"
bādiǎn sānkè	"8:45"

There are some Chinese speakers who, for "8:45," prefer **bādiǎn sìshiwǔfēn** to **bādiǎn sānkè**.

e. **Chà**, literally "lack," can be used to indicate a point of time between the 31st minute and the 59th minute before the next hour. For "(number of minutes) to (an hour)," some speakers say (hour) + **chà** + (number of minutes) while other speakers put the expression with **chà** before the hour and say: **chà** + (number of minutes) + (hour). Examples: "12:55" could be either **yīdiǎn chà wǔfēn** or **chà wǔfēn yīdiǎn**; "11:45" could be either **shí'èrdiǎn chà yíkè** or **chà yíkè shí'èrdiǎn**.

f. For number of minutes past the hour, some speakers use **guò**. Example: "3:05" could be either **sāndiǎn líng wǔfēn** or **sāndiǎn guò wǔfēn**.

g. In giving clock times, it is common to use a sentence-final particle **le**, since clock times—like age—by their very nature imply change.

h. The question for "What time is it?" is **Xiànzài jǐdiǎn zhōng le?** or just **Xiànzài jǐdiǎn le?** It is common to add the time word **xiànzài** "now" in Chinese questions and answers about time (compare the addition of **jīnnián** with questions on age). One reason why time words like **xiànzài** are used more in Chinese than in English is because Chinese does not have explicit tense.

i. As in Europe, for official purposes (e.g., for train, bus, television, and radio schedules), the twenty-four-hour clock is used, beginning with **língdiǎn zhōng** "zero o'clock," **yīdiǎn zhōng** "1:00 A.M.," etc. For example, **shísāndiǎn** would be 1:00 P.M., **èrshidiǎn** would be 8:00 P.M., and **èrshisāndiǎn** would be 11:00 P.M.

To summarize the most important points above, we can say that the pattern for telling time, in its full form, is:

XIÀNZÀI	Hour	DIǍN	Minutes	FĒN	LE
Xiànzài	liǎng	diǎn	sānshibā	fēn	le.

"(Now) it's 2:38."

The other important things to remember are that if a whole hour is involved (e.g., "2:00"), drop the "minutes" and **fēn** in the pattern; and if the minutes equal 15, 30, or 45, also drop the "minutes" and **fēn** and use **yíkè**, **bàn**, or **sānkè** in their place, as explained above.

2B. In the second sentence of this utterance, the first **le** is present because a clock time is involved and, moreover, the adverb **yǐjīng** "already" cooccurs (it is very common to have a **le** after **yǐjīng** "already" because of the implied change). The second **le** involves anticipated change (cf. 3-2: 6D); the speaker anticipates that the traveler will no longer be able to get on the train on time because it is already too late.

2C. **Kǒngpà**, with the meaning "I'm afraid that," "I suppose that," "I think that," or "probably," is very common in spoken Chinese. No pronoun for "I" is added. Here are some more examples with **kǒngpà**:

Kǒngpà tā tài mángle.	"I think she's probably too busy."
Kǒngpà yǐjīng sāndiǎn le.	"It's probably already three o'clock."

Kǒngpà is the first example we have had of a word class called moveable adverb. Moveable adverbs constitute a large group of adverbs that can directly precede the verb, but they are "moveable" in that they may also stand at the beginning of the sentence, before a place word or the subject of the verb. For example, one could say either of the following to mean "I'm afraid he's no longer going to come":

> **Tā kǒngpà bù láile.**
>
> **Kǒngpà tā bù láile.**

All moveable adverbs are bisyllabic, though not all bisyllabic adverbs are moveable. If one is not sure whether a given adverb is a regular adverb or a moveable adverb, the safest course of action is to place the adverb after the subject and immediately before the verb, since that position is always correct.

3. The conjunction **Nèmme, ...** "then, in that case, well then" is a discourse marker that introduces a change in the topic. Much like the conjunction **Nà, ...** , to which you were introduced previously, **Nèmme, ...** serves to connect different parts of a conversation, often introducing a new sentence or drawing a conclusion. Appropriate use of conjunctions like **nèmme** and **nà** will make your Chinese seem more fluent and give you extra time to think of what to say next.

5A. The **jiù** here means "then" in the sense of "then, in that case."

5B. Pay special attention to the verb **zuò** which, in addition to its basic meaning of "sit" also means "travel by" or "take" some means of transportation. For example, **zuò** would be used for riding in a car, taking a bus or street car, taking a train, taking a boat, and taking an airplane. However, **zuò** is not used for any means of transportation that one straddles, e.g., riding a bicycle or motorcycle or riding a horse.

5C. -DE to Create Nominal Phrases. Compare the following two phrases:

shídiǎn bànde huǒchē	"the 10:30 train"
shídiǎn bànde	"the 10:30 one"

If the noun following a -de is dropped, the phrase that remains can substitute for the missing noun and has a meaning such as "the...one" or "the one that..." Here are some more examples:

wǒ mǎide	"the ones I bought"
tā yàode	"what she wanted"
xìng Gāode	"the one who is surnamed Gao"
mài bēizide	"the one who sells cups" or "the cup seller"

7. Why is there no question particle **ma** at the end of the question **Dào Tiānjīn yào duō cháng shíjiān?** "How long does it take to get to Tianjin?" ANSWER: Because of the presence of the question word **duō** "how, to what extent?" Literally, this question could be translated as "To Tianjin it takes how long (a) time?"

8A. Be very careful about the pronunciation of the syllable **duō** in **chàbuduō**. You must not pronounce it as **dōu** and say *chàbudōu, which does not exist!

8B. Number of Hours. To express the number of hours, say the number followed by the general measure **ge** followed by the noun **zhōngtóu** "hour." The pattern is:

Number	GE	ZHŌNGTÓU
sān	ge	zhōngtóu
"three hours"		

Some more examples:

yíge zhōngtóu	"one hour"
liǎngge zhōngtóu	"two hours"

èrshisìge zhōngtóu	"twenty-four hours"
Jǐge zhōngtóu?	"How many hours?"

Carefully contrast and memorize the following pair of expressions with **zhōngtóu** that are easily confused:

bàn'ge zhōngtóu	"half an hour"
yíge bàn zhōngtóu	"an hour and a half"

How would one say "two hours and a half"? The answer is: **liǎngge bàn zhōngtóu**.

Also, be careful to distinguish both **bàn'ge zhōngtóu** and **yíge bàn zhōngtóu** from **yīdiǎn bàn**, which means "1:30" (as a clock time, not to indicate for how long something takes place).

Unit 3: Review and Study Guide

New Vocabulary

ADVERBS

chàbuduō	almost, about
jiù	then
yǐjīng	already
yígòng	in all
zài	again
zhǐ	only

CONJUNCTIONS

nèmme	then, in that case, well

INTERJECTIONS

yò	"gosh," "wow"

MEASURES

diǎn	o'clock, hour
fēn	minute
fēn	penny
kè	quarter of an hour
kuài	dollar (monetary unit)
máo	ten cents, dime
suì	year of age
tàng	(for runs by trains, buses)

MOVEABLE ADVERBS

kǒngpà	"I'm afraid that"; probably

NOUNS

bān	class
bēibāo	knapsack, backpack
bēizi	cup
chē	vehicle (car, cab, bus, bicycle)
dàizi	bag

dìdi	younger brother
fùqin	father
gēge	older brother
gōngshìbāo	briefcase, attache case
huǒ	fire
huǒchē	train
jiějie	older sister
mèimei	younger sister
mǔqīn	mother
nánde	man, male
nánlǎoshī	male teacher
nánshēng	male student
niánji	age
nǚde	woman, female
nǚlǎoshī	female teacher
nǚshēng	female student
qián	money
shíjiān	time
yuè	month
zhōng	clock, o'clock; bell
zhōngtóu	hour

NUMBERS

bā	eight
-bǎi	hundred
bàn(r)	half
èr	two
jiǔ	nine
liǎng-	two
líng	zero
liù	six
qī	seven
-qiān	thousand

sān	three
shí	ten
sì	four
wǔ	five
yī	one

PARTICLES

ba	(indicates suggestions)

PLACE WORDS

Déguo	Germany
Fǎguo	France
Tiānjīn	Tianjin

QUESTION WORDS

duō	how
duōshǎo	how much, how many
jǐ-	how many

RESULTATIVE COMPOUNDS

láibují	not have enough time

RESULTATIVE ENDINGS

-jí	reach a goal in time

SPECIFIERS

shàng-	last
xià-	next

STATIVE VERBS

cháng	be long
dà	be big; old (of people)
duì	be correct
guì	be expensive
kě'ài	be loveable, cute

piányi	be cheap	chà	lack	mài	sell
TIME WORDS		dào	arrive, reach	méiyou	not have; there is/ are not
jīnnián	this year	jiā	add; plus		
xiànzài	now	jiǎn	subtract; minus	xiǎng	think
		kāi	depart (of a train, bus, ship)	yào	want, need, cost, take
VERBS					
ài	love; like	kàn	look, see	yǒu	there is, there are
cāi	guess	mǎi	buy	zuò	travel by, take

Major New Grammar Patterns

Place word + YǑU + noun phrase to indicate existence: Bānshang yǒu shíge tóngxué. "In the class there are ten classmates." (3-1)

Numbers from One to Ten (3-1)

Age: Nǐ duō dà niánji le? "How old are you?"; **Nǐ jǐsuì le?** "How old are you?" (of children); **Wǒ jīnnián shíbāsuì le.** "I'm eighteen years old." (3-2)

Reduplicated monosyllabic verbs + KÀN: xiángxiang kàn "try and think" (3-2)

Numbers from 11 to 99 with SHÍ (3-2)

Tag questions: Zhè shi nǐ mèimei, duì bu dui? "This is your younger sister, right?"; **Zhè shi nǐ dìdi, shì bu shì?** "This is your younger brother, isn't it?" (3-2)

LE to indicate anticipated change in a situation: Tā xiàge yuè jiù jiǔsuì le "Next month she will be nine years old." (3-2)

MÉIYOU "not have; there is not/ there are not" as the negative of YǑU: **Wǒ méiyou gēge.** "I don't have (any) brothers." (3-2)

ZHÈIGE "this/this one" and **NÈIGE** "that/that one" (3-3)

Numbers from 100 to 999 with -bǎi "hundred" (3-3)

LE after TÀI in affirmative sentences: tài guìle "too expensive" (3-3)

YÀO to indicate price: Nèige bēizi yào sānkuài wǔ. "That cup costs three fifty." (3-3)

Reduplication of Verbs: kàn → kànkan "take a look" (3-3)

BA to indicate suggestions: Nín kàn ba. "Why don't you take a look?" (3-3)

Monetary system: liùkuài wǔmáo jiǔfēn qián "six dollars and fifty-nine cents" (3-3)

Numbers from 1,000 to 9,999 with -qiān "thousand" (3-3)

-DE following long phrases to indicate modification: xiàyítàng dào Tiānjīnde huǒchē "the next train that goes to Tianjin" (3-4)

Time when before the verb: Wǒ bādiǎn zhōng qù. "I go at eight o'clock." (3-4)

Clock times: liǎngdiǎn sānshibāfēn zhōng "2:38" (3-4)

-DE to create nominal phrases: shídiǎn bànde "the 10:30 one," **wǒ mǎide** "the ones I bought" (3-4)

Number of hours: sān'ge zhōngtóu "three hours" (3-4)

Numbers, Dates, Time, and Money (II)

COMMUNICATIVE OBJECTIVES

Once you have mastered this unit, you will be able to use Chinese to:

1. Count from 10,000 to one billion.

2. Express ordinal numbers: first, second, third, etc.

3. Talk across time: today (morning, noon, afternoon, evening, night), tomorrow, yesterday, day before yesterday, day after tomorrow, this year, next year, last year, year before last, year after next.

4. Ask when someone was born (day/month/year) and answer when you are asked.

5. Ask about the days of the week and hours of the day when an establishment is open or closed.

6. Ask what someone's address is and answer when you are asked.

7. Discuss the population of various countries and cities.

8. Ask if someone has ever been to various countries and cities and answer when you are asked. If they have been there before, how many times? If not, do they want to go? When? And how long do they want to stay?

Inquiring About Opening and Closing Times

Jessica Osbourne, an American student who has just arrived in Taipei, walks up to the language lab attendant at the Mandarin Training Center of National Taiwan Normal University to ask about the language lab schedule.

 Basic Conversation 4-1

1. AMERICAN

Qǐng wèn, yǔyán shíyànshì měitiān jǐdiǎn zhōng kāimén, jǐdiǎn zhōng guānmén?

Excuse me, what time every day does the language lab open and what time does it close?

2. LANGUAGE LAB ATTENDANT

Zǎoshang bādiǎn kāimén, wǎnshang jiǔdiǎn bàn guānmén.

It opens at 8:00 in the morning and closes at 9:30 at night.

3. AMERICAN

Xīngqīliù kāi bu kāi?

Is it open on Saturdays?

4. LANGUAGE LAB ATTENDANT

Xīngqīliù kāi bàntiān. Shàngwǔ kāi, xiàwǔ bù kāi.

Saturdays it's open half-days. It's open in the morning but not in the afternoon.

5. AMERICAN

Xīngqītiān ne?

And on Sundays?

6. LANGUAGE LAB ATTENDANT

Xīngqītiān xiūxi.

It's closed on Sundays.

7. AMERICAN

Xièxie nǐ.

Thank you.

8. LANGUAGE LAB ATTENDANT

Náli.

Sure.

Build Up

1. American
yǔyán	language [N]
shíyàn	experiment [N]
shíyànshì	laboratory [N]
yǔyán shíyànshì	language lab [PH]
měi-	each, every [SP]
tiān	day [M]
měitiān	every day
měitiān jǐdiǎn zhōng	every day at what time
kāi	open [V]
mén(r)	door, gate [N]
kāimén	open a door, open [VO]
jǐdiǎn zhōng kāimén	opens at what time
guān	close [V]
guānmén	close a door, close [VO]
jǐdiǎn zhōng guānmén	closes at what time

Qǐng wèn, yǔyán shíyànshì měitiān jǐdiǎn zhōng kāimén, jǐdiǎn zhōng guānmén?

Excuse me, what time every day does the language lab open and what time does it close?

2. Language lab attendant
zǎoshang	in the morning [TW]
zǎoshang bādiǎn	at 8:00 in the morning
wǎnshang	in the evening [TW]
wǎnshang jiǔdiǎn bàn	at 9:30 in the evening

Zǎoshang bādiǎn kāimén, wǎnshang jiǔdiǎn bàn guānmén.

It opens at 8:00 in the morning and closes at 9:30 at night.

3. American
xīngqīliù	Saturday [TW]
kāi bu kāi	opens or not opens

Xīngqīliù kāi bu kāi?

Is it open on Saturdays?

4. Language lab attendant
bàntiān	half the day
kāi bàntiān	(it) is open for half the day
shàngwǔ	morning, A.M. [TW]
shàngwǔ kāi	in the morning it opens
xiàwǔ	afternoon, P.M. [TW]
xiàwǔ bù kāi	in the afternoon it doesn't open

Xīngqīliù kāi bàntiān. Shàngwǔ kāi, xiàwǔ bù kāi.

Saturdays it's open half-days. It's open in the morning but not in the afternoon.

5. American
xīngqītiān	Sunday [TW]

Xīngqītiān ne?

And on Sundays?

6. Language lab attendant
xiūxi	rest, take time off [V]

Xīngqītiān xiūxi.

It's closed on Sundays.

7. American

Xièxie nǐ.

Thank you.

8. Language lab attendant
    náli   "not at all" [IE]
Náli.   Sure.

 ## Supplementary Vocabulary

A. GENERAL

1. **píngcháng**   usually, ordinarily [MA]
    qǐchuáng   get up from bed, rise [VO]
    zǎoshang jǐdiǎn qǐchuáng in the morning at what time rise
    Nǐ píngcháng zǎoshang jǐdiǎn qǐchuáng? What time do you usually get up in the morning?

2. **shuìjiào**   sleep, go to bed [VO]
    wǎnshang jǐdiǎn shuìjiào in the evening at what time sleep
    Nǐ píngcháng wǎnshang jǐdiǎn shuìjiào? What time do you usually go to bed at night?

3. **shuì**   sleep [V]
    měitiān shuì jǐge zhōngtóu every day sleep how many hours
    Nǐ píngcháng měitiān shuì jǐge zhōngtóu? How many hours do you usually sleep each day?

4. **xīngqī (B)**   week [N]
    shàngge xīngqī   last week
    zhèige xīngqī   this week
    Shi shàngge xīngqī, bú shi zhèige xīngqī. It was last week, not this week.

5. **lǐbài**   week [N]
    xiàge lǐbài   next week
    dào Táiwān qù   go to Taiwan
    Tā xiàge lǐbài dào Táiwān qù. She's going to Taiwan next week.

B. DAYS OF THE WEEK (WITH XĪNGQĪ)

6. **xīngqīyī**   Monday [TW]

7. **xīngqī'èr**   Tuesday [TW]

8. **xīngqīsān**   Wednesday [TW]

9. **xīngqīsì**   Thursday [TW]

10. **xīngqīwǔ**   Friday [TW]

11. **xīngqīliù**   Saturday [TW]

12. **xīngqītiān**   Sunday [TW]

13. **xīngqīrì**   Sunday [TW]

14. **xīngqījǐ**   which day of the week [QW]

C. DAYS OF THE WEEK (WITH LǏBÀI)

15. **lǐbàiyī**   Monday [TW]

16. **lǐbài'èr**   Tuesday [TW]

17. **lǐbàisān**   Wednesday [TW]

18. **lǐbàisì**   Thursday [TW]

19. **lǐbàiwǔ**   Friday [TW]

20. **lǐbàiliù**   Saturday [TW]

21. **lǐbàitiān**   Sunday [TW]

22. lǐbàirì	Sunday [TW]
23. lǐbàijǐ	which day of the week [QW]

Grammatical and Cultural Notes

1A.   There is some variation in the pronunciation of the word for "language lab." In addition to the form in the Basic Conversation, **yǔyán shíyànshì**, there are also some speakers who say **yǔyán shíyànshǐ**, with Tone Three on the last syllable, and there are yet other speakers say **yǔyán shìyànshì**, with Tone Four on the first syllable of the second word.

1B.   **TIĀN** as Measure Meaning "Day." Even though in English the word "day" is obviously a noun, in Chinese **tiān** functions grammatically as a measure, not as a noun. Therefore, to say "every day," you place the specifier **měi-** directly before **tiān** and say **měitiān**. Because **tiān** is itself a measure, nothing is inserted between **měi-** and **tiān**. Similarly, to say "one day," you place the number **yī** directly before **tiān** and say **yìtiān** (it would be a big mistake to say *****yíge tiān**). This is very different from the situation with nouns, where a measure must be inserted between the number or specifier and the noun (e.g., **yíge xīngqī** "one week" or **měige yuè** "every month"). Study the following carefully:

TIĀN (A MEASURE)	**XĪNGQĪ** (A NOUN)	**YUÈ** (ALSO A NOUN)
yìtiān	**yíge xīngqī**	**yíge yuè**
"one day"	"one week"	"one month"
liǎngtiān	**liǎngge xīngqī**	**liǎngge yuè**
"two days"	"two weeks"	"two months"
jǐtiān	**jǐge xīngqī**	**jǐge yuè**
"how many days?"	"how many weeks?"	"how many months?"
měitiān	**měige xīngqī**	**měige yuè**
"every day"	"every week"	"every month"

1C.   Observe the order of the various elements in this utterance: **Yǔyán shíyànshì měitiān jǐdiǎn zhōng kāimén, jǐdiǎn zhōng guānmén?** "The language lab every day at what time opens, at what time closes?" Both **měitiān** "every day" and **jǐdiǎn zhōng** "at what time" are adverbial expressions, so they precede the verb **kāimén** "open." The reason that **měitiān** precedes **jǐdiǎn zhōng** is that it is the larger and more general time expression.

1D.   The expression **kāimén** "open" (lit. "open the door") is your first example of a verb-object compound or [VO]. These are verbal compounds composed of a one-syllable verb plus a one-syllable object, which are ordinarily written together and are often best translated into English as a verb without an object. There are several other verb-object compounds in this lesson:

guānmén	"close" (lit. "close a door")
qǐchuáng	"get up" (lit. "rise from bed")
shuìjiào	"sleep" (lit. "sleep a sleep")

Verb-object compounds will be discussed in more detail in 5-2: SV2.

1E.   Some speakers avoid using **guānmén** "close" to ask about closing times for stores, since this term literally means "closes (its) doors" and some business people feel it is therefore inauspicious, since for a shop to "close its doors" can also mean that it is going out of business. For this reason, some Chinese use a separate term to talk about the closing times of shops: **dǎyáng**.

2A. **Zǎoshang** refers to early morning, generally before 9:00 A.M. Between 9:00 A.M. and noon is called **shàngwǔ** (see line 4).

2B. Here, as in 1C, the larger and more general time expressions precede the more specific ones. Thus, **zǎoshang** "in the morning" precedes **bādiǎn** "8:00," and **wǎnshang** "in the evening" precedes **jiǔdiǎn bàn** "9:30." Note that this is the opposite of English, since we say "eight in the morning" and "9:30 at night."

2C. In English, we often use the demonstrative adjective "this" with time words like "morning" and "afternoon," saying "this morning," "this evening" and so on. In Chinese you CANNOT use **zhèige** in this way and say *zhèige zǎoshang or *zhèige wǎnshang. Instead of **zhèige**, you should use **jīntiān** "today" and say **jīntiān zǎoshang** "this morning" (lit. "today in the morning") and **jīntiān wǎnshang** "this evening" (lit. "today in the evening").

3-6, SV4, SV6-14. An alternate pronunciation of **xīngqīliù** "Saturday" that you will hear in Taiwan and occasionally elsewhere is **xīngqíliù**, with Tone Two on the second syllable. This is how the word is pronounced in the recording of this Basic Conversation. This alternate pronunciation applies to all the words containing **xīngqī** "week" that are introduced in this lesson.

4A. Time Spent After the Verb. In line 4 of this lesson, you will notice that the time expression **bàntiān** "for half the day" follows the verb **kāi** "open," but that the time words **xīngqīliù** "Saturday," **shàngwǔ** "in the morning," and **xiàwǔ** "in the afternoon" all precede **kāi**. The reason for this is that there is a very important rule in Chinese grammar, as we saw in 3-4: 1E, that time expressions indicating when something happens ("time when") precede the verb; but that, as we now see in this lesson for the first time, time expressions indicating for how long something happens ("time spent") follow the verb. Both patterns are contained in the following example sentence, which you should study carefully:

Subject	Time When	Verb	Time Spent
Yǔyán shíyànshì	xīngqīliù	kāi	bàntiān.

"The language lab is open for half the day on Saturday."

4B. You cannot use **zhèige** "this" with **shàngwǔ** and **xiàwǔ** but must use **jīntiān** "today'; say **jīntiān shàngwǔ** "this morning" and **jīntiān xiàwǔ** "this afternoon" (cf. 2C above).

6. Here the verb **xiūxi**, lit. "rest," is used to indicate that the language lab is closed on Sundays. However, this verb is also frequently used in its literal sense; so on an arduous hike, for example, you could say to a friend:

Wǒ lèile! Nǐ yě lèile ba? Wǒmen xiūxi shífēn zhōng, hǎo ma?

"I'm tired. You must be tired, too? Let's rest for 10 minutes, O.K.?"

8. The literal meaning of **nǎli** is "where?"; in fact, it is frequently used as an equivalent of **nǎr**. However, **nǎli** can also, as is here the case, be used as a polite response to thanks or compliments to ritually deny the need for thanks or the validity of a compliment, much like English "you're welcome," "it's nothing," or "don't mention it." The implication of **nǎli** is "Your saying thanks or paying me a compliment, these are words from where?," i.e., "Why do you say that?" Many Northern speakers prefer the term **bú kèqi** "you're welcome" (1-4).

SV6-23. Days of the Week. The Western concept of the seven-day week did not exist in traditional Chinese society, so until about two hundred years ago, there was no word for "week."

Main entrance to National Taiwan Normal University in Taipei

Xīngqī, literally "star period," is a common word for "week" which has come into increased spoken use in China in recent years. As was mentioned above, in Taiwan and occasionally in China, **xīngqī** is pronounced **xīngqí**, with Tone Two on the second syllable. The words for the days of the week are formed by suffixing to **xīngqī-** the number for the particular day of the week, from **yī** "one" to **liù** "six," with "Monday" being considered the first day and counting in this manner up to "Saturday," the sixth day. "Sunday" is different, with two possible forms: **xīngqītiān** and **xīngqīrì** (notice that the basic meaning of the bound form **rì** is "sun," as in "Sunday"). Be careful to contrast the pronunciations and meanings of **xīngqī'èr** "Tuesday" and **xīngqīrì** "Sunday," because they sound somewhat similar and American students of Chinese tend to confuse them.

The question word for "which day of the week?" is **xīngqījǐ**. To ask "What day of the week is it today?," one can say either **Jīntiān shi xīngqījǐ?** or simply **Jīntiān xīngqījǐ?** without a verb **shi** (the question is then a topic-comment structure, i.e., "Talking about today, which day of the week?")

An older word for "week" is **lǐbài**, which literally means "worship" and was introduced by Western missionaries in the nineteenth century. As with **xīngqī**, the number for the day of the week is suffixed to **lǐbài-**, there being two forms for "Sunday," **lǐbàitiān** and **lǐbàirì**, as well as a question form **lǐbàijǐ** "which day of the week?" Both the series with **xīngqī** and that with **lǐbài** are common everywhere Chinese is spoken. In general, **xīngqī** is considered more modern, while **lǐbài** is considered a little more traditional and colloquial; also, **lǐbài** is seldom written. We recommend that you use the **xīngqī** series in your own speech and writing, but you should be prepared to understand **lǐbài** when you hear it.

When mentioning several days of the week at a time, abbreviations such as **yī-sān-wǔ** "M W F" and **èr-sì-liù** "T Th Sat" are possible and fairly common, in both speech and writing. Examples:

Wǒ yī-sān-wǔ jiǔdiǎn shàng Zhōngwén. Nǐ ne?

"I have Chinese on Mondays, Wednesdays, and Fridays at 9:00. And you?"

Tā èr-sì-liù dōu méiyou kè.

"She doesn't have any classes on Tuesdays, Thursdays, and Saturdays."

In SV4-5, you learn how to say "last week" and "next week": **shàngge xīngqī** or **shàngge lǐbài** "last week," and **xiàge xīngqī** or **xiàge lǐbài** "next week." To remember which one means next and which one means last, think of how Chinese is traditionally written, from top to bottom: the past (including last week) is ABOVE (**shàng**) where you are reading currently, while the future (including next week) is BELOW (**xià**) where you are. Or remember this mnemonic: "the top of the inning comes before the bottom."

These expressions for "last week" and "next week" can be combined with specific days of the week, as in **shàngge xīngqīsān** "last Wednesday" or **xiàge xīngqīwǔ** "next Friday." In Chinese, Monday is considered the first day of the week and Sunday the last day of the week, unlike in English, where the week begins on Sunday.

Chinese speakers are very precise in using the terms **shàngge** and **xiàge**. If today is Monday and one is referring to this coming Friday, one must say **zhèige xīngqīwǔ** "this Friday" and not *****xiàge xīngqīwǔ**, which would mean Friday of the next week. On the other hand, if today is Saturday and one is referring to the following Friday, one must say **xiàge xīngqīwǔ** "next Friday" and not *****zhèige xīngqīwǔ**. In English, the words "last" and "next" can refer either to the week or the day (i.e., "next Friday" could mean either Friday of the next week, or it could mean the next Friday to arrive, including a Friday yet to arrive in this week). Chinese is unambiguous in this regard: **shàng** and **xià** always refer only to the last or next week.

Personal Information

Vernice Johns, an American student in Taipei, has had an upset stomach for several days, so she goes to a neighborhood clinic to see a doctor. Since she can't yet write Chinese very well, a nurse helps her fill out the registration form.

 ## Basic Conversation 4-2

1. NURSE **Nǐ jiào shémme míngzi?**
What's your name?

2. JOHNS **Wǒ jiào Zhāng Wényīng. Zhāng shi "gōng" "cháng" Zhāng, wén shi "wénhuà"de wén, yīng shi "Yīngguo"de yīng.**
My name is Zhāng Wényīng. The Zhāng is the Zhāng made up of "bow" and "long," the wén is the wén in the word for "culture," and the yīng is the yīng in the word for "England."

3. NURSE **Nǐ shi něinián chūshēngde?**
Which year were you born?

4. JOHNS **Yī-jiǔ-bā-líng-nián, jiù shi Mínguó liùshijiǔnián.**
In 1980, the sixty-ninth year of the Republic.

5. NURSE **Jǐyuè jǐhào?**
Which month and which day?

6. JOHNS **Sìyuè shísānhào.**
April 13th.

7. NURSE **Nǐde dìzhǐ shi...**
Your address is...

8. JOHNS **Hépíng Dōng Lù yīduàn, èrshiqīxiàng, sānnòng, yībǎi wǔshisìhào, bālóu.**
Heping East Road Section One, Lane 27, Alley 3, Number 154, Eighth Floor.

9. NURSE **Hǎo, qǐng děng yíxià.**
All right, please wait a moment.

Build Up

----

1. Nurse

Nǐ jiào shémme míngzi?   What's your name?

----

2. Johns

Zhāng   Zhang [SN]

Wényīng   (Chinese for the first name "Vernice")

gōng   bow (the weapon) [N]

"gōng" "cháng" Zhāng   the surname Zhāng that is written with the characters "bow" and "long"

wénhuà   culture [N]

"wénhuà"de wén   the character wén as in wénhuà

Wǒ jiào Zhāng Wényīng. Zhāng shi "gōng"   My name is Zhāng Wényīng. The Zhāng is the Zhāng
"cháng" Zhāng, wén shi "wénhuà"de wén,   made up of "bow" and "long," the wén is the wén in
yīng shi "Yīngguo"de yīng.   the word for "culture," and the yīng is the yīng in the word for "England."

----

3. Nurse

nián   year [M]

něinián   which year

chūshēng   be born [V]

něinián chūshēngde   born in what year

Nǐ shi něinián chūshēngde?   Which year were you born?

----

4. Johns

yī-jiǔ-bā-líng-nián   the year 1980

jiù   precisely, exactly [A]

jiù shi   be precisely, be none other than

Mínguó   the Republic (of China) [TW]

Mínguó liùshijiǔnián   the 69th year of the Republic

Yī-jiǔ-bā-líng-nián, jiù shi Mínguó liùshijiǔnián. In 1980, the sixty-ninth year of the Republic.

----

5. Nurse

jǐyuè   which month of the year [QW]

hào   day of the month [M]

jǐhào   which day of the month [QW]

Jǐyuè jǐhào?   Which month and which day?

----

6. Johns

sìyuè   April [TW]

shísānhào   the thirteenth day of the month

Sìyuè shísānhào.   April 13th.

----

7. Nurse

dìzhǐ   address [N]

Nǐde dìzhǐ shi...   Your address is...

----

8. Johns

hépíng   peace [N]

dōng   east [L]

lù   road [N]

Hépíng Dōng Lù   Heping East Road [PW]

duàn   section [M]

yīduàn   section one

-xiàng   lane [BF]

èrshiqīxiàng	Lane 27
-nòng	alley [BF]
sānnòng	Alley 3
hào	number (in addresses, sizes) [M]
yībǎi wǔshisìhào	Number 154
lóu	floor (of a building) [N]
bālóu	eighth floor
Hépíng Dōng Lù yīduàn, èrshiqīxiàng, sānnòng, yībǎi wǔshisìhào, bālóu.	Heping East Road Section One, Lane 27, Alley 3, Number 154, Eighth Floor.

9. Nurse

děng	wait, wait for [V]
děng yíxià	wait a moment
Hǎo, qǐng děng yíxià.	All right, please wait a moment.

Supplementary Vocabulary

A. DAYS AND YEARS

1. **jīntiān**	today [TW]
2. **míngtiān**	tomorrow [TW]
3. **zuótiān**	yesterday [TW]
4. **jīnnián**	this year [TW]
5. **míngnián**	next year [TW]
6. **qùnián**	last year [TW]

B. MONTHS OF THE YEAR

7. **yīyuè**	January [TW]
8. **èryuè**	February [TW]
9. **sānyuè**	March [TW]
10. **sìyuè**	April [TW]
11. **wǔyuè**	May [TW]
12. **liùyuè**	June [TW]
13. **qīyuè**	July [TW]
14. **bāyuè**	August [TW]
15. **jiǔyuè**	September [TW]
16. **shíyuè**	October [TW]
17. **shíyīyuè**	November [TW]
18. **shí'èryuè**	December [TW]

C. GENERAL

19. **shēngrì**	birthday [N]
Nǐde shēngrì shi jǐyuè jǐhào?	What day and month is your birthday?

Grammatical and Cultural Notes

2.   When hearing someone's name, a Chinese person will often not be able to tell with which characters it is written, since there are many homophonous characters in Chinese. For example, there are two fairly common surnames pronounced **Zhāng: gōng cháng Zhāng** "the Zhang made up of bow and long" and **lì zǎo Zhāng** "the Zhang made up of stand and early." This is the reason for the kind of name description illustrated here. Some characters are described according to their component parts while others are described in terms of common words in which they occur. This could be compared to English oral spellings of names such as "B" as in "Baker." You should ask your instructor how to describe your own Chinese name as soon as possible, since this is often done during introductions when one does not have a name card available.

3A.   **SHI...-DE** to express time or place of known past actions. The **shi...-de** pattern is frequently used to indicate the time or place of known past actions. When using **shi...-de**, you and your interlocutor are already aware of the fact that something has happened in the past; what you don't know is when or where the known past action took place. The **shi** is placed before the time or place, while the **-de** is usually placed at the end of the sentence. The pattern for expressing the time of known past actions is:

Subject	SHI	Time	Verb	-DE
Wǒ	shi	yī-jiǔ-bā-wǔ-nián	chūshēng	de.

"I was born in 1985."

The pattern for expressing the place of known past actions is:

Subject	SHI	Place	Verb	-DE
Wǒ	shi	zài Měiguo	chūshēng	de.

"I was born in America."

In the pattern for expressing place, note there is a coverb **zài** "in, at, on" before the place word. We will be taking up the **shi...-de** pattern and also the coverb **zài** in more detail later in the course. For now, memorize the following two questions along with the appropriate responses for yourself:

Question #1:   **Nǐ shi něinián chūshēngde?**   **Response: Wǒ shi...nián chūshēngde.**

"In what year were you born?"   "I was born in the year..."

Question #2:   **Nǐ shi zài nǎr chūshēngde?**   **Response: Wǒ shi zài...chūshēngde.**

"Where were you born?"   "I was born in (place)."

3B.   **NIÁN** as Measure Meaning "Year." As in the case of **tiān** "day" (cf. 4-1: 1B), the Chinese word **nián** "year" is a measure, not a noun. This means that, when specified or counted, **nián** is preceded directly by a number and not first by a measure like **ge**. Also, unlike most measures, **nián** and **tiān** are not normally followed by nouns. Thus, for "three years" say **sānnián** (one could NEVER say *sān'ge nián). The following examples contrast the use of **nián** and **tiān**, which are measures, with that of **yuè** and **xīngqī**, which are nouns. Study them carefully, noting which are preceded by **ge** and which are not:

NIÁN	TIĀN	XĪNGQĪ	YUÈ
yìnián	**yìtiān**	**yíge xīngqī**	**yíge yuè**
"one year"	"one day"	"one week"	"one month"
liǎngnián	**liǎngtiān**	**liǎngge xīngqī**	**liǎngge yuè**
"two years"	"two days"	"two weeks"	"two months"
jǐnián	**jǐtiān**	**jǐge xīngqī**	**jǐge yuè**
"how many years?"	"how many days?"	"how many weeks?"	"how many months?"
měinián	**měitiān**	**měige xīngqī**	**měige yuè**
"every year"	"every day"	"every week"	"every month"

3C.   The expression for "half a year" is **bànnián**. Distinguish this carefully from **bānián** "eight years." "A year and a half" would be **yìnián bàn**, "two and a half years" would be **liǎngnián bàn**, etc.

3D.   Be careful to distinguish **nián** "year (of the calendar or of time in general)" from **suì** "year of age (of a human being or other living creature)," which you had in 3-2. In questions and answers about age, one could use only **suì** and never **nián**. Similarly, in a sentence like "He is three years younger than I," the Chinese would say "He compared to me is smaller by three **suì**."

3E.   Instead of **něinián** "which year?," some speakers (including the speaker who recorded this conversation) say **nǎnián**. There are also other speakers who add **yī** "one" in the middle and say **něiyìnián** or **nǎyìnián**. The meaning of all of these is the same.

3F.   Time When Before Place. If you want to ask or state not only when but also where someone was born, the time expression must come before the place. For example, you would ask: **Qǐng wèn, nǐ shi něinián zài nǎr chūshēngde?** "Excuse me, when and where were you born?" (lit. "You are which year where born?") The other person might then reply: **Wǒ shi yī-jiǔ-jiǔ-sān-nián zài Měiguo chūshēngde** "I was born in 1993 in America." Note that in both the question and the answer, the time when comes before the place. To sum up the pattern:

Subject	SHI	Time When	Place	Verb	DE
Wǒ	shi	yī-jiǔ-jiǔ-sān-nián	zài Měiguo	chūshēng	de.

"I was born in 1993 in America."

4A.   Years of the Calendar with **NIÁN**. To create the words for the years of the calendar, the numbers representing the year are usually read off one digit at a time followed by **nián** "year." The pattern is:

Digits of the Year	NIÁN
yī-jiǔ-jiǔ-qī	nián

"1997" (lit. "the year 1997")

Examples:

yī-jiǔ-jiǔ-bā-nián	"the year 1998"
èr-líng-líng-líng-nián	"the year 2000"
èr-líng-líng-wǔ-nián	"the year 2005"
èr-líng-yī-sān-nián	"the year 2013"

In English the word "year" is often omitted, but in Chinese **nián** is usually included, so you should always add **nián**. For "the year 2000," there are some speakers who say **liǎngqiānnián**. Also, one may occasionally hear longer forms such as **yìqiān jiǔbǎi jiǔshibānián** "nineteen hundred and ninety-eight," but these are rather rare.

4B.   Calendar. For most purposes, China has adopted the Western calendar or **yánglì**, including the custom of reckoning years according to their order before or after the Christian era. The official way of reckoning years in Taiwan is according to what year it is since the founding of the Republic of China in 1911 (this follows the traditional Chinese custom of dating events according to the year of the emperor's reign in which they occurred). To convert Western-style years into **Mínguó** years as used in Taiwan or in China from 1911-49, subtract 1911 from the Western year. Thus, 1998 would be 1998 - 1911 = the 87th year of the Republic of China. To convert Republic of China years into Western years, add 1911 (e.g., the 80th year of the Republic would be 80 + 1911 = 1991). Especially when dealing with foreigners or discussing foreign history, the Western calendar is also used in Taiwan. In China, in the study of history, the Western calendar is ordinarily used, though the **Mínguó** forms can be used for dates before 1950. However, years later than **Mínguó sānshibānián** "1949" are not said using the **Mínguó** forms, since that is the year when the Republic of China ceased to exist, according to the People's Republic. Traditional Chinese holidays such as the Chinese New Year, Dragon Boat Festival, and Mid-Autumn Festival follow the traditional lunar calendar, called **yīnlì**. The lunar calendar, which is still used in the countryside, is based on the 29-30 day cycle of the moon, from one full moon to the next. There are twelve lunar months in a year, with an extra month once every four years.

5-6.   Days of the Month with **HÀO**. The days of the month are indicated by the number of the day plus the measure **hào**, which literally means "number." The expression for "Which day of the month?" is **Jǐhào?** The pattern for expressing day of the month is:

Number of Day	HÀO
shíliù	hào

"16th day of month"

Here are the words for first to thirty-first day of the month:

yīhào "1st day of month"	shíyīhào "11th day of month"	èrshiyīhào "21st day of month"
èrhào "2nd day of month"	shí'èrhào "12th day of month"	èrshi'èrhào "22nd day of month"
sānhào "3rd day of month"	shísānhào "13th day of month"	èrshisānhào "23rd day of month"
sìhào "4th day of month"	shísìhào "14th day of month"	èrshisìhào "24th day of month"
wǔhào "5th day of month"	shíwǔhào "15th day of month"	èrshiwǔhào "25th day of month"
liùhào "6th day of month"	shíliùhào "16th day of month"	èrshiliùhào "26th day of month"
qīhào "7th day of month"	shíqīhào "17th day of month"	èrshiqīhào "27th day of month"
bāhào "8th day of month"	shíbāhào "18th day of month"	èrshibāhào "28th day of month"
jiǔhào "9th day of month"	shíjiǔhào "19th day of month"	èrshijiǔhào "29th day of month"
shíhào "10th day of month"	èrshihào "20th day of month"	sānshihào "30th day of month"
sānshiyīhào "31st day of month"		

6.   Dates. When discussing categories of things in Chinese, there is a general habit of first mentioning the more general category and then moving to the more specific category, which is exactly the opposite of the English habit of moving from the specific to the general. You have already seen this in Chinese names, where the surname precedes the given name (since the category of people sharing the same surname is larger than the category of people with the same given name). The order of dates in Chinese is also the opposite of that in English. In Chinese, one begins with the largest category—the year, and then, in succession, mentions the month, day of the month, and day of the week. To sum up, the Chinese pattern is:

Year	Month	Day of the Month	Day of the Week
èr-líng-líng-wǔ nián	shíyīyuè	èrhào	xīngqīyī

"Monday, November 2, 2005" (lit. "2005 November 2 Monday")

If an even smaller category like the time of day were to be added (e.g., **xiàwǔ sìdiǎn bàn** "4:30 P.M."), then that would be added at the end, after the day of the week.

7.   **Nǐde dìzhǐ shi...** "Your address is..." is an incomplete sentence used as a question. It is left incomplete so as to avoid seeming overly direct. It would sound strange to say in Chinese ***Nǐde dìzhǐ shi shémme?**

8A.   Addresses. As with dates, the order of the elements in a Chinese address is the opposite of English. Again, in Chinese one moves from the largest category to the smallest one. What in English is "2nd Floor, 40 Whitman Street, Williamstown, Massachusetts, U.S.A.," would in Chinese be (translated back into English literally) "U.S.A., Massachusetts, Williamstown, Whitman Street, Number 40, 2nd floor." The formula for Chinese addresses is:

COUNTRY	PROVINCE	CITY	STREET	NUMBER	FLOOR
Zhōngguó	Guǎngdōng	Guǎngzhōu	Zhōngshān Lù	wǔhào	sānlóu

"3rd floor, No. 5, Zhongshan Road, Guangzhou, Guangdong, China"

8B.   Sections of roads are called **duàn**. Roads are called **lù**. Side lanes off roads are called **-xiàng**, and side alleys off lanes are called **-nòng**. House numbers are **hào** (note that the same word, **hào**, can mean both house number and day of the month). Usually odd numbers are on one side of a road, with even numbers on the opposite side. Lanes are numbered as if they were houses or stores on the main road, so that if the previous house or store was number 56 and then there is a lane, that lane will be lane number 58. Then the first house or store on the next block on the main road is number 60. This same system applies to alleys located off lanes.

8C.   Some people pronounce **-nòng** "alley" as **-lòng**. In fact, due to influence from other Chinese dialects, there is a fair amount of confusion between **n-** and **l-** among speakers of non-standard Mandarin, especially if the syllable ends in a nasal sound like **-n** or **-ng**.

8D.   Floors of Buildings with **LÓU**. The floors of buildings are indicated by the number of the floor followed by the measure **lóu** "floor." The expression for "Which floor?" is **Jǐlóu?** The pattern for expressing which floor of a building is:

Number of Floor	LÓU
sān	**lóu**
"third floor"	

"First floor" to "tenth floor" would be expressed as follows:

yīlóu	"first floor"	**liùlóu**	"sixth floor"
èrlóu	"second floor"	**qīlóu**	"seventh floor"
sānlóu	"third floor"	**bālóu**	"eighth floor"
sìlóu	"fourth floor"	**jiǔlóu**	"ninth floor"
wǔlóu	"fifth floor"	**shílóu**	"tenth floor"

Contrast the pronunciations of **j-** and **q-** (as well as the tones of the first syllable) in the following conversational exchange, being sure to give the **q-** a big puff of breath:

Chinese elevator operator:	**Jǐlóu?**	"Which floor?"
American visitor:	**Qīlóu!**	"Seventh floor!"

Note that the ordinal prefix **dì-** is not attached to **lóu** (or to **duàn**, **-xiàng**, **-nòng**, or **hào**). So for "third floor," say **sānlóu**, NOT *****dìsānlóu**.

Some buildings, especially hospitals, may not have a "fourth floor," because the number **sì** "four" sounds somewhat like the word **sǐ** "die" and is therefore considered inauspicious. In mainland China and Taiwan, stories of a building are numbered from the ground level up, as in the U.S. But in Hong Kong, through English influence, our "second floor" is their "first floor."

To express "floor of a building," there are some Chinese speakers who use the measure **céng** instead of **lóu**. These speakers would say **yīcéng** "first floor," **èrcéng** "second floor," **sāncéng** "third floor," etc.

9.   **Qǐng děng yíxià** "Please wait a moment" is a very common and useful expression for politely asking someone to wait briefly. Here are some common variants of this imperative:

Qǐng nǐ děng yíxià.	"Please wait a moment."
Nǐ děng yíxià.	"Wait a moment."
Děng yíxià.	"Wait a moment."

SV6.   To remember **qùnián** "last year," think of it as the **nián** "year" that has **qù** "gone" by.

SV7–18.   Months of the Year with **YUÈ**. The months of the year are indicated by the number of the month plus the word **yuè** "month," which literally means "moon." The expression for "Which month?" is **Jǐyuè?** as in line 5 of the conversation. The pattern for month of the year is:

Number of Month	YUÈ
shí	**yuè**
"October"	

The names of the months are:

yīyuè	"January"	**qīyuè**	"July"
èryuè	"February"	**bāyuè**	"August"
sānyuè	"March"	**jiǔyuè**	"September"
sìyuè	"April"	**shíyuè**	"October"
wǔyuè	"May"	**shíyīyuè**	"November"
liùyuè	"June"	**shí'èryuè**	"December"

Be sure to distinguish carefully between the names of the months, on the one hand, and the expressions for numbers of months, on the other. Examples:

yīyuè	"January"	**BUT**	**yíge yuè**	"one month"
èryuè	"February"	**BUT**	**liǎngge yuè**	"two months"
jǐyuè	"which month?"	**BUT**	**jǐge yuè**	"how many months?"

To say "this month" say **zhèige yuè**; to say "last month" say **shàngge yuè**; and to say "next month" say **xiàge yuè**.

When indicating a month in a preceding year, in the present year, or in a following year, in English we can say "last April," "this March," or "next May." In Chinese, you could not use **shàngge** "last," **zhèige** "this," or **xiàge** "next" in this way. Instead, you would have to say **qùnián** "last year," **jīnnián** "this year," or **míngnián** "next year" plus the name of the month. Examples:

qùnián sìyuè	"last April"	**or**	"April of last year" (NOT *shàngge sìyuè)
jīnnián sānyuè	"this March"	**or**	"March of this year" (NOT *zhèige sānyuè)
míngnián wǔyuè	"next May"	**or**	"May of next year" (NOT *xiàge wǔyuè)

SV19.   The verb **shi** in **Nǐde shēngrì shi jǐyuè jǐhào?** could be omitted, the question then becoming **Nǐde shēngrì jǐyuè jǐhào?** The meaning would be exactly the same, and this would then become a topic-comment construction ("Talking about your birthday, which month which day?").

Heping East Road Section One, Taipei

Second Trip to China

Ben Ross, an American from Louisiana who is in Beijing on business, is staying at the Swisshotel. While waiting for the elevator, he encounters the hotel bellhop who helped him move his luggage into his room the previous day.

Basic Conversation 4-3

1. ROSS   **Nǐ hǎo!**
How are you?

2. BELLHOP   **Nǐ hǎo! Nǐ shi Měiguo rén ma?**
How are you? Are you American?

3. ROSS   **Duì, wǒ shi Měiguo rén.**
Yes, I'm American.

4. BELLHOP   **Zhè shi nǐ dìyīcì dào Zhōngguo lái ma?**
Is this your first time in China?

5. ROSS   **Bù, zhè shi dì'èrcì. Wǒ qùnián láiguo yícì.**
No, this is the second time. I came once before last year.

6. BELLHOP   **M, nǐ zhèicì yào zhù duō jiǔ?**
Uh, how long are you going to stay this time?

7. ROSS   **Dàyuē bàn'ge yuè. Wǒ shí'èrhào huíguó.**
About half a month. I return home on the 12th.

8. BELLHOP   **Nǐ zhù něige fángjiān?**
Which room are you staying in?

9. ROSS   **Wǒ zhù sān líng liù.**
I'm staying in 306.

10. BELLHOP   *(sees another guest approaching)*

     Ò, duìbuqǐ, wǒ děi zǒule. Zàijiàn!
Oh, sorry, I have to go now. Goodbye!

11. ROSS   **Zàijiàn!**
Goodbye!

 **Build Up**

1. Ross
Nǐ hǎo!   How are you?

2. Bellhop
Nǐ hǎo! Nǐ shi Měiguo rén ma?   How are you? Are you American?

3. Ross
Duì, wǒ shi Měiguo rén.   Yes, I'm American.

4. Bellhop
dì-   (forms ordinal numbers) [SP]
dìyī   number one, the first
cì   time [M]
dìyīcì   the first time
nǐ dìyīcì dào Zhōngguo lái   the first time you come to China
Zhè shi nǐ dìyīcì dào Zhōngguo lái ma?   Is this your first time in China?

5. Ross
dì'èrcì   the second time
zhè shi dì'èrcì   this is the second time
-guo   (indicates experience) [P]
láiguo   have come before
wǒ qùnián láiguo yícì   last year I came once
Bù, zhè shi dì'èrcì. Wǒ qùnián   No, this is the second time.
láiguo yícì.   I came once before last year.

6. Bellhop
m   (hesitation sound; pause filler) [I]
yào   be going to, will [AV]
zhù   live (in), stay (in) [V]
yào zhù   will live, will stay
jiǔ   be long (of time) [SV]
duō jiǔ   for how long
yào zhù duō jiǔ   will stay how long
M, nǐ zhèicì yào zhù duō jiǔ?   Uh, how long are you going to stay this time?

7. Ross
dàyuē   approximately, about [A]
bàn'ge yuè   half a month
dàyuē bàn'ge yuè   approximately half a month
huíguó   return to one's home country [VO]
wǒ shí'èrhào huíguó   I return to my country on the twelfth
Dàyuē bàn'ge yuè. Wǒ shí'èrhào huíguó.   About half a month. I return home on the 12th.

8. Bellhop
fángjiān   room [N]
něige fángjiān   which room
Nǐ zhù něige fángjiān?   Which room are you staying in?

9. Ross
Wǒ zhù sān líng liù.   I'm staying in 306.

....

10. Bellhop

Ò, duìbuqǐ, wǒ děi zǒule. Zàijiàn!   Oh, sorry, I have to go now. Goodbye!

....

11. Ross

Zàijiàn!   Goodbye!

Supplementary Vocabulary

A. GENERAL

1. shuō   say, speak [V]

  ránhòu   afterward, then [MA]

  Tā xiān shuōle shémme?   What did he say first?

  Ránhòu shuōle shémme?   And what did he say then?

2. jiā   family, home [PW]

  huíjiā   return to one's home [VO]

  Nǐ míngtiān huí bu huíjiā?   Are you returning home tomorrow?

B. MORE TIME WORDS

3. zhōngwǔ   noon [TW]

4. báitiān   in the daytime [TW]

5. yèli   at night [TW]

6. qiántiān   day before yesterday [TW]

7. hòutiān   day after tomorrow [TW]

8. qiánnián   year before last [TW]

9. hòunián   year after next [TW]

Grammatical and Cultural Notes

4A.   **DÌ-** To Create Ordinal Numbers. To create ordinal numbers (e.g., "first," "second," "third"), where you designate the place occupied by an item in an ordered sequence, place the specifier **dì-** before the number. The number is then often, but not always, followed by a measure. The pattern is:

Dì-	Number	Measure
dì	yī	cì

"the first time"

Some examples with **dì-** followed by a number only (these might be said, for example, when reciting the points of an argument):

dìyī	"first"
dì'èr	"second" (NEVER say *dìliǎng)
dìsān	"third"

Now some examples with **dì-** followed by number and measure, or **dì-** followed by number, measure, and noun:

dìshítiān	"the 10th day"
dì'èrnián	"the second year"

dìyíge rén	"the first person"
dìyíge	"the first one"
dì'èrwèi xiānsheng	"the second gentleman"
dì'èrwèi	"the second one"

The question form is **dìjǐ**, e.g., **Dìjǐge?** "The number which one?" or **Dìjǐcì** "The number which time?" All of the preceding examples take **dì-** to create ordinal numbers, but note that to express which floor of a building, as you saw in 4-2, you simply say number + **lóu**, as in **qīlóu** "seventh floor"; you could NOT say *****dìqīlóu**. Also, note that in narrating past events, where in English we would say "the next day" or "the next year," in Chinese one would say **dì'èrtiān** "the second day" and **dì'èrnián** "the second year." One could not use **xià-** "next" in this sense, nor could one say **míngtiān** or **míngnián**.

4B. Contrast the following constructions with the measure **cì** "time," noting especially when **liǎng-** is used and when **èr** is used:

jǐcì "how many times?"	BUT	**dìjǐcì** "the number which time?"
yícì "one time, once"	BUT	**dìyícì** "the first time"
liǎngcì "two times, twice"	BUT	**dì'èrcì** "the second time"
sāncì "three times"	BUT	**dìsāncì** "the third time"

Also, be very careful to distinguish the pronunciation of **cì** "time" from the number **sì** "four." For practice, try saying the following:

sìcì	"four times"
dìsìcì	"the fourth time"
sìshicì	"forty times"
sìshisìcì	"forty-four times"
dìsìshisìcì	"the forty-fourth time"

4C. The literal translation of line 4, **Zhè shi nǐ dìyícì dào Zhōngguo lái ma?**, would be: "This is your number-one time to China come?"

5A. **-GUO** to Express Experience. The common and very important particle **-guo**, which has the basic meaning "go through, pass," stresses that the subject of the sentence has in the past gone through the experience of performing the action of the verb. The particle **-guo** is usually suffixed to verbs, though it can occasionally be suffixed to whole sentences. The pattern is:

Subject	Verb	-GUO
Wǒ	**qù**	**guo.**

"I've gone there." or "I've been there."

Some more examples with the particle **-guo**:

Wǒ qùguo Zhōngguo.	"I've been to China."
Tā zuòguo huǒchē.	"She has been on a train before."
Wǒ yě shíqī, shíbāsuìguo.	"I also was once 17 or 18."

Since past time is involved, the negative of **-guo** is always with **méi**, never with **bù**. The **méi** stands right before the verb, with the **-guo** coming right after the verb. The English translation usually contains the word "never" or "haven't ever." Example:

Wǒ méi zuòguo huǒchē.	"I've never ridden on a train before."

A student relaxes on the campus of Beijing University

To make questions with verbs that have a **-guo** attached, you can either add **ma** at the end or use the affirmative-negative question pattern. The English translation of questions containing **-guo** usually contains the word "ever." Examples:

Nǐ zuòguo huǒchē ma?	"Have you ever taken a train?" or "Have you ever been on a train?"
Nǐ zuòguo méi zuòguo huǒchē?	"Have you ever taken a train?" or "Have you ever been on a train?"

Instead of **Nǐ zuòguo méi zuòguo huǒchē?**, some speakers will use the abbreviated form **Nǐ zuò méi zuòguo huǒchē?**

Also, due to dialectal influence, some Chinese from southern China and Taiwan will add a **yǒu** to sentences with **-guo**, e.g., ***Wǒ yǒu zuòguo** "I've been on one (i.e., a train)"; however, this is not considered standard usage. One should say **Wǒ zuòguo**.

5B. To ask "How many times have you been to China?," some speakers will say **Nǐ qùguo Zhōngguo jǐcì?** and other speakers will say **Nǐ qùguo jǐcì Zhōngguo?** Either way is correct.

6A. The interjection **m** is a pause filler or hesitation sound. It fills in the pause while the speaker thinks of what to say next and also holds the speaker's place in the conversation, that is, makes clear to the listener that the speaker is not yet done speaking.

6B. In **Nǐ zhèicì yào zhù duō jiǔ?** "How long will you stay this time?," notice that **zhèicì** precedes the verb expression (**yào zhù**), but **duō jiǔ** follows it. This is because **zhèicì** "this time" expresses "time when," which always comes before the verb, while **duō jiǔ** "how long" expresses "time spent," which always comes after the verb (3-4: 1E and 4-1: 4A).

6C. In lesson 3-3, we previously encountered the verb **yào** with the meaning "cost" and in 3-4 we saw it again with the meaning "take (time)." Now, in this line of this lesson, we learn a new meaning of **yào** as an auxiliary verb, namely, "be going to, will." Compare:

Nèige zhǐ yào sānkuài wǔ.	"That only costs $3.50."
Dào Tiānjīn yào duō cháng shíjiān?	"How long does it take to get to Tianjin?"
Nǐ yào zhù duō jiǔ?	"How long are you going to stay?"

7A. Contrast these two expressions carefully:

bàn'ge yuè	"half a month"
yíge bàn yuè	"a month and a half"

7B. Note, in this line, **huíguó** "return to one's home country" and, in SV2 in this lesson, **huíjiā** "return to one's home." Both of these verb-object compounds are, of course, formed with the verb **huí** "go back to, return," which you learned in 1-1 in the phrase **huí sùshè** "return to one's dorm." Chinese speakers are quite sensitive to the meaning of **huí** as "go back" or "return" to a place you have a clear connection with, so you need to be careful about how you use this verb. For example, in English we might say "Next week I'm going home for a few days" but in Chinese one would have to use **huíjiā**, one could NEVER say ***qù jiā** or ***dào wǒde jiā qù**. Similarly, if you're an American based in China and next week you're going to the U.S. on a one-week business trip after which you'll return to China, you shouldn't say ***Wǒ xiàge lǐbài qù Měiguo** or ***Wǒ xiàge lǐbài dào Měiguo qù**, but rather you should say **Wǒ xiàge lǐbài huí Měiguo qù**, because America is where you are originally from, so you are considered to be "returning" to it.

SV1A. **Ránhòu** "afterward, then" can be used in ordering either past or future events. Some speakers use this word in a very loose way to try to connect thoughts that are not really very connected, a little like English "and then..."

SV1B. The **-le** on **shuōle** indicates completed action (2-4: 7B).

SV3–5. The following chart will help you review the time words relating to the divisions of the day that you learned in this and the preceding lessons:

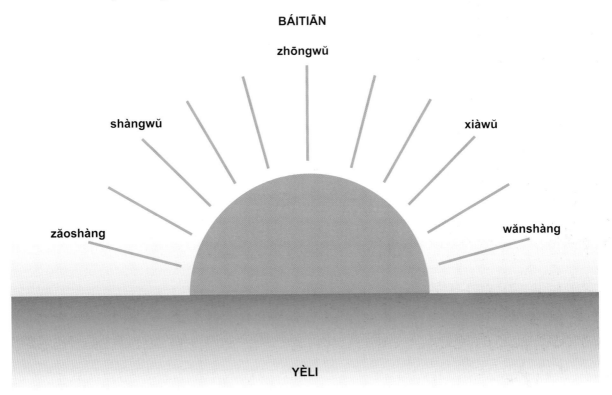

SV5. For "tonight," say **jīntiān yèli**. What do you think "tomorrow night" and "last night" would be? (Answers: **zuótiān yèli** and **míngtiān yèli**.)

SV6–7. The following chart will help you review the time words for "today" and the days preceding and following "today" that you learned in this and the preceding lessons:

QIÁNTIĀN	ZUÓTIĀN	JĪNTIĀN	MÍNGTIĀN	HÒUTIĀN
"day before yesterday"	"yesterday"	"today"	"tomorrow"	"day after tomorrow"

SV8–9. The following chart will help you review the time words for "this year" and the years preceding and following "this year" that you learned in this and the preceding lessons:

QIÁNNIÁN	QÙNIÁN	JĪNNIÁN	MÍNGNIÁN	HÒUNIÁN
"year before last"	"last year"	"this year"	"next year"	"year after next"

PART 4

Asking About Population

Derek Miller, a student in a study abroad program in Beijing, asks his teacher, Mr. Sun, about the population of China and several Chinese cities.

 Basic Conversation 4-4

1. MILLER **Sūn Lǎoshī, qǐng wèn, Zhōngguo yǒu duōshǎo rén?**
Excuse me, Mr. Sun, how many people are there in China?

2. SUN **Zhōngguo chàbuduō yǒu shísānyì rén.**
China has about one billion three hundred million people.

3. MILLER **Běijīng yǒu duōshǎo rén?**
How many people are there in Beijing?

4. SUN **Běijīng yǒu yìqiānduōwàn rén.**
Beijing has more than ten million people.

5. MILLER **Nèmme, Nánjīng ne?**
And what about Nanjing?

6. SUN **Nánjīngde rénkǒu bǐjiào shǎo. Hǎoxiàng zhǐ yǒu wǔbǎiwàn.**
The population of Nanjing is smaller. It seems it has only five million.

 Build Up

. . . .

1. Miller
Sūn   Sun [SN]
Sūn Lǎoshī   Teacher Sun, Mr. Sun
yǒu duōshǎo rén   there are how many people
Sūn Lǎoshī, qǐng wèn, Zhōngguo yǒu   Excuse me, Mr. Sun, how many people are there in
duōshǎo rén?   China?

2. Sun

-yì	hundred million [NU]
shísānyì	one billion three hundred million
shísānyì rén	one billion three hundred million people
Zhōngguo chàbuduō yǒu shísānyì rén.	China has about one billion three hundred million people.

3. Miller

Běijīng	Beijing [PW]
Běijīng yǒu duōshǎo rén?	How many people are there in Beijing?

4. Sun

-wàn	ten thousand [NU]
-qiānwàn	ten million [NU]
yìqiānwàn	ten million
duō	be many, much, more [SV/NU]
yìqiānduōwàn	more than ten million
yìqiānduōwàn rén	more than ten million people
Běijīng yǒu yìqiānduōwàn rén.	Beijing has more than ten million people.

5. Miller

Nánjīng	Nanjing [PW]
Nèmme, Nánjīng ne?	And what about Nanjing?

6. Sun

rénkǒu	population [N]
bǐjiào	comparatively, relatively [A]
shǎo	be few, less [SV]
rénkǒu bǐjiào shǎo	population is comparatively few
hǎoxiàng	apparently, it seems to me [MA]
zhǐ yǒu	it only has, there only are
-bǎiwàn	million [NU]
wǔbǎiwàn	five million
zhǐ yǒu wǔbǎiwàn	there are only five million
hǎoxiàng zhǐ yǒu wǔbǎiwàn	seems there are only five million
Nánjīngde rénkǒu bǐjiào shǎo.	The population of Nanjing is smaller.
Hǎoxiàng zhǐ yǒu wǔbǎiwàn.	It seems it has only five million.

Supplementary Vocabulary

1. **shíwàn** — one hundred thousand [NU]
   sānshiwàn rén — three hundred thousand people

2. **kè** — class [N]
   shàngkè — have class [VO]
   shàng Zhōngwén kè — have Chinese class
   Wǒmen měitiān dōu shàng Zhōngwén kè. — We have Chinese class every day.

3. **chídào** — arrive late, be late [V]
   chídàoguo jǐcì — have been late how many times
   Nǐ Zhōngwén kè chídàoguo jǐcì? — How many times have you been late to Chinese class?

4. **chángcháng** — often [A]
   táokè — skip class [VO]
   Nèige tóngxué chángcháng táokè. — That classmate often skips class.

5. Guǎngzhōu
    Shànghǎi
Guǎngzhōu, Shànghǎi nǐ dōu qùguo ba?

Guangzhou [PW]
Shanghai [PW]
I suppose you've been to both Guangzhou and Shanghai?

6. Táiběi
    Xī'ān
Wǒ qùguo Táiběi gēn Xiānggǎng, kěshi méi qùguo Xī'ān.

Taipei [PW]
Xian [PW]
I've been to Taipei and Hong Kong, but I've never been to Xian.

Grammatical and Cultural Notes

1. Notice that the grammatical structure of the question **Zhōngguó yǒu duōshǎo rén?** "In China there are how many people?" is based on the pattern Place Word + **yǒu** + Noun, which is used to indicate the existence of something in a certain place (3-1: 1B).

2A. Some speakers prefer the order **Zhōngguó chàbuduō yǒu shísānyì rén** while other speakers prefer **Zhōngguó yǒu chàbuduō shísānyì rén**.

2B. Large Numbers. There are two main differences between Chinese and English in the larger numbers: (1) Chinese has special words for "ten thousand" (**-wàn**) and "one hundred million" (**-yì**) which English lacks (we have to use two or three words to say this); and (2) English has a separate word for "million," which Chinese lacks (in Chinese one says **yībǎiwàn** "one hundred ten thousands").

The basic units for the Chinese higher numbers are **-wàn** "ten thousand" and **-yì** "one hundred million"; like **-bǎi** "hundred" and **-qiān** "thousand," these are never said alone. The secondary units are formed as follows: **yíwàn** "ten thousand," **shíwàn** "one hundred thousand" (lit. "ten ten thousands"), **yìbǎiwàn** "one million" (lit. "one hundred ten thousands"), **yìqiānwàn** "ten million" (lit. "one thousand ten thousands"), **yíyì** "one hundred million," and **shíyì** "one billion" (lit. "ten one hundred millions"). While it helps to understand the underlying logic, it is best to memorize the preceding as set expressions rather than trying to construct them on the spot. Examples of some key Chinese larger numbers:

yíwàn	"10,000"	**shíwàn**	"100,000"	**yìbǎiwàn**	"1,000,000"
liǎngwàn	"20,000"	**èrshiwàn**	"200,000"	**liǎngbǎiwàn**	"2,000,000"
sānwàn	"30,000"	**sānshiwàn**	"300,000"	**sānbǎiwàn**	"3,000,000"
sìwàn	"40,000"	**sìshiwàn**	"400,000"	**yìqiānwàn**	"10,000,000"
wǔwàn	"50,000"	**wǔshiwàn**	"500,000"	**liǎngqiānwàn**	"20,000,000"
liùwàn	"60,000"	**liùshiwàn**	"600,000"	**wǔqiānwàn**	"50,000,000"
qīwàn	"70,000"	**qīshiwàn**	"700,000"	**yíyì**	"100,000,000"
bāwàn	"80,000"	**bāshiwàn**	"800,000"	**sānyì**	"300,000,000"
jiǔwàn	"90,000"	**jiǔshiwàn**	"900,000"	**shíyì**	"one billion"
shíwàn	"100,000"	**yìbǎiwàn**	"1,000,000"	**sānshiyì**	"three billion"

Remember that the word **líng** "zero" must be inserted whenever there is an intermediate zero in a number, as in **yìqiān líng shíyī** "1,011" and **yìqiān yìbǎi líng yī** "1,101." When there are two or more consecutive intermediate zeros, **líng** can stand for all of them without having to be repeated, e.g., **yìqiān líng yī** "1,001."

With the larger numbers, while it is always correct to use **liǎng** as in **liǎngwàn** "20,000" and **liǎngbǎiwàn** "two million," there are some speakers who use **èr** and say **èrwàn** "20,000" or **èrbǎiwàn** "two million."

4A. DUŌ to Express "More Than." When it occurs after a numerical expression, **duō** indicates "more than" the amount stated. Examples:

    yìbǎiduō rén   "more than a hundred people"

yīqiānduōkuài	"more than a thousand dollars"
yíge duō zhōngtóu	"more than an hour"
yíwèi yībǎiduōsuìde lǎo tàitai	"an old woman more than a hundred years old"

Contrast expressions where the **duō** comes before the measure, such as **èrshiduōkuài** "more than twenty dollars (but less than thirty dollars)," with expressions where it comes after the measure, such as **èrshikuài duō** "more than twenty dollars (but less than twenty-one dollars)". In the former expression, the **duō** comes after the number and before **kuài**, so listeners know one is talking about "twenty and more dollars"; in the latter expression, the **duō** comes after the measure **kuài**, so listeners know one is talking about twenty dollars and an amount less than the next **kuài**.

4B.   Either **yīqiānduōwàn** or **yìqiānduōwàn**, with a tone change on the **yī**, are possible.

4C.   The stative verb **duō** is very common and useful. Some more examples with its regular meaning of "be many, be much, be more":

> **Hǎo rén bù duō.**
>
> "There are not many good people." (lit. "Good people are not many.")

> **Lǎo Lǐ rènshi hěn duō rén.**
>
> "Old Li knows lots of people." (lit. "Old Li knows very many people.")

> **Chídàode tóngxué duō ma?**
>
> "Are there many classmates who arrive late?" (lit. "Are the classmates who arrive late many?")

Duō must be preceded by an adverb when used to modify a noun (one could never say *Tā yǒu duō qián to mean "She has much money"). The combination **hěn duō** frequently occurs before other nouns. Examples:

hěn duō rén	"lots of people"
hěn duō qián	"much money"
hěn duō shíjiān	"much time"

4D.   With large numbers like **-qiān** and **-wàn**, and also with the question word **duōshǎo**, the general measure **ge** is optional before the noun **rén**. So one could say:

yìqiān rén or **yìqiān'ge rén**	"a thousand people"
yíwàn rén or **yíwàn'ge rén**	"ten thousand people"
yíwànduō rén or **yíwànduōge rén**	"more than ten thousand people"
duōshǎo tóngxué or **duōshǎoge tóngxué**	"how many students?"

4E.   Be careful about the pronunciation of the stative verb **duō** "be many, much, more." Be sure you distinguish **duō** from **dōu** "all, both".

5.   Notice the use of **nèmme** as a discourse marker to introduce a new topic, **Nánjīng** (3-4: 3).

6A.   As regards the pronunciation of the adverb **bǐjiào** "comparatively, relatively," the standard pronunciation is **bǐjiào**, with the second syllable in Tone Four, but there are speakers who pronounce the word as **bǐjiǎo**, with the second syllable in Tone Three.

6B.   The stative verb **shǎo** "be few, be less" is very important. Some more examples with **shǎo**:

Outdoor market in Beijing

Kiosk on Xizhimenwai Avenue in Beijing

Rén hěn shǎo.

"There weren't many people." (lit. "People were very few.")

Qùde rén bù shǎo.

"Quite a few people went." (lit. "The people who went were not few.")

Bù duō yě bù shǎo.

"Neither many nor few." (lit. "Not many also not few.")

6C. HǍOXIÀNG. The adverb **hǎoxiàng** "apparently, it seems to me" is very common and useful when one wishes, as is common in Chinese, not to be overly direct and emphatic, or when one wants to avoid committing oneself too strongly to a certain viewpoint so as to save one's own or someone else's face. Chinese speakers will sometimes use **hǎoxiàng** even when they are completely sure of the facts. **Hǎoxiàng** is an example of a Moveable Adverb, which means it may, like all adverbs, occur directly before the verb, or it may also occur at the beginning of the sentence. Some examples with **hǎoxiàng**:

Tāmen hǎoxiàng hái méi lái.	"It seems they haven't come yet."
Hǎoxiàng tā xìng Zhào.	"Apparently her surname is Zhao."
Tā hǎoxiàng bù dǒng.	"It seems he doesn't understand."
Nǐ hǎoxiàng bú tài gāoxìng.	"It seems as though you're not very happy."
Tā hǎoxiàng méi qùguo Zhōngguo.	"I think she has never been to China before."

Be careful to distinguish the adverb **hǎoxiàng** "it seems to me that, apparently" from the verb **xiǎng** "think," which was introduced in 3-2. Contrast:

Hǎoxiàng wǒ qùguo.	"It seems like I've been there before."
Wǒ xiǎng wǒ qùguo.	"I think I've been there before."

SV2A.   Note that **shàngkè** is a verb-object compound meaning "have a class" (either attending one as a student or teaching one as a teacher); it does NOT mean "a class," which would just be **kè**. Thus, to say "I like my classes," one should say **Wǒ xǐhuan wǒde kè**, and CANNOT say * **Wǒ xǐhuan wǒde shàngkè**.

SV2B.   Note the **dōu** after **měitiān** in **Wǒmen měitiān dōu shàng Zhōngwén kè** "We have Chinese class every day." In a statement with a preceding **měi-** "each, every," the adverb **dōu** usually follows to stress the absence of exceptions.

SV6.   In correct Pinyin, the geographical term *Xian* must be written as **Xī'ān**, with an apostrophe, so as to differentiate it from the word **xiān** "first."

Unit 4: Review and Study Guide

New Vocabulary

ADVERBS

bǐjiào	comparatively, relatively
chángcháng	often
dàyuē	approximately, about
jiù	precisely, exactly

AUXILIARY VERBS

yào	be going to, will

BOUND FORMS

-nòng	alley
-xiàng	lane

IDIOMATIC EXPRESSIONS

náli	"not at all"

INTERJECTIONS

m	(hesitation sound; pause filler)

LOCALIZERS

dōng	east

MEASURES

cì	time
duàn	section
hào	day of the month; number (in addresses, sizes)
nián	year
tiān	day

MOVEABLE ADVERBS

hǎoxiàng	apparently, it seems to me
píngcháng	usually, ordinarily
ránhòu	afterward, then

NOUNS

dìzhǐ	address
fángjiān	room
gōng	bow (the weapon)
hépíng	peace
kè	class
lǐbài	week
lóu	floor (of a building)
mén(r)	door, gate
rénkǒu	population
shēngrì	birthday
shíyàn	experiment
shíyànshì	laboratory
wénhuà	culture
xīngqī	week

yǔyán	language

NUMBERS

-bǎiwàn	million
-qiānwàn	ten million
shíwàn	hundred thousand
-wàn	ten thousand
-yì	hundred million

PARTICLES

-guo	(indicates experience)

PHRASES

yǔyán shíyànshì	language lab

PLACE WORDS

Běijīng	Beijing
Guǎngzhōu	Guangzhou, Canton
jiā	family, home
Nánjīng	Nanjing
Shànghǎi	Shanghai
Táiběi	Taipei
Xī'ān	Xian

QUESTION WORDS

jǐhào	which day of the month
jǐyuè	which month of the year
lǐbàijǐ	which day of the week
xīngqījǐ	which day of the week

SPECIFIERS

dì-	(forms ordinal numbers)
měi-	each, every

STATIVE VERBS

duō	be many, much, more
jiǔ	be long (of time)
shǎo	be few, less

SURNAMES

Sūn	Sun
Zhāng	Zhang

TIME WORDS

báitiān	in the daytime
báyuè	August
èryuè	February
hòunián	year after next
hòutiān	day after tomorrow

jīnnián	this year
jīntiān	today
jiǔyuè	September
lǐbài'èr	Tuesday
lǐbàiliù	Saturday
lǐbàirì	Sunday
lǐbàisān	Wednesday
lǐbàisì	Thursday
lǐbàitiān	Sunday
lǐbàiwǔ	Friday
lǐbàiyī	Monday
liùyuè	June
míngnián	next year
míngtiān	tomorrow
Mínguó	the Republic (of China)
qiánnián	year before last
qiántiān	day before yesterday
qíyuè	July
qùnián	last year
sānyuè	March
shàngwǔ	morning, A.M.
shí'èryuè	December
shíyīyuè	November
shíyuè	October
sìyuè	April
wǎnshang	in the evening
wǔyuè	May
xiàwǔ	afternoon, P.M.
xīngqī'èr	Tuesday
xīngqīliù	Saturday
xīngqīrì	Sunday
xīngqīsān	Wednesday
xīngqīsì	Thursday
xīngqītiān	Sunday
xīngqīwǔ	Friday
xīngqīyī	Monday
yèli	at night
yīyuè	January
zǎoshang	in the morning
zhōngwǔ	noon
zuótiān	yesterday

VERBS

chídào	arrive late, be late
chūshēng	be born
děng	wait, wait for
guān	close

kāi	open	**VERB-OBJECT COMPOUNDS**		kāimén	open a door, open
shuì	sleep	guānmén	close a door, close	qǐchuáng	get up from bed, rise
shuō	say, speak	huíguó	return to one's home country		
xiūxi	rest, take time off			shàngkè	have class
zhù	live (in), stay (in)	huíjiā	return to one's home	shuìjiào	sleep, go to bed
				táokè	skip class

Major New Grammar Patterns

TIĀN as measure meaning "day": **yìtiān** "one day," **liǎngtiān** "two days," **jǐtiān** "how many days?," **měitiān** "every day" (4-1)

Time spent after the verb: **Yǔyán shíyànshì xīngqīliù kāi bàntiān.** "On Saturday the language lab is open for half the day." (4-1)

Days of the week: **xīngqīyī** or **lǐbàiyī** "Monday," etc. (4-1)

SHÌ...-DE to express time or place of known past actions: **Wǒ shì yī-jiǔ-bā-wǔ-nián chūshēng de.** "I was born in 1985." **Wǒ shì zài Měiguo chūshēng de.** "I was born in America." (4-2)

NIÁN as measure meaning "year": **yìnián** "one year," **liǎngnián** "two years," **jǐnián** "how many years?" **měinián** "every year" (4-2)

Time when before place: **Wǒ shì yī-jiǔ-bā-wǔ-nián zài Měiguo chūshēngde** "I was born in 1985 in America." (4-2)

Years of the calendar with NIÁN: **yī-jiǔ-bā-wǔ-nián** "1985" (4-2)

Days of the month with HÀO: **wǔhào** "the fifth day of the month," **jǐhào** "which day of the month?" (4-2)

Dates: èr-líng-líng-wǔ nián shíyīyuè èrhào xīngqīyī "Monday, November 2, 2005" (4-2)

Addresses: Zhōngguo Guǎngdōng Guǎngzhōu Zhōngshān Lù wǔhào sānlóu "3rd floor, No. 5, Zhong Shan Rd., Guangzhou, China" (4-2)

Floors of buildings with LÓU: **yīlóu** "first floor," **èrlóu** "second floor," **sānlóu** "third floor," **jǐlóu?** "which floor?" (4-2)

Months of the year with YUÈ: **sānyuè** "March," **wǔyuè** "May," **shí'èryuè** "December," **jǐyuè** "which month of the year?" (4-2)

DÌ- to create ordinal numbers: **dìyī** "first," **dì'èrge** "the second one," **dìsāncì** "the third time" (4-3)

-GUO to express experience: Wǒ qùguo. "I've gone there." or "I've been there." (4-3)

**Large numbers: yíwàn "ten thousand," shíwàn "one hundred thousand," yìbǎiwàn "one million," yìqiānwàn "ten million," yíyì "one hundred million," shíyì "billion" (4-4)

DUŌ to express "more than": **yìbǎiduō rén** "more than a hundred people," **yìqiānduōkuài** "more than a thousand dollars" (4-4)

HǍOXIÀNG: Tāmen hǎoxiàng hái méi lái. "It seems they haven't come yet." (4-4)

Locating Persons, Places, and Things

COMMUNICATIVE OBJECTIVES

Once you have mastered this unit, you will be able to use Chinese to:

1. Discuss where someone or something is located relative to someone or something else: here, there, right, left, front, back, top, bottom, above, below, inside, outside, underneath, next to.

2. Talk about the direction in which a certain place is located with reference to another place: north, south, east, west.

3. Inquire if someone is in or not and, in case they are not in, ask if you may leave a note.

4. Inquire about where someone lives or is staying and reply when you are asked.

5. Ask where the bathroom is and answer when you are asked.

6. Ask if a seat is taken and answer when you are asked.

7. Talk about where you eat breakfast, lunch, and dinner.

8. Apologize for your limited Chinese, or for keeping someone waiting a long time.

9. Discuss people's Chinese and English names.

Searching for Mary Wang

Sarah Eng, who is teaching English at a college in Beijing, recently met a young Chinese woman whom she knows only as "Mary Wang." To visit her, she goes to the address the woman gave her.

Basic Conversation 5-1

1. **CHINESE** **Qǐng jìn!**
   Come in, please!

2. **AMERICAN** **Duìbuqǐ, wǒ xiǎng zhǎo yixiar Wáng Xiáojie. Qǐng wèn, tā zài bu zai?**
   Excuse me, I'd like to find Ms. Wang. May I ask, is she in?

3. **CHINESE** **Něiwèi Wáng Xiáojie?**
   Which Ms. Wang?

4. **AMERICAN** **Shízài bàoqiàn. Wǒ shi Měiguo Huáqiáo, Zhōngwén bú tài hǎo. Wǒ bù zhīdào tāde Zhōngwén míngzi. Búguò, tāde Yīngwén míngzi jiào "Mary Wang."**
   I'm really sorry. I'm an overseas Chinese from America and my Chinese is not too good. I don't know her Chinese name. But her English name is "Mary Wang."

5. **CHINESE** **Ò, wǒ zhīdaole. Shi Wáng Guólì. Búguò, tā xiànzài bú zài zhèr.**
   Oh, now I know. It's Wang Guoli. But she's not here right now.

6. **AMERICAN** **Qǐng wèn, nǐ zhīdao tā zài nǎr ma?**
   Excuse me, would you know where she is?

7. **CHINESE** **Tā zài lǎobǎnde bàngōngshì.**
   She's in the boss's office.

8. **AMERICAN** **Nà, wǒ kě bu kéyi gěi tā liú yíge tiáozi?**
   In that case, may I leave her a note?

9. **CHINESE** **Dāngrán kéyi.**
   Of course you may.

10. **AMERICAN** **Xièxie.**
    Thanks.

 **Build Up**

---

1. Chinese

Qǐng jìn!   Come in, please!

---

2. American

    xiǎng   want to, would like to [AV]

    zhǎo   look for [V]

    zhǎo yixiar   look for

    xiǎng zhǎo yixiar   would like to find

    zài   be present; be located at [V]

    tā zài bu zai   is she present

Duìbuqǐ, wǒ xiǎng zhǎo yixiar Wáng Xiáojie.   Excuse me, I'd like to find Ms. Wang.

Qǐng wèn, tā zài bu zai?   May I ask, is she in?

---

3. Chinese

Něiwèi Wáng Xiáojie?   Which Ms. Wang?

---

4. American

    shízài   really, truly [A]

    bàoqiàn   feel sorry, regret [V]

    shízài bàoqiàn   really sorry

    Huáqiáo   overseas Chinese [N]

    Měiguo Huáqiáo   overseas Chinese from America

    zhīdao   know [V]

    Zhōngwén bú tài hǎo   (my) Chinese is not very good

    bù zhīdào   not know

    Zhōngwén míngzi   Chinese name

    tāde Zhōngwén míngzi   her Chinese name

    búguò   however [CJ]

    Yīngwén   English (language) [N]

    Yīngwén míngzi   English name

    tāde Yīngwén míngzi   her English name

Shízài bàoqiàn. Wǒ shi Měiguo Huáqiáo,   I'm really sorry. I'm an overseas Chinese from America

Zhōngwén bú tài hǎo.   and my Chinese is not too good.

Wǒ bù zhīdào tāde Zhōngwén míngzi.   I don't know her Chinese name.

Búguò, tāde Yīngwén míngzi jiào "Mary Wang."   But her English name is "Mary Wang."

---

5. Chinese

    wǒ zhīdaole   now I know

    Wáng Guólì   Wang Guoli (Chinese name)

    zhèr   here [PW]

    zài zhèr   (she) is here

    bú zài zhèr   (she) is not here

    tā xiànzài bú zài zhèr   she's not here right now

Ò, wǒ zhīdaole. Shi Wáng Guólì.   Oh, now I know. It's Wang Guoli.

Búguò, tā xiànzài bú zài zhèr.   But she's not here right now.

---

6. American

    nǐ zhīdao   you know

    tā zài nǎr   where is she

Qǐng wèn, nǐ zhīdao tā zài nǎr ma?   Excuse me, would you know where she is?

7. Chinese

lǎobǎn	boss, owner [N]
bàngōngshì	office [PW]
lǎobǎnde bàngōngshì	the boss's office
Tā zài lǎobǎnde bàngōngshì.	She's in the boss's office.

8. American

kéyi	may, can [AV]
kě bu kéyi	may or may not
liú	leave (someone something) [V]
gěi tā liú	leave for her
tiáozi	note [N]
gěi tā liú yíge tiáozi	leave a note for her
Nà, wǒ kě bu kéyi gěi tā liú yíge tiáozi?	In that case, may I leave her a note?

9. Chinese

dāngrán	of course [MA]
Dāngrán kéyi.	Of course you may.

10. American

Xièxie.	Thanks.

Supplementary Vocabulary

1. yàoshi	if [MA]
yàoshi nǐ zhǎo yíge rén	if you are looking for a person
zěmme bàn	"what should be done?" [IE]
Yàoshi nǐ zhǎo yíge rén, kěshi tā bú zài, nǐ zěmme bàn?	If you look for someone, but she isn't there, what do you do?
2. zhuōzi	table [N]
yǐzi	chair [N]
nàr	there [PW]
Zhuōzi zài zhèr, yǐzi zài nàr.	The tables are here, the chairs are over there.
3. zhāng	(for tables, name cards) [M]
zhèizhāng zhuōzi	this table
bǎ	(for chairs, umbrellas) [M]
nèibǎ yǐzi	that chair
Wǒ yào mǎi zhèizhāng zhuōzi gēn nèibǎ yǐzi.	I want to buy this table and that chair.

Grammatical and Cultural Notes

2A.   In the sense of "want to" or "would like to," **xiǎng** is usually followed by a main verb. So you can say **Wǒ xiǎng qù** "I want to go" but you could not, for example, say *Wǒ xiǎng yíge fángjiān** "I want a room." For the latter, you would have to use **yào**: **Wǒ yào yíge fángjiān.** It is also possible to use **xiǎng** and **yào** together and say **Wǒ xiǎng yào yíge fángjiān**.

2B.   Note the **yixiar** in **zhǎo yixiar** "look for." As was mentioned in 2-2: 3C when we learned **jièshao yixiar** "introduce," **yixia(r)** is often added after verbs to soften them and make them sound less abrupt.

2C.   **ZÀI** as Main Verb. **Zài** "be present" or "be located at" is one of the most common and important verbs in Chinese. It has a number of different functions and usages. You have seen it before used as a coverb in sentences like **Nín zài něige dānwèi gōngzuò?** "In which organization do you work?" (cf. 2-3).

In line 2 of this conversation, **Tā zài bu zài?** "Is she present?," **zài** is used as a main verb, without any object, to mean "be present" or "be there." When you want to ask if a certain person is present, either in person or on the telephone, use this pattern:

Polite Phrase	Name of Person	ZÀI BU ZÀI?
Qǐng wèn,	Wáng Xiáojie	zài bu zài?

"Excuse me, is Ms. Wang in?"

The answers to this question would be either **Tā zài** "He/she is present" or **Tā bú zài** "He/she is not present." As another example, when roll is called in Chinese schools or places of work, as the person in charge reads off each person's name, that person answers with a loud **Zài!** meaning "Present!"

In lines 5, 6, and 7 of this conversation, **zài** is also used as a main verb but with a place word as object. When **zài** has an object, it is usually best translated as "be located at" or "be at." So we could translate **Tā xiànzài bú zài zhèr** as "She is not here now," **Tā zài nǎr?** as "Where is she?," and **Tā zài lǎobǎnde bàngōngshì** as "She is in the boss's office." To sum up, this pattern works like this:

Subject	ZÀI	Place Word
Yǐzi	zài	nàr.

"The chairs are over there."

Even though **zài** often translates into English with a form of the verb "to be," be careful to use **zài** and not **shì** for sentences expressing location. For example, English "Where are my namecards?" would have to be expressed as **Wǒde míngpiàn zài nǎr?** and could NEVER be said as ***Wǒde míngpiàn shi nǎr?** Contrast the following three sentences, all of which use forms of the verb "to be" in English but which use three very different constructions in Chinese:

Tā shi lǎoshī.

"She is a teacher." (here, **lǎoshī** EQUALS **tā**)

Tā hěn máng.

"She is busy." (here, **hěn máng** DESCRIBES **tā**)

Tā zài Shànghǎi.

"She is in Shanghai." (here, **zài Shànghǎi** LOCATES **tā**)

Finally, be aware that when the subject of **bú zài** is a person and **bú zài** is followed by **le**, this has a special meaning of "not being there any longer," i.e., "dead." Example: **Tā yǐjīng bú zàile** "He/she has already passed away."

4A. The verb **bàoqiàn**, which is used to express regret to others, is similar in meaning to **duìbuqǐ**. It can be used alone; or one can say **Hěn bàoqiàn** or **Shízài bàoqiàn** followed by a sentence of explanation; or one can have a sentence of explanation followed by **hěn bàoqiàn** or **shízài bàoqiàn**. Examples:

Bàoqiàn!	"Sorry!"
Hěn bàoqiàn, wǒ chídàole.	"I'm very sorry, I arrived late." or "I'm very sorry to arrive late."
Wǒ chídàole, shízài bàoqiàn.	"I arrived late, I'm very sorry."

4B. The important and very common verb **zhīdao** means "know" in the sense of knowing a fact or knowing of a person. Be careful not to confuse it with **rènshi**, which means "know" in the sense of knowing a person, i.e., being or becoming acquainted with her or him. These two verbs are nicely distinguished in the following sentence:

Wǒ zhīdao zhèige rén, kěshi wǒ bú rènshi ta.

"I know of this person, but I'm not acquainted with him." (**ta** is here neutral tone because it is a verb object)

Note that verbs like **zhīdao** that express states ("knowing") rather than actions are NOT compatible with the **shi...-de** pattern; do NOT take the suffix **-le** for completed action; and do NOT take **méi** for past negative (instead they take **bù**). Thus, for example, one would say **Wǒ zhīdao tā shi Rìběn rén** "I knew she was Japanese" (and could NOT say *Wǒ shi zhīdaode tā shi Rìběn rén, or *Wǒ zhīdaole tā shi Rìběn rén); and one would say **Wǒmen qùnián hái bù zhīdào** "We didn't know yet last year" (and could NOT say *Wǒmen qùnián hái méi zhīdào).

4C.   Be careful about the pronunciation of **zhīdao** "know" as opposed to **bù zhīdào** "not know." Contrast the full Tone Four on the syllable **-dào** in the negative form **bù zhīdào** "not know" with the neutral tone **-dao** in the affirmative form **zhīdao**. The commonly asked affirmative-negative question would be **Nǐ zhīdao bù zhīdào?** "Do you know?" A useful phrase for you to use when disagreeing with someone or when introducing new information into a conversation is **Kěshi, nǐ zhīdao ma, ...** "But, you know, ..." or simply **Nǐ zhīdao, ...** "You know, ..." These phrases help make your following comment less abrupt, since they imply that the other person may already share the same knowledge (even if that is not true). Introductory phrases like this can help make you sound more fluent.

4D.   In 1-3 you learned **Zhōngwén** "Chinese language." Here are some common collocations that begin with **Zhōngwén**, with **Zhōngwén** standing before another noun and modifying it:

Zhōngwén bān	"Chinese class" (the section itself with students and teacher)
Zhōngwén kè	"Chinese class" (as on a schedule)
Zhōngwén lǎoshī	"Chinese language teacher"
Zhōngwén míngzi	"Chinese name"
Zhōngwén zhuōzi	"Chinese language table" (i.e., in schools for foreigners for the purpose of practicing Chinese language; some native Chinese speakers might not be familiar with this expression)

4E.   It is common for people in Taiwan and Hong Kong who frequently have contact with foreigners to choose English given names. High school and college students also often do this in their English classes. This custom exists in China but is less common there.

Entrance to the Forbidden City in Beijing

5. The **le** on **zhīdaole** indicates there has been a sudden realization that the speaker knows whom the other person is talking about, i.e., that this is a changed situation.

6. Embedded Questions. Examine the question **Qǐng wèn, nǐ zhīdao tā zài nǎr ma?** "Excuse me, do you know where she is?" This sentence is an example of an embedded question, or question within a question; that is, the question **Tā zài nǎr?** "Where is she?" has here been embedded within the question **Nǐ zhīdao ma?** "Do you know?" In other words:

Nǐ zhīdao ma? + Tā zài nǎr? →
Nǐ zhīdao (Tā zài nǎr?) ma? →
Nǐ zhīdao tā zài nǎr ma?

The fact that this is an embedded question is the reason why there are both a question word (**nǎr**) and the question particle **ma** present in the same sentence. In normal, unembedded questions, one could never have both a question word and **ma**. Here are some more examples of embedded questions with **zhīdao**:

Nǐ zhīdao tā shi shéi ma?	"Do you know who she is?"
Nǐ zhīdao jīntiān jǐhào ma?	"Do you know what the date is today?"
Nǐmen zhīdao zhè shi shémme ma?	"Do you know what this is?"
Nǐ zhīdao zhèige duōshǎo qián ma?	"Do you know how much this is?"

Also, note that the word order in Chinese questions is the same as in Chinese statements, while in English the word order in questions often changes. Compare:

Chinese Statement:	**Tā zhīdao wǒ zài nǎr.**
Chinese Question:	**Tā zhīdao wǒ zài nǎr ma?**
English Statement:	"She knows where I am."
English Question:	"Does she know where I am?"

7.   Be careful to distinguish **bàngōngshì** "office" from **gōngshìbāo** "briefcase" (3-3).

8A.   *Deletion of Second Syllable of Bisyllabic Verbs in Affirmative Part of Affirmative-Negative Questions.* In line 8, look at the question **Wǒ kě bu kéyi gěi tā liú yíge tiáozi?** "May I leave her a note?" The **kě bu kéyi** here is an abbreviation of the full form **kéyi bu kéyi**. It would not be incorrect to use the full form, but when forming affirmative-negative questions involving two-syllable verbs (including regular verbs, auxiliary verbs, and stative verbs), Chinese speakers frequently drop the second syllable of the affirmative part of the question. To illustrate:

a b **BU** a b	→	a **BU** a b
kéyi bu kéyi	→	**kě bu kéyi**
"may or may not"		

Examples:

Full Form		Abbreviated Form	
zhīdao bu zhīdào	→	**zhī bu zhīdào**	"know or don't know?"
kéyi bu kéyi	→	**kě bu kéyi**	"may or may not?"
yīnggāi bu yīnggāi	→	**yīng bu yīnggāi**	"should or should not?"
gāoxìng bu gāoxìng	→	**gāo bu gāoxìng**	"happy or unhappy?"
hǎochī bu hǎochī	→	**hǎo bu hǎochī**	"good or not good to eat?"
jǐnzhāng bu jǐnzhāng	→	**jǐn bu jǐnzhāng**	"nervous or not nervous?"

The pattern where bisyllabic verbs in the affirmative part of affirmative-negative questions are abbreviated in this way most likely developed in Mandarin due to influence from Southern Chinese dialects. Older speakers in Beijing tend to prefer the full forms. However, the pattern with the abbreviations is common throughout China, even among younger speakers from Beijing.

Beijing residents and tourists outside the wall of the Forbidden City

8B.   **GĚI** *as a Coverb.* The literal meaning of **gěi** is "give," but as a coverb (i.e., when it co-occurs with other verbs), **gěi** often translates as English "for." Thus, in this line, we have **Wǒ gěi tā liú yíge tiáozi** "I am going to leave a note for her." The negative of this sentence would be formed by placing **bù** or **méi** right before the **gěi**: **Wǒ bù gěi tā liú yíge tiáozi** "I'm not going to leave a note for her." We actually have encountered **gěi** as a coverb meaning "for" previously in the sentence **wǒ gěi nǐ jièshao yixiar** "let me introduce you" (lit. "I introduce for you") in 2-2. Here are some more examples of **gěi** used as a coverb meaning "for":

Wǒ gěi nǐ mǎile yíge xīnde gōngshìbāo.	"I bought a new briefcase for you."
Nǐ kàn, Xiǎo Lǐ gěi Xiǎo Bái kāimén le!	"Look, Little Li opened the door for little Bai!"
Nǐ yào zhǎo Gāo Xiáojie, shì ma?	"You're looking for Ms. Gao, right?
Nǐ děng yixia, wǒ gěi nǐ zhǎo.	Wait a minute, I'll look for her for you."

8C.   Be sure you are clear on how to use the verb **liú** "leave (someone something)." The pattern is **gěi** (PERSON) **liú** (THING). Literally, this means "for (PERSON) leave (THING)."

8D.   In pronouncing the verb **liú**, remember that the syllable which is spelled as **liu** in Pinyin is pronounced as if it were written **liou**, so that it rhymes with English "yo" as in "yo-yo" but not with "few."

SV1.   **YÀOSHI**. The very common and useful moveable adverb **yàoshi** "if" can occur either before or after the subject or topic of the sentence to express a condition. For example, to say "If you look for a person but they are not there, what would you do?," you could say either:

> **Yàoshi nǐ zhǎo yíge rén kěshi tā bú zài, nǐ zuò shémme?** or
>
> **Nǐ yàoshi zhǎo yíge rén kěshi tā bú zài, nǐ zuò shémme?**

Attention: Do not use **yàoshi** in the sense of English "whether." If you wish to express the "if" that means "whether," you should use an affirmative-negative verb construction. To illustrate this, let's say you want to translate "I don't know if he's coming"; this really means "I don't know whether he's coming." This sentence could NEVER be translated as ***Wǒ bù zhīdào yàoshi tā lái.** Instead, the correct translation should be **Wǒ bù zhīdào tā lái bu lái.**

SV2A.   **-ZI** as a Noun Suffix. Note the **-zi** at the end of **zhuōzi** "table" and **yǐzi** "chair." This is a noun suffix that occurs as the final syllable of many nouns. You have already seen the noun suffix **-zi** in the following nouns:

háizi	"child"	(1-2)
yàngzi	"way"	(1-2)
bēizi	"cup"	(3-3)
dàizi	"bag"	(3-3)
tiáozi	"note"	(5-1)
zhuōzi	"table"	(5-1)
yǐzi	"chair"	(5-1)

In the future, whenever you see a **-zi** at the end of a word, you can be sure that the word is a noun.

SV2B.   Be sure to distinguish **nàr** "there" from **nǎr** "where?"

SV2C.   Regarding **zhèr** and **nàr**, the **zh-** series has to do with something close to the speaker, while the **n-** series has to do with something away from the speaker. Contrast the following:

Close to speaker:	**zhè** "this" (as a pronoun)	**zhèige** "this, this one"	**zhèr** "here"
Away from speaker:	**nà** "that" (as a pronoun)	**nèige** "that, that one"	**nàr** "there"

Some speakers make **zhèr** sound almost as if it were spelled "zhàr," and other speakers make **nàr** sound almost as if it were spelled "nèr." Also, there are some speakers who add a light **he** sound in the middle of **zhèr** and **nàr**, making them sound almost as if they were spelled **zhèher** and **nàher**.

SV3.   Though we recommend the measure **bǎ** for the noun **yǐzi** "chair," there are some speakers who will use **zhāng** for both **zhuōzi** "table" and **yǐzi** "chair."

Conversation at a Noodle Stand

Cindy Han, an American from Texas who is studying Chinese in Beijing, has ordered noodles at a noodle stand in Beijing. She decides to sit down at a table with a young Chinese woman about her age whom she has never met before. After asking if the seat is free, Han tries striking up a conversation.

Basic Conversation 5-2

1. AMERICAN   **Qǐng wèn, zhèige wèizi yǒu rén ma?**
Excuse me, is there anyone in this seat?

2. CHINESE   **Méiyou, méiyou. Nín zuò ba.**
No. Go ahead and sit down.

3. AMERICAN   **Nín cháng lái zhèr chī wǔfàn ma?**
Do you often come here to eat lunch?

4. CHINESE   **Wǒ cháng lái. Nín ne?**
I come often. And you?

5. AMERICAN   **Wǒ yě cháng zài zhèr chī. Nín shi xuésheng ma?**
I eat here often, too. Are you a student?

6. CHINESE   **Bù, wǒ shi gōngrén, zài Běijīng Dìyī Píxié Chǎng gōngzuò. Nín ne?**
No, I'm a laborer. I work at Beijing Number One Shoe Factory. How about you?

7. AMERICAN   **Wǒ zài Měiguo shi dàxuéshēng, xiànzài zài zhèr xué Zhōngwén.**
I'm a college student in America, now I'm learning Chinese here.

8. CHINESE   **Nín zài nǎr xuéxí?**
Where are you studying?

9. AMERICAN   **Zài Běidàde Hànyǔ péixùn zhōngxīn.**
At the Chinese language training center at Peking University.

10. CHINESE   *(looking at her watch)* **Yò! Kuài yīdiǎn le. Wǒ děi zǒule. Zàijiàn!**
Gosh! It'll soon be one o'clock. I have to be going now. So long!

11. AMERICAN   **Zàijiàn!**
So long!

Build Up

---

1. American

wèizi	seat, place [N]

Qǐng wèn, zhèige wèizi yǒu rén ma?   Excuse me, is there anyone in this seat?

---

2. Chinese

Méiyou, méiyou. Nín zùo ba.   No. Go ahead and sit down.

---

3. American

cháng	often [A]
cháng lái zhèr	often come here
chī	eat [V]
wǔfàn	lunch [N]
chī wǔfàn	eat lunch

Nín cháng lái zhèr chī wǔfàn ma?   Do you often come here to eat lunch?

---

4. Chinese

Wǒ cháng lái. Nín ne?   I come often. And you?

---

5. American

cháng zài zhèr chī	often eat here
xuésheng	student [N]
nín shi xuésheng ma	are you a student

Wǒ yě cháng zài zhèr chī. Nín shi xuésheng ma?   I eat here often, too. Are you a student?

---

6. Chinese

gōngrén	worker, laborer [N]
pí	leather, skin [N]
xié	shoe [N]
píxié	leather shoe [N]
chǎng	factory [N]
píxié chǎng	leather shoe factory
Běijīng Dìyī Píxié Chǎng	Beijing First Shoe Factory

Bù, wǒ shi gōngrén, zài Běijīng Dìyī Píxié Chǎng gōngzuò. Nín ne?   No, I'm a laborer. I work at Beijing Number One Shoe Factory. How about you?

---

7. American

dàxuéshēng	college student [N]
wǒ shi dàxuéshēng	I'm a college student
xué	learn, study [V]
xué Zhōngwén	learn Chinese
zài zhèr xué Zhōngwén	study Chinese here

Wǒ zài Měiguo shi dàxuéshēng, xiànzài zài zhèr xué Zhōngwén.   I'm a college student in America, now I'm learning Chinese here.

---

8. Chinese

Nín zài nǎr xuéxí?   Where are you studying?

---

9. American

Běidà	Peking University [PW]
Hànyǔ	Chinese (language) [N]
péixùn	train [V]
zhōngxīn	center [N]
Hànyǔ péixùn zhōngxīn	Chinese language training center

| Zài Běidàde Hànyǔ péixùn zhōngxīn. | At the Chinese language training center at Peking University. |

10. Chinese

kuài	soon, quickly [A]
kuài yīdiǎn le	soon it will be one o'clock
Yò! Kuài yīdiǎn le. Wǒ děi zǒule. Zàijiàn!	Gosh! It'll soon be one o'clock. I have to be going now. So long!

11. American

| **Zàijiàn!** | So long! |

Supplementary Vocabulary

1. zǎofàn   breakfast [N]
   zhōngfàn   lunch [N]
   wǎnfàn   dinner, evening meal [N]
   zài dàxuéde shítáng chī   eat at the college's dining halls
   Zǎofàn, zhōngfàn, wǎnfàn, wǒ dōu zài   I eat breakfast, lunch, and dinner in the
   dàxuéde shítáng chī.   college dining halls.

2. fàn   rice (cooked); food [N]
   chīfàn   eat food, eat [VO]
   Nǐ píngcháng zài něige shítáng chīfàn?   In which dining hall do you usually eat?

3. cài   food [N]
   Zhōngguo cài   Chinese food
   chī Zhōngguo cài   eat Chinese food
   Wǒ cháng chī Zhōngguo cài.   I often eat Chinese food.

Grammatical and Cultural Notes

1.   The noun **wèizi** "seat, place" must be carefully distinguished from the noun **yǐzi** "chair." The former refers to the place where one sits, whereas the latter refers to a piece of furniture. Note that **wèizi**, like **yǐzi**, is a noun with the noun suffix **-zi**.

3A.   **Cháng** "often" means the same as, and is usually interchangeable with, **chángcháng**, which we encountered in 4-4. The negative of both of these is **bù cháng** "not often"; one cannot say *__bù chángcháng__. Examples:

   Wǒ cháng lái zhèr. or **Wǒ chángcháng lái zhèr.**

   "I often come here." or "I often came here."

   Wǒ bù cháng lái zhèr.

   "I don't often come here." or "I didn't often come here."

Because **cháng** and **chángcháng** express habitual action over a period of time, they are incompatible with the verb suffix **-le** that expresses completed action or the verb suffix **-guo** that expresses experience. So you can say **Wǒ cháng qù tā jiā** "I often go/went to her house" but CANNOT say *__Wǒ cháng qùle tā jiā__ or *__Wǒ cháng qùguo tā jiā__. Also, **hěn** "very" and **bú tài** "not very" are incompatible with **cháng** and **chángcháng**, so you CANNOT say *__hěn cháng__ or *__hěn chángcháng__ to mean "very often," and you CANNOT say *__bú tài cháng__ to mean "not very often."

Contrast **cháng** and **chángcháng** "often" with **píngcháng** "usually" (4-1). Not only is the meaning different, but **cháng** and **chángcháng** are adverbs while **píngcháng** is a moveable adverb, meaning it can stand before the subject or before the verb.

3B.   **LÁI** + Verb to Indicate Purpose. In 1-1: SV2C, we mentioned that **qù** followed by another verb can indicate the purpose for which one is going to a certain place. In this line, we see that **lái** followed by another verb can also indicate purpose: **Nín cháng lái zhèr chī wǔfàn ma?** "Do you often come here in order to eat lunch?" A place word, such as **zhèr**, is frequently inserted after the **lái** and before the second verb. The pattern is:

Subject	LÁI	(Place Word)	Verb Phrase
Tā	lái	zhèr	xué Zhōngwén.

"She's coming here to study Chinese."

Some more examples of **lái** indicating purpose:

Yǎwén lái Běijīng zhǎo tāde tóngxué.

"Yawen came to Beijing to look for her classmates."

Lín Tàitai měige xīngqīliù lái Táiběi mǎi cài.

"Mrs. Lin comes to Taipei every Saturday to buy food."

Nèige Měiguo dàxuéshēng lái wǒmen jiā zuò shémme?

"What is that American college student coming to our house for?" (lit. "That American college student comes to our house to do what?")

5.   **ZÀI** as Coverb. Examine the following sentence: **Wǒ zài yìjiā gōngsī gōngzuò** "I work at a company" (lit. "I am located at a company work"). There are two verbs in this sentence, **zài** "be located at" and **gōngzuò** "work." When **zài** occurs first in a sentence followed by another verb, it is said to be a coverb. Though from the Chinese point of view **zài** is a verb, from the English point of view it often corresponds to prepositions like "in," "at," or "on." One important thing to remember concerning **zài** as a coverb is that in English, the phrase with the "in," "at," or "on" usually occurs after the verb; but in Chinese, the phrase with **zài** always occurs BEFORE the main verb. To sum up, the pattern with **zài** as coverb is:

Subject	ZÀI	Place	Verb
Wǒ	zài	yìjiā gōngsī	gōngzuò.

"I work at a company."

Now look carefully at the first sentence in utterance 5 of this Basic Conversation: **Wǒ yě cháng zài zhèr chī** "I often eat here, too" (lit. "I also often am located here eat"). This also is a coverb sentence with **zài** used before the place word **zhèr**. Utterances 6, 7, and 8 are all coverb sentences with **zài** occurring as a coverb before a place word; utterance 9 also contains **zài**, though the main verb there must be assumed from the context. Here now are some more examples of **zài** used as a coverb:

Nǐmen zài nǎr shàngkè?

"Where do you have class?" (one could NEVER say ***Nǐmen shàngkè zài nǎr?**)

Tā zài Zhōngguo xuéxí Hànyǔ.

"She's studying Chinese in China." (one could NEVER say ***Tā xuéxí Hànyǔ zài Zhōngguo.**)

Wǒ bú zài shítáng chīfàn.

"I don't eat in the cafeteria." (one could NEVER say ***Wǒ bù chīfàn zài shítáng.**)

In the last example above, note that the negative **bù** is placed before the coverb **zài**, not before the main verb **chīfàn**.

Be careful not to confuse the pattern **zài** + place word + verb, on the one hand, with the pattern **dào** + place word + verb, on the other (1-1: 3B and 2-2: 4B). The pattern with **zài** indicates location in a place while the pattern with **dào** indicates motion to a place. Examples:

> **Tā yào zài shítáng chīfàn.**   "She wants to eat in the dining hall."
>
> **Tā yào dào shítáng qù chīfàn.**   "She wants to go to the dining hall to eat."

6A. Examine the name of this factory: **Běijīng Dìyī Píxié Chǎng** "Beijing Number One Shoe Factory." In China, factories of the same type that are located in the same city are often referred to by number. The formula is: name of city + **dì** "number" + number (representing the order of the factory's founding) + type of factory.

6B. Notice that **pí** means "leather," **xié** means "shoe," and when the two words are combined as **píxié**, the meaning is "leather shoe." In China, shoes are traditionally made of cloth, so the default term **xié** usually refers to cloth shoes. On the other hand, in European and American culture, the default term "shoe" usually refers to leather shoes. For this reason, the best translation of **píxié** is usually "shoe(s)," though you should be sure to know what the constituents mean.

7. The verb **xué** "learn, study" is similar in meaning to **xuéxí**, which you learned as a verb meaning "learn, study" in 2-3. The differences between the two include: (1) **xuéxí** functions both as a verb and as a noun meaning "studies" (1-3), while **xué** functions only as a verb; (2) **xué** is a transitive verb and thus must have an object present or clear from the context while **xuéxí** can be transitive as well as intransitive (e.g., one can say **Wǒ zài túshūguǎn xuéxí** "I study at the library" or **Wǒ zài Běidà xuéxí** "I'm studying at Beijing University," but one could not substitute **xué** for **xuéxí** in these sentences); (3) **xué** is a more traditional, colloquial expression, while **xuéxí** is newer and more formal; (4) **xué** can be used everywhere Chinese is spoken while **xuéxí** is used primarily in China (it is uncommon in conversation in Taiwan).

Students walking to class at Beijing University

9A. College and University Abbreviations. Most Chinese college and university names consist of four syllables—a two-syllable word indicating a place, person, or thing after which the university was named, followed by the two-syllable word **dàxué** "college, university." The usual way to abbreviate college and university names is to retain the first and third syllables but drop the second and fourth syllables, i.e., 1234 → 13. This type of abbreviation may be compared to English abbreviations like "Cal Tech" (for "California Institute of Technology") or "hazmats" (for "hazardous materials"), where syllables from two different words are combined into one new, shorter word that blends the meanings of the original terms. The linguistic term for such words is portmanteau. Due to influence from Classical Chinese and the desire to save time and space, such portmanteau expressions are especially common in Chinese. Examples of Chinese college and university abbreviations:

Full Form		Abbreviation	
Běijīng Dàxué	→	**Běidà**	"Peking University"
Táiwān Dàxué	→	**Táidà**	"Taiwan University"
Zhōngshān Dàxué	→	**Zhōngdà**	"Sun Yat-sen University"

9B. The capital of China, which was formerly spelled in English as Peking, is now spelled Beijing, following the conventions of Pinyin except for tones. For historical reasons, those in charge have chosen to retain the former English spelling Peking University.

9C. **Hànyǔ** means "Chinese language" in the sense of the language of the Han majority people of China as opposed to a minority language like Tibetan or Uighur. **Hànyǔ** usually refers to spoken Chinese as opposed to written Chinese. While the various Chinese dialects are technically all different varieties of **Hànyǔ**, when the term **Hànyǔ** is used by ordinary people, it usually refers to Mandarin.

10A. KUÀI (YÀO)...LE to Indicate an Imminent Action or Situation. In this utterance, consider the sentence **Kuài yīdiǎn le** "Soon it will be one o'clock." The adverb **kuài** here means "soon," with the **le** at the end of the sentence indicating anticipated change in a situation (3-2: 6D). **Kuài yīdiǎn le** means something like "Soon it will be one o'clock and, once it is, the situation will be different than it is now." The auxiliary verb **yào** "will" is commonly added after kuài to emphasize the imminent future situation. The pattern is:

Topic	KUÀI (YÀO)	Verb	LE
Tā	kuài yào	zǒu	le.

"She will be leaving soon."

Here are some more examples of **kuài (yào)...le** to indicate an imminent action or situation:

Tā kuài sānsuì le.	"Soon he'll be three years old."
Kuài shàngkèle.	"Class will start soon."
Wèizi kuài méiyǒu le.	"The seats will soon be gone."
Tā kuài yào huíguóle.	"She's about to go back to her native country."
Kuài yidianr chī, nǐ kuài yào chídào le!	"Eat faster, you'll soon be late!"

Bronze ceremonial vessel, Forbidden Palace, Beijing

10B. Notice there is no tone change on the **yīdiǎn** "one o'clock" (which would normally be pronounced **yìdiǎn**, with a tone change on the **yī**). The younger generation in Beijing commonly omits this tone change, especially for clock times and addresses.

SV1A. Zhōngfàn "lunch" is a synonym of **wǔfàn**, introduced in line 3 of this Basic Conversation.

SV1B. Zǎofàn, zhōngfàn, wǎnfàn, wǒ dōu zài dàxuéde shítáng chī literally means "Breakfast, lunch, dinner, I all of them located at the university's dining hall eat." This is an example of a sentence with a preposed object ("breakfast, lunch, dinner") that functions as the topic of the sentence; the rest of the sentence is a comment about that topic (1-3: 5F). Notice the **dōu** "all of them" in the comment that refers back to the topic.

SV2.   Verb-Object Compounds. Chinese verb phrases consisting of a one-syllable verb plus a one-syllable object are called verb-object compounds, e.g., **kāimén** "open a door" or "open." In verb-object compounds, the verb and the object are in this textbook written together, unless other words intervene. Some English verbs without an object correspond to a verb-object compound expression in Chinese. For example, "eat" would normally be said as **chīfàn**, literally "eat rice." To say only **chī** without an object would sound incomplete or unclear, unless there were already a linguistic or real world context that had been established that made it clear what was being eaten. There follows a list of the verb-object compounds that have been introduced so far:

kāimén	"open a door" (4-1)
guānmén	"close a door (4-1)
qǐchuáng	"get up from bed" (4-1)
shuìjiào	"sleep" (4-1)
huíguó	"return to one's native country" (4-3)
huíjiā	"return home" (4-3)
shàngkè	"go to class, have class" (4-4)
táokè	"skip class" (4-4)
chīfàn	"eat" (5-2)

Important note regarding verb-object compounds: Since verb-object compounds already have "built-in" objects, they cannot take additional objects. Therefore, if a more specific object is expressed, the general object is dropped and the specific object is substituted for it. For example, "I want to eat" is **Wǒ yào chīfàn**, but "I want to eat noodles" would be **Wǒ yào chī miàn**; you could NOT say *Wǒ yào chīfàn miàn.

"Where Are You Staying?"

Adam Norris, an American business-man who is on a brief trip to Beijing, has a lunch appoint-ment with his Chinese friend, Li Zongxian. Twenty minutes late due to a traffic jam, he finally arrives at the restau-rant. He first asks the cashier where the restroom is, then joins his friend for lunch.

Basic Conversation 5-3

1. NORRIS **Qǐng wèn, cèsuǒ zài nǎr?**
Excuse me, where's the bathroom?

2. CASHIER **Zài nèibianr.**
It's over there.

3. NORRIS *(emerges from the restroom and walks over to his friend's table)*

Xiǎo Lǐ, dùibuqǐ, ràng nǐ jiǔ děngle.
Little Li, sorry, I made you wait a long time.

4. LI **Méi shìr, méi shìr. Xiǎo Luó, hǎo jiǔ bú jiànle! Nǐ kě shòule yidianr. Nǐ zhèihuí lái Běijīng zhùzai nǎr?**
That's O.K. Adam, haven't seen you for a long time! You sure have gotten thinner. Where are you staying on this trip to Beijing?

5. NORRIS **Zhùzai Cháng Chéng Fàndiàn, qī-yāo-wǔ-hào fángjiān. Nǐ hái shi zhùzai lǎo dìfang ma?**
I'm staying at the Great Wall Hotel, room 715. Are you still living where you were before?

6. LI **Bù, wǒmen qùnián jiù bāndao Xiāng Shān le.**
No, last year we moved to Fragrant Hills.

7. NORRIS **Xiāng Shān zài nǎr?**
Where is Fragrant Hills?

8. LI **Zài Běijīng chéngde běibiānr.**
To the north of Beijing city.

Build Up

---

1. Norris

cèsuǒ	toilet [PW]
cèsuǒ zài nǎr	where is the toilet
Qǐng wèn, cèsuǒ zài nǎr?	Excuse me, where's the bathroom?

---

2. Cashier

nèibian(r)	that side, there [PW]
Zài nèibianr.	It's over there.

---

3. Norris

Xiǎo Lǐ	Little Li
ràng	let, cause, make [V/CV]
ràng nǐ jiǔ děngle	"made you wait a long time" [IE]
Xiǎo Lǐ, dùibuqǐ, ràng nǐ jiǔ děngle.	Little Li, sorry, I made you wait a long time.

---

4. Li

méi shì(r) (B)	"it's nothing," "never mind" [IE]
kě	indeed, certainly [A]
shòu	be thin, lean, skinny [SV]
nǐ kě shòule yidianr	you really have become a little thinner
huí	time [M]
zhèihuí	this time
lái Běijīng	come to Beijing
nǐ zhèihuí lái Běijīng	you this time come to Beijing
-zài	at, in, on [PV]
zhùzai	live in, live at; stay in, stay at [V+PV]
nǐ zhùzai nǎr	where do you live
Méi shìr, méi shìr. Xiǎo Luó, hǎo jiǔ bú jiànle!	That's O.K. Adam, haven't seen you for a long time!
Nǐ kě shòule yidianr.	You sure have gotten thinner.
Nǐ zhèihuí lái Běijīng zhùzai nǎr?	Where are you staying on this trip to Beijing?

---

5. Norris

Cháng Chéng	Great Wall [PW]
fàndiàn	hotel [PW]
Cháng Chéng Fàndiàn	Great Wall Hotel [PW]
zhùzai Cháng Chéng Fàndiàn	stay at the Great Wall Hotel
yāo (B)	one [NU]
qī-yāo-wǔ-hào fángjiān	room number seven one five
dìfang	place [N]
lǎo dìfang	old place, same place as before
hái shi zhùzai lǎo dìfang	still live at the old place
Zhùzai Cháng Chéng Fàndiàn, qī-yāo-wǔ-hào fángjiān.	I'm staying at the Great Wall Hotel, room 715.
Nǐ hái shi zhùzai lǎo dìfang ma?	Are you still living where you were before?

---

6. Li

bān	move (a thing or one's home) [V]
-dào	arrive at, to [PV]
bāndao	move to [V+PV]
xiāng	be fragrant, smell good [SV]
shān	mountain, hill [N]
Xiāng Shān	Fragrant Hills [PW]
bāndao Xiāng Shān	move to Fragrant Hills
Bù, wǒmen qùnián jiù bāndao Xiāng Shān le.	No, last year we moved to Fragrant Hills.

7. Norris

Xiāng Shān zài nǎr?	Where is Fragrant Hills?

8. Li

chéng	city [N]
Běijīng chéng	the city of Beijing
běibiān(r)	north [PW]
Běijīng chéngde běibiānr	the north of the city of Beijing
Zài Běijīng chéngde běibiānr.	To the north of Beijing city.

Supplementary Vocabulary

1. něibiān(r)   which side, where [QW]
    Zhōngguode něibiānr   what part of China
Xiānggǎng zài Zhōngguode něibiānr?   Hong Kong is in which part of China?

2. nánbiān(r)   south [PW]
    zài Zhōngguode nánbiānr   in China's south
Xiānggǎng zài Zhōngguode nánbiānr.   Hong Kong is in the south of China.

3. dōngbiān(r)   east [PW]
    yě jiù shi shuō   that is to say
    xībiān(r)   west [PW]
Rìběn zài Zhōngguode dōngbiānr, yě jiù shi shuō   Japan is to the east of China, which is to say that
Zhōngguo zài Rìběnde xībiānr.   China is to the west of Japan.

4. zhèibian(r)   this side, here [PW]
    zài zhèibianr zhǎo   look over here
    qù něibianr zhǎo   go over there to search
Wǒmen xiān zài zhèibianr zhǎo, ránhòu   We'll first search over here, and then
qù něibianr zhǎo.   go over there to search.

5. pàng   be fat (of people or animals) [SV]
    shízài tài pàng   really too fat
Nèige háizi shízài tài pàngle!   That child really is too fat!

Grammatical and Cultural Notes

3A.   As you know from earlier lessons, "time when" precedes the verb while "time spent" follows the verb. It is true that in **ràng nǐ jiǔ děngle** "made you wait a long time," the **jiǔ** involves "time spent" and yet it precedes the verb. The reason is that **jiǔ děng** has become a set phrase, which operates differently than normal grammar rules would dictate. Converting this to conversational style would give the normal grammatical sequence: **Ràng nǐ děngle hěn jiǔ le** "(I) have been making you wait for a long time."

3B.   The **le** in the idiomatic expression **ràng nǐ jiǔ děngle** is a new kind of **le** that indicates that an action has been continuing for some time and has continued up through the present. For now, simply memorize this expression as is; we will take up this new **le** later, in 11-1.

3C.   In China to be five or ten minutes late for a lunch appointment is not a problem. However, being twenty minutes late is excessive and calls for a serious apology.

4A.   **Méi shìr** "it's nothing," "never mind," "that's O.K." is a very common expression, especially in northern China. It literally means "there is no matter" and can serve as a polite response to an apology or to thanks. In Taiwan **méi guānxi** (2-4), which can also be used in China, is usually used instead.

4B.   While most Americans would probably find it impolite to comment to someone they haven't seen in a long time that they had "gotten thinner," Chinese people frequently make personal comments of this nature in the belief that such comments, far from being impolite, indicate caring and concern for the other person. If someone should say this to you—or the opposite, that you have gained weight—don't take offense; the comment is no doubt meant well.

4C.   The adverb **kě** "indeed, certainly" is commonly used in Northern Chinese speech as an intensifier to indicate emphasis. Sentences containing a **kě** frequently have a **le** at the end. Some examples with **kě**:

Nàrde fàn kě hǎochīle.	"The food there really is delicious."
Zhèihuí nǐ kě cāiduile!	"This time you really did guess right!"
Háizi kě xǐhuan chī táng le.	"Kids really do like to eat candy."
Nǐ kě bié wàngle!	"And don't you forget it!"

4D.   In China **shòu** "be thin" has traditionally had negative connotations of being sickly and not in good health while **pàng** "be fat" (cf. SV5) has had positive connotations of being healthy and well-fed. Among younger, educated people in the larger cities, these notions have begun to change as the result of Western influence. Note that **shòu** can mean "thin" only in the sense of lacking fatty tissue. There is a completely different word to express "thin" in dimensions, as in "a thin piece of wood."

4E.   Stative Verb + **(YÌ)DIǍN(R)** to Express "A Little More...." This common pattern means "a little more STATIVE VERB." This is how the comparative degree (e.g., "bigger," "better," "faster") is formed in Chinese. The **yìdiǎn(r)** often loses its tones to become neutral tone **yidian(r)** and the syllable **yi** is often dropped in rapid speech; the final (**r**) suffix is, of course, optional. The pattern is:

Stative Verb	(YÌ)DIǍN(R)
shòu	yidianr
"a little skinnier"	

Examples:

Nèige guì dianr.	"That one is a little more expensive."
Zhèige piányi yidianr.	"This one is a little cheaper."
Yǒu hǎo yìdiǎnde ma?	"Are there better ones?"
Nǐ pàngle yidianr!	"You've gotten a little fatter!"
Wǒ jīntiān hǎole yidian.	"I'm a little better today."

4F.   -**ZÀI** as Postverb. You have previously learned **zài** as a main verb and as a coverb. Now, in this lesson, you will learn **zài** as a postverb. A postverb is a type of verb that is suffixed onto the main verb of a sentence to link the action of the main verb to a following object. For example, in the sentence **Wǒ zhùzai Cháng Chéng Fàndiàn** "I'm staying at the Great Wall Hotel," **zhù** "live, stay" is the main verb and -**zài** "at, in, on" is the postverb. The number of postverbs is limited, -**zài** and -**dào** (cf. 6B below) being two of the most common ones. In rapid conversation, postverbs frequently lose their tone (i.e., become neutral tone) in their position after the main verb. The pattern with -**zài** as postverb is:

Main Verb	Postverb
zhù	zai
"live in"	

Here are some more examples of the postverb -**zài**:

Lǐ Tàitai zhùzai nǎr?	"Where does Mrs. Li live?"
Wǒ zhùzai Nánjīng.	"I live in Nanjing."
Nín zuòzai zhèr, hǎo ma?	"Why don't you sit here, all right?"
Tā chūshēngzai Měiguo.	"She was born in America."

Postverbs normally attach only to monosyllabic main verbs. **Chūshēngzai** "be born in," as in the last example above, is one of the very few bisyllabic verbs that can take the postverb **-zài**. With the great majority of bisyllabic verbs, like **gōngzuò** "to work," a coverb construction would be employed, as in **Yǒu hěn duō Měiguo rén zài Běijing gōngzuò** "There are many Americans who work in Beijing"; one could NEVER say ***Yǒu hěn duō Měiguo rén gōngzuòzai Běijing**.

It would be possible to transform all of the example sentences above with the post verb **-zài** into coverb sentences with the coverb **zài**. For example: **Lǐ Tàitai zhùzai nǎr? → Lǐ Tàitai zài nǎr zhù?** "Where does Mrs. Li live?" However, you should be aware that the pattern with the postverb **-zài** is quite common.

Postverbs cannot be added to other verbs at will. The particular combinations have to be learned on a case-by-case basis. The combination **zhùzai** is particularly common. However, with **zhùzai**, be aware that if there is a "time spent" expression, then one cannot use **zhùzai** but must put the **zài** before the place word. Example:

Great Wall Hotel, Beijing

> **Wǒ zài Běijīng zhùle liǎngge yuè.**
>
> "I lived in Beijing for two months."
> (It would be incorrect to say ***Wǒ zhùzai Běijīng liǎngge yuè.**)

Also, note that in rapid, colloquial speech, the postverb **-zài** is sometimes omitted. The exchange you heard in 4-3 was an example of this:

Chinese:	**Nǐ zhù něige fángjiān?**	"Which room are you staying in?"
American:	**Wǒ zhù sān líng liù.**	"I'm staying in 306."

A fuller form of this, with the postverb **-zài** added back in, would be:

Chinese:	**Nǐ zhùzai něige fángjiān?**	"Which room are you staying in?"
American:	**Wǒ zhùzai sān líng liù.**	"I'm staying in 306."

5A. Remember that the Chinese verb **zhù** that you first encountered in lesson 4-3 can mean either "live" or "stay." One can use **zhù** to say "live in a certain city or country," "stay in a hotel," or "be in a hospital."

5B. **Cháng Chéng** "Great Wall" literally means "long wall." In 3-4 you learned the stative verb **cháng** "be long" and in this lesson in utterance 8 you learn **chéng** "city"; **chéng** gained the meaning "city" from the city wall that used to surround all cities in traditional China. The Great Wall is in Chinese also called the **Wàn Lǐ Cháng Chéng** "10,000 li long wall" (a **lǐ** or "Chinese mile" is a traditional Chinese unit of distance that is the equivalent of half a kilometer).

5C. **Yāo** is an alternate word for **yī** "one" that is frequently used in China when referring to numbers, for example, in addresses and telephone numbers. The reason **yāo** is used is so as to prevent any possible confusion between **yī** "one" and **qī** "seven," since in rapid conversation (for example, on the telephone) these could sound similar. **Yāo** is not commonly used in Taiwan. Also, **yāo** is never used in dates, so one can say only **yīyuè** "January" and **èr-líng-yī-yī-nián** "the year 2011."

6A. The **jiù** here means "then, that early" or "already then."

6B. **-DÀO** as Postverb. In the sentence **Wǒmen qùnián jiù bāndao Xiāng Shān le** "Last year we moved to Xiang Shan," we encounter our second postverb, **-dào**. In this sentence, **bān** "move" is the main verb, **-dào** is a postverb meaning "to" (cf. 4F above), and **Xiāng Shān** is the object of the postverb **-dào**. As in the case of the postverb **-zài** (cf. 4F above), in rapid conversation **-dào** often becomes neutral tone, then being pronounced as **-dao**. The pattern with **-dào** as postverb is:

Main Verb	Postverb
bān	dao
"move to"	

Some more examples with the postverb **-dào**:

Tāmen bāndao nǎr le?	"Where did they move to?"
Tāmen bāndao Táiběi le.	"They moved to Taipei."
Wǒ yào zuòdao Tiān'ānmén.	"I'm going to take it (e.g., a bus or a trolley) to Tiananmen."
Wǒ xiǎng zhùdao xià xīngqī'èr.	"I'd like to stay until next Tuesday."
Yǔyán shíyànshì xiàwǔ kāidao wǔdiǎn zhōng.	"The language lab is open in the afternoon until five o'clock."

Sometimes stative verbs can combine with the postverb **-dào**. Example:

Wǒ shízài bù zhīdào yào mángdao shémme shíhou.

"I really don't know until when I'm going to be busy"

6C.   **Xiāng Shān** "Fragrant Hills" is a suburb to the northwest of Beijing.

8A AND SV2-3. Points of the Compass. The words for the four basic points of the compass or directions, in the order they are usually said in Chinese (which is different from the English order!), are:

dōng	"east"
nán	"south"
xī	"west"
běi	"north"

Grammatically speaking, the above terms are localizers and, except in a limited number of patterns that will be taken up later, cannot ordinarily be said alone but are combined with the suffix **-biān(r)** "side" to create:

dōngbiān(r)	"east, east side"
nánbiān(r)	"south, south side"
xībiān(r)	"west, west side"
běibiān(r)	"north, north side"

Mythical dragon turtle, Forbidden City, Beijing

The names of many countries, provinces, and cities contain **dōng**, **nán**, **xī**, or **běi**. Examples:

Countries: **Yuènán** "Vietnam," **Nánhán** "South Korea," **Běihán** "North Korea"

Provinces: **Shāndōng** ("to the mountains' east"), **Shānxī** ("to the mountains' west"), **Hú'nán** ("to the lake's south"), **Húběi** ("to the lake's north"), **Hé'nán** ("to the river's south"), **Héběi** ("to the river's north"), **Guǎngdōng** ("to Guang's east"), **Guǎngxī** ("to Guang's west"), **Xīzàng** ("Western scriptures"), **Yúnnán** ("to the clouds' south")

Cities: **Nánjīng** ("Southern capital"), **Běijīng** ("Northern capital"), **Táidōng** "Taitung" ("Taiwan's east"), **Táinán** "Tainan" ("Taiwan's south"), **Táiběi** "Taipei" ("Taiwan's north")

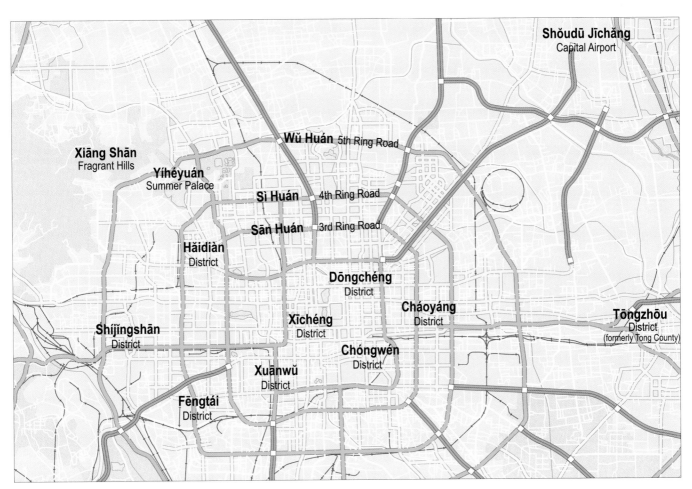

Běijīng and environs

8B.   **Zài Běijīng chéngde běibiānr** could mean either "It is to the north of Beijing city" or "It is in the northern part of Beijing city." The context will usually make clear what is meant. See also the next three notes.

SV1.   Examine the question **Xiānggǎng zài Zhōngguode něibiānr?** "Hong Kong is in which part of China?" Be aware that this could also mean "Hong Kong is to which side of China," but that translation would not make sense, since Hong Kong is part of China. However, if we asked **Yuènán zài Zhōngguode něibiānr?**, that question should be translated as "Vietnam is to which side of China?," since everyone knows that Vietnam is not in China.

SV2.   **Xiānggǎng zài Zhōngguode nánbiānr** is translated as "Hong Kong is *in* the south of China," but **Yuènán zài Zhōngguode nánbiānr** would be translated as "Vietnam is *to* the the south of China" (cf. SV1 above).

SV3A.   Grammatically speaking, the sentence **Rìběn zài Zhōngguode dōngbiānr** could mean "Japan is in the east of China" but, again, common sense tells us that interpretation is not appropriate and only the interpretation "Japan is to the east of China" makes sense.

SV3B.   **Yě jiù shi shuō** literally means "also precisely is to say."

New Computer

Guo Zhiwen, a middle-aged Taipei businessman, has invited Peter Walters, a 25-year-old American who works part-time at Guo's office, to visit him at his home. The two men, who know each other fairly well, are chatting in the living room of Guo's condominium when Guo suggests they go to his study to look at the new computer he has just bought.

Basic Conversation 5-4

1. GUO **Peter, wǒ mǎile yìtái xīn diànnǎo, zài shūfángli. Nǐ yào bu yao kànkan?**
Peter, I bought a new computer, it's in the study. Do you want to see it?

2. WALTERS **Hǎo a!**
Sure!

(they enter Guo's study and Walters looks at the new computer)

E, shi yìtái wǔ-bā-liù ma? Lǐmiàn yǒu duōshǎo RAM?
Uh, is it a Pentium? How much RAM is there in it?

3. GUO **Sānshi'èrge.**
32.

4. WALTERS *(sits down at computer and tries to turn it on)*

Kāiguān yīnggāi zài pángbiān ba?
The switch ought to be on the side, I suppose?

5. GUO **Bú duì, zài qiánmian.**
No, it's in front.

6. WALTERS **Ò. E, wǒ kě bu kéyi kànkan shǐyòng shǒucè?**
Oh. Uh, could I see the operating manual?

7. GUO **Dāngrán kéyi. Jiù zài nǐ zuǒbiānde nèige shūjiàshang—ò, bú duì, bú duì, shi zài nǐ hòumiande nèibǎ yǐzishang.**
Of course you can. It's right on that bookcase to your left—oh, no, it's on that chair in back of you.

8. WALTERS **Āiyò, zhuōzi dǐxia shi shémme dōngxi a?**
Hey, what is that under the table?

9. GUO **Ò, shi Láifú, wǒmen jiāde gǒu. Nǐ búyào guǎn ta.**
Oh, it's Laifu, our family's dog. Don't worry about him.

Build Up

1. Guo

tái	(for computers, TV sets) [M]
diànnǎo	computer [N]
yìtái diànnǎo	a computer
yìtái xīn diànnǎo	a new computer
wǒ mǎile yìtái xīn diànnǎo	I bought a new computer
shūfáng	study [PW]
lǐ	in, inside [L]
shūfángli	in the study
zài shūfángli	(it) is in the study
yào	want to [AV]
yào bu yao kànkan	do (you) want to see (it)
Peter, wǒ mǎile yìtái xīn diànnǎo, zài shūfángli.	Peter, I bought a new computer, it's in the study.
Nǐ yào bu yao kànkan?	Do you want to see it?

2. Walters

Hǎo a!	Sure!
e	(hesitation sound; pause filler) [I]
wǔ-bā-liù	Pentium® (brand of computer) [N]
yìtái wǔ-bā-liù	a Pentium
lǐmiàn	in, inside [PW]
lǐmiàn yǒu duōshǎo RAM	inside there is how much RAM
E, shi yìtái wǔ-bā-liù ma?	Uh, is it a Pentium? How much RAM is there in it?
Lǐmiàn yǒu duōshǎo RAM?	

3. Guo

Sānshí'èrge.	32.

4. Walters

kāiguān	switch [N]
pángbiān(r)	at or on the side, next to [PW]
yīnggāi zài pángbiān	should be located on the side
Kāiguān yīnggāi zài pángbiān ba?	The switch ought to be on the side, I suppose?

5. Guo

bú duì	not correct, no
qiánmian	in front, front [PW]
zài qiánmian	(it) is in front
Bú duì, zài qiánmian.	No, it's in front.

6. Walters

kě bu kéyi kànkan	may or may not see
shǐyòng	use, employ [V]
shǒucè	handbook, manual [N]
shǐyòng shǒucè	operating manual [PH]
Ò. E, wǒ kě bu kéyi kànkan shǐyòng shǒucè?	Oh. Uh, could I see the operating manual?

7. Guo

zuǒbian(r)	left side, left [PW]
shūjià	bookshelf, bookcase [N]
shàng	on top, on [L]
shūjiàshang	on the bookshelf
zuǒbiānde nèige shūjiàshang	on that bookshelf to the left

hòumian	in back, back [PW]
hòumiande nèibǎ yǐzishang	on that chair which is in back

Dāngrán kéyi. Jiù zài nǐ zuǒbiānde nèige shūjiàshang—ò, bú duì, bú duì, shi zài nǐ hòumiande nèibǎ yǐzishang.

Of course you can. It's right on that bookcase to your left—oh, no, it's on that chair in back of you.

----

8. Walters

āiyò	(indicates surprise) [I]
dǐxia	underneath [PW]
zhuōzi dǐxia	underneath the table
dōngxi	thing [N]
shémme dōngxi	what thing
shi shémme dōngxi	it is what thing

Āiyò, zhuōzi dǐxia shi shémme dōngxi a?

Hey, what is that under the table?

----

9. Guo

Láifú	Laifu ("Bring luck"; dog's name)
gǒu(r)	dog [N]
wǒmen jiāde gǒu	our family's dog
guǎn	concern oneself with [V]
tā	it (animal or thing) [PR]
búyào guǎn ta	don't concern yourself with it

Ò, shi Láifú, wǒmen jiāde gǒu. Nǐ búyào guǎn ta.

Oh, it's Laifu, our family's dog. Don't worry about him.

Supplementary Vocabulary: Place Words and Localizers

1. qián	in front, front [L]
2. qiántou	in front, front [PW]
3. qiánbian(r)	in front, front [PW]
4. qiánmian	in front, front [PW]
5. hòu	in back, back [L]
6. hòutou	in back, back [PW]
7. hòubian(r)	in back, back [PW]
8. hòumian	in back, back [PW]
9. lǐ	in, inside [L]
10. lǐtou	in, inside [PW]
11. lǐbian(r)	in, inside [PW]
12. lǐmiàn	in, inside [PW]
13. wài	outside [L]
14. wàitou	outside [PW]
15. wàibian(r)	outside [PW]
16. wàimian	outside [PW]
17. shàng	on top, on [L]
18. shàngtou	on top, on [PW]
19. shàngbian(r)	on top, on [PW]
20. shàngmian	on top, on [PW]
21. xià	on the bottom, under, below [L]
22. xiàtou	on the bottom, under, below [PW]

23. **xiàbian(r)**	on the bottom, under, below [PW]
24. **xiàmian**	on the bottom, under, below [PW]
25. **zuǒ**	left [L]
26. **zuǒbian(r)**	left side, left [PW]
27. **yòu**	right [L]
28. **yòubian(r)**	right side, right [PW]

Grammatical and Cultural Notes

1A.   Note that at the beginning of the video, as soon as the guest has entered and sat down, the host offers him something to drink. This is typical in Chinese society. One does not ask, as Americans would: "Would you like something to drink?," because social etiquette would require the guest to answer in the negative. The guest is under no obligation to drink what is offered. In fact, it is common to take a sip or two and let the rest stand; to drink everything is a signal for the host to pour more. In this video, the American guest drinks even before the Chinese host has finished pouring his own glass; this is rather rude. It would have been more polite for the guest to wait until the host invites him to drink.

1B.   **-LE** in Sentences with Quantified Objects to Indicate Completed Action. In 2-4: 7B, we first took up the particle **-le** to indicate completed action, as in **Wǒ gǎocuòle** "I got it wrong." Notice that that sentence, as well as all of the sentences with **-le** that we discussed back then, did not have an object. If there is a sentence with a verb and a quantified object and we wish to indicate completed action, we must attach a **-le** to the verb, but there is no **le** at the end of the sentence. (A quantified object means an object that has a quantity expression before it; for example, "a table," "two chairs," and "very many books" are all quantified objects, while "tables," "chairs," and "books" are not quantified objects.) Now look at the first sentence of this Basic Conversation: **Wǒ mǎile yìtái xīn diànnǎo** "I bought a new computer." Because there is a verb with a quantified object ("a new computer") and the speaker intends to indicated completed action, a **-le** is attached to **mǎi**, forming **mǎile**, and there is no **le** at the end of the sentence. Here are some more examples of **-le** in sentences with quantified objects to indicate completed action:

Lǎo Bái liúle yíge tiáozi.	"Old Bai left a note."
Lǎobǎn jīntiān mǎile wǔtái diànnǎo.	"Today the boss sold five computers."
Xiǎo Chén chīle hěn duō dōngxi.	"Little Chen ate a lot of things."

1C.   **Tái** is the measure for computers, television sets, and radios. Remember that in Chinese, you must insert a measure between a number and a noun if you want to say how many of something. Examples:

| **Nǐ jiāli yǒu jǐtái diànnǎo?** | "How many computers do you have at home?" |
| **Wǒ jiāli yǒu liǎngtái diànnǎo.** | "I have two computers at home." |

Diànnǎo gōngsīde lǎobǎn shuō tāmen zhèige yuè děi mài yìbǎi wǔshítái diànnǎo.
"The owner of the computer company said that they have to sell 150 computers this month."

1D.   Localizers and Place Words. Localizers are noun-like forms that are used in combination with other words to indicate location. In the sentence **Xīn diànnǎo zài shūfángli** "The new computer is in the study," **lǐ** "in" (often pronounced with a neutral tone as **li**) is a localizer which is attached to the noun **shūfáng** "study" to create the place word **shūfángli** "in the study." The two most common localizers are **lǐ** "in" and **shàng** "on." These two localizers, which often lose their tones to become **li** and **shang**, are often suffixed onto nouns to form place words. Examples:

with **lǐ**:	**shūfángli** "in the study"
	fángjiānli "in the room"
	shítángli "in the cafeteria"

with **shàng**:	**zhuōzishang**	"on the table"
	diànnǎoshang	"on the computer"
	yǐzishang	"on the chair"

Various localizers combine with the suffixes **-miàn** "side," **-tou** (noun suffix), and **-biān(r)** "side" to create place words. These suffixes frequently, but not always, lose their tone to become neutral tone. Examples:

Group One (three forms for each):

miàn	-tou	-biān(r)	English
lǐmiàn	lǐtou	lǐbian(r)	"inside"
wàimian	wàitou	wàibian(r)	"outside"
qiánmian	qiántou	qiánbian(r)	"in front"
hòumian	hòutou	hòubian(r)	"in back"
shàngmian	shàngtou	shàngbian(r)	"on top"
xiàmian	xiàtou	xiàbian(r)	"on the bottom"

Group Two (one form each in common use):

zuǒbian(r)	"left side"
yòubian(r)	"right side"
pángbiān(r)	"on the side, next to"
dǐxia	"underneath"

Place words are always placed directly AFTER the noun they refer to. Examples: **zhuōzi dǐxia** "underneath the table," **túshūguǎn wàimian** "outside the library." This is the opposite order from English. For those place words where there are alternate forms available, the forms ending in **-miàn** are considered more "written-style" and are more common in Southern China, while the forms ending in **-tou** or **-biānr** are considered more conversational and are more common in Northern China. Where alternate forms are available, we recommend that you use the forms in **-miàn**, but be sure to learn how to understand the other forms. In addition to the common place words listed above, there are also certain other forms which some people use, such as **zuǒmiàn** "left side" and **yòumian** "right side," etc. However, there are many speakers who don't use these, so we will not practice them here.

1E.   Notice that the English equivalent of **zài shūfángli** is "it's in the study." Frequently, Chinese sentences will have no subject at all, if the subject is clear from the context.

1F.   In this line you learn a new meaning for **yào**, namely, "want to." Review these meanings of **yào** that you have previously learned: "want, need, cost, take" (3-3) and "be going to, will" (4-3).

2A.   The interjection **e** is a pause filler or hesitation sound. Like **m** in 4-3: 6A, it fills the pause while the speaker thinks of what to say next, and also prevents what is said next from seeming too direct or blunt.

2B.   In the Mandarin of educated Chinese, it is not at all uncommon to hear English abbreviations like RAM, especially when referring to technical terms.

4A.   As you may have guessed, the noun **kāiguān** "switch" is composed of two verbs that you learned in lesson 4-1: **kāi** "open" and **guān** "close." So a literal meaning of **kāiguān** would be something like "an opener and closer."

4B.   The English auxiliary verb "should" can indicate either obligation (as in "You should listen to your parents") or probability (as in "You shouldn't have any problems"). The Chinese auxiliary verb **yīnggāi** works exactly the same way.

7A.   The **jiù** here means "precisely, exactly." In colloquial English, "right" is sometimes a good translation.

7B.   Be sure you understand the structure of **nǐ zuǒbiande nèige shūjiàshang**. Beginning with the skeleton of this clause, and then fleshing it in piece by piece, we have:

shūjiàshang	"on the bookshelf"
nèige shūjiàshang	"on that bookshelf"
zuǒbiande nèige shūjiàshang	"on that bookshelf to the left"
nǐ zuǒbiande nèige shūjiàshang	"on that bookshelf to your left"

There is no **-de** after **nǐ** because when you would have two **-de** in the same phrase (**nǐde zuǒbiande nèige shūjiàshang**), the first **-de** is usually dropped. Chinese native speakers generally feel it doesn't sound pleasant to have too many **-de** in close proximity.

7C.   Be sure to distinguish carefully the pronunciations of these three words, which American speakers of Chinese often confuse:

zǒu	"leave, depart" (1-2)
zuò	"sit" (1-4)
zuǒ	"left" (5-4)

7D.   The grammatical structure of **nǐ hòumiande nèibǎ yǐzishang** "on that chair in back of you" is similar to that of **nǐ zuǒbiande nèige shūjiàshang** that was described in 7B above.

8A.   **Āiyò** is a common interjection that expresses surprise, astonishment, or disappointment. It can be translated as "oh," "gosh," etc. Depending on the speaker, on the amount of emotion, and on the context, the exact pronunciation of this interjection may vary, so that one can say **āiyò** as in this lesson, **āiyà** (as in 10-1), or **āiya** (as in 19-3). Examples:

Āiyò, nǐ yě láile!	"Oh, you're here, too!"
Āiyò, yǐjīng jiǔdiǎn shífēn le!	"Oh dear, it's already 9:10!"
Āiyò, Hé lǎo xiānsheng yǐjīng bú zàile!	"Gosh, old Mr. He has already passed away!"

8B.   The English noun "thing" corresponds to two Chinese nouns: **shì(r)**, which you learned in 1-1, and **dōngxi**, which you learn in this lesson. The difference is that **shì(r)** refers to non-material entities, matters, affairs, or abstract things; while **dōngxi** refers to material objects or concrete things.

9A.   For a dog to have a name such as **Láifú** "bring luck, luck comes" is considered very auspicious. Many Chinese believe that saying an auspicious word frequently will bring good fortune to them and their families. Another common dog's name which both makes good Chinese sense and is an almost perfect rendering of the English original is **Láixǐ** "Lassie," literally "bring happiness" or "happiness comes."

Taipei residents performing early morning exercises in a city park

9B.   **Tā** is the pronoun for "it" when referring to animals (as here) or, more rarely, things. According to the rules of traditional Northern Mandarin spoken grammar, **tā** in the sense of "it" can be used only as an object, not as a subject. In any case, **tā** is used much less frequently than English "it." Usually, the Chinese equivalent of English "it" is nothing at all, e.g., **Wǒ méi mǎi** "I didn't buy it"; one could NEVER say ***Wǒ méi mǎi tā** to mean "I didn't buy it."

9C.   In the sentence **Nǐ búyào guǎn ta** "Don't concern yourself with him," the pronoun **tā** has lost its tone to become neutral tone **ta**. This often happens to pronoun objects (cf. section on neutral tones in "Pronunciation and Romanization" at the beginning of this volume).

SV1-28. Notice that the majority of the localizers and place words listed here divide into four pairs of opposites based on the following word roots:

qián	"front"	**hòu**	"back"
lǐ	"inside"	**wài**	"outside"
shàng	"above"	**xià**	"below"
zuǒ	"left"	**yòu**	"right"

While the order of the constituents in the first three pairs is the same as in English ("front and back, inside and outside, above and below"), the order of the constituents in the last pair is the opposite of English (**zuǒ yòu** "left and right" instead of normal English "right and left").

Supplement for Unit 5: A Never-Ending Story

Perhaps you have heard the following English story:

The night was dark and stormy,

The air was full of ice and sleet,

The captain cried "Reynaldo, tell us a story,"

And Reynaldo began...

After "and Reynaldo began...," of course, one returns to the beginning of this never-ending story.

Below is a similar never-ending story in Chinese which uses two of the localizers you have learned in this unit (can you find them?):

Shānshang yǒu yízuò miào,	"On a mountain there was a temple,
Miàoli yǒu yíge héshang,	In the temple there was a monk,
Héshang zài zuò shémme ne?	What was the monk doing?
Tā shuō gùshi. Tā shuō...	He was telling a story. He said..."

After **Tā shuō**, of course, one goes back to the beginning of the story. So, did you find the two localizers? (Answer: The two localizers are **shang** in **shānshang** "on the mountain" and **li** in **miàoli** "in the temple." The **shang** in **héshang** "monk" looks like a localizer but actually is part of the word for "monk.")

Unit 5: Review and Study Guide

New Vocabulary

ADVERBS
cháng — often
kě — indeed, certainly
kuài — soon, quickly
shízài — really, truly

AUXILIARY VERBS
kéyi — may, can
xiǎng — want to, would like to
yào — want to

CONJUNCTIONS
búguò — however

COVERBS
ràng — let, cause, make

IDIOMATIC EXPRESSIONS
méi shì(r) — "it's nothing," "never mind"
ràng nǐ jiǔ děngle — "made you wait a long time"
zěmme bàn — "what should be done?"

INTERJECTIONS
āiyò — (indicates surprise)
e — (hesitation sound; pause filler)

LOCALIZERS
hòu — in back, back
lǐ — in, inside
qián — in front, front
shàng — on top, on
wài — outside
xià — on the bottom, under, below
yòu — right
zuǒ — left

MEASURES
bǎ — (for chairs, umbrellas)
huí — time
tái — (for computers, TV sets)
zhāng — (for tables, name cards)

MOVEABLE ADVERBS
dāngrán — of course
yàoshi — if

NOUNS
cài — food
chǎng — factory
chéng — city
dàxuéshēng — college student
diànnǎo — computer
dìfang — place
dōngxi — thing
fàn — rice (cooked); food
gōngrén — worker, laborer
gǒu(r) — dog
Hànyǔ — Chinese (language)
Huáqiáo — overseas Chinese
kāiguān — switch
lǎobǎn — boss, owner
pí — leather, skin
píxié — leather shoe
shān — mountain, hill
shǒucè — handbook, manual
shūjià — bookshelf, bookcase
tiáozi — note
wǎnfàn — dinner, evening meal
wèizi — seat, place
wǔ-bā-liù — Pentium® (brand of computer)
wǔfàn — lunch
xié — shoe
xuésheng — student
Yīngwén — English (language)
yǐzi — chair
zǎofàn — breakfast
zhōngfàn — lunch
zhōngxīn — center
zhuōzi — table

NUMBERS
yāo — one

PHRASES
shǐyòng shǒucè — operating manual

PLACE WORDS
bàngōngshì — office
běibiān(r) — north
Běidà — Peking University
cèsuǒ — toilet
Cháng Chéng — Great Wall
Cháng Chéng Fàndiàn — Great Wall Hotel
dōngbiān(r) — east
fàndiàn — hotel
hòubian(r) — in back, back
hòumian — in back, back
hòutou — in back, back
lǐbian(r) — in, inside
lǐmiàn — in, inside
lǐtou — in, inside
nánbiān(r) — south
nàr — there
nèibian(r) — that side, there
pángbiān(r) — next to
qiánbian(r) — in front, front
qiánmian — in front, front
qiántou — in front, front
shàngbian(r) — on top, on
shàngmian — on top, on
shàngtou — on top, on
shūfáng — study
wàibian(r) — outside
wàimian — outside
wàitou — outside
xiàbian(r) — on the bottom, under, below
xiàmian — on the bottom, under, below
xiàtou — on the bottom, under, below
xībiān(r) — west
Xiāng Shān — Fragrant Hills
yòubian(r) — right side, right
zhèibian(r) — this side, here
zhèr — here
zuǒbian(r) — left side, left

POSTVERBS
-zài — at, in, on
-dào — arrive at, to

PRONOUNS
tā — it (animal or thing)

QUESTION WORDS
něibiān(r) — which side, where

STATIVE VERBS
pàng — be fat (of people or animals)
shòu — be thin, lean, skinny
xiāng — be fragrant, smell good

VERBS
bān — move (a thing or one's home)
bàoqiàn — feel sorry, regret

chī	eat	péixùn	train	zhīdao	know
guǎn	concern oneself with	shǐyòng	use, employ	zhǎo	look for
		xué	learn, study		
liú	leave (someone something)	zài	be present; be located at	**VERB-OBJECT COMPOUNDS**	
				chīfàn	eat food, eat

Major New Grammar Patterns

ZÀI as main verb: Tā zài bu zài? "Is she present?," **Tā zài Niǔyuē.** "She is in New York." (5-1)

Embedded questions: Nǐ zhīdao tā zài nǎr ma? "Do you know where she is?" (5-1)

Deletion of second syllable of bisyllabic verbs in affirmative part of affirmative-negative questions: kéyi bu kéyi → kě bu kéyi "may I or may I not?" (5-1)

GĚI as coverb: Wǒ gěi tā liú yíge tiáozi "I'm going to leave a note for her." (5-1)

YÀOSHI: Yàoshi nǐ zhǎo yíge rén.../Nǐ yàoshi zhǎo yíge rén... "If you're looking for a person..." (5-1)

-ZI as a noun suffix: zhuōzi "table," **yǐzi** "chair" (5-1)

LÁI + Verb to indicate purpose: Tā lái zhèr xué Zhōngwén. "She's coming here to study Chinese." (5-2)

ZÀI as coverb: Wǒ zài yìjiā gōngsī gōngzuò. "I work at a company." (5-2)

College and university abbreviations: Běijīng Dàxué → Běidà "Beijing University" (5-2)

KUÀI (YÀO)...LE to indicate an imminent action or situation: Tā kuài yào zǒu le. "She will be leaving soon." (5-2)

Verb-Object Compounds: chīfàn "eat rice" → "eat," **shuìjiào** "sleep" (5-2)

Stative Verb + (YÌ)DIǍN(R): piányi yidianr "a little cheaper," **hǎo yìdiǎn** "a little better" (5-3)

-ZÀI as postverb: Wǒ zhùzai Nánjīng. "I live in Nanjing." (5-3)

-DÀO as postverb: Tāmen qùnián bāndao Táiběi le. "Last year they moved to Taipei." (5-3)

Points of the compass: dōngbiān(r) "east, east side," **nánbiān(r)** "south, south side," **xībiān(r)** "west, west side," **běibiān(r)** "north, north side" (5-3)

-LE in sentences with quantified objects to indicate completed action: Wǒ mǎile yìtái xīn diànnǎo "I bought a new computer." (5-4)

Localizers and Place Words (5-4):

lǐ: fángjiānli "in the room"

shàng: zhuōzishang "on the table"

lǐmiàn/lǐtou/lǐbian(r) "inside"

wàimian/wàitou/wàibian(r) "outside"

qiánmian/qiántou/qiánbian(r) "in front"

hòumian/hòutou/hòubian(r) "in back"

shàngmian/shàngtou/shàngbian(r) "on top"

xiàmian/xiàtou/xiàbian(r) "on the bottom"

zuǒbian(r) "left side"

yòubian(r) "right side"

pángbian(r) "on the side, next to"

dǐxia "underneath"

Biographical Information (I)

COMMUNICATIVE OBJECTIVES

Once you have mastered this unit, you will be able to use Chinese to:

1. Ask where someone is from and answer when you are asked.

2. Inquire about where someone was born and grew up and reply to the same questions when you are asked.

3. Ask if someone is married and answer when you are asked.

4. Ask if someone has children: if so, how many? Daughter(s) or son(s)? Are they in school?

5. Talk in greater detail about your family: your siblings, parents, grandparents.

6. Express the reason(s) why someone does something or why something is as it is.

7. Talk about different levels of the educational system: elementary school, junior high, middle school, senior high, college or university.

8. Ask in which grade or year of what kind of school someone is, and answer the same questions when you are asked.

9. Present a gift to someone.

10. Ask what a given Chinese word means.

11. Talk about intermediate directions: northeast, northwest, southeast, southwest.

Conversation with a Six-year-old

Harvey Rosenthal, who is spending his junior year studying Chinese language and culture in Beijing, has been invited to visit the home of one of his Chinese teachers. Rosenthal is sitting in the living room of his teacher's apart- ment while his teacher is preparing some refreshments in the kitchen. Suddenly, the teacher's six-year-old son enters the room.

Basic Conversation 6-1

1. CHILD   **Shūshu, nǐ hǎo!**
                Hello, uncle!

2. ROSENTHAL   **Nǐ hǎo! Nǐ jiào shémme míngzi?**
                How are you? What's your name?

3. CHILD   **Wǒ jiào Dōngdong.**
                My name is Dongdong.

4. ROSENTHAL   **Dōngdong, nǐ jǐsuì le?**
                Dongdong, how old are you?

5. CHILD   **Liùsuì le.**
                Six.

6. ROSENTHAL   **Nǐ shàng xiǎoxué le ba?**
                I guess you already go to elementary school?

7. CHILD   **Duì, yǐjīng shàng yīniánjí le.**
                Yes, I'm already in first grade.

8. ROSENTHAL   *(takes a package from his backpack)*
                Dōngdong, zhè shi wǒ sònggěi nǐde xiǎo lǐwù.
                Dongdong, this is a little present for you.

9. CHILD   *(opens the package, finds chocolate inside, and tries a piece)*
                Xièxie shūshu.
                Thank you, uncle.

10. ROSENTHAL   **Bú kèqi.**
                You're welcome.

11. CHILD   **M, zhēn hǎochī!**
                Mm, it's really delicious!

🔵 **Build Up**

---

1. **Child**

    shūshu   uncle (father's younger brother) **[N]**

Shūshu, nǐ hǎo!   Hello, uncle!

---

2. **Rosenthal**

Nǐ hǎo! Nǐ jiào shémme míngzi?   How are you? What's your name?

---

3. **Child**

    Dōngdong   Dongdong (child's nickname)

Wǒ jiào Dōngdong.   My name is Dongdong.

---

4. **Rosenthal**

Dōngdong, nǐ jǐsuì le?   Dongdong, how old are you?

---

5. **Child**

Liùsuì le.   Six.

---

6. **Rosenthal**

    shàng   go to, attend **[V]**

    xiǎoxué   elementary school **[PW]**

    shàng xiǎoxué   attend elementary school

Nǐ shàng xiǎoxué le ba?   I guess you already go to elementary school?

---

7. **Child**

    niánjí   grade, level (in school) **[N]**

    yīniánjí   first grade **[TW]**

Duì, yǐjīng shàng yīniánjí le.   Yes, I'm already in first grade.

---

8. **Rosenthal**

    sòng   give (as a present) **[V]**

    -gěi   give; for, to **[PV]**

    sònggěi   give (someone as a present) **[V+PV]**

    lǐwù   gift, present **[N]**

    xiǎo lǐwù   a small present

    wǒ sònggěi nǐde xiǎo lǐwù   a small present that I give you

Dōngdong, zhè shi wǒ sònggěi nǐde xiǎo lǐwù.   Dongdong, this is a little present for you.

---

9. **Child**

Xièxie shūshu.   Thank you, uncle.

---

10. **Rosenthal**

Bú kèqi.   You're welcome.

---

11. **Child**

    m   (indicates something tastes delicious) **[I]**

    zhēn   really **[A]**

    hǎochī   be good to eat, delicious **[SV]**

    zhēn hǎochī   really good-tasting

M, zhēn hǎochī!   Mm, it's really delicious!

Supplementary Vocabulary

A. GENERAL

1. **péngyou**   friend [N]
   wǒ gěi nǐ jièshao   I'll introduce to/for you
   Wǒ gěi nǐ jièshao yíge péngyou.   Let me introduce a friend to you.

2. **yǒu méiyou**   have or not have, do you have
   nánpéngyou   boyfriend, male friend [N]
   Nǐ yǒu méiyou nánpéngyou?   Do you have a boyfriend?

3. **nǚpéngyou**   girlfriend, female friend [N]
   hǎokàn   be good-looking [SV]
   Nǐde nǚpéngyou hěn hǎokàn.   Your girlfriend is good-looking.

4. **āyí**   aunt (mother's sister) [N]
   Tāde āyí zài yìjiā màoyì gōngsī gōngzuò.   His aunt works at a trading company.

5. **xǐhuan**   like [V/AV]
   xǐhuan chī   like to eat
   táng   candy; sugar [N]
   Méiyou háizi bù xǐhuan chī táng.   All kids like to eat candy.

B. SCHOOLS AND YEAR IN SCHOOLS

6. **chūzhōng**	junior high school [PW]
7. **gāozhōng**	senior high school [PW]
8. **zhōngxué**	middle school [PW]
9. **chūyī**	first year in junior high school [TW]
10. **chū'èr**	second year in junior high school [TW]
11. **chūsān**	third year in junior high school [TW]
12. **gāoyī**	sophomore year in high school [TW]
13. **gāo'èr**	junior year in high school [TW]
14. **gāosān**	senior year in high school [TW]
15. **dàyī**	first year in college [TW]
16. **dà'èr**	sophomore year in college [TW]
17. **dàsān**	junior year in college [TW]
18. **dàsì**	senior year in college [TW]

Grammatical and Cultural Notes

1A. Chinese children are from an early age taught to acknowledge adults by calling out the appropriate kinship term for them. Children (up through the age of 20 or so) call men who are approximately the same age as or younger than their fathers **shūshu** (lit. "father's younger brother, uncle"), and they call women who are approximately the age of their mothers or younger **āyí** (lit. "mother's younger sister, aunt," cf. SV4). Children call older men **lǎo yéye** (lit. "old paternal grandfather") and older women **lǎo nǎinai** (lit. "old paternal grandmother"). Adults can call a child by her or his given name or nickname, if known, or else can refer to the child as **dìdi** (if a boy, lit. "younger brother"), **mèimei** (if a girl, lit. "younger sister"), or **xiǎo péngyou** "little friend."

1B. An alternate pronunciation of **shūshu** that you will hear in Taiwan and occasionally elsewhere is **shúshu**.

1C. Some native speakers of Chinese, especially those from the Beijing area, would criticize the little boy in this video for using **nǐ** instead of **nín**. These speakers think it would have been more polite for the boy to say **Shūshu, nín hǎo!**

3. Many children's nicknames consist of reduplicated single syllables. Examples: **Dōngdong, Dīngding, Fēifei,**

Hónghong, Jiājia, Lìli, Lùlu. Other children's names have **Xiǎo** "little" as the first syllable followed by part of their given name. Examples: **Xiǎo Kuí, Xiǎo Míng, Xiǎo Yún**.

6-7. School System and Grade in School.

a. The Chinese educational system is divided into **xiǎoxué** "elementary school," **zhōngxué** "middle school," and **dàxué** "university." **Zhōngxué** is in turn divided into **chūzhōng** "junior high school" and **gāozhōng** "senior high school." The verb **shàng** can be used with all of these to mean "go to, attend."

b. Year or grade in a school is expressed by the appropriate number followed by **niánjí** "grade in school." Examples:

yìniánjí	"first grade"	**sìniánjí**	"fourth grade"
èrniánjí	"second grade"	**wǔniánjí**	"fifth grade"
sānniánjí	"third grade"	**liùniánjí**	"sixth grade"

The tone change on **yī** is optional. Note that "second grade" is **èrniánjí** and NOT *liǎngniánjí*. Do NOT use **dì-** with grades in school (never say *dìsānniánjí*). The question word is **jǐniánjí** "which grade?"; for example, **Nǐ dàxué jǐniánjí?** "What year in college are you?" Finally, distinguish carefully the two very different words **niánjí** "grade" and **niánji** "age" (3-2).

Two students chatting at Beijing University

c. If you wish to indicate the grade in a certain type of school, then first give the name of the type of school followed by the grade. As we saw before with addresses, names, and dates, it is always the larger category which precedes the smaller one. Examples:

xiǎoxué sānniánjí	"third grade in elementary school"
chūzhōng èrniánjí	"second year in junior high school, 8th grade"
dàxué sìniánjí	"fourth year at the university, senior year"

d. For junior high school and above, it is very common to abbreviate the full expressions for grade in a certain type of school by means of this formula: first syllable of the type of school + the number of the year in school. In other words, **chū-, gāo-,** or **dà-** plus the appropriate number. Specifically:

chūyī	"seventh grade"	**gāoyī**	"tenth grade"	**dàyī**	"first year in college"
chū'èr	"eighth grade"	**gāo'èr**	"eleventh grade"	**dà'èr**	"sophomore year in college"
chūsān	"ninth grade"	**gāosān**	"twelfth grade"	**dàsān**	"junior year in college"
				dàsì	"senior year in college"

For "sophomore in college," be sure to say **dà'èr** and NOT *dàliǎng*. The following chart may help to summarize the above:

CHINESE (FULL FORM)	CHINESE (SHORT FORM)	ENGLISH
xiǎoxué yìniánjí	--	first grade
xiǎoxué èrniánjí	--	second grade
xiǎoxué sānniánjí	--	third grade
xiǎoxué sìniánjí	--	fourth grade
xiǎoxué wǔniánjí	--	fifth grade
xiǎoxué liùniánjí	--	sixth grade
chūzhōng yìniánjí	chūyī	seventh grade
chūzhōng èrniánjí	chū'èr	eighth grade
chūzhōng sānniánjí	chūsān	ninth grade

CHINESE (FULL FORM)	CHINESE (SHORT FORM)	ENGLISH
gāozhōng yīniánjí	gāoyī	tenth grade
gāozhōng èrniánjí	gāo'èr	eleventh grade
gāozhōng sānniánjí	gāosān	twelfth grade
dàxué yīniánjí	dàyī	first year of college
dàxué èrniánjí	dà'èr	second year of college
dàxué sānniánjí	dàsān	third year of college
dàxué sìniánjí	dàsì	fourth year of college

8A. In China, when visiting someone at their home for the first time, you should always bring a gift. Fruit is always a good choice, as is imported liquor or food items such as fine teas, coffee, a box of cookies, or cake. If there is a child in the family, you might bring a gift for the child, for example, a toy or game from the U.S., some new U.S. coins in a red envelope, or English language learning materials.

8B. **Sònggěi** "give (something to someone as a present)" is composed of the verb **sòng** "give (as a present)" plus the postverb **-gěi** "give." Here are some more examples of **sònggěi**:

> **Zhè shi wǒ sònggěi nǐde táng.**   "This is some candy that I am giving you."
>
> **Wǒ sònggěile tā hěn duō lǐwù.**   "I gave him lots of presents."

The postverb **-gěi** can be attached to other verbs as well, for example:

dàigěi	"carry something to someone"
liúgěi	"leave something for someone"
màigěi	"sell something to someone"
shuōgěi	"say something for someone"
xiěgěi	"write something for someone"
zuògěi	"make something for someone"

Students on campus of Beijing University

9. Note that the child, looking at the foreign "uncle," says **Xièxie shūshu** "Thank you, uncle" rather than **Xièxie nǐ** "Thank you." This is because it is considered more courteous to refer to a person by his or her title than to use **nǐ** or **nín**. For example, to thank the general manager of a company, one would usually say **Xièxie zǒngjīnglǐ** rather than **Xièxie nín**.

SV1. In China, the word **péngyou** "friend" often means more than in America, where the word "friend" is sometimes used casually. Chinese people sometimes tell stories of Americans who told them they were their **péngyou**, but when they passed each other on campus several weeks later, the American did not even recognize the Chinese.

SV2-3. For traditional Chinese speakers, the terms **nánpéngyou** and **nǚpéngyou** often indicate more serious relationships and commitments than American "boyfriend" and "girlfriend." Indeed, a sentence like **Tā yǐjīng yǒu péngyou le**, literally "He/she already has a friend," could mean "He/she is already engaged."

SV3. Compare **hǎochī** "be good to eat" in utterance 11 with **hǎokàn** "be good-looking" here. **Hǎokàn** can be used to describe people, scenery, and objects of all kinds. **Hǎo** can be prefixed to a number of verbs in this way to create stative verbs meaning "be good to..." or "be easy to...." Another example is **hǎotīng** "be nice to listen to, pretty (of music, voices, or sounds)."

Library of Beijing University

SV5.   The Chinese verb **xǐhuan** "like" is very important and very useful. Be careful with the pronunciation: take your time and pronounce the first syllable, **xǐ**, as low as you can; then pronounce the second syllable, **huan**, more lightly. Notice that **xǐhuan** can function both as a regular verb (with **xǐhuan** being the only verb in the sentence) and as an auxiliary verb (where another main verb comes after **xǐhuan**), so you could say either of the following:

As a regular verb:	**Wǒ xǐhuan táng.**	"I like candy."
As an auxiliary verb:	**Wǒ xǐhuan chī táng.**	"I like to eat candy."

The English verb "like" requires an object; in other words, you can't just say "I like," you have to say "I like it," "I don't like it," "I like this book," "I like that person," etc. The Chinese verb **xǐhuan**, whether in the affirmative or negative, does not require an object. For example, consider this conversation:

Speaker A:	**Nǐ xǐhuan zhèige dàizi ma?**	"Do you like this bag?"
Speaker B:	**Wǒ xǐhuan.**	"I like it."

Chat at the Chiang Kai-shek Memorial

Wayne Hammond, a consular officer at the American Institute in Taiwan, is sitting on a bench at the Chiang Kai-shek Memorial in Taipei reading a newspaper, when a Taiwanese man whom he doesn't know sits down next to him and begins conversing with him.

 Basic Conversation 6-2

1. TAIWANESE MAN **Hello! Nǐ hǎo! Nǐ shi Měiguo rén ma?**
Hello! How are you? Are you American?

2. HAMMOND **Duì, wǒ shi Měiguo rén.**
Yes, I'm an American.

3. TAIWANESE MAN **Měiguo shémme dìfang?**
What place in America?

4. HAMMOND **Wǒ zài Niǔyuē chūshēng, ránhòu zài Jiùjīnshān zhǎngdàde. Nǐ shi náli rén?**
I was born in New York and then grew up in San Francisco. Where are you from?

5. TAIWANESE MAN **Wǒ shi Táiběi rén. Nǐ kànqilai hěn niánqīng ei! Hái bú dào sānshí ba?**
I'm a native of Taipei. You sure look young! I suppose you must be under 30?

6. HAMMOND **Wǒ jīnnián èrshijiǔ.**
I'm twenty-nine.

7. TAIWANESE MAN **Jiéhūnle ma?**
Are you married?

8. HAMMOND **Yǐjīng jiéhūnle.**
Yes, I'm married.

9. TAIWANESE MAN **Yǒu méiyǒu xiǎohái?**
Do you have kids?

10. HAMMOND **Yǒu, wǒmen yǒu liǎngge háizi. Yíge érzi, yíge nǚ'ér.**
Yes, we have two children. One son and one daughter.

🔘 Build Up

---

1. Taiwanese man

Hello! Nǐ hǎo! Nǐ shi Měiguo rén ma? | Hello! How are you? Are you American?

---

2. Hammond

Duì, wǒ shi Měiguo rén. | Yes, I'm an American.

---

3. Taiwanese man

shémme dìfang | what place, where
Měiguo shémme dìfang? | What place in America?

---

4. Hammond

Niǔyuē	New York [PW]
wǒ zài Niǔyuē chūshēng	I was born in New York
jiù	be old (of things) [SV]
jīn	gold [BF/SN]
Jiùjīnshān	San Francisco [PW]
zhǎng	grow [V]
-dà	big [RE]
zhǎngdà	grow up [RC]
wǒ zài Jiùjīnshān zhǎngdàde	I grew up in San Francisco
náli	where [QW]
náli rén	a person from where
nǐ shi náli rén	you are a person from where

Wǒ zài Niǔyuē chūshēng, ránhòu zài Jiùjīnshān zhǎngdàde. Nǐ shi náli rén? | I was born in New York and then grew up in San Francisco. Where are you from?

---

5. Taiwanese man

-qǐlai	in the VERBing [RE]
kànqilai	in the looking [RC]
niánqīng	be young [SV]
nǐ kànqilai hěn niánqīng	you look very young
ei (T)*	(indicates liveliness) [P]
bú dào	not arrive at, not reach
hái bú dào sānshí	have not yet reached 30

Wǒ shi Táiběi rén. Nǐ kànqilai hěn niánqīng ei! Hái bú dào sānshí ba? | I'm a native of Taipei. You sure look young! I suppose you must be under 30?

---

6. Hammond

Wǒ jīnnián èrshijiǔ. | I'm twenty-nine.

---

7. Taiwanese man

jiéhūn | marry, get married [VO]
Jiéhūnle ma? | Are you married?

---

8. Hammond

Yǐjīng jiéhūnle. | Yes, I'm married.

---

9. Taiwanese man

xiǎohái(r) | small child, kid [N]
Yǒu méiyǒu xiǎohái? | Do you have kids?

---

* Remember that, as indicated on the list of abbreviations on page 70, (T) indicates that a vocabulary item is used mainly in Taipei or Taiwan.

....

10. Hammond

érzi	son [N]
nǚ'ér	daughter [N]

Yǒu, wǒmen yǒu liǎngge háizi. Yíge érzi, yíge nǚ'ér.   Yes, we have two children. One son and one daughter.

 ## Supplementary Vocabulary

1. zěmme kéyi   how is it permitted, how can
zhèli   here [PW]
zài zhèli shuìjiào   sleep here
Nǐ zěmme kéyi zài zhèli shuìjiào?   How can you sleep here?

2. zuòzai   sit in, sit at, sit on [V+PV]
nàli   there [PW]
tā zuòzai nàli   she sits there
zuò   do, make [V]
zuò shémme   do what
Tā zuòzai nàli zuò shémme?   What is she doing sitting there?

3. bānjiā   move one's home [VO]
bānguo jiā   have the experience of having moved
Nǐ bānguo jiā ma?   Have you ever moved?

4. jiéguo sāncì hūn   have married three times
líhūn   divorce, get divorced [VO]
líguo sāncì hūn   have divorced three times
Tā jiéguo sāncì hūn, yě líguo sāncì hūn.   He has married three times and also gotten divorced three times.

5. yìsi   meaning [N]
"líhūn" shi shémme yìsi   what does **líhūn** mean
Qǐng wèn, "líhūn" shi shémme yìsi?   Excuse me, what is the meaning of **líhūn**?

Grammatical and Cultural Notes

1.   The Chiang Kai-shek Memorial (called **Zhōngzhèng Jìniàntáng** in Chinese) is a large memorial hall, built in Classical Chinese architectural style, that is located in the middle of downtown Taipei. A walled park with several traditional arched gates, lily ponds, and the National Theatre and National Concert Hall surround the memorial. Chiang Kai-shek (**Jiǎng Jièshí** in Mandarin, 1887-1975) was an important general and statesman in mainland China from the 1920s through the 1940s who served as the first president of the Republic of China in 1948-49. In 1949, after the Republic of China lost the civil war with the Communists, he relocated the ROC government to Taiwan, where he resumed the presidency of the Republic of China from 1950 until his death. The spelling of his last name, Chiang, is Wade-Giles romanization for Jiang. The spelling of his first name, Kai-shek, represents the Cantonese pronunciation of the characters read in Mandarin as **Jièshí**, since he first came to prominence in Guangdong province, where Cantonese is the local language. Chiang Kai-shek is a controversial figure in Taiwan, since some appreciate his successful protection of Taiwan from the forces of Communism over four decades, while others are critical of his administration because of its harsh repression. In 2007, over the strong objections of the Taipei City government, the memorial was renamed National Taiwan Democracy Memorial Hall as a memorial to human rights abuses committed under Chiang's authoritarian rule; a little over a year later, the original name was restored.

1B. The speaker who recorded the Build Up has Standard Mandarin pronunciation, but the two speakers in the Basic Conversation audio and video for this part and the next two parts (6-3 and 6-4) have a moderate Taiwanese accent in their Mandarin. Typical features of a Taiwanese accent include the initials **zh-**, **ch-** and **sh-** dropping the **h** to become **z-**, **c-**, and **s-**; and the finals **-ing** and **-eng** dropping the **g** to become **-in** and **-en**. Actually, this kind of pronunciation is very common in much of southern mainland China as well. We urge you to use Standard Mandarin pronunciation in your own speech, but you should try to understand such non-standard pronunciation when you hear it.

4A. The basic grammatical structure of the first sentence in utterance 4 is that of a **shi...-de** sentence with the **shi** deleted. A fuller form of the sentence would be **Wǒ shi zài Niǔyuē chūshēng, ránhòu zài Jiùjīnshān zhǎngdàde** "I was born in New York, and then I grew up in San Francisco." Remember that the **shi...-de** construction expresses time or (as here) place of known past actions (4-2: 3A). As for why there is no **-de** after **chūshēng**, the reason is that **zài Niǔyuē chūshēng** is a dependent clause that is part of the whole sentence and could not be said alone. However, you could add a **-de** to **chūshēng** if you wanted to and say: **Wǒ zài Niǔyuē chūshēngde. Ránhòu zài Jiùjīnshān zhǎngdàde**. In this case, it would seem a little like two separate sentences: "I was born in

Liberty Square, Taipei, with Shin Kong Life Tower in background

New York. And then I grew up in San Francisco." If someone asks you **Nǐ shi zài nǎr zhǎngdàde?** "Where did you grow up?," be sure you answer with this sentence structure: **Wǒ shi zài** (NAME OF PLACE) **zhǎngdàde** "I grew up in (NAME OF PLACE)." You absolutely could NOT follow the English word order and say ****Wǒ zhǎngdà zài** (NAME OF PLACE).

4B. **Niǔyuē** "New York" is a borrowing from English. Since the early Chinese immigrants to New York spoke different dialects of Cantonese, they rendered the name "New York" by means of the closest-sounding syllables in their dialect, which were **Náuyeuk** in standard Cantonese. However, when the two characters for **Náuyeuk** are read off in Mandarin, they are pronounced as **Niǔyuē**, which is even further removed from the sounds of the original.

4C. **Jiùjīnshān** "San Francisco" literally means "old gold mountain."

4D. **Jiù** means "be old, used, worn, out of date" and describes THINGS. Contrast **jiù** with **lǎo**, which means "be old" and describes PEOPLE. Examples:

> **Wǒde bēibāo jiùle.**   "My backpack has gotten old."
>
> **Wǒde fùmǔ lǎole.**   "My parents have gotten old."

4E. **Jīn** means "gold"; however, it is a bound form, so you cannot say it alone (**jīnzi**, with the noun suffix **-zi**, is one word for "gold" that is a free form and can be said by itself). Note that **Jīn** is also a surname; in fact, the common Korean surname Kim is written with this character.

4D. Notice the structure of the resultative compound verb **zhǎngdà** "grow up" (lit. "grow with the result that one gets big, grow big"). We will be discussing resultative compounds in more detail later.

5A. **-QILAI** to Indicate "in the (Verb)-ing." The resultative verb ending **-qilai** means "in the (performing of the action of some verb)." The pattern is:

Verb	-QILAI
kàn	qilai

"in the looking at"

Examples:

Tā kànqilai hěn lǎo.

"She looks very old." (lit. "She in the looking at is very old.")

Nǐ kànqilai hěn shòu!

"You look thin!" (lit. "You in the looking at are very thin!")

Diànnǎo xuéqilai bù nán.

"Computing is not hard to learn." (lit. "Computers in the learning are not difficult.")

Zhōngwén xuéqilai hěn yǒu yìsi.

"Chinese is interesting to learn." (lit. "Chinese in the learning of it is interesting.")

Shuōqilai róngyi, zuòqilai nán.

"Easier said than done." (lit. "Talking about it is easy, doing it is hard.")

Zhèige gōngzuò zuòqilai tǐng róngyide.

"This job is quite easy." ("This job in the doing of it is very easy.")

Shítángde fàn kànqilai hěn hǎochī, búguò chīqilai bú tài hǎochī.

"The food in the dining hall looks tasty, but in eating it, it doesn't taste very good."

Zhèige càide míngzi tīngqilai bú tài hǎotīng, kěshi chīqilai zhēn hǎochī!

"The name of this food doesn't sound very nice, but it really tastes great!"

5B.   The phrase **hái bú dào** means "not yet arrive at" or "not yet reach." It is used to indicate an amount is smaller than might be expected, or that a certain time is still early. The question in the Basic Conversation **Hái bú dào sānshí ba?** means "I guess you have not yet reached the age of 30?" Here are some more examples of **hái bú dào**:

Wǒ xiǎng wǒmende xīn xiàozhǎng hái bú dào wǔshisuì.

"I think our new president is not yet fifty years old."

Zhèige fángjiān yìtiān hái bú dào liǎngbǎikuài? Tài piányile!

"This room is not even 200 yuan per day? That's unbelievably cheap!"

Huǒchē shídiǎn kāi, xiànzài hái bú dào jiǔdiǎn bàn, yīnggāi láidejí.

"The train departs at 10:00, and it's now not yet 9:30, we should be able to make it."

5C.   Notice how the Taiwanese man finds out the American man's age. Instead of asking point-blank how old he is, he says "You sure look young. I suppose you must be under 30?" This almost forces the American to reveal what his age is.

7A.   **Jiéhūn** is a verb-object compound which means "get married." A fuller form of the question **Jiéhūnle ma?** would be **Nǐ jiéhūnle ma?** "Are you married?" The **-le** here is completed action **-le** (cf. 2-4: 7B).

7B.   Note that the syllable **hūn** in **jiéhūn** sounds as if it were written **hwūn**; there is a **w** sound after the **h**. Moreover, the **h** should be pronounced with a good deal of guttural friction.

8. **Yǐjīng jiéhūnle** literally means "Already have married." A fuller form of this would be **Wǒ yǐjīng jiéhūnle** "I already have married." To say "marry someone," add the coverb **gēn** "with" and say **gēn…jiéhūn**. Study carefully the following examples of different usages involving **jiéhūn**:

Nǐ jiéhūnle ma?	"Have you gotten married?" or "Are you married?"
Wǒ jiéhūnle.	"I got married." or "I'm married."
Wǒ hái méi jiéhūn.	"I haven't gotten married yet." or "I'm not yet married."
Wǒ yào gēn tā jiéhūn, kěshi tā bú yào gēn wǒ jiéhūn.	"I want to marry him, but he doesn't want to marry me."
Tā yǐjīng jiéguo sāncì hūn le.	"He's already been married three times."

Notice that the usual way to say "I'm not married" is **Wǒ hái méi jiéhūn** "I haven't gotten married yet." The reason for the **hái méi** "not yet" is that in Chinese society, everyone is expected to marry. If you say **Wǒ bù jiéhūn**, that would NOT mean "I'm not married"; instead, it would mean "I'm not going to get married."

Chinese people frequently ask "personal" questions such as if one is married or how many children one has. If one is of marriageable age and is not yet married, or if one is married but does not yet have children, one is likely to be asked why. The assumption in Chinese society is that everyone older than 25 to 30 should marry and have children, so that the family line will continue. A famous quotation from the Classic of Filial Piety reads **Bú xiào yǒu sān, wú hòu wéi dà** "There are three ways not to be filial, of which the worst is not to have children" (lit. "Not be filial has three, not having those who come later is biggest").

9. In 1-2 you had **háizi**, which is the general word for "child" of whatever age. For example, we are always the **háizi** of our parents, even when we are fifty or sixty years old. In this lesson you learn **xiǎohái(r)**, which means "small child" or "young child." In Beijing one says **xiǎoháir**; in Taiwan one says **xiǎohái**.

SV1-2. You have now learned these three place words ending in **-li**:

zhèli	"here"
nàli	"there"
náli	"where?"

The above three words are synonymous with the following three place words ending in **-r** which you have learned previously:

zhèr	"here"
nàr	"there"
nǎr	"where?"

In terms of usage, the series ending in **-r** is typical of Beijing and other parts of North China. The series ending in **-li** is common everywhere that Chinese is spoken and, moreover, is what is normally used in standard written Chinese.

Note how the series that begins with **zh-** plus Tone Four means "close to the speaker":

zhè	"this" (2-2)
zhèr	"here" (5-2)
zhèli	"here" (6-2)
zhèi-	"this" (2-1)
zhèibian(r)	"this side, here" (5-3)
zhèmme	"like this, in this way, so" (2-2)

Da An Park, Taipei, with Taipei 101 visible in the distance

And note how the series that begins with **n-** plus Tone Four means "away from the speaker":

nà	"that; in that case" (2-2)
nàr	"there" (5-1)
nàli	"there" (6-2)
nèi-	"that" (2-1)
nèibiān(r)	"that side, there" (5-3)
nèmme	"like that, in that case, so" (3-4, 7-3)

SV2A. Watch your pronunciation and use of the very common Chinese verb **zuò** "do, make," contrasing it carefully with **zuò** "sit" (1-4) or "travel by" (3-4), **zuǒ** "left" (5-4), and **zǒu** "leave" (1-2).

SV2B. Here are some common collocations with **zuò** "do, make":

Conversation with a Chinese native speaker can at first seem daunting, but you have at your disposal phrases and strategies that can help you take control of a conversation!

zuò'ài	"make love" (be careful how you use)
zuòcài	"cook"
zuòfàn	"cook"
zuòshì	"work, have a job"
zuò gōngkè	"do homework"
zuò péngyou	"make friends"

SV3. How would you say "I've moved twice"? Since **bānjiā** "move" (lit. "move home") is a verb-object compound, you would put **liǎngcì** "twice" in between the verb **bān** and the object **jiā** and say: **Wǒ bānguo liǎngcì jiā.** Also note the noun phrase **bānjiā gōngsī** "moving company."

SV4. To say "get divorced FROM," one says in Chinese **gēn...líhūn** (lit. "get divorced WITH"). So remember: for both "marry someone" and "divorce someone," you say **gēn...** followed by the verb. An example with **gēn...líhūn**:

Tā gēn tā xiānsheng líhūnle.   "She has gotten divorced from her husband."

SV5. Communication Strategies. Engaging in conversation with a Chinese native speaker can at first be daunting, but you should realize that when conversing with someone (unlike when listening to a lecture or watching a movie), you do have a certain amount of control over the conversation. For example, you can ask for repetition of key points, you can confirm meanings, you can to some extent choose the subjects you want to talk about or change subjects, and you can end the conversation.

It can be helpful for you to have at your disposal phrases and strategies that will help you control a conversation. For example, in the Classroom Expressions section of this textbook, you learned the expression **Qǐng nǐ zài shuō yíbiàn** "Please say it again." If someone has said something you don't understand, you can use this phrase to ask them to repeat, perhaps expanded a bit into the less abrupt:

Duìbuqǐ, wǒde Zhōngwén hái bú tài hǎo, kě bu kéyi qǐng nín zài shuō yíbiàn?

"Sorry, my Chinese is not very good yet, could I ask you to say it again?"

However, even more natural than asking someone to repeat something word for word would be to confirm your understanding of what the other person has said by using a pattern such as **"X'de yìsi shi "Y"** (lit. "the meaning of X is Y"). For example:

Ò, suóyi nínde yìsi shì...

"Oh, so what you mean is..." (lit. "Oh, so your meaning is...")

Similarly, it's important to learn useful phrases—sometimes called metalanguage—for facilitating and managing your own language learning. Some of these you learned in the Classroom Expressions section, such as **Dìjǐshēng?** "Which tone is it?," **Duì bu dui?** "Is it correct?," **Qǐng nǐ dà shēng yidianr** "A little louder, please," **Qǐng nǐ kuài yidianr** "A little faster, please," and **Qǐng nǐ màn yidianr** "A little slower, please." It can also be useful to be able to ask the meaning of something. A common formula for doing this, as illustrated in SV 5, is:

Qǐng wèn, X shi shémme yìsi?

"Excuse me, what does X mean?" (lit. "Excuse me, X is what meaning?")

The answer to this question would be:

"X" shi "Y" de yìsi.

"The meaning of X is Y." (lit. "X is Y's meaning.")

Circumlocution, that is, using other, simpler words to "talk around" the more difficult word you don't know or have forgotten, can likewise be a useful communication strategy. You could say:

Wǒde yìsi shi shuō...

"What I mean is..." (lit. "My meaning is to say...")

We hope that most of the time you will manage to cope without resorting to English. However, if you need to know the Chinese equivalent of an English term and you have access to a Chinese native speaker who knows English, you could use the following question to ask:

Qǐng wèn, X Zhōngwén zěmme shuō?

"Excuse me, how do you say X in Chinese?"

Finally, it can be useful for you to have at your disposal "escape clauses" to rely on when a conversation breaks down or you become linguistically stressed or exhausted and need a quick out. In such a situation, you could, for example, look at your watch and say:

Āiyò, yǐjīng bādiǎnle! Wǒ wàngle wǒ hái yǒu shì. Duìbuqǐ, wǒ děi zǒule!

"Oh, gosh, it's already eight o'clock! I forgot I still have something to do. I'm sorry, I have to be leaving!"

Man being wheeled on an outing in front of National Theatre, Taipei

Chat at the Chiang Kai-shek Memorial (cont.)

The Taiwanese man asks Hammond questions about his children and about where Hammond and his wife work (continued from the previous conversation).

 ### Basic Conversation 6-3

1. TAIWANESE MAN   **Háizi jǐsuì le? Yǐjīng shàngxuéle ma?**
   How old are your kids? Already in school?

2. HAMMOND   **Méiyou, tāmen hái xiǎo. Érzi sānsuì, nǚ'ér jiǔge yuè dà, suóyi hái méi shàngxué.**
   No, they're still small. My son is 3, my daughter is 9 months old, so they're not in school yet.

3. TAIWANESE MAN   **Nǐ zài náli gōngzuò?**
   Where do you work?

4. HAMMOND   **Wǒ zài Měiguo Zài Tái Xiéhuì fúwù.**
   I work at the American Institute in Taiwan.

5. TAIWANESE MAN   **Ò. Nǐ tàitai yě shàngbān ma?**
   Oh. Does your wife work, too?

6. HAMMOND   **Tā zài Táiběi Měiguo Xuéxiào jiāoshū. Búguò, yīnwei háizi hái xiǎo, suóyi tā zhǐ néng gōngzuò bàntiān.**
   She teaches at Taipei American School. However, because our kids are still small, she can only work half-time.

 ### Build Up

1. Taiwanese man

shàngxué	attend school [VO]
Háizi jǐsuì le? Yǐjīng shàngxuéle ma?	How old are your kids? Already in school?

2. Hammond

méiyou	(indicates past negative of action verbs) [AV]
jiǔge yuè dà	be nine months old
suóyi	therefore, so [CJ]

méi shàngxué	didn't attend school
hái méi shàngxué	haven't attended school yet
Méiyou, tāmen hái xiǎo. Érzi sānsuì, nǚ'ér jiǔge yuè dà, suóyi hái méi shàngxué.	No, they're still small. My son is 3, my daughter is 9 months old, so they're not in school yet.

3. Taiwanese man

Nǐ zài náli gōngzuò?	Where do you work?

4. Hammond

xiéhuì	association, society [N]
Měiguo Zài Tái Xiéhuì	American Institute in Taiwan [PW]
fúwù	serve [V]
Wǒ zài Měiguo Zài Tái Xiéhuì fúwù.	I work at the American Institute in Taiwan.

5. Taiwanese man

shàngbān(r)	work, go to work [VO]
Ò. Nǐ tàitai yě shàngbān ma?	Oh. Does your wife work, too?

6. Hammond

xuéxiào	school [PW]
Táiběi Měiguo Xuéxiào	Taipei American School [PW]
jiāo	teach [V]
jiāoshū	teach [VO]
yīnwei	because [CJ]
yīnwei háizi hái xiǎo	because the kids are still small
néng	be able to, can [AV]
suóyi tā zhǐ néng gōngzuò bàntiān	therefore she can only work half days
Tā zài Táiběi Měiguo Xuéxiào jiāoshū.	She teaches at Taipei American School.
Búguò, yīnwei háizi hái xiǎo, suóyi tā zhǐ néng gōngzuò bàntiān.	However, because our kids are still small, she can only work half-time.

🖸 Supplementary Vocabulary

A. INTERMEDIATE DIRECTIONS

1. **dōngnán**	southeast [PW]
2. **dōngběi**	northeast [PW]
3. **xī'nán**	southwest [PW]
4. **xīběi**	northwest [PW]

B. GENERAL

5. **hángkōng**	aviation [N]
hángkōng gōngsī	airline [PH]
Xī'nán Hángkōng Gōngsī	Southwest Airlines® [PW]
Tā zài Xī'nán Hángkōng Gōngsī gōngzuòguo.	She has worked at Southwest Airlines.
6. **xiàbān(r)**	get off from work [VO]
Nǐ mǔqin měitiān jǐdiǎn shàngbān, jǐdiǎn xiàbān?	What time every day does your mother go to work and what time does she get off from work?
7. **wèishemme**	why [QW]
nán xué	be hard to learn
Zhōngwén hěn nán xué	Chinese is hard to learn
Tāmen wèishemme shuō Zhōngwén hěn nán xué?	Why do they say Chinese is hard to learn?

Grammatical and Cultural Notes

2A.   **MÉIYOU** to Indicate Past Negative of Action Verbs. You have already learned **méiyou** "not have, there is not/there are not" as the negative form of **yǒu** "have" (3-2: SV2A). **Méiyou** can also function, very much like **méi** (cf. 2-4: 2A), as an auxiliary verb that indicates the past negative of action verbs and means "did not," "has not," or "have not." This **méiyou** ordinarily occurs before the main verb to which it refers but if the context is clear, as here, it can occur alone. (In this line, **Méiyou** is a short form of the fuller form **Háizi hái méiyou shàngxué** "The children have not yet started attending school.") In many cases, **méi** and **méiyou** are synonymous. However, there are two differences: (1) **méiyou** can occur alone or at the ends of sentences while **méi** cannot; (2) **méiyou** is used all over China while **méi** is more common in the North. The pattern is:

Subject	MÉIYOU	Action Verb
Tāmen	**méiyou**	**lái.**

"They didn't come."

Here are some more examples of **méiyou** to indicate past negative of action verbs:

Huǒchē hái méiyou dào.	"The train has not yet arrived."
Wǒ méiyou dài míngpiàn.	"I didn't bring name cards."
Tāmen méiyou sòng lǐwù.	"They didn't give a gift."

We could even have a dialog like this:

Speaker A: **Tā qùle ma?**	"Did she go?"
Speaker B: **Méiyou.**	"No."
Speaker A: **Tā méiyou qù ma?**	"She didn't go?"
Speaker B: **Duì, tā méiyou qù.**	"Right, she didn't go."

In the dialog above, the **méiyou** in the third and fourth lines could be replaced by **méi**, but not the **méiyou** in the second line. Also, notice that **méiyou** and **méi** to indicate past negative of action verbs are the exact opposite of **-le** to indicate completed action; **-le** indicates that an action has been completed, while **méiyou** and **méi** indicate that the action did not take place.

2B.   Examine **nǚ'ér jiǔge yuè dà** "my daughter is nine months old" (lit. "daughter nine months big"). To indicate how many months old an infant is, say: (number of months) + **ge yuè dà**. Examples:

Tā sān'ge yuè dà.	"She is three months old."
Wǒ cāi nèige xiǎoháir chàbuduō liùge yuè dà.	"I would guess that child is about six months old."

2C.   **Suóyi** is a conjunction that means "therefore, for this reason, so." It cannot mean "so" in the sense of "so that" or "in order to," for which there is another word. In other words, one could NEVER use **suóyi** to say *Tā qùle Zhōngguo suóyi tā kéyi xué Zhōngwén "She went to China so she could learn Chinese." That sentence could be corrected to this one: **Tā yào xué Zhōngwén, suóyi tā qùle Zhōngguo** "She wanted to learn Chinese, so she went to China."

4.   The American Institute in Taiwan (AIT) is the name of the unofficial organization in Taiwan and the U.S. that was created to succeed the former U.S. Embassy to the Republic of China when the U.S. recognized the PRC in 1979.

5.   **Shàngbān** refers to going to work in an office or other organization where there are set starting times and set ending times. This term would be used of a secretary, for example, but not of a laborer. Also, be careful not to confuse these two expressions:

shàngbān	"work, go to work" (e.g., **Tā zài yìjiā gōngsī shàngbān** "She works at a company.")
bānshang	"in a class" (e.g., **Tā bānshang yǒu shíge tóngxué** "She has 10 students in her class.")

6A.   Taipei American School (TAS) is a large, English-language international school located in suburban Taipei that educates children from the international community from kindergarten through high school.

6B.   **JIĀO** and **JIĀOSHŪ**. When teaching in general is meant, the usual equivalent of the English word "teach" is the verb-object compound **jiāoshū**, which literally means "teach books." For example:

Wǒ xǐhuan jiāoshū.   "I like to teach."

Taipei American School

You could not just say ***Wǒ xǐhuan jiāo**, without the addition of the object **shū**, since that would be unclear and sound incomplete. Now, as with other verb-object compounds, if a specific object is meant (e.g., the teaching of a certain subject, or a certain level, or a certain person), then the general object **shū** is dropped and the specific object is added. Examples:

Tā jiāo Yīngwén.	"She teaches English."
Wáng Lǎoshī jīnnián jiāo yīniánjí le.	"Teacher Wang is teaching first grade this year."
Shéi jiāo nǐmen?	"Who is teaching you?"

Finally, note that **jiāo** is one of a small group of verbs that can take two objects. Examples:

Lǐ Lǎoshī jiāo wǒmen Zhōngwén.	"Professor Li is teaching us Chinese."
Shéi jiāo nǐmen Rìwén?	"Who is teaching you Japanese?"

6C.   **YĪNWEI...SUÓYI...** Yīnwei...suóyi... "because..." is our first example of so-called paired conjunctions or paired adverbs, of which there are many in Chinese. The thing to remember is that whereas in English one conjunction or one adverb usually suffices, in Chinese it often "takes two to tango," a conjunction or adverb in the first clause and another conjunction or adverb in the second clause being necessary to express the complete meaning. **Yīnwei** means "because"; **suóyi** when it occurs alone (as in line 2 of this conversation) means "therefore." However, the pattern **yīnwei...suóyi...**, lit. "because...therefore...," usually translates into English simply as "because." The **yīnwei** clause gives the reason and the **suóyi** clause tells the result. In Chinese, the "because" clause almost always comes first, while in English the clause with "because" often comes last. **Yīnwei** is like a moveable adverb and, if the subject of both clauses is the same, it may precede or follow the subject of the first clause; **suóyi** is unmovable and always appears at the beginning of the second clause. To sum up, the pattern is:

YĪNWEI	**First Clause (Reason)**	**SUÓYI**	**Second Clause (Result)**
Yīnwei	jīntiān shi xīngqītiān,	suóyi	yǔyán shíyànshì bù kāi.

"Because today is Sunday, (therefore) the language lab is closed."

Examples:

Tā yīnwei hěn máng, suóyi bù néng lái.

"She can't come because she's busy." (lit. "She because very busy, therefore not can come.")

Tā yīnwei méi xuéguo Zhōngwén, suóyi bù néng qù Zhōngguo.

"He can't go to China because he has never studied Chinese."

Yīnwei Xiǎo Wáng chángcháng chídào, suóyi jīnglǐ hěn bù gāoxìng.

"The manager is upset because Little Wang is often late."

Notice in the last example above that because the subject of the first clause is different from that of the second, the **yīnwei** must be placed before the first subject.

Always be careful to distinguish **yīnwei** "because" from **suóyi** "therefore"; don't mix up the two parts of this construction!

6D. **Néng** "be able, can" usually refers to physical ability. Compare **néng** with **kéyi** "can, may, be permitted" (5-1), which often refers to permission.

6E. The reason that **bàntiān** "half the day" occurs after the verb **gōngzuò** rather than before it is that it refers to "time spent" ("for half the day") rather than "time when" (4-1: 4A). We could add a "time when" expression to this sentence and say: **Wǒ míngtiān zhǐ néng gōngzuò bàntiān** "Tomorrow I can only work for half the day."

SV1-4. Intermediate Points of the Compass. The intermediate points of the compass are stated in Chinese in the opposite order from English. Chinese takes **nán** "south" and **běi** "north" as the two main points of reference while English takes "east" and "west" as its main points of reference. The terms for the intermediate points can be said alone or with the suffix **biān(r)** added at the end. Compare:

> When discussing the intermediate points of the compass, Chinese takes **nán** "south" and **běi** "north" as the two main points of reference while English takes "east" and "west" as its main points of reference.

dōngnán	or	**dōngnánbiān(r)**	"southeast" (lit. "east south")
dōngběi	or	**dōngběibiān(r)**	"northeast" (lit. "east north")
xī'nán	or	**xī'nánbiān(r)**	"southwest" (lit. "west south")
xīběi	or	**xīběibiān(r)**	"northwest" (lit. "west north")

SV7A. The question word **wèishemme** "why?" also functions as a moveable adverb and can, therefore, occur before either the verb or the subject of the sentence (unlike in Chinese, in English "why" must always precede the subject). At the end of questions containing **wèishemme**, there is frequently a sentence-final particle **ne**, which softens the tone of the question. Examples:

> **Nǐ wèishemme bù xué Zhōngwén ne?**
>
> "Why don't you learn Chinese?"

> **Wèishemme tā shuō Xiǎo Liú bú shi hǎo rén ne?**
>
> "Why did she say that Little Liu was not a good person?"

SV7B. Note **nán xué** "hard to learn." The stative verb **nán** followed by another verb can mean "hard to." Here is another example:

> **Lǎoshīde bàngōngshì hěn nán zhǎo.**   "The teacher's office is hard to find."

Sometimes **nán** followed by another verb can mean "be unpleasant to...." Examples: **nánchī** "be unappetizing," **nánkàn** "be ugly," and **nántīng** "be unpleasant to listen to."

Chat at the Chiang Kai-shek Memorial (cont.)

The Taiwanese man and Hammond continue talking about each other's families, then part company (continued from the previous conversation).

Basic Conversation 6-4

1. **TAIWANESE MAN**   Nǐ yǒu méiyou xiōngdì jiěmèi?
Do you have brothers or sisters?

2. **HAMMOND**   Wǒ yǒu yíge jiějie. Nǐ ne?
I have an older sister. And you?

3. **TAIWANESE MAN**   Wǒ zài wǒmen jiā páiháng lǎodà. Wǒ yǒu yíge dìdi, liǎngge mèimei.
I'm the oldest in our family. I have a younger brother and two younger sisters.

4. **HAMMOND**   Tāmen dōu zhùzai Táiběi ma?
Do they all live in Taipei?

5. **TAIWANESE MAN**   Wǒ dàmèi zhùzai Táiběi. Xiǎomèi zài Yīngguo liúxué. Wǒ dìdi yímín Àozhōu le.
My older younger sister lives in Taipei. My little sister is studying in England. My younger brother emigrated to Australia.

6. **HAMMOND**   Ò, duìbuqǐ, wǒ hái děi qù bàn yìdiǎn shì. Xiān zǒule.
Oh, sorry, I still have to go do something. I'll be on my way.

7. **TAIWANESE MAN**   Ò, wàngle zìwǒ jièshaole. Wǒ jiào Zhèng Détiān. Zhè shi wǒde míngpiàn.
Oh, I forgot to introduce myself. My name is Zheng Detian. This is my name card.

8. **HAMMOND**   Wǒ jiào Huáng Wén. Wǒ yě gěi nǐ yìzhāng míngpiàn
My name is Huang Wen. I'll also give you a name card.

9. **TAIWANESE MAN**   Yǐhòu yǒu jīhui zài liáo ba!
In the future if there's a chance let's chat again!

10. **HAMMOND**   Hǎo a.
Sure.

Build Up

1. Taiwanese man

xiōngdì	older and younger brothers [N]
jiěmèi	older and younger sisters [N]
xiōngdì jiěmèi	brothers and sisters, siblings
Nǐ yǒu méiyou xiōngdì jiěmèi?	Do you have brothers or sisters?

2. Hammond

Wǒ yǒu yíge jiějie. Nǐ ne?	I have an older sister. And you?

3. Taiwanese man

wǒmen jiā	our family
páiháng	one's seniority among siblings [N]
lǎo-	(indicates rank among siblings) [BF]
lǎodà	oldest (among siblings) [N]
páiháng lǎodà	rank is the oldest among one's siblings
Wǒ zài wǒmen jiā páiháng lǎodà.	I'm the oldest in our family.
Wǒ yǒu yíge dìdi, liǎngge mèimei.	I have a younger brother and two younger sisters.

4. Hammond

Tāmen dōu zhùzai Táiběi ma?	Do they all live in Taipei?

5. Taiwanese man

dàmèi	older younger sister [N]
xiǎomèi	younger younger sister [N]
liúxué	study as a foreign student [VO/V]
zài Yīngguo liúxué	study abroad in England
yímín	immigrate, emigrate [V]
Àozhōu (T)	Australia [PW]
yímín Àozhōu	immigrate to Australia
Wǒ dàmèi zhùzai Táiběi.	My older younger sister lives in Taipei.
Xiǎomèi zài Yīngguo liúxué.	My little sister is studying in England.
Wǒ dìdi yímín Àozhōu le.	My younger brother emigrated to Australia.

6. Hammond

Ò, duìbuqǐ, wǒ hái děi qù bàn yìdiǎn shì.	Oh, sorry, I still have to go do something.
Xiān zǒule.	I'll be on my way.

7. Taiwanese man

wàng	forget [V]
wàngle	forgot
zìwǒ jièshao	introduce oneself [PH]
wàngle zìwǒ jièshaole	(I) forgot to introduce myself
Zhèng	Zheng [SN]
Détiān	Detian (given name)
wǒ jiào Zhèng Détiān	my name is Zheng Detian
Ò, wàngle zìwǒ jièshaole. Wǒ jiào Zhèng Détiān.	Oh, I forgot to introduce myself. My name is Zheng
Zhè shi wǒde míngpiàn.	Detian. This is my name card.

8. Hammond

Huáng	Huang (lit. "yellow") [SN]
Wén	Wen (given name)
wǒ jiào Huáng Wén	my name is Huang Wen
gěi	give [V]

| gěi nǐ yìzhāng míngpiàn | give you a business card |
| Wǒ jiào Huáng Wén. Wǒ yě gěi nǐ yìzhāng míngpiàn. | My name is Huang Wen. I'll also give you a name card. |

9. **Taiwanese man**

yǐhòu	in the future [TW]
jīhui	opportunity, chance [N]
yǐhòu yǒu jīhui	in the future if there's a chance
liáo	chat [V]
zài liáo	chat again
Yǐhòu yǒu jīhui zài liáo ba!	In the future if there's a chance let's chat again!

10. **Hammond**

| Hǎo a. | Sure. |

Supplementary Vocabulary

A. KINSHIP TERMS

1. fùmǔ	parents [N]
2. zǔfù	paternal grandfather [N]
3. zǔmǔ	paternal grandmother [N]
4. wàizǔfù	maternal grandfather [N]
5. wàizǔmǔ	maternal grandmother [N]

B. GENERAL

6. Àodàlìyà (B)	Australia [PW]
7. gēn	with [CV]
liáotiān	chat [VO]
gēn péngyou liáotiān	chat with friends
Wǒ hěn xǐhuan gēn péngyou liáotiān.	I very much like to chat with friends.

Additional Vocabulary

1. dàgē	oldest brother [N]
2. dàjiě	oldest sister [N]
3. dà dìdi	older younger brother [N]
4. xiǎodì	little brother [N]

Grammatical and Cultural Notes

1.   The phrase **xiōngdì jiěmèi** literally means "older brother, younger brother, older sister, younger sister" but is often best translated as "siblings."

3A.   In Chinese families, one's rank in the family, in the order from oldest to youngest, is very important. This is the reason for expressions such as **páiháng** "one's seniority among siblings." The question form with **páiháng** is: **Nǐ zài nǐmen jiā páiháng lǎojǐ?** "In your family what is your seniority among your siblings?" If you get asked this question, be sure to answer **Wǒ zài wǒmen jiā páiháng…** "In our family I'm…" and be sure not to mix up **wǒ** and **nǐ**, as some foreign students of Chinese have done! Grammatically, the noun **páiháng** is the topic in all of these sentences and **lǎodà** or **lǎojǐ**, etc. is the comment.

3B.   **Lǎodà** means "oldest." **Lǎo'èr** would mean "second-oldest" (some male speakers prefer **lǎoliǎng** as **lǎo'èr** can have another meaning), **lǎosān** would be "third-oldest," and so forth. For "youngest in the family," some speakers say **lǎoyāo** while others say **lǎoxiǎo**. Distinguish carefully between **lǎodà, lǎo'èr, lǎosān,** and **lǎosì,** which indicate relative age in the family, and **dàyī, dà'èr, dàsān,** and **dàsì,** which indicate year in college.

5A.   The verb **liúxué** "study as a foreign student, study abroad" can function either as a verb-object compound (as in **Wǒ liúguo sānnián xué** "I studied abroad for three years") or as a regular verb (as in **Wǒ liúxuéguo sānnián,** with the same meaning). Recently it has even come to be used as a transitive verb, as in **liúxué Zhōngguo** "study abroad in China."

5B.   **Yímín** can also be used as a transitive verb: **yímín Àozhōu** "immigrate to Australia."

7A.   The verb **wàng** "forget" is common and useful; be sure not to forget it! Probably due to the nature of "forgetting," it frequently has a completed action **-le** attached to it. **Wàng** can also be used with the postverb **-zai** to create **wàngzai** "forget something in some place." Examples:

Duìbuqǐ, wǒ wàngle!	"Sorry, I forgot!"
Wǒ wàngle wǒ yào shuō shémme le.	"I forgot what I was going to say."
Nǐ bié wàngle dài nǐde míngpiàn, hǎo bu hǎo?	"Don't forget to bring your name cards, OK?"
Nǐ shuōde nèige dàizi, nǐ xiǎng nǐ wàngzai nǎr le?	"That bag you mentioned, where do you think you forgot it?"
Wǒ hǎoxiàng wàngzai péngyou jiā le.	"I think I forgot it at a friend's house."

7B.   The phrase **zìwǒ jièshao** "to self-introduce, to introduce oneself" is quite useful. If you wish to establish contact with someone and it is not feasible to have someone else introduce you, one formula you can make use of goes like this: **Nín hǎo! Wǒ zìwǒ jièshao yixia. Wǒ xìng ..., wǒ jiào ..., wǒ zài ... gōngzuò. Zhè shi wǒde míngpiàn, qǐng duō zhǐjiào! Qǐngwèn, nín guìxìng?** "How do you do? Let me introduce myself. My last name is ... , my full name is ... , I work at .... This is my name card, I'm much obliged. Excuse me, what is your last name?"

7C.   **-LE...LE** in Sentences with Non-Quantified Objects to Indicate Completed Action. There are two **le** in the sentence **Wǒ wàngle zìwǒ jièshao le** "I forgot to introduce myself." When there is an action verb in an affirmative sentence with a simple, non-quantified object present and the action of the verb has been completed, two **le** are employed. ("I bought a car" would be a sentence with a non-quantified object, while "I bought two cars" involves a quantified object, cf. 5-4: 1B.) The first **-le** is attached to the main verb while the second **le** occurs at the end of the sentence. The pattern is:

Subject	Verb Phrase	-LE	Object	LE
Wǒ	yǐjīng mǎi	le	bēibāo	le.

"I have already bought a backpack."

Some more sentences with the **-le...le** pattern:

Wǒ mǎile chē le.	"I bought a car."
Tā yǐjīng chīle fàn le.	"He already ate."
Tāmen yǐjīng dàole Běijīng le.	"They have already arrived in Beijing."
Wǒ guānle diànnǎo le.	"I turned off the computer."

The first **-le** (the verb **-le**) in double **le** sentences is often dropped, but we recommend that for now you use both **le**.

8A.   Be sure you pronounce the common surname **Huáng** "Yellow" differently from the even more common surname **Wáng** "King." The only—but important—difference between the two is strong friction deep in your throat on the **h** in **Huáng**.

8B.   In the sentence **Wǒ yě gěi nǐ yìzhāng míngpiàn** "I'll also give you a name card," **gěi** functions as a regular verb meaning "give." Notice that **gěi** here has two objects: the indirect object **nǐ** and the direct object **míngpiàn**.

You have now encountered these three different usages of **gěi**:

As a coverb meaning "for" (5-1: 8B):

> **Qǐng nǐ gěi wǒ mǎi yíge bēizi, hǎo ma?**
>
> Please buy a cup for me, all right?"

As a postverb meaning "give, for, to" (6-1: 8B):

> **Duìbuqǐ, wǒmen bù néng màigěi nǐ.**
>
> "Sorry, we can't sell it to you."

As a main verb meaning "give" (6-4: 8B):

> **Wǒ jīntiān xiān gěi nǐ èrshikuài, xíng ma?**
>
> "I'll give you twenty bucks for today, O.K.?"

9.   There is an implied conditional in the sentence **Yǐhòu yǒu jīhui zài liáo ba!** This sentence literally means "In the future there is a chance, let's chat again!," but here it must be understood as "In the future, IF there is a chance, let's chat again!" While there are specific words in Chinese for "if," it is very common to imply conditional meanings in this way. The **ba** at the end of the sentence is the **ba** indicating suggestions.

SV1-5, AV1-4. The Chinese Kinship System. The Chinese kinship system is very complex. However, due to the wide availability of birth control, the gradual urbanization of China, and the one-child policy of the Chinese government, the number of brothers, sisters, and other relatives that children have are rapidly diminishing, and occasions calling for the use of words like "aunt," "uncle," "cousin," "nephew," "niece" and so forth will gradually recede. Therefore, the words expressing these kinship relationships will in the future most likely reduce in frequency and number, meaning that the learning of Chinese will become somewhat easier. Indeed, it appears that the only relatives many Chinese children will have will be parents and two sets of grandparents vying to outdo each other in spoiling their grandchild!

The terms for grandparents given in supplementary vocabulary SV2-5 are the formal ones. There are also colloquial terms as follows:

yéye	"paternal grandfather"
nǎinai	"paternal grandmother"
lǎoye	"maternal grandfather"
lǎolao	"maternal grandmother"
wàipó	"maternal grandmother"

In the above Chinese kinship terms, notice the crucial distinction between paternal and maternal.

In AV1-4, below **dàgē** "eldest brother" there would be **èrgē** "older brother number two," **sān'gē** "older brother number three" and so on. Below **dàjiě** "eldest sister" there would be **èrjiě** "older sister number two," **sānjiě** "older sister number three" and so on. Younger brothers and sisters are also referred to by number in this way, e.g., **sāndì** "third-oldest younger brother" and **sìmèi** "fourth-oldest younger sister." Notice that, in all these cases, the ordinal number prefix **dì-** is not used.

SV7A.   The difference between **liáo** "chat" in line 9 and the verb-object compound **liáotiān** "chat" is that, if you have already said **liáotiān** or, from the context, it is clear that you mean "chatting," then it is sufficient to say only **liáo**. Otherwise, you should say **liáotiān**.

SV7B.   To say "chat with someone," one uses the coverb **gēn**, as in **gēn péngyou liáotiān** "chat with friends."

AV3.   Instead of **dà dìdi** "older younger brother," there are also some speakers who say **dàdì**.

Unit 6: Review and Study Guide

New Vocabulary

ADVERBS

zhēn	really

AUXILIARY VERBS

méiyou	(indicates past negative of action verbs)
néng	be able to, can
xǐhuan	like

BOUND FORMS

jīn	gold
lǎo-	(indicates rank among siblings)

CONJUNCTIONS

suóyi	therefore, so
yīnwei	because

COVERBS

gēn	with

INTERJECTIONS

m	(indicates something tastes delicious)

NOUNS

āyí	aunt (mother's sister)
dàmèi	older younger sister
érzi	son
fùmǔ	parents
hángkōng	aviation
jiěmèi	older and younger sisters
jīhui	opportunity, chance
lǎodà	oldest (among siblings)
lǐwù	gift, present
nánpéngyou	boyfriend, male friend
niánjí	grade, level (in school)
nǚ'ér	daughter
nǚpéngyou	girlfriend, female friend
páiháng	one's seniority among siblings
péngyou	friend
shūshu	uncle (father's younger brother)
táng	candy; sugar
wàizǔfù	maternal grandfather
wàizǔmǔ	maternal grandmother
xiǎohái(r)	small child, kid
xiǎomèi	younger younger sister
xiéhuì	association, society
xiōngdì	older and younger brothers
yìsi	meaning
zǔfù	paternal grandfather
zǔmǔ	paternal grandmother

PARTICLES

ei	(indicates liveliness)

PHRASES

hángkōng gōngsī	airline
zìwǒ jièshao	introduce oneself

PLACE WORDS

Àodàliyà	Australia
Àozhōu	Australia
chūzhōng	junior high school
dōngběi	northeast
dōngnán	southeast
gāozhōng	senior high school
Jiùjīnshān	San Francisco
Měiguo Zài Tái Xiéhuì	American Institute in Taiwan
nàli	there
Niǔyuē	New York
Táiběi Měiguo Xuéxiào	Taipei American School
xiǎoxué	elementary school
xīběi	northwest
xī'nán	southwest
Xī'nán Hángkōng Gōngsī	Southwest Airlines®
xuéxiào	school
zhèli	here
zhōngxué	middle school

POSTVERBS

-gěi	give; for, to

QUESTION WORDS

náli	where
wèishemme	why

RESULTATIVE COMPOUNDS

kànqilai	in the looking
zhǎngdà	grow up

RESULTATIVE ENDINGS

-dà	big
-qǐlai	in the VERBing

STATIVE VERBS

hǎochī	be good to eat, delicious
hǎokàn	be good-looking
jiù	be old (of things)
niánqīng	be young

SURNAMES

Huáng	Huang (lit. "yellow")
Jīn	gold
Zhèng	Zheng

TIME WORDS

chū'èr	second year in junior high school
chūsān	third year in junior high school
chūyī	first year in junior high school
dà'èr	sophomore year in college
dàsān	junior year in college
dàsì	senior year in college
dàyī	first year in college
gāo'èr	junior year in high school
gāosān	senior year in high school
gāoyī	sophomore year in high school
yǐhòu	in the future
yìniánjí	first grade

VERBS

fúwù	serve
gěi	give
jiāo	teach
liáo	chat
shàng	go to, attend
sòng	give (as a present)
wàng	forget
xǐhuan	like
yímín	immigrate, emigrate
zhǎng	grow
zuò	do, make

VERB-OBJECT COMPOUNDS

bānjiā	move one's home
jiāoshū	teach
jiéhūn	marry, get married
liáotiān	chat
líhūn	divorce, get divorced
liúxué	study as a foreign student
shàngbān(r)	work, go to work
shàngxué	attend school
xiàbān(r)	get off from work

Major New Grammar Patterns

School system and grade in school: xiǎoxué sānniánjí "third grade in elementary school," **chūyī** "seventh grade," **gāo'èr** "eleventh grade," **dàsān** "junior year in college," **jǐniánjí** "which grade?" (6-1)

-QILAI to indicate "in the (verb) -ing": Tā kànqilai hěn lǎo. "She looks very old." (6-2)

MÉIYOU to indicate past nega- tive of action verbs: **Tā méiyou qù.** "She didn't go." (6-3)

JIĀO and JIĀOSHŪ: Wǒ xǐhuan jiāoshū. "I like to teach." **Shéi jiāo nǐmen Yīngwén?** "Who is teaching you English?" (6-3)

YĪNWEI...SUÓYI...: Tā yīnwei hěn máng, suóyi bù néng lái. "Because she's busy, she can't come." (6-3)

Intermediate points of the compass: dōngnán "southeast," **dōngběi** "northeast," **xī'nán** "southwest," **xīběi** "northwest" (6-3)

...-LE...LE in sentences with non-quantified objects to indicate completed action: Wǒ wàngle zìwǒ jièshaole. "I forgot to introduce myself." (6-4)

Biographical Information (II)

COMMUNICATIVE OBJECTIVES

Once you have mastered this unit, you will be able to use Chinese to:

1. Inquire when and with whom someone arrived in a certain place and reply to the same questions when you are asked.

2. Ask people what languages they know and where they learned them, and answer the same questions when you are asked.

3. Discuss how well you speak, read, and write Chinese and other languages.

4. Respond appropriately if someone should praise your Chinese language proficiency.

5. Ask someone what they think of a certain country or city, and answer the same questions when you are asked.

6. Contrast different time periods and talk about the order of events: before, after, in the beginning, originally, formerly, later, etc.

7. Talk about your own and other people's cousins: male and female, older and younger, on your father's side and on your mother's side.

More Questions About One's Family

John Niu, a young Chinese-American who has just arrived in Beijing to study Chinese medicine, has been invited to have dinner with several of his relatives. Over dinner, he chats with an older cousin of his he has never met before who has come from out of town to see him.

Basic Conversation 7-1

1. AMERICAN **Biǎojiě, nǐmen jiā zhùzai nǎr a?**
Cousin, where does your family live?

2. CHINESE **Wǒmen zhùzai Tōng Xiàn, zài Běijīng chéngde dōngbianr.**
We live in Tong County, to the east of Beijing city.

3. AMERICAN **Ò. Nǐmen jiā dōu yǒu shémme rén a?**
Oh. Who all is there in your family?

4. CHINESE **Wǒ hé nǐ biǎojiěfu, hái yǒu yíge háizi.**
My husband and me, and also one child.

5. AMERICAN **Nánháir, nǚháir a? Duō dàle?**
Is it a boy or a girl? How old?

6. CHINESE **E, nǚháir, jīnnián jiǔsuì le.**
Uh, a girl, nine years old.

7. AMERICAN **Biǎojiě, nín zài nǎr gōngzuò a?**
Cousin, where do you work?

8. CHINESE **E, wǒ zài yòu'éryuán gōngzuò.**
Uh, I work in a kindergarten.

9. AMERICAN **Biǎojiěfu ne?**
And your husband?

10. CHINESE **Nǐ biǎojiěfu yuánlái zài yìjiā gōngchǎng gōngzuò. Yīnwei shēnti bú tài hǎo, suóyi ne, xiànzài gǎiháng le, zuò diǎnr xiǎo mǎimài.**
My husband used to work in a factory. Because his health isn't very good, he has now switched jobs and is in business for himself.

Build Up

1. American

biǎojiě — older female cousin of different surname [N]

Biǎojiě, nǐmen jiā zhùzai nǎr a? — Cousin, where does your family live?

2. Chinese

xiàn — county [N]

Tōng Xiàn — Tong County [PW]

Wǒmen zhùzai Tōng Xiàn, — We live in Tong County,

zài Běijīng chéngde dōngbianr. — to the east of Beijing city.

3. American

Ò. Nǐmen jiā dōu yǒu shémme rén a? — Oh. Who all is there in your family?

4. Chinese

hé — and [CJ]

biǎojiěfu — husband of older female cousin of different surname [N]

wǒ hé nǐ biǎojiěfu — I and your cousin's husband

hái — in addition [A]

hái yǒu — in addition there is

Wǒ hé nǐ biǎojiěfu, hái yǒu yíge háizi. — My husband and me, and also one child.

5. American

nánháir — boy [N]

nǚháir — girl [N]

Nánháir, nǚháir a? Duō dàle? — Is it a boy or a girl? How old?

6. Chinese

E, nǚháir, jīnnián jiǔsuì le. — Uh, a girl, nine years old.

7. American

Biǎojiě, nín zài nǎr gōngzuò a? — Cousin, where do you work?

8. Chinese

yòu'éryuán (B) — kindergarten [PW]

E, wǒ zài yòu'éryuán gōngzuò. — Uh, I work in a kindergarten.

9. American

Biǎojiěfu ne? — And your husband?

10. Chinese

yuánlái — originally, formerly [MA]

gōngchǎng — factory [PW]

yuánlái zài yìjiā gōngchǎng — formerly was at a factory

shēnti — body [N]

shēnti bú tài hǎo — be in poor health

ne — (pause filler) [P]

suóyi ne — therefore

gǎiháng — change one's line of work [VO]

mǎimài — buying and selling, business [N]

zuò mǎimài — do or engage in business [PH]

zuò xiǎo mǎimài — conduct business on a small scale

diǎn(r) — (short for **yìdiǎn[r]** "a little")

zuò diǎnr xiǎo mǎimài   do some small-scale business
Nǐ biǎojiěfu yuánlái zài yìjiā gōngchǎng gōngzuò.   My husband used to work in a factory.
Yīnwei shēnti bú tài hǎo, suóyi ne,   Because his health isn't very good, he has now
xiànzài gǎiháng le, zuò diǎnr xiǎo mǎimài.   switched jobs and is in business for himself.

Supplementary Vocabulary

    1. kǒu   (for people; lit. "mouth") [M]
    Tāmen jiā sānkǒu rén.   There are three people in their family.

    2. cóngqián   in the past, formerly [TW]
    Wǒ cóngqián zài yìjiā hěn dàde màoyì   I used to work at a large trading company.
    gōngsī gōngzuò.

Additional Vocabulary: More Cousins

    1. biǎogē   older male cousin of different surname [N]
    2. biǎodì   younger male cousin of different surname [N]
    3. biǎomèi   younger female cousin of different surname [N]
    4. tánggē   older male cousin of same surname [N]
    5. tángjiě   older female cousin of same surname [N]
    6. tángdì   younger male cousin of same surname [N]
    7. tángmèi   younger female cousin of same surname [N]

Grammatical and Cultural Notes

1A.   Note that the speaker addresses his cousin neither by the cousin's given name, nor as "Mrs.," but by the appropriate kinship term. This is evidence of the importance of kinship relationships in Chinese society.

1B.   Phonetic Changes in Sentence-Final Particle **A**. Note the varying pronunciations in this conversation of the sentence-final particle **a** (cf. 1-1: 3D). At the end of line 1, after the word **nǎr**, a sounds like **ra**. At the end of line 3, after the word **rén**, a sounds like **na**. At the end of line 5, after **nǚháir**, it again sounds like **ra**. In the next lesson (7-2), after the word **huà**, you will encounter another form of **a**, namely, **ya**. And in a later lesson, after the word **xíng**, we will see that **a** has yet one other common variant, **nga**. The basic principle behind these phonetic changes (called "assimilation" in linguistics) is that the sound directly preceding the **a** influences the pronunciation of **a** and is carried forward as the initial sound of **a**. Below are the rules for these phonetic changes of **a**. You don't need to learn the rules, but you should always listen carefully, remain receptive, and try your best to reproduce in your own speech what you hear Chinese native speakers say. In time, many of these phonetic changes will come naturally to you.

PRECEDING SYLLABLE ENDS IN	A CHANGES INTO	EXAMPLES
a, e, i, o, ai, ei, yu	ya	Hē ya! Nǐ ya! Wǒ ya! Mǎi ya! Qù ya!
u, ao, ou	wa	Zhū wa! Nǐ hǎo wa! Gǒu wa!
chi, r, ri, shi, zhi	ra	Chī ra! Nǎr ra? Xīngqīrì ra! Shì ra! Zhǐ ra!
n	na	Tā shi nǎrde rén na?
ng	nga	Zěmmeyàng nga?

2.   **Tōng Xiàn** "Tong County" was in 1997 upgraded into a district of Beijing, known as Tongzhou District. It is considered the eastern gateway to Beijing. However, as in this conversation, many speakers still use the former term.

Forbidden City, Beijing

3.   Notice the use of **dōu** in the question **Nǐmen jiā dōu yǒu shémme rén a?** "Who all is there in your family? or "Who all do you have in your family?" You had **dōu** previously to "look backward" to the subject or topic of a sentence and sum up a plurality of things or people that are in some way the same, e.g., **Tāmen dōu láile** "They all came," where the **dōu** refers to the preceding **tāmen**. The **dōu** in **Nǐmen jiā dōu yǒu shémme rén a?** is a different **dōu** which appears in questions only. It is a special "forward-looking" use of **dōu**, where **dōu** refers to the following object **rén**, not to the preceding subject **nǐmen**, with an answer consisting of more than one person expected. IMPORTANT WARNING: While **dōu** is used in the question, **dōu** cannot be used in the answer. In other words, you cannot answer the question **Nǐmen jiā dōu yǒu shémme rén?** with *Wǒmen jiā dōu yǒu... Instead, you should just answer: **Wǒmen jiā yǒu...** Another example of this kind of "forward-looking" **dōu** is: **Nǐmen dōu mǎile xiē shémme?** "What all did you buy?" And again, you would answer such a question **Wǒmen mǎile...** and could not answer it with *Wǒmen dōu mǎile...

4A.   Notice that in **Wǒ hé nǐ biǎojiěfu** "I and your cousin's husband (=my husband)" the **wǒ** occurs first and the other person afterwards. This is, of course, the reverse of the polite English order where one mentions the other person first; however, there is nothing impolite about the Chinese.

4B.   The conjunction **hé** "and" is similar in meaning to **gēn**, which you had in 2-4. Unlike **gēn**, which is used primarily in speech, **hé** can be used in speech or writing. Both of these conjunctions can ordinarily be used only to connect nouns or pronouns, not to connect verbs or clauses. So you CAN say **wǒ hé nǐ** "you and I" or **bēibāo gēn gōngshìbāo** "backpacks and briefcases," but you CANNOT say *Wǒ xǐhuan chīfàn hé wǒ xǐhuan shuìjiào "I like to eat and I like to sleep" (instead you could say **Wǒ xǐhuan chīfàn, yě xǐhuan shuìjiào**).

4C.   Many Chinese speakers in Taiwan pronounce the conjunction **hé** as **hàn**.

4D.   Notice in this line that, when the cousin refers to her husband, she uses neither his name nor the kinship term in relation to herself ("my husband"), but rather the kinship term in relation to the person to whom she is speaking ("your cousin's husband"). To use kinship terms from the point of view of the listener rather than that of the speaker is very common, especially when a more senior person is speaking to a more junior person.

5.   Choice-Type Questions with Choice Implied. There are several ways to indicate choice in Chinese. While there are explicit words for "or" which will be introduced later, one of the most common ways to indicate alternatives is simply by listing them, one directly after another. Such questions are called choice-type questions with choice implied. The pattern is:

Choice1	Choice2
Nánháir	nǚháir?

"A boy or a girl?" (lit. "Boy girl?")

Some more examples of choice-type questions with choice implied:

Nǐ yào zhèige yào nèige?

"Do you want this one or do you want that one?" (lit. "You want this one want that one?")

> **Zhèr hǎo nàr hǎo?**
>
> "Is it better here (in China) or there (in America)?"

8.   An alternate word for **yòu'éryuán** "kindergarten" that you will hear in Taiwan and occasionally elsewhere is **yòuzhìyuán**.

10A.   While English employs verb endings to indicate time, Chinese often employs adverbs. One common moveable adverb that can indicate time is **yuánlái** "originally, formerly." Some more examples:

> **Wǒ yuánlái zài zhōngxué jiāoshū.**
>
> "I used to teach at a middle school."

> **Lǎo Liú yuánlái zhùzai Nánjīng, qùnián bāndao Běijīng le.**
>
> "Old Liu used to live in Nanjing. Last year he moved to Beijing."

10B.   Note the phrase **suóyi ne, ...** "therefore, ..." The particle **ne** is here a pause filler after the **suóyi**. Using it gives the speaker more time to plan the rest of her utterance and makes her speech seem smoother, since a pause after **suóyi** would sound abrupt and awkward. Here are some other common examples of **ne** as a pause filler after introductory expressions:

> **Xiànzài ne, ...**   "Now, ..."
>
> **Kěshi ne, ...**   "But, ..."
>
> **Búguò ne, ...**   "However, ..."

10C.   In the conversation for listening for this part, the term **gǎiháng** "change one's line of work" is pronounced with an (**r**) suffix as **gǎihángr**. This is an example of Beijing dialect. We recommend that in your own speech, you use the Standard Mandarin pronunciation **gǎiháng**.

10D.   Note in this line the expression **zuò mǎimài** "do or engage in business" (lit. "do buy-sell"). A colloquial word for "business person" is **zuò mǎimàide**, lit. "one who does business." On the same pattern we can create **mài dōngxide** "someone who sells things, a vendor" and **zuòfànde** "someone who makes food, a cook."

SV1A.   The measure **kǒu** means "mouth" in Classical Chinese and is, in Modern Chinese, often used when discussing numbers of people or population (since one more person is one more "mouth" to feed). While it is fine to say **sān'ge rén** "three people," when discussing how many people there are in one's family, many Chinese will say **sānkǒu rén**. Here is another example with **kǒu**:

> **Nǐmen jiāli yǒu jǐkǒu rén?**   "How many people are there in your family?"

SV1B.   This sentence can be analyzed as a topic (**tāmen jiā**) followed by a comment (**sānkǒu rén**); the meaning is something like "As for their family, it's a situation of three people." It would, of course, also be quite correct to add a verb **yǒu** and say **Tāmen jiā yǒu sānkǒu rén** "Their family has three people"; that sentence would be a subject + predicate sentence like the English.

SV2.   The moveable adverb **cóngqián** means "in the past, formerly." Be careful about the pronunciation of this word; remember that Pinyin **c-** sounds like a strong English "ts" and that Pinyin **q-** sounds somewhat like a strong English "ch." **Yuánlái**, which you saw in line 10 of this conversation, overlaps in meaning with **cóngqián**, but **yuánlái** can also have the meaning "originally."

AV1-7.   Given the one-child per family policy in China, the various words meaning cousin are now used less than before. In fact, the terms for sibling (**gēge, dìdi, jiějie, mèimei**) are now often used to replace those for cousin. We recommend you still use the traditional terms for cousin, but if you hear, for example, **jiějie**, be aware that **biǎojiě** may actually be meant.

"You Can Speak Chinese!"

Lisa Olsen, a young American woman who is working and studying in Beijing, has been invited to a dinner banquet. Next to her is sitting a Chinese woman whom she has never met before. The woman has smiled at her shyly several times as if she would like to start a conversation. Olsen plucks up her courage and decides to say something to the woman.

Basic Conversation 7-2

| 1. OLSEN | **Nín hǎo!** |
| | How are you? |

| 2. CHINESE WOMAN | **Nín hǎo! Nín huì shuō Zhōngguo huà ya!** |
| | How are you? You can speak Chinese! |

| 3. OLSEN | **Huì yìdiǎnr.** |
| | I know a little. |

| 4. CHINESE WOMAN | **Ò, nín shuōde bú cuò ma! Shi zài nǎr xuéde?** |
| | Oh, you really speak quite well! Where did you learn? |

| 5. OLSEN | **Yuánlái wǒ zài Měiguo xuéguo yìdiǎnr. Xiànzài zài Běijīng Yǔyán Wénhuà Dàxué jìxù xué.** |
| | I learned some in America before. Now I'm continuing my study of it at Beijing Language and Culture University. |

| 6. CHINESE WOMAN | **Nín huì xiě Zhōngguo zìr ma?** |
| | Do you know how to write Chinese characters? |

| 7. OLSEN | **Wǒ rènshi jǐbǎige Zhōngguo zì. Yǒude yě huì xiě, yǒude bú huì.** |
| | I recognize several hundred Chinese characters. Some I can also write, others I can't. |

| 8. CHINESE WOMAN | **Nín hái huì qítāde yǔyán ma?** |
| | Do you know any other languages? |

| 9. OLSEN | **Wǒ yǐqián huì shuō yìdiǎnr Xībānyáyǔ, kěshi xiànzài quán wàngle.** |
| | I used to be able to speak a little Spanish, but now I've completely forgotten. |

PART 2

Build Up

---

1. Olsen

Nín hǎo!	How are you?

---

2. Chinese woman

huì	know how to, can [AV]
huà	word, language [N]
shuōhuà	speak words, speak [VO]
Zhōngguo huà	spoken Chinese [PH]
huì shuō Zhōngguo huà	can speak Chinese
ya	(form of the particle **a** used after words ending in **-a** or **-i**) [P]
Nín hǎo! Nín huì shuō Zhōngguo huà ya!	How are you? You can speak Chinese!

---

3. Olsen

Huì yìdiǎnr.	I know a little.

---

4. Chinese woman

-de	(verb suffix that indicates manner) [P]
bú cuò	"not bad," "quite good" [IE]
shuōde bú cuò	speak quite well
ma	(indicates something obvious) [P]
Ò, nín shuōde bú cuò ma! Shi zài nǎr xuéde?	Oh, you really speak quite well! Where did you learn?

---

5. Olsen

Běijīng Yǔyán Wénhuà Dàxué	Beijing Language and Culture University [PW]
jìxù	continue [V/AV]
jìxù xué	continue to learn
Yuánlái wǒ zài Měiguo xuéguo yìdiǎnr.	I learned some in America before. Now I'm
Xiànzài zài Běijīng Yǔyán Wénhuà Dàxué jìxù xué.	continuing my study of it at Beijing Language and Culture University.

---

6. Chinese woman

xiě	write [V]
zì(r)	character, word [N]
xiězì(r)	write characters, write [VO]
Zhōngguo zì(r)	Chinese character [PH]
xiě Zhōngguo zì(r)	write Chinese characters
Nín huì xiě Zhōngguo zìr ma?	Do you know how to write Chinese characters?

---

7. Olsen

rènshi	recognize [V]
jǐ-	a few, several [NU]
jǐbǎige	several hundred
yǒude	some [AT/PR]
yǒude yě huì xiě	some I also can write
yǒude bú huì	others I don't know
Wǒ rènshi jǐbǎige Zhōngguo zì. Yǒude yě huì xiě, yǒude bú huì.	I recognize several hundred Chinese characters. Some I can also write, others I can't.

---

8. Chinese woman

qítā	other [AT]
qítāde yǔyán	other languages
Nín hái huì qítāde yǔyán ma?	Do you know any other languages?

9. Olsen

yǐqián	before, formerly [TW]
wǒ yǐqián huì shuō	I used to know how to speak
Xībānyáyǔ	Spanish (language) [N]
yìdiǎnr Xībānyáyǔ	a little Spanish
quán	completely [A]
quán wàngle	completely forgot
Wǒ yǐqián huì shuō yìdiǎnr Xībānyáyǔ, kěshi xiànzài quán wàngle.	I used to be able to speak a little Spanish, but now I've completely forgotten.

Supplementary Vocabulary: Talking About Languages

1. **Yīngyǔ**	English (language) [N]
Nǐde Yīngyǔ shi zài nǎr xuéde?	Where did you learn your English?
2. **Fǎyǔ**	French (language) [N]
Tā huì bú huì shuō Fǎyǔ?	Does he speak French?
3. **yǒu rén**	there are people, some people
yǒu rén shuō	some people say that
Déyǔ	German (language) [N]
Yǒu rén shuō Déyǔ hěn nán xué.	Some people say German is hard to learn.
4. **Rìyǔ**	Japanese (language) [N]
Wǒde Rìyǔ quán wàngle.	I completely forgot my Japanese.
5. **Pǔtōnghuà (B)**	Mandarin (language) [N]
Nǐde Pǔtōnghuà shuōde bú cuò.	You speak Mandarin very well.
6. **Hànzì**	Chinese character [N]
Nǐ huì xiě duōshǎo Hànzì?	How many characters can you write?

Additional Vocabulary: More Languages

A. MODERN LANGUAGES

1. **Ālābóyǔ**	Arabic (language) [N]
2. **Xībóláiyǔ**	Hebrew (language) [N]
3. **Yìdàlìyǔ**	Italian (language) [N]
4. **Hányǔ**	Korean (language) [N]
5. **Éyǔ**	Russian (language) [N]
6. **Yuènányǔ**	Vietnamese (language) [N]

B. CLASSICAL LANGUAGES

7. **Gǔdài Hànyǔ**	Classical Chinese (language) [N]
8. **Xīlàwén**	Greek (language) [N]
9. **Lādīngwén**	Latin (language) [N]

C. CHINESE DIALECTS

10. **fāngyán**	dialect [N]
11. **Guǎngdōng huà**	Cantonese [PH]
12. **Fúzhōu huà**	Fuzhou [PH]
13. **Kèjiā huà**	Hakka [PH]
14. **Shànghǎi huà**	Shanghai [PH]

15. **Táiwān huà**   Taiwanese [PH]
16. **Cháozhōu huà**   Teochew [PH]
17. **Táishān huà**   Toishan [PH]

Grammatical and Cultural Notes

1. Notice how the American student plucks up her courage and takes the initiative in speaking to the Chinese woman seated next to her. You will often have to take the first step in communicating in Chinese with Chinese people; the Chinese persons next to you may be just as eager to converse with you as you are to converse with them, but they could be shy and may be terrified that you speak only English and that communication will falter.

2A. Chinese Equivalents of English "Know." **Huì** is the verb for "know" in the sense of "know how to, have learned how to, can." Distinguish it from two other verbs which you have had that also often translate as "know": **zhīdao** "know a fact" or "know of someone" (5-1) and **rènshi** "know someone, be acquainted with someone" (2-2). Contrast the following sentences:

Nǐ huì shuō Zhōngguo huà ma?	"Do you know how to speak Chinese?"
Nǐ zhīdao Chéngdū zài nǎr ma?	"Do you know where Chengdu is?"
Nǐ rènshi nèige rén ma?	"Do you know that person?"

In English we sometimes use the verb "speak" in the sense of "know how to speak," e.g., "Do you speak Chinese?" In Chinese, this is best rendered with **huì** as **Nǐ huì shuō Zhōngguo huà ma?** or **Nǐ huì bu huì shuō Zhōngguo huà?** One would ordinarily not omit **huì** and say *Nǐ shuō Zhōngguo huà ma? or *Nǐ shuō bu shuō Zhōngguo huà? Also, note that, as with most other main verbs and auxiliary verbs that express states and emotions, **huì** can express past time without the use of any verb suffixes like **-le**. So to say "Were you able to speak Chinese last year?," you would say **Qùnián nǐ huì bu huì shuō Zhōngguo huà?**

When pronouncing **huì**, be sure to make the initial **h-** strong and "rough" enough, so that **huì** does not sound like **wèi**. To help with that, practice saying the following sentence: **Zhèiwèi bú huì!** "This one doesn't know how!" The **huì** should sound very different from the **wèi**.

2B. Chinese Equivalents of English "Can." In addition to translating as "know how," **huì** can also be translated as "can." Be careful to distinguish it from two other verbs you have had that also often translate as "can"; these are **kéyi**, which means "can" in the sense of "may, be permitted to" and **néng**, which means "can" in the sense of "be physically able to." Contrast the following:

Tā huì shuōhuà ma?

"Can she speak?" (e.g., has that baby already learned how to speak)

Tā néng shuōhuà ma?

"Can she speak?" (e.g., is that person physically able to speak, after her recent case of laryngitis)

Tā kéyi shuōhuà ma?

"Can she speak?" (e.g., may she or does she have permission to speak)

If you want to say that you know a certain language, don't say *Wǒ kéyi shuō...; instead, you should say **Wǒ huì shuō...**

2C. Note the very important and common verb-object compound **shuōhuà** "speak, talk" (lit. "say words"). Example:

Nèige rén bù cháng shuōhuà. "That person doesn't often speak."

As we noted in note 5-2: SV2 on verb-object compounds, if a specific object is used (that is to say, if you want to say not only that someone is speaking but that they are speaking something, like a language), then the general object (here **huà**) is dropped. Thus, to say "I like to speak Chinese," one would say:

> **Wǒ xǐhuan shuō Zhōngguo huà.**

You could NEVER say ***Wǒ xǐhuan shuōhuà Zhōngguo huà.**

2D.   Terms for "Chinese Language." Due to the linguistic and political history of China over the past century, there have come to be in common use several competing terms to refer to "Chinese language" or "Mandarin," which can be rather confusing for the beginning student. The traditional term for spoken Chinese, which is still used in non-technical conversation wherever Chinese is spoken, is **Zhōngguo huà** "Chinese speech." The traditional term for written Chinese, which can also be used everywhere, is **Zhōngwén** (some people use **Zhōngwén** to refer to spoken Chinese as well, though purists would criticize such usage). In China, and increasingly in Hong Kong and Macao, the official term for "Mandarin" is **Pǔtōnghuà** "common speech." **Hànyǔ** "language of the Han people" is also often used in China as an equivalent of **Pǔtōnghuà** although, strictly speaking, **Hànyǔ** includes the other Chinese dialects as well as Mandarin. The term **Guóyǔ** "national language" was used in all of China from 1918 until the 1950s to refer to Mandarin and is still so used in Taiwan, Hong Kong, and Macao. **Huáyǔ** "Chinese language" is the term used for Mandarin in Singapore and Malaysia. Thus, all of the following are possible equivalents of "You speak Chinese quite well":

> **Nǐde Zhōngguo huà shuōde bú cuò!** (everywhere; colloquial and a bit old-fashioned)
>
> **Nǐde Zhōngwén shuōde bú cuò!** (everywhere, but purists believe **Zhōngwén** should refer only to written Chinese)
>
> **Nǐde Pǔtōnghuà shuōde bú cuò!** (China, Hong Kong, Macao)
>
> **Nǐde Hànyǔ shuōde bú cuò!** (China)
>
> **Nǐde Guóyǔ shuōde bú cuò!** (Taiwan, Hong Kong, Macao)
>
> **Nǐde Huáyǔ shuōde bú cuò!** (Singapore, Malaysia)

Our recommendation to you is: (1) be prepared to understand any of the above terms when you hear them; (2) if you are aware of what terms your interlocutors prefer, follow their usage; (3) when in doubt, use **Zhōngguo huà** for "spoken Chinese" and **Zhōngwén** for "written Chinese."

2E.   Although the situation is beginning to change, many Chinese are still surprised when a foreigner can speak Chinese. The assumption is often that foreigners can speak only English. Also, while in this conversation the Chinese lady is willing to speak in Chinese, some Chinese who have studied English will answer the non-native's Chinese questions in English, and other Chinese who don't know much English may reply by saying: "Sorry, no English!" (meaning "Sorry, I don't speak any English"). What to do if you would like to speak Chinese but your Chinese interlocutor prefers speaking English? Of course, we encourage you to use your Chinese as much as possible, since this is the only way to become fluent. However, if the other party's proficiency in English is clearly superior to your own proficiency in Chinese and they prefer using English, it would be rude for you to insist on speaking to them in Chinese. (This could be interpreted as meaning "I think that your English is poor and my Chinese is better" and might cause them and you to lose face.) Don't worry, you will meet plenty of Chinese who will be willing to speak Chinese with you, especially once your Chinese is above the beginning level. At the same time, even if you're speaking in English to a Chinese person, be aware that your knowledge of Chinese language, society, and culture is still relevant and important; you should not talk to them in exactly the same way you would speak to an American. To some degree, the conventions of cross-cultural communication are required for effective interaction.

3.   To say "I know a little Chinese," say **Wǒ huì shuō yidianr Zhōngguo huà** or **Wǒ huì yidianr Zhōngguo huà** (you CANNOT put the **yidianr** at the end of the sentence and say ***Wǒ huì shuō Zhōngguo huà yidianr**). To say "I know (a) very little," say **Wǒ huì yìdiǎndiǎn** (you CANNOT say ***Wǒ huì hěn yìdiǎnr** since, in Chinese, adverbs like **hěn** may only precede verbs or other adverbs).

4A.   **-DE** After Verbs to Indicate Manner. In this line, examine the phrase **nín shuōde bú cuò** "you speak well."

The particle **-de** occuring after a verb and before a complement expressing manner indicates the manner in which the action of the verb is, was, or will be performed. The pattern is:

Topic	Verb	-DE	Complement
Nín	shuō	de	bú cuò.

"You speak well."

Here are some more examples:

Nǐ láide tài zǎo.	"You came too early."
Xiǎoháir zhǎngde tài kuàile!	"Kids grow up too quickly!"
Wǒ zuótiān yèli shuìde bú tài hǎo.	"Last night I didn't sleep very well."
Zhèige lǐbài bēibāo màide hěn hǎo.	"This week backpacks have been selling very well."

If you want to express manner and the main verb of the sentence consists of a verb-object compound, you should first state the topic with the verb-object compound in its basic form, and then repeat only the verb (not the object), followed by **-de** and the complement expressing manner. Examples:

Topic	Verb	-DE	Complement
Tā chīfàn	chī	de	hěn dà shēng.

"He eats very loudly."

Topic	Verb	-DE	Complement
Tā xiě Zhōngguo zì	xiě	de	hěn hǎokàn.

"Her Chinese characters look good." (lit. "She writes Chinese characters very attractively.")

Some more examples:

Tāmen xué Zhōngwén xuéde hěn màn.	"They are learning Chinese very slowly."
Liú Lǎoshī jiāoshū jiāode bú cuò.	"Mr. Liu teaches quite well."
Wǒmen liáotiān liáode hěn gāoxìng.	"We chatted very happily."
Tā shuō Zhōngguo huà shuōde hěn hǎo.	"He speaks Chinese very well."

4B.   The expression **bú cuò**, literally "not bad," is actually the equivalent of English "pretty good." Chinese speakers in general have a strong preference for indicating meaning indirectly through understatement or double negatives rather than directly. They often feel that speaking too directly could embarrass the other party if he or she should disagree, or cause loss of face for the speaker if he or she should later be proven wrong. Some more examples of this phenomenon:

bù duō	"not many"	= "few"
bù shǎo	"not few"	= "many"
bù hǎochī	"not good-tasting"	= "tastes bad"
bù hǎokàn	"not good-looking"	= "ugly"
bù gāoxìng	"not happy"	= "upset, angry"
bú tài hǎo	"not too good"	= "quite bad"
bú tài guì	"not too expensive"	= "rather inexpensive"

4C.   **MA** to Indicate an Obvious Situation. The particle **ma** occurring at the end of a sentence can indicate that something is obvious to the speaker, and that the speaker believes it must also be obvious to the listener. The pattern is:

Statement	MA
Nàrde dōngxi tǐng guì	ma!

"The things there are quite expensive, you know!"

While the question particle **ma** which you were introduced to in 1-2 is accompanied by high pitch, the **ma** which indicates obviousness is accompanied by low pitch. Contrast:

Question **ma** accompanied by high pitch:

> **Tā bú huì ma?** "She doesn't know how?"

Obvious Situation **ma** accompanied by low pitch:

> **Tā bú huì ma!** "She doesn't know how (and that's pretty obvious to me, and I'd think it would be obvious to you as well)!"

Be aware that very frequent use of this new low-pitch **ma** that indicates an obvious situation is considered by some speakers as effeminate.

4D. **(Nín) shi zài nǎr xuéde?** "Where did you learn?" This is an example of **shi...-de** expressing the place of a known past action (4-2: 3A). The reason you don't use completed action **-le** here is because the fact that the learning has occurred is already known; the focus here is on where that known action, i.e., the learning, took place. Be careful to distinguish the **-de** of the **shi...-de** pattern from the **-de** after verbs that indicates manner, as in **nín shuōde bú cuò** "you speak well" (cf. 4A in this lesson).

5. With over 13,000 students, **Běijīng Yǔyán Wénhuà Dàxué** "Beijing Language and Culture University," commonly abbreviated in Chinese as **Běiyǔ**, is the largest institution in China specializing in language instruction. One of its best known programs specializes in teaching Mandarin to speakers of other languages. While the official English name of this institution is still "Beijing Language and Culture University," the official Chinese name was recently abbreviated to **Běijīng Yǔyán Dàxué** (lit. "Beijing Language University"), resulting in the popular joke that "**Běijīng Yǔyán Dàxué méiyou wénhuà le!**" "Beijing Language University doesn't have culture anymore!"

6. The expression for "Chinese character" is **Zhōngguo zì(r)** or, as introduced in SV6, **Hànzì**. It is NOT possible to say *Zhōngwén zì. As a noun, **zì(r)** must preceded by the general measure **ge** when it is counted or specified. So to say "I know about 200 Chinese characters," you should say **Wǒ rènshi chàbuduō liǎngbǎige Zhōngguo zì**. You could NOT omit the **ge** and say *Wǒ rènshi chàbuduō liǎngbǎi Zhōngguo zì.

7A. In this line we encounter a new usage of **rènshi**, namely, "recognize" (in this case, recognizing Chinese characters). To render the English "I don't know this character," in Chinese one would say **Wǒ bú rènshi zhèige zì** "I don't recognize this character"; it would NOT be correct to say *Wǒ bù zhīdào zhèige zì (cf. note 2A above). However, if you recognized a character but didn't know its meaning, you could say **Wǒ rènshi zhèige zì, búguò wǒ bù zhīdào zhèige zì zài zhèli shi shémme yìsi** "I recognize this character, but I don't know what its meaning is here." By the way, the expression for "to be literate" is **rènshi zì** (lit. "recognize characters"); so to say "That old man is illiterate," you would say **Nèiwèi lǎo xiānsheng bú rènshi zì**.

7B. Question Words Used as Indefinites. Question words when spoken with light stress and normal (rather than high) pitch may have indefinite meanings rather than be indicating questions. This is usually clear from the context. Your first example of a question word used as an indefinite is **jǐ-**, which normally means "how many" but can, when used as an indefinite, mean "some" or "several." Contrast:

> **(1) a. Nǐ rènshi jǐbǎige Zhōngguo zì?** (question, high pitch)
>
> "How many hundred Chinese characters do you know?"
>
> **b. Wǒ rènshi jǐbǎige Zhōngguo zì.** (statement, normal pitch)
>
> "I know several hundred Chinese characters."
>
> **(2) a. Nǐ yǒu jǐkuài qián?** (question, high pitch)
>
> "How many dollars do you have?"
>
> **b. Wǒ zhǐ yǒu jǐkuài qián.** (statement, normal pitch)
>
> "I only have a couple of dollars."

Note that **jǐ-** must always be used with a measure. Thus, for "several hundred characters," one must say **jǐbǎige zì** and could NEVER say *****jǐbǎi zì**. Also, contrast carefully the pronunciation of the first syllable of the following question and answer:

> **Jǐbǎige?** "How many hundred?"
>
> **Qībǎige!** "Seven hundred!"

7C.   YǑUDE...YǑUDE... "some...others..." The pattern **yǒude...yǒude...** that occurs for the first time in this sentence is both common and useful. Let's first take a look at **yǒude** alone. One way to express "some" in Chinese is with the expression **yǒude** preceding a noun. For example:

yǒude rén	"some people"
yǒude lǎoshī	"some teachers"
yǒude zì	"some characters."

In the case of all of these noun expressions consisting of **yǒude** plus a noun, you can also leave off the noun, and what then remains is the pronoun **yǒude** "some." **Yǒude** derives, as you may have guessed, from the verb **yǒu** "there is/are." So if one says **yǒude zì** "some characters," one is literally saying "characters which there are"; and if one says **yǒude**, one is literally saying "those which there are."

IMPORTANT NOTE: **Yǒude** can be used only before the subject or topic of a sentence; it CANNOT be used in front of the object. Therefore, while you CAN say **Yǒude Zhōngguo zì wǒ huì xiě** "Some Chinese characters I can write," you CANNOT say *****Wǒ huì xiě yǒude Zhōngguo zì** "I can write some Chinese characters."

Yǒude frequently occurs in the pattern **yǒude...yǒude...** "some...some..." or "some...others...." The basic pattern is:

Topic1	Comment1	Topic2	Comment2
Yǒude zì	wǒ huì xiě,	yǒude	hái bú huì.

"Some of the characters I know how to write, others I don't know yet."

Here, now, are several additional examples of this common pattern:

Yǒude láile, yǒude méi lái.	"Some came, some didn't come."
Yǒude huì, yǒude bú huì.	"Some (e.g., people) know it, others don't." or "Some (e.g., Chinese characters) I know, others I don't."
Yǒude wǒ mǎile, yǒude wǒ méi mǎi.	"I bought some, I didn't buy others."
Yǒude shi wǒde, yǒude bú shi wǒde.	"Some are mine, some are not mine."
Yǒude rén yǐjīng zhīdao, yǒude hái bù zhīdào.	"Some people already know, others don't know yet."
Yǒude dìfang hěn nán, yǒude dìfang bú tài nán.	"Some parts were hard, other parts were not too hard." (e.g., of a book or movie)

8.   Carefully distinguish the different pronunciations and meanings of **hái** "in addition" and **huì** "can."

9.   **Xībānyáyǔ** "Spanish language" is sometimes abbreviated as **Xīyǔ**.

SV1-6 AND AV1-17. Names of Languages. The traditional way of referring to spoken languages is to give the name of the country followed by **huà** "speech," e.g., **Déguo huà** "spoken German," **Fǎguo huà** "spoken French," etc. This usage is still common in everyday, non-technical conversation. Note that **Yīngguo huà** "spoken English" is not often said; usually **Yīngwén** or **Yīngyǔ** is used instead. To specify "American English," you can say **Měiyǔ**.

The more modern and "scientific" way to refer to different languages is by means of the final syllable **-yǔ** "language." In general, to create the name of the language from the name of the country, drop **guo** (if present) and add **-yǔ**:

Yīngguo	→	Yīngyǔ	"English"
Yìdàlì	→	Yìdàlìyǔ	"Italian"
Déguo	→	Déyǔ	"German"

But note that you can NEVER say *Zhōngyǔ for "Chinese."

When reference is primarily to the written language, the syllable **-wén** is often used in conjunction with the first syllable of the name of the country, e.g., **Yīngwén** "English." Some speakers also use the terms ending in **-wén** to refer to the spoken language, while other speakers would consider that poor usage. In general, to use **-wén** to create the name of the written language from the name of the country, drop **guo** (if present) and add **-wén**:

Yīngguo	→	Yīngwén	"(written) English"
Yìdàlì	→	Yìdàlìwén	"(written) Italian"
Déguo	→	Déwén	"(written) German"
Zhōngguo	→	Zhōngwén	"(written) Chinese"

SV2. An alternate pronunciation of **Fǎyǔ** "French (language)" that you will hear in Taiwan and occasionally elsewhere is **Fàyǔ**.

SV3. Note that **shuō** means not only "speak" but also "say," in the sense that "(someone) says (something)."

SV5. **Pǔtōnghuà**, literally "common speech," is the word used in China for "Mandarin." It is composed of the stative verb **pǔtōng** "be common" plus the noun **huà** "speech."

AV1-17. The names of these modern languages, classical languages, and Chinese dialects are arranged in alphabetical order of the English equivalents within each group.

AV4. There are several words for Korean. Besides **Hányǔ**, another common term for "spoken Korean" is **Hánguo huà**. If you mean "written Korean," you can say **Hánwén**. Yet another term for "Korean language" that is sometimes encountered is **Cháoxiǎnyǔ**.

AV5. An alternate pronunciation of **Éyǔ** "Russian" that you will hear in Taiwan and occasionally elsewhere is **Èyǔ**.

AV7. Synonyms for **Gǔdài Hànyǔ** "Classical Chinese" that you will hear occasionally include **Gǔ Hànyǔ**, **Gǔwén**, and **Wényánwén**.

AV10-17. As was discussed in the introduction to this volume, these so-called Chinese "dialects" are really different languages, from a linguistic point of view.

The Nosy Professor

Eric Bigelow, an American graduate student, is speaking with one of his professors outside the Foreign Students Guest House on the campus of Capital University of Economics and Business in Beijing. Although Bigelow has been taking one of the professor's classes for several weeks, this is the first time the two have spoken at any length.

Basic Conversation 7-3

1. CHINESE PROFESSOR **Nǐ shémme shíhou dào Běijīngde?**
   When did you arrive in Beijing?

2. BIGELOW **Wǒ shi jīnnián èr yuèfen dàode.**
   I arrived in February of this year.

3. CHINESE PROFESSOR **Nǐ yíge rén láide ma?**
   Did you come alone?

4. BIGELOW **Bù, hé wǒ àirén yìqǐ láide.**
   No, I came together with my wife.

5. CHINESE PROFESSOR **Nǐ zài nǎr xuéde Zhōngwén? Shì bu shi yǐqián zài Zhōngguo xuéguo?**
   Where did you learn Chinese? Had you learned it in China before?

6. BIGELOW **Kāishǐ shi zài Měiguo xuéde. Hòulái yòu zài Táiwān xuéle yíduànr shíjiān.**
   At first I studied it in the States. Later I studied for a while in Taiwan.

7. CHINESE PROFESSOR **Nánguài nǐde Hànyǔ jiǎngde zhèmme hǎo.**
   No wonder you speak Chinese so well.

8. BIGELOW **Náli, náli. Hái chàde hěn yuǎn ne!**
   Not at all. I still have a long ways to go!

Build Up

1. Chinese professor
   shíhou(r) — time [N]
   shémme shíhou — what time
   Nǐ shémme shíhou dào Běijīngde? — When did you arrive in Beijing?

2. Bigelow

yuèfen(r)	month [N]
èr yuèfen	February
jīnnián èr yuèfen	this year in February
Wǒ shi jīnnián èr yuèfen dàode.	I arrived in February of this year.

3. Chinese professor

yíge rén	by oneself, alone [PH]
yíge rén lái	come alone
Nǐ yíge rén láide ma?	Did you come alone?

4. Bigelow

hé	with [CV]
yìqǐ	together [A/PW]
hé wǒ àirén yìqǐ	together with my wife
hé wǒ àirén yìqǐ lái	come together with my wife
Bù, hé wǒ àirén yìqǐ láide.	No, I came together with my wife.

5. Chinese professor

nǐ shi zài nǎr xuéde	where did you learn (it)
nǐ shi zài nǎr xuéde Zhōngwén	where did you learn Chinese
shì bu shi	is it or is it not the case that
yǐqián zài Zhōngguo xuéguo	before in China had learned
Nǐ zài nǎr xuéde Zhōngwén?	Where did you learn Chinese?
Shì bu shi yǐqián zài Zhōngguo xuéguo?	Had you learned it in China before?

6. Bigelow

kāishǐ	in the beginning [TW]
hòulái	afterward, later [TW]
yòu	again [A]
duàn(r)	section, segment, period [M]
yíduànr shíjiān	a stretch or period of time
xuéle yíduànr shíjiān	learned for a period of time
Kāishǐ shi zài Měiguo xuéde.	At first I studied it in the States.
Hòulái yòu zài Táiwān xuéle yíduànr shíjiān.	Later I studied for a while in Taiwan.

7. Chinese professor

nánguài...	no wonder... [PT]
jiǎng	speak, say [V]
zhèmme hǎo	to this extent good, so good
jiǎngde zhèmme hǎo	speak so well
Nánguài nǐde Hànyǔ jiǎngde zhèmme hǎo.	No wonder you speak Chinese so well.

8. Bigelow

yuǎn	be far away [SV]
chàde hěn yuǎn	be very much lacking
hái chàde hěn yuǎn ne	still be very deficient
Náli, náli. Hái chàde hěn yuǎn ne!	Not at all. I still have a long ways to go!

 **Supplementary Vocabulary**

1. kāishǐ		begin [V]
Wǒde gōngzuò yǐjīng kāishǐle.		My work has already begun.
2. nèmme		like that, so [A]
nèmme duō		so much, that much
Wǒ bù néng chī nèmme duō.		I can't eat that much.
3. yǒude shíhou(r)		sometimes [PH]
jiǎnghuà		speak, talk [VO]
tā huà jiǎngde tài duō		she talks too much
Yǒude shíhou tā huà jiǎngde tài duō.		Sometimes she talks too much.

Grammatical and Cultural Notes

1.   In the question **Nǐ shémme shíhou dào Běijīngde?** "When did you arrive in Beijing?," note that **shémme shíhou** "what time?" or "when?" functions as a Question Word expression. This is the reason why there is no question particle **ma** at the end of the sentence.

1-6.   **SHI...-DE** to Express Attendant Circumstances of Known Past Actions. As we saw in 4-2: 3A, the **shi...-de** pattern can indicate the time or place of known past actions. If you now look at lines 1-6 of this conversation, you will see that **shi...-de** can indicate not only time and place of past actions but also other attendant circumstances accompanying past actions such as whether one went alone to a certain place or with someone else. The pattern is:

Subject	SHI	Attendant Circumstances	Verb	-DE
Wǒ	shi	hé wǒ àirén yìqǐ	lái	de.

"I came together with my wife."

When using **shi...-de**, you and your interlocutor are already aware of the fact that something has happened in the past; what you don't know is under what circumstances the past action took place. **Shi...-de** stresses the circumstances under which a past action occurred, e.g., when, where, with whom, by what means, or how something happened. The negative of **shi...-de** is **bú shi...-de**. As an example of the positive and negative forms, consider the following dialog:

Speaker A: **Nǐ shi zuótiān dàode ma?**

"Did you arrive yesterday?"

Speaker B: **Wǒ bú shi zuótiān dàode. Wǒ shi jīntiān dàode.**

"I didn't arrive yesterday. I arrived today."

In rapid speech, the **shi** part of the **shi...-de** pattern in a POSITIVE SENTENCE is often omitted. Instead of saying **Wǒ shi gēn tā yìqǐ qùde** "I went together with him," many Chinese would simply say **Wǒ gēn tā yìqǐ qùde**. In the Basic Conversation for this lesson, the **shi...-de** pattern happens to occur with **shi** in lines 2 and 6, and without **shi** in lines 1, 3, 4, and 5 (though it could be reinserted into those lines). Our advice to you is to use the full **shi...-de** pattern for now. As your exposure to and proficiency in Chinese increases, you will probably begin dropping some occurrences of **shi** in **shi...-de** naturally. But note carefully that in a NEGATIVE SENTENCE with **bú shi...-de**, the **shi** can never be dropped.

Now look at the question in line 1: **Nǐ shémme shíhou dào Běijīngde?** "When did you arrive in Beijing?" There are some speakers who would say this as **Nǐ shémme shíhou dàode Běijīng?** with the **-de** after the verb **dào** rather than after the object **Běijīng**. Also look at the question in line 5: **Nǐ zài nǎr xuéde Zhōngwén?** "Where did you learn Chinese?" There are some speakers who would say this as **Nǐ zài nǎr xué Zhōngwénde?** The point is this: in the case of a sentence with a verb and an object, if you use a **(shi)...-de** construction in the sentence, the object of the verb can come either before or after the **-de**. The only exception is when the object is a PRONOUN object, in which case the **-de** must come after the pronoun. Examples:

Part 3   The Nosy Professor   **271**

Either:	**Nǐ shémme shíhou dào Běijīngde?**
Or:	**Nǐ shémme shíhou dàode Běijīng?**

Either:	**Nǐ shi zài nǎr xuéde Zhōngwén?**
Or:	**Nǐ shi zài nǎr xué Zhōngwénde?**

But only:	**Nǐ shi zài nǎr rènshi tāde?**
(INCORRECT:	****Nǐ shi zài nǎr rènshide tā?**)

Finally, remember that **shi...-de** can only be used with known past actions. If you are asking whether somebody went to some place, you can't use **shi...-de** because the past action is not known (instead you would use completed action **-le**). Similarly, if you are asking whether someone was a student or was in some place or lived in some place, you also can't use **shi...-de** because "being" and "living" are states, not actions (instead you would use neither **shi...-de** nor **-le** but possibly add an adverb or time word). If you're still unclear about when to use **shi...-de**, look at the following two sentences, which are the same in English (except for intonation), but which are very different in Chinese:

a.   **Tā fùmǔ qùnián líhūnle.** "His parents got divorced last year." (the assumption by the speaker is that this is new information for the listener; the emphasis is on what the person's parents did, i.e., the action of getting divorced)

b.   **Tā fùmǔ shi qùnián líde hūn.** "His parents got divorced last year." (the assumption by the speaker is that the listener already knew that the person's parents got divorced but not when they got divorced; in this sentence, the emphasis is on the time of the divorce)

2A.   Remember that an expression describing when something happens ("time when") always precedes the verb in Chinese, but often follows the verb in English. Contrast:

Chinese:	**Wǒ shi jīnnián èr yuèfen dàode.**
Literal translation:	"I this year February arrived."
Idiomatic English:	"I arrived in February of this year."

2B.   The noun **yuèfen(r)** in **èr yuèfen** "February" is here a synonym for **yuè**, which could have been used instead. But note that if you use **yuèfen**, you cannot add the day of the month with **hào**. So while "February" could be either **èryuè** or **èr yuèfen**, "February 5" can be only **èryuè wǔhào**.

3.   The phrase **yíge rén** "one person—alone" is extremely common. This whole phrase functions as an adverb, so it occurs before the verb it modifies. Thus, be sure to say **Wǒ yíge rén qù** "I'll go alone," NOT ****Wǒ qù yíge rén**.

4A.   Learn the common Mandarin adverb **yìqǐ** "together," e.g., **Wǒmen yìqǐ chīfàn ba** "Let's eat together." **Yìqǐ** can also serve as a place word, e.g., **Jīntiān wǒmen dōu zài yìqǐ** "Today we're all together."

4B.   In lesson 7-1 you were introduced to **hé** as a conjunction meaning "and," as in **wǒ hé nǐ** "you and I." In this lesson you are introduced to **hé** as a coverb meaning "with" (see next note).

4C.   **HÉ...YÌQǏ** and **GĒN...YÌQǏ**. **Hé...yìqǐ** "together with..." is a useful and common pattern for expressing that one undertook some action together with someone else. A fuller form of this sentence would be **Bù, wǒ shi hé wǒ àirén yìqǐ láide** "No, I came together with my wife." The basic pattern is:

Subject	HÉ	Noun/Pronoun	YÌQǏ	Verb
Wǒ	**hé**	**nǐ**	**yìqǐ**	**qù.**

"I'll go together with you."

Besides **hé...yìqǐ**, you can also use the coverb **gēn** "with" which we learned in 6-4 to say **gēn...yìqǐ**, which has exactly the same meaning and is used exactly the same way. Example:

> **Wǒmen gēn tāmen yìqǐ zǒu ba!**   "Let's go together with them!"

5A.   Note **(Nǐ) shì bu shi yǐqián zài Zhōngguo xuéguo?** "Had you learned (it, the Chinese language) in China before?" The **shì bu shi** here means "is it or is it not the case that...." **Shì bu shi** is often used to create questions in this way.

5B.   The suffix **-guo** on **xuéguo** indicates past experience (4-3: 5A). **Xuéguo** may here be translated as "had learned."

6A.   Distinguish the pronunciation of **kāishǐ** "in the beginning" from **kǎoshì** "test" or "take a test."

6B.   The time word **hòulái** means "afterward, later, later on"; it always refers to past events. To express "in the future," use **yǐhòu**, which you learned in 6-4.

6C.   **Yòu** is an adverb meaning "again"; it is usually used for past actions and indicates a realized repetition. You have previously been introduced to the adverb **zài**, which also means "again"; **zài** is usually used for future actions and indicates an unrealized repetition. Examples:

> **Tā zuótiān yòu láile.**   "She came again yesterday."
>
> **Wǒ míngtiān zài lái.**   "I'll come again tomorrow."

Occasionally **yòu** can be used for future repetition which is bound to come true, or when the future repetition is part of a regular pattern that began in the past. Examples:

> **Míngtiān yòu shi xīngqīyī le.**   "Tomorrow is again Monday."
>
> **Xīngqīwǔ wǒmen yòu yào kǎoshìle.**   "On Friday we will again be testing."
>
> **Tā míngtiān yòu yào láile.**   "She is coming again tomorrow."

6D.   The **-le** on **xuéle** indicates completed action. To indicate completed action with verbs that are followed by quantified objects (**yíduànr shíjiān** "a period of time" in this sentence), there is only a **-le** on the verb and no **le** at the end of the sentence (5-4: 1B). Notice that the speaker uses the **shi...-de** construction to answer the question about where he learned Chinese, and then starts a new line of thought about what he did elsewhere.

7A.   NÁNGUÀI... The pattern **nánguài...** means "no wonder (that)...." The literal meaning of this common and useful expression is "hard to blame." The **nánguài** is placed directly before the sentence about which the speaker wants to express "no wonder." The pattern is:

NÁNGUÀI	Sentence
Nánguài	**nǐde Hànyǔ jiǎngde zhèmme hǎo.**

"No wonder that you speak Chinese so well."

Examples:

> **Xiǎo Wángde tàitai shi Měiguo rén, nánguài tāde Yīngwén nèmme hǎo.**
>
> "Little Wang's wife is American, no wonder his English is so good."

> **Tā shi gāozhōng Zhōngwén lǎoshī, nánguài tāde Hànyǔ jiǎngde nèmme hǎo.**
>
> "She is a high school Chinese teacher, no wonder she speaks Chinese so well."

> **Zhèrde fàn zhēn hǎochī, nánguài nǐ měitiān dōu lái zhèr chī wǔfàn!**
>
> "The food here is really good, no wonder you come here every day to eat lunch!"

7B.   **Jiǎng** is a synonym for **shuō** "speak." In the same way that **shuō** combines with **huà** to form the verb-object compound **shuōhuà** "say words, speak" (cf. last lesson), one can also combine **jiǎng** with **huà** to create

jiǎnghuà (cf. SV3). In Southern China and Taiwan, **jiǎnghuà** is even more common than **shuōhuà**.

Entrance to Main Library of Beijing University

8A.   How to Handle Compliments and Praise. In formal situations or between people who do not know each other well, it is customary in China when receiving a compliment or praise not to accept it or even to deny it. This is why the speaker in this conversation says **nǎli** "not at all" when her Chinese interlocutor praises her Chinese (**nǎli** literally means "where," the implication being "where are those words of praise of yours coming from, they're not at all deserved"). It is very common to repeat **nǎli** as **nǎli, nǎli** and then add some explanatory comment, or perhaps say something nice about the other person. Recently, probably under Western influence, some Chinese speakers of the younger generation have begun accepting praise and answering with **xièxie** "thanks" as in English. However, we recommend that, especially in formal situations or with older people, you follow traditional usage.

Here are some other things to keep in mind regarding compliments: In English, we often make compliments from the point of view of the speaker, for example, "I really love your new hair-style!" (with "I" as the topic of the sentence). In Chinese, on the other hand, one would usually say, "Your new hair-style looks really nice!" (with "your new hair-style" as the topic), which is felt by Chinese speakers to be a more objective statement. Chinese people in general compliment each other more often on performance than on appearance, whereas Americans often compliment others on appearance. In China, females in general tend to compliment each other more than males do. Finally, being very polite and making or refusing to accept compliments shows social distance between you and the other speaker. Once you get close to someone, there is no need to compliment them so much, and if you are complimented, you can say nothing or accept the compliment, perhaps with an amendment ("thanks, but..."). If you know someone well and are still very formal in your dealings with them, it can create distance.

A final comment on cross-cultural communication. Let's say you are a proud parent and someone else makes a flattering comment about your son. In such a situation, a Chinese person might say **Nǎli, tā tiáopí dǎodàn** "Not at all, he's a naughty boy." And yet, in English, you might say "Thanks, I'm proud of him, too." How far does one go in acculturation? Would you be willing to make negative comments about your own children, when you know they are not true, just to "play along" with Chinese culture? This is a very personal decision; understanding how Chinese society works is one thing, but to act completely in accordance with the conventions of that society is quite another. In general, among modern, western-educated Chinese, it can sound silly for you as a non-Chinese if you try to go too far in the Chinese direction. The goal for most of you should be to become a successful foreigner in Chinese society and to be able to accomplish those things that need to be accomplished. It is unrealistic (and may be self-defeating) to pretend to be Chinese when you clearly are not.

8B.   **Hái chàde hěn yuǎn ne**, literally "still lacks very far," is a modest reply to the compliment about the speaker's Chinese language proficiency. The **-de** after the verb **chà** is the **-de** that indicates manner (7-2: 4A). This is a very useful expression; add it to your conversational arsenal!

SV3A.   **Yǒude shíhou(r)** is a very common phrase meaning "sometimes." It literally means "the times which there are." The **-de** is optional, so you will also hear this said as **yǒu shíhou(r)**. This phrase functions like a moveable adverb, in that it can precede or follow the topic or subject of a sentence. It can also be used in a pair, for example:

Wǒ yǒude shíhou zài túshūguǎn xuéxí, yǒude shíhou zài fángjiānli xuéxí.

"I sometimes study in the library, and sometimes study in my room."

SV3B.   The phrase **tā huà jiǎngde tài duō** literally means "she, words, says too many" → "she says too many words" → "she talks too much."

Conversation with a Waitress

An American college student who is studying Chinese decides to try out his Mandarin on the waitress at a Chinese restaurant in Massachusetts.

 Basic Conversation 7-4

1. AMERICAN

Qǐng wèn, nǐ shi cóng Zhōngguo láide ma?
Excuse me, are you from China?

2. WAITRESS

Shì a. Nǐ qùguo Zhōngguo ma? Nǐde Zhōngguo huà shuōde tǐng bàng ma!
Yes. Have you been to China? You really speak Chinese very well!

3. AMERICAN

Náli. Nǐ jiā zài Zhōngguo shémme dìfang?
Thanks. Where in China is your home?

4. WAITRESS

Xī'ān. Shì ge gǔ chéng. Nǐ tīngshuōguo ma?
Xian. It's an ancient city. Have you heard of it?

5. AMERICAN

Tīngshuōguo. Lái Měiguo zhīqián, nǐ zài shémme dānwèi gōngzuò?
Yes, I have. Where did you work before you came to the U.S.?

6. WAITRESS

Wǒ dàxué bìyè yǐhòu, zài yíge zhōngxué jiāole jǐnián shū (Ò.), ránhòu jiù shēnqǐng lái Měiguo niàn yánjiūshēng le.
After graduating from college, I taught for a few years at a middle school (Oh.), then I applied to come to the States to attend graduate school.

7. AMERICAN

Ò, shi zhèiyang. Nèmme, nǐ juéde Měiguo zěmmeyàng?
Oh, so that's how it was. So what do you think of America?

8. WAITRESS

Bú cuò. Měiguo tǐng fùyu, dà duōshù rén gōngzuò dōu hěn nǔlì, jiù shi zhì'ān chàle dianr (Ò.).
Not bad. America is very prosperous and the majority of people work very hard; the only thing is there's a little too much crime (Oh.).

Build Up

1. American
cóng	from [CV]
cóng Zhōngguo lái	come from China
nǐ shi cóng Zhōngguo láide	you came from China
Qǐng wèn, nǐ shi cóng Zhōngguo láide ma?	Excuse me, are you from China?

2. Waitress
bàng	be great, wonderful [SV]
shuōde tǐng bàng	speak very well
Shì a. Nǐ qùguo Zhōngguo ma?	Yes. Have you been to China?
Nǐde Zhōngguo huà shuōde tǐng bàng ma!	You really speak Chinese very well!

3. American
Náli. Nǐ jiā zài Zhōngguo shémme dìfang?	Thanks. Where in China is your home?

4. Waitress
gǔ	be ancient [SV]
gǔ chéng	ancient city
shì ge gǔ chéng	(it) is an ancient city
tīngshuō	hear of, hear it said that [V]
nǐ tīngshuōguo ma	have you ever heard of it
Xī'ān. Shì ge gǔ chéng. Nǐ tīngshuōguo ma?	Xian. It's an ancient city. Have you heard of it?

5. American
...zhīqián	before..., ...ago [PT]
lái Měiguo zhīqián	before (you) came to America
Tīngshuōguo. Lái Měiguo zhīqián, nǐ zài shémme dānwèi gōngzuò?	Yes, I have. Where did you work before you came to the U.S.?

6. Waitress
bìyè	graduate [VO]
dàxué bìyè	graduate from a university
...yǐhòu	after... [PT]
dàxué bìyè yǐhòu	after graduating from college
jiāole jǐnián shū	taught several years of school
shēnqǐng	apply [V]
shēnqǐng lái Měiguo	apply to come to America
niàn	study [V]
yánjiūshēng	graduate student [N]
niàn yánjiūshēng	study as a graduate student
Wǒ dàxué bìyè yǐhòu, zài yíge zhōngxué jiāole jǐnián shū (Ò.), ránhòu jiù shēnqǐng lái Měiguo niàn yánjiūshēng le.	After graduating from college, I taught for a few years at a middle school (Oh.), then I applied to come to the States to attend graduate school.

7. American
zhèiyang(r)	this way, like this [MA]
shi zhèiyang	it was like this
juéde	feel [V]
nǐ juéde Měiguo zěmmeyàng	you feel America is how
Ò, shi zhèiyang. Nèmme, nǐ juéde Měiguo zěmmeyàng?	Oh, so that's how it was. So what do you think of America?

8. Waitress

fùyu	be prosperous [SV]
duōshù	the majority [N]
dà duōshù	the great majority
dà duōshù rén	the great majority of people
nǔlì	be diligent, work hard [SV]
jiù	only [A]
jiù shi	it's only that
zhì'ān	public order, public security [N]
chà	be lacking, deficient [SV]
zhì'ān chàle dianr	public order is a little deficient

Bú cuò. Měiguo tǐng fùyu, dà duōshù rén
gōngzuò dōu hěn nǔlì,
jiù shi zhì'ān chàle dianr (Ò.).

Not bad. America is very prosperous and the
majority of people work very hard;
the only thing is there's a little too much crime (Oh.).

 ## Supplementary Vocabulary

1. nèiyang(r)   that way, like that [MA]
nèiyangr xiě   write like that
Zhèige zì nèiyangr xiě bú duì.   It's not correct to write this character like that.

2. ...yǐqián   before..., ...ago [PT]
yíge yuè yǐqián   one month ago
Yíge yuè yǐqián wǒmen hái zài Zhōngguo.   One month ago, we were still in China.

3. ...zhīhòu   after... [PT]
bìyè zhīhòu   after graduating
Nǐ dàxué bìyè zhīhòu xiǎng zuò shémme?   What do you want to do after you graduate from college?

Grammatical and Cultural Notes

1A.   The coverb **cóng** "from" is very common and useful. Like all coverbs, it comes BEFORE the main verb of a sentence. So to say "I'm going to see a friend who comes from California," you would in Chinese have to say the equivalent of "I'm going to see a from-California-come friend": **Wǒ qù kàn yíge cóng Jiāzhōu láide péngyou. Cóng** often pairs off, as here, with the main verb **lái**, creating the pattern **cóng...lái** "come from...."

1B.   Note the use of **shi...-de** in this sentence. This is to express attendant circumstances of a known past action (7-3: 1-6). In this case, the person asking the question already knows that his interlocutor came from somewhere, but wants to find out from exactly where the person came.

4A.   Xian, the capital of Shaanxi Province, is famous for the Han Dynasty terracotta warriors that were discovered there in 1974. Note that in Pinyin Xian must be written as **Xī'ān**, with an apostrophe, so as to differentiate it from the word **xiān** "first."

4B.   In the sentence **Shì ge gǔ chéng** "It is an ancient city," **ge** is an abbreviated form of **yíge** "one, an." In rapid conversation, it is common to abbreviate **yíge** as **ge**.

4C.   **Tīngshuō** "hear of, hear it said that" is an extremely common and useful verb. It literally means "hear-say"; cf. the English expression "hearsay" as in "hearsay evidence."

5.   In the question **Nǐ zài shémme dānwèi gōngzuò** "Where did you work?," there is no grammatical indication of the tense or aspect of the verb (such as **-le**, **-guo**, or **shi...-de**). In Chinese, if one is talking about past events that extended over a period of time and the time is clear from the context (the previous phrase was **lái Měiguo**

zhīqián "before you came to America"), then it is not necessary to add any grammatical marker indicating tense or aspect.

5-6.   Phrase + **YĬQIÁN/ZHĪQIÁN** and Phrase + **YĬHÒU/ZHĪHÒU** There is a pair of words in Chinese for "before" or "ago": **yǐqián** and **zhīqián**; and there is a pair of words for "after": **yǐhòu** and **zhīhòu**. The difference between the members of each pair is in part stylistic (the series beginning in **yǐ-** is considered by some speakers to be less formal while that beginning in **zhī-** is considered somewhat more formal) and in part simply a matter of personal preference. Whichever word is used, it is (in the meaning of "before" or "after" some event) placed at the END of the clause to which it belongs. Note that in English we place the words "before" and "after" at the beginning of the clause. The basic patterns in Chinese are:

Clause	YĬQIÁN/ZHĪQIÁN
wǒ shàng dàxué	yǐqián
"before I go/went to college"	

Clause	YĬHÒU/ZHĪHÒU
tāmen qù Zhōngguo	zhīhòu
"after they go/went to China"	

Here are some additional things to note concerning **yǐqián/zhīqián** and **yǐhòu/zhīhòu**:

a.   In Chinese, an independent clause always follows the dependent clause with **yǐqián/zhīqián** or **yǐhòu/zhīhòu**. For example, take **Wǒ shàng dàxué yǐqián, gōngzuòle liǎngnián** "Before I went to college, I worked for two years," where **gōngzuòle liǎngnián** is the independent clause. In English, the order of the dependent and independent clauses can be reversed without any change in meaning ("I worked for two years before I went to college"). However, in Chinese, the clause containing "before" or "after" must always come first!

b.   **Yǐhòu/zhīhòu** can sometimes be used for future events. In that case, they are sometimes best translated as "in" (see the fourth and fifth examples in the example section below).

c.   Instead of **yǐqián/zhīqián** and **yǐhòu/zhīhòu**, there are some speakers who sometimes use only **qián** and **hòu** with the same meanings (see the last two examples below). This is also very common in writing.

d.   In addition to the patterns above, **yǐqián/zhīqián** can also be used as time words alone at the beginning of a sentence to mean "before, formerly, in the past" (7-2). Example: **Yǐqián Měiguo méiyou rén xué Zhōngwén** "In the past, nobody in America studied Chinese." Similarly, **yǐhòu/zhīhòu** can be used as time words at the beginning of a sentence to mean "in the future" (6-4). Example: **Yǐhòu wǒ yào xué Gǔdài Hànyǔ** "In the future I want to study Classical Chinese."

Now let's look at some more examples of sentences with **yǐqián/zhīqián/qián** and **yǐhòu/zhīhòu/hòu**:

1. **Tā shi yìnián yǐqián qù Zhōngguode.**	"He went to China one year ago."
2. **Wǒ lái zhèr yǐqián jiù tīngshuōguo.**	"I had heard about it before I came here."
3. **Tā chīle fàn yǐhòu jiù qù túshūguǎn xuéxí.**	"After eating, he went to the library to study."
4. **Chén Xiānsheng liǎngge yuè zhīhòu yào jiéhūnle.**	"Mr. Chen is going to get married in two months."
5. **Tā sāntiān hòu yào huí Táiwān.**	"In three days she's going to return to Taiwan."
6. **Lín Xiáojie shi yíge xīngqī qián lái Měiguode.**	"Ms. Lin came to America one week ago."

6A.   **BÌYÈ**. The verb **bìyè** "graduate" is somewhat complicated. Examine the phrase in the conversation **wǒ dàxué bìyè yǐhòu** "after I graduate(d) from college." In English, we say "graduate from" some school or institution, but in Chinese, most speakers don't use **cóng** but rather say the name of the school or institution followed directly by the verb **bìyè**. The pattern is:

Institution	**BÌYÈ**
Běidà	**bìyè**

"graduate from Beijing university"

This can then be placed into a sentence such as **Nǐ Běidà bìyè yǐhòu yào zuò shémme?** "What do you want to do after you graduate from Beijing University?" or **Tā jiějie shi Běidà bìyède** "Her sister graduated from Beijing University."

Learn thoroughly the following questions with **bìyè**, which you will often have occasion to ask or be asked:

Nǐ shi něige dàxué bìyède?	"What college did you graduate from?"
Nǐ shi něinián dàxué bìyède?	"What year did you graduate from college?"
Nǐ dàxué bìyè yǐhòu yào zuò shémme?	"What do you want to do after you graduate from college?"

Here are some additional notes about the verb **bìyè** for future reference (you needn't learn this now):

a.   Some speakers consider **bìyè** a verb-object compound while others consider it a regular verb, so either of the following is possible for "She graduated the year before last": **Tā shi qiánnián bìyède** or **Tā shi qiánnián bìde yè**.

b.   Some speakers add a **zài** "at" before the institution (e.g., **Nǐ shi zài něige dàxué bìyède?** "(At) what college did you graduate from?"); however, we don't recommend that you use **zài** in this way.

c.   There are some speakers who use **cóng** "from" before the institution, as we do in English (e.g., **Wǒ shi yī-jiǔ-qī-èr nián cóng Kāngnài'ěr Dàxué bìyède** "I graduated from Cornell University in 1972"); but, again, we don't recommend you say this.

6B.   Notice how the verb-object compound **jiāoshū** is here split up as **jiāole jǐnián shū** "taught for a few years," with the expression indicating the amount of time spent inserted in between **jiāo** and **shū**. Many verb-object compounds operate this way; another example is **jiéle sāncì hūn** "married three times."

6C.   Backchannel Comments. When Chinese people listen to someone speak, they frequently punctuate the speaker's language with backchannel comments like **Ò** "Oh" and **Zhèiyang** "So that's how it is," which you see in lines 6, 7, and 8 of this conversation. Other common Chinese backchannel comments include **Èi** "Uh-huh" and **Ng** "Yeah." Of course, more substantive expressions like **Shì** "It is thus," **Shìde** "Yes," and **Duì** "Correct" can also serve as backchannel comments. The basic meaning of backchannel comments is simply "I hear you, I'm listening, I understand," not necessarily "I agree with you." Many misunderstandings and failed business deals have resulted from the misinterpretation by Westerners of backchannel comments by Chinese people speaking in Chinese or English! To facilitate comprehension by your Chinese interlocutors, we recommend that you make judicious use of backchannel comments in your own speech. This is especially important on the telephone, where there is a lack of visual clues. Appropriate use of backchannel comments can make you sound more proficient and natural and can serve to assure your interlocutor that you are listening and following what the speaker is saying. This is especially important because, since you are a non-native speaker of Chinese, your interlocutor is likely to worry that you may not always understand everything.

6D.   The word **yánjiū** "research" can, as in English, function both as a verb and a noun. The verb **yánjiū** is sometimes also used as a perfunctory response to inconvenient requests, as in:

Zhèijiàn shì ma, wǒmen yánjiū yanjiu zài shuō ba.

"As for this matter, we'll look into it and see."

6E.   The verb **niàn** means "study." Here are some common collocations with **niàn**:

niàn Zhōngwén	"study Chinese" (or any other academic subject)
niàn dàxué	"study at college, attend a university"
niàn Běidà	"study at Beijing University" (or any other academic institution)
niàn yánjiūshēng	"study as a graduate student"

Niàn can also mean "read out loud" as in **Xiànzài qǐng nǐ niàn** "Now you please read out loud."

7A.   Instead of **zhèiyang(r)** "this way, like this," some speakers say, with the same meaning, **zhèyang(r)** while yet other speakers say **zhèiyangzi**.

7B.   Notice the use of **nèmme** here as a discourse marker to change the subject.

7C.   In this utterance you are introduced to the common and useful verb **juéde** "feel." Here are some more examples with **juéde**:

> **Nǐ juéde zěmmeyàng?**
>
> "How do you feel?" (e.g., is your headache gone now?) or "How do you feel about it?" (e.g., do you agree with our business proposition?)
>
> **Wǒ juéde hěn hǎo.**
>
> "I feel fine." or "I feel it's fine."
>
> **Wǒ jīntiān juéde hěn lèi.**
>
> "I feel very tired today."
>
> **Wǒ juéde zhèrde dōngxi tài guìle.**
>
> "I feel the things here are too expensive."
>
> **Wǒ juéde nǐ bù yīnggāi qù.**
>
> "I feel you shouldn't go." or "I don't feel you should go."

Notice in the last example that the negative **bù** comes before **yīnggāi qù** and not before **juéde**. So English "I don't feel that…" is usually translated positively as if it were "I feel that…not." As we saw earlier in 3-2: 2A, the verb **xiǎng** "think" operates similarly.

8A.   Distinguish the pronunciation of **dà duōshù** "the great majority" from **duō dà** "how old" (3-2).

8B.   Besides **zhǐ** (3-3), another way to express "only" is with the adverb **jiù**, e.g., **Wǒ jiù yǒu yíkuài qián** "I have only $1.00." Remember that **jiù** has a number of other meanings: "then" (3-2) and "precisely, exactly" (4-2). In the sense of "only," **jiù** is used mainly in North China, while **zhǐ** can be used wherever Chinese is spoken.

Unit 4: Review and Study Guide

New Vocabulary

ADVERBS		CONJUNCTIONS		MOVEABLE ADVERBS	
hái	in addition	hé	and	nèiyang(r)	that way, like that
jiù	only			yuánlái	originally, formerly
nèmme	like that, so	COVERBS		zhèiyang(r)	this way, like this
quán	completely	cóng	from		
yìqǐ	together	hé	with	NOUNS	
yòu	again			biǎojiě	older female cousin of different surname
		IDIOMATIC EXPRESSIONS			
ATTRIBUTIVES		bú cuò	"not bad," "quite good"		
qítā	other			biǎojiěfu	husband of older female cousin of different surname
yǒude	some	MEASURES			
		duàn(r)	section, segment, period (of time)		
AUXILIARY VERBS				Déyǔ	German (language)
huì	know how to, can	kǒu	(for people; lit. "mouth")		
				duōshù	the majority

Fǎyǔ	French (language)	ya	(form of particle **a** used after words ending in **-a** or **-i**)	gǔ	be ancient
Hànzì	Chinese character			nǔlì	be diligent, work hard
huà	word, language				
mǎimài	business	**PATTERNS**		yuǎn	be far away
nánháir	boy	nánguài...	no wonder...		
nǔháir	girl	...yǐhòu	after...	**TIME WORDS**	
Pǔtōnghuà	Mandarin (language)	...yǐqián	before..., ...ago	cóngqián	in the past, formerly
		...zhīhòu	after...		
Rìyǔ	Japanese (language)	...zhīqián	before..., ...ago	hòulái	afterward, later
		bìyè	graduate	kāishǐ	in the beginning
shēnti	body			yǐqián	before, formerly
shíhou(r)	time	**PHRASES**			
xiàn	county	yíge rén	by oneself, alone	**VERBS**	
Xībānyáyǔ	Spanish (language)	yǒude shíhou(r)	sometimes	jiǎng	speak, say
		Zhōngguo huà	spoken Chinese	jìxù	continue
yánjiū	research	Zhōngguo zì(r)	Chinese character	juéde	feel
yánjiūshēng	graduate student	zuò mǎimài	do or engage in business	kāishǐ	begin
Yīngyǔ	English (language)			niàn	study
yuèfen(r)	month	**PLACE WORDS**		rènshi	recognize
zhì'ān	public order, public security	Běijīng Yǔyán Wénhuà Dàxué		shēnqǐng	apply
			Beijing Language and Culture University	tīngshuō	hear of, hear it said that
NUMBERS		gōngchǎng	factory	xiě	write
jǐ-	a few, several	yòu'éryuán	kindergarten	yánjiū	research
PARTICLES		**STATIVE VERBS**		**VERB-OBJECT COMPOUNDS**	
-de	(verb suffix that indicates manner)	bàng	be great, wonderful	gǎiháng	change one's line of work
ma	(indicates something obvious)	chà	be lacking, deficient	jiǎnghuà	speak, talk
				shuōhuà	speak words, speak
ne	(pause filler)	fùyu	be prosperous	xiězì(r)	write characters, write

Major New Grammar Patterns

Choice-type questions with choice implied: Nánháir nǔháir? "A boy or a girl?" **Nǐ yào zhèige yào nèige?** "Do you want this one or do you want that one?" (7-1)

Chinese equivalents of English "know": Nǐ huì shuō Zhōngguo huà ma? "Do you know how to speak Chinese?" **Nǐ zhīdao Chéngdū zài nǎr ma?** "Do you know where Chengdu is?" **Nǐ rènshi tā ma?** "Do you know him?" (7-2)

Chinese equivalents of English "can": Tā huì shuōhuà ma? "Can she speak?" (i.e., has the baby already learned how to) **Tā néng shuōhuà ma?** "Can she speak?" (i.e., physically able, after her recent illness) **Tā kéyǐ shuōhuà ma?** "Can she speak?" (i.e., may she or does she have permission to) (7-2)

Terms for "Chinese language" (7-2)

-DE after verbs to indicate man-

ner: **Tā Zhōngguo huà shuōde hěn hǎo.** "She speaks Chinese very well." **Tā xiě Zhōngguo zì xiěde hěn hǎokàn.** "He writes Chinese characters very attractively." (7-2)

MA to indicate an obvious situation: Nínde Hànyǔ shuōde tǐng bú cuò ma! "You speak Chinese quite well, you know!" (7-2)

Question Words used as indefinites: Wǒ rènshi jǐbǎige Zhōngguo zì. "I know a few hundred Chinese characters." **Wǒ zhǐ yǒu jǐkuài qián.** "I only have a few dollars." (7-2)

YǑUDE...YǑUDE...: Yǒude láile, yǒude méi lái. "Some came, some didn't come." **Yǒude wǒ mǎile, yǒude méi mǎi.** "I bought some, I didn't buy others." (7-2)

Names of languages (7-2)

SHI...-DE to express attendant circumstances of known past actions: Wǒ shi hé wǒ àirén yìqǐ

lái de. "I came together with my spouse." (7-3)

HÉ...YÌQǏ and GEN...YÌQǏ: Wǒmen hé tāmen yìqǐ qù ba! "Let's go together with them!" (7-3)

NÁNGUÀI...: Nánguài nǐde Hànyǔ jiǎngde zhèmme hǎo. "No wonder that you speak Chinese so well." (7-3)

Phrase + YǏQIÁN/ZHĪQIÁN and Phrase + YǏHÒU/ZHĪHÒU: Tā shi yìnián yǐqián qù Zhōngguode. "He went to China one year ago." **Tā liǎngge yuè zhīhòu yào jiéhūn.** "She's going to get married in two months." (7-4)

BÌYÈ: Tā shi Běidà bìyède. "She graduated from Beijing University." (7-4)

Backchannel comments: Ò. "Oh.," **Zhèiyang.** "So this is how it is." (7-4)

Getting Around Beijing (I)

COMMUNICATIVE OBJECTIVES

Once you have mastered this unit, you will be able to use Chinese to:

1. Ask how to get to a certain place.

2. Understand and give simple directions.

3. Inquire if a certain place is near or far from where you are, or if a certain place is near or far from some other place.

4. Call a taxi and give appropriate instructions to the taxi company or driver: from where to where, when, how many people, how many pieces of luggage, etc.

5. Complain to the taxi company if the taxi you requested has not yet arrived.

6. Discuss alternate routes if traffic should be congested.

7. Express exasperation: "Darn it!"

"How Do I Get to the Beijing Hotel?"

Patricia Nguyen, an American studying Chinese at a study abroad program in Beijing, asks a pedestrian how to get to the Beijing Hotel.

Basic Conversation 8-1

1. AMERICAN   **Láojià, qù Běijīng Fàndiàn zěmme zǒu?**
Excuse me, how do I get to the Beijing Hotel?

2. PEDESTRIAN   **Běijīng Fàndiàn, shi ma? Yìzhí wàng qián zǒu, guòle Tiān'ānmén jiù dàole.**
The Beijing Hotel? Go straight ahead,it's right after Tiananmen.

3. AMERICAN   **Lí zhèr hěn yuǎn ma?**
Is it very far from here?

4. PEDESTRIAN   **Lí zhèr bú tài yuǎn.**
It's not too far from here.

5. AMERICAN   **Dàgài yào duō jiǔ?**
About how long will it take?

6. PEDESTRIAN   **Zǒulùde huà, dàgài yào èrshifēn zhōng zuǒyòu, huòzhě nín dǎ ge dī gèng kuài, wǔfēn zhōng jiù dàole.**
If you walk, it will probably take about twenty minutes, or if you take a cab it'll be even faster, you'll be there in five minutes.

7. AMERICAN   **Hǎo, xièxie nín.**
O.K., thanks.

8. PEDESTRIAN   **Bú kèqi.**
You're welcome.

Build Up

1. American

láojià (B)	"excuse me" [IE]
Běijīng Fàndiàn	Beijing Hotel [PW]
zǒu	go, walk [V]

zěmme zǒu	how do you go
Láojià, qù Běijīng Fàndiàn zěmme zǒu?	Excuse me, how do I get to the Beijing Hotel?

2. Pedestrian

yìzhí	straight [A]
wàng	to, toward [CV]
wàng qián zǒu	go toward the front, walk ahead
yìzhí wàng qián zǒu	go straight ahead
guò	pass, go by [V]
Tiān'ānmén	Tiananmen [PW]
guòle Tiān'ānmén	(when you) have passed Tiananmen
jiù dàole	then (you) will have arrived
Běijīng Fàndiàn, shi ma? Yìzhí wàng qián zǒu, guòle Tiān'ānmén jiù dàole.	The Beijing Hotel? Go straight ahead, it's right after Tiananmen.

3. American

lí	be distant from, from [CV]
Lí zhèr hěn yuǎn ma?	Is it very far from here?

4. Pedestrian

Lí zhèr bú tài yuǎn.	It's not too far from here.

5. American

dàgài	probably, about [MA]
Dàgài yào duō jiǔ?	About how long will it take?

6. Pedestrian

zǒulù	walk [VO]
zǒulùde huà	if you walk
zuǒyòu	about, approximately [PW]
èrshifēn zhōng zuǒyòu	approximately twenty minutes
huòzhě	or [CJ]
dǎdī	take a taxi [VO]
nín dǎ ge dī	you take a taxi
gèng	even more, more [A]
kuài	be fast [SV]
gèng kuài	even faster, faster
nín dǎ ge dī gèng kuài	(if) you take a taxi it will be even faster
Zǒulùde huà, dàgài yào èrshifēn zhōng zuǒyòu, huòzhě nín dǎ ge dī gèng kuài, wǔfēn zhōng jiù dàole.	If you walk, it will probably take about twenty minutes, or if you take a cab it'll be even faster, you'll be there in five minutes.

7. American

Hǎo, xièxie nín.	O.K., thanks.

8. Pedestrian

Bú kèqi.	You're welcome.

Supplementary Vocabulary: Distance and Directions

1. jìn	be close, near [SV]
lí wǒ jiā hěn jìn	close to my home
Tā jiā lí wǒ jiā hěn jìn.	Her home is close to my home.
2. wàng dōng zǒu	walk toward the east

nán	south [L]
wàng nán zǒu	walk toward the south
Qǐng nǐ xiān wàng dōng zǒu,	Please first head toward the east,
ránhòu wàng nán zǒu.	then head toward the south.

3. **xī**	west [L]
kāi	drive (a vehicle) [V]
wàng xī kāi	drive toward the west
běi	north [L]
wàng běi kāi	drive toward the north
Nín xiān wàng xī kāi,	First drive toward the west,
ránhòu wàng běi kāi.	then drive toward the north.

4. **dōngfāng**	east, the East [PW]
dào dōngfāng lái	come to the East
xīfāng	west, the West [PW]
dào xīfāng qù	go to the West
Wǒ yào dào dōngfāng lái,	I wanted to come to the East,
nǐ yào dào xīfāng qù.	you wanted to go to the West.

5. **nánfāng**	south, the South [PW]
cóng nánfāng lái	come from the South
běifāng	north, the North [PW]
cóng běifāng lái	come from the North
Lǎo Lǐ shi cóng nánfāng láide,	Old Li came from the South,
bú shi cóng běifāng láide.	not from the North.

6. **Dōngfāng rén**	Asian [PH]
Xīfāng rén	Westerner [PH]
Yīngwén lǎoshī shi Dōngfāng rén,	The English teacher is an Asian,
Zhōngwén lǎoshī shi Xīfāng rén, hěn yǒu yìsi!	and the Chinese teacher is a Westerner, it's interesting!

7. **nánfāng rén**	Southerner [PH]
nánfāng huà	southern speech [PH]
běifāng rén	Northerner [PH]
běifāng huà	northern speech [PH]
Nánfāng rén jiǎng nánfāng huà,	Southerners speak southern speech,
běifāng rén jiǎng běifāng huà.	and Northerners speak northern speech.

Grammatical and Cultural Notes

1A.   **Láojià** "excuse me" is a polite expression frequently used in Beijing and environs when you need to disturb someone to ask a question. **Láojià** is said first, as an apology and to get the other person's attention, and **Láojià** is then followed by the request for information or assistance. **Láojià** is not used in southern China and Taiwan, where **qǐngwèn**, with approximately the same meaning, would be used instead (the main difference between the two is that after **qǐngwèn** you must ask a question, while **láojià** can sometimes also be used as an independent statement). Note that **duìbuqǐ** also translates as "excuse me," but in Chinese it is used mostly as an apology and would not often be used to seek information.

1B.   **QÙ...ZĚMME ZǑU?** The pattern for asking "How does one get to such-and-such a place?" is **qù** + name of place + **zěmme zǒu?** This literally means "go to (name of place) how to go?" Frequently there will be a polite phrase like **láojià** or **qǐngwèn** before the **qù**.

Polite Phrase	QÙ	Place	ZĔMME ZŎU
Láojià,	qù	Tiān'ānmén	zĕmme zŏu?

"Excuse me, how do I get to Tiananmen?"

Some more examples:

Láojià, qù Wàijiāobù zĕmme zŏu?

"Excuse me, how do you get to the Foreign Ministry?"

Láojià, qù Cháng Chéng Fàndiàn zĕmme zŏu?

"Excuse me, how does one get to the Great Wall Hotel?"

Qǐngwèn, qù Táidà zĕmme zŏu?

"Excuse me, how do you get to National Taiwan University?"

1C.   In 1-2 you learned **zŏu** with the meaning "leave, depart." Now you learn another meaning of **zŏu**: "walk."

2A.   Note that the pedestrian here confirms the American's question: **Bĕijīng Fàndiàn, shi ma?** "The Beijing Hotel, is it?" It is very common to repeat questions in this way with **shi ma**. Besides confirming that one has understood correctly, doing so also fills what might otherwise be awkward empty moments and gives one extra time to think of the answer; we suggest you also get in the habit of doing this.

2B.   The adverb **yìzhí** "straight" is very common. It can also mean "keep straight on doing something." Some more examples:

Qǐng nǐ yìzhí zŏu.   "Please go straight."

Qǐng nǐ yìzhí wàng zuŏ zŏu.   "Please keep on walking toward the left."

2C.   **WÀNG** to Express Movement toward a Certain Direction. The coverb **wàng** "to, toward" expresses movement toward a certain direction. It is followed by a localizer and a verb. The basic pattern is:

Subject	Localizer	Verb
wàng	qián	zŏu

"go toward the front, walk ahead"

Though we recommend the colloquial pronunciation **wàng**, there are also many speakers who use the more formal, literary pronunciation **wǎng**; both pronunciations are correct. Some more examples:

Qǐng nǐ xiān wàng dōng zŏu, ránhòu zài wàng xī zŏu.

"Please first walk toward the east, and then walk toward the west."

Tā zhǐ huì wàng qián kāi, hái bú huì wàng hòu kāi.

"He can only drive straight ahead, he can't yet drive backwards."

Wàng lǐ jǐ, wàng lǐ jǐ!

"Squeeze toward the inside, squeeze toward the inside!" (said by the conductor to passengers on a bus)

Xiān wàng zuŏ kàn, zài wàng yòu kàn!

"First look toward the left, and then look toward the right!"

Note that, in giving directions, where we would say "turn right" or "go left," many Chinese would use the localizers **dōng** "east," **nán** "south," **xī** "west," **bĕi** "north" and say "turn to the east" or "go toward the north."

2D. The verb **guò** means "pass, go by" both in the sense of "physically pass by (e.g., a building)" and in the sense of "time passes" or "goes by." So one could also say:

> **Shíjiān guòde tài kuàile!**   "Time passes too quickly!"

2E. Tiananmen is composed of the words **tiān** "heaven," **ān** "peace," and **mén** "gate" (which you have learned), so the name means "gate of heavenly peace." It is the front gate to the Imperial Palace, built in 1417 during the Ming Dynasty.

2F. A literal translation of the sentence **Yìzhí wàng qián zǒu, guòle Tiān'ānmén jiù dàole** would be "Straight toward ahead go, having passed Tiananmen then have arrived."

3.   **Lí** to Express Distance From. The coverb **lí** literally means "be separated from." There are two common patterns with **lí** that involve the stative verbs **yuǎn** "be far" and **jìn** "be close": **lí...yuǎn** "be far from..." and **lí... jìn** "be close to..." (cf. SV1). Although **lí** is used most commonly to indicate physical distance, it is sometimes used abstractly, for example, to indicate how distant in time something is or was. The two patterns can be diagrammed as follows:

Place1	LÍ	Place2	HĚN YUĂN
Zhōngguo	lí	Měiguo	hěn yuǎn.

"China is far from America."

Place1	LÍ	Place2	HĚN JÌN
Jiānádà	lí	Měiguo	hěn jìn.

"Canada is close to America."

Examples:

Nǐ jiā lí zhèr yuǎn ma?	"Is your home far from here?"
Nǐ jiā lí zhèr yuǎn bu yuǎn?	"Is your home far from here?"
Wǒ jiā lí zhèr hěn jìn.	"My home is close to here."

Lí cannot be made negative. So, unlike other coverbs, in constructions with **lí** it is the main verb that is made negative. The most common negative patterns are **A lí B bù yuǎn** "A is not far from B" and **A lí B bú jìn** "A is not close to B." Examples:

> **Wǒ jiā lí zhèr bù yuǎn.**
>
> "My home is not far from here."

> **Hángzhōu lí Shànghǎi bù yuǎn yě bú jìn.**
>
> "Hangzhou is neither far from nor close to Shanghai."

Even though **yuǎn** and **jìn** occur very commonly with **lí**, other types of complements are also possible. For example:

> **Xiànzài lí shàngkè hái yǒu shífēn zhōng.**
>
> "Now there are still ten minutes from the time class starts."

Attention: Be careful not to confuse **lí** "be separated from" with **cóng** (7-4), which simply means "from (one place)." When you want to express distance between two points (i.e., how close or how far away some place is), you must use **lí**. If you want to express origin (e.g., where someone came from) or direction ("from...to..."), you should use **cóng**. Here are some sentences that contrast **lí** and **cóng**:

Tāmen lí Běijīng hěn jìn.	"They are close to Beijing."
Tāmen cóng Běijīng lái.	"They are coming from Beijing."
Wǒ jiā lí nǐ jiā bú tài yuǎn.	"My home is not very far from your home."
Cóng wǒ jiā dào nǐ jiā zěmme zǒu?	"How do you get from my home to your home?"

Remember that **yuǎn** "be far" and **jìn** "be close" are stative verbs, with the English verb "to be" built in. Therefore, there is no need to add a **shì**, except in cases of unusual stress. So ordinarily one would say **Xuéxiào lí wǒ jiā hěn jìn** "School is close to my home," NOT *Xuéxiào shi lí wǒ jiā hěn jìn.

6A.　Conditional Clauses with **-DE HUÀ**. The addition of **-de huà** (lit. "the words that...") at the end of a clause emphasizes that the clause is conditional ("if so-and-so..."). For example, **zǒulùde huà**, literally "if it is the words that one walks," or in good English "if you walk." The pattern with **-de huà** is often used after **yàoshi** and other adverbs meaning "if"; or it can be used alone, as here. Examples:

> **Zǒulùde huà, dàgài yào bàn'ge zhōngtóu zuǒyòu.**
>
> "If you walk, it will probably take about half an hour."

> **Yàoshi dǎdīde huà, dàgài yào shífēn zhōng zuǒyòu.**
>
> "If you take a cab, it will probably take about ten minutes."

6B.　**ZUǑYÒU**. The place word **zuǒyòu**, literally "to the left or right of—slightly more or slightly less," means "approximately, about" and is placed after a numerical expression to indicate an approximate quantity. Distinguish **zuǒyòu** from **chàbuduō** and **dàyuē**, which have approximately the same meaning but are placed before the numerical expression. The pattern is:

Beijing Hotel on East Chang An Avenue

Numerical Expression	ZUǑYÒU
èrshifēn zhōng	**zuǒyòu**
"approximately twenty minutes"	

Compare the following three phrases, all of which mean "about two months":

> **chàbuduō liǎngge yuè**
>
> **dàyue liǎngge yuè**
>
> **liǎngge yuè zuǒyòu**

Also, note that when "right and left" are referred to together, the Chinese order is the opposite of English: **zuǒyòu** "left and right." More examples of **zuǒyòu** used to mean "approximately, about":

> **Yào bànnián zuǒyòu.**
>
> "It will take about half a year."

> **Táiběide rénkǒu yǒu sānbǎiwàn zuǒyòu.**
>
> "The population of Taipei is about three million."

> **Cóng Běijīng dào Chángchéng hěn kuài; zhǐ yào yíge zhōngtóu zuǒyòu.**
>
> "It's very fast to get from Beijing to the Great Wall; it takes only approximately one hour."

6C.　The term **dī** in **dǎdī** "take a taxi" is an abbreviation of **dīshì** "taxi." Actually, **dīshì** is the Mandarin pronunciation of the Cantonese word **dīksí**, which in turn derives from English "taxi."

6D.　Be sure you master the very common adverb **gèng** "even, even more." It commonly occurs before stative verbs and auxiliary verbs. Some more examples:

> **Zhèige bú cuò, kěshi nèige gèng hǎo.**
>
> "This one is not bad, but that one is even better."

> **Wǒ yě xǐhuan chī Měiguo cài, búguò wǒ gèng xǐhuan chī Zhōngguo cài.**
>
> "I also like American food, but I like Chinese food even more."

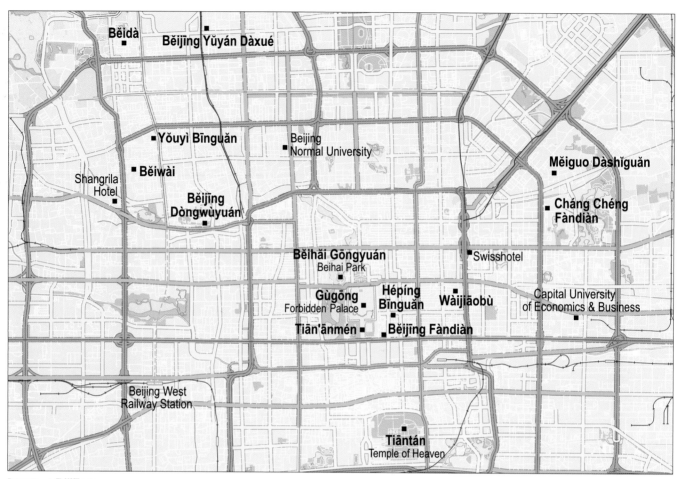

Downtown **Běijīng**

6E.   Note the grammar of the sentence **Nín dǎ ge dī gèng kuài**. Literally, this means "you take a cab, even faster" or, in better English, "If you take a cab, it would be even faster." The topic of the sentence is **Nín dǎ ge dī**; the comment is **gèng kuài**.

SV2-3.   There are in Chinese set orders for many groups of related terms, with some of these orders different from English. In English we say "north, south, east, and west," but in Chinese the correct order is:

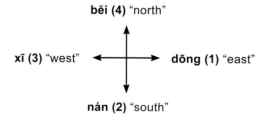

SV3.   One of the many meanings of the verb **kāi** is "to operate (a car, bus, streetcar, subway, boat, airplane, etc.)." Obviously, the best English translation will depend on the particular mode of transportation, so that sometimes **kāi** is best translated as "drive," sometimes as "fly," etc.

Calling for a Taxi to the Airport

Linda Fuentes, a graduate student in Art History who has spent the past year conducting research in Beijing, calls a taxi company for a cab to take her from the Foreign Experts Building at Beijing Foreign Studies University to Capital Airport.

Basic Conversation 8-2

1. DISPATCHER **Nín hǎo! Yǒuyì Bīnguǎn Qìchē Gōngsī.**
Hello. Friendship Hotel Taxi Company.

2. FUENTES **Wéi? Nǐ hǎo. Wǒ yào yíliàng chē qù Shǒudū Jīchǎng.**
Hello? Hi. I'd like a car to go to Capital Airport.

3. DISPATCHER **Nín xiànzài zài nǎr?**
Where are you now?

4. FUENTES **Zài Běijīng Wàiguóyǔ Dàxuéde zhuānjiā lóu.**
In the foreign experts building at Beijing Foreign Studies University.

5. DISPATCHER **Jǐge rén?**
How many people?

6. FUENTES **Jiù wǒ yíge rén.**
Just me alone.

7. DISPATCHER **Shémme shíhou yào chē?**
What time would you like the car?

8. FUENTES **Xiànzài jiù yào.**
Right now.

9. DISPATCHER **Xíng. Nín guìxìng?**
All right. What's your last name?

10. FUENTES **Wǒ shi Měiguo rén, wǒde Zhōngguó xìngmíng shi Fù Líndá.**
I'm an American, my Chinese name is **Fù Líndá**.

11. DISPATCHER **Hǎode. Chēzi shífēn zhōng yǐhòu jiù dào. Nín zài Běiwài zhuānjiā lóu ménkǒur děng ba.**
All right. The car will be there in ten minutes. Wait at the entrance to the foreign experts building at BFSU.

◉ Build Up

1. Dispatcher

yǒuyì (B)	friendship [N]
bīnguǎn	guest house, hotel [PW]
Yǒuyì Bīnguǎn	Friendship Hotel [PW]
qìchē	car, vehicle [N]
qìchē gōngsī	car company, taxi company
Nín hǎo! Yǒuyì Bīnguǎn Qìchē Gōngsī.	Hello. Friendship Hotel Taxi Company.

2. Fuentes

wéi	"hello" (on the telephone) [I]
liàng	(for land vehicles) [M]
yíliàng chē	a car, a taxi
shǒudū	capital [N]
jīchǎng	airport [PW]
Shǒudū Jīchǎng	Capital Airport [PW]
Wéi? Nǐ hǎo. Wǒ yào yíliàng chē qù Shǒudū Jīchǎng.	Hello? Hi. I'd like a car to go to Capital Airport.

3. Dispatcher

Nín xiànzài zài nǎr?	Where are you now?

4. Fuentes

wàiguo	foreign country [N]
wàiguoyǔ	foreign language [N]
Běijīng Wàiguoyǔ Dàxué	Beijing Foreign Studies University [PW]
zhuānjiā	expert [N]
lóu	building (with two or more floors) [N]
zhuānjiā lóu	(foreign) experts building [PH]
Zài Běijīng Wàiguoyǔ Dàxuéde zhuānjiā lóu.	In the foreign experts building at Beijing Foreign Studies University.

5. Dispatcher

Jǐge rén?	How many people?

6. Fuentes

Jiù wǒ yíge rén.	Just me alone.

7. Dispatcher

Shémme shíhou yào chē?	What time would you like the car?

8. Fuentes

Xiànzài jiù yào.	Right now.

9. Dispatcher

Xíng. Nín guìxìng?	All right. What's your last name?

10. Fuentes

xìngmíng	first and last name [N]
Zhōngwén xìngmíng	Chinese name
wǒde Zhōngwén xìngmíng	my Chinese name
Fù	Fu [SN]
Líndá	(Chinese for "Linda")

Wǒ shi Měiguo rén, wǒde Zhōngwén xìngmíng shi Fù Líndá.	I'm an American, my Chinese name is Fù Líndá.

11. **Dispatcher**

hǎode	"all right," "O.K." [IE]
chēzi	car, vehicle [N]
shífēn zhōng yǐhòu	after/in ten minutes
shífēn zhōng yǐhòu jiù dào	after 10 minutes then it'll arrive
Běiwài	(abbreviation for Beijing Foreign Studies University or BFSU) [PW]
Běiwài zhuānjiā lóu	foreign experts building at BFSU
ménkǒu(r)	doorway, entrance [PW]
Běiwài zhuānjiā lóu ménkǒur	entrance to the foreign experts building at BFSU
zài ménkǒur děng	wait at the entrance
Hǎode. Chēzi shífēn zhōng yǐhòu jiù dào. Nín zài Běiwài zhuānjiā lóu ménkǒur děng ba.	All right. The car will be there in ten minutes. Wait at the entrance to the foreign experts building at BFSU.

Supplementary Vocabulary

1. **wàiguo rén**	foreigner [PH]
wàiguo huà	foreign language [PH]
Zhōngguo rén jiǎng Zhōngguo huà, wàiguo rén jiǎng wàiguo huà.	Chinese people speak Chinese, and foreigners speak foreign languages.
2. **chūzū**	rent out [V]
chūzū qìchē	taxi [PH]
liǎngliàng chūzū qìchē	two taxis
Wǒ yào liǎngliàng chūzū qìchē.	I'd like two taxis.

Grammatical and Cultural Notes

1A.   There are various phrases with **yǒuyì** "friendship," such as **Zhōng-Měi yǒuyì** "Chinese-American friendship," a term you will commonly encounter in China.

1B.   An alternate pronunciation of **yǒuyì** that you will sometimes hear is **yǒuyí**.

2A.   **Wéi** is the expression for "hello" that is used when speaking on the telephone. Some speakers pronounce this more like **wái**.

2B.   **Liàng** is the measure for all kinds of land vehicles that end in **-chē**. Examples:

yíliàng chē	"a car"
zhèiliàng qìchē	"this automobile"
nèiliàng qìchē	"that car"
jǐliàng chēzi?	"how many cars?"
něiliàng chūzū qìchē?	"which taxi?"

2C.   Pivot Sentences. The sentence **Wǒ yào yíliàng chē qù Shǒudū Jīchǎng** "I want a car to go to Capital Airport" is an example of a so-called pivot sentence. This sentence is actually composed of the following two sentences:

Wǒ yào yíliàng chē.	+	**Chē qù Shǒudū Jīchǎng.**
"I want a car."	+	"The car goes to Capital Airport."

In the first sentence above, **chē** is the object, while in the second sentence, **chē** is the subject. When the two sentences are combined, the second **chē** is deleted and the first **chē** acts as a "pivot," serving simultaneously as the object of the first sentence and as the subject of the second sentence. Other common verbs in pivot sentences besides **yào** include **qǐng**, **yǒu**, and **zhǎo**. More examples of pivot sentences:

Wǒ qǐng nǐ chī wǔfàn.	"I'd like to invite you for lunch."
Wǒ yǒu ge péngyou xìng Lǐ.	"I have a friend who is surnamed Li."
Wǒmen zhǎo yíge tóngxué gēn wǒmen yìqǐ qù.	"We're looking for a classmate to go together with us."
Wǒ rènshi yíge rén yǒu shí'èrge háizi!	"I know a man who has twelve kids!"

4A.   **Wàiguoyǔ** "foreign language" can be shortened to **wàiyǔ**. Another, even more colloquial term for "foreign language" is **wàiguo huà** (cf. SV1 of this lesson).

4B.   **Zhuānjiā** "expert" here refers to **wàiguo zhuānjiā** "foreign expert." These are foreign technical, medical, and educational personnel who are invited to China by the Chinese government or other official organizations for a period of time to help China modernize. This system, adopted from the former Soviet Union, was begun in the 1950s. The **wàiguo zhuānjiā** often live in special buildings called **zhuānjiā lóu**.

6.   Examine **jiù wǒ yíge rén** "only I alone, just me." Normally, adverbs cannot appear before pronouns. In the sense of "only" (but not in the sense of "then"), **jiù** does sometimes appear before pronouns, as here. We could analyze the sentence as deriving from **jiù yǒu wǒ yíge rén** "there was only I alone," from which the verb **yǒu** has been deleted.

10A.   **Xìngmíng** "given name plus surname" is a more specific and formal term than **míngzi** "name." Remember that **míngzi** could refer to someone's given name or to someone's given name plus surname. **Xìngmíng** is commonly used when filling out forms or when identifying someone in a formal situation. In normal conversation, one would usually just say **míngzi** "name."

10B.   You may have noticed that in the video and the conversation for listening, the speakers say **wǒde Zhōngguo xìngmíng** "my Chinese name," but in the Build Up, that speaker says **wǒde Zhōngwén xìngmíng**, lit. "my Chinese language name." Both expressions are possible, but we recommend you say **wǒde Zhōngwén xìngmíng**.

11A.   Learn **hǎode** "all right, O.K.," which is very common as a brief reply. In a number of common short replies to questions, **-de** is frequently added for emphasis. The two most common of these are **hǎode** and **shìde** "yes." Others include **kéyide** "it's O.K.," **duìde** "right," and **xíngde** "O.K."

11B.   **Chēzi shífēn zhōng yǐhòu jiù dào** "The car will arrive in ten minutes." We learned in 7-4: 5-6 that phrase + **yǐhòu**, literally "after...," can be used for future events to indicate "in a certain amount of time." Another example:

Wǒ wǔfēn zhōng yǐhòu lái zhǎo nǐ.   "I'll come looking for you in five minutes."

11C.   Review the two common uses of **jiù** illustrated in this conversation. In line 11, as well as in line 8, **jiù** means "as early as..., that quickly." But in line 6, **jiù** means "only."

11D.   Imperative sentences (i.e., sentences that make commands or requests) often have a **ba** at the end of the sentence. This is the **ba** that indicates a suggestion, which helps tone down or soften the request.

SV1.   To many Chinese speakers, there are basically two types of people, **Zhōngguo rén** "Chinese" and **wàiguo rén** "foreigners." This usually applies no matter in which country the Chinese speaker is located. Therefore, some Chinese who have lived in the U.S. for many years will still refer to non-Chinese Americans as **wàiguo rén** "foreigners."

Calling for a Taxi to the Airport (cont.)

Almost half an hour has passed but the taxi has still not arrived, so Fuentes—who is becoming increasingly worried about missing her flight—decides to get up and call the taxi company again to ask why her cab is not yet there (continued from the previous conversation).

 ## Basic Conversation 8-3

1. DISPATCHER **Nǐ hǎo! Yǒuyì Bīnguǎn Qìchē Gōngsī.**
Hello. Friendship Hotel Taxi Company.

2. FUENTES **Wéi? Wǒ bàn'ge xiǎoshí yǐqián dǎ diànhuà yàoguo yíliàng chē. Nǐmen shuō shífēn zhōng jiù dào. Zěmme dào xiànzài hái méi lái a?**
Hello? Half an hour ago I called and requested a cab. You said it would arrive in ten minutes. How come it still hasn't come until now?

3. DISPATCHER **Duìbuqǐ, xiànzài shi shàngxiàbān shíjiān, jiāotōng bǐjiào yōngjǐ. Chē wǒmen yǐjīng pàiqule, qǐng nín zài nàixīn děng yìhuǐr.**
I'm sorry, it's rush hour now and traffic is quite congested. We've already dispatched the cab, please be patient and wait a bit longer.

4. FUENTES **Hái yào děng duō jiǔ a?**
How much longer do I have to wait?

5. DISPATCHER **Nín bié zháojí, wǒ xiǎng yìhuǐr jiù huì dào.**
Don't worry, I think it will be there soon.

6. FUENTES **Máfan nín kuài yidianr, hǎo ma? Wǒ kuài yào láibujíle!**
Please try to hurry, will you? Soon I'll be late!

7. DISPATCHER **Hǎo, wǒ mǎshàng tōngzhī sījī jìnkuài gǎndào.**
O.K., I'll immediately notify the driver to rush there as fast as he can.

Build Up

1. Dispatcher

Nǐ hǎo! Yǒuyì Bīnguǎn Qìchē Gōngsī.   Hello. Friendship Hotel Taxi Company.

2. Fuentes

xiǎoshí	hour [N]
bàn'ge xiǎoshí	half an hour
bàn'ge xiǎoshí yǐqián	half an hour ago
dǎ	hit [V]
diànhuà	telephone [N]
dǎ diànhuà	make a telephone call [PH]
yào	request [V]
yàoguo yíliàng chē	had requested a car
zěmme	how come, why [QW]
zěmme hái méi lái	how come (it) hasn't come yet
dào xiànzài	up until now, by now
dào xiànzài hái méi lái	until now (it) still hasn't come

Wéi? Wǒ bàn'ge xiǎoshí yǐqián dǎ diànhuà   Hello? Half an hour ago I called and requested a cab.
yàoguo yíliàng chē. Nǐmen shuō shífēn zhōng   You said it would arrive in ten minutes. How come it
jiù dào. Zěmme dào xiànzài hái méi lái a?   still hasn't come until now?

3. Dispatcher

shàngxiàbān shíjiān	the time when one goes to or gets off from work
jiāotōng	traffic [N]
yōngjǐ	be crowded [SV]
jiāotōng bǐjiào yōngjǐ	traffic is relatively crowded
pài	dispatch, send [V]
-qu	(indicates motion away from the speaker) [RE]
pàiqu	dispatch, send out [RC]
chē wǒmen yǐjīng pàiqule	we've already dispatched the car
nàixīn	be patient [SV]
yìhuǐr	a while [N]
nàixīn děng yìhuǐr	patiently wait a while
zài nàixīn děng yìhuǐr	patiently wait a while longer

Duìbuqǐ, xiànzài shi shàngxiàbān shíjiān,   I'm sorry, it's rush hour now and traffic is quite
jiāotōng bǐjiào yōngjǐ. Chē wǒmen yǐjīng pàiqule,   congested. We've already dispatched the cab,
qǐng nín zài nàixīn děng yìhuǐr.   please be patient and wait a bit longer.

4. Fuentes

yào	need to, have to, should [AV]

Hái yào děng duō jiǔ a?   How much longer do I have to wait?

5. Dispatcher

zháojí	worry, get excited [VO/SV]
nín bié zháojí	don't you worry
huì	be likely to, will [AV]
yìhuǐr jiù huì dào	in a little while it will arrive

Nín bié zháojí, wǒ xiǎng yìhuǐr jiù huì dào.   Don't worry, I think it will be there soon.

6. Fuentes

máfan	trouble, disturb [V]
máfan nín	(I) trouble you to, please
kuài yidianr	a little faster
kuài yào láibujíle	soon won't have enough time
Máfan nín kuài yidianr, hǎo ma?	Please try to hurry, will you? Soon I'll be late!
Wǒ kuài yào láibujíle!	

7. Dispatcher

mǎshàng	immediately, right away [A]
tōngzhī	notify [V]
sījī	driver, chauffeur [N]
wǒ mǎshàng tōngzhī sījī	I'll notify the driver right away
jìnkuài	as fast as possible [A]
gǎn	rush, hurry [V]
gǎndào	rush or hurry to a place [V+PV]
jìnkuài gǎndào	rush there as fast as possible
Hǎo, wǒ mǎshàng tōngzhī sījī jìnkuài gǎndào.	O.K., I'll immediately notify the driver to rush there as fast as he can.

Supplementary Vocabulary

1. **juédìng** — decide [V]

   juédìng zuò shémme — decide to do what

   Chūzū qìchē hái méi lái, tā juédìng zuò shémme? — When the taxi still hadn't come, what did she decide to do?

2. **fázi** — means, method, way [N]

   yǒu fázi — have a way, have a method

   shàng — go to, come to [CV]

   shàng zhèr lái — to here come, come here

   ràng tā shàng zhèr lái — cause him to come here

   Nǐ yǒu fázi ràng tā shàng zhèr lái ma? — Do you have a way to make him come here?

Grammatical and Cultural Notes

2A.   **Xiǎoshí** "hour" can be used as a noun with the measure **ge**, as here, or as a measure itself. In other words, it's correct to say either **yíge xiǎoshí** or **yìxiǎoshí**, and one can say **bàn'ge xiǎoshí** or **bànxiǎoshí**, etc. On the other hand, **zhōngtóu**, which you had in lesson 3-4 and which also means "hour," must always be used with the measure **ge**.

2B.   **Dǎ diànhuà** is the expression for "make a telephone call." **Dǎ** by itself means "hit" (e.g., **Bié dǎ wǒ!** "Don't hit me!") while **diànhuà** literally means "electric speech," this being the term that came to be used after the importation of the telephone into China in the 19th century. If the person to whom the call is being made is mentioned, this is done with the coverb **gěi** "give, to, for" followed by the appropriate noun or pronoun. Negative **bù** or **méi** precedes the **gěi**. Examples:

> **Qǐng nǐ gěi tā dǎ ([yí]ge) diànhuà.**
>
> "Please call her on the telephone."

> **Wǒ gěi tā dǎle hǎojǐcì diànhuà, kěshi méi rén zài.**
>
> "I called him quite a few times, but there was nobody there."

> **Wǒ méi gěi tā dǎ diànhuà.**
>
> "I didn't call her on the telephone."

For "I called him," always say **Wǒ gěi tā dǎ diànhuà le**. Never say **Wǒ dǎ tā le** (unless you mean it), because that means "I hit him"!

2C.   Pay attention to the different meanings of the verb **yào**. Here in line 2, **yào** means "request." In line 4, **yào** is introduced in the meaning "need to, have to, should." And in line 6, **yào** means "be going to, will." You have also encountered **yào** previously with the meanings "want, need, cost take" (3-3) and "want to" (5-4). Compare:

Nǐ yào shémme?	"What do you want?"
Zhèige yào duōshǎo qián?	"How much does this cost?"
Wǒ yào qù Zhōngguo le!	"I'm going to go to China!"
Wǒ yě yào kàn!	"I want to see it, too!"
Wǒ yàoguo liǎngliàng chē.	"I requested two cars."
Hái yào děng duō jiǔ?	"How much longer do we have to wait?"

2D.   **Nǐmen shuō shífēn zhōng jiù dào** "You said that it would arrive in ten minutes." Notice that there is no verb suffix **-le** here on the verb **shuō** even though this involves completed action. This is the normal situation in quotations. So if you wish to say, for example, "She said that she has been very busy recently," you should say **Tā shuō tā zuìjìn hěn máng** and you should NOT say *Tā shuōle tā zuìjìn hěn máng.

2E.   You learned back in 2-2 that **zěmme** can mean "how"; now you learn it in its other sense of "how come, why." In this latter sense, it is often interchangeable with **wèishemme** (6-3), except that **zěmme** is more colloquial and a little stronger—it often expresses the speaker's astonishment or incredulity. As with **wèishemme**, questions containing **zěmme** frequently (but not necessarily) end in a sentence-final particle **ne**, which softens the tone of the question. Examples:

Nǐ zěmme méi gàosu wǒ ne?	"How come you didn't tell me?"
Wǒmen zěmme bù qǐng tā ne?	"How come we're not inviting her?"
Tā zěmme měicì dōu chídào ne?	"How come he arrives late every time?"

3A.   **Shàngxiàbān(r)** "go to work and get off from work" is a compressed form of **shàngbān(r)** "go to work" and **xiàbān(r)** "get off from work." Compressed forms like this are common in Chinese.

3B.   **Chē wǒmen yǐjīng pàiqule** literally means "As for the car, we have already sent it out." **Chē** is here an example of a preposed object which becomes the topic of the sentence.

3C.   Resultative Compounds. In this line, notice the resultative compound verb **pàiqu** "dispatch, send out," which is composed of the verb **pài** "send" plus the resultative ending **-qu** (lit. "go"), which indicates motion away from the speaker. Also notice, in line 6 of this Conversation, the resultative compound **láibují** "not be able to make it on time," which you first saw in 3-4. In addition, in 2-4, you had **gǎocuò** "get wrong," composed of the action verb **gǎo** "get" and the resultative verb ending **-cuò** "wrong"; and in 6-2, you had **zhǎngdà** "grow up" (lit. "grow big"). All of these verbs are examples of resultative verbs, a very important verb type in Chinese. A resultative compound is a verb compound composed of an action verb followed by a resultative ending (usually a verb or stative verb) which indicates the result of the action. For example, **zhǎngdà** "grow with the result that one becomes big, grow up" is composed of the action verb **zhǎng** "grow" plus the resultative ending **-dà** "big." Some resultative compounds are composed of verbs indicating direction or motion plus the resultative endings **-lái** "come" or **-qù** "go"; **pàiqu** "dispatch, send out" belongs to this group. In the lessons to come, you will see many more resultative compounds.

3D.   Note that the stative verb **nàixīn** "be patient" can also function as a noun meaning "patience." Example: **Nǐ zěmme zhèmme méiyou nàixīn?** "How come you're so impatient?" (lit. "You how come so not have patience?") As you have seen before, it is not uncommon for a Chinese word to belong to more than one word class.

3E.   There are some people who pronounce **yìhuǐr** "a while" as **yíhuìr**.

5-6.   Notice the auxiliary verb **huì** "be likely to, will" in line 5 and compare it with the auxiliary verb **yào** "will" in line 6. Both of these auxiliary verbs can mean "will" but there is a difference: **huì**, which often implies "be likely to," is not as emphatic as **yào**.

6A.   The polite introductory phrase **máfan nín**, literally "(I) trouble you (to...)," is very common at the beginning of all kinds of requests. It softens the tone of an otherwise direct request and "recognizes" the troubles the person asked must go through to comply with the request.

6B.   Notice the use of **yidianr** "a little" after the stative verb **kuài** "fast." **Kuài yidianr**, which literally means "faster by a little bit," is best translated into English as "a little faster" (5-3: 4E). Note that you CANNOT say *yìdiǎnr kuài.

6C.   Look at **Wǒ kuài yào láibùjíle!** "Soon I'll be late!" As we saw in 5-2: 10A, the pattern **kuài yào...le** indicates that an action is about to take place. The **kuài** in this pattern is an adverb meaning "soon." Some more examples of the pattern **kuài yào...le** to indicate imminent action:

Kuài yào kāishǐle!	"It's about to start!"
Xiàozhǎng kuài yào jiǎnghuàle.	"The president is about to speak."
Wǒ tīngshuō tāmen kuài yào líhūnle.	"I've heard they're about to divorce."

Notice that there are two **kuài** in line 6, with different meanings and usages. The first **kuài** is a stative verb meaning "be fast," while the second **kuài** is an adverb meaning "soon," as discussed above.

7A.   **Tōngzhī** "notify" implies from superior to subordinate. While a teacher could say to her or his students **Wǒ huì tōngzhī nǐmen** "I'll notify you," students could not say this to their teacher.

7B.   The adverb **mǎshàng** "immediately" literally means "on a horse, horseback" and dates from Mongol times, i.e., the Yuan Dynasty (1271–1368).

7C.   **Wǒ mǎshàng tōngzhī sījī jìnkuài gǎndào** "I'll notify the driver immediately to hurry there as fast as he can" is another example of a pivot sentence (8-2: 2C). This sentence is actually composed of the following two sentences:

Wǒ mǎshàng tōngzhī sījī.	+	**Sījī jìnkuài gǎndào.**
"I'll immediately notify the driver."	+	"The driver will hurry there as fast as he can."

When the two sentences are combined, **sījī** serves as a pivot, serving simultaneously as the object of the first sentence and the subject of the second sentence, the second **sījī** being deleted.

SV2.   The verb **shàng** can mean "go to" or "come to." **Shàng** and **qù** can both mean "go" but there are several differences: (1) **shàng** is more common in northern China and little used in the south, while **qù** can be used everywhere; (2) **shàng** is more colloquial while **qù** is standard written or spoken Chinese; (3) **shàng** is always followed by a place word or question word, while **qù** can also be followed by other verbs (e.g., **Wǒ qù mǎi dōngxi**); and (4) **qù** can be a one-word answer to a question, but **shàng** cannot. Examples:

Nǐmen shàng nǎr a?

"Where are you going?"

Nǐ shàng wǒ zhèr lái zuò shémme?

"What did you come over here for?" (lit. "You came to me here came to do what?")

The taxi finally arrives and, after loading the luggage, the driver takes Fuentes to Capital Airport. On arrival, she pays the driver his fare and enters the terminal building (continued from the previous conversation).

 Basic Conversation 8-4

1. DRIVER   Shi nín yào chē dào Shǒudū Jīchǎng ma?
             Was it you who requested a cab to Capital Airport?

2. FUENTES   Duì, shì wǒ.
             Yes, it was me.

3. DRIVER   Jiù zhèiliǎngjiàn xíngli ma?
             Just these two pieces of luggage?

4. FUENTES   Duì.
             Yes.

             (after they start off)

             Cóng zhèr dào jīchǎng xūyào duōshǎo shíjiān?
             How long does it take to get from here to the airport?

5. DRIVER   Sìshifēn zhōng zuǒyòu ba.
             Probably about forty minutes.

             (notices heavy traffic)
             Zāogāo, zhèr yòu dǔchē le, wǒmen zhǐhǎo huàn tiáo biéde lù zǒule.
             Darn, there's a traffic jam here again, we'll have to change to a different route.

6. FUENTES   *(when they arrive at the airport)*

             Duōshǎo qián?
             How much is it?

7. DRIVER   Yìbǎi èrshibākuài sì.
             RMB 128.40.

8. FUENTES   Gěi nín yìbǎi wǔshikuài. Nín zhǎo wǒ èrshikuài jiù hǎole.
             Here's a hundred fifty dollars. Give me twenty bucks in change and that will be fine.

9. DRIVER   Xièxie.
                 Thanks.

10. FUENTES   Zàijiàn.
                 Goodbye.

11. DRIVER   Zàijiàn.
                 Bye.

Build Up

1. Driver

Shi nín yào chē dào Shǒudū Jīchǎng ma?   Was it you who requested a cab to Capital Airport?

2. Fuentes

Duì, shì wǒ.   Yes, it was me.

3. Driver

jiàn	(for luggage, matters) [M]
zhèiliǎngjiàn	these two pieces
xíngli	luggage, baggage [N]
zhèiliǎngjiàn xíngli	these two pieces of luggage
Jiù zhèiliǎngjiàn xíngli ma?	Just these two pieces of luggage?

4. Fuentes

Duì.	Yes.
cóng zhèr dào jīchǎng	from here to the airport
xūyào	need [V]
xūyào duōshǎo shíjiān	takes how much time
Cóng zhèr dào jīchǎng xūyào duōshǎo shíjiān?	How long does it take to get from here to the airport?

5. Driver

Sìshifēn zhōng zuǒyòu ba.	Probably about forty minutes.
zāogāo	"darn it"; be a mess [IE/SV]
dǔchē	be clogged up with cars [VO]
zhèr yòu dǔchē le	there's a traffic jam here again
zhǐhǎo	have no choice but [A]
huàn	change to, exchange [V]
tiáo	(for streets, alleys) [M]
biéde	other, another [AT]
biéde lù	another road
zhǐhǎo huàn tiáo biéde lù	the only thing (we) can do is change to another road
Zāogāo, zhèr yòu dǔchē le,	Darn, there's a traffic jam here again,
wǒmen zhǐhǎo huàn tiáo biéde lù zǒule.	we'll have to change to a different route.

6. Fuentes

Duōshǎo qián?   How much is it?

7. Driver

Yìbǎi èrshibākuài sì.   RMB 128.40.

8. Fuentes

zhǎo	give in change [V]
Gěi nín yìbǎi wǔshikuài. Nín zhǎo	Here's a hundred fifty dollars. Give me
wǒ èrshikuài jiù hǎole.	twenty bucks in change and that will be fine.

9. Driver
Xièxie.   Thanks.

10. Fuentes
Zàijiàn.   Goodbye.

11. Driver
Zàijiàn.   Bye.

 Supplementary Vocabulary

1. kāichē   drive a car [VO]
yīngdāng   should, ought to [AV]
Nǐ hái bú huì kāichē? Yīngdāng xué ma!   You don't yet know how to drive a car? You should learn, you know?

2. zhǎoqián   give (someone) change [VO]
Zhèige dōngxi mài jiǔkuài wǔ, wǒ gěi nǐ shíkuài,   This thing sells for $9.50 and I gave you ten dollars.
nǐ dāngrán yīngdāng zhǎoqián!   Of course you should give change!

3. qīng   be light (not heavy) [SV]
zhòng   be heavy [SV]
Nǐ bān qīngde ba, wǒ kéyi bān zhòngde.   Why don't you move the light ones, I can move the heavy ones.

4. gōngjīn   kilo [M]
Nǐ duō zhòng? –Wǒ jiǔshíbāgōngjīn.   How heavy are you? –I weigh 98 kilos.

5. mǐ   meter [M]
Nǐ duō gāo? –Wǒ yīmǐ bā èr.   How tall are you? –I'm one meter eighty-two.

6. bàntiān   "half the day," a long time [NU+M]
zuìhòu   in the end, finally [TW]
Wǒ zuótiān xiàwǔ děng nǐ děngle bàntiān,   I waited for you for a long time yesterday afternoon.
zuìhòu wǒ zhǐhǎo zǒule.   In the end, I had no choice but to leave.

7. shīfu   master; driver [N]
sāichē   be clogged up with cars [VO]
Shīfu, yàoshi sāichēde huà, shì bu shi   Driver, if there's a traffic jam, would it be better to
huàn biéde lù bǐjiào hǎo?   change to a different road?

Grammatical and Cultural Notes

2.   Note **Duì, shì wǒ** "Yes, it was me." In normal usage, the verb **shì** "be" is in the neutral tone (**shi**). When it is stressed, however, as here, it is pronounced with a full fourth tone. Contrast the following conversation involving three speakers:

   Speaker A: **Túshūguǎn wàitou nèige rén shi Xiǎo Liú ma?**

                 "Is that Little Liu outside the library?"

   Speaker B: **Bú shi, bú shi Xiǎo Liú.**

                 "No, it isn't Little Liu."

   Speaker C: **Shì tā, shì Xiǎo Liú!**

                 "It is him, it is Little Liu!"

3A. Specifier + Number + Measure + Noun. You have seen before the pattern Specifier + Measure + Noun (e.g., **zhèijiàn xíngli** "this piece of luggage"). You have also seen the pattern Number + Measure + Noun (e.g., **liǎngjiàn xíngli** "two pieces of luggage"). Now you see a new pattern where these two old patterns have been combined. The new pattern is:

Specifier	Number	Measure	Noun
zhèi	liǎng	jiàn	xíngli

"these two pieces of luggage."

Here are some additional examples of specifier + number + measure + noun:

zhèisānzhāng zhuōzi	"these three tables"
zhèibáge rén	"these eight people"
nèiwǔge shūjiàzi	"those five bookshelves"
nèijǐjiā gōngchǎng	"those several factories"
něiliǎngliàng chē?	"which two cars?"
měishíge yuè	"every ten months"
"péngyou" zhèiliǎngge zì	"the word 'friend'" (lit. "the two characters **péngyou**")

3B. In the audio recording, the speaker says **zhèliǎngjiàn** instead of **zhèiliǎngjiàn**. This type of variation between **zhè-** and **zhèi-** is very common. Both pronunciations are correct.

4A. When a single passenger takes a taxi, in Taiwan he or she would normally sit in the back, on the right side. In China, it is fine to sit in the back, but some people consider it more "proletarian" and better form to sit up front next to the driver and chat. This is also definitely better for your Chinese language development, but can be frightening and even dangerous!

4B. **CÓNG...DÀO...** The pattern **cóng...dào...** "from...to..." is a very common pattern for expressing the beginning and ending points when talking about places, directions, destinations, times, dates, etc. The pattern can be diagrammed like this:

CÓNG	Place1	DÀO	Place2
cóng	Běijīng	dào	Tiānjīn

"from Beijing to Tianjin"

Examples:

Cóng zhèr dào Tiān'ānmén bú tài yuǎn.

"It's not too far from here to Tiananmen."

Cóng shítáng dào túshūguǎn zěmme zǒu?

"How do you get from the cafeteria to the library?"

Cóng wǒ jiā dào xuéxiào yào chàbuduō shífēn zhōng.

"From my home to the school it takes about ten minutes."

Wǎnfàn shi cóng jǐdiǎn dào jǐdiǎn?

"Dinner is from what time until what time?"

Cóng wǔdiǎn bàn dào qīdiǎn.

"From 5:30 until 7:00."

Tā cóng yī-jiǔ-bā-yī-nián dào yī-jiǔ-bā-qī-nián zài Běidà xuéxí.

"From 1981 to 1987 she studied at Beijing University."

Tā měitiān cóng zǎoshang dào wǎnshang yìzhí dōu hěn máng.

"He's busy every day all the time from morning to evening."

4C. Instead of **Cóng zhèr dào jīchǎng xūyào duōshǎo shíjiān?** "How much time does it take to get from here to the airport?," some speakers prefer **Cóng zhèr dào jīchǎng xūyào duōcháng shíjiān?** "How long does it take to get from here to the airport?" Either wording can be considered correct.

5A. Slang. Chinese, like all languages, has its share of slang. **Zāogāo** "darn it, dang, what a mess" is a very common and quite acceptable way to indicate frustration or consternation about something unfortunate that has happened. Sometimes the pronunciation is drawn out very long so that it sounds like this: **z-ā-o-g-ā-o. Zāogāo,** which literally means "rotten cake," can also function as a stative verb, e.g., **Nà zhēnde hěn zāogāo** "That is really a mess."

5B. ZHǏHǍO. The adverb **zhǐhǎo** "have no choice but, can only" (lit. "only good") is commonly used to indicate that no alternative is available and one must choose a less desirable course of action. The pattern is:

Subject	ZHǏHǍO	Verb Phrase
Wǒmen	zhǐhǎo	míngtiān zài lái.

"We have no choice but to come again tomorrow."

Examples:

Túshūguǎn yǐjīng guānle, wǒmen zhǐhǎo huí sùshè.

"The library has already closed, we have no choice but to return to our dorm."

Xiǎo Wáng bú zài, wǒmen zhǐhǎo gěi tā liú ge tiáozi.

"Little Wang is not here, the only thing we can do is leave him a note."

5C. The verb **huàn** means "change, exchange." **Huàn lù,** as in the Basic Conversation, means "change roads," which doesn't really mean that you are "changing" the road but rather that you are "exchanging" it, i.e., changing from one road to another. Here are some other things and people that one can change with **huàn:**

huàn chē	"change buses, change trains"
huàn fángjiān	"change rooms"
huàn gōngzuò	"change jobs"
huàn nánpéngyou	"change boyfriends"
huàn nǚpéngyou	"change girlfriends"
huàn lǎoshī	"change teachers" (normally not to be recommended!)
huàn qián	"change money"
huàn rén	"change people" (e.g., on the staffs of companies or on athletic teams)

Note that you cannot use **huàn** to say that someone has changed.

5D. You are introduced here to the attributive **biéde** "other, another," as in **huàn tiáo biéde lù** "change to another road." Compare this with the attributive **qítā** "other" as in **huì qítāde yǔyán** "know other languages," which you learned in 7-2. The difference between the two is that **qítāde** involves the remainder of a known quantity, some of which have been previously discussed, while **biéde** is more general and involves an unknown quantity. The difference is somewhat like the difference between English "the other" vs. "another."

5E. Be sure to give the **h-** on **huàn** "change" sufficient friction, so it sounds different from the **w-** in **wàn** "ten thousand."

5F. **Tiáo** is the measure for long and narrow things such as streets, roads, alleys, rivers, snakes, fish, and (for some speakers) dogs.

5G.   **Tiáo** is here short for **yìtiáo**. The **yī** before measures is often omitted in rapid, colloquial conversation. Examples:

yǒu yíge rén	→ **yǒu ge rén**	"there was a person"
huàn yìtái xīnde	→ **huàn tái xīnde**	"exchange it (e.g., a computer) for a new one"
gěi tā dǎ yíge diànhuà →	**gěi tā dǎ ge diànhuà**	"call her on the telephone"
wǒ yǒu yìdiǎnr shì	→ **wǒ yǒu diǎnr shì**	"I have a little something to do"

7.   The speaker on the audio recording says **bākuài** without a tone change on the **bā**, rather than **bákuài**, with a tone change before the fourth-tone syllable **kuài**. Both pronunciations are common and both are correct.

SV1A.   **Nǐ hái bú huì kāichē?** "You don't know how to drive yet?" is an intonation question (2-3: 1C), so in this case there is no affirmative-negative verb construction or question particle **ma**.

SV1B.   The auxiliary verb **yīngdāng** "should" means the same as **yīnggāi** (2-2).

SV1C.   **Yīngdāng xué ma!** "You should learn, for heaven's sakes!" The **ma** at the end of this line is the **ma** that indicates an obvious situation (7-2: 4C).

Great Hall of the People, Beijing

SV3.   You previously encountered the stative verb **qīng** "be light" in the noun **qīngshēng** "neutral tone" in the Classroom Expressions at the beginning of this volume.

SV3-5. Height and Weight. Learn the stative verb **zhòng** "be heavy." You can now ask how much a person weighs and reply when you are asked. The question is:

Nǐ duō zhòng?   "How heavy are you?"

To answer questions about weight, use the measure **gōngjīn** "kilo." No verb is needed. For example:

Wǒ liùshisāngōngjīn. "I weigh 63 kilos." (lit. "I'm 63 kilos.")

Some common weights are listed below in five pound increments with their equivalent in kilograms. If you don't find your weight, you can compute it yourself (one kilo = 2.2 pounds).

90 lbs.	=	41 kilos	130 lbs.	=	59 kilos	170 lbs.	=	77 kilos
95 lbs.	=	43 kilos	135 lbs.	=	61 kilos	175 lbs.	=	80 kilos
100 lbs.	=	45 kilos	140 lbs.	=	64 kilos	180 lbs.	=	82 kilos
105 lbs.	=	48 kilos	145 lbs.	=	66 kilos	185 lbs.	=	84 kilos
110 lbs.	=	50 kilos	150 lbs.	=	68 kilos	190 lbs.	=	86 kilos
115 lbs.	=	52 kilos	155 lbs.	=	70 kilos	195 lbs.	=	89 kilos
120 lbs	=	55 kilos	160 lbs.	=	73 kilos	200 lbs.	=	91 kilos
125 lbs.	=	57 kilos	165 lbs.	=	75 kilos	205 lbs.	=	93 kilos

You already know the stative verb **gāo** "be tall." To ask how tall someone is, ask:

Nǐ duō gāo?   "How tall are you?"

To answer questions about height, use the appropriate number followed by the measure **mǐ** "meter." For the number of centimeters, simply read off one digit after another, in telephone number style. For example:

Wǒ yìmǐ bā èr.   "I'm one meter eighty-two."

Some common heights are listed below in feet and inches with their equivalents in meters and centimeters. If your height is not given, you can compute it yourself (one inch = 2.54 centimeters).

4'8"	=	1.43 M	5'4"	=	1.63 M	6'	=	1.83 M
4'9"	=	1.45 m	5'5"	=	1.65 m	6'1"	=	1.85 m
4'10"	=	1.48 m	5'6"	=	1.68 m	6'2"	=	1.88 m
4'11"	=	1.5 m	5'7"	=	1.7 m	6'3"	=	1.91 m
5'	=	1.53 m	5'8"	=	1.73 m	6'4"	=	1.93 m
5'1"	=	1.55 m	5'9"	=	1.75 m	6'5"	=	1.96 m
5'2"	=	1.58 m	5'10"	=	1.78 m	6'6"	=	1.98 m
5'3"	=	1.6 m	5'11"	=	1.8 m	6'7"	=	2.01 m

SV7A. **Shīfu** traditionally means "master worker (in some trade)" as opposed to an apprentice worker. In addition to that traditional meaning, **shīfu** is used in China (though not in Taiwan or Hong Kong) as a polite way to address a professional driver of some vehicle. It can be used for males or females. **Sījī xiānsheng** would be another polite way to address a male driver.

SV7B. The verb-object compound **sāichē** is a common synonym of **dǔchē**. Both mean "be clogged up with cars, congested."

Unit 8: Review and Study Guide

New Vocabulary

ADVERBS

gèng	even more, more
jìnkuài	as fast as possible
mǎshàng	immediately, right away
yìzhí	straight
zhǐhǎo	have no choice but

ATTRIBUTIVES

biéde	other, another

AUXILIARY VERBS

huì	be likely to, will
yào	need to, have to, should
yīngdāng	should, ought to

CONJUNCTIONS

huòzhě	or

COVERBS

lí	be distant from, from
shàng	go to, come to, to
wàng	to, toward

IDIOMATIC EXPRESSIONS

hǎode	"all right," "O.K."
láojià	excuse me
zāogāo	"darn it," "what a mess"

INTERJECTIONS

wéi	"hello"

LOCALIZERS

běi	north
nán	south
xī	west

MEASURES

gōngjīn	kilo
jiàn	(for luggage, matters)
liàng	(for land vehicles)
mǐ	meter
tiáo	(for streets, alleys)

MOVEABLE ADVERBS

dàgài	probably, about

NOUNS

chēzi	car, vehicle
diànhuà	telephone
fázi	means, method, way
jiāotōng	traffic
lóu	building (with two or more floors)
nàixīn	patience
qìchē	car, vehicle
shīfu	master; driver
shǒudū	capital
sījī	driver, chauffeur
wàiguo	foreign country
wàiguoyǔ	foreign language
xiǎoshí	hour
xíngli	luggage, baggage
xìngmíng	first and last name
yìhuǐr	a while
yǒuyì	friendship
zhuānjiā	expert

NUMBER + MEASURE

bàntiān	"half the day," a long time

PHRASES

běifāng huà	northern speech
běifāng rén	Northerner
chūzū qìchē	taxi
dǎ diànhuà	make a telephone call
Dōngfāng rén	Asian
nánfāng huà	southern speech
nánfāng rén	Southerner
wàiguo huà	foreign language
wàiguo rén	foreigner
Xīfāng rén	Westerner
zhuānjiā lóu	(foreign) experts building

PLACE WORDS

běifāng	north, the North
Běijīng Fàndiàn	Beijing Hotel
Běijīng Wàiguoyǔ Dàxué	Beijing Foreign Studies University
Běiwài	(abbreviation for Beijing Foreign Studies University)
bīnguǎn	guest house, hotel
dōngfāng	east, the East
jīchǎng	airport
ménkǒu(r)	doorway, entrance
nánfāng	south, the South
Shǒudū Jīchǎng	Capital Airport
Tiān'ānmén	Tiananmen
xīfāng	west, the West
Yǒuyì Bīnguǎn	Friendship Hotel
zuǒyòu	about, approximately

QUESTION WORDS

zěmme	how come, why

RESULTATIVE COMPOUNDS

pàiqu	dispatch, send out

RESULTATIVE ENDINGS

-qu	(indicates motion away from the speaker)

STATIVE VERBS

jìn	be close, near
kuài	be fast
nàixīn	be patient
qīng	be light (not heavy)
yōngjǐ	be crowded
zāogāo	be a mess
zháojí	worry, get excited
zhòng	be heavy

SURNAMES

Fù	Fu

TIME WORDS

zuìhòu	in the end, finally

VERBS

chūzū	rent out
dǎ	hit
gǎn	rush, hurry
guò	pass, go by
huàn	change to, exchange
juédìng	decide
kāi	drive, operate a vehicle
máfan	trouble, disturb
pài	dispatch, send
tōngzhī	notify
xūyào	need
yào	request
zhǎo	give in change
zǒu	go, walk

VERB-OBJECT COMPOUNDS

dǎdī	take a taxi
dǔchē	be clogged up with cars
kāichē	drive a car
sāichē	be clogged up with cars
zháojí	worry, get excited
zhǎoqián	give (someone) change
zǒulù	walk

Major New Grammar Patterns

QÙ...ZĚMME ZǑU: Láojià, qù Wàijiāobù zěmme zǒu? "Excuse me, how do you get to the Foreign Ministry?" (8-1)

WÀNG to express movement toward a certain direction: wàng xī zǒu "walk toward the west," **wàng qián kāi** "drive forward" (8-1)

LÍ to express distance from: Nǐ jiā lí zhèr yuǎn bu yuǎn? "Is your home far from here?," **Wǒ jiā lí zhèr hěn jìn.** "My home is close to here." (8-1)

ZUǑYÒU: liǎngge yuè zuǒyòu "about two months" (8-1)

Conditional clauses with -DE HUÀ: Zǒulùde huà, dàgài yào bàn'ge zhōngtóu zuǒyòu. "If you walk, it will probably take about half an hour." (8-1)

Pivot sentences: Wǒ yào yíliàng chē qù Shǒudū Jīchǎng "I want a car to go to Capital Airport" (8-2)

Resultative compounds: pàiqu "send out," **láibují** "not be able to make it on time" (8-3)

Specifier + Number + Measure + Noun: zhèiliǎngjiàn xíngli "these two pieces of luggage" (8-4)

CÓNG...DÀO...: Cóng sāndiǎn bàn dào wǔdiǎn. "From 3:30 until 5:00." (8-4)

ZHǏHAO: Wǒmen zhǐhǎo huí sùshè. "We have no choice but to return to our dorm." (8-4)

Height and weight: Nǐ duō zhòng? "How heavy are you?" **Wǒ liùshisāngōngjīn.** "I weigh 63 kilos." **Nǐ duō gāo?** "How tall are you?" **Wǒ yīmǐ bā èr.** "I'm one meter eighty-two." (8-4)

Getting Around Beijing (II)

COMMUNICATIVE OBJECTIVES

Once you have mastered this unit, you will be able to use Chinese to:

1. Understand and give more complicated directions: go straight, pass a certain place, turn right at the third traffic light, etc.

2. Ask about taking a bus or streetcar: which number to take, where the stop is, where to get off, where to change to another bus or streetcar.

3. Converse with a bus or streetcar conductor: tell the conductor where you got on and where you wish to go, buy the ticket, ask the conductor to let you know when you arrive at your stop, ask how many stops there are until your stop, etc.

4. Discuss whether or not someone is able to do something: can find/can't find, can fall asleep/can't fall asleep, can understand/can't understand, etc.

5. Talk about colors.

6. Talk about pets.

Lost in Beijing

Cindy Han, a young American woman from Texas who is studying Chinese in Beijing, is looking for the Peace Hotel. She is worried that she has gotten lost, so she asks a pedestrian for directions.

Basic Conversation 9-1

1. AMERICAN	**Duìbuqǐ, qǐng wèn, qù Hépíng Bīnguǎn zěmme zǒu?** Excuse me, how do you get to the Peace Hotel?
2. FIRST CHINESE PEDESTRIAN	**Duìbuqǐ, wǒ bú shi běndì rén, wǒ yě bú tài qīngchu. Nàr yǒu yíwèi jiāotōngjǐng, nín qù wèn tā ba.** Sorry, I'm not from here, I'm not sure either. Over there is a traffic policeman, why don't you go ask him.
3. AMERICAN	*(asks another pedestrian)* **Láojià, qǐng wèn, qù Hépíng Bīnguǎn zěmme zǒu?** Pardon me, how do you get to the Peace Hotel?
4. SECOND CHINESE PEDESTRIAN	**Cóng zhèr yìzhí wàng qián zǒu. Guòle dì'èrge hónglǜdēng, wàng běi guǎi. Zài zǒu chàbuduō wǔfēn zhōng jiù dàole.** From here keep going straight. When you pass the second traffic light, turn to the north. Go another five minutes or so and you'll be there.
5. AMERICAN	**Xièxie.** Thanks.
6. SECOND CHINESE PEDESTRIAN	**Bú yòng xiè.** Don't mention it.

Build Up

1. American

Hépíng Bīnguǎn	Peace Hotel [PW]

Duìbuqǐ, qǐng wèn, qù Hépíng Bīnguǎn zěmme zǒu? Excuse me, how do you get to the Peace Hotel?

2. First Chinese Pedestrian

běndì	this place, here [N]
běndì rén	a person from this area, a local
wǒ bú shi běndì rén	I'm not a person from this area
qīngchu	be clear, clear about [SV]
wǒ bú tài qīngchu	I'm not too clear (about that)
jiāotōngjǐng (B)	traffic police [N]
nàr yǒu yíwèi jiāotōngjǐng	there's a traffic policeman over there
Duìbuqǐ, wǒ bú shi běndì rén, wǒ yě bú tài qīngchu.	Sorry, I'm not from here, I'm not sure either.
Nàr yǒu yíwèi jiāotōngjǐng, nín qù wèn tā ba.	Over there is a traffic policeman, why don't you go ask him.

3. American

Láojià, qǐng wèn, qù Hépíng Bīnguǎn zěmme zǒu?	Pardon me, how do you get to the Peace Hotel?

4. Second Chinese Pedestrian

hóng	be red [SV]
lǜ	be green [SV]
dēng	light, lamp [N]
hónglǜdēng	traffic light [N]
guòle dì'èrge hónglǜdēng	have passed the second traffic light
guǎi (B)	turn [V]
wàng běi guǎi	turn toward the north
zài zǒu chàbuduō wǔfēn zhōng	again go for about five minutes
Cóng zhèr yìzhí wàng qián zǒu. Guòle dì'èrge hónglǜdēng, wàng běi guǎi. Zài zǒu chàbuduō wǔfēn zhōng jiù dàole.	From here keep going straight. When you pass the second traffic light, turn to the north. Go another five minutes or so and you'll be there.

5. American

Xièxie.	Thanks.

6. Second Chinese Pedestrian

bú yòng	not need to, don't need to [A+AV]
xiè	thank [V]
bú yòng xiè	"don't mention it" [IE]
Bú yòng xiè.	Don't mention it.

 # Supplementary Vocabulary

A. GENERAL

1. lùkǒu(r)	intersection [PW]
xiàyíge lùkǒu	the next intersection
zhuǎn	turn [V]
zuǒ zhuǎn	turn left
Zài xiàyíge lùkǒu zuǒ zhuǎn.	Turn left at the next intersection.

2. jǐngchá	police, policeman [N]
jiāotōng jǐngchá (T)	traffic police [PH]
Kuài, wǒmen xūyào yíwèi jiāotōng jǐngchá!	Quick, we need a traffic policeman!

B. COLORS

3. yánsè	color [N]
Nǐ xǐhuan shémme yánsè?	What color do you like?

4. **hēi**   be black [SV]
   bái   be white [SV]
   Wǒ yào hēide, bú yào báide.   I want black ones, not white ones.

5. **lán**   be blue [SV]
   huáng   be yellow [SV]
   Wǒ mǎile lán xié, tā mǎile huáng xié.   I bought blue shoes and she bought yellow shoes.

6. **hóngsè**   the color red [N]
   lánsè   the color blue [N]
   Wǒ xǐhuan hóngsè gēn lánsè.   I like red and blue.

7. **hēisè**   the color black [N]
   báisè   the color white [N]
   Wǒ yào hēisède, bú yào báisède.   I want black-colored ones, I don't want white-colored ones.

8. **lǜsè**   the color green [N]
   huángsè   the color yellow [N]
   Lǜsède bēibāo hé huángsède dàizi dōu shi wǒde.   The green backpack and the yellow bag are both mine.

Additional Vocabulary: More Colors

1. **huīsè**   grey color [N]
2. **zǐsè**   purple color [N]
3. **zōngsè**   brown color [N]
4. **kāfēisè**   coffee color [N]
5. **júhóngsè**   orange color [N]
6. **fěnhóngsè**   pink color [N]

Grammatical and Cultural Notes

2A.   When asked where the Peace Hotel is, the first Chinese speaker says **wǒ yě bú tài qīngchu** "I'm not too clear either." This is really just a euphemism for **wǒ bù zhīdào** "I don't know." Most speakers want to be helpful and some will even take the trouble to draw a map or escort one to the place for which one is looking. On the other hand, other speakers may not like to admit they don't know something, which would result in loss of face, and they therefore may sometimes say something very general or even inaccurate. For this reason, it is always good practice to ask a second person and possibly even a third after a few minutes of searching. In general, younger, educated, urban residents are more accustomed to speaking with foreigners and are more likely to give helpful answers.

2B.   **Jiāotōngjǐng** is the expression used in China for "traffic policeman" or "traffic policewoman"; it is sometimes abbreviated to **jiāojǐng**. In Taiwan, the expression **jiāotōng jǐngchá** is used instead (cf. SV2).

2C.   Chinese Equivalents of English "Ask." **Wèn** means "ask" in the sense of asking someone a question. For example:

   Nǐ yàoshi bù dǒngde huà, yào wèn lǎoshī a!

   "If you don't understand, you should ask the teacher!"

If the sense is politely asking or requesting someone to do something (as in "Ask him to come again tomorrow") or inviting someone to some event (as in "Ask her over to dinner"), then one cannot use **wèn** but must use **qǐng** "invite" instead. For example:

   Qǐng tā míngtiān zài lái.   "Ask him to come again tomorrow."

   Qǐng tā dào wǒmen jiā lái chī fàn.   "Ask her over to our house for dinner."

If a superior asks an inferior to do something, then **qǐng** is considered too polite and **jiào** "tell (someone to do something)" or **ràng** "have (someone do something)" are used instead. Example:

> **Lǎoshī jiào wǒmen zuò zuòyè.**   "The teacher asked us to do our homework."

2D.   Notice that in **Nín qù wèn tā ba** "Why don't you go ask him," the **qù** indicates the purpose for which one is going to a certain place (1-1, SV2c).

4.   **Guǎi** is the verb for "turn" commonly used in northern China. In all of Mainland China and Taiwan, the verb **zhuǎn** can be used to mean "turn" (cf. SV1).

6.   **Bú yòng xiè** "don't need to thank, don't mention it, you're welcome" is very common. Besides the verb **xiè** "thank," this expression is made up of **bú** "not" and **yòng**, an auxiliary verb meaning "need to" (as in **Wǒ yòng qù ma?** "Do I need to go?"). The negative **bú yòng** is much more common than the affirmative **yòng**. Note that **bú yòng** is one way to express the negative of **děi** "must." In Beijing dialect, **bú yòng** is often abbreviated into **béng**. **Bú yòng** can be used with verbs other than **xiè**. Examples:

Nǐ bú yòng shuō.	"You don't need to say it."
Nǐ bú yòng gěi tā qián.	"You don't need to give her money."
Nǐ bú yòng gēn wǒ qù.	"You don't have to go with me."
Bú yòng zhǎo.	"Keep the change." (lit. "Don't need to make change.")

SV4-8, AV1-6. Color Terms. Most of the various color terms are stative verbs. To transform them into nouns, the bound form **-sè** "color" is added (e.g., **hóngsè** "the color red"). To make adjectives out of the forms with **-sè**, a **de** can be added, e.g., **hóngsède xíngli** "red-colored luggage." To ask "What color is it?," say **Shì shémme yánsède?** In Beijing dialect, the word **yánsè** "color" is often pronounced **yánshar** and, instead of the bound form **-sè** in the various color words, many speakers say **-shǎr**, e.g., **shēn lǜshǎrde qúnzi** "a deep green–colored skirt."

Color stative verbs work differently from other stative verbs in that to say that something is a certain color, such as green, you say that it is "a green one." For example, in English we can say "The grass is green" but in Chinese, if you say **Cǎo hěn lǜ**, that stresses the intensity of the color green (as in "The grass is really green!"). If you simply wish to comment that "The grass is green," then the normal way to say this in Chinese is **Cǎo shi lǜde**. Similarly, "The sky is blue" is **Tiān shi lánde** and "The book is black" is **Nèiběn shū shi hēide**.

Typical Beijing street scene on Chengfu Road

Color words are often reduplicated to indicate greater vividness or intensity of color, e.g., **hónghóngde**, **lánlánde**, **báibáide**, **hēihēide**. This is somewhat similar to English "red all over." Color terms and their connotations are not the same across languages. While Chinese color symbolism is complex, the main things you should remember are:

Hóng "red" signifies good luck, prosperity, and happiness. In the PRC, red also connotes a revolutionary spirit. At Chinese New Year, children and servants are given red envelopes (**hóngbāo**) with money inside. If you wrap presents, red is the best color for the wrapping paper. Though the color red is felicitous in many contexts, avoid writing in red ink, as this may be interpreted as meaning you wish to end your relationship with the person to whom you are writing. (Of course, it is fine for teachers to correct their students' papers in red ink.)

Hēi "black" can have negative connotations (e.g., death, disaster, evil), much as it does in the West. Therefore, be careful about wearing clothes that are all black.

Bái "white" is in China associated with mourning. When wrapping gifts, avoid white wrapping paper or white ribbons; use red instead. Also, avoid outfits that are entirely white, as well as white hats and white flowers.

Huáng "yellow" sometimes means "pornographic" (for example, when describing novels or movies). The demarcation between yellow and brown is different in Chinese from English. For example, shoes that we would describe as brown might in Chinese be called **huángsède xié**, or the color of earth might be considered as **huáng**.

Different cultures and their languages analyze and describe the world in different ways. Do not expect Chinese words to have the same ranges of meaning as English words. A concept which is expressed by a single word in one language may be expressed by two words in another language and have to be explained in a sentence or two in yet a third language. Words or features that are considered unrelated in one language may be subsumed under a single linguistic category in another language. This obviously dooms "word-for-word" translation from English to Chinese or from Chinese to English.

By Bus and Street Car to the Summer Palace

Rick Price, an American graduate student who has recently arrived in Beijing, wants to visit the Summer Palace. He asks a pedestrian which bus to take.

Basic Conversation 9-2

1. PRICE	**Duìbuqǐ, qǐng wèn, qù Yíhéyuán zuò jǐlù chē?**
	Excuse me, to get to the Summer Palace, what bus number do you take?

2. PEDESTRIAN	**Yíhéyuán a? Wǒ děi xiángxiang. Nín xiān zuò sān-èr-sān-lù gōnggòng qìchē, ránhòu huàn yāo-yāo-yāo-lù diànchē, zuòdao zhōngdiǎn zhàn jiù shi Yíhéyuán le.**
	The Summer Palace? Let me think. First take bus number 323, and then transfer to street car number 111. Take it to the last stop, which is the Summer Palace.

3. PRICE	**Nà, wǒ zuòdao nǎr huàn yāo-yāo-yāo-lù ne?**
	And where do I transfer to 111?

4. PEDESTRIAN	**Zuòdao Dòngwùyuán huàn chē.**
	You transfer at Zoo.

5. PRICE	**Xièxie.**
	Thanks.

6. PEDESTRIAN	**Bú kèqi.**
	You're welcome.
	(sees the bus coming)
	Chē láile! Kuài shàngchē ba.
	The bus is coming! Get on quick.

Build Up

1. Price

Yíhéyuán	Summer Palace [PW]
lù	(for bus routes) [M]
jǐlù chē	the number-which bus
zuò jǐlù chē	take bus number what

Duìbuqǐ, qǐng wèn, qù Yíhéyuán zuò jǐlù chē?	Excuse me, to get to the Summer Palace, what bus number do you take?

2. Pedestrian

xiángxiang	think a bit
wǒ děi xiángxiang	I must think a bit
gōnggòng	public [AT]
gōnggòng qìchē	public bus, bus [PH]
diànchē	street car, trolley, tram [N]
xiān zuò gōnggòng qìchē	first take the bus
ránhòu huàn diànchē	then change to a trolley
sān-èr-sān-lù gōnggòng qìchē	public bus number 323
yāo-yāo-yāo-lù diànchē	trolley number 111
zuòdao	take (a vehicle) to [V+PV]
zhōngdiǎn	final or terminal point [N]
zhàn	station, stop [N/M]
zhōngdiǎn zhàn	last station, last stop [PH]
zuòdao zhōngdiǎn zhàn	take to the last station
Yíhéyuán a? Wǒ děi xiángxiang.	The Summer Palace? Let me think.
Nín xiān zuò sān-èr-sān-lù gōnggòng qìchē,	First take bus number 323, and then
ránhòu huàn yāo-yāo-yāo-lù diànchē,	transfer to street car number 111. Take it to
zuòdao zhōngdiǎn zhàn jiù shi Yíhéyuán le.	the last stop, which is the Summer Palace.

3. Price

Nà, wǒ zuòdao nǎr huàn yāo-yāo-yāo-lù ne?	And where do I transfer to 111?

4. Pedestrian

dòngwù	animal [N] (M: **zhī**)
dòngwùyuán(r)	zoo [PW]
Dòngwùyuán(r)	Zoo (name of bus and street car station near Beijing Zoo) [PW]
Zuòdao Dòngwùyuán huàn chē.	You transfer at Zoo.

5. Price

Xièxie.	Thanks.

6. Pedestrian

Bú kèqi.	You're welcome.
shàngchē	get on a vehicle [VO]
kuài shàngchē ba	you better get on the bus quickly
Chē láile! Kuài shàngchē ba.	The bus is coming! Get on quick.

Supplementary Vocabulary

1. chēzhàn	bus stop; bus station [PW]
búbì	don't need to, not be necessary [AV]
búbì dào ménkǒur	don't need to go to the doorway
Chēzhàn hái méi dào, nín xiān búbì dào ménkǒur děng.	We haven't arrived at the bus stop yet, you don't yet need to go to the doorway to wait.
2. nǐmen jiāli	at your home
yǎng	raise, keep [V]
xiǎo dòngwù	small animal
Nǐmen jiāli yǎng xiǎo dòngwù ma?	Do you keep any small animals at home?

3. **zhī**	(for most animals) [M]
yìzhī gǒu	one dog
māo(r)	cat [N] (M: **zhī**)
yìzhī māo	one cat
niǎo(r)	bird [N] (M: **zhī**)
liǎngzhī niǎo	two birds
yú(r)	fish [N] (M: **tiáo**)
jǐtiáo yú	several fish
Wǒmen jiā yǎngle yìzhī gǒu, yìzhī māo, liǎngzhī niǎo gēn jǐtiáo yú.	At our home we have a dog, a cat, two birds and some fish.

Grammatical and Cultural Notes

1A.   **Yíhéyuán**, the Summer Palace, is located in the northwestern suburbs of Beijing. This is where the Qing dynasty emperors spent their summers. It is now the largest park in Beijing.

1B.   As you learned in 4-2, **lù** is basically a noun meaning "road." Here **lù** is used as a measure meaning bus route. The bus and street car routes mentioned in this conversation are only examples for language practice and are not intended to be up-to-date or accurate.

2A.   **Diànchē** "street car" literally means "electric car." Two other words you have had that contain the word **diàn** "electricity" are **diànhuà** "telephone" (lit. "electric speech") and **diànnǎo** "computer" (lit. "electric brain").

2B.   **XIĀN...RÁNHÒU...** The pattern **xiān...ránhòu...** "first...then..." is commonly used for indicating the order in which two actions occur. There is often, but not always, a **zài** "again, then" after the **ránhòu**. The pattern is:

XIĀN	Action1	RÁNHÒU (ZÀI)	Action2
Xiān	zuò gōnggòng qìchē,	ránhòu (zài)	huàn diànchē.

"First take the bus, then change to a street car."

Here are two additional examples:

| **Xiān chīfàn, ránhòu zài qù mǎi dōngxi.** | "First eat and then go shopping." |
| **Xiān xué shuōhuà, ránhòu zài xué xiězì.** | "First learn speaking, then learn writing." |

2C.   **Zuòdao**, literally "take (some means of transportation) to," is composed of the main verb **zuò** "take" plus the postverb **-dào** "to."

3.   This line literally means "in that case, I take it (the bus) to where to change to (trolley) line 111?"

4.   Beginning with this lesson, the measure for each new noun that takes a specific measure will be indicated in bold print in parentheses after the English explanation and word class. Thus, (M: **zhī**) after **dòngwù** "animal" means that **zhī** is the measure used with the noun **dòngwù**. We will be taking up measures in more detail in lesson 12-2 (for a definition of a measure, see the section on measures in "Word Classes of Spoken Chinese" near the end of this volume).

SV1A.   **Chēzhàn hái méi dào** literally means "the station hasn't yet arrived." Notice how in Chinese the focus is on the station, while in English the focus is on the speakers: "We haven't yet arrived."

SV1B.   **Búbì** "don't need to" is a common way to express the negative of **děi** "must" (*bù děi is not possible, nor can *bì be said alone in this sense). Contrast:

| **Nǐ děi qù.** | "You must go." |
| **Nǐ búbì qù.** | "You don't need to go." |

Instead of **Nǐ búbì qù**, one could also say **Nǐ bú yòng qù**, with the same meaning (9-1).

SV3.   A common measure for "dog" that we recommend you use is **zhī**, which is the most common measure for animals; for example, **yìzhī gǒu** "one dog, a dog." However, be aware that there are also speakers who use the measure **tiáo** "long and thin strip of something," as in **yìtiáo gǒu** "one dog, a dog."

By Bus and Street Car to the Summer Palace (cont.)

Price gets on the bus and buys a ticket from the conductress (continued from the previous conversation).

 Basic Conversation 9-3

1. CONDUCTRESS	**Yǒu mǎi piàode ma? Méi piàode mǎi piào!**	
	Is anybody buying a ticket? Those who don't have a ticket, buy a ticket!	
2. PRICE	**Yìzhāng dào Dòngwùyuánrde.**	
	One ticket to Zoo.	
3. CONDUCTRESS	**Nín shi zài nǎr shàngde?**	
	Where did you get on?	
4. PRICE	**Gāng shàngde.**	
	I just got on.	
5. CONDUCTRESS	**Wǔmáo.**	
	Fifty cents.	
6. PRICE	**Gěi nín qián. Dào Dòngwùyuánr máfan nín jiào wo yixia.**	
	Here's the money. When we get to Zoo, please call me.	
7. CONDUCTRESS	**Xíng.**	
	O.K.	

 Build Up

1. **Conductress**

piào	ticket [N] (M: **zhāng**)
mǎi piàode	one who buys a ticket
yǒu mǎi piàode ma	is there someone who buys a ticket
méi	not have [V]
méi piàode	one who doesn't have a ticket
Yǒu mǎi piàode ma? Méi piàode mǎi piào!	Is anybody buying a ticket? Those who don't have a ticket, buy a ticket!

2. **Price**
Yìzhāng dào Dòngwùyuánrde.   One ticket to Zoo.

3. **Conductress**
  shàng   get on [V]
Nín shi zài năr shàngde?   Where did you get on?

4. **Price**
  gāng   just now, just [A]
Gāng shàngde.   I just got on.

5. **Conductress**
Wŭmáo.   Fifty cents.

6. **Price**
  gěi nín qián   (I) give you the money
  jiào   call (someone) [V]
  jiào wo   call me
  jiào wo yixia   call me
  máfan nín jiào wo yixia   trouble you to call me
Gěi nín qián. Dào Dòngwùyuánr máfan nín   Here's the money. When we get to Zoo,
jiào wo yixia.   please call me.

7. **Conductress**
Xíng.   O.K.

 ## Supplementary Vocabulary

A. COMMON ANTONYMS

1. **cōngming**   be smart [SV]
   bèn   be stupid [SV]
Wŏ xĭhuan hé cōngmingde rén zài yìqĭ, bù   I like to be with smart people, I don't like to be with
xĭhuan hé bènde rén zài yìqĭ.   stupid people.

2. **lăn**   be lazy [SV]
   yònggōng   be hardworking, studious [SV]
   yònggōng yìdiănr   a little more studious
Nĭ shízài tài lănle; yĭhòu děi yònggōng yidianr. You really are too lazy; in the future you must study
                                                harder.

3. **gānjìng**   be clean [SV]
   tĭng gānjìngde   quite clean
   zhĭ yŏu nĭde fángjiān   there is only your room
   zāng   be dirty [SV]
   nèmme zāng   be so dirty
Tāmende fángjiān dōu tĭng gānjìngde,   Their rooms are all quite clean, why is only
wèishemme zhĭ yŏu nĭde fángjiān nèmme zāng?   your room so dirty?

4. **zhěngqí**   be in order, neat [SV]
   yŏude hěn zhěngqí   some are orderly
   luàn   be disorderly, messy [SV]
   yŏude hěn luàn   some are messy
Xuéshēng zhùde sùshè, yŏude hěn zhěngqí,   Some of the dorms the students live in are in good
yŏude hěn luàn.   order, others are a mess.

B. GENERAL

5. shòupiàoyuán — ticketseller, conductor [N]
gānggāng — just now, just [A]
Shòupiàoyuán gānggāng zǒu. — The conductor just left.

6. búdàn — not only [A]
érqiě — moreover, and, also [CJ]
búdàn cōngming érqiě hěn yònggōng — not only smart but also very studious
Xiǎo Zhèng búdàn cōngming érqiě hěn yònggōng. — Little Zheng is not only smart but also very hard-working.

7. tā zhīdaole — when he comes to know
shēngqì — get angry [VO/SV]
huì bu huì shēngqì — be likely to get angry or not
Nǐ xiǎng tā zhīdaole, huì bu huì shēngqì? — Do you think he'll get angry when he finds out?

8. wánxiào — joke [N]
kāi wánxiào — joke around, play a prank [PH]
gēn tā kāi wánxiào — joke around with him
Nǐ bié gēn tā kāi wánxiào. — Don't joke around with him.

9. shuō xiàohua(r) — tell a joke [PH]
Tā cháng shuō xiàohuar. — She often tells jokes.

10. xīwàng — hope [V]
néng yǒu jīhui — can have an opportunity
Wǒ xīwàng yǐhòu néng yǒu jīhui rènshi nǐmende xiàozhǎng. — I hope in the future to be able to have an opportunity to meet your school president.

Grammatical and Cultural Notes

1. Note the **méi** "not have" in **méi piàode** "one who doesn't have a ticket." **Méi** is an abbreviated form of **méiyou**, so a fuller form of **méi piàode** would be **méiyou piàode rén**. You've actually seen this use of **méi** to mean **méiyou** before; consider:

   méi yìsi — "not be interesting" (1-4)
   méi guānxi — "never mind," "it doesn't matter" (2-4)
   méi shì(r) — "it's nothing," "never mind" (5-3)

   So now you should realize that there are actually two **méi**: (1) the one that indicates past negative of action verbs (**Wǒ méi qù** "I didn't go"); and the one that means "not have, there is/are not," as in **méi piàode**. Note that while **méiyou** can occur at the end of a sentence or question, the abbreviated form **méi** ordinarily cannot.

2. **Yìzhāng dào Dòngwùyuánrde** literally means "one (ticket) to Zoo (station)." A fuller form would be **yìzhāng dào Dòngwùyuánrde piào** "one ticket to Zoo (station)." An even shorter form would be **yìzhāng Dòngwùyuánr** "one, Zoo."

3. Common variants of this question include: **Zài nǎr shàngde?**, **Cóng nǎr shàngde?**, and **Nǎr shàngde?** All of these mean "Where did you get on?" The **shàng**, of course, here means **shàngchē** "get on the bus."

4. **Gāng** "just now, just" is a common and useful adverb that refers to the immediate past, or to a past action that occurred or was to occur immediately prior to some other past action. There is usually no **-le** at the end of verbs occurring after **gāng**. To negate a sentence with **gāng**, place **bú shi** before the **gāng**; do not use **méi**. Examples of sentences with **gāng**:

   Tā gāng dào.   "He just arrived."

Lǎoshī gāng zǒu.	"The teacher just left."
Wǒ gāng yào zǒu tā jiù láile.	"I was just about to leave when she came."
Nǐ gāng cóng Měiguo lái, dàgài hái bù xíguàn.	"You just came from America, probably you aren't used to it yet."
Wǒ bú shi gāng láide, wǒ yǐjīng láile yíge duō zhōngtóu le!	"I didn't just come, I've been here for over an hour!"

6A.   **Gěi nín qián** literally means "(I) give you the money." This is commonly said when paying money to someone so as to draw attention to the fact—and state for the record—that money is in fact being paid.

6B.   The literal meaning of **Dào Dòngwùyuánr máfan nín jiào wo yixia** is "Arrive zoo, trouble you call me."

6C.   In this utterance, you learn a new usage of the verb **jiào**, namely, "to call (over to someone)," that is, to say something in a loud and distinct voice so as to be heard at a distance and draw someone else's attention. You previously saw the verb **jiào** in 2-1, where it meant "to be called or named," and in 2-2, where it meant "to call (someone a certain name)." These usages are all semantically related but not entirely the same. Contrast these three examples:

> **Wǒ jiào Bái Jiéruì.**
> "I am called/named/my name is Bai Jierui." (here **jiào** means "be called or named a certain name")

> **Nǐ hái shi jiào wǒ Xiǎo Chén hǎole.**
> "It would be better if you called me Little Chen." (here **jiào** means "call someone else a certain name")

> **Máfan nín jiào wo yixia.**
> "Please (you) call me." (here **jiào** means "call over to someone")

6D.   Pronouns in object position often lose their tone. That is the reason why the **wo** in **jiào wo yixia** "call me" is neutral tone.

6E.   Notice that the **yixia** in **jiào wo yixia** comes after the object **wo**. What would be the difference between **jiào wo** and **jiào wo yixia**? As we saw in 2-2: 3C, use of **yixia** after verbs makes them sound more conversational, more polite, and less abrupt.

SV2.   The stative verb **yònggōng** "be hardworking, be studious" can refer only to how a student pursues his or her studies. On the other hand, the stative verb **nǔlì** "be diligent, work hard," which you learned in lesson 7-4, can refer to how a person pursues studies or any kind of work.

SV5A.   **Shòupiàoyuán** literally means "sell-ticket-person."

SV5B.   **Gānggāng** is a close synonym of **gāng**. In addition to "just now, just," it can also mean "just exactly," as in **gānggāng yìqiān kuài** "exactly one thousand dollars." As with **gāng**, there is usually no **-le** at the end of verbs occurring after **gānggāng**.

SV6.   **BÚDÀN...ÉRQIĚ...**   The pattern **búdàn...érqiě...** "not only...but also..." is a common and useful pattern that emphasizes the information contained in the second part of the sentence (the part that follows the **érqiě**). The meanings of the two parts of the sentence must logically build upon and reinforce each other; the two parts must either both be positive or else both be negative. The same way it would not make sense to say in English "He is not only intelligent but also very lazy," one could NOT say in Chinese *Tā búdàn cōngming, érqiě hěn lǎn. The basic pattern is:

Topic	BÚDÀN	Verb Phrase1	ÉRQIĚ	Verb Phrase2
Xiǎo Zhèng	búdàn	cōngming,	érqiě	hěn yònggōng.

"Little Zheng is not only smart but also very hard-working."

Some more examples of the **búdàn...érqiě...** pattern:

> **Tā búdàn lǎn, érqiě hěn bèn.**
>
> "He's not only lazy, but also very stupid."

> **Tā búdàn niánqīng, érqiě cōngming.**
>
> "She's not only young but also smart."

> **Wǒmen búdàn shi tóngshì, érqiě yě shi péngyou, duì bu dui?**
>
> "We're not only colleagues, but also friends, right?"

Sometimes **búdàn** can occur with **hái** instead of **érqiě**. Example:

> **Tā búdàn huì shuō Guóyǔ, hái huì shuō qítāde wàiyǔ.**
>
> "He can not only speak Mandarin, he can also speak other foreign languages."

SV8.   **Kāi wánxiào** can also be used in the sense of "kid." For example:

> **Nǐ zài kāi wánxiào ba?**
>
> "I guess you must be kidding?"

SV10.   Be careful to distinguish the pronunciation of **xīwàng** "hope" from **xǐhuan** "like."

Bicycles and street car on a sunny winter day in Beijing

Price prepares to get off the bus but discovers he has misplaced his ticket. He tells the conductress he can't find his ticket (continued from the previous conversation).

Basic Conversation 9-4

| 1. PRICE | **Kuài dàole ba?** |
| | I suppose we're almost there? |

| 2. CONDUCTRESS | **Zǎozhe ne, hái yǒu sìzhàn. Dào shíhou wǒ jiào nín.** |
| | It's still early, there are still four stops. When the time comes, I'll call you. |

(after a while)

Wèi, xiàyízhàn jiù shi Dòngwùyuánr le. Nín gāi zhǔnbèi xiàchē le.
Hey, the next station is Zoo. You should prepare to get off.

| 3. PRICE | **Hǎo, xièxie nín.** |
| | O.K., thank you. |

| 4. CONDUCTRESS | *(to all passengers)* |

Xiàchēde tóngzhì qǐng chūshì chēyuèpiào.
Comrades who are getting off, please show your individual or monthly tickets.

| 5. PRICE | *(about to get off the bus, searching for his ticket)* |

Duìbuqǐ, wǒde piào zhǎobuzháole.
I'm sorry, I can't find my ticket.

| 6. CONDUCTRESS | **Méi guānxi, wǒ jìde nín mǎiguo piào le. Yǐhòu kě děi xiǎoxīn diǎnr!** |
| | That's all right, I remember you bought a ticket. In the future you really should be more careful! |

Build Up

1. Price
Kuài dàole ba?   I suppose we're almost there?

2. Conductress

zǎo	be early [SV]
-zhe	(indicates continuous aspect) [P]
ne	(indicates continuous aspect) [P]
zǎozhe ne	"it is being early," it's early
hái yǒu sìzhàn	there are still four stations
dào shíhou	when the time comes

Zǎozhe ne, hái yǒu sìzhàn. Dào shíhou wǒ jiào nín.   It's still early, there are still four stops. When the time comes, I'll call you.

wèi	"hey" [I]
xiàyízhàn	the next station
gāi	should [AV]
zhǔnbèi	prepare, get ready, plan [V/AV]
xiàchē	get off a vehicle [VO]
nín gāi zhǔnbèi xiàchē le	you should prepare to get off

Wèi, xiàyízhàn jiù shi Dòngwùyuánr le.   Hey, the next station is Zoo.
Nín gāi zhǔnbèi xiàchē le.   You should prepare to get off.

3. Price

Hǎo, xièxie nín.   O.K., thank you.

4. Conductress

tóngzhì	comrade [N]
xiàchēde tóngzhì	comrades who are getting off
chūshì	show, produce [V]
chēpiào	bus ticket [N] (M: **zhāng**)
yuèpiào	monthly ticket [N] (M: **zhāng**)
chēyuèpiào	individual and/or monthly tickets
qǐng chūshì chēyuèpiào	please show individual and/or monthly tickets

Xiàchēde tóngzhì qǐng chūshì chēyuèpiào.   Comrades who are getting off, please show your individual or monthly tickets.

5. Price

-zháo	(indicates action of verb is realized) [RE]
zhǎozháo	look for and find, find [RC]
zhǎobuzháo	not be able to find, can't find
wǒde piào zhǎobuzháole	my ticket can't be found now

Duìbuqǐ, wǒde piào zhǎobuzháole.   I'm sorry, I can't find my ticket.

6. Conductress

jìde	remember [V]
wǒ jìde	I remember
nín mǎiguo piào le	you have bought a ticket
xiǎoxīn	be careful [SV]
xiǎoxīn diǎnr	be a little more careful
yǐhòu kě děi xiǎoxīn diǎnr	in the future really must be a little more careful

Méi guānxi, wǒ jìde nín mǎiguo piào le.   That's all right, I remember you bought a ticket.
Yǐhòu kě děi xiǎoxīn diǎnr!   In the future you really should be more careful!

 Supplementary Vocabulary

1. shuìzháo   fall asleep [RC]
shuìbuzháo   not be able to fall asleep

Lǎo Hóu yǐjīng shuìle, kěshi wǒ shuìbuzháo.   Old Hou is already asleep, but I can't fall asleep.

2. -dào	(indicates action of verb is realized) [RE]
zhǎodào	look for and find, find [RC]
zhǎobudào	not be able to find, can't find
Tāde chēpiào zhǎodàole, kěshi zāogāo,	She found her bus ticket, but darn it,
wǒde zhǎobudào!	I can't find mine!
3. tīng	hear, listen [V]
dǒng	understand [V]
-dǒng	understand [RE]
tīngdǒng	hear and understand [RC]
tīngdedǒng	hear and be able to understand
tīngbudǒng	hear and not be able to understand
Wǒ yǒude shíhou tīngdedǒng,	I sometimes can understand,
yǒude shíhou tīngbudǒng.	but sometimes I can't understand.
4. kàn	read [V]
kàndǒng	read and understand [RC]
kàndedǒng	read and be able to understand
kànbudǒng	read and not be able to understand
Zhōngguo zì, yǒude wǒ kàndedǒng,	Some Chinese characters I can read,
yǒude wǒ kànbudǒng.	others I can't read.

Grammatical and Cultural Notes

2A. **-ZHE** As Continuous Aspect Suffix. In this line of the conversation, note **zǎozhe ne** "it is continuing being early" or "it's still early." The verb suffix **-zhe** can be attached to various kinds of verbs to indicate continuous aspect, i.e., that some action or state (in this case "earliness") is continuing over a period of time. This is Northern Chinese-style usage; in other parts of China one would just say **Hái zǎo** "It's still early." The Chinese continuous aspect suffix **-zhe** sometimes corresponds to the "-ing" form of the verb in English. Sentence final particle **ne** is often added at the end of the sentence to further emphasize the continuous aspect. We will take up other uses of **-zhe** later. The basic pattern is:

Verb	ZHE	(NE)
Zǎo	zhe	ne.

"It's early" (lit. "It's continuing being early")

Here are two more examples of verbs with the continuous aspect suffix **-zhe**:

Mén hái kāizhe ne.

"The door is still open." (lit. "The door is continuously being open.")

Tāmen dōu hái zài fángjiānli zuòzhe ne.

"They are all still sitting in the room."

2B. There is a discrepancy between the video software, which says **hái yǒu liǎngzhàn** "there are still two stops," and the text and audio, which says **hái yǒu sìzhàn** "there are still four stops."

2C. The auxiliary verb **gāi** "should" is a synonym of **yīnggāi** (2-2) and **yīngdāng** (8-4). However, **gāi** also has another meaning of "be someone's turn," as in **Xiànzài gāi nǐ le** "Now it's your turn."

4A. The gender-neutral term **tóngzhì** "comrade" (lit. "same aspiration") was introduced to China with the advent of Communism in the early years of the twentieth century. From the 1950s through the 1980s, **tóngzhì** was used commonly throughout China, supplanting the more traditional terms of address **xiānsheng**, **tàitai**, and **xiáojie**. In recent years, due to the opening of Chinese society and influence from Taiwan and Hong Kong, where the traditional terms continued to be used, **xiānsheng** and (to a lesser extent) **tàitai** and **xiáojie** have made a come-back. While the word **tóngzhì** is now used less commonly than before, it is still used to refer to people in the Communist Party and is sometimes encountered on other occasions as well. In recent years, **tóngzhì** has gained an additional meaning of "gay person" or "homosexual." **Tóngzhì** can be added to your list of **tóng-** words:

tóngshì	"colleague" (lit. "same job," 2-3)
tóngwū(r)	"roommate" (lit. "same room," 2-2)
tóngxué	"classmate" (lit. "same learning," 2-1)
tóngzhì	"comrade" (lit. "same aspiration," 9-4)

4B.   **Chēpiào**, a very common term, refers to an individual bus, streetcar, or train ticket bought for one particular trip. The noun **yuèpiào** means "monthly ticket," in other words, a ticket that is good for one month. **Chēyuèpiào** is an abbreviated form for **chēpiào hé yuèpiào** "individual bus tickets and monthly bus tickets."

5.   Potential Resultative Compounds. A resultative compound like **zhǎozháo** "find" in the middle of which has been added the infix **-de-** means "be able to..." (e.g., **zhǎodezháo** "can find"); it is called an affirmative potential resultative compound. A resultative verb in the middle of which has been added the infix **-bu-** means "not be able to..." (e.g., **zhǎobuzháo** "can't find"); it is called a negative potential resultative compound. Study the following examples carefully:

BASE VERB	RESULTATIVE COMPOUND	AFFIRMATIVE POTENTIAL RESULTATIVE COMPOUND	NEGATIVE POTENTIAL RESULTATIVE COMPOUND
zhǎo	**zhǎozháo**	**zhǎodezháo**	**zhǎobuzháo**
"look for"	"look for and find"	"be able to find"	"be unable to find"
mǎi	**mǎidào**	**mǎidedào**	**mǎibudào**
"buy"	"buy"	"be able to buy"	"be unable to buy"
kàn	**kàndào**	**kàndedào**	**kànbudào**
"see"	"see"	"be able to see"	"be unable to see"
tīng	**tīngdào**	**tīngdedào**	**tīngbudào**
"hear"	"hear"	"be able to hear"	"be unable to hear"
zhǎng	**zhǎngdà**	**zhǎngdedà**	**zhǎngbudà**
"grow"	"grow up"	"be able to grow up"	"be unable to grow up"

The affirmative and negative potential resultative compounds can be used together to form affirmative-negative questions, e.g., **Nǐ kàndedào kànbudào?** "Are you able to see it?"

Actually, the apology **duìbuqǐ** "excuse me," which you learned in 2-3, is itself a negative potential resultative compound, with the literal meaning "be unable to face (because of shame)"; in fact, **duìbuqǐ** can even have an object, e.g., **Nǐ zhèiyangr zuò duìbuqǐ wǒ** "Your doing things that way is doing wrong by me" (i.e., "you are unable to face me").

Pay careful attention to the difference between negative potential resultative compounds (e.g., **zhǎobudào** "can't find, couldn't find") and resultative compounds with **méi** (e.g., **méi zhǎodào** "didn't find"). The former indicate inability ("can't, couldn't, wasn't able to") while the latter simply indicate that some action did not take place. Some more examples:

NEGATIVE POTENTIAL RESULTATIVE COMPOUND		NEGATIVE RESULTATIVE COMPOUND WITH MÉI	
kànbudào	"couldn't see, can't see"	**méi kàndào**	"didn't see"
tīngbudào	"couldn't hear, can't hear"	**méi tīngdào**	"didn't hear"
zhǎngbudà	"couldn't grow up, can't grow up"	**méi zhǎngdà**	"didn't grow up"

There are some defective resultative compounds. For example, in 3-4 you learned the negative potential resultative compound **láibují** "not have enough time," formed with the resultative ending **-jí** "reach a goal in time." The corresponding affirmative potential resultative compound **láidejí** "have enough time" is common, but the plain resultative compound *láijí does not exist.

Although **néng** and **kéyi** can also be used to express ability and inability, potential resultative compounds are particularly common and idiomatic in Chinese, and you should make an effort to incorporate them into your speech.

6A.   Be sure you remember the verb **jìde** "remember"! It is high in frequency and can be used alone or with either a preposed or a following object. Here are some more examples of **jìde**:

Nǐ hái jìde wǒ ma?	"Do you still remember me?"
Nǐ jìde bu jìde?	"Do you remember?"
Wǒ yǐjīng bú jìdele.	"I don't remember anymore."
Wǒ xiǎo shíhoude shìr hái jìde hěn qīngchu.	"I still remember things from my childhood very clearly."
Tā yǐqián shuōde huà wǒ hái jìde hěn qīngchu.	"I still remember clearly what he said."

6B.   **Yǐhòu kě děi xiǎoxīn diǎnr** "in the future you really should be more careful." The adverb **kě** here serves as an intensifier of the auxiliary verb **děi** to indicate emphasis (cf. 5-3: 4C), so we could translate **kě děi** as "really must."

SV1.   To say someone "is asleep" or "has started sleeping," say **Tā shuìle**. The sentence **Tā shuìzháole** means "He/she has fallen asleep." One could NEVER say *Tā shi shuì to mean "He/she is asleep."

SV2.   The resultative ending **-dào** indicates that the action of the verb has been realized. Besides **zhǎodào**, another common example with this resultative ending is **mǎidào** "succeed in buying something, buy something." With a number of verbs you can use either **-zháo** or **-dào**, but with the verb **shuì** "sleep," you can use only the resultative ending **-zháo**, never **-dào**. Example:

Nǐ mǎidào nèiběn shū méiyou?

"Were you able to buy that book?" or "Did you buy that book?"

Unit 9: Review and Study Guide

New Vocabulary

ADVERBS		AUXILIARY VERBS		CONJUNCTIONS	
búdàn	not only	**búbì**	don't need to, not be necessary	**érqiě**	moreover, and, also
gāng	just now, just				
gānggāng	just now, just	**bú yòng**	not need to, don't need to	**IDIOMATIC EXPRESSIONS**	
				bú yòng xiè	"don't mention it"
ATTRIBUTIVES		**gāi**	should	**INTERJECTIONS**	
gōnggòng	public			**wèi**	"hey"

MEASURES

lù	(for bus routes)
zhī	(for most animals)

NOUNS

báisè	the color white
běndì	this place, here
chēpiào	bus ticket
dēng	light, lamp
diànchē	street car, trolley, tram
dòngwù	animal
hēisè	the color black
hónglǜdēng	traffic light
hóngsè	the color red
huángsè	the color yellow
jiāotōngjǐng	traffic police
jǐngchá	police
lánsè	the color blue
lǜsè	the color green
māo(r)	cat
niǎo(r)	bird
piào	ticket
shòupiàoyuán	ticketseller, conductor
tóngzhì	comrade
wánxiào	joke
yánsè	color
yú(r)	fish
yuèpiào	monthly ticket
zhàn	station, stop
zhōngdiǎn	final or terminal point

PARTICLES

ne	(indicates continuous aspect)
-zhe	(indicates continuous aspect)

PHRASES

gōnggòng qìchē	public bus, bus
jiāotōng jǐngchá	traffic police
kāi wánxiào	joke around, play a prank
shuō xiàohua(r)	tell a joke
zhōngdiǎn zhàn	last station, last stop

PLACE WORDS

chēzhàn	bus stop; bus station
dòngwùyuán(r)	zoo
Hépíng Bīnguǎn	Peace Hotel
lùkǒu(r)	intersection
Yíhéyuán	Summer Palace

RESULTATIVE COMPOUNDS

kàndǒng	read and understand
shuìzháo	fall asleep
tīngdǒng	hear and understand
zhǎodào	look for and find, find
zhǎozháo	look for and find, find

RESULTATIVE ENDINGS

-dào	(indicates action of verb is realized)
-dǒng	understand
-zháo	(indicates action of verb is realized)

STATIVE VERBS

bái	be white
bèn	be stupid
cōngming	be smart
gānjìng	be clean
hēi	be black
hóng	be red
huáng	be yellow
lán	be blue
lǎn	be lazy
lǜ	be green
luàn	be disorderly, messy
qīngchu	be clear, clear about
shēngqì	get angry
xiǎoxīn	be careful
yònggōng	be hardworking, studious
zāng	be dirty
zǎo	be early
zhěngqí	be in order, neat

VERBS

chūshì	show, produce
dǒng	understand
guǎi	turn
jiào	call (someone)
jìde	remember
kàn	read
méi	not have
shàng	get on
tīng	hear, listen
xiè	thank
xīwàng	hope
yǎng	raise, keep
zhuǎn	turn
zhǔnbèi	prepare, get ready, plan

VERB-OBJECT COMPOUNDS

shàngchē	get on a vehicle
shēngqì	get angry
xiàchē	get off a vehicle

Major New Grammar Patterns

Chinese equivalents of English "ask": Nǐ yàoshi bù dǒngde huà, yào wèn lǎoshī a! "If you don't understand, you should ask the teacher!"; Qǐng tā míngtiān zài lái. "Ask him to come again tomorrow."; Lǎoshī jiào wǒmen zuò zuòyè. "The teacher asked us to do our homework." (9-1)

Color terms: (listed in the New Vocabulary section) (9-1)
XIĀN...RÁNHÒU... "first... then...": Xiān chīfàn ránhòu zài qù mǎi dōngxi. "First eat and then go shopping." (9-2)
BÚDÀN...ÉRQIĚ... "not only... but also...": Tā búdàn niánqīng, érqiě cōngming. "She's not only young, but also smart." (9-3)

-ZHE as continuous aspect suffix: zǎozhe ne "it's (continuing being) early" (9-4)
Potential resultative compounds: zhǎo "look for," zhǎozháo "look for and find," zhǎodezháo "be able to find," zhǎobuzháo "be unable to find" (9-4)

Weather

COMMUNICATIVE OBJECTIVES

Once you have mastered this unit, you will be able to use Chinese to:

1. Talk about the weather and weather forecasts: hot, warm, cool, cold; high and low temperatures; dry vs. humid air; clear vs. cloudy skies; thunder, lightning, rain, fog, snow, typhoons, etc.

2. Discuss climates: Beijing, Taipei, your hometown.

3. Talk about the four seasons.

4. Make comparisons and contrasts: "San Francisco is colder than Taipei, but not so cold as Beijing," etc.

A Weather Forecast

Holly Young, an American college student who is studying Chinese and teaching English in Taipei, has just gotten up. She walks into the living room of the apartment she and her Taiwanese friend, Su Ning, share. As she sees Su reading the morning newspaper, she asks what the weather forecast for that day is.

 ## Basic Conversation 10-1

1. YOUNG   **Zǎo! Jīntiān tiānqi yùbào zěmme shuō?**
            Good morning! What's the weather forecast for today?

2. SU   *(looking at the weather forecast in the newspaper)*

            Wǒ kànkan. Jīntiān shàngwǔ shi qíngtiān, xiàwǔ kěnéng huì biànchéng yīntiān.
            Let me see. This morning will be clear, this afternoon it's possible it will become cloudy.

3. YOUNG   **Ò.**
            Oh.

4. SU   *(continues summarizing the weather forecast)*

            Cóng míngtiān kāishǐ huì yuè lái yuè rè. Jīntiān zuì gāo wēndù shi èrshibādù, zuì dī wēndù shi èrshisìdù.
            Starting tomorrow it's going to get hotter and hotter. Today's high will be 28 degrees, the low will be 24 degrees.

5. YOUNG   *(hears sound of thunder and rain)*

            Éi? Hǎoxiàng dǎléi le! Shì bu shì yào xiàyǔ?
            Huh? I think I heard thunder. Is it going to rain? *(goes to window to look)*

            Āiyà! Yǐjīng xiàle, hái xiàde bù xiǎo ei!
            Gosh! It's already started raining, and pretty heavily, too!

6. SU   **Suóyi shuō, tiānqi yùbào yě zhǐ shi yùbào éryǐ, bù yídìng zhǔn.**
            That's why weather forecasts are merely forecasts, and not necessarily accurate.

 ## Build Up

1. **Young**
   zǎo   "good morning" [IE]
   tiānqi   weather [N]

yùbào	forecast [N]
tiānqi yùbào	weather forecast [PH]
zěmme shuō	how does it say, what does it say
Zǎo! Jīntiān tiānqi yùbào zěmme shuō?	Good morning! What's the weather forecast for today?

2. Su

qíngtiān	fine day, sunny day [N]
kěnéng	be possible [AV]
kěnéng huì	it's possible it will
biàn	change [V]
-chéng	become; into [PV]
biànchéng	change into, become [V+PV]
yīntiān	cloudy or overcast weather [N]
Wǒ kànkan. Jīntiān shàngwǔ shi qíngtiān, xiàwǔ kěnéng huì biànchéng yīntiān.	Let me see. This morning will be clear, this afternoon it's possible it will become cloudy.

3. Young

| Ò. | Oh. |

4. Su

cóng míngtiān kāishǐ	starting tomorrow
yuè lái yuè...	more and more... [PT]
rè	be hot [SV]
yuè lái yuè rè	hotter and hotter
zuì	most [A]
zuì gāo	highest
wēndù	temperature [N]
zuì gāo wēndù	highest temperature
dù	degree (of temperature) [M]
èrshibādù	28 degrees
dī	be low [SV]
zuì dī	lowest
zuì dī wēndù	low(est) temperature
Cóng míngtiān kāishǐ huì yuè lái yuè rè.	Starting tomorrow it's going to get hotter and hotter.
Jīntiān zuì gāo wēndù shi èrshibādù,	Today's high will be 28 degrees,
zuì dī wēndù shi èrshisìdù.	the low will be 24 degrees.

5. Young

éi	(introduces questions) [I]
dǎléi	thunder [VO]
hǎoxiàng dǎléi le	it seems it has thundered
yǔ	rain [N]
xiàyǔ	rain [VO]
yào xiàyǔ	it's going to rain
shì bu shi yào xiàyǔ	is it going to rain
Éi? Hǎoxiàng dǎléi le! Shì bu shi yào xiàyǔ?	Huh? I think I heard thunder. Is it going to rain?
āiyà	"oh," "gosh" [I]
xiàde bù xiǎo	it's raining quite a lot
Āiyà! Yǐjīng xiàle, hái xiàde bù xiǎo ei!	Gosh! It's already started raining, and pretty heavily, too!

6. Su

suóyi shuō	so, therefore [PH]
...éryǐ	...and that's all [PT]
zhǐ shi yùbào éryǐ	only are forecasts and that's all
yídìng	definitely [A]

bù yídìng	not necessarily
zhǔn	be accurate [SV]
bù yídìng zhǔn	not necessarily accurate
Suóyi shuō, tiānqi yùbào yě zhǐ shi yùbào éryǐ, bù yídìng zhǔn.	That's why weather forecasts are merely forecasts, and not necessarily accurate.

 ## Supplementary Vocabulary

1. tiān	sky [N]
tiānshang	in the sky
yún	cloud [N] (M: **duǒ**)
Tiānshang hǎo duō yún.	There are lots of clouds in the sky.
2. shǎndiàn	lightning strikes [VO]
Tāmen jiā yǎngde xiǎo gǒu pà shǎndiàn.	The puppy they keep at their house is scared of lightning.

Grammatical and Cultural Notes

1. **Tiānqi yùbào zěmme shuō** "What does the weather forecast say?" literally means "How does the weather forecast say?" Here is another example of **zěmme shuō**:

    Nà, nǐde fùmǔ zěmme shuō ne?   "So, what do/did your parents say?"

2A. **Kěnéng** is an auxiliary verb meaning "be possible" or "it's possible that...." It can be used alone as a brief response, or within a longer sentence. Examples:

    Kěnéng.   "It's possible."

    Bù kěnéng!   "Impossible!"

    Míngtiān kěnéng huì xiàyǔ.

    "Tomorrow it's possible it will rain."

    Tā yǒu kěnéng wàngle shíjiān.

    "It's possible that she forgot the time."

    Nǐ kěnéng hái méi tīngshuō: tāmen liǎngge líhūnle.

    "You may not have heard yet: the two of them got divorced."

    Nèiliàng qìchē tài jiùle, mài yíwàn kuài shi bù kěnéngde.

    "That car is too old, it's not going to be possible for you to sell it for ten thousand dollars."

    A: Nǐ juéde tā míngtiān huì lái ma?

    A: "Do you think she'll come tomorrow?"

    B: Bú tài kěnéng.

    B: "It's not very likely."

Sometimes Chinese speakers will use **kěnéng** even when they know something to be a fact but don't wish to speak too directly. For example, even if you know someone didn't come to some event because they had other things to do, you might still say **Tā kěnéng yǒu diǎnr shìr** "It's possible that she had something she had to do."

2B.   **Huì** is here an auxiliary verb meaning "be likely to, will" (8-3: 5-6). So we have two auxiliary verbs in a row (**kěnéng huì** "it's possible that it will") preceding the main verb **biànchéng** "become."

2C.   **Biànchéng** "change into, be transformed into, become" is composed of the main verb **biàn** "change," to which has been attached the postverb **-chéng** "become; into." **Biànchéng** would be used for weather changing from one type to another or, in science fiction, for humans transforming into animals; but one could not use **biàn-chéng** in the sense of "become" to say "I want to become a teacher." Some other examples of constructions with the postverb **-chéng**:

kànchéng	"look at something and interpret it as (something else)"
shuōchéng	"say something so that it becomes (something else)"
tīngchéng	"hear something as (something else)"
xiěchéng	"write one thing as (another)"

Here is an example sentence with **xiěchéng**:

Wǒ yuánlái xiǎng xiě yíge "dà" zì, kěshi bù xiǎoxīn xiěchéng "tài" zì le!

"I originally wanted to write the character **dà**, but I wasn't careful and wrote it as the character **tài**!"

4A.   **CÓNG...KĀISHǏ.** As you learned earlier, the coverb **cóng** means "from" and the verb **kāishǐ** means "begin." The pattern **cóng...kāishǐ** means "beginning from..." or "starting from...." A time expression is inserted in between **cóng** and **kāishǐ**. The basic pattern is:

CÓNG	Time Expression	KĀISHǏ
cóng	míngtiān	kāishǐ

"starting from tomorrow"

Some more examples of the **cóng...kāishǐ** pattern:

cóng xià xīngqī kāishǐ	"starting next week"
cóng míngnián wǔyuè yīhào kāishǐ	"starting on May 1 of next year"

4B.   **YUÈ LÁI YUÈ...** The common and useful pattern **yuè lái yuè...** "more and more..." can be followed by a stative verb, auxiliary verb, or regular verb to mean "more and more...." In good English, this construction is often translated by two adjectives ending in "-er," e.g., **yuè lái yuè gāo** "higher and higher." If the verb or adjective is negative, the Chinese can sometimes be translated by "less and less." Examples:

YUÈ LÁI YUÈ	Verb
yuè lái yuè	rè

"hotter and hotter" (lit. "more and more hot")

Yǔ xiàde yuè lái yuè dà.

"It's raining more and more heavily." (lit. "The rain comes down more and more big.")

Nǐde Hànyǔ yuè lái yuè hǎo!

"Your Chinese is getting better and better!"

Zuìjìn wēndù yuè lái yuè gāo.

"Recently the temperature has been getting higher and higher."

Xuéxí Zhōngwénde Měiguo dàxuéshēng yuè lái yuè duō.

"More and more American college students are studying Chinese."

Tā yuè lái yuè huì zuò Zhōngguo cài le.

"He can cook Chinese food better and better." (lit. "He more and more can make Chinese food.")

Wǒ yuè lái yuè bù xǐhuan ta.

"I more and more dislike him." or "I like him less and less."

Zuìjìn tiānqi yùbào yuè lái yuè bù zhǔn.

"Recently weather forecasts have been less and less accurate."

After **yuè lái yuè...** one cannot add an adverb of degree such as **hěn** or **bǐjiào**. So one could NOT say ***Tāde Zhōngwén yuè lái yuè hěn hǎo**. Due to influence from English, **Yuè lái yuè duōde...** "More and more..." is now sometimes used at the beginning of a sentence to modify the subject or topic. For example:

Yuè lái yuè duōde Zhōngguo rén huì shuō Yīngwén.

"More and more Chinese people can speak English."

The more traditional way of saying this is:

Huì shuō Yīngwénde Zhōngguo rén yuè lái yuè duō.

"The Chinese people who can speak English are getting to be more and more."

4C.   Contrast the pronunciation of **rè** "be hot" with **rì** as in **Rìběn** "Japan" or **xīngqīrì** "Sunday." For **rè** your mouth should be half open, while for **rì** your teeth are together and your mouth is nearly closed. Also contrast both the pronunciation and the Pinyin spelling of **rè** and **rì** with the number **èr** "two."

4D.   Note the adverb **zuì** "most" as in **zuì gāo wēndù** "highest temperature" (lit. "most high temperature") and **zuì dī wēndù** "lowest temperature." The adverb **zuì** is very common and important. Here are some more examples:

Tài Shān shi wǒ zuì xǐhuande dìfang.

"Mt. Tai is the place I like most." (Mt. Tai, located in central Shandong, is one of the five sacred Taoist mountains of China)

Wǒde péngyou lǐtou, wǒ juéde Xiǎo Báide Zhōngwén zuì hǎo.

"Among my friends, I feel that Little Bai's Chinese is the best." (notice how **lǐtou** is used here)

4E.   For "highest temperature" and "lowest temperature," many speakers say **zuì gāo wēndù** and **zuì dī wēndù**, respectively. However, there are also speakers who use the abbreviations **zuìgāowēn** and **zuìdīwēn**, with exactly the same meanings. Either set of expressions is correct. Note that in the Build Up, the longer forms are used, but in the conversation audio and video, the abbreviations are used.

4F.   **DÙ** to Express Temperatures. **Dù** "degree of temperature" is a measure. The pattern is:

Number	DÙ
èrshíbā	**dù**
"twenty-eight degrees"	

Study the following examples:

yídù	"one degree"	**shíbādù**	"eighteen degrees"
liǎngdù	"two degrees"	**sānshi'èrdù**	"thirty-two degrees"
sāndù	"three degrees"	**jǐdù**	"how many degrees?"

In both Mainland China and Taiwan, the Centigrade or Celsius scale (referred to as **Shèshì**) is used, as opposed to the Fahrenheit scale (referred to as **Huáshì**) which is more common in the U.S. The formulas for converting between Centigrade and Fahrenheit are:

(Centigrade temperature + 40) x 9/5 - 40 = Fahrenheit temperature

(Fahrenheit temperature + 40) x 5/9 - 40 = Centigrade temperature

Thus, the high temperature of **èrshibādù** that is mentioned in the Basic Conversation would be 28 + 40 = 68 multiplied by 9/5 = 122.4 minus 40 = 82.4° Fahrenheit, and the low temperature of **èrshisìdù** would be 24 + 40 = 64 multiplied by 9/5= 115.2 minus 40 = 75.2° Fahrenheit.

Detail of a Taoist temple in Penghu, Taiwan

4G.   Keep in mind that while the meaning of **dī** is "be low," the tone of this word is Tone One and HIGH!

5A.   In Chinese as in many other languages, meteorological phenomena fall outside the regular patterns of the language. In English, for example, we say "it rains" but what, exactly, is the "it"? In Chinese, most meteorological terms involve verb-object compounds without a subject, e.g., **dǎléi** "hits thunder—to thunder" and **xiàyǔ** "drops rain—to rain."

5B.   **Shì bu shì yào xiàyǔ?** "Is it the case or isn't it the case that it's going to rain—is it going to rain?" This question could be answered either by **Duì, yào xiàyǔ** or by **Bú huì xiàyǔ.** The affirmative-negative verb construction **Shì bu shì...** is sometimes used to create questions in this way. Another example: **Tā shì bu shì bù láile?** "Is it the case that he's not coming any more? or "Is he no longer coming?"

5C.   Be careful to differentiate the pronunciation of **xiàyǔ** "rain" from that of **xiàwǔ** "afternoon." For pronunciation practice, you might try saying the following as quickly as you can: **Jīntiān xiàwǔ yào xiàyǔ** "This afternoon it's going to rain."

5D.   **Xiàde bù xiǎo** "rains not small" or "rains quite heavily." This is an abbreviation of the full form **xiàyǔ xiàde bù xiǎo.** Compare also **xiàyǔ xiàde hěn xiǎo** "it's raining very little" and **xiàyǔ xiàde hěn dà** "it's raining a lot." Also, note the understatement contained in **hái xiàde bù xiǎo**, literally "even falls not small" or "and it's raining not just a little." While it would not be incorrect to say **xiàde hěn dà** "it's raining heavily," Chinese people have a cultural preference for understatement.

6A.   **...ÉRYǏ.** **Éryǐ** can occur at the end of a sentence to express "and that's all" or "nothing more." **Éryǐ** may be used alone or in combination with a preceding adverb like **zhǐ** "only" or **jiù** "only." The pattern is:

Sentence	...ÉRYǏ
Tiānqi yùbào zhǐ shi yùbào	**éryǐ.**

"Weather forecasts are only forecasts and that's all."

Some more examples of **...éryǐ**:

Wǒ zhǐ yǒu yìbǎikuài éryǐ.

"I have only one hundred dollars and that's all."

Tā shuō tā jiù yǒu liǎngge hǎo péngyou éryǐ.

"She says she has only two good friends, no more."

Wǒmen bù yídìng zhēn xiǎng mǎi shémme, zhǐ shi kànkan éryǐ.

"We don't necessarily really want to buy something, we're just looking, that's all."

6B.   Learn the common adverbial expressions **yídìng** "definitely" and **bù yídìng** "not necessarily." Less common than these two expressions but still heard sometimes is **yídìng bù** "definitely not." Compare the following three examples, which range on a scale from strongly positive through noncommittal to strongly negative:

Wǒ yídìng lái.	"I'll definitely come." or "I'll be sure to come."
Wǒ bù yídìng lái.	"I won't necessarily come." or "I may or may not come."
Wǒ yídìng bù lái.	"I will definitely not come." or "I'm definitely not coming."

Remember that **yídìng** and **bù yídìng** are adverbs, so they can occur only before a verb or occasionally before another adverb. One must say **Wǒ yídìng lái** "I will definitely come" and could NOT say *Yídìng wǒ lái. Note that **Bù yídìng** "Not necessarily" frequently occurs by itself as an answer to or comment on what someone else has said.

SV1.   Consider the sentence **Tiānshang hǎo duō yún** "There are lots of clouds in the sky." This is a topic-comment construction (cf. 1-3, 5F). A literal translation might be: "Regarding the sky, lots of clouds." Not all Chinese sentences have verbs. Of course, a verb **yǒu** "there are" could also be inserted into this sentence, to give **Tiānshang yǒu hǎo duō yún**.

SV2.   The word **diàn** can mean either "electricity" or "lightning." **Shǎndiàn** literally means "flash lightning." Review your collection of words containing **diàn**:

diànchē	"street car"
diànhuà	"telephone"
diànnǎo	"computer"
shǎndiàn	"there flashes lightning"

Courtyard of a traditional-style home in Penghu, Taiwan

Beijing Weather

Oliver Kerr is chatting with a Chinese classmate on the campus of Beijing Foreign Studies University one fine October morning. Kerr, an American college student who is spending his junior year in China, just arrived in Beijing a few weeks earlier. He and his Chinese classmate, who are both 21 years old, know each other fairly well.

Basic Conversation 10-2

1. KERR	Běijīngde tiānqi bú cuò ma! Bù lěng yě bú rè, tǐng shūfu.	
	Hey, the weather in Beijing is not bad! It's neither cold nor hot, quite comfortable.	

2. CHINESE CLASSMATE　Yě jiù shi qiūtiān hái kéyi. Xiàtiān rède yào sǐ. Dōngtiān yòu gān yòu lěng, hěn shǎo xiàxuě.
Fall is pretty good. Summers are extremely hot. Winters are both dry and cold, and it seldom snows.

3. KERR　Nà, chūntiān ne?
Well, what about the spring?

4. CHINESE CLASSMATE　Rúguǒ bú shi fēngshā tài dà jiù hǎole. Yào xiǎng zài Běijīng wánr yě jiù shi qiūtiān zuì héshì.
If there weren't so much wind and sand, it would be O.K. If you want to have a good time in Beijing, the fall is best.

5. KERR　Zhèmme shuō, wǒ láide zhèng shi shíhou le.
Then I've come at just the right time.

6. CHINESE CLASSMATE　Duì.
Right.

Build Up

1. Kerr
lěng	be cold [SV]
bù lěng yě bú rè	neither cold nor hot
shūfu	be comfortable [SV]
Běijīngde tiānqi bú cuò ma!	Hey, the weather in Beijing is not bad!
Bù lěng yě bú rè, tǐng shūfu.	It's neither cold nor hot, quite comfortable.

2. Chinese classmate

qiūtiān	fall, autumn [TW]
xiàtiān	summer [TW]
sǐ	die [V]
rède yào sǐ	be extremely hot
dōngtiān	winter [TW]
gān	be dry [SV]
yòu gān yòu lěng	both dry and cold
hěn shǎo	seldom [PH]
xuě	snow [N]
xiàxuě	snow [VO]
hěn shǎo xiàxuě	it seldom snows

Yě jiù shi qiūtiān hái kéyi. Xiàtiān rède yào sǐ.   Fall is pretty good. Summers are extremely hot.
Dōngtiān yòu gān yòu lěng, hěn shǎo xiàxuě.   Winters are both dry and cold, and it seldom snows.

3. Kerr

chūntiān	spring [TW]

Nà, chūntiān ne?   Well, what about the spring?

4. Chinese classmate

rúguǒ	if [MA]
fēng	wind [N]
shā	sand, gravel [N]
fēngshā	wind and sand; blowing sand [N]
rúguǒ bú shi fēngshā tài dà jiù hǎole	if it weren't that the blowing sand is too great then it would be all right
yào	if [MA]
wán(r)	play, have a good time [V]
yào xiǎng zài Běijīng wánr	if you want to have a good time in Beijing
héshì	be appropriate [SV]
qiūtiān zuì héshì	the fall is the most appropriate

Rúguǒ bú shi fēngshā tài dà jiù hǎole.   If there weren't so much wind and sand, it would be O.K.

Yào xiǎng zài Běijīng wánr yě jiù shi qiūtiān zuì héshì.   If you want to have a good time in Beijing, the fall is best.

5. Kerr

zhèmme shuō	saying it like this; then [PH]
zhèng	just [A]
zhèng shi shíhou	be just the time

Zhèmme shuō, wǒ láide zhèng shi shíhou le.   Then I've come at just the right time.

6. Chinese classmate

Duì.   Right.

 ## Supplementary Vocabulary

1. jìjié   season [N]
Nǐ zuì xǐhuande jìjié shi něige jìjié?   The season you like most is which season?

2. tàiyáng   sun [N]
    chū tàiyáng   the sun comes/is out [PH]
Nǐ kàn, chū tàiyáng le!   Look, the sun came out!

Grammatical and Cultural Notes

1A. The **ma** here expresses obviousness (7-2: 4C). The speaker feels that his comments about the weather in Beijing being pretty good should be obvious to his interlocutor, given the lovely weather that day. Remember that this **ma** expressing obviousness is pronounced with low sentence intonation and is very different in intonation and meaning from the question particle **ma**, which is pronounced with rising sentence intonation.

1B. **BÙ...YĚ BÙ...** Note in this sentence the pattern **bù...yě bù...** "neither...nor...." Although Chinese speakers can be very direct and precise if they wish, there is a general preference, as we have noted before, for indirectness and approximation. One main reason for such indirectness and approximation is so as not to lose face, or cause another to lose face, in case one's answer is later proved to be incorrect. The pattern is:

Subject	BÙ	Verb Phrase1	YĚ BÙ	Verb Phrase2
Tā	bù	gāo	yě bù	ǎi.

"She is neither tall nor short."

Some more examples:

Jīntiān tiānqi bù lěng yě bú rè.	"Today the weather is neither cold nor hot."
Wǒde péngyou bù duō yě bù shǎo.	"My friends are neither many nor few."
Tā shuō Zhōngwén bù nán yě bù róngyi.	"He said that Chinese was neither hard nor easy."

1C. The stative verb **shūfu** "be comfortable" is very common and useful. It can be used of things (e.g., weather, furniture, rooms) or people. Examples:

Zhèibǎ yǐzi zuòqilai hěn shūfu.

"This chair is comfortable." (lit. "This chair in the sitting of it is very comfortable.")

Zhèige fángjiān zhùqilai hěn shūfu.

"This room is very comfortable to stay in." (lit. "This room in the living of it is very comfortable.")

Wǒ jīntiān bú tài shūfu.

"I don't feel very good today." (i.e., "I'm sick.")

Tāmen nèiyang jiǎnghuà ràng wǒ juéde hěn bù shūfu.

"Their talking that way made me feel very uncomfortable."

2A. In pronouncing the noun **qiūtiān** "fall, autumn," remember that the syllable which is spelled as **qiu** in Pinyin is pronounced as if it were written **qiou** (so that it rhymes with English "show" but not with "shoe").

2B. **Rède yào sǐ** literally means "be hot to the extent that one is going to die" or "so hot you're going to die," in other words, "extremely hot." This **-de**, which expresses extent ("so...that..."), is often attached to stative verbs. We will discuss it in more detail later. The expression **...yào sǐ ...** "going to die" is used in informal speech for unpleasant matters; some Chinese people think it is crude because it refers to death (for that reason, some speakers would avoid saying this on Chinese New Year). Some more examples of **...yào sǐ**:

Wǒ lèide yào sǐ.	"I'm extremely tired."
Tā zuìjìn mángde yào sǐ.	"She's extremely busy."
Kuài yào kǎoshìle, wǒ jǐnzhāngde yào sǐ!	"Soon we'll be testing, I'm incredibly nervous!"

2C. **YÒU...YÒU...** As you have already learned, the adverb **yòu** means "again." With affirmative verbs, the paired adverb pattern **yòu...yòu...** means "both...and...." Each of the **yòu** is followed by a verb phrase, which can include a stative verb, auxiliary verb, regular verb, or resultative verb. This pattern indicates that several states or actions exist at the same time. Therefore, the two expressions that come after the two **yòu** must logically be able to complement each other and cannot contradict each other. For example, you could say **yòu hǎo yòu**

piányi "both good and cheap" but you could not normally say ****yòu hǎo yòu guì** "both good and expensive." The word "both" can sometimes be omitted in the English translation. The pattern is:

Subject/Topic	YÒU	Verb Phrase1	YÒU	Verb Phrase2
Tāmen màide dōngxi	yòu	hǎo	yòu	piányi.

"The things they sell are both good and cheap."

Yòu...yòu... is stronger and "tighter" than **yě...yě...**, which can also be used to express "both...and..." (cf. **Wǒ yě shi Měiguo rén yě shi Zhōngguo rén** "I'm both American and Chinese"). When two stative verbs are present, **yòu...yòu...** is generally preferred over **yě...yě...** Note that after **yòu** there is usually no adverb **hěn** "very." Here are some more examples of the **yòu...yòu...** construction:

Nèige xuésheng yòu cōngming yòu yònggōng.

"That student is both smart and diligent."

Tā shuōhuà yòu kuài yòu bù qīngchu, shízài tīngbudǒng.

"She speaks both fast and unclearly, I really can't understand her."

The **yòu...yòu...** pattern can be negated by placing a **bù** or **méi** after each **yòu**. In English, a sentence with **yòu bù...yòu bù...** or **yòu méi...yòu méi...** often translates as "neither...nor...." Examples:

Zhèrde cài yòu bù hǎochī yòu bù hǎokàn.

"The food here is neither good-tasting nor does it look appetizing."

Tā yòu bú huì shuō Zhōngguo huà, yòu bú huì xiě Zhōngguo zì.

"He can neither speak Chinese nor write it."

2D. You previously learned **shǎo** as a stative verb meaning "to be few, to be little." As the predicate of a sentence, **hěn shǎo** would mean that the subject or topic is "very few" or "very little." For example:

Tāde péngyou hěn shǎo.

"His friends are very few." or "He has very few friends."

Now, when it precedes a verb, the phrase **hěn shǎo** (lit. "very few" or "very little") can also function as an adverb and mean "seldom." Examples:

Tā hěn shǎo qù.	"She seldom goes."
Zhèr hěn shǎo xiàyǔ.	"It seldom rains here."
Wǒmen hěn shǎo zài nàr chīfàn.	"We seldom eat there."

Below we shall list the adverbs of frequency that you have learned so far in descending order:

cháng or **chángcháng**	"often"
yǒude shíhou(r)	"sometimes"
bù cháng	"not often"
hěn shǎo	"seldom"

3. You have now learned the names of the four seasons in Chinese. As in English, they are usually said in the order **chūntiān, xiàtiān, qiūtiān, dōngtiān**, which can be abbreviated to **chūn-xià-qiū-dōng**. In English we often use "this," "next," and "last" to refer to seasons in the current, following, or previous years. In Chinese, one usually first gives the year—**jīnnián, míngnián**, or **qùnián**—followed by the season. Examples:

jīnnián xiàtiān	"this summer"
míngnián chūntiān	"next spring"
qùnián qiūtiān	"last fall"

4A.   Conditional Sentences with **RÚGUŎ...JIÙ...** This pattern, which means "if...then...," is a common way to express a condition. The pattern is:

RÚGUŎ	Condition	Subject	JIÙ	Result
Rúguǒ	xiàxuě,	wǒ	jiù	bú qù.

"If it snows, I (then) won't come."

Rúguǒ...jiù... is equivalent in meaning to **yàoshi...jiù...**, except that the pattern with **yàoshi** is more colloquial and is used mainly in Northern China. The pattern with **rúguǒ**, on the other hand, can be written as well as spoken and is common throughout the Chinese-speaking world. Note that in English there must be an "if," but the "then" is optional. In Chinese, on the other hand, there is usually a "then" (**jiù**), but the "if" (**rúguǒ** or **yàoshi**) is optional. It is also possible to have a conditional **-de huà** at the end of the first clause (8-1: 6A) in conjunction with the **rúguǒ**. Be sure that the **jiù** follows the subject and stands before the verb.

Some more examples:

Rúguǒ tā lái, wǒ jiù bù lái.	"If she comes, (then) I won't come."
Rúguǒ nǐ bù xǐhuan, wǒ jiù bù mǎi.	"If you don't like it, (then) I won't buy it."
Rúguǒ xiàyǔde huà, wǒmen jiù bú qù.	"If it should rain, (then) we won't go."

4B.   Learn the noun **fēng** "wind." The stative verb **dà** "to be big" is used with **fēng**. Example:

Jīntiān fēng hěn dà.   "Today there's a strong wind." (lit. "Today the wind is very big.")

4C.   Examine the sentence **Rúguǒ bú shi fēngshā tài dà jiù hǎole.** The literal meaning of this sentence is: "If not is wind-sand too big, then become-good." In normal English, one translation would be: "If it weren't that the blowing sand is too great, then it would be all right."

4D.   This **yào** "if" means the same as **yàoshi**, which is really composed of **yào** plus **shi** "be."

4E.   The Chinese verb **wán(r)** "play, have a good time, have fun, amuse oneself" is very common and useful. Unlike English "play," **wán(r)** can be used of adults as well as children. More examples:

Huānyíng nǐ dào wǒ jiā lái wánr.

"You're welcome to come to my home to have a good time."

Xièxie nín, wǒ jīntiān wánrde hěn gāoxìng.

"Thank you, I had a great time today." (e.g., said by a guest to the host when leaving a dinner party)

4F.   Note **zuì héshì** "most appropriate." In lesson 10-1, you were introduced to the very common adverb **zuì** "most." You have previously encountered **zuì** in these expressions:

zuì dī wēndù	"lowest temperature"
zuì gāo wēndù	"highest temperature"
zuìjìn	"recently"
zuìhòu	"in the end, finally"

In comparing different degrees of appropriateness, we could say:

Zhèige héshì, nèige gèng héshì, kěshi nèibiān nèige zuì héshì.

"This one is appropriate, that one is more appropriate, but that one over there is the most appropriate."

Here are some more examples with **zuì**:

zuì guìde qìchē	"the most expensive car(s)"
zuì nán xiěde zì	"the characters that are the hardest to write"
wǒ kànguo zuì gāode shān	"the tallest mountain I've ever seen"
wǒ zuì nán wàngde yíge rén	"the person that is the hardest for me to forget"

Taiwan Weather

Eileen Thompson is in Taipei for several days, staying at the Japanese-style home of her Taiwanese friend, Wu Xiaoling. The two middle-aged women are chatting in the living room when Thompson sees heavy fog right outside the screen door.

Basic Conversation 10-3

1. THOMPSON		**Jīntiān zǎoshàng zěmme yòu yǒu wù? Hǎoxiàng shi cóng shāchuāng piāojìnláide yàngzi.**
		How come there's fog again this morning? It seems like it floated in through the window screen.
2. WU		**M. Yángmíng Shān dōngtiān chángcháng shi zhèiyangzi. Kōngqì hěn cháoshī, yě cháng xià máomáoyǔ. Qíshí, xiànzài jiù zài xià dànshi yīnwei yǒu wù, suóyi kànbuchūlái.**
		Yeah. Yangming Mountain is often like this in the winter. The air is humid and it often drizzles. Actually, it's drizzling right now, but because of the fog, you can't tell.
3. THOMPSON		**Wǒ yùnqi zhēn shi bù hǎo. Shàngcì lái Táiwān pèngshang dà táifēng. Zhèicì tiāntiān xiàyǔ, gēnběn méi bànfǎ chūmén!**
		I'm really unlucky. When I came to Taiwan last time, I encountered a big typhoon. This time it's been raining every day, so I can't go out at all!

Build Up

1. Thompson

wù	fog [N]
shāchuāng	screen window [N]
piāo	float [V]
-lái	(indicates motion toward speaker) [RE]
jìnlái	come in [RC]
-jìnlái	come in [RE]
piāojìnlái	float in [RC]
hǎoxiàng shi cóng shāchuāng piāojìnláide yàngzi	it seems like it floated in from the window screen
Jīntiān zǎoshàng zěmme yòu yǒu wù?	How come there's fog again this morning?
Hǎoxiàng shi cóng shāchuāng piāojìnláide yàngzi.	It seems like it floated in through the window screen.

2. Wu

m	(indicates agreement) [I]
Yángmíng Shān	Yangming Mountain [PW]
zhèiyangzi	this way, like this [MA]
kōngqì	air [N]
cháoshī	be humid [SV]
máomáoyǔ	light rain [N]
xià máomáoyǔ	drizzle [PH]
qíshí	actually [MA]
zài	(indicates progressive aspect) [AV]
zài xià	it's drizzling
xiànzài jiù zài xià	right now it's drizzling
dànshi	but [CJ]
chūlái	come out [RC]
-chūlái	come out [RE]
kànchūlái	know something by looking [RC]
kànbuchūlái	be unable to know something by looking

M. **Yángmíng Shān dōngtiān chángcháng shi zhèiyangzi.**
Yeah. Yangming Mountain is often like this in the winter.

Kōngqì hěn cháoshī, yě cháng xià máomáoyǔ.
The air is humid and it often drizzles.

Qíshí, xiànzài jiù zài xià dànshi yīnwei yǒu wù, suóyi kànbuchūlái.
Actually, it's drizzling right now, but because of the fog, you can't tell.

3. Thompson

yùnqi	luck [N]
yùnqi bù hǎo	have bad luck
yùnqi zhēn shi bù hǎo	really have bad luck
shàngcì lái Táiwān	when I came to Taiwan last time
pèng	bump, run into [V]
-shàng	up, on [RE]
pèngshang	run into, encounter [RC]
táifēng	typhoon [N]
pèngshang dà táifēng	run into a big typhoon
tiāntiān	every day
tiāntiān xiàyǔ	it rains every day
gēnběn (+ NEGATIVE)	(not) at all [A]
bànfǎ(r)	way of doing something, method [N]
méi bànfǎ(r)	have no way to do something
gēnběn méi bànfǎ	there is no way at all
chūmén(r)	go outside [VO]

Wǒ yùnqi zhēn shi bù hǎo. Shàngcì lái Táiwān pèngshang dà táifēng.
I'm really unlucky. When I came to Taiwan last time, I encountered a big typhoon.

Zhèicì tiāntiān xiàyǔ, gēnběn méi bànfǎ chūmén!
This time it's been raining every day, so I can't go out at all!

 Supplementary Vocabulary

1. jìnqu
go in [RC]
Nǐ jìnqu kànkan, hǎo ma?
Could you go in and take a look?

2. chūqu
go out [RC]
Zhèige dìfang zěmme chūqu?
How do you get out of this place?

3. nèiyangzi
that way, like that [MA]
Nǐ búyào nèiyangzi kàn wǒ!
Don't look at me like that!

Grammatical and Cultural Notes

1A. This conversation takes place in a Japanese-style house on Yangming Mountain, a famous resort area and national park that is located about 10 miles to the north of downtown Taipei. Taiwan was occupied by Japan for 51 years, from 1895 until 1945. During this period, many Japanese-style houses were built. While some survive, most have been replaced by more modern concrete structures.

1B. As we saw in 10-3, to say "it's raining heavily" one uses **dà: xiàyǔ xiàde hěn dà**. Similarly, to say "there is heavy fog," say **wù hěn dà** "the fog is great." Most other meteorological phenomena work the same way: **fēng hěn dà** "there's a strong wind," **xiàxuě xiàde hěn dà** "it's snowing heavily."

1C. **HǍOXIÀNG...-DE YÀNGZI**. Early in this course, you learned the moveable adverb **hǎoxiàng** "seem" and the noun **yàngzi** "way, appearance" (as in **lǎo yàngzi** "old way"). Now, in this lesson, we combine the two into the pattern **hǎoxiàng...-de yàngzi**, which means "seem like..." or "seem as though...." The meaning of **yàngzi** is "appearance," so the literal meaning of the whole pattern would be "seem like the appearance of...." A sentence is placed between the **hǎoxiàng**, which can precede or follow the subject, and the **-de yàngzi**. The meaning is similar to **hǎoxiàng** when used alone. The pattern is:

HǍOXIÀNG	Sentence	-DE YÀNGZI
Hǎoxiàng	wù cóng shāchuāng piāojìnlái	de yàngzi.

"It seems as though the fog floats in through the window screen."

Remember that in Chinese there is often a tendency to make statements that are more tentative and less direct than in English, lest the speaker lose face if he or she is later proven wrong, and to reduce possible conflict with the listener if he or she should disagree. Some more examples of the pattern **hǎoxiàng...-de yàngzi**:

Hǎoxiàng tā xiànzài bú zàide yàngzi.   "It seems she's not here now."

Hǎoxiàng zhèiyàng bǐjiào hǎokànde yàngzi.   "It would seem to look better like this."

1D. Directional Verbs. In line 1 of the Basic Conversation for this lesson, note the verb **piāojìnlái** "float in" and in line 2 note the verb **kànbuchūlái** "be unable to tell something by looking." Also, in the Basic Conversation Build Up and Supplementary Vocabulary, note the four very important verbs **jìnlái** "come in," **jìnqu** "go in," **chūlái** "come out," and **chūqu** "go out."

All of the above verb forms are examples of a type of resultative verb called directional verb. A directional verb is a resultative compound verb composed of a base verb indicating direction or motion to which is attached one of two resultative endings: either **-lái**, which indicates motion toward the speaker, or **-qù**, which indicates motion away from the speaker. For example, take the base verb **jìn** meaning "enter" (you learned it in lesson 1-4 in the phrase **qǐng jìn**). If we attach to it the resultative ending **-lái**, then we can create the directional verb **jìnlái** "come in." That is:

BASE VERB	VERB ENDING	ENGLISH
jìn	lái	come in
chū	lái	come out
jìn	qù	go in
chū	qù	go out

The negatives of the above are all with **bù** or **méi**: **bú jìnlái** "doesn't come in," **bú jìnqù** "doesn't go in," **méi chūlái** "didn't come out," and **méi chūqu** "didn't go out."

Sometimes resultative compounds composed of directional verbs can themselves function as resultative endings and be attached onto other verbs. That is the case in the verbs **piāojìnlái** and **kànchūlái**, where the verb endings **jìnlái** and **chūlái** themselves function as verb endings that are attached to the base verbs **piāo** "float" and **kàn** "look." To diagram this:

BASE VERB	VERB ENDING	ENGLISH
piāo	jìnlái	float in (lit. "float and come in")
kàn	chūlái	know something by looking (lit. "look and it comes out")

The negatives of the above are with **méi**: **méi piāojìnlái** "didn't float in" and **méi kànchūlái** "didn't know by looking."

Finally, the infixes **-de-** or **-bu-** can be inserted between the base verb and the verb ending of directional verbs to indicate whether the result indicated by the resultative ending can or cannot be achieved (cf. 9-4). Examples:

BASE VERB	INFIX	VERB ENDING	ENGLISH
jìn	de	lái	can come in
jìn	bu	lái	can't come in
jìn	de	qù	can go in
jìn	bu	qù	can't go in
chū	de	lái	can come out
chū	bu	lái	can't come out
chū	de	qù	can go out
chū	bu	qù	can't go out
piāo	de	jìnlái	can float in
piāo	bu	jìnlái	can't float in
kàn	de	chūlái	can know something by looking
kàn	bu	chūlái	can't know something by looking

2A.   **ZÀI** as Auxiliary Verb to Indicate Progressive Aspect. Look at the phrase in the Basic Conversation **xiànzài jiù zài xià** "it is falling right now" (the topic **máomáoyǔ** "light rain" was mentioned in the previous sentence). The auxiliary verb **zài** when used before a main verb frequently indicates progressive aspect, i.e., that an action is in progress. The meaning is similar to English "be" followed by "VERB + -ing" as in "is eating." The action can be present, past, or future, depending on the context. To sum up, this pattern, which usually translates into "to be doing something," is:

Subject	ZÀI	Verb Phrase
Tā	**zài**	**chīfàn.**

"He's eating."

Examples:

Tā zài xiězì.	"She's writing."
Tā zài kāichē.	"She's driving a car."
Tā zài jiǎnghuà.	"He's speaking."
Nǐ zài zuò shémme ne?	"And what are you doing?"
Wǒ zài xuéxí ne!	"I'm studying!"

2C.   The literal meaning of the resultative compound **kànchūlái** is "look and it comes out" or "know something by looking." The negative **kànbuchūlái**, as in the Basic Conversation, would therefore mean "be unable to know something by looking." Here are some more examples:

Nǐ shuō tā yǐjīng bāshi duō suìle? Zhēn shì kànbuchūlái!

"You say she's already over 80? You really can't tell from looking at her!"

Tā shi nánde, bú shi nǔde! Nǐ kànbuchūlái ma?

"He's a man, not a woman. You can't tell?"

Another example with the resultative ending **-chūlái is shēngbuchūlái** "be unable to give birth" (lit. "try to give birth but it can't come out"):

Tāmen yuánlái yào shēng sìge háizi, dànshi shēngbuchūlái.

"They originally wanted to have (lit. "give birth to") four children, but they couldn't."

3A.   Here you learn how to say "be lucky" and "be unlucky." The Chinese equivalents are **yùnqi hěn hǎo** "luck is good" and **yùnqi bù hǎo** "luck is not good." The topic of the sentence precedes these phrases. Here are two examples:

       Nǐde yùnqi zhēn hǎo!   "You are really lucky!"

       Wǒ zuìjìn yùnqi bú tài hǎo.   "Recently I've been having bad luck."

3B.   Notice the topic **wǒ** "I" in the first sentence. The following two sentences do not have an explicit topic, but **wǒ** is understood from the context. As we have seen before, pronouns—especially the first person pronoun—are often omitted in Chinese where they would be present in English. Often, as here, the topic is referred to in the first sentence of a discourse but omitted in succeeding sentences, until such time as the topic changes.

3C.   The English word "typhoon" is a borrowing from Cantonese **daih fùng** "big wind," which is also the original source (probably via English) of Mandarin **táifēng**.

3D.   Reduplication of Measures and Nouns to Indicate "Every."   Certain measures and nouns may be reduplicated to mean "every." For example, the measure **tiān** "day" when reduplicated as **tiāntiān** gains the meaning "every day." A few other measures and nouns operate similarly. Compare:

tiān	"day"	→	**tiāntiān**	"every day"
nián	"year"	→	**niánnián**	"every year"
rén	"person"	→	**rénrén**	"everybody"

Such reduplicated forms are often, though not always, followed by **dōu**. For example:

       Tāmen tiāntiān dōu lái.   "They come every day."

3E.   The adverb **gēnběn** followed by **bù** or **méi** means "not at all" or "not in the slightest way." Examples:

Tā gēnběn bú huì.

"He doesn't have the slightest idea of how to do it."

Tā gēnběn méiyou lái shàngkè.

"She didn't come to class at all."

Nǐ gēnběn bù zhīdào wǒ zài shuō shémme!

"You don't have the foggiest notion of what I'm talking about!"

3F.   The Noun Suffix **-FĂ**. The noun **bànfǎ(r)** is composed of the verb **bàn** "do," which you learned in 1-1, plus the noun suffix **-fǎ**, which means "way" or "method of doing something." Numerous other verbs may also be followed by the suffix **-fǎ(r)** to create nouns. The pattern is:

Verb	FĂ(R)
bàn	**fǎ(r)**

"way of doing something"

Bànfǎ(r) is a common and useful noun meaning "way or method of doing something." It often refers to a way of dealing with a difficult situation. The expression **méi bànfǎ(r)** "have no way to do something" is frequently used in an idiomatic way to mean "no way" or "there's nothing that can be done." Some examples with **bànfǎ(r)**:

Duìbuqǐ, méi bànfǎr.	"Sorry, there's nothing that can be done."
Wǒ shízài méi bànfǎ.	"There was really nothing I could do."
Wǒmen yídìng yào xiǎng ge bànfǎ a!	"We've got to think of a way!"

Here are some other common examples of verbs that you have previously learned to which the suffix **-fǎ** has been added so as to create nouns:

chīfǎ	"way of eating"
jiǎngfǎ	"way of speaking"
jiāofǎ	"way of teaching"
kànfǎ	"way of looking at things, opinion"
shuōfǎ	"way of speaking"
xiǎngfǎ	"way of thinking, opinion"
xiěfǎ	"way of writing"
xuéfǎ	"way of learning"
zuòfǎ	"way of doing things"

Family outing on Yangming Mountain, Taipei County

Talking About the Weather in Your Hometown

In a park in Beijing, a local Chinese man sees what appears to him to be an overseas Chinese man reading a foreign magazine. He decides to sit down and strike up a conversation.

 Basic Conversation 10-4

1. CHINESE
Nǐ hǎo!
Hi!

2. AMERICAN
Nǐ hǎo!
Hello!

3. CHINESE
Qǐng wèn, nǐ shi Zhōngguo rén ma?
Excuse me, are you Chinese?

4. AMERICAN
Wǒ shi Huáyìde Měiguo rén.
I'm Chinese-American.

5. CHINESE
Ò, nǐ shi Měijí Huárén. Éi, nǐ jiā zài Měiguo shémme dìfang?
Oh, you're an American Chinese. So, where in the U.S. do you live?

6. AMERICAN
Zài Měiguo xī'àn, Jiāzhōu, lí Jiùjīnshān bù yuǎn.
On the U.S. west coast, California, not far from San Francisco.

7. CHINESE
Nàrde qìhou zěmmeyàng?
What's the climate like there?

8. AMERICAN
Tǐng bú cuòde. Dōngtiān bǐ Běijīng nuǎnhuo, yě méiyou zhèr zhèmme gānzào; érqiě xiàtiān hái bǐ zhèr liángkuai. Kéyi shuō shi dōng-nuǎn-xià-liáng.
Pretty nice. Winters are warmer than in Beijing, and not as dry as here; and summers are cooler than here. One could say it's "warm in the winter and cool in the summer."

9. CHINESE
Nà, nǐ lái Běijīng zhèmme jiǔ le, xiànzài yǐjīng xíguàn Běijīngde qìhou le ba?
Well, you've been in Beijing so long, by now you must be used to Beijing's climate?

10. AMERICAN
M, gāng láide shíhou, bú tài shìyìng. Xiànzài chàbuduōle.
Yeah, when I had just come, I wasn't very much used to it. Now it's pretty much O.K.

Build Up

1. Chinese	
Nǐ hǎo!	Hi!

2. American	
Nǐ hǎo!	Hello!

3. Chinese	
Qǐng wèn, nǐ shi Zhōngguo rén ma?	Excuse me, are you Chinese?

4. American	
Wǒ shi Huáyìde Měiguo rén.	I'm Chinese-American.

5. Chinese

Měijí Huárén	Chinese with U.S. nationality [PH]
Ò, nǐ shi Měijí Huárén.	Oh, you're an American Chinese.
Éi, nǐ jiā zài Měiguo shémme dìfang?	So, where in the U.S. do you live?

6. American

xīàn	west coast [PW]
Jiāzhōu	California [PW]
Zài Měiguo xīàn, Jiāzhōu, lí Jiùjīnshān bù yuǎn.	On the U.S. west coast, California, not far from San Francisco.

7. Chinese

qìhou	climate [N]
Nàrde qìhou zěmmeyàng?	What's the climate like there?

8. American

tǐng bú cuòde	not at all bad
bǐ	compare [V/CV]
nuǎnhuo	be warm [SV]
bǐ Běijīng nuǎnhuo	compared to Beijing are warmer
gānzào	be dry [SV]
méiyou zhèr zhèmme gānzào	not as dry as here
liángkuai	be comfortably cool [SV]
dōng-nuǎn-xià-liáng	"warm in winter, cool in summer" [EX]
Tǐng bú cuòde. Dōngtiān bǐ Běijīng nuǎnhuo,	Pretty nice. Winters are warmer than in Beijing,
yě méiyou zhèr zhèmme gānzào;	and not as dry as here;
érqiě xiàtiān hái bǐ zhèr liángkuai.	and summers are cooler than here.
Kéyi shuō shi dōng-nuǎn-xià-liáng.	One could say it's "warm in the winter and cool in the summer."

9. Chinese

xíguàn	be accustomed to [V]
xíguàn Běijīngde qìhou	be accustomed to Beijing's climate
Nà, nǐ lái Běijīng zhèmme jiǔ le,	Well, you've been in Beijing so long,
xiànzài yǐjīng xíguàn Běijīngde qìhou le ba?	by now you must be used to Beijing's climate?

10. American

...-de shíhou(r)	at the time when... [PT]
gāng láide shíhou	when I had just come
shìyìng	adapt, get used to [V]

bú tài shìyìng	not be very well adapted to
chàbuduō	not lack much, be good enough [IE]
M, gāng láide shíhou, bú tài shìyìng.	Yeah, when I had just come, I wasn't very much used
Xiànzài chàbuduōle.	to it. Now it's pretty much O.K.

 ## Supplementary Vocabulary

1. dōngàn
Měiguode dōngàn bǐ xī'àn lí Zhōngguo yuǎn.

east coast [PW]
The East Coast of the U.S. is farther from China than the West Coast.

2. Àomén
Àomén méiyou Xiānggǎng nèmme dà.

Macao [PW]
Macao is not as large as Hong Kong.

3. fēngjǐng
  měi
Nàrde fēngjǐng hěn měi.

scenery [N]
be beautiful [SV]
The scenery there is beautiful.

4. wǎn
Tā bǐ wǒ wǎn dào shífēn zhōng.

be late [SV/A]
She arrived ten minutes later than I.

5. nánguò
Nǐ bié nánguò, zhè shi méiyou bànfǎde.

be sad [SV]
Don't be sad, there's nothing that can be done about this.

Grammatical and Cultural Notes

5. **Měijí Huárén** (lit. "American nationality Chinese person") is the most common term for "Chinese-American" in the PRC. It emphasizes that the person is basically a Chinese, though of U.S. citizenship. In Taiwan the term **Měiguo Huáqiáo** "overseas Chinese from America" is often used. The term **Huáyì(de) Měiguo rén** "Chinese-American" that we learned in 2-1 is based on the American perspective that one is basically an American but of Chinese ethnicity.

6. **Jiāzhōu** "California" is a common abbreviation of **Jiālìfúníyà zhōu** "California state."

8A. The sentence **Dōngtiān bǐ Běijīng nuǎnhuo** "Winters are warmer than Beijing" is an abbreviated version of the fuller sentence **Nàrde dōngtiān bǐ Běijīngde dōngtiān nuǎnhuo** "The winters there are warmer than the winters in Beijing."

8B. **Bǐ** to Express Unequal Comparison. In Chinese, as in English, there are equal comparisons ("this one is as good as that one") and unequal comparisons ("this one is better than that one"). We take up in this lesson unequal comparison with the coverb **bǐ**, which forms one of the most basic and most common grammatical patterns in Chinese. As a regular verb, **bǐ** means "compare," e.g., **Nǐ bié gēn rénjia bǐ** "Don't always compare (yourself) to others." Strictly speaking, **bǐ** has this same meaning when used as a coverb in a sentence like **Tā bǐ wǒ gāo** "She is taller than me"; literally, this sentence means "She compared to me is tall." Coverbal phrases with **bǐ** and an object frequently modify stative verbs, as in the previous example, but they can also modify auxiliary verbs (e.g., **Tā bǐ wǒ huì wánr** "He knows how to have fun more than I do") or regular verbs (e.g., **Tā bǐ wǒ zǎo láile yíge zhōngtóu** "She came an hour earlier than I"). The basic pattern is:

Topic	Bǐ	Object	Comment
Tā	bǐ	wǒ	gāo.

"She is taller than me." (lit. "She compared to me is tall.")

Here are some more examples of **bǐ** to express unequal comparison:

> **Xiānggǎng bǐ Àomén dà.**
>
> "Hong Kong is bigger than Macao."

> **Zhèrde xuésheng bǐ nàrde xuésheng cōngming.**
>
> "The students here are smarter than the students there."

> **Nǐ jiā lí wǒ jiā bǐ tā jiā lí wǒ jiā hái yuǎn ma?**
>
> "Is your home even further from my home than his home is?"

The pattern with **bǐ** can also be used to indicate that someone is older or younger than someone else. To say "a certain number of years older" one uses **dà**, literally "big," NOT *lǎo; and for "a certain number of years younger" one uses **xiǎo**, literally "small," NOT *niánqīng. For how many years older or younger someone is, one uses **suì**, NOT *nián. Examples:

> **Wǒ jiějie bǐ wǒ dà yísuì.**   "My older sister is one year older than I am."
>
> **Wǒ dìdi bǐ wǒ xiǎo liǎngsuì.**   "My little brother is two years younger than me."

Attention: In the **bǐ** pattern you CANNOT use adverbs like **hěn** or **tài** or **fēicháng** before the verb. You could NEVER say *Zhèige bǐ nèige hěn hǎo for "This one is better than that one." Instead, one would simply say **Zhèige bǐ nèige hǎo** "This one is better than that one," without any **hěn** or other adverb.

The negative of sentences with **bǐ** can be formed by adding a **bù** directly before the **bǐ**. Examples:

> **Zhèige bù bǐ nèige hǎo!**   "This one is NOT better than that one!"
>
> **Gōngchē bù bǐ qìchē màn!**   "Buses are NOT slower than cars!"

The **bù** is always placed directly before the **bǐ**; you could never say *Zhèige bǐ nèige bù hǎo. You should note that the negative with **bù bǐ** is not all that commonly used except when you wish to negate the whole construction, as in direct contradictions of what someone else has said. The normal way to negate unequal comparisons (that is, to say "This is not as good as that") is by means of a different pattern that we will take up in note 8D below.

8C.   Some speakers pronounce **nuǎnhuo** "to be warm" as **nuǎnhé** or **nuǎnhe**, even though these pronunciations are not considered standard.

8D.   A **MÉIYOU** B **NÈMME/ZHÈMME** C. The very common pattern **A méiyou B nèmme** (or **zhèmme**) **C** means "A is not as C as B is." This pattern is what is normally used as the negative of the pattern with **bǐ** that is introduced in 8B above. Compare the following two sentences:

POSITIVE: **Zhèige bǐ nèige hǎo.**

                        "This one is better than that one." (lit. "This one compared to that one is good.")

NEGATIVE: **Zhèige méiyou nèige nèmme hǎo.**

                        "This one is not as good as that one." (lit. "This one does not have that one so good.")

In general, if one is talking about something close to one, **zhèmme** is used; otherwise, **nèmme** is used. To sum up, the pattern is:

A	MÉIYOU	B	ZHÈMME/NÈMME	C
Zhōngwén	méiyou	Rìwén	nèmme	nán.

"Chinese is not as hard as Japanese." (lit. "Chinese doesn't have Japanese so hard.")

Examples:

> **Tā méiyou wǒ zhèmme gāo.**   "She is not so tall as I am."
>
> **Wǒ méiyou tā nèmme cōngming.**   "I am not as smart as she is."

Attention: To say "This is not as good as that," you could never say *Zhèige bǐ nèige bù hǎo. Instead, you should say **Zhèige méiyou nèige nèmme hǎo.**

8E. Note **érqiě** "moreover, and, also," which you learned in 9-3. This conjunction, which always occurs at the beginning of a clause, is very useful for combining phrases or sentences.

8F. Notice the use of **yě** and **érqiě** to mean "and" in the sentence **Dōngtiān bǐ Běijīng nuǎnhuo, yě méiyou zhèr zhèmme gānzào; érqiě xiàtiān hái bǐ zhèr liángkuai** "Winters are warmer than in Beijing, and not as dry as here; and summers are cooler than here." You could NOT use **gēn** as the word for "and" in this sentence, since **gēn** connects nouns (as in **gōngshìbāo gēn bēibāo** "briefcases and backpacks") but not phrases.

8G. Four-character Expressions. There exist in both spoken and written Chinese a great number of four-character expressions, which are called **chéngyǔ** in Chinese. These often allude to famous stories or events in Chinese history, or may be direct quotations from famous works of Chinese literature. Such four-character expressions are usually composed in Classical Chinese and thus often have a different grammatical structure from Modern Chinese (to reflect this, we will hyphenate the constituent syllables of four-character expressions in our transcriptions). Chinese speakers frequently use **chéngyǔ**, since they often sum up succinctly a meaning which it would take many words of ordinary spoken Chinese to express and, moreover, they convey the impression that one is a learned and eloquent person. **Dōng-nuǎn-xià-liáng**, which literally means "winter warm summer cool," is your first example of a **chéngyǔ**. Familiarity with **chéngyǔ** is useful for the nonnative in gaining credibility in Chinese society; nothing impresses Chinese more than an aptly used **chéngyǔ** coming from the mouth of a foreigner! Appropriate use of **chéngyǔ** is a hallmark of the educated Chinese speaker and, what is more, **chéngyǔ** can really be very helpful in expressing succinctly a complicated idea.

9A. Carefully distinguish the pronunciation of **xíguàn** "be accustomed to" from **xǐhuan** "like."

9B. The **le** in **nǐ lái Běijīng zhèmme jiǔ le** "you've come to/been in Beijing so long" indicates time continuing up through the present. Actually, this phrase is a shortened form of the more complete **nǐ lái Běijīng láile zhèmme jiǔ le**, with the same meaning. More later on this use of **le** to indicate time continuing up through the present.

9C. **(Nǐ) xiànzài yǐjīng xíguàn Běijīngde qìhou le ba?** "I suppose you now already have gotten accustomed to Beijing's climate?" This is an example of a double **le** construction where the first **-le** has been omitted. Normally, there would be a completed action **-le** after **xíguàn**, but so long as there is a **le** at the end of the sentence, then the **-le** in the middle of the sentence can optionally be omitted. It would, however, be quite correct to keep both of the **le** and say **Nǐ xiànzài yǐjīng xíguànle Běijīngde qìhou le ba?**

10A. ...-DE SHÍHOU(R). The pattern **...-de shíhou(r)** at the end of a dependent clause means "at the time when..." or "when..." or "while....." Speakers from Beijing and environs often add (**r**) and pronounce this as **...-de shíhour**. The pattern is:

Dependent Clause	-DE SHÍHOU,	Main Clause
Tā zài Běijīng	de shíhou,	yǒu hěn duō péngyou.

"When she was in Beijing, she had many friends."

Actually, **...-de shíhou** is a noun phrase meaning "the...time," so the above example could also be translated literally as "The she-was-in-Beijing time, she had many friends" or "At the time when she was in Beijing, she had many friends."

Note the following concerning the pattern **...-de shíhou**:

a. You would not use this pattern when "when" is a question word, as in the question "When was she in Beijing?." That sentence would be rendered in Chinese as **Tā shémme shíhou zài Běijīng?**

b. In English, the "when" clause can precede or follow the dependent clause; in other words, one could say either "When I went in, he was still sleeping" or "He was still sleeping when I went in." In Chinese, however, the clause with **...-de shíhou** ordinarily comes first, before the main clause.

c. In English, we use "when" more loosely than **...-de shíhou** is used in Chinese. Our use of "when" to mean "during the same time that" correlates to the Chinese use of **...-de shíhou**. However, we also use "when" to mean "immediately after," for example, "When the bell rings, everyone must go outside" or "When I got to Shanghai, I saw that life there is more modern than I had imagined." For these latter cases, one normally would not use **...-de shíhou** in Chinese but would instead use **...yǐhòu** or nothing at all. Example:

> **Wǒ shàngle dàxué yǐhòu, rènshile hěn duō cóng Zhōngguo láide péngyou.**
>
> "When I went to college, I met a lot of friends from China."

d. Completed action **-le** does not co-occur with **...-de shíhou**. So one would say:

> **Tā mǎile yìzhāng chēpiào.**   "She bought a bus ticket."
>
> **Tā mǎi chēpiàode shíhou, ...**   "When she bought the bus ticket, ..."

One could NOT say ***Tā mǎile chēpiàode shíhou, ...**

Here are some more examples of good usage of **...-de shíhou**:

> **Tā gàosu wǒde shíhou, yǐjīng tài wǎnle.**
>
> "When he told me, it was already too late."

> **Wǒ tīngbudǒngde shíhou, zěmme bàn?**
>
> "What should I do when I don't understand?"

> **Měicì kǎoshìde shíhou, tā dōu huì jǐnzhāngde yào sǐ.**
>
> "Every time when we have tests, he gets incredibly nervous."

Note that the subject of the dependent clause with **...-de shíhou** may be the same as or different from the subject of the main clause. In other words, you can have:

> **(a) Wǒ dàode shíhou, hái bù zhīdào.**   "When I arrived, I didn't yet know."

but you can also have:

> **(b) Wǒ dàode shíhou, tā hái bù zhīdào.**   "When I arrived, he didn't yet know."

If the subject in the second clause is the same as the subject in the first clause, as in example (a) above, the subject is commonly omitted.

10B. The verbs **shìyìng** "adapt, get used to" (in this line) and **xíguàn** "be accustomed to" (in line 9) are near synonyms, but there is a slight difference in meaning. In the case of **shìyìng**, you change yourself and adapt to a new situation; in the case of **xíguàn**, you don't change yourself but simply become accustomed to a new situation.

SV2. **Àomén** "Macao" is one of two special administrative regions of the PRC. Located about 40 miles west of Hong Kong, Macao consists of a peninsula that borders Guangdong province to the north and two islands that face the South China Sea. Macao was a Portuguese colony from the sixteenth century until 1999, when it reverted to Chinese control. Cantonese is the main language spoken there, though knowledge of Mandarin is becoming increasingly common, and there is still a small population that speaks Portuguese or Macanese creole.

SV4. The stative verb **wǎn** "be late" is common and useful. Examples:

> **Yǐjīng hěn wǎnle.**   "It's already gotten to be very late."
>
> **Xiànzài tài wǎnle.**   "It's too late now."

Wǎn is one of a limited number of stative verbs that can also serve as an adverb, as in the example sentence given in the Supplementary Vocabulary section: **Tā bǐ wǒ wǎn dào shífēn zhōng** "She arrived ten minutes later than me."

Unit 10: Review and Study Guide

New Vocabulary

ADVERBS

gēnběn (+ NEGATIVE)	(not) at all
yídìng	definitely
zhèng	just
zuì	most

AUXILIARY VERBS

kěnéng	be possible
zài	(indicates progressive aspect)

CONJUNCTIONS

dànshi	but

COVERBS

bǐ	compare

EXPRESSIONS

dōng-nuǎn-xià-liáng	"warm in winter, cool in summer"

IDIOMATIC EXPRESSIONS

chàbuduō	not lack much, be good enough
zǎo	"good morning"

INTERJECTIONS

āiyà	"oh," "gosh"
éi	(introduces questions)
m	(indicates agreement)

MEASURES

dù	degree (of temperature)

MOVEABLE ADVERBS

nèiyangzi	that way, like that
qíshí	actually
rúguǒ	if
yào	if
zhèiyangzi	this way, like this

NOUNS

bànfǎ(r)	way of doing something, method
fēng	wind
fēngjǐng	scenery
fēngshā	wind and sand; blowing sand
jìjié	season
kōngqì	air
máomáoyǔ	light rain
qìhou	climate

qíngtiān	fine day, sunny day
shā	sand, gravel
shāchuāng	screen window
táifēng	typhoon
tàiyáng	sun
tiān	sky
tiānqi	weather
wēndù	temperature
wù	fog
xuě	snow
yīntiān	cloudy or overcast weather
yǔ	rain
yùbào	forecast
yún	cloud
yùnqi	luck

PATTERNS

...-de shíhou(r)	when...
...éryǐ	only
yuè lái yuè...	more and more...

PHRASES

chū tàiyáng	the sun comes/is out
hěn shǎo	seldom
Měijí Huárén	Chinese with U.S. nationality
suóyi shuō	so, therefore
tiānqi yùbào	weather forecast
xià máomáoyǔ	drizzle
zhèmme shuō	saying it like this; then

PLACE WORDS

Àomén	Macao
dōngàn	east coast
Jiāzhōu	California
xī'àn	west coast
Yángmíng Shān	Yangming Mountain

POSTVERBS

-chéng	become; into

RESULTATIVE COMPOUNDS

chūlái	come out
chūqu	go out
jìnlái	come in
jìnqu	go in
kànchūlái	know something by looking

pèngshang	run into, meet with, encounter
piāojìnlái	float in

RESULTATIVE ENDINGS

-chūlái	come out
-jìnlái	come in
-shàng	up, on

STATIVE VERBS

cháoshī	be humid
dī	be low
gān	be dry
gānzào	be dry
héshì	be appropriate
lěng	be cold
liángkuai	be comfortably cool
měi	be beautiful
nánguò	be sad
nuǎnhuo	be warm
rè	be hot
shūfu	be comfortable
wǎn	be late
zhǔn	be accurate

TIME WORDS

chūntiān	spring
dōngtiān	winter
qiūtiān	fall, autumn
xiàtiān	summer

VERBS

bǐ	compare
biàn	change
pèng	bump, run into
piāo	float
shìyìng	adapt, get used to
sǐ	die
wán(r)	play, have a good time
xíguàn	be accustomed to

VERB-OBJECT COMPOUNDS

chūmén(r)	go outside
dǎléi	thunder
shǎndiàn	lightning strikes
xiàxuě	snow
xiàyǔ	rain

Major New Grammar Patterns

CÓNG...KĀISHǏ: cóng míngtiān kāishǐ "starting from tomorrow" (10-1)

YUÈ LÁI YUÈ... "more and more": **Tiānqi yuè lái yuè rè.** "The weather has been getting hotter and hotter." (10-1)

DÙ to express temperatures: shíbādù "eighteen degrees" (10-1)

...ÉRYǏ "and that's all": Wǒ zhǐ yǒu yìbǎikuài éryǐ. "I only have one hundred dollars and that's all." (10-1)

BÙ...YĚ BÙ... "neither...nor...": Tā shuō Zhōngwén bù nán yě bù róngyi. "She said that Chinese was neither hard nor easy." **(10-2)**

YÒU...YÒU... "both...and...": Nèige xuésheng yòu cōngming yòu yònggōng. "That student is both smart and diligent." (10-2)

RÚGUǑ...JIÙ... "if...then...": Rúguǒ xiàyǔde huà, wǒmen jiù bú qù. "If it should rain, we (then) won't go." (10-2)

HǍOXIÀNG...-DE YÀNGZI "seem like...": Hǎoxiàng wù cóng shāchuāng piāojìnláide yàngzi. "It seems as though the fog is floating in through the window screen." (10-3)

Directional verbs: jìnlái "come in," **jìnqu** "go in," **chūlái** "come out," **chūqu** "go out," **piāojìnlái** "float in," **kànbuchūlái** "be unable to know something by looking" (10-3)

ZÀI as auxiliary verb to indicate progressive aspect: Tā zài chīfàn. "He's eating." (10-3)

Reduplication of measures and nouns to indicate "every": tiān "day" → **tiāntiān** "every day," **nián** "year" → **niánnián** "every year,"

rén "person" → **rénrén** "everybody" (10-3)

The noun suffix -FǍ "way of doing something": bànfǎ "way of doing something," **kànfǎ** "way of looking at things," **xiǎngfǎ** "way of thinking," **xiěfǎ** "way of writing," etc. (10-3)

BǏ to express unequal comparison: Tā bǐ wǒ gāo. "He is taller than me." (10-4)

A MÉIYOU B NÈMME/ZHÈMME C "A is not as C as B": Wǒ méiyou tā nèmme gāo. "I'm not as tall as him." (10-4)

...DE SHÍHOU(R) "when": Tā gàosu wǒde shíhou, yǐjīng tài wǎnle. "When he told me, it was already too late." (10-4)

Word Classes of Spoken Chinese

Adverb [A]

Adverbs are words that modify verbs and answer questions such as how, when, or to what degree. For example, in the sentence **Zhèige tài guì** "This is too expensive," **tài** "too" is an adverb modifying the stative verb **guì** "be expensive." Some adverbs can modify predicates that themselves begin with adverbs, e.g, **Tāmen dōu hěn lèi** "They were all very tired," where the adverb **dōu** "all" modifies the predicate **hěn lèi**, which itself begins with the adverb **hěn** "very." Besides **dōu**, **hěn**, **tài**, and **yě**, other common adverbs include **bù** "not," **cái** "not until," **cháng** "often," **gāng** "just," **gèng** "even more," **hái** "still," **jiù** "then," **xiān** "first," **yòu** "again (in the past)," **zài** "again (in the future)," **zhēn** "really," **zhǐ** "only," and **zuì** "most."

In English, adverbs may occur in various positions in the sentence (cf. "Often I go swimming," "I often go swimming," "I go swimming often"), but in Chinese, adverbs are more limited as to their position in the sentence (for the preceding English sentences, one can say only **Wǒ cháng qù yóuyǒng** "I often go swimming"). There are in Chinese two main groups of adverbs. The first group, which is called regular adverbs [A] and which includes all monosyllabic adverbs and some bisyllabic ones like **bǐjiào** "comparatively" and **yídìng** "definitely," must occur after the subject and before the verb. The second group, which is called moveable adverbs [**MA**] and all of whose members are bisyllabic, can occur either before or after the subject but, again, must always occur before the verb. Some common examples of moveable adverbs are **dàgài** "probably," **dāngrán** "of course," **píngcháng** "usually," and **yěxǔ** "perhaps." If one is not sure whether a given adverb is a regular adverb or a moveable adverb, the safest course of action is to place the adverb after the subject and immediately before the verb, since that position is always correct. In any case, monosyllabic adverbs like **dōu** and **yě** must never be used before a noun or pronoun.

There is a small number of exceptions to the rule that adverbs always occur before the verb. These include the pattern **...-de hěn** "very" as in **hǎode hěn** "very good," where **hěn** occurs at the end of a sentence; and informal Beijing dialect, where adverbs occasionally occur at the ends of sentences, e.g., **Tā wǔsuì cái** "She's only five years old" instead of the standard Mandarin **Tā cái wǔsuì**.

Attributive [AT]

Attributives are a small group of adjective-like words that modify a following noun, e.g., **gōnggòng** "public," **guójì** "international," and **Zhōng-Měi** "Sino-American." The important thing to remember about attributives is that though they can function as adjectives before nouns (as in **guójì xuéxiào** "international school"), they cannot be used as stative verbs in the predicate (one could ordinarily not say ***Zhèige xuéxiào hěn guójì** "This school is very international").

Auxiliary Verb [AV]

Chinese auxiliary verbs are similar to English so-called "helping verbs" like "can," "may," or "must." Auxiliary verbs always co-occur with a main verb, which they precede, and serve to modify the meaning of the main verb in various ways. For example, in the sentence **Nǐ yīnggāi gàosu wǒ** "You should have told me," the auxiliary **yīnggāi** "should" modifies the meaning of the main verb **gàosu** "tell" by adding the sense of obligation. Common Chinese auxiliary verbs include **ài** "love to," **děi** "must," **gāi** "should," **gǎn** "dare to," **huì** "know how to," **kěnéng** "be possible," **kéyi** "may," **néng** "be able to," **xiǎng** and **yào** "want to," **yīngdāng** and **yīnggāi** "should," and **yuànyi** "like to." There are some auxiliary verbs that occur only in the negative, such as **méi** and **méiyou** "didn't," **bié** and **búyào** "don't," and **búbì** "don't need to."

Characteristics of auxiliary verbs include:

1. In affirmative-negative questions, it is the auxiliary that is used to form the question, not the main verb of the sentence, e.g., **Nǐ yuànyi bu yuanyi qù?** "Would you like to go?" Such questions are answered by repeating the affirmative or negative form of the auxiliary verb (not of the main verb), as in **Yuànyi!** "I would!" or **Bú yuànyi** "I wouldn't."

2. Unlike most other verbs, auxiliary verbs cannot take the verb suffixes **-le**, **-guo**, and **-zhe** (except that **-le** is possible if the main verb is omitted). Moreover, auxiliary verbs rarely take the past negative **méi**, which is itself an auxiliary (however one does occasionally hear **méi néng** "couldn't"). To say "You shouldn't have gone," say **Nǐ bù yīnggāi qù**; and to say "Two years ago I didn't yet know how to speak Chinese" say **Liǎngnián qián wǒ hái bú huì shuō Hànyǔ**.

3. Unlike most regular verbs (but like stative verbs), auxiliary verbs can be preceded by adverbs such as **hěn** or **tài** and can be followed by complements such as **-jíle**. Examples: **Tā hěn ài chī làde** "She very much likes to eat hot food," **Wǒ xǐhuanjíle!** "I like it extremely much!"

4. Auxiliary verbs typically are followed immediately by the main verb. However, sometimes other words can occur between the auxiliary and the main verb. For example, in the question **Nǐ xǐhuan zài zhèr shàng dàxué ma?** "Do you like attending college here?," the coverb phrase **zài zhèr** "here" comes between the auxiliary **xǐhuan** "like" and the main verb **shàng** "attend." Sometimes there can be two or more auxiliary verbs in succession, as in **Tā kěnéng bú huì yuànyi gēn nǐ qù** "She might not want to go with you," which contains three auxiliary verbs!

5. Many auxiliary verbs can also function alone as regular verbs, e.g., **yào** "want" in **Wǒ yào zhèige, bú yào nèige** "I want this one but not that one" or **xǐhuan** "like" in **Wǒ hěn xǐhuan nǐ** "I like you very much."

Bound Form [BF]

A bound form is a syllable that has a meaning of its own but cannot be spoken alone. Bound forms must always be attached to another syllable or word in order to be used independently. This is rather like the English prefix "anti-" in "anti-war" or "antisocial," which clearly has a meaning of its own ("against") but is ordinarily not said by itself. Examples of Chinese bound forms include **wū** "room" as in the words **wūzi** "room" and **tóngwū** "roommate"; or **cān** "meal" as in the words **cāntīng** "restaurant," **cānzhuō** "dining table," **jùcān** "get together for a meal," **wǎncān** "dinner," and **Xīcān** "Western-style food."

Conjunction [CJ]

Conjunctions are words that connect two or more words, phrases, clauses, or sentences. Examples: **búguò** "however," **dànshi** "but," and **gēn** "and." Since many conjunctions have developed from other word classes, it is sometimes difficult to distinguish conjunctions from moveable adverbs and coverbs. A key difference between conjunctions and moveable adverbs is that the former must precede the subject, while the latter may either precede the subject or come between the subject and the verb. For this reason, **dànshi** "but" is a conjunction while **kěshi**, which can also be translated as "but," is a moveable adverb.

Coverb [CV]

A coverb is a type of verb which "co"-occurs (hence the name) with the main verb of a sentence, the meaning of which it supplements by adding information about how, where, for whom, with whom, etc. the action of the verb takes place. A coverb is normally followed by a noun or pronoun object, together with which it creates a coverb phrase, much like a prepositional phrase in English. The coverb phrase always precedes the main verb of the sentence. For example, in the sentence **Wǒ měitiān zài shítáng chī wǔfàn** "I eat lunch in the dining hall every day," **zài** "in" is a coverb, which has as its object the noun **shítáng** "dining hall." The coverb phrase **zài shítáng** "in the dining hall" occurs before the main verb **chī** "eat" and provides information about where the eating takes place.

There are two groups of coverbs. Members of the first group can function only as coverbs; common members of this group are **bǎ** (moves object before the verb), **bèi** (indicates passive), **cóng** and **lí** "from," and **wàng** "toward." Members of the second group of coverbs can serve both as coverbs and as main verbs, though their meaning as coverbs often differs somewhat from their meaning as main verbs. Common members of the second group are **dào** "to; arrive," **gěi** "for; give," **yòng** "with; use"; **zài** "at, in, on; be present," and **zuò** "by (car, boat, train, airplane); sit."

Coverbs have the following characteristics:

1. In the negative forms, **bù** and **méi(you)** normally stand before the coverb rather than before the main verb of the sentence. Examples: **Wǒ yǐhòu bù gěi ta mǎi dōngxi le** "In the future I won't buy things for her" or **Wǒ méi bǎ nǐ gěi wàngle!** "I didn't forget you!"

2. In the case of affirmative-negative questions, it is normally the coverb that is used to form the question, not the main verb. For example, one would say **Nǐ gēn bu gēn wǒ lái?** "Are you coming with me?" and could not say *__Nǐ gēn wǒ lái bu lái?__

3. Coverbs usually do not take verb suffixes like **-le** or **-guo**, which are attached instead to the main verb of the sentence. However, a few coverbs can take the progressive suffix **-zhe**, as in **Qǐng nǐ gēnzhe wǒ zǒu** "Please follow me."

4. It is possible to have more than a single coverb in a sentence. For example, the following sentence has three coverbs: **Tā yào zuò chuán cóng Xiānggǎng dào Fúzhōu qù** "He's going to go from Hong Kong to Fuzhou by boat."

One important thing to remember about coverbs is that the phrase with the coverb and its object goes BEFORE the main verb rather than after it. So English "She studies in the library" would in Chinese be **Tā zài túshūguǎn xuéxí** and could NEVER be *__Tā xuéxí zài túshūguǎn.__ Actually, the Chinese sequence of coverb before main verb would seem to be the more "logical" one, since one has to be in the library (**zài túshūguǎn**) before one can begin studying (**xuéxí**).

Equative Verb [EV]

An equative verb equates or connects two nouns, pronouns, or noun phrases. **Shì** "be," which when unstressed is normally pronounced without a tone as **shi**, is by far the most common equative verb. For example, in the sentence **Wǒ shi Měiguo rén** "I'm an American," the equative verb **shì** connects the pronoun **wǒ** "I" with the noun phrase **Měiguo rén** "American." Equative verbs are limited in number. Besides **shì**, there are only two other common equative verbs in spoken Chinese: **jiào** "be called or named" and **xìng** "be surnamed."

Expression [EX]

Expressions are set phrases with conventionalized meanings which Chinese speakers frequently utter on appropriate occasions. Expressions consist of two types. The first type involves set phrases from Classical Chinese, called **chéngyǔ**, which usually consist of four syllables and tend to make a pithy remark about some topic. In the Pinyin transcription in this text, each syllable of a **chéngyǔ** is separated by a hyphen so as to make the meaning and syllable division more transparent. Examples: **jiào-xué-yǒu-fāng** "have an effective method in one's teaching," **yì-yán-wéi-dìng** "be agreed with one word."

The second type of expression involves common sayings from colloquial Chinese, called **súyǔ**, which are not necessarily four syllables in length. Examples: **Bú dào Cháng Chéng fēi hǎohàn** "If you don't go to the Great Wall you're not a brave man," **Gōngjìng bù rú cóng mìng** "Showing respect is not as good as following orders."

Idiomatic Expression [IE]

Some Chinese words or phrases have meanings and usages that cannot be derived from the combined meanings of their constituents. In other words, the meaning of the whole is greater—or different—than the sum of the parts. For this reason, idiomatic expressions must be learned as wholes and are not amenable to analysis. Idiomatic expressions, which may consist of greetings, courtesy expressions, or other conventionalized sayings, are frequently said two or more times in succession. Examples: **duìbuqǐ** "excuse me," **gānbēi** "bottoms up," **jiùmìng** "help!," **méi shìr** "never mind," **nǐ hǎo** "how are you?," **zàijiàn** "goodbye."

Interjection [I]

An interjection is a word lacking a direct grammatical connection to the rest of the sentence that is used as an exclamation, hesitation sound, pause filler, or "back channel comment" (to indicate that one is listening to and following someone else's conversation). Interjections are most frequently used by themselves or at the beginnings of sentences, but sometimes they may occur in other positions. The tones of interjections are more fluid than the tones of other words, there being considerable variation from speaker to speaker, or even from one occurrence of an interjection to the next occurrence in the speech of the same person. Common interjections include **āiyà** "gosh," **e** (hesitation sound), **èi** "yeah," **hài** (indicates exasperation), **m** (indicates agreement), **ò** "oh," **wà** "wow," and **yò** "gosh."

Localizer [L]

Localizers are noun-like forms that are used in combination with other words to indicate location. Except in very limited circumstances (cf. no. 3 below), they cannot be used alone but must be attached to other elements. The most common localizers include: **běi** "north," **dōng** "east," **hòu** "back," **lǐ** "in," **nán** "south," **qián** "front," **shàng** "on," **wài** "outside," **xī** "west," **xià** "under," **yòu** "right," and **zuǒ** "left."

Localizers have the following characteristics:

1. They may be suffixed onto nouns to form place words. Examples: **guówài** "outside of the country," **shūjiàshang** "on the bookshelf," **wūzili** "in the room."

2. They can be combined with the prefix **yǐ-** or with the suffixes **-biān(r)**, **-bù**, **-miàn**, or **-tou** to form place words. Examples: **yǐxī** "to the west of," **zuǒbianr** "on the left side," **nánbù** "in the southern part of an area," **lǐmiàn** "inside," **wàitou** "outside."

3. Localizers may be used alone after the coverbs **wàng/wǎng**, **xiàng**, and **cháo**, all of which mean "to" or "toward." Examples: **wàng qián zǒu** "walk toward the front, walk ahead," **wàng lǐ jǐ** "squeeze toward the inside," **xiàng dōng zǒu** "walk toward the east."

Measure [M]

Measures, also called "classifiers" by some grammarians, are noun-like forms that are used immmediately after a specifier and/or number to quantify nouns. For example, in the phrase **zhèisānzhāng zhuōzi** "these three tables," **zhèi-** is the specifier meaning "this" or "these," **sān** is a number meaning "three," **zhāng** is the measure for tables, and **zhuōzi** is the noun meaning "table."

There are various kinds of measures. Some measures can indicate duration or frequency of occurrence, e.g., **tiān** "day" in **Tā shuìle yìtiān jiào** "She slept for one whole day" or **cì** "time" in **Wǒ qùguo liǎngcì** "I've been there twice." Others indicate weight and length, e.g., **jīn** "catty" in **liǎngjīn xiāngjiāo** "two catties of bananas" or **gōnglǐ** "kilometer" in **wǔshi gōnglǐ** "50 kilometers." Yet other measures involve time, money, or dates.

In rapid speech, the number **yī** "one" when occurring before a measure is sometimes omitted, e.g., **Wǒ mǎi (yí)ge hóngde** "I'll buy a red one." Also, if understood from the context, the noun after a measure can often be omitted, e.g., **Wǒ yào zhèitái, bú yào nèitái** "I want this one, not that one" (referring to **diànnǎo** "computers," for which the measure is **tái**). Some measures can be reduplicated to mean "every," e.g., **tiān** "day" in **Tā tiāntiān dōu lái** "She comes every day" or **zhāng** (measure for flat things) in **Wǒ zhāngzhāng dōu yào** "I want every single one of them" (referring to **dìtú** "maps," for which the measure is **zhāng**). Since a few Chinese measures translate as English nouns (e.g., **tiān** "day" and **nián** "year"), be careful not to put measures in front of these. Say **yìtiān** "one day" and **yìnián** "one year;" NEVER say *yíge tiān or *yíge nián.

Moveable Adverb [MA]

Like regular adverbs, moveable adverbs can occur after the subject of a sentence, and before the verb, to modify the verb. Unlike regular adverbs, moveable adverbs can also occur before the subject of the sentence.

For example, **shízài** "really" is a regular adverb, so it must always occur after the subject and one can say only **Wǒ shízài yǒu diǎnr hòuhuǐ** "I really regret it a little" and never *****Shízài wǒ yǒu diǎnr hòuhuǐ**. On the other hand, **xiànzài** "now" is a moveable adverb, so one can say either **Xiànzài wǒ yǒu diǎnr hòuhuǐ** "Now I regret it a little" or **Wǒ xiànzài yǒu diǎnr hòuhuǐ** "I now regret it a little."

All moveable adverbs are bisyllabic, though not all bisyllabic adverbs are moveable. Common moveable adverbs include **běnlái** "originally," **dàgài** "probably," **dāngrán** "of course," **gānghǎo** "just," **kěshi** "but," **píngcháng** "usually," **xiànzài** "now," and **yěxǔ** "perhaps." If one is not sure whether a given adverb is a regular adverb or a moveable adverb, the safest course of action is to place the adverb after the subject and immediately before the verb, since that position is always correct. See also the entry on adverb.

Noun [N]

As in English, in Chinese a noun is a word that represents a person, animal, thing, or abstraction, e.g., **dàgē** "oldest brother," **gǒu** "dog," **fēijī** "airplane," **hépíng** "peace." Grammatically, any word that can be preceded by a number plus a measure (e.g., **yìběn shū** "a book") or that can be preceded by a pronoun plus **de** (**wǒde diànnǎo** "my computer") is a noun. Some nouns can also be identified through characteristic suffixes like **-jiā** as in **huàjiā** "painter," **-tou** as in **shítou** "stone," or **-zi** as in **háizi** "child."

A noun may stand directly before another noun to modify it, as in **mùtou zhuōzi** "wood(en) table" or **Zhōngguo zì** "Chinese character." Unlike English, Chinese nouns cannot be counted by adding numbers directly before them. For example, one can't say *****liǎng yǐzi** for "two chairs"; instead, a measure must be inserted between the number and the noun, as in **liǎngbǎ yǐzi**. Also, with the exception of a small number of nouns referring to people that can optionally take the plural marker **-men** (e.g., **péngyoumen** "friends," **tóngxuémen** "comrades"), Chinese nouns are ordinarily not marked for number, so a noun like **bǐ** "pen" could, depending on the context, mean either "pen" or "pens."

Number [NU]

Numbers are noun-like forms that function to count, enumerate, or measure. Examples include **jiǔ** "nine," **wǔshisān** "53," **liǎngqiānwàn** "20 million." Numbers can be spoken alone only in counting, in reading off single digits (as in phone numbers or years), or in a mathematical context; otherwise, numbers are always bound to measures.

Some numbers are never used alone. For example, **-bǎi** "hundred," **-qiān** "thousand," **-wàn** "ten thousand," and **-yì** "one hundred million" must always be preceded by another number (e.g., **sānbǎi** "three hundred," **wǔqiān** "five thousand," **báwàn** "eighty thousand," **shísānyì** "one billion three hundred million"). The number **liǎng-** "two" must always be followed by a measure or number. Usually, numbers precede measures, but sometimes they follow, e.g., **yíge bàn** "one and one-half" and **jiǔkuài wǔ** "$9.50." When used in the indefinite sense of "a few, several," the question word **jǐ-** "how many" is considered a number and is usually pronounced with a neutral tone (e.g., **Wǒ yǒu jige wèntí** "I have a few questions"). Similarly, when used in the indefinite sense of "more than...," the stative verb **duō** "be much, more" may also be considered a number (e.g., **liǎngbǎiduōge** "more than two hundred").

Particle [P]

Particles, which never occur alone, are used at the ends of words, phrases, or sentences to indicate particular grammatical functions. There are two main types of particles: (1) particles that are used as word suffixes, e.g., **-de, -le, -guo, -zhe**; and (2) sentence-final particles, e.g., **a, ba, le, ma, ne**.

Pattern [PT]

A pattern involves two or more words in a set grammatical order that convey a specific meaning. Patterns usually constitute major or minor grammatical constructions and should be paid special attention, since they tend to be productive in the language. Examples: **chúle...** "except," **...-de shíhou** "when...," **...fēnzhī...** (for fractions), **nándào...** "don't tell me that...," **...shemmede** "...and so on," **yuè lái yuè...** "more and more...."

Phrase [PH]

For the purposes of this textbook, a phrase is considered to be a group of words which are commonly used together which are well worth learning as a unit. Grammatically, phrases can consist of two nouns, where the first describes the second, e.g., **diànyǐng míngxīng** "movie star" and **tiānqi yùbào** "weather forecast"; or a verb plus an object, e.g., **dǎ diànhuà** "make a telephone call" and **xià máomáoyǔ** "drizzle"; or combinations of words belonging to various other word classes that frequently occur together, e.g., **hěn shǎo** "seldom," **yíge rén** "alone," **yǒude shíhou** "sometimes."

Place Word [PW]

Place words are a specialized class of nouns that indicate or name places. All geographical names—such as names of towns, cities, counties, provinces, and countries—are place words, as are nouns which refer to buildings, institutions, organizations, parks, mountains, bodies of water, and other specific locations. Examples of place words: **Àodàlìyà** "Australia," **bàngōngshì** "office," **Běidà** "Beijing University," **Běifāng** "North," **Cháng Chéng** "Great Wall," **Cháng Chéng Fàndiàn** "Great Wall Hotel," **dàshǐguǎn** "embassy," **gébì** "next door," **Hépíng Dōng Lù** "Heping East Road," **jiā** "home," **Jiāzhōu** "California," **kètīng** "living room," **lǐtou** "inside," **lóushàng** "upstairs," **Shànghǎi** "Shanghai," **shàngmian** "top," **tǐyùguǎn** "gymnasium," **yòubiān** "right side," **zhèli** "here."

Place words can indicate place, location, or position without the need of a localizer or other word indicating location. All place words can precede the verb **yǒu** "there is/are" and follow the verbs **zài** "be located at" and **dào** "arrive at." They can also be inserted into the patterns **cóng...lái** "come from..." and **dào...qù** "go to...." Since they are nouns, place words can serve as the subject, topic, or object of a verb, e.g., **Zhèr tài chǎo** "It's too noisy here" (lit. "Here is too noisy") or **Tā zài Guǎngzhōu** "She's in Guangzhou." Place words can also modify or be modified by other nouns, e.g., **qiánmiànde sùshè** "the dormitory which is in front" vs. **sùshède qiánmiàn** "the front of the dormitory."

Remember especially these two things about place words: (1) since all geographical names are considered to be place words, geographical names do not take the localizer **lǐ** to express "in" (say **Tāmen dōu zài Zhōngguo** "They're all in China" but NEVER *Tāmen dōu zài Zhōngguoli); (2) if a noun or pronoun is preceded by **zài**, **cóng**, or **dào** and is not itself a place word, then either a localizer must be attached to it or else **zhèr** or **nàr** must follow it (say **zài zhuōzishang** "on the table" but NEVER *zài zhuōzi; and say **Qǐng dào tā nar qù** "Please go to him over there" but NEVER *Qǐng dào tā qù).

Postverb [PV]

A postverb is a type of verb that is suffixed onto the main verb to link the action of the main verb to a following object. Postverbs often imply movement toward a certain place. For example, in the sentence **Wǒmen bāndao Xiāng Shān le** "We moved to Fragrant Hills," **bān** "move" is the main verb, **-dào** "to" is the postverb, and **Xiāng Shān** "Fragrant Hills" is the object of the postverb **-dào**. In the sentence **Qǐng nǐ bǎ míngzi xiězai zhèr** "Please write your name here," **xiě** "write" is the main verb, **-zài** is the postverb, and **zhèr** "here" is the object of the postverb **-zài**. Or again, in **Tā bǎ "shí" zì xiěcheng "qiān" zì le** "She wrote the character for 'ten' so that it looked like the character for 'thousand,'" **xiě** "write" is the main verb, **-chéng** "become, into" is the postverb, and **"qiān" zì** "the character for 'thousand'" is the object of the postverb **-chéng**. Postverbs are limited in number, the most common ones being **-chéng** "into," **-dào** "to," **-gěi** "to, for," and **-zài** "at, in, on."

Additional comments on postverbs:

1. Postverbs frequently lose their tone (i.e., become neutral tone) in their position after the main verb.

2. For a few main verb-postverb combinations, such as **zhùzai** "live in" and **shēngzai** "be born in," no movement toward a place is implied, and the meaning is the same as alternate constructions with the coverb **-zài**. So for "She lives in Shanghai," one could say either **Tā zhùzai Shànghǎi** or **Tā zài Shànghǎi zhù**; and for "He was born in Beijing," one could say either **Tā shēngzai Běijīng** or **Tā zài Běijīng shēngde**. However, most postverbs do not have coverb alternates, and most postverbs do indicate movement.

3. Sometimes stative verbs can combine with postverbs, e.g., **Wǒ zhēn bù zhīdào yào mángdao shémme shíhou** "I really don't know until when I'll be busy" or **Nǐ kàn nǐ lèicheng zhèige yàngzi!** "Look at how tired you've become!"

4. With the postverbs **-zài** and **-gěi**, one cannot have potential forms (that is, one CANNOT say *xiědegei or *zhùbuzai).

5. Particles normally occur after the object and are not attached to the postverb, so one says **Xiǎoháir diàozai shuǐlǐ le** "The child fell into the water" and NOT *Xiǎoháir diàozaile shuǐlǐ.

6. Postverbs normally attach only to monosyllabic main verbs, as in **zhùzai** "live in" or **bāndao** "move to." There are a few bisyllabic main verbs that can take postverbs, e.g., **chūshēngzai** "be born in" or **shēnghuozai** "live in," but these must be learned on a case-by-case basis. With the great majority of bisyllabic verbs, like **gōngzuò** "to work," a coverb construction would be employed, as in **Yǒu hěn duō Měiguo rén zài Běijing gōngzuò** "There are many Americans who work in Beijing"; one would NEVER say *Yǒu hěn duō Měiguo rén gōngzuòzai Běijing.

7. Occasionally one finds quasi-postverb constructions like **xiě xìn gěi tā** "write her a letter" or **dǎ diànhuà gěi wǒ** "call me on the phone" where **gěi** follows a main verb plus its direct object to indicate the indirect object. However, since the direct object intervenes between the main verb and **gěi**, we will not consider these as postverbs per se.

Pronoun [PR]

A pronoun is a word that is used as a substitute for a noun and refers to persons or things named or understood from the context. The largest class of pronouns in Chinese is personal pronouns, which include **wǒ** "I," **nǐ** "you (singular)," **nín** "you (polite)," **tā** "he, she, it," **wǒmen** "we," **zámmen** "we (inclusive)," **nǐmen** "you (plural)," and **tāmen** "they."

Besides the personal pronouns, there are also other pronouns referring to humans such as **biérén** "others," **dàjiā** "everybody," and the reflexive pronoun **zìjǐ** "oneself." In addition, there are the demonstrative pronouns **zhè** "this" and **nà** "that," which may occur as topics or subjects but never as objects, so one can say **Nà shi shémme?** "What is that?" but could NEVER say *Wǒ bú yào nà "I don't want that."

Chinese pronouns do not change depending on case as English pronouns do (cf. "I, me, my, mine"). Chinese pronouns can be used as topics, subjects, or objects of sentences. With the addition of a **-de** (which can be dropped before relatives or body parts), they can also serve as modifiers of nouns, for example, **wǒde qián** "my money," **nǐde gōngsī** "your company," **tā bàba** "her dad," and **wǒ shǒu** "my hand."

Question Word [QW]

A question word is a word or, in some cases, a bound form that is used to form a question that cannot be answered by "yes" or "no." For example, in the question **Tā shi shéi?** "Who is she?," **shéi** "who?" is a question word. Other examples of question words include **duō** "how?," **duōshǎo** "how much?," **jǐ-** "how many?," **nǎr** "where?," **nǎli** "where?," **něi-** "which?," **shémme** "what?," **wèishemme** "why?," and **zěmme** and **zěmmeyàng** "how?."

Many question words are simultaneously members of other word classes. For example, **shéi** and **shémme** are also pronouns, **jǐ-** and **něi-** are also specifiers, and **zěmme** and **zěmmeyàng** are also adverbs. Some question words can be used to form exclamations, e.g., **Duō hǎo wa!** "How wonderful!," **Nèmme dàde fángzi yào huā duōshǎo qián na!** "How much money you have to spend for such a huge house!," or **Zěmme zhèmme guì ya!** "How can it be so expensive!"

Be sure to keep in mind that if a question word is present in a Chinese sentence and the intent is to ask a question, no question particle **ma** is added at the end of the sentence. Also, remember that while English questions with "who?," "what?" etc. have a different word order from the corresponding affirmative statement, Chinese question words occupy the same position in the sentence as the word which replaces them in the answer. For example, compare the English word order in the question "What is he buying?" with the statement "He is buying a book"; in Chinese, the word order in question and statement are the same: **Tā mǎi shémme?** as opposed to **Tā mǎi shū.**

Under certain conditions, many question words become indefinites, translating as English "whoever, whatever, whichever, wherever, however"; "everybody, everything, everywhere"; "somebody, something, some place, some way"; "anyone, anybody, anyplace, anywhere, any way"; or "a few." Those conditions include:

1. When they are followed by **dōu** or **yě**, e.g., **Nǎr dōu xíng** "Anywhere is fine," **Shéi yě méi qù** "Nobody went."

2. When they are preceded by **bù** or **méi(you)**, e.g., **Bù zěmme guì** "Not particularly expensive," or **Méiyou shéi bǐ nǐ cōngming** "Nobody is smarter than you" (lit. "There isn't anybody who is smarter than you").

3. When they are unstressed in statements or in questions that are already questions because of affirmative-negative verb constructions or a final **ma**. For example: **Tā yǒu jige hǎo péngyou** "He has a few good friends," **Mǎi diǎnr shémme ma?** "Would you like to buy something?" **Nǐ yào bu yao dào nar qù hē diar shémme?** "Would you like to go somewhere and drink something?"

4. When repeated in parallel constructions in two clauses of a complex sentence, e.g., **Shéi yùnqi hǎo, shéi jiù yíng** "Whoever is lucky will win" or **Nǐ dào nǎr qù, wǒ jiù dào nǎr qù** "I'll go wherever you go."

Resultative Compound [RC]

A resultative compound is a verb compound composed of an action verb followed by a resultative ending (usually a verb or stative verb) which indicates the result of the action. For example, **zhǎngdà** "grow with the result that one becomes big, grow up" is a resultative compound composed of the action verb **zhǎng** "grow" plus the resultative ending **-dà** "big." Or again, **kàndǒng** "look at with the result that one understands" is a resultative compound composed of the action verb **kàn** "look" plus the resultative ending **-dǒng** "understand."

For most verbs, there are actual resultative forms and potential resultative forms, each of which may be either affirmative or negative. The actual forms indicate whether the result indicated by the resultative ending is or is not achieved. The potential forms, which insert the infix **-de-** or **-bu-** between the verb and the resultative ending, indicate whether the result indicated by the resultative ending can or cannot be achieved. Some verbs have only some of these forms. Examples:

Actual resultative (affirmative): tīngdǒngle "listened with the result that one understands, understood"

Actual resultative (negative): méi tīngdǒng "did not listen with the result that one understands, didn't understand"

Potential resultative (affirmative): tīngdedǒng "able to listen with the result that one understands, can/could/will be able to understand"

Potential resultative (negative): tīngbudǒng "not able to listen with the result that one understands, can't/couldn't/won't be able to understand"

Some resultative compounds are composed of verbs indicating direction or motion plus the resultative endings **-lái** "come" or **-qù** "go," e.g., **jìnlái** "come in," **chūqu** "go out." These also have actual and potential forms, for example, **jìndelái** "can come in," **chūbuqù** "can't go out." Sometimes resultative compounds composed of directional verbs can themselves function as resultative endings and be suffixed onto other action verbs. For example, the resultative ending **-jìnlái** "come in" can be suffixed onto the action verb **pǎo** "run" to create **pǎojìnlái** "run in." If there is an object, it is inserted before the **-lái** or the **-qù**, as in **pǎojìn fángzili lái** "run into the house."

Resultative Ending [RE]

A resultative ending is an ending in a resultative compound which indicates the result of the action of the first verb. For example, the resultative compound **chībǎo** "eat with the result that one becomes full," is composed of the verb **chī** "eat" plus the resultative ending **-bǎo** "full." Some resultative endings indicate direction, e.g., the resultative ending **-lái** "come" in **huílai** "come back." Most resultative endings are either stative verbs or regular verbs. While the majority of resultative endings consist of a single syllable, there are also some common resultative endings like **-qǐlai**, **-jìnlai**, and **-jìnqu** that consist of two syllables.

Examples of other resultative endings include **-bǎo** "full" (as in **chībǎo** "eat one's fill"), **-dìng** "fixed" (as in **shuōbudìng** "not be able to say for sure"), **-guàn** "be used to" (as in **chīdeguàn** "can get used to eating something"), **-hǎo** "good" (as in **náhǎo** "hold well"), **-qilai** (as in **kànqilai** "in the looking" or **xiángqilai** "think of "), **-liǎo** "be able to" (as in **shòubuliǎo** "not be able to endure"), **-míngbai** "understand" (as in **tīngbutàimíngbai** "can't understand very well"), **-sǐ** "to the point of death" (as in **xiàsǐ** "frighten to death"), **-wán** "finish" (as in **màiwán** "finish selling, sold out"), and **-zháo** (as in **shuìbuzháo** "not be able to fall asleep"). For more information on resultative endings, see the entry for Resultative Compound.

Specifier [SP]

Specifiers are adjectival expressions like **zhèi-** "this" or **nèi-** "that" that "specify" or point to a definite thing or things. The order is usually specifier + number + measure + noun, e.g., **zhèisānběn shū** "these three (volumes of) books." If the number is **yī** "one," it is usually deleted, e.g., **nèitái diànnǎo** "that computer" (instead of **nèi yìtái diànnǎo**). If the noun is understood from the context, it also is often deleted; for example, when talking about books, one could say simply **nèiběn** "that volume." Other common specifiers besides **zhèi-** and **nèi-** include **dì-** (for ordinal numbers), **gè-** "each, every," **měi-** "each, every," **shàng-** "last," and **xià-** "next." **Něi-** "which?" is both a question word and a specifier.

Stative Verb [SV]

A stative verb is a verb that describes a state, quality, or condition of the topic or subject. For example, in the sentence **Nǐ máng ma?** "Are you busy?," **máng** is a stative verb meaning "to be busy." Other examples of stative verbs include **chǎo** "be noisy," **dǎoméi** "be out of luck," **dà** "be big," **gāoxìng** "be happy," **hǎo** "be good," **hǎochī** "be good to eat," **lǜ** "be green," **yǒumíngr** "be famous," and **yǒuqián** "be rich."

In English, the great majority of Chinese stative verbs translate as "to be + adjective." Note that in Chinese, the "to be" is embedded in the meaning of the stative verb, so it is important not to add a **shì** "to be" (except in cases of unusual emphasis). For example, to say "I'm busy," one would normally say **Wǒ hěn máng** and NOT *****Wǒ shi máng**.

Characteristics of stative verbs include:

1. Stative verbs can serve as a complete predicate or as the main word of the predicate, e.g., **Wǒ hěn hǎo** "I'm fine."

2. Unlike regular verbs, stative verbs can be (and frequently are) preceded by the adverb **hěn** "very," e.g., **Rìwén hěn nán** "Japanese is (very) hard." In a statement consisting of **hěn** + stative verb, the **hěn** often loses its meaning of "very" unless it is pronounced with stress. Without an adverb like **hěn**, stative verbs in statements often have a comparative sense, e.g., **Zhōngguo hǎo, Měiguo hǎo?** "Is China better, or is America better?"

3. Stative verbs almost always take **bù** for the negative and only very rarely take **méi**. (The exception to this is stative verbs that begin with **yǒu**, which always take **méi** or **méiyou** as the negative.)

4. Stative verbs can be followed by **le** to indicate change of state, e.g., **Tā èle** "She has gotten hungry." A negative adverb plus a stative verb plus a final **le** indicates that a certain state no longer exists; this can often be translated as "no longer" or "isn't... anymore," e.g., **Tā bù gāoxìngle** "She's no longer happy" or "She has become unhappy."

5. Besides serving in the predicate, stative verbs can also be used as adjectives before nouns, e.g., **hǎo háizi** "a good child," **hǎokànde huār** "pretty flowers." This capability to serve as an adjective is one of the characteristics that distinguish stative verbs from regular verbs, since what follows a regular verb would usually be considered as its object.

6. Stative verbs can be followed by **(yi)dian(r)** "(a little) more" to indicate the comparative degree, e.g., **hǎo yidian** "better," **guì dianr** "a little more expensive."

7. Stative verbs can also be followed by certain suffixes and constructions indicating extreme degree, such as **-jíle** or **...-de hěn**, e.g., **lèijíle** "extremely tired," **hǎode hěn** "very good."

8. Stative verbs frequently occur within resultative verb constructions, either as the first verb (e.g., **hǎobuliǎo** "unable to get well") or as a resultative verb ending, e.g., **nònghuàile** "messed it up."

9. Stative verbs can be reduplicated to create adverbs, e.g., **mànmàn chī** "eat slowly," **hǎohāor zuò** "do it well," **gāogaoxìngxìngde huíjiā** "return home happily."

10. Stative verbs can sometimes serve as adverbial modifiers of verbs, e.g., **hěn nǔlìde xuéxí** "study very hard."

As has been pointed out, most Chinese stative verbs correspond to English "be + adjective," but there are exceptions, so be careful. For example, English "to be sick" corresponds to the Chinese regular (not stative) verb **bìng** "to get sick," so one must say **Tā bìngle** "She got sick" or **Tā bìngde hěn lìhai** "She is very sick" and cannot say *Tā hěn bìng. Similarly, for "be lucky" one normally says **yùnqi hěn hǎo** "luck is good," for example, **Tā yùnqi hěn hǎo** "She is very lucky" (lit. "As for her, the luck is very good").

Surname [SN]

A Chinese surname, like an English surname, is a word that indicates the family name of a person. The majority of Chinese surnames consists of only one syllable, but there is a small number of surnames that contains two syllables. Common one-syllable surnames include **Bái, Chén, Gāo, Mǎ, Lǐ, Lín, Wáng,** and **Zhāng.** Common two-syllable surnames are **Duānmù, Ōuyáng, Sīmǎ,** and **Sītú.** Depending on the degree of formality, the two-syllable surnames can be used alone or in combination with a title, but the one-syllable surnames can not be used alone and must be used with a title. Common titles include **Lǎo** "Old" and **Xiǎo** "Little," both of which precede the surname; and **Xiānsheng** "Mr.," **Tàitai** "Mrs.," **Xiáojie** "Miss" or "Ms.," **Tóngzhì** "Comrade," and **Lǎoshi** "Teacher," all of which follow the surname.

Time Word [TW]

Time words constitute a specialized class of nouns referring to time. They include periods of the day, days of the week, months of the year, seasons, years, and certain other adverbs of time. Examples: **shàngwǔ** "A.M.," **lǐbàisān** "Wednesday," **míngtiān** "tomorrow," **èryuè** "February," **chūntiān** "spring," **jīnnián** "this year," **dàsì** "senior year in college," **xiànzài** "now."

What distinguishes time words from regular nouns is that, in addition to functioning as subjects, objects, and noun modifiers, they can also function as moveable adverbs. Observe the different usages of the time word **xīngqīyī** "Monday" in the following:

As subject: Xīngqīyī shi wǔyuè wǔhào. "Monday is May 5th."

As object: Wǒ bù xǐhuan xīngqīyī. "I don't like Mondays."

As noun modifier: xīngqīyī wǎnshang "Monday evening"

As moveable adverb before the subject: Xīngqīyī wǒ hěn máng. "On Monday I'll be busy."

As moveable adverb after the subject: Wǒ xīngqīyī hěn máng. "On Monday I'll be busy."

Verb [V]

The term verb as used in this text refers to a "regular verb," as distinct from several other types of verb such as auxiliary verb, coverb, equative verb, postverb, resultative verb compound, resultative verb ending, stative verb, and verb-object compound.

In Chinese, a regular verb is a word that expresses an action, event, occurrence, or function. Chinese verbs may be transitive (e.g., **cāi** "guess," **jiǎnchá** "inspect," **kāishǐ** "begin," **mǎi** "buy," **pà** "fear") or intransitive (e.g., **bìng** "get sick," **chūshēng** "be born," **gǎnmào** "catch cold," **sǐ** "die," **tǎng** "lie down").

Grammatically, all regular verbs can take the negative **bù** or **méi** as well as the completed action suffix **-le**. Chinese verbs are not inflected in person, number or tense as in English (cf. "go, goes, went, gone, going"). There are no irregular verbs in Chinese except for the verb **yǒu** "have," the negative of which is **méiyou** rather than the expected *****bù yǒu**, which is never said.

Verb-Object Compound [VO]

Chinese verb phrases consisting of a one-syllable verb plus a one-syllable object are called verb-object compounds, e.g., **fùqián** "pay money, pay," **kāichē** "drive a car, drive." In verb-object compounds, the verb and the object are (in this textbook) written together in Pinyin, unless other words happen to intervene (cf. below). Although from the Chinese point of view all verb-object compounds are basically alike, through the prism of English we can say that there are two types.

The first type of verb-object compound involves generalized objects the translations of which would normally be dropped when translating into English. Though in English the objects are unnecessary, in Chinese the verb would sound incomplete or unclear without an object. For example, in English we can say "speak," but in Chinese one usually says **shuōhuà** "speak words"; or in English we say "eat," but in Chinese one usually says **chīfàn** "eat food." Other examples of this type of verb-object compound include **chōuyān** "smoke tobacco—to smoke," **huàhuàr** "paint paintings—to paint," **jiāoshū** "teach a book—to teach," **kànshū** "look at a book—to read," **shuìjiào** "sleep a sleep—to sleep," **xiàyǔ** "there descends rain—to rain," **xiězì** "write characters—to write," and **zǒulù** "walk a road—to walk."

In the case of the second type of verb-object compound, even from the point of view of English one can clearly see a specific object, so with these one does translate the object. Examples of this type of verb-object compound include **chīsù** "eat vegetarian food," **dǎdī** "take a taxi," **dǎqiú** "play a ball game," **diǎncài** "order dishes of food," **pàochá** "steep tea," and **tuōxié** "take off one's shoes."

Verb-object compounds can be split by grammatical suffixes and other words. For example, **jiéhūn** "marry" is split in **tā hái jiézhe hūnde shíhou** "when she was still married," or **bìyè** "graduate" is split in **Tā kěnéng bìbuliǎo yè** "He may not be able to graduate," or **jiāoshū** "teach" is split in **Tā jiāoguo hǎojǐniánde shū** "She has taught for quite a few years."

One important thing to remember about verb-object compounds is that since their objects are already "built in," they cannot take additional objects. Therefore, if one wishes to express a specific object, the general object must first be deleted. For example, **chīfàn** means "eat," so one can say **Wǒ yào chīfàn** "I want to eat." But if one wishes to say "I want to eat fish," one cannot say *****Wǒ yào chīfàn yú**. Instead, one must first drop from **chīfàn** the general object **fàn**, and then add the specific object **yú**, giving: **Wǒ yào chī yú**.

Chinese-English Glossary

This glossary contains all the Chinese vocabulary introduced in the Basic Conversation and Supplementary Vocabulary sections of units 1 to 10 of *Basic Spoken Chinese*. The following information is included for each entry: the Chinese word, spelled in Pinyin, printed in bold; one or more English equivalents; the word class of the Chinese word [in brackets]; and the numbers of the unit and part where the Chinese word was introduced (in parentheses). For example:

Chinese	English	Word Class	Unit & Part
róngyi	be easy	[SV]	(1-3)

The entries are arranged in alphabetical order of the Pinyin spellings, spelled one syllable at a time, with the vowel **u** preceding **ü**. Syllables are listed in order of tone, i.e., in the order Tone One, Tone Two, Tone Three, Tone Four, followed by Neutral Tone. For entries consisting of more than one syllable, we go through the first syllable tone by tone before considering the second syllable. For example:

bā	bān
bá	bānjiā
báyuè	bàn(r)
bǎ	bàngōngshì
bà	bāng
ba	bāngmáng
-bǎi	

Capitalization, hyphens (-), apostrophes ('), periods (...), and the optional (**r**) suffix are disregarded for purposes of alphabetization. In the case of two entries with identical spelling, order is determined based on order of introduction in the textbook. If two or more different items are spelled identically and are written with the same character(s), they are treated as different usages of one entry rather than as two separate entries.

The purpose of this glossary is to refresh your memory of words that have previously been introduced but which you may have forgotten. Since each entry includes the number of the unit and part in the textbook where the item first occurred, you are encouraged to refer back to that part for more detailed information. Do not attempt to learn new words from this glossary; keep in mind that a Chinese word means something only in a certain grammatical and semantic context and that English translations can be misleading.

A
āyí aunt (mother's sister) [N] (6-1)
à "oh" [I] (2-4)
a (softens the sentence) [P] (1-1)
ǎi be short (not tall) [SV] (1-3)
ài love; like [V/AV] (3-2)
àirén spouse, husband, wife [N] (1-2)
āiyà "oh," "gosh" [I] (10-1)
āiyò (indicates surprise) [I] (5-4)
Àodàlìyà Australia [PW] (6-4)
Àomén Macao [PW] (10-4)
Àozhōu Australia [PW] (6-4)

B
bā eight [NU] (3-1)

báyuè August [TW] (4-2)
bǎ (for chairs, umbrellas) [M] (5-1)
bàba dad, daddy [N] (1-2)
ba (indicates suggestions) [P] (3-3); (indicates supposition) [P] (2-3)
Bái Bai (lit., "white") [SN] (2-1)
bái be white [SV] (9-1)
báisè the color white [N] (9-1)
báitiān in the daytime [TW] (4-3)
-bǎi hundred [NU] (3-3)
-bǎiwàn million [NU] (4-4)
bān class [N] (3-1)
bān move (a thing or one's home) [V] (5-3)
bāndào move to [V+PV] (5-3)

bānjiā move one's home [VO] (6-2)
bānshang in a class [N+L] (3-1)
bàn take care of, do [V] (1-1)
bàn(r) half [NU] (3-1)
bànfǎ(r) way of doing something, method [N] (10-3)
bàngōngshì office [PW] (5-1)
bàntiān "half the day," a long time [NU+M] (8-4)
bàng be great, wonderful [SV] (7-4)
bàoqiàn feel sorry, regret [V] (5-1)
bēibāo knapsack, backpack [N] (3-3)
bēizi cup [N] (3-3)
běi north [L] (8-1)
běibiān(r) north [PW] (5-3)

Běidà Peking University [PW] (5-2)

Běifāng north, the North [PW] (8-1)

Běifāng huà northern speech [PH] (8-1)

Běifāng rén Northerner [PH] (8-1)

Běijīng Beijing [PW] (4-4)

Běijīng Fàndiàn Beijing Hotel [PW] (8-1)

Běijīng Wàiguóyǔ Dàxué Beijing Foreign Studies University [PW] (8-2)

Běijīng Yǔyán Wénhuà Dàxué Beijing Language and Culture University [PW] (7-2)

Běiwài (abbreviation for Beijing Foreign Studies University) [PW] (8-2)

běndì this place, here [N] (9-1)

bèn be stupid [SV] (9-3)

bǐ compare [V/CV] (10-4)

bǐjiào comparatively, relatively [A] (4-4)

bìyè graduate [VO] (7-4)

biàn change [V] (10-1)

biànchéng change into, become [V+PV] (10-1)

biǎojiě older female cousin of different surname [N] (7-1)

biǎojiěfū husband of older female cousin of different surname [N] (7-1)

bié don't [AV] (2-2)

biéde other, another [AT] (8-4)

bīnguǎn guest house, hotel [PW] (8-2)

bú cuò "not bad," "quite good" [IE] (7-2)

bú duì not correct, no (5-4)

bú kèqi "you're welcome" [IE] (1-4)

bú yòng not need to, don't need to [A+AV] (9-1)

bú yòng xiè "don't mention it" [IE] (9-1)

búbì don't need to, not be necessary [AV] (9-2)

búdàn not only [A] (9-3)

búguò however [CJ] (5-1)

búyào don't [AV] (2-2)

bù not [A] (1-3)

C

cāi guess [V] (3-2)

cài food [N] (5-2)

cèsuǒ toilet [PW] (5-3)

chà lack [V] (3-4); be lacking, deficient [SV] (7-4)

chàbuduō almost, about [A] (3-4); not lack much, be good enough [IE] (10-4)

cháng be long [SV] (3-4)

cháng often [A] (5-2)

Cháng Chéng Great Wall [PW] (5-3)

Cháng Chéng Fàndiàn Great Wall Hotel [PW] (5-3)

chángcháng often [A] (4-4)

chǎng factory [N] (5-2)

cháoshī be humid [SV] (10-3)

chē vehicle (car, cab, bus, bicycle) [N] (3-4)

chēpiào bus ticket [N] (9-4)

chēzhàn bus stop; bus station [PW] (9-2)

chēzi car, vehicle [N] (8-2)

Chén Chen [SN] (2-1)

chēnghu address [V] (2-2)

chéng city [N] (5-3)

-chéng become; into [PV] (10-1)

chī eat [V] (5-2)

chīfàn eat food, eat [VO] (5-2)

chídào arrive late, be late [V] (4-4)

chū tàiyáng the sun comes/is out [PH] (10-2)

chū'èr second year in jr. high school [TW] (6-1)

chūmén(r) go outside [VO] (10-3)

chūlái come out [RC] (10-3)

-chūlái come out [RE] (10-3)

chūqu go out [RC] (10-3)

chūsān third year in jr. high school [TW] (6-1)

chūshēng be born [V] (4-2)

chūshì show, produce [V] (9-4)

chūyī first year in jr. high school [TW] (6-1)

chūzhōng junior high school [PW] (6-1)

chūzū rent out [V] (8-2)

chūzū qìchē taxi [PH] (8-2)

chūntiān spring [TW] (10-2)

cì time [M] (4-3)

cōngming be smart [SV] (9-3)

cóng from [CV] (7-4)

cóngqián in the past, formerly [TW] (7-1)

cuò be wrong [SV] (2-4)

-cuò wrong [RE] (2-4)

D

dǎ hit [V] (8-3)

dǎ diànhuà make a telephone call [PH] (8-3)

dǎdī take a taxi [VO] (8-1)

dǎléi thunder [VO] (10-1)

dà be big; old (of people) [SV] (3-2)

-dà big [RE] (6-2)

dà'èr sophomore year in college [TW] (6-1)

dàgài probably, about [MA] (8-1)

dàmèi older younger sister [N] (6-4)

dàsān junior year in college [TW] (6-1)

dàshǐguǎn embassy [PW] (2-3)

dàsì senior year in college [TW] (6-1)

dàxué university, college [PW] (2-3)

dàxuéshēng college student [N] (5-2)

dàyī first year in college [TW] (6-1)

dàyuē approximately, about [A] (4-3)

dài take along, bring [V] (2-4)

dàizi bag [N] (3-3)

dānwèi work unit, organization [PW] (2-3)

dànshi but [CJ] (10-3)

dāngrán of course [MA] (5-1)

dào to [CV] (1-1); arrive, reach [V] (3-4)

-dào arrive at, to [PV] (5-3); (indicates action of verb realized) [RE] (9-4)

Déguo Germany [PW] (3-1)

Déyǔ German (language) [N] (7-2)

-de (in tǐng...-de pattern) [P] (1-3); (indicates possession) [P] (2-2); (indicates that what precedes describes what follows) [P] (2-4)

-de (verb suffix that indicates manner) [P] (7-2)

...-de shíhou(r) when... [PT] (10-4)

děi must [AV] (1-4)

dēng light, lamp [N] (9-1)

děng wait, wait for [V] (4-2)

dī be low [SV] (10-1)

dīxia underneath [PW] (5-4)

dì- (forms ordinal numbers) [SP] (4-3)

dìdi younger brother [N] (3-2)

dìfang place [N] (5-3)

dìzhǐ address [N] (4-2)

diǎn o'clock, hour [M] (3-4)

diànchē street car, trolley, tram [N] (9-2)

diànhuà telephone [N] (8-3)

diànnǎo computer [N] (5-4)

dōng east [L] (4-2)

dōngàn east coast [PW] (10-4)

dōngběi northeast [PW] (6-3)

dōngbiān(r) east [PW] (5-3)

dōngfāng east, the East [PW] (8-1)

Dōngfāng rén Asian [PH] (8-1)

dōngnán southeast [PW] (6-3)

dōng-nuǎn-xià-liáng "warm in winter and cool in summer" [EX] (10-4)

dōngtiān winter [TW] (10-2)

dōngxi thing [N] (5-4)

dǒng understand [V] (9-4)

-dǒng understand [RE] (9-4)

dòngwù animal [N] (9-2)

dòngwùyuán(r) zoo [PW] (9-2)

Dòngwùyuán(r) Zoo (name of bus and street car station) [PW] (9-2)

dōu all, both [A] (1-2)

dǔchē be clogged up with cars [VO] (8-4)

dù degree (of temperature) [M] (10-1)

duàn section (of a road) [M] (4-2); period (of time) [M] (7-3)

duì be correct [SV] (3-2)

duìbuqǐ "excuse me, sorry" [IE] (2-3)

duō how [QW] (3-2); be many, much, more [SV/NU] (4-4)

duōshǎo how much, how many [QW] (3-3)

duōshù the majority [N] (7-4)

E

e (hesitation sound; pause filler) [I] (5-4)

éi (introduces questions) [I] (10-1)

èi "hey, hi" [I] (1-3)

ei (indicates liveliness) [P] (6-2)

érqiě moreover, and, also [CJ] (9-3)

...éryǐ and that's all [PT] (10-1)

érzi son [N] (6-2)

èr two [NU] (3-1)

èryuè February [TW] (4-2)

F

fázi means, method, way [N] (8-3)

Fǎguo France [PW] (3-1)

Fǎyǔ French (language) [N] (7-2)

fàn rice (cooked); food [N] (5-2)

fàndiàn hotel [PW] (5-3)

fángjiān room [N] (4-3)

fēn penny [M] (3-3); minute [M] (3-4)

fēng wind [N] (10-2)

fēngjǐng scenery [N] (10-4)

fēngshā wind and sand; blowing sand [N] (10-2)

fúwù serve [V] (6-3)

Fù Fu [SN] (8-2)

fùmǔ parents [N] (6-4)

fùqin father [N] (3-2)

fùyu be prosperous [SV] (7-4)

G

gāi should [AV] (9-4)

gǎiháng(r) change one's line of work [VO] (7-1)

gān be dry [SV] (10-2)

gānjìng be clean [SV] (9-3)

gānzào be dry [SV] (10-4)

gǎn rush, hurry [V] (8-3)

gǎndào rush or hurry to a place [V+PV] (8-3)

gāng just now, just [A] (9-3)

gānggāng just now, just [A] (9-3)

gāo be tall, high [SV] (1-3)

Gāo Gao (lit., "tall") [SN] (1-3)

gāo'èr junior year in high school [TW] (6-1)

gāosān senior year in high school [TW] (6-1)

gāoxìng be happy [SV] (2-2)

gāoyī sophomore year in high school [TW] (6-1)

gāozhōng senior high school [PW] (6-1)

gǎo get, do [V] (2-4)

gǎocuò get or do something wrong [RC] (2-4)

gēge older brother [N] (3-2)

ge (general measure) [M] (2-3)

gěi for [CV] (2-2); give [V] (6-4)

-gěi give; for, to [PV] (6-1)

gēn and [CJ] (2-4)

gēn with [CV] (6-4)

gēnběn (+ NEGATIVE) (not) at all [A] (10-3)

gèng even more, more [A] (8-1)

gōng bow (the weapon) [N] (4-2)

gōngchǎng factory [PW] (7-1)

gōnggòng public [AT] (9-2)

gōnggòng qìchē public bus, bus [PH] (9-2)

gōngjīn kilo [M] (8-4)

gōngrén worker, laborer [N] (5-2)

gōngshìbāo briefcase, attache case [N] (3-3)

gōngsī company, firm [PW] (2-3)

gōngzuò work [N] (1-3); work [V] (2-3)

gǒu(r) dog [N] (5-4)

gǔ be ancient [SV] (7-4)

guǎi turn [V] (9-1)

guān close [V] (4-1)

guānmén close a door, close [VO] (4-1)

guǎn concern oneself with [V] (5-4)

Guǎngzhōu Guangzhou [PW] (4-4)

H

guì be expensive [SV] (3-3)

guìxìng "what's your honorable surname?" [IE] (2-3)

guò pass, go by [V] (8-1)

-guo (indicates experience) [P] (4-3)

H

hái still [A] (1-2); in addition [A] (7-1)

háizi child, children [N] (1-2)

Hànyǔ Chinese (language) [N] (5-2)

Hànzì Chinese character [N] (7-2)

hángkōng aviation [N] (6-3)

hángkōng gōngsī airline [PH] (6-3)

hǎo be good [SV] (1-2); "all right" [IE] (2-2)

hǎo jiǔ bú jiànle "long time no see" [IE] (1-2)

hǎochī be good to eat, delicious [SV] (6-1)

hǎode "all right," "O.K." [IE] (8-2)

hǎokàn be good-looking [SV] (6-1)

hǎoxiàng apparently, it seems to me [MA] (4-4)

hào number (in addresses, sizes) [M] (4-2); day of the month [M] (4-2)

Hé He [SN] (1-3)

hé and [CJ] (7-1); with [CV] (7-3)

hépíng peace [N] (4-2)

Hépíng Bīnguǎn Peace Hotel [PW] (9-1)

Hépíng Dōng Lù Heping East Road [PW] (4-2)

héshì be appropriate [SV] (10-2)

hēi be black [SV] (9-1)

hēisè the color black [N] (9-1)

hěn very [A] (1-2)

hěn shǎo seldom [PH] (10-2)

hóng be red [SV] (9-1)

hónglǜdēng traffic light [N] (9-1)

hóngsè the color red [N] (9-1)

Hóu Hou [SN] (2-4)

hòu in back, back [L] (5-4)

hòubian(r) in back, back [PW] (5-4)

hòulái afterward, later [TW] (7-3)

hòumian in back, back [PW] (5-4)

hòunián year after next [TW] (4-3)

hòutiān day after tomorrow [TW] (4-3)

hòutou in back, back [PW] (5-4)

Huáqiáo overseas Chinese [N] (5-1)

Huáyì person of Chinese descent [N] (2-1)

Huáyì Měiguo rén Chinese-American [PH] (2-1)

huà word, language [N] (7-2)

huānyíng "welcome" [IE] (1-4); welcome [V] (2-2)

huàn change to, exchange [V] (8-4)

Huáng Huang (lit., "yellow") [SN] (6-4)

huáng be yellow [SV] (9-1)

huángsè the color yellow [N] (9-1)

huí go back to [V] (1-1); time [M] (5-3)

huíguó return to one's home country [VO] (4-3)

huíjiā return to one's home [VO] (4-3)

huì know how to, can [AV] (7-2); be likely to, will [AV] (8-3)

huǒ fire [N] (3-4)

huǒchē train [N] (3-4)

huòzhě or [CJ] (8-1)

J

jīchǎng airport [PW] (8-2)

jīhui opportunity, chance [N] (6-4)

-jí reach a goal in time [RE] (3-4)

jǐ- how many [QW] (3-1); a few, several [NU] (7-2)

jǐge how many [QW+M] (3-1)

jǐhào which day of the month [QW] (4-2)

jǐyuè which month of the year [QW] (4-2)

jìde remember [V] (9-4)

jìjié season [N] (10-2)

jìxù continue [V/AV] (7-2)

jiā (for companies, factories) [M] (2-3); family, home [PW] (4-3)

jiā add; plus [V] (3-3)

Jiā'nádà Canada [PW] (2-1)

Jiāzhōu California [PW] (10-4)

jiǎn subtract; minus [V] (3-3)

jiàn (for luggage, matters, etc.) [M] (8-4)

jiǎng speak, say [V] (7-3)

jiǎnghuà speak, talk [VO] (7-3)

jiāo teach [V] (6-3)

jiāoshū teach [VO] (6-3)

jiāotōng traffic [N] (8-3)

jiāotōng jǐngchá traffic police [PH] (9-1)

jiāotōngjǐng traffic police [N] (9-1)

jiào be called or named [EV] (2-1); call (someone a name) [V] (2-2); call (someone) [V] (9-3)

jiéhūn marry, get married [VO] (6-2)

jiějie older sister [N] (3-2)

jiěmèi older and younger sisters [N] (6-4)

jièshao introduce [V] (2-2)

jīn gold [BF/SN] (6-2)

jīnnián this year [TW] (3-2)

jīntiān today [TW] (4-2)

jǐnzhāng be nervous, intense [SV] (1-3)

jìn enter [V] (1-4)

jìn be close, near [SV] (8-1)

jìnkuài as fast as possible [A] (8-3)

jìnlái come in [RC] (10-3)

-jìnlái come in [RE] (10-3)

jìnqu go in [RC] (10-3)

jīnglǐ manager [N] (2-4)

jǐngchá police [N] (9-1)

jiǔ nine [NU] (3-1)

jiǔ be long (of time) [SV] (4-3)

jiǔyuè September [TW] (4-2)

jiù then [A] (3-2); precisely, exactly [A] (4-2); only [A] (7-4)

jiù be old (of things) [SV] (6-2)

Jiùjīnshān San Francisco [PW] (6-2)

juéde feel [V] (7-4)

juédìng decide [V] (8-3)

K

kāi depart (of a train, bus, ship) [V] (3-4); open [V] (4-1); drive (a vehicle) [V] (8-1)

kāi wánxiào joke around, play a prank on [PH] (9-3)

kāichē drive a car [VO] (8-4)

kāiguān switch [N] (5-4)

kāimén open a door, open [VO] (4-1)

kāishǐ begin [V] (7-3); in the beginning [TW] (7-3)

kàn look, see [V] (3-2); read [V] (9-4)

kànchūlái know something by looking [RC] (10-3)

kàndǒng read and understand [RC] (9-4)

kànqilai in the looking [RC] (6-2)

Kē Ke [SN] (1-1)

kéyi be O.K. [SV] (1-3); may, can [AV] (5-1)

kě indeed, certainly [A] (5-3)

kě'ài be loveable, cute [SV] (3-2)

kěnéng be possible [AV] (10-1)

kěshi but [MA] (2-1)

kè quarter of an hour [M] (3-4)

kè class [N] (4-4)

kōngqì air [N] (10-3)

kǒngpà "I'm afraid that'; probably [MA] (3-4)

kǒu(r) (for people; lit., "mouth") [M] (7-1)

kuài dollar (monetary unit) [M] (3-3)

kuài soon, quickly [A] (5-2); be fast [SV] (8-1)

kùn be sleepy [SV] (1-3)

L

lái come [V] (2-2)

-lái (indicates motion toward speaker) [RE] (10-3)

láibují not have enough time [RC] (3-4)

lán be blue [SV] (9-1)

lánsè the color blue [N] (9-1)

lǎn be lazy [SV] (9-3)

láojià "excuse me" [IE] (8-1)

lǎo be old (of people) [SV] (1-3)

lǎo- (indicates one's rank among siblings) [BF] (6-4)

lǎobǎn boss, owner [N] (5-1)

lǎodà oldest (among siblings) [N] (6-4)

lǎoshī teacher [N] (1-4)

le (indicates changed status) [P] (1-2)

-le (indicates completed action) [P] (2-4)

lèi be tired, fatigued [SV] (1-2)

lěng be cold [SV] (10-2)

lí be distant from, from [CV] (8-1)

líhūn divorce, get divorced [VO] (6-2)

Lǐ Li [SN] (1-4)

lǐ in, inside [L] (5-4)

lǐbài week [N] (4-1)

lǐbài'èr Tuesday [TW] (4-1)

lǐbàijǐ which day of the week [QW] (4-1)

lǐbàiliù Saturday [TW] (4-1)

lǐbàirì Sunday [TW] (4-1)

lǐbàisān Wednesday [TW] (4-1)

lǐbàisì Thursday [TW] (4-1)

lǐbàitiān Sunday [TW] (4-1)

lǐbàiwǔ Friday [TW] (4-1)

lǐbàiyī Monday [TW] (4-1)

lǐbian(r) in, inside [PW] (5-4)

lǐmiàn in, inside [PW] (5-4)

lǐtou in, inside [PW] (5-4)

lǐwù gift, present [N] (6-1)

liángkuai be comfortably cool [SV] (10-4)

liǎng- two [NU] (3-1)

liàng (for land vehicles) [M] (8-2)

liáo chat [V] (6-4)

liáotiān chat [VO] (6-4)

Lín Lin [SN] (1-4)

líng zero [NU] (3-3)

liú leave (someone something) [V] (5-1)

liúxué study as a foreign student [VO/V] (6-4)

liù six [NU] (3-1)

liùyuè June [TW] (4-2)

lóu floor (of a building) [N] (4-2); building (of two or more floors) [N] (8-2)

lù road [N] (4-2); (for bus routes or lines) [M] (9-2)

lùkǒu(r) intersection [PW] (9-1)

lǜ be green [SV] (9-1)

lǜsè the color green [N] (9-1)

luàn be disorderly, messy [SV] (9-3)

Luó Luo [SN] (2-4)

M

m (hesitation sound; pause filler) [I] (4-3); (indicates that something tastes delicious) [I] (6-1); (indicates agreement) [I] (10-3)

Mǎláixīyà Malaysia [PW] (2-1)

māma mom, mommy [N] (1-2)

máfan trouble [V] (8-3)

Mǎ Ma (lit., "horse") [SN] (2-1)

mǎshàng immediately, right away [A] (8-3)

ma (indicates questions) [P] (1-2)

ma (indicates something obvious) [P] (7-2)

mǎi buy [V] (3-3)

mǎimài buying and selling, business [N] (7-1)

mài sell [V] (3-3)

màn zǒu "take care" [IE] (1-4)

máng be busy [SV] (1-2)

māo(r) cat [N] (9-2)

máo ten cents, dime [M] (3-3)

máomáoyǔ light rain [N] (10-3)

màoyì trade [N] (2-4)

màoyì gōngsī trading company [PH] (2-4)

méi (indicates past negative of action verbs) [AV] (2-4); not have [V] (9-3)

méi guānxi "never mind," "it doesn't matter" [IE] (2-4)

méi shì(r) "it's nothing," "never mind" [IE] (5-3)

méi yìsi not be interesting [PH] (1-4)

méiyou not have; there is/are not [V] (3-2); (indicates past negative of action verbs) [AV] (6-3)

měi be beautiful [SV] (10-4)

Měiguo America [PW] (2-1)

Měiguo Zài Tái Xiéhuì American Institute in Taiwan [PW] (6-3)

měi- each, every [SP] (4-1)

Měijí Huárén Chinese with U.S. nationality [PH] (10-4)

mèimei younger sister [N] (3-2)

mén(r) door, gate [N] (4-1)

ménkǒu(r) doorway, entrance [PW] (8-2)

mǐ meter [M] (8-4)

Mínguó the Republic (of China) [TW] (4-2)

míngnián next year [TW] (4-2)

míngpiàn name card, business card [N] (2-4)

míngtiān tomorrow [TW] (4-2)

míngzi name [N] (2-1)

mǔqin mother [N] (3-2)

N

nà that [PR] (2-2); in that case, so [CJ] (2-2)

nǎli "not at all" [IE] (4-1); where [QW] (6-2)

nàli there [PW] (6-2)

nàixīn be patient; patience [SV/N] (8-3)

nán be difficult, hard [SV] (1-3)

nán south [L] (8-1)

nánbiān(r) south [PW] (5-3)

nánde man, male [N] (3-1)

Nánfāng south, the South [PW] (8-1)

Nánfāng huà southern speech [PH] (8-1)

Nánfāng rén Southerner [PH] (8-1)

nánguài... no wonder... [PT] (7-3)

nánguò be sad [SV] (10-4)

nánháir boy [N] (7-1)

Nánjīng Nanjing [PW] (4-4)

nánlǎoshī male teacher [N] (3-1)

nánpéngyou boyfriend, male friend [N] (6-1)

nánshēng male student [N] (3-1)

nǎr where [QW] (1-1)

nàr there [PW] (5-1)

ne and how about, and what about [P] (1-1); (pause filler) [P] (7-1); (indicates continuous aspect) [P] (9-4)

něi- which [QW] (2-1)

něibiān(r) which side, where [QW] (5-3)

něiguó which country [QW] (2-1)

nèi- that [SP] (2-1)

nèibian(r) that side, there [PW] (5-3)

nèiyang(r) that way, like that [MA] (7-4)

nèiyangzi that way, like that [MA] (10-3)

nèmme then, in that case, well [CJ] (3-4); like that, so [A] (7-3)

néng be able to, can [AV] (6-3)

nǐ you [PR] (1-1)

nǐ hǎo "how are you?," "hi" [IE] (1-1)

nǐmen you (plural) [PR] (1-4)

nián year [M] (4-2)

niánji age [N] (3-2)

niánjí grade, level (in school) [N] (6-1)

niánqīng be young [SV] (6-2)

niàn study [V] (7-4)

niǎo(r) bird [N] (9-2)

nín you (singular, polite) [PR] (1-4)

Niǔyuē New York [PW] (6-2)

nòng alley [BF] (4-2)

nǔlì be diligent, work hard [SV] (7-4)

nǚde woman, female [N] (3-1)

nǚ'ér daughter [N] (6-2)

nǚháir girl [N] (7-1)

nǚlǎoshī female teacher [N] (3-1)

nǚpéngyou girlfriend, female friend [N] (6-1)

nǚshēng female student [N] (3-1)

nǚshì madam, lady [N] (2-3)

nuǎnhuo be warm [SV] (10-4)

O

ò "oh" [I] (2-2)

P

páiháng one's seniority among siblings [N] (6-4)

pài dispatch, send [V] (8-3)

pàiqu dispatch, send out [RC] (8-3)

pángbiān(r) at or on the side, next to [PW] (5-4)

pàng be fat (of people or animals) [SV] (5-3)

péixùn train [V] (5-2)

péngyou friend [N] (6-1)

pèng bump, run into [V] (10-3)

pèngshang run into, encounter [RC] (10-3)

pí leather, skin [N] (5-2)

píxié leather shoe [N] (5-2)

piányi be cheap [SV] (3-3)

piāo float [V] (10-3)

piāojìnlái float in [RC] (10-3)

piào ticket [N] (9-3)

píngcháng usually, ordinarily [MA] (4-1)

Pǔtōnghuà Mandarin (language) [N] (7-2)

Q

qī seven [NU] (3-1)

qíshí actually [MA] (10-3)

qítā other [AT] (7-2)

qíyuè July [TW] (4-2)

qǐchuáng get up from bed, rise [VO] (4-1)

-qǐlai in the VERBing [RE] (6-2)

qìchē car, vehicle [N] (8-2)

qìhou climate [N] (10-4)

-qiān thousand [NU] (3-3)

-qiānwàn ten million [NU] (4-4)

qián money [N] (3-3)

qián in front, front [L] (5-4)

qiánbian(r) in front, front [PW] (5-4)

qiánmian in front, front [PW] (5-4)

qiánnián year before last [TW] (4-3)

qiántiān day before yesterday [TW] (4-3)

qiántou in front, front [PW] (5-4)

qīng be light (not heavy) [SV] (8-4)

qīngchu be clear, clear about [SV] (9-1)

qíngtiān fine day, sunny day [N] (10-1)

qǐng "please" [IE] (1-4)

qǐng jìn "please come in" [IE] (1-4)

qǐng wèn "excuse me," "may I ask" [IE] (2-1)

qǐng zuò "please sit down" [IE] (1-4)

qiūtiān fall, autumn [TW] (10-2)

qù go, go to [V] (1-1)

-qù (indicates motion away from the speaker) [RE] (8-3)

qùnián last year [TW] (4-2)

quán completely [A] (7-2)

R

ránhòu afterward, then [MA] (4-3)

ràng let, cause, make [V/CV] (5-3)

ràng nǐ jiǔ děngle "made you wait a long time" [IE] (5-3)

rè be hot [SV] (10-1)

rén person [N] (2-1)

rénkǒu population [N] (4-4)

rènshi become acquainted with, know [V] (2-2); recognize [V] (7-2)

Rìběn Japan [PW] (2-1)

Rìyǔ Japanese (language) [N] (7-2)

róngyi be easy [SV] (1-3)

rúguǒ if [A] (10-2)

S

sān three [NU] (3-1)

sānyuè March [TW] (4-2)

sāichē be clogged up with cars [VO] (8-4)

shā sand, gravel [N] (10-2)

shāchuāng screen window [N] (10-3)

shān mountain, hill [N] (5-3)

shǎndiàn lightning strikes [VO] (10-1)

shàng- last [SP] (3-2)

shàng on top, on [L] (5-4); go to, attend [V] (6-1); go to, come to, to [CV] (8-3); get on (a vehicle, etc.) [V] (9-3)

-shàng up, on [RE] (10-3)

shàngbān(r) work, go to work [VO] (6-3)

shàngbian(r) on top, on [PW] (5-4)

shàngchē get on a vehicle [VO] (9-2)

Shànghǎi Shanghai [PW] (4-4)

shàngkè have class [VO] (4-4)

shàngmian on top, on [PW] (5-4)

shàngtou on top, on [PW] (5-4)

shàngwǔ morning, A.M. [TW] (4-1)

shàngxué attend school [VO] (6-3)

shǎo be few, less [SV] (4-4)

shéi who, whom [QW] (2-2)

shémme what [QW] (2-1)

shēnqǐng apply [V] (7-4)

shēnti body [N] (7-1)

shēngqì get angry [VO/SV] (9-3)

shēngrì birthday [N] (4-2)

Shī Shi [SN] (2-4)

shīfu master, driver [N] (8-4)

shí ten [NU] (3-1)

shí'èryuè December [TW] (4-2)

shíhou(r) time [N] (7-3)

shíjiān time [N] (3-4)

shítáng cafeteria, dining hall [PW] (1-1)

shíwàn hundred thousand [NU] (4-4)

shíyàn experiment [N] (4-1)

shíyànshì laboratory [N] (4-1)

shíyīyuè November [TW] (4-2)

shíyuè October [TW] (4-2)

shízài really, truly [A] (5-1)

shǐyòng use, employ [V] (5-4)

shǐyòng shǒucè operating manual [PH] (5-4)

shì(r) matter, thing (abstract) [N] (1-1)

shì be [EV] (1-3)

shìyìng adapt, get used to [V] (10-4)

shǒucè handbook, manual [N] (5-4)

shǒudū capital [N] (8-2)

Shǒudū Jīchǎng Capital Airport [PW] (8-2)

shòu be thin, lean [SV] (5-3)

shòupiàoyuán ticketseller, conductor [N] (9-3)

shūfáng study [PW] (5-4)

shūfu be comfortable [SV] (10-2)

shūjià bookshelf, bookcase [N] (5-4)

shūshu uncle (father's younger brother) [N] (6-1)

shuì sleep [V] (4-1)

shuìjiào sleep, go to bed [VO] (4-1)

shuìzháo fall asleep [RC] (9-4)

shuō say, speak [V] (4-3)

shuō xiàohua(r) tell a joke [PH] (9-3)

shuōhuà speak words, speak [VO] (7-2)

sījī driver, chauffeur [N] (8-3)

sǐ die [V] (10-2)

sì four [NU] (3-1)

sìyuè April [TW] (4-2)

sòng give (as a present) [V] (6-1)

sònggěi give (someone as a present) [V+PV] (6-1)

sùshè dormitory [PW] (1-1)

suì year of age [M] (3-2)

Sūn Sun [SN] (4-4)

suóyi therefore, so [CJ] (6-3)

suóyi shuō so, therefore [PH] (10-1)

T

tā he, she; him, her [PR] (1-2); it (animal or thing) [PR] (5-4)

tāmen they, them [PR] (1-2)

tái (for computers, TV sets) [M] (5-4)

Táiběi Taipei [PW] (4-4)

Táiběi Měiguo Xuéxiào Taipei American School [PW] (6-3)

táifēng typhoon [N] (10-3)

Táiwān Taiwan [PW] (2-1)

tài too, excessively [A] (1-3)

tàitai Mrs. [N] (1-4); wife [N] (2-3); married woman, lady [N] (2-4)

tàiyáng sun [N] (10-2)

táng candy; sugar [N] (6-1)

tàng (for runs by trains and buses) [M] (3-4)

táokè skip class [VO] (4-4)

tiān day [M] (4-1); sky [N] (10-1)

Tiān'ānmén Tiananmen [PW] (8-1)

Tiānjīn Tianjin [PW] (3-4)

tiānqi weather [N] (10-1)

tiānqi yùbào weather forecast [PH] (10-1)

tiáo (for streets, alleys) [M] (8-4)

tiáozi note [N] (5-1)
tīng hear, listen [V] (9-4)
tīngdǒng hear and understand [RC] (9-4)
tīngshuō hear of, hear it said that [V] (7-4)
tǐng quite, very [A] (1-3)
Tōng Xiàn Tong County [PW] (7-1)
tōngzhī notify [V] (8-3)
tóngshì colleague [N] (2-3)
tóngwū(r) roommate [N] (2-2)
tóngxué classmate [N] (2-1)
tóngzhì comrade [N] (9-4)
túshūguǎn library [PW] (1-1)

W

wài outside [L] (5-4)
wàibian(r) outside [PW] (5-4)
wàiguo foreign country [N] (8-2)
wàiguo huà foreign language [PH] (8-2)
wàiguo rén foreigner [PH] (8-2)
wàiguoyǔ foreign language [N] (8-2)
wàijiāobù foreign ministry [PW] (2-3)
wàimian outside [PW] (5-4)
wàitou outside [PW] (5-4)
wàizǔfù maternal grandfather [N] (6-4)
wàizǔmǔ maternal grandmother [N] (6-4)
wán(r) play, have a good time [V] (10-2)
wánxiào joke [N] (9-3)
wǎn be late [SV/A] (10-4)
wǎnfàn dinner, evening meal [N] (5-2)
wǎnshang in the evening [TW] (4-1)
-wàn ten thousand [NU] (4-4)
Wáng Wang [SN] (1-1)
wàng forget [V] (6-4)
wàng to, toward [CV] (8-1)
wéi "hello" (on the telephone) [I] (8-2)
wèi (polite measure for people) [M] (2-1)
wèi "hey" [I] (9-4)
wèishemme why [QW] (6-3)
wèizi seat, place [N] (5-2)
wénhuà culture [N] (4-2)
wèn ask [V] (2-1)
wēndù temperature [N] (10-1)
wǒ I, me [PR] (1-1)
wǒmen we, us [PR] (1-4)
Wú Wu [SN] (2-3)
wǔ five [NU] (3-1)

wǔ-bā-liù Pentium® (brand of computer) [N] (5-4)
wǔfàn lunch [N] (5-2)
wǔyuè May [TW] (4-2)
wù fog [N] (10-3)

X

xī west [L] (8-1)
Xī'ān Xian [PW] (4-4)
xī'àn west coast [PW] (10-4)
Xībānyá Spain [PW] (2-1)
Xībānyáyǔ Spanish (language) [N] (7-2)
xīběi northwest [PW] (6-3)
xībiān(r) west [PW] (5-3)
xīfāng west, the West [PW] (8-1)
Xīfāng rén Westerner [PH] (8-1)
xī'nán southwest [PW] (6-3)
Xī'nán Hángkōng Gōngsī Southwest Airlines® [PW] (6-3)
xīwàng hope [V] (9-3)
xíguàn be accustomed to [V] (10-4)
xǐhuan like [V/AV] (6-1)
xià- next [SP] (3-2)
xià on the bottom, under, below [L] (5-4)
xià máomáoyǔ drizzle [PH] (10-3)
xiàbān(r) get off from work [VO] (6-3)
xiàbian(r) on the bottom, under, below [PW] (5-4)
xiàchē get off a vehicle [VO] (9-4)
xiàmian on the bottom, under, below [PW] (5-4)
xiàtiān summer [TW] (10-2)
xiàtou on the bottom, under, below [PW] (5-4)
xiàwǔ afternoon, P.M. [TW] (4-1)
xiàxuě snow [VO] (10-2)
xiàyǔ rain [VO] (10-1)
xiān first, before someone else [A] (1-2)
xiānsheng Mr. [N] (1-4); husband [N] (2-3); gentleman [N] (2-4)
xiàn county [N] (7-1)
xiànzài now [TW] (3-4)
xiāng be fragrant, smell good [SV] (5-3)
Xiāng Shān Fragrant Hills [PW] (5-3)
Xiānggǎng Hong Kong [PW] (2-3)
Xiānggǎng Zhōngwén Dàxué Chinese University of Hong Kong [PW] (2-3)
xiǎng think [V] (3-2); want to, would like to [AV] (5-1)
-xiàng lane [BF] (4-2)

xiáojie Miss, Ms. [N] (1-4); young lady [N] (2-4)
xiǎo be small, little, young [SV] (1-3)
xiǎohái(r) small child, kid [N] (6-2)
xiǎomèi younger younger sister [N] (6-4)
xiǎoshí hour [N] (8-3)
xiǎoxīn be careful [SV] (9-4)
xiǎoxué elementary school [PW] (6-1)
xiàozhǎng head of a school [N] (2-3)
xié shoe [N] (5-2)
xiéhuì association, society [N] (6-3)
xiě write [V] (7-2)
xiězì(r) write characters, write [VO] (7-2)
Xiè (lit., "thank") [SN] (1-4)
xiè thank [V] (9-1)
xièxie "thank you" [IE] (1-2); thank [V] (1-4)
xīn be new [SV] (2-2)
Xīnjiāpō Singapore [PW] (2-1)
xīngqī week [N] (4-1)
xīngqī'èr Tuesday [TW] (4-1)
xīngqījǐ which day of the week [QW] (4-1)
xīngqīliù Saturday [TW] (4-1)
xīngqīrì Sunday [TW] (4-1)
xīngqīsān Wednesday [TW] (4-1)
xīngqīsì Thursday [TW] (4-1)
xīngqītiān Sunday [TW] (4-1)
xīngqīwǔ Friday [TW] (4-1)
xīngqīyī Monday [TW] (4-1)
xíng be all right, O.K. [V] (1-2)
xíngli luggage, baggage [N] (8-4)
xìng be surnamed [EV] (2-3)
xìngmíng first and last name [N] (8-2)
xiōngdì older and younger brothers [N] (6-4)
xiūxi rest, take time off [V] (4-1)
xūyào need [V] (8-4)
xué learn, study [V] (5-2)
xuésheng student [N] (5-2)
xuéxí study, studies [N] (1-3); learn, study [V] (2-3)
xuéxiào school [PW] (6-3)
xuě snow [N] (10-2)

Y

ya (form of **a** used after words ending in **-a** or **-i**) [P] (7-2)
yánjiū research [N/V] (7-4)
yánjiūshēng graduate student [N] (7-4)
yánsè color [N] (9-1)

Yángmíng Shān Yangming Mountain [PW] (10-3)

yǎng raise, keep [V] (9-2)

yàngzi way, appearance [N] (1-3)

yāo one [NU] (5-3)

yào want, need, cost, take [V] (3-3); be going to, will [AV] (4-3); want to [AV] (5-4); request [V] (8-3); need to, should [AV] (8-3); if [MA] (10-2)

yàoshi if [MA] (5-1)

yě also, too [A] (1-1)

yèli at night [TW] (4-3)

yī one, a [NU] (2-3)

yīyuè January [TW] (4-2)

yídìng definitely [A] (10-1)

yíge rén by oneself, alone [PH] (7-3)

yígòng in all [A] (3-1)

Yíhéyuán Summer Palace [PW] (9-2)

yímín immigrate, emigrate [V] (6-4)

yíxià(r) (softens the verb) [NU+M] (2-2)

yǐhòu in the future [TW] (6-4)

...yǐhòu after... [PT] (7-4)

yǐjīng already [A] (3-4)

yǐqián before, formerly [TW] (7-2)

...yǐqián before..., ...ago [PT] (7-4)

yǐzi chair [N] (5-1)

-yì hundred million [NU] (4-4)

yìdiǎn(r) a little, some [NU+M] (1-1)

yìhuǐr a while [N] (8-3)

yìniánjí first grade [TW] (6-1)

yìqǐ together [A/PW] (7-3)

yìsi meaning [N] (6-2)

yìzhí straight [A] (8-1)

yīntiān cloudy or overcast weather [N] (10-1)

yīnwei because [CJ] (6-3)

yīngdāng should, ought to [AV] (8-4)

yīnggāi should [AV] (2-2)

Yīngguo England [PW] (2-4)

Yīngwén English (language) [N] (5-1)

Yīngyǔ English (language) [N] (7-2)

yò "gosh, wow" [I] (3-3)

yōngjǐ be crowded [SV] (8-3)

yònggōng be hardworking, studious [SV] (9-3)

yǒu have [V] (1-2); there is, there are [V] (3-1)

yǒu yìsi be interesting [PH] (1-4)

yǒude some [AT/PR] (7-2)

yǒude shíhou(r) sometimes [PH] (7-3)

yǒuyì friendship [N] (8-2)

Yǒuyì Bīnguǎn Friendship Hotel [PW] (8-2)

yòu right [L] (5-4)

yòu again [A] (7-3)

yòubian(r) right side, right [PW] (5-4)

yòu'éryuán kindergarten [PW] (7-1)

yú(r) fish [N] (9-2)

yǔ rain [N] (10-1)

yǔyán language [N] (4-1)

yǔyán shíyànshì language lab [PH] (4-1)

yùbào forecast [N] (10-1)

yuánlái originally, formerly [MA] (7-1)

yuǎn be far away [SV] (7-3)

yuè month [N] (3-2)

yuè lái yuè... more and more... [PT] (10-1)

yuèfen(r) month [N] (7-3)

yuèpiào monthly ticket [N] (9-4)

yún cloud [N] (10-1)

yùnqi luck [N] (10-3)

Z

zài be located at, at [CV] (2-3); be present, be located at [V] (5-1); (indicates progressive aspect) [AV] (10-3)

zài again [A] (3-4)

-zài at, in, on [PV] (5-3)

zàijiàn "goodbye" [IE] (1-2)

zāng be dirty [SV] (9-3)

zāogāo "darn it"; be a mess [IE/SV] (8-4)

zǎo be early [SV] (9-4); "good morning" [IE] (10-1)

zǎofàn breakfast [N] (5-2)

zǎoshang in the morning [TW] (4-1)

zěmme how [QW] (2-2); how come, why [QW] (8-3)

zěmme bàn "what should be done?" [IE] (5-1)

zěmmeyàng how, in what way [QW] (1-2)

zhàn station, stop [N/M] (9-2)

Zhāng Zhang [SN] (4-2)

zhāng (for tables, name cards) [M] (5-1)

zhǎng grow [V] (6-2)

zhǎngdà grow up [RC] (6-2)

-zháo (indicates action of verb is realized) [RE] (9-4)

zháojí worry, get excited [VO/SV] (8-3)

zhǎo look for [V] (5-1); give in change [V] (8-4)

zhǎodào look for and find, find [RC] (9-4)

zhǎoqián give (someone) change [VO] (8-4)

zhǎozháo look for and find, find [RC] (9-4)

Zhào Zhao [SN] (1-2)

-zhe (indicates continuous aspect) [P] (9-4)

zhè this [PR] (2-2)

zhèli here [PW] (6-2)

zhèibian(r) this side, here [PW] (5-3)

zhèi- this [SP] (2-1)

zhèiyang(r) this way, like this [MA] (7-4)

zhèiyangzi this way, like this [MA] (10-3)

zhèmme like this, in this way, so [A] (2-2)

zhèmme shuō saying it like this; then [PH] (10-2)

zhēn really [A] (6-1)

zhěngqí be in order, neat [SV] (9-3)

Zhèng Zheng [SN] (6-4)

zhèng just [A] (10-2)

zhèr here [PW] (5-1)

zhī (for most animals) [M] (9-2)

zhīdao know [V] (5-1)

...zhīhòu after... [PT] (7-4)

...zhīqián before..., ...ago [PT] (7-4)

zhǐ only [A] (3-3)

zhǐhǎo have no choice but [A] (8-4)

zhì'ān public order, public security [N] (7-4)

zhōng clock, o'clock; bell [N] (3-4)

zhōngdiǎn final or terminal point [N] (9-2)

zhōngdiǎn zhàn last station, last stop [PH] (9-2)

zhōngfàn lunch [N] (5-2)

Zhōngguo China [PW] (2-1)

Zhōngguo huà spoken Chinese [PH] (7-2)

Zhōngguo zì(r) Chinese character [PH] (7-2)

Zhōng-Měi Sino-American [AT] (2-4)

zhōngtóu hour [N] (3-4)

Zhōngwén Chinese (language) [N] (1-3)

zhōngwǔ noon [TW] (4-3)

zhōngxīn center [N] (5-2)

zhōngxué middle school [PW] (6-1)

zhòng be heavy [SV] (8-4)

zhù live (in), stay (in) [V] (4-3)

zhùzai live in, live at; stay in, stay at [V+PV] (5-3)

zhuānjiā expert [N] (8-2)

zhuānjiā lóu (foreign) experts building [PH] (8-2)

zhuǎn turn [V] (9-1)

zhǔn be accurate [SV] (10-1)

zhǔnbèi prepare, get ready, plan [V/AV] (9-4)

zhuōzi table [N] (5-1)

zì(r) character, word [N] (7-2)

zìwǒ jièshao introduce oneself [PH] (6-4)

zǒngjīnglǐ general manager [N] (2-4)

zǒu leave, depart [V] (1-2); go, walk [V] (8-1)

zǒulù walk [VO] (8-1)

zǔfù paternal grandfather [N] (6-4)

zǔmǔ paternal grandmother [N] (6-4)

zuì most [A] (10-1)

zuìhòu in the end, finally [TW] (8-4)

zuìjìn recently [MA] (1-3)

zuótiān yesterday [TW] (4-2)

zuǒ left [L] (5-4)

zuǒbian(r) left side, left [PW] (5-4)

zuǒyòu about, approximately [PW] (8-1)

zuò sit [V] (1-4); travel by, take [V] (3-4)

zuò do, make [V] (6-2)

zuò mǎimài do or engage in business [PH] (7-1)

zuòdào take (a vehicle) to [V+PV] (9-2)

zuòzai sit in, sit at [V+PV] (6-2)

English-Chinese Glossary

This glossary contains the English equivalents of the Chinese vocabulary introduced in the Basic Conversation and Supplementary Vocabulary sections of units 1 to 10 of *Basic Spoken Chinese*. Certain Chinese words whose English equivalents users are not likely to look up (such as Chinese surnames, particles, verb endings, and some measures) have been omitted.

The following information is included for each entry: the English word; a Chinese equivalent, spelled in Pinyin; the word class of the Chinese word [in brackets]; and the numbers of the unit and part where the Chinese word was introduced (in parentheses). For example:

English	Chinese	Word Class	Unit & Part
easy	róngyi	[SV]	(1-3)

The purpose of the English-Chinese glossary, which is arranged in alphabetical order of the English words, is to refresh your memory of Chinese words that have previously been introduced but which you may have forgotten. Since each entry includes the number of the unit and part in the textbook where the Chinese equivalent first occurred, you are encouraged to refer back to that part for more detailed information. Do not attempt to learn new words from this glossary; keep in mind that a Chinese word means something only in a certain grammatical and semantic context and that English translations can be misleading.

A

a yī [NU] (2-3)

a few jǐ- [NU] (7-2)

a little yìdiǎn(r) [NU+M] (1-1)

a while yìhuǐr [N] (8-3)

able néng [AV] (6-3)

about chàbuduō [A] (3-4); dàgài [MA] (8-1); dàyuē [A] (4-3); zuǒyòu [PW] (8-1)

accurate zhǔn [SV] (10-1)

accustomed to xíguàn [V] (10-4)

actually qíshí [MA] (10-3)

adapt shìyìng [V] (10-4)

add jiā [V] (3-3)

address chēnghu [V] (2-2); dìzhǐ [N] (4-2)

afraid kǒngpà [MA] (3-4)

after ...yǐhòu [PT] (7-4); ...zhīhòu [PT] (7-4)

afternoon xiàwǔ [TW] (4-1)

afterward hòulái [TW] (7-3); ránhòu [MA] (4-3)

again yòu [A] (7-3); zài [A] (3-4)

age niánji [N] (3-2)

ago ...yǐqián [PT] (7-4); ...zhīqián [PT] (7-4)

air kōngqì [N] (10-3)

airport jīchǎng [PW] (8-2)

all dōu [A] (1-2)

all right hǎo [IE] (2-2); hǎode [IE] (8-2); xíng [V] (1-2)

alley nòng [BF] (4-2)

almost chàbuduō [A] (3-4)

alone yíge rén [PH] (7-3)

already yǐjīng [A] (3-4)

also érqiě [CJ] (9-3); yě [A] (1-1)

A.M. shàngwǔ [TW] (4-1)

America Měiguo [PW] (2-1)

ancient gǔ [SV] (7-4)

and érqiě [CJ] (9-3); gēn [CJ] (2-4); hé [CJ] (7-1)

animal dòngwù [N] (9-2)

another biéde [AT] (8-4)

apparently hǎoxiàng [MA] (4-4)

appearance yàngzi [N] (1-3)

apply shēnqǐng [V] (7-4)

appropriate héshì [SV] (10-2)

approximately dàyuē [A] (4-3); zuǒyòu [PW] (8-1)

April sìyuè [TW] (4-2)

arrive dào [V] (3-4)

arrive at -dào [PV] (5-3)

arrive late chídào [V] (4-4)

as fast as possible jìnkuài [A] (8-3)

Asian (person) Dōngfāng rén [PH] (8-1)

ask wèn [V] (2-1)

association xiéhuì [N] (6-3)

at zài [CV] (2-3); -zài [PV] (5-3)

at night yèli [TW] (4-3)

attend shàng [V] (6-1)

attend school shàngxué [VO] (6-3)

August báyuè [TW] (4-2)

aunt (mother's sister) āyí [N] (6-1)

Australia Àodàlìyà [PW] (6-4); Àozhōu [PW] (6-4)

autumn qiūtiān [TW] (10-2)

aviation hángkōng [N] (6-3)

B

back hòu [L] (5-4); hòubian(r) [PW] (5-4); hòumian [PW] (5-4); hòutou [PW] (5-4)

backpack bēibāo [N] (3-3)

bag dàizi [N] (3-3)

baggage xíngli [N] (8-4)

be shì [EV] (1-3)

beautiful měi [SV] (10-4)

because yīnwei [CJ] (6-3)

become biànchéng [V+PV] (10-1); -chéng [PV] (10-1)

before yǐqián [TW] (7-2); ...yǐqián [PT] (7-4); ...zhīqián [PT] (7-4)

begin kāishǐ [V] (7-3)

Beijing Běijīng [PW] (4-4)

bell zhōng [N] (3-4)

below xià [L] (5-4); xiàbian(r) [PW] (5-4); xiàmian [PW] (5-4); xiàtou [PW] (5-4)

big dà [SV] (3-2)

bird niǎo(r) [N] (9-2)

birthday shēngrì [N] (4-2)

black hēi [SV] (9-1)

black color hēisè [N] (9-1)

blue lán [SV] (9-1)

blue color lánsè [N] (9-1)

body shēnti [N] (7-1)

bookcase shūjià [N] (5-4)

bookshelf shūjià [N] (5-4)

born chūshēng [V] (4-2)

boss lǎobǎn [N] (5-1)

both dōu [A] (1-2)

bottom xià [L] (5-4); xiàbian(r) [PW] (5-4); xiàmian [PW] (5-4); xiàtou [PW] (5-4)

bow (the weapon) gōng [N] (4-2)

boy nánháir [N] (7-1)

boyfriend nánpéngyou [N] (6-1)

breakfast zǎofàn [N] (5-2)

briefcase gōngshìbāo [N] (3-3)

bring dài [V] (2-4)

brother (older) gēge [N] (3-2); (younger) dìdi [N] (3-2)

brothers (older and younger) xiōngdì [N] (6-4)

building (of two or more floors) lóu [N] (8-2)

bump pèng [V] (10-3)

bus gōnggòng qìchē [PH] (9-2)

bus station chēzhàn [PW] (9-2)

bus stop chēzhàn [PW] (9-2)

bus ticket chēpiào [N] (9-4)

business mǎimài [N] (7-1)

business card míngpiàn [N] (2-4)

busy máng [SV] (1-2)

but dànshi [CJ] (10-3); kěshi [MA] (2-1)

buy mǎi [V] (3-3)

by oneself yíge rén [PH] (7-3)

C

cafeteria shítáng [PW] (1-1)

California Jiāzhōu [PW] (10-4)

call (someone) jiào [V] (9-3); (call someone a name) jiào [V] (2-2)

called jiào [EV] (2-1)

can huì [AV] (7-2); kéyi [AV] (5-1); néng [AV] (6-3)

Canada Jiā'nádà [PW] (2-1)

candy táng [N] (6-1)

Capital Airport Shǒudū Jīchǎng [PW] (8-2)

capital shǒudū [N] (8-2)

car chēzi [N] (8-2); qìchē [N] (8-2)

careful xiǎoxīn [SV] (9-4)

cat māo(r) [N] (9-2)

cause ràng let [V] (5-3)

cent fēn [M] (3-3)

center zhōngxīn [N] (5-2)

certainly kě [A] (5-3)

chair yǐzi [N] (5-1)

chance jīhui [N] (6-4)

change biàn [V] (10-1); huàn [V] (8-4); (into) biànchéng [V+PV] (10-1); (one's line of work) gǎiháng(r) [VO] (7-1)

character zì(r) [N] (7-2)

chat liáo [V] (6-4); liáotiān [VO] (6-4)

chauffeur sījī [N] (8-3)

cheap piányi [SV] (3-3)

child háizi [N] (1-2); xiǎohái(r) [N] (6-2)

China Zhōngguo [PW] (2-1)

Chinese (language) Hànyǔ [N] (5-2);

Zhōngwén [N] (1-3); (spoken Chinese) Zhōngguo huà [PH] (7-2)

Chinese character Hànzì [N] (7-2); Zhōngguo zì(r) [PH] (7-2)

Chinese with U.S. nationality Měijí Huárén [PH] (10-4)

Chinese-American Huáyì Měiguo rén [PH] (2-1)

city chéng [N] (5-3)

class bān [N] (3-1); kè [N] (4-4)

classmate tóngxué [N] (2-1)

clean gānjìng [SV] (9-3)

clear qīngchu [SV] (9-1)

clear about qīngchu [SV] (9-1)

climate qìhou [N] (10-4)

clock zhōng [N] (3-4)

clogged up with cars dǔchē [VO] (8-4); sāichē [VO] (8-4)

close (not open) guān [V] (4-1); guānmén [VO] (4-1)

close (not far) jìn [SV] (8-1)

cloud yún [N] (10-1)

cloudy weather yīntiān [N] (10-1)

cold lěng [SV] (10-2)

colleague tóngshì [N] (2-3)

college dàxué [PW] (2-3)

college student dàxuéshēng [N] (5-2)

color yánsè [N] (9-1)

come lái [V] (2-2)

come in jìnlái [RC] (10-3)

come to shàng [CV] (8-3)

come out chūlái [RC] (10-3)

comfortable shūfu [SV] (10-2)

company gōngsī [PW] (2-3)

comparatively bǐjiào [A] (4-4)

compare bǐ [V/CV] (10-4)

completely quán [A] (7-2)

computer diànnǎo [N] (5-4)

comrade tóngzhì [N] (9-4)

concern oneself with guǎn [V] (5-4)

conductor shòupiàoyuán [N] (9-3)

continue jìxù [V/AV] (7-2)

cool liángkuai [SV] (10-4)

correct duì [SV] (3-2)

cost yào [V] (3-3)

county xiàn [N] (7-1)

cousin (older female cousin of different surname) biǎojiě [N] (7-1)

crowded yōngjǐ [SV] (8-3)

culture wénhuà [N] (4-2)

cup bēizi [N] (3-3)

cute kě'ài [SV] (3-2)

D
dad bàba [N] (1-2)
darn it zāogāo [IE/SV] (8-4)
daughter nǚ'ér [N] (6-2)
day tiān [M] (4-1)
day after tomorrow hòutiān [TW] (4-3)
day before yesterday qiántiān [TW] (4-3)
day of the month hào [M] (4-2)
December shí'èryuè [TW] (4-2)
decide juédìng [V] (8-3)
deficient chà [SV] (7-4)
definitely yídìng [A] (10-1)
degree (of temperature) dù [M] (10-1)
delicious hǎochī [SV] (6-1); m [I] (6-1)
depart kāi [V] (3-4); zǒu [V] (1-2)
die sǐ [V] (10-2)
difficult nán [SV] (1-3)
diligent nǔlì [SV] (7-4)
dime máo [M] (3-3)
dining hall shítáng [PW] (1-1)
dinner (evening meal) wǎnfàn [N] (5-2)
dirty zāng [SV] (9-3)
disorderly luàn [SV] (9-3)
dispatch pài [V] (8-3); pàiqu [RC] (8-3)
disturb máfan [V] (8-3)
divorce líhūn [VO] (6-2)
do bàn [V] (1-1); gǎo [V] (2-4); zuò [V] (6-2)
do business zuò mǎimài [PH] (7-1)
do something wrong gǎocuò [RC] (2-4)
dog gǒu(r) [N] (5-4)
dollar kuài [M] (3-3)
don't bié [AV] (2-2); búyào [AV] (2-2)
don't need to bú yòng [A+AV] (9-1); búbì [AV] (9-2)
door mén(r) [N] (4-1)
doorway ménkǒu(r) [PW] (8-2)
dormitory sùshè [PW] (1-1)
drive (a vehicle) kāi [V] (8-1)
drive a car kāichē [VO] (8-4)
driver shīfu [N] (8-4); sījī [N] (8-3)
drizzle xià máomáoyǔ [PH] (10-3)
dry gān [SV] (10-2); gānzào [SV] (10-4)

E
each měi- [SP] (4-1)
early zǎo [SV] (9-4)
east dōng [L] (4-2); dōngbiān(r) [PW] (5-3); dōngfāng [PW] (8-1)
east coast dōngàn [PW] (10-4)
easy róngyi [SV] (1-3)
eat chī [V] (5-2); chīfàn [VO] (5-2)
eight bā [NU] (3-1)
elementary school xiǎoxué [PW] (6-1)
embassy dàshǐguǎn [PW] (2-3)
emigrate yímín [V] (6-4)
employ shǐyòng [V] (5-4)
encounter pèngshang [RC] (10-3)
engage in business zuò mǎimài [PH] (7-1)
England Yīngguo [PW] (2-4)
English (language) Yīngwén [N] (5-1); Yīngyǔ [N] (7-2)
enter jìn [V] (1-4)
entrance ménkǒu(r) [N] (8-2)
even (more) gèng [A] (8-1)
evening wǎnshang [TW] (4-1)
every měi- [SP] (4-1)
exactly jiù [A] (4-2)
exchange huàn [V] (8-4)
excited zháojí [VO/SV] (8-3)
excuse me duìbuqǐ [IE] (2-3); láojià [IE] (8-1); qǐng wèn [IE] (2-1)
expensive guì [SV] (3-3)
experiment shíyàn [N] (4-1)
expert zhuānjiā [N] (8-2)

F
factory chǎng [N] (5-2); gōngchǎng [PW] (7-1)
fall qiūtiān [TW] (10-2)
fall asleep shuìzháo [RC] (9-4)
family jiā [PW] (4-3)
far away yuǎn [SV] (7-3)
fast kuài [SV] (8-1)
fat (of people or animals) pàng [SV] (5-3)
father fùqin [N] (3-2)
February èryuè [TW] (4-2)
feel juéde [V] (7-4)
feel sorry bàoqiàn [V] (5-1)
female nǚde [N] (3-1)
female friend nǚpéngyou [N] (6-1)
female teacher nǚlǎoshī [N] (3-1)
fen fēn [M] (3-3)
few shǎo [SV] (4-4)
final point zhōngdiǎn [N] (9-2)
finally zuìhòu [TW] (8-4)
find zhǎodào [RC] (9-4); zhǎozháo [RC] (9-4)
fine day qíngtiān [N] (10-1)

fire huǒ [N] (3-4)
firm gōngsī [PW] (2-3)
first xiān [A] (1-2)
first and last name xìngmíng [N] (8-2)
first grade yìniánjí [TW] (6-1)
first year in college dàyī [TW] (6-1)
first year in jr. high school chūyī [TW] (6-1)
fish yú(r) [N] (9-2)
five wǔ [NU] (3-1)
float piāo [V] (10-3)
float in piāojìnlái [RC] (10-3)
floor (of a building) lóu [N] (4-2)
fly (an airplane) kāi [V] (4-3)
fog wù [N] (10-3)
food fàn [N] (5-2); cài [N] (5-2)
for gěi [CV] (2-2); -gěi [PV] (6-1)
forecast yùbào [N] (10-1)
foreign country wàiguo [N] (8-2)
foreign language wàiguo huà [PH] (8-2); wàiguoyǔ [N] (8-2)
foreign experts building zhuānjiā lóu [PH] (8-2)
foreign ministry wàijiāobù [PW] (2-3)
foreigner wàiguo rén [PH] (8-2)
forget wàng [V] (6-4)
formerly cóngqián [TW] (7-1); yǐqián [TW] (7-2); yuánlái [MA] (7-1)
four sì [NU] (3-1)
fragrant xiāng [SV] (5-3)
France Fǎguo [PW] (3-1)
French (language) Fǎyǔ [N] (7-2)
Friday lǐbàiwǔ [TW] (4-1); xīngqīwǔ [TW] (4-1)
friend péngyou [N] (6-1)
friendship yǒuyì [N] (8-2)
from cóng [CV] (7-4); lí [CV] (8-1)
front qián [L] (5-4); qiánbian(r) [PW] (5-4); qiánmian [PW] (5-4); qiántou [PW] (5-4)

G
gate mén(r) [N] (4-1)
general manager zǒngjīnglǐ [N] (2-4)
gentleman xiānsheng [N] (2-4)
German (language) Déyǔ [N] (7-2)
Germany Déguo [PW] (3-1)
get gǎo [V] (2-4)
get angry shēngqì [VO/SV] (9-3)
get off a vehicle xiàchē [VO] (9-4)
get off from work xiàbān(r) [VO] (6-3)
get on (a vehicle, etc.) shàng [V] (9-3)
get on a vehicle shàngchē [VO] (9-2)

get ready zhǔnbèi [V/AV] (9-4)

get something wrong gǎocuò [RC] (2-4)

get up from bed qǐchuáng [VO] (4-1)

get used to shìying [V] (10-4)

gift lǐwù [N] (6-1)

girl nǚháir [N] (7-1)

girlfriend nǚpéngyou [N] (6-1)

give gěi [V] (6-4); -gěi [PV] (6-1); (as present) sòng [V] (6-1); (to someone as present) sònggěi [V+PV] (6-1)

give in change zhǎo [V] (8-4); zhǎoqián [VO] (8-4)

go qù [V] (1-1); zǒu [V] (8-1)

go back to huí [V] (1-1)

go by guò [V] (8-1)

go in jìnqu [RC] (10-3)

go out chūqu [RC] (10-3)

go outside chūmén(r) [VO] (10-3)

go to qù [V] (1-1); shàng [V] (6-1), [CV] (8-3)

go to bed shuìjiào [VO] (4-1)

go to work shàngbān(r) [VO] (6-3)

going to yào [AV] (4-3)

gold jīn [BF/SN] (6-2)

good hǎo [SV] (1-2)

good enough chàbuduō [PH] (10-4)

good morning zǎo [IE] (10-1)

good to eat hǎochī [SV] (6-1)

goodbye zàijiàn [IE] (1-2)

good-looking hǎokàn [SV] (6-1)

gosh āiyà [I] (10-1); yò [I] (3-3)

grade (in school) niánjí [N] (6-1)

graduate bìyè [VO] (7-4)

graduate student yánjiūshēng [N] (7-4)

grandfather (maternal) wàizǔfù [N] (6-4); (paternal) zǔfù [N] (6-4)

grandmother (maternal) wàizǔmǔ [N] (6-4); (paternal) zǔmǔ [N] (6-4)

gravel shā [N] (10-2)

great (i.e., wonderful) bàng [SV] (7-4)

Great Wall Cháng Chéng [PW] (5-3)

green lǜ [SV] (9-1)

green color lǜsè [N] (9-1)

grow zhǎng [V] (6-2)

grow up zhǎngdà [RC] (6-2)

Guangzhou Guǎngzhōu [PW] (4-4)

guess cāi [V] (3-2)

guest house bīnguǎn [PW] (8-2)

H

half bàn(r) [NU] (3-1)

handbook shǒucè [N] (5-4)

happy gāoxìng [SV] (2-2)

hard nán [SV] (1-3)

hardworking yònggōng [SV] (9-3)

have yǒu [V] (1-2)

have a good time wán(r) [V] (10-2)

have class shàngkè [VO] (4-4)

have no choice but zhǐhǎo [A] (8-4)

have to yào [AV] (8-3)

he tā [PR] (1-2)

head of a school xiàozhǎng [N] (2-3)

hear tīng [V] (9-4); (hear it said that) tīngshuō [V] (7-4)

heavy zhòng [SV] (8-4)

hello (on the telephone) wéi [I] (8-2)

here běndì [N] (9-1); zhèli [PW] (6-2); zhèr [PW] (5-1); zhèibian(r) [PW] (5-3)

hey èi [I] (1-3); wèi [I] (9-4)

hi èi [I] (1-3); nǐ hǎo [IE] (1-1)

high gāo [SV] (1-3)

hill shān [N] (5-3)

hit dǎ [V] (8-3)

home jiā [PW] (4-3)

Hong Kong Xiānggǎng [PW] (2-3)

hope xīwàng [V] (9-3)

hot rè [SV] (10-1)

hotel bīnguǎn [PW] (8-2); fàndiàn [PW] (5-3)

hour diǎn [M] (3-4); xiǎoshí [N] (8-3); zhōngtóu [N] (3-4)

how duō [QW] (3-2); zěnme [QW] (2-2); zěnmeyàng [QW] (1-2)

how come zěnme [QW] (8-3)

how many duōshǎo [QW] (3-3); jǐ- [QW] (3-1); jǐge [QW+M] (3-1)

how much duōshǎo [QW] (3-3)

however búguò [CJ] (5-1)

humid cháoshī [SV] (10-3)

hundred -bǎi [NU] (3-3)

hundred million -yì [NU] (4-4)

hundred thousand shíwàn [NU] (4-4)

hurry gǎn [V] (8-3); gǎndào [V+PV] (8-3)

husband àirén [N] (1-2); xiānsheng [N] (2-3)

I

I wǒ [PR] (1-1)

if rúguǒ [MA] (10-2); yào [MA] (10-2); yàoshi [MA] (5-1)

immediately mǎshàng [A] (8-3)

immigrate yímín [V] (6-4)

in lǐ [L] (5-4); lǐbian(r) [PW] (5-4); lǐmiàn [PW] (5-4); lǐtou [PW] (5-4); -zài [PV] (5-3)

in addition hái [A] (7-1)

in all yígòng [A] (3-1)

in that case nà [CJ] (2-2); nèmme [CJ] (3-4)

in the beginning kāishǐ [TW] (7-3)

in the daytime báitiān [TW] (4-3)

in the end zuìhòu [TW] (8-4)

in the future yǐhòu [TW] (6-4)

in the past cóngqián [TW] (7-1)

in what way zěmmeyàng [QW] (1-2)

indeed kě [A] (5-3)

inside lǐ [L] (5-4); lǐbian(r) [PW] (5-4); lǐmiàn [PW] (5-4); lǐtou [PW] (5-4)

intense jǐnzhāng [SV] (1-3)

interesting yǒu yìsi [PH] (1-4)

intersection lùkǒu(r) [PW] (9-1)

introduce jièshao [V] (2-2)

introduce oneself zìwǒ jièshao [PH] (6-4)

it (animal or thing) tā [PR] (5-4)

J

January yīyuè [TW] (4-2)

Japan Rìběn [PW] (2-1)

Japanese (language) Rìyǔ [N] (7-2)

joke wánxiào [N] (9-3)

joke around kāi wánxiào [PH] (9-3)

July qíyuè [TW] (4-2)

June liùyuè [TW] (4-2)

junior high school chūzhōng [PW] (6-1)

junior year in college dàsān [TW] (6-1)

junior year in high school gāo'èr [TW] (6-1)

just gāng [A] (9-3); gānggāng [A] (9-3); zhèng [A] (10-2)

K

kid xiǎohái(r) [N] (6-2)

kilo gōngjīn [M] (8-4)

kindergarten yòu'éryuán [PW] (7-1)

knapsack bēibāo [N] (3-3)

know rènshi [V] (2-2); zhīdao [V] (5-1)

know how huì [AV] (7-2)

L

laboratory shíyànshì [N] (4-1)

laborer gōngrén [N] (5-2)

lack chà [V] (3-4); (not lack much) chàbuduō [RC] (10-4)

lacking chà [SV] (7-4)

lady nǚshì [N] (2-3); tàitai [N] (2-4)

lamp dēng [N] (9-1)

lane xiàng [BF] (4-2)

language huà [N] (7-2); yǔyán [N] (4-1)

language lab yǔyán shíyànshì [PH] (4-1)

last shàng- [SP] (3-2)

last station zhōngdiǎn zhàn [PH] (9-2)

last stop zhōngdiǎn zhàn [PH] (9-2)

last year qùnián [TW] (4-2)

late wǎn [SV/A] (10-4)

later hòulái [TW] (7-3)

lazy lǎn [SV] (9-3)

lean shòu [SV] (5-3)

learn xué [V] (5-2); xuéxí [V] (2-3)

leather pí [N] (5-2)

leather shoe píxié [N] (5-2)

leave liú [V] (5-1); zǒu [V] (1-2)

left zuǒ [L] (5-4); zuǒbian(r) [PW] (5-4)

less shǎo [SV] (4-4)

level (in school) niánjí [N] (6-1)

library túshūguǎn [PW] (1-1)

light (lamp) dēng [N] (9-1); (not heavy) qīng [SV] (8-4)

lightning strikes shǎndiàn [VO] (10-1)

like ài [V/AV] (3-2); xǐhuan [V/AV] (6-1); xiǎng [AV] (5-1)

like this zhèmme [A] (2-2); zhèiyang(r) [MA] (7-4); zhèiyangzi [MA] (10-3)

like that nèmme [A] (7-3); nèiyang(r) [MA] (7-4); nèiyangzi (10-3)

likely to huì [AV] (8-3)

listen tīng [V] (9-4)

little xiǎo [SV] (1-3)

live zhù [V] (4-3)

live at zhùzai [V+PV] (5-3)

live in zhùzai [V+PV] (5-3)

located at zài [CV] (2-3); zài [V] (5-1)

long cháng [SV] (3-4); (of time) jiǔ [SV] (4-3)

long time bàntiān [NU+M] (8-4)

look kàn [V] (3-2)

look for zhǎo [V] (5-1)

love ài [V/AV] (3-2)

low dī [SV] (10-1)

luck yùnqi [N] (10-3)

luggage xíngli [N] (8-4)

lunch wǔfàn [N] (5-2); zhōngfàn [N] (5-2)

M

Macao Àomén [PW] (10-4)

madam nǚshì [N] (2-3)

majority duōshù [N] (7-4)

make ràng [V] (5-3); zuò [V] (6-2)

make a telephone call dǎ diànhuà [PH] (8-3)

Malaysia Mǎláixīyà [PW] (2-1)

male nánde [N] (3-1)

male friend nánpéngyou [N] (6-1)

male teacher nánlǎoshī [N] (3-1)

man nánde [N] (3-1)

manager jīnglǐ [N] (2-4)

Mandarin (language) Pǔtōnghuà [N] (7-2)

manual shǒucè [N] (5-4)

many duō [SV] (4-4)

March sānyuè [TW] (4-2)

marry jiéhūn [VO] (6-2)

master shīfu [N] (8-4)

matter shì(r) [N] (1-1)

may kéyǐ [AV] (5-1)

May wǔyuè [TW] (4-2)

meaning yìsi [N] (6-2)

means fázi [N] (8-3)

messy luàn [SV] (9-3)

meter mǐ [M] (8-4)

method bànfǎ(r) [N] (10-3); fázi [N] (8-3)

middle school zhōngxué [PW] (6-1)

million -bǎiwàn [NU] (4-4)

minus jiǎn [V] (3-3)

minute fēn [M] (3-4)

Miss xiáojie [N] (1-4)

mom māma [N] (1-2)

Monday lǐbàiyī [TW] (4-1); xīngqīyī [TW] (4-1)

money qián [N] (3-3)

month yuè [N] (3-2); yuèfen(r) [N] (7-3)

monthly ticket yuèpiào [N] (9-4)

more duō [SV/NU] (4-4); gèng [A] (8-1)

more and more... yuè lái yuè... [PT] (10-1)

moreover érqiě [CJ] (9-3)

morning shàngwǔ [TW] (4-1); in the morning zǎoshang [TW] (4-1)

most zuì [A] (10-1)

mother mǔqin [N] (3-2)

mountain shān [N] (5-3)

move (a thing or one's home) bān [V] (5-3); (one's home) bānjiā [VO] (6-2); (to) bāndào [V+PV] (5-3)

Mr. xiānsheng [N] (1-4)

Mrs. tàitai [N] (1-4)

Ms. xiáojie [N] (1-4)

much duō [SV] (4-4)

must děi [AV] (1-4)

N

name míngzi [N] (2-1)

name card míngpiàn [N] (2-4)

named jiào [EV] (2-1)

Nanjing Nánjīng [PW] (4-4)

near jìn [SV] (8-1)

neat zhěngqí [SV] (9-3)

need xūyào [V] (8-4); yào [V] (3-3)

need to yào [AV] (8-3)

nervous jǐnzhāng [SV] (1-3)

never mind méi guānxi [IE] (2-4); méi shì(r) [IE] (5-3)

new xīn [SV] (2-2)

New York Niǔyuē [PW] (6-2)

next xià- [SP] (3-2)

next to pángbiān(r) [PW] (5-4)

next year míngnián [TW] (4-2)

nine jiǔ [NU] (3-1)

no bú duì (5-4)

no wonder... nánguài... [PT] (7-3)

noon zhōngwǔ [TW] (4-3)

north běi [L] (8-1); běibiān(r) [PW] (5-3); Běifāng [PW] (8-1)

northeast dōngběi [PW] (6-3)

northern speech Běifāng huà [PH] (8-1)

Northerner Běifāng rén [PH] (8-1)

northwest xīběi [PW] (6-3)

not bù/bú [A] (1-3)

not at all gēnběn (+ NEGATIVE) [A] (10-3)

not bad bú cuò [IE] (7-2)

not correct bú duì (5-4)

not have méi [V] (9-3); méiyou [V] (3-2)

not have enough time láibují [RC] (3-4)

not interesting méi yìsi [PH] (1-4)

not necessary búbì [AV] (9-2)

not need to bú yòng [A+AV] (9-1)

not only búdàn [A] (9-3)

note tiáozi [N] (5-1)

notify tōngzhī [V] (8-3)

November shíyīyuè [TW] (4-2)

now xiànzài [TW] (3-4)

number hào [M] (4-2)

O

o'clock diǎn [M] (3-4); zhōng [N] (3-4)

October shíyuè [TW] (4-2)

of course dāngrán [MA] (5-1)

office bàngōngshì [PW] (5-1)

often cháng [A] (5-2); chángcháng [A] (4-4)

oh à [I] (2-4); āiyà [I] (10-1); ò [I] (2-2)

O.K. hǎo [IE] (2-2); hǎode [IE] (8-2); kéyi [SV] (1-3); xíng [V] (1-2)

old (of people) dà [SV] (3-2); lǎo [SV] (1-3) (of things) jiù [SV] (6-2)

oldest (among siblings) lǎodà [N] (6-4)

on shàng [L] (5-4); shàngbian(r) [PW] (5-4); shàngmian [PW] (5-4); shàng-tou [PW] (5-4); -zài [PV] (5-3)

one yāo [NU] (5-3); yī [NU] (2-3)

only ...éryǐ [PT] (10-1); jiù [A] (7-4); zhǐ [A] (3-3)

open kāi [V] (4-1); kāimén [VO] (4-1)

operating manual shǐyòng shǒucè [PH] (5-4)

opportunity jīhui [N] (6-4)

or huòzhě [CJ] (8-1)

ordinarily píngcháng [MA] (4-1)

organization dānwèi [PW] (2-3)

originally yuánlái [MA] (7-1)

other biéde [AT] (8-4); qítā [AT] (7-2)

ought yīngdāng [AV] (8-4)

outside wài [L] (5-4); wàibian(r) [PW] (5-4); wàimian [PW] (5-4); wàitou [PW] (5-4)

overseas Chinese Huáqiáo [N] (5-1)

owner lǎobǎn [N] (5-1)

P

parents fùmǔ [N] (6-4)

pass guò [V] (8-1)

patient nàixīn [SV] (8-3)

patience nàixīn [N] (8-3)

peace hépíng [N] (4-2)

Pentium® (brand of computer) wǔ-bā-liù [N] (5-4)

period (of time) duàn [M] (7-3)

person rén [N] (2-1)

place dìfang [N] (5-3); wèizi [N] (5-2)

plan zhǔnbèi [V/AV] (9-4)

play wán(r) [V] (10-2)

please qǐng [IE] (1-4)

plus jiā [V] (3-3)

P.M. xiàwǔ [TW] (4-1)

police jǐngchá [N] (9-1)

population rénkǒu [N] (4-4)

precisely jiù [A] (4-2)

prepare zhǔnbèi [V/AV] (9-4)

present lǐwù [N] (6-1); zài [V] (5-1)

probably dàgài [MA] (8-1); kǒngpà [MA] (3-4)

produce chūshì [V] (9-4)

prosperous fùyu [SV] (7-4)

public gōnggòng [AT] (9-2)

public security zhì'ān [N] (7-4)

Q

quarter of an hour kè [M] (3-4)

quickly kuài [A] (5-2)

quite tǐng [A] (1-3)

R

rain xiàyǔ [VO] (10-1); yǔ [N] (10-1); (light) máomáoyǔ [N] (10-3)

raise yǎng [V] (9-2)

reach dào [V] (3-4)

read kàn [V] (9-4)

really shízài [A] (5-1); zhēn [A] (6-1)

recently zuìjìn [TW] (1-3)

recognize rènshi [V] (7-2)

red hóng [SV] (9-1)

red color hóngsè [N] (9-1)

regret bàoqiàn [V] (5-1)

relatively bǐjiào [A] (4-4)

remember jìde [V] (9-4)

rent out chūzū [V] (8-2)

Republic of China Mínguó [TW] (4-2)

request yào [V] (8-3)

research yánjiū [N/V] (7-4)

rest xiūxi [V] (4-1)

return to one's home huíjiā [VO] (4-3)

return to one's home country huíguó [VO] (4-3)

rice (cooked) fàn [N] (5-2)

right yòu [L] (5-4); yòubian(r) [PW] (5-4)

right away mǎshàng [A] (8-3)

rise qǐchuáng [VO] (4-1)

road lù [N] (4-2)

room fángjiān [N] (4-3)

roommate tóngwū(r) [N] (2-2)

run (into) pèng [V] (10-3), pèngshang [RC] (10-3)

rush gǎn [V] (8-3); gǎndào [V+PV] (8-3)

S

sad nánguò [SV] (10-4)

San Francisco Jiùjīnshān [PW] (6-2)

sand shā [N] (10-2)

Saturday lǐbàiliù [TW] (4-1); xīngqīliù [TW] (4-1)

say jiǎng [V] (7-3); shuō [V] (4-3)

scenery fēngjǐng [N] (10-4)

school xuéxiào [PW] (6-3)

screen window shāchuāng [N] (10-3)

season jìjié [N] (10-2)

seat wèizi [N] (5-2)

second year in jr. high school chū'èr [TW] (6-1)

section duàn [M] (4-2)

see kàn [V] (3-2)

seem hǎoxiàng [MA] (4-4)

seldom hěn shǎo [PH] (10-2)

sell mài [V] (3-3)

send pài [V] (8-3)

senior high school gāozhōng [PW] (6-1)

senior year in college dàsì [TW] (6-1)

senior year in high school gāosān [TW] (6-1)

September jiǔyuè [TW] (4-2)

serve fúwù [V] (6-3)

seven qī [NU] (3-1)

several jǐ- [NU] (7-2)

Shanghai Shànghǎi [PW] (4-4)

she tā [PR] (1-2)

shoe xié [N] (5-2)

short (not tall) ǎi [SV] (1-3)

should gāi [AV] (9-4); yào [AV] (8-3); yīngdāng [AV] (8-4); yīnggāi [AV] (2-2)

show chūshì [V] (9-4)

Singapore Xīnjiāpō [PW] (2-1)

Sino-American Zhōng-Měi [AT] (2-4)

sister (younger) mèimei [N] (3-2); (younger younger) xiǎomèi [N] (6-4); (older) jiějie [N] (3-2); (older younger) dàmèi [N] (6-4)

sisters (older and younger) jiěmèi [N] (6-4)

sit zuò [V] (1-4); (in, at, on) zuòzai [V+PV] (6-2)

six liù [NU] (3-1)

skip class táokè [VO] (4-4)

sleep shuì [V] (4-1); shuìjiào [VO] (4-1)

sleepy kùn [SV] (1-3)

small xiǎo [SV] (1-3)

smart cōngming [SV] (9-3)

smell good xiāng [SV] (5-3)

snow xuě [N] (10-2); xiàxuě [VO] (10-2)

so nèmme [A] (7-3); suǒyi [CJ] (6-3); suǒyi shuō [PH] (10-1); zhèmme [A] (2-2)

society xiéhuì [N] (6-3)

some yìdiǎn(r) [NU+M] (1-1); yǒude [AT/PR] (7-2)

sometimes yǒude shíhou(r) [PH] (7-3)
son érzi [N] (6-2)
soon kuài [A] (5-2)
sophomore year in college dà'èr [TW] (6-1)
sophomore year in high school gāoyī [TW] (6-1)
south nán [L] (8-1); nánbiān(r) [PW] (5-3); Nánfāng [PW] (8-1)
southeast dōngnán [PW] (6-3)
southern speech Nánfāng huà [PH] (8-1)
Southerner Nánfāng rén [PH] (8-1)
southwest xī'nán [PW] (6-3)
Spain Xībānyá [PW] (2-1)
Spanish (language) Xībānyáyǔ [N] (7-2)
speak jiǎnghuà [VO] (7-3); jiǎng [V] (7-3); shuō [V] (4-3); shuōhuà [VO] (7-2)
spouse àirén [N] (1-2)
spring chūntiān [TW] (10-2)
station zhàn [N/M] (9-2)
stay zhù [V] (4-3)
still hái [A] (1-2)
stop zhàn [N/M] (9-2)
straight yìzhí [A] (8-1)
street car diànchē [N] (9-2)
student xuésheng [N] (5-2); (female) nǚshēng [N] (3-1); (male) nánshēng [N] (3-1)
studies xuéxí [N] (1-3)
studious yònggōng [SV] (9-3)
study niàn [V] (7-4); shūfáng [PW] (5-4); xué [V] (5-2); xuéxí [N] (1-3), [V] (2-3); (as a foreign student) liúxué [VO/V] (6-4)
stupid bèn [SV] (9-3)
subtract jiǎn [V] (3-3)
sugar táng [N] (6-1)
summer xiàtiān [TW] (10-2)
Summer Palace Yíhéyuán [PW] (9-2)
sun tàiyáng [N] (10-2)
sun comes out chū tàiyáng [PH] (10-2)
Sunday lǐbàirì [TW] (4-1); lǐbàitiān [TW] (4-1); xīngqīrì [TW] (4-1); xīngqītiān [TW] (4-1)
sunny day qíngtiān [N] (10-1)
surnamed xìng [EV] (2-3)
switch kāiguān [N] (5-4)

T

table zhuōzi [N] (5-1)
Taipei Táiběi [PW] (4-4)

Taiwan Táiwān [PW] (2-1)
take yào [V] (3-3); (travel by) zuò [V] (3-4)
take a taxi dǎdī [VO] (8-1)
take along dài [V] (2-4)
take care màn zǒu [IE] (1-4)
take care of bàn [V] (1-1)
take (a vehicle) to zuòdào [V+PV] (9-2)
talk jiǎnghuà [VO] (7-3)
tall gāo [SV] (1-3)
taxi chūzū qìchē [PH] (8-2)
teach jiāo [V] (6-3); jiāoshū [VO] (6-3)
teacher lǎoshī [N] (1-4)
telephone diànhuà [N] (8-3)
tell a joke shuō xiàohua(r) [PH] (9-3)
temperature wēndù [N] (10-1)
ten thousand -wàn [NU] (4-4)
ten shí [NU] (3-1)
ten million -qiānwàn [NU] (4-4)
thank xiè [V] (9-1); xièxie [V] (1-4)
thank you xièxie [IE] (1-2)
that nà [PR] (2-2); nèi- [SP] (2-1)
that way nèiyang(r) [MA] (7-4); nèi-yangzi [MA] (10-3)
then jiù [A] (3-2); nèmme [CJ] (3-4); ránhòu [MA] (4-3); zhèmme shuō [PH] (10-2)
there nàli [PW] (6-2); nàr [PW] (5-1); nèibian(r) [PW] (5-3)
there is/there are yǒu [V] (3-1)
there is not/there are not méiyou [V] (3-2)
therefore suóyi [CJ] (6-3); suóyi shuō [PH] (10-1)
they tāmen [PR] (1-2)
thin (lacking fatty tissue) shòu [SV] (5-3)
thing dōngxi [N] (5-4); (abstract) shì(r) [N] (1-1)
think xiǎng [V] (3-2)
third year in jr. high school chūsān [TW] (6-1)
this zhè [PR] (2-2); zhèi- [SP] (2-1)
this place běndì [N] (9-1)
this way zhèiyang(r) [MA] (7-4); zhèi-yangzi [MA] (10-3)
this year jīnnián [TW] (3-2)
thousand -qiān [NU] (3-3)
three sān [NU] (3-1)
thunder dǎléi [VO] (10-1)
Thursday lǐbàisì [TW] (4-1); xīngqīsì [TW] (4-1)
Tiananmen Tiān'ānmén [PW] (8-1)
Tianjin Tiānjīn [PW] (3-4)

ticket piào [N] (9-3)
ticketseller shòupiàoyuán [N] (9-3)
time cì [M] (4-3); huí [M] (5-3); shíhou(r) [N] (7-3); shíjiān [N] (3-4)
tired lèi [SV] (1-2)
to dào [CV] (1-1); -dào [PV] (5-3); -gěi [PV] (6-1); shàng [CV] (8-3); wàng [CV] (8-1)
today jīntiān [TW] (4-2)
together yìqǐ [A/PW] (7-3)
toilet cèsuǒ [PW] (5-3)
tomorrow míngtiān [TW] (4-2)
too (also) yě [A] (1-1); (excessively) tài [A] (1-3)
top shàng [L] (5-4); shàngbian(r) [PW] (5-4); shàngmian [PW] (5-4); shàng-tou [PW] (5-4)
toward wàng [CV] (8-1)
trade màoyì [N] (2-4)
trading company màoyì gōngsī [PH] (2-4)
traffic jiāotōng [N] (8-3)
traffic light hónglǜdēng [N] (9-1)
traffic police jiāotōng jǐngchá [PH] (9-1); jiāotōngjǐng [N] (9-1)
train huǒchē [N] (3-4); péixùn [V] (5-2)
tram diànchē [N] (9-2)
trolley diànchē [N] (9-2)
trouble máfan [V] (8-3)
truly shízài [A] (5-1)
Tuesday lǐbài'èr [TW] (4-1); xīngqī'èr [TW] (4-1)
turn guǎi [V] (9-1); zhuǎn [V] (9-1)
two èr [NU] (3-1); liǎng- [NU] (3-1)
typhoon táifēng [N] (10-3)

U

uncle (father's younger brother) shūshu [N] (6-1)
under xià [L] (5-4); xiàbian(r) [PW] (5-4); xiàmian [PW] (5-4); xiàtou [PW] (5-4)
underneath dǐxia [PW] (5-4)
understand dǒng [V] (9-4)
university dàxué [PW] (2-3)
use shǐyòng [V] (5-4)
usually píngcháng [MA] (4-1)

V

vehicle chē [N] (3-4); chēzi [N] (8-2); qìchē [N] (8-2)
very hěn [A] (1-2); tǐng [A] (1-3)

W

wait děng [V] (4-2)

walk zǒu [V] (8-1); zǒulù [VO] (8-1)

want xiǎng [AV] (5-1); yào [V] (3-3); yào [AV] (5-4)

warm nuǎnhuo [SV] (10-4)

way bànfǎ(r) [N] (10-3); fázi [N] (8-3); yàngzi [N] (1-3)

we wǒmen [PR] (1-4)

weather tiānqi [N] (10-1)

weather forecast tiānqi yùbào [PH] (10-1)

Wednesday lǐbàisān [TW] (4-1); xīngqīsān [TW] (4-1)

week lǐbài [N] (4-1); xīngqī [N] (4-1)

welcome huānyíng [IE] (1-4); huānyíng [V] (2-2)

well nèmme [CJ] (3-4)

west xī [L] (8-1); xībiān(r) [PW] (5-3); xīfāng [PW] (8-1)

west coast xī'àn [PW] (10-4)

Westerner Xīfāng rén [PH] (8-1)

what shémme [QW] (2-1)

when ...de shíhou(r) [PT] (10-4); jǐdiǎn (3-4); shémme shíhou (7-3)

where nǎr [QW] (1-1); náli [QW] (6-2); nèibiān(r) [QW] (5-3)

which něi- [QW] (2-1)

which country něiguó [QW] (2-1)

which day of the month jǐhào [QW] (4-2)

which day of the week lǐbàijǐ [QW] (4-1); xīngqījǐ [QW] (4-1)

which month of the year jǐyuè [QW] (4-2)

white bái [SV] (9-1)

white color báisè [N] (9-1)

who(m) shéi [QW] (2-2)

why wèishemme [QW] (6-3); zěmme [QW] (8-3)

wife àirén [N] (1-2); tàitai [N] (2-3)

will huì [AV] (8-3); yào [AV] (4-3)

wind fēng [N] (10-2)

wind and sand fēngshā [N] (10-2)

winter dōngtiān [TW] (10-2)

with gēn [CV] (6-4); hé [CV] (7-3)

woman nǚde [N] (3-1); (married) tàitai [N] (2-4); (unmarried) xiáojie [N] (2-4)

wonderful bàng [SV] (7-4)

word huà [N] (7-2); zì(r) [N] (7-2)

work gōngzuò [N] (1-3); gōngzuò [V] (2-3); shàngbān(r) [VO] (6-3)

work hard nǔlì [SV] (7-4)

work unit dānwèi [PW] (2-3)

worker gōngrén [N] (5-2)

worry zháojí [VO/SV] (8-3)

wow yò [I] (3-3)

write xiě [V] (7-2); xiězì(r) [VO] (7-2)

wrong cuò [SV] (2-4)

X

Xian Xī'ān [PW] (4-4)

Y

year nián [M] (4-2); (of age) suì [M] (3-2)

year after next hòunián [TW] (4-3)

year before last qiánnián [TW] (4-3)

yellow huáng [SV] (9-1)

yellow color huángsè [N] (9-1)

yesterday zuótiān [TW] (4-2)

you nǐ [PR] (1-1); (plural) nǐmen [PR] (1-4); (singular, polite) nín [PR] (1-4)

you're welcome bú kèqi [IE] (1-4)

young niánqīng [SV] (6-2); xiǎo [SV] (1-3)

Z

zero líng [NU] (3-3)

zoo dòngwùyuán(r) [PW] (9-2)